# SOUTH·WESTERN

# COLLEGE
# KEYBOARDING

Lessons 1-180

## WordPerfect® Office 2000
### Complete Course

**Susie H. VanHuss, Ph.D.**
University of South Carolina

**Charles H. Duncan, Ed.D.**
Eastern Michigan University

**Connie M. Forde, Ph.D.**
Mississippi State University

**Donna L. Woo**
Cypress College, California

VISIT US ON THE INTERNET
**www.swep.com**
www.thomson.com

## South-Western
### Thomson Learning™

Cincinnati • Albany, NY • Belmont, CA • Bonn • Boston • Detroit • Johannesburg • London • Madrid
Melbourne • Mexico City • New York • Paris • Singapore • Tokyo • Toronto • Washington

**Team Leader:** Karen Schmohe
**Project Manager—Keyboarding:** Jane Phelan
**Consulting Editor:** Diane Bowdler
**Production:** D&G Limited, LLC
**Copy Editor:** Gary Morris
**Editor:** Martha Conway
**Production Coordinator:** Jane Congdon
**Marketing Manager:** Tim Gleim
**Marketing Coordinator:** Lisa Barto
**Designer:** Ann Small, a small design studio
**Photo Editors:** Michelle Kunkler, Linda Ellis
**Art/Design Coordinator:** Michelle Kunkler
Cover and Special Page Illustrations by Elvira Regine

---

**Photo Credits:**

p. 189 © CORBIS

p. 58 © Digital Stock

p. xv © EyeWire, Inc.

pp. 3, 5, 8, 9, 11, 12, 13, 14, 15, 16, 18, 19, 20, 21, 22, 23, 24, 37, 38, 40, 42, 44, 46, 48, 50, 52, 54, A20, A21, A22, RG12 Greg Grosse

pp. 144, 191, 192, 243 Photo by Alan Brown/Photonics Graphics

pp. xii, xv, 43, 45, 59, 65, 83, 243, 251, 316, 322 © PhotoDisc, Inc.

---

Copyright © 2000
by SOUTH-WESTERN EDUCATIONAL PUBLISHING
Cincinnati, Ohio

South-Western Educational Publishing is a division of Thomson Learning.
Thomson Learning is a trademark used herein under license.

# preface

COLLEGE KEYBOARDING, *WordPerfect® 2000 Complete Course* is a learning package designed for the new millennium. This exceedingly successful package combines *Windows 98*, a state-of-the-art operating system; *WordPerfect 9*, an excellent word processing software; *Keyboarding Pro Multimedia*, an ideal all-in-one keyboarding instruction program; and well-written text materials presented in a concise, easy-to-learn format. This winning combination ensures that you will develop the skills needed for success in the automated office.

Keyboarding is a skill needed for success in virtually every career! Students, administrative employees, managers, attorneys, physicians, scientists, engineers, musicians, and factory workers use their keyboard to compose e-mails and memos, access databases, manipulate numbers, and communicate with coworkers. The keyboard provides access to critical information—and information is power.

Industry integrates and requires employees to use tools that facilitate communication. To function effectively in their jobs, most employees need basic skill using all applications in the suite and in-depth skill in one or more applications. *College Keyboarding* combines the learning of keyboarding, word processing, Internet usage, and the other *WordPerfect 2000* applications to help you develop the skills needed in today's

[...]. As with any skill, you will be successful if you apply proper
[...] practice in each session. And your keyboarding practice
[...] *Multimedia* will teach you the alphabetic, numeric, and
[...] When you're ready, *Skill Builder* is on your desktop to
[...] th 20 lessons that can be completed in either speed or
[...] along with progress graphs, colored photos, sound
[...]sor will keep you motivated.

In the new millennium, the skills needed for success in virtually every career include keyboarding skills, skills using the Internet, basic skills in all applications in software suites such as WordPerfect Office 2000, and in-depth skill in one or more applications in the suite.

## ...earning Goals

...organized into five carefully
...ed levels.

...1-30, you will:
...e alphabetic and numeric keys "by
...appropriate techniques.

...strong keyboarding skill.

...*boarding Pro Multimedia* software, which is
...ed to teach and build your keyboarding skills.

...vel 2, Lessons 31-60, you will:
...ontinue to build keyboarding skill—improving both
your speed and accuracy.

- Format letters, using *WordPerfect 9* functions for creating, editing, and formatting documents.

- Learn to use the Internet.

In Level 3, Lessons 61-93, you will:
- Expand formatting skills to two-page letters and memos, letters with special features, tables, and formal reports using advanced functions such as headers and footers; endnotes and footnotes; and tables with rotated text, formulas, and other options.

- Continue to build strong keyboarding skills.

In Level 4, Lessons 94-120, you will:
- Enhance documents with columns and graphics such as clipart, shapes, and TextArt.

- Use mail merge to create mass mailings, envelopes, and labels.

- Prepare effective employment documents to showcase your skills.

In Level 5, Modules A-H, you will:
- Expand your word processing skills to create a newsletter with a desktop publishing appearance and word processing features that support collaborative writing and team documents.

- Learn the basics of the other software applications (*Presentations, Quattro Pro, Paradox*) so that information created in these programs can be integrated into *WordPerfect* documents.

- Create documents for Web pages using *WordPerfect*.

- Learn the basics of speech recognition, a new emerging technology that interfaces with keyboarding.

## Features That Enhance Learning

*COLLEGE KEYBOARDING, WordPerfect 9* incorporates numerous design features that simplify learning and ensure mastery of keyboarding, word processing, and document formatting.

**Skillbuilding.** Skillbuilding activities are an integral part of most lessons, and four Skillbuilding Workshops provide extra practice. The Skill Builder module of *Keyboarding Pro* can also be used on an ongoing basis once the alphabetic keys have been learned.

**Formatting.** Major emphasis is placed on applying principles of good design and utilizing software features that allow you to maximize productivity. Full-page models introduce all new document formats and help you apply good design principles.

**Word processing.** Colorful graphics and extensive screen captures supplement the step-by-step procedures for each new function. Preapplication drills apply functions before you encounter them in documents.

**E-mail and Internet activities.** You will embark on the superhighway of communications—the Internet. Optional Internet activities are integrated throughout the text. Activities progress from opening a Web site, setting up an e-mail account, downloading files, and using search engines. Individual and team activities are included.

**News and views.** These segments highlight topics of current interest that will broaden your knowledge of workforce trends and issues.

**Checkpoints.** Beginning in Level 2, modules conclude with an objective and performance assessment to help you gauge whether you have mastered the skills and knowledge presented in the module before taking the assessment.

**Projects.** Six realistic projects reinforce the software skills, communication skills, and decision making applied to that point. A project follows Lessons 60 and 120; four projects are integrated into Modules A-H.

**Workshops and special features.** Skillbuilding, communication, file management, editing, and numeric keypad workshops supplement the lessons.

**Formatting Template.** The CD-ROM included in the back of this book includes files required to complete various documents. These documents are identified in the text with a disk or CD-ROM icon.

**Software and supplements**. Additional products that supplement this text are displayed on the next page.

# *family* of Products

## Technology Solutions

### Keyboarding Pro Multimedia
New key learning on CD-ROM with enhanced graphics, 3-D viewer, and video clips. Easy-to-use Send feature for distance education students. Timed writing options and a *Windows* word processor with a timer add flexibility. See pp. xvi–xx for more information.

### CheckPro 2000
Combined skillbuilding and document checking software for Lessons 31–120. Easy-to-use Send feature for distance education. Students key from the textbook; it verifies the speed and accuracy of documents and production tests. Separate versions are available for *Word 2000* and *WordPerfect 9*.

### Online Learning
Browser-based instruction designed for student use. Appropriate for distance education or as a supplement to classroom instruction. Available in either HTML format or as a WebCT cartridge.
* Includes instructional lesson slides, quizzes, Web links, enrichment activities, flashcards, online quizzes, interactive documents for mastering formatting, and online reference of model documents.
* WebCT version also offers access to e-mail, online chat, course calendar, announcements, and more.

### World Class Course: Thomson World Class Course
Offers an online syllabus for distance or distributed learning at www.worldclasslearning.com.

## Other Software Solutions

### MicroPace Pro
Timed writing, error diagnostics, and paced skill development software. Timings are keyed from *College Keyboarding*. The *College Keyboarding* template offers the option for one or two spaces following end-of-sentence punctuation.

### KeyChamp
A unique program certain to increase keyboarding speed. *KeyChamp* pinpoints the keys that slow students down and assigns practice specifically for their needs. For use after keys are learned.

## Instructor Support

**Instructor's Editions**   Lessons 1–60 and 61–120

**Instructor's Manual and Key**   Modules A–H

**Instructor's Resource Kit**   Includes the following:
Keys for Lessons 1–120          Multicultural Projects
Transparency Masters            Poster
Objective and Performance Tests

## Simulations and Projects

Simulations apply skills ranging from entry-level keyboarding to word processing and integrated applications.

**The Candidate**   Beginning word processing simulation. 20–25 hours.

**SBI**   Advanced word processing. 20–25 hours.

**Sports Connection Integrated Simulation**   35–40 hours

# table
## of contents

# summary of functions

| LESSON | FUNCTION |
|---|---|
| **Module A  Desktop Publishing** | |
| A1 | Columns |
| A2-A3 | Wrap text around graphic |
| | Hyphenation |
| A4 | Charts |
| A5 | Shapes |
| | Group objects |
| | Drop cap |
| **Module B  Presentations** | |
| B1 | Create presentation |
| B2 | Slide layout |
| | Transitions |
| | Animation |
| B3 | Views, speaker notes, printing |
| **Module C  Spreadsheet Basics** | |
| C1 | Create spreadsheet |
| | Move within a spreadsheet |
| | Enter data |
| C2 | Fit column width |
| | Enter text, values, and formulas |
| | Copy data |
| | Zoom, QuickFill |
| | Functions |
| C3 | Charts |
| **Module D  Compound Documents** | |
| D1 | Embed objects/Paste special |
| D2 | Link objects |
| D4 | Embed screen capture |
| **Module E  Paradox** | |
| E1 | Enter and edit records |
| | Navigate tables |
| | Use form |

| LESSON | FUNCTION |
|---|---|
| E2 | Create and design tables |
| | Define fields |
| | Add validity checks |
| E3 | Create queries |
| | Sort |
| | Query using criteria |
| E4 | Report Expert |
| | Modify report |
| E5 | Merge with database query |
| | Labels |
| **Module F  Working Collaboratively** | |
| F1 | QuickCorrect |
| | Smart Quotes |
| | Format-As-You-Go |
| | SpeedLinks |
| | QuickWords |
| F2 | Styles |
| | QuickStyle |
| F3 | Tables of contents |
| F4 | Comments |
| F5 | Document review |
| | Master documents and subdocuments |
| **Module G  Web Publishing** | |
| G1 | Internet Publisher |
| G2 | Link web pages |
| G3 | Publish files to the Web |
| **Module H  Speech Recognition Software** | |
| H1 | Dragon NaturallySpeaking basics |
| H2 | Punctuation and commands |
| H3 | Correct text |
| H4 | Train the system |
| | QuickTour |

# welcome
## to Windows 98

**Exploring Windows**

*Windows 98* is the operating system software you are using to control the operation of your computer and the peripherals such as the mouse and printer. Software applications that run under *Windows 98* have many common features. They all use similar icons and consistent menus. A typical *Windows* desktop is shown below. Your *Windows* desktop will have most of the icons shown, and you may have additional icons. Note in particular three icons:

My Computer — My computer
Network Neighborhood — Network Neighborhood
Recycle Bin — Recycle Bin
Start button — Start button
Taskbar — Taskbar

**My Computer** displays the disk drives, CD-ROM, and printers that are attached to your computer.

**Network Neighborhood** allows you to view the available resources if your computer is connected to a network environment.

**Recycle Bin** stores documents that have been deleted from the hard drive. Documents in the Recycle Bin may be restored and returned to their folders. When the Recycle Bin is emptied, the documents are deleted and cannot be restored.

*Windows* enables you to choose the classic desktop shown or an active desktop that resembles an Internet Web page. You will learn about using the active desktop in a later module. The gray bar at the bottom of the desktop is the **taskbar**. The taskbar contains the **Start button** on the left and the system clock on the right. The Start button is always visible when *Windows* is running. The Start button is used to run the *Windows* application software that you will use such as *Windows Explorer* or *Microsoft Word*. The taskbar may have shortcut buttons near the Start button as shown in the figure above, and it may also have buttons for software applications such as *Windows Explorer* that may be running.

In the next few pages, you will learn the basics of *Windows 98*. These basic concepts can be used with all *Windows 98* application software. If you have access to the CD-ROM disk containing your *Windows 98* software, you should view the *Windows 98* overview and work through the brief tutorial.

## Using the mouse

*Windows 98* software requires the use of a mouse or other pointing device. The pointing device may be separate or may be built into your keyboard. Note that the mouse contains a left button and a right button. The left button is used to select, open, or drag objects. The right button is used to display a shortcut or context menu. In *Windows 98*, you can also use it to drag objects. If you have used previous versions of *Windows* software, you will note that the right mouse button is used more extensively in *Windows 98* than in previous versions.

## Mouse pointer

The mouse pointer changes in appearance depending on its location on the desktop and the task that it is doing.

I   The I-beam indicates that the mouse pointer is located in the text area. When you pause, it blinks.

The arrow selects items. It displays when the mouse is located outside the text area. You can position or hover this arrow over a toolbar icon to display the function of that icon.

The hourglass indicates that *Windows* is processing your command. You must wait until *Windows* finishes what it is doing before keying text or entering another command.

↔   A double-headed arrow appears when the pointer is at the border of a window or object and is used to change its size.

The pointer is moved by moving the mouse on a padded, flat surface called a mouse pad. The pointer can be repositioned by picking up the mouse and placing it in another spot on the mouse pad. If you have a touch pad on your keyboard, the pointer is moved by moving your finger on the touch pad. The mouse performs four basic actions:

**Point:** Move the pointer so that it touches an icon or text. Positioning the pointer on some items such as those on the Start menu will display the options available.

**Click:** Point to a desired item, and then press the mouse button once and release. Pressing the left mouse button selects the item; pressing the right mouse button provides quick access to menus or commands.

**Double-click:** Point to a desired item; then quickly press and release the left mouse button twice. This action opens an object or issues a command.

**Drag:** Point to the desired item; hold down the mouse button and drag the item to a new location on the desktop; then release the button.

## Working with Windows 98

To run an application, click the Start button on the opening *Windows 98* screen. Notice that the Start menu appears. The Start menu is divided into three sections:

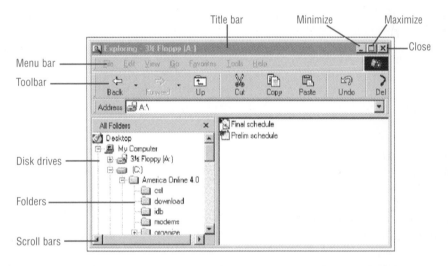

The *top* portion of the menu contains applications that you may add such as *America Online* or *WordPerfect*.

The *center* portion of the menu contains a list of options such as Help, Documents, or Programs. Note that the Programs option is highlighted.

The *lower* portion of the menu contains basic commands such as Log On and Shut Down.

The right triangular arrows indicate that a cascading or submenu is available for that option. When you point to one of the triangular arrows, a list of options appears at the right side of the Start menu.

To open an application that appears in the list, move the pointer to the application and click it. Note that *Windows Explorer* is highlighted. *Windows Explorer* is an application used to manage files and folders. If you click *Windows Explorer*, the following **window** will display.

**Window:** A work area on the desktop that can be resized or moved. To resize a window, point at the border. When the pointer changes to a double arrowhead, drag the window to the desired size. To move a window, point to the title bar and drag it to the new position. Release the mouse button when the window has been moved to the desired position.

**Title bar:** Displays the name of the application that is currently open. Provides other information such as folder or filename.

**Minimize button:** Minimizes window. By clicking the minimize button, the window disappears and becomes a button on the taskbar. It can be restored by clicking the button.

**Maximize button**: Maximizes window. By clicking the maximize button, the window enlarges to full-screen size.

**Close button:** Closes the application.

**Scroll bars:** Allow you to see information that requires more space than is available on one screen. Click the Up or Down arrow to view additional information.

**Windows Explorer**

Files can be managed by using a program called *Windows Explorer*. To access Windows, all documents and programs are stored in **folders**. In *Windows Explorer*, you can see the hierarchy of folders and all the files and folders within selected folders. *Windows Explorer* is especially useful for creating folders, and moving, copying, or renaming files. To open *Windows Explorer*, click *Start*, then click *Programs*, then click *Windows Explorer*.

**Creating folders and subfolders**

Folders and subfolders can be set up on your hard disk drive or on a floppy disk. The example shown below illustrates setting up folders for a Keyboarding and an English class. Each class folder has two subfolders—one for classwork and one for homework.

**To create a folder:**

1. Select the drive you wish to use (in the example, Drive A).

2. From the File menu bar, choose *File*, then click **New** and then **Folder**.

3. Key the name of the folder and press ENTER.

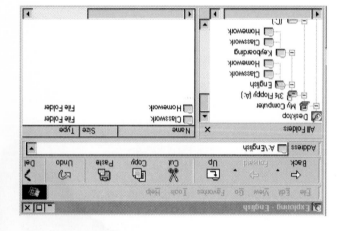

**Deleting and renaming folders**

If you change your English class to a Spanish class, you could simply rename the folder. To rename a file, click on the folder to be renamed (English) then click *File*, and then *Rename*. Key the new filename (Spanish). To delete a file or a folder, click on the folder to be deleted and press DELETE. Respond Yes to the inquiry, *Are you sure you want to remove the folder Classwork and all its contents?*

**Moving and copying files**

When a file is copied, the original file remains in place, and another copy of the file is placed at the destination. When a file is moved, the original file is removed from its original location and placed at the destination.

• Folders and files are moved by dragging the object from the Contents pane to its destination. If you drag a folder on the same disk, it will be moved. If you drag a file to another disk (from Drive A to C), it will be copied.

• To copy a file/folder, use the CTRL key while dragging the file.

• To move a file/folder, use the SHIFT key.

The file or folder that is to be copied is referred to as the **source copy**; the location where the copy is to be moved is called the **destination**. Folders and files that are moved or copied by mistake can be restored to their original location by using Undo in the Edit menu.

# *know your* computer

--------------------------------------------------------------------------------

**Computers consist of these essential parts:**

1. **Central processing unit:** The internal operating unit, including the processing unit, memory chips, disk drives, etc.

2. **Disk drive:** A unit that reads and writes onto disks.

3. **Monitor:** A screen that displays information as it is keyed and messages from the computer called *prompts*.

4. **Mouse:** Input device. *Windows* software is designed to be used with a mouse.

5. **Keyboard:** Input device for entering alphabetic and numeric characters and symbols as well as special keys for entering commands.

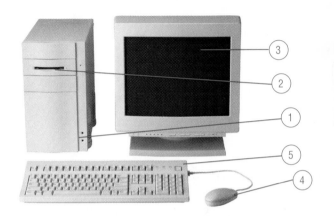

## Keyboard arrangement

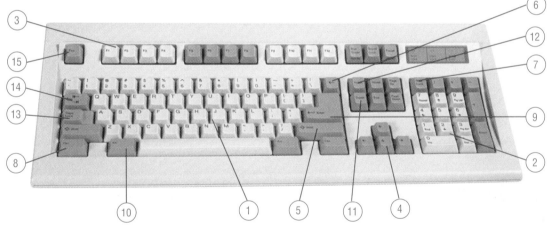

1. **Alphanumeric keys:** Center portion of the keyboard.

2. **Numeric keypad:** Calculator type keys used for entering statistical data. To turn on the keypad, press the NUMLOCK key.

3. **Function keys:** Perform a software function; used by themselves or with other keys.

4. **Arrow keys:** Move the insertion point.

5. **SHIFT key:** Makes lowercase letters uppercase.

6. **BACKSPACE:** Deletes the character to the left of the insertion point.

7. **NUMLOCK:** Switches the numeric keypad between numeric and editing.

8. **CTRL (Control):** Expands the use of function keys.

9. **ENTER:** Advances the insertion point to the next line. ENTER is often used to execute a command.

10. **ALT (Alternate) key:** Used with another key to execute a function.

11. **DELETE key:** Erases text to the right of the insertion point.

12. **Insert key:** Toggles the software between insert mode and typeover/overstrike mode.

13. **CAPS LOCK:** Capitalizes all alphabetic characters.

14. **TAB:** Moves the cursor to a preset position.

15. **ESC (Escape):** Exits a menu or dialog box in word processing software.

# welcome
# to Keyboarding Pro

With the full-featured *Keyboarding Pro* software, you can use the power of your computer to learn alphabetic and numeric keyboarding and the keypad. The 30 alphabetic and numeric software lessons correlate with the first 30 lessons in the *College Keyboarding* textbook. After you complete Lesson 13, you can use Skill Builder to boost your speed and accuracy.

Your computer should be turned on, and either *Windows 98* or *Windows 95* should be displayed.

1. Open *Keyboarding Pro*.

   *Windows 98 or Windows 95:*

   • Click the **Start** button.
   • Point to the Programs menu; a submenu displays to the right listing all the programs.
   • Click **Keyboarding Pro** in the programs submenu.

2. Click anywhere in the opening screen to remove it and bring up the Log In dialog box.

3. Select the appropriate name from the list that appears in the Log In dialog box. Then enter the correct password to continue. Click the **Guest** button only if instructed. (See Figure 1.)

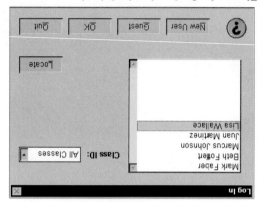

**Figure 1:** Student Log In dialog box

When using the program for the first time, you click the **New User** button and complete the New Student Registration dialog box (as described on the next page).

4. After you log in, the program will either display the Main menu or prompt you to continue where you left off. If the Main menu appears, choose the appropriate lesson. A check mark appears next to each lesson that you have completed unless you used the Guest option to log in. Check marks also appear on the Notebook tabs to show which exercises have been completed.

## New student registration

The first time you use *Keyboarding Pro*, you must enter the following information: name, class ID, and password. You must also identify where to store the data.

1. Click the **New User** button shown in the Log In dialog box. The New Student dialog box appears. (See Figure 2.)

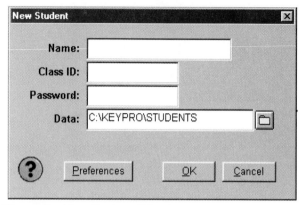

**Figure 2:** New Student dialog box

2. Enter user name (first name, last name).

3. Record the class ID.

4. Enter a password. Write the password on a piece of paper and store it in a safe place.

5. Specify the data location if necessary. For example, the path may already be set to **c:\keypro\students.** If you have your own subdirectory, which was created previously, you must set the path accordingly (e.g., **c:\keypro\students\lopez**). You can click on the **Folder** icon to browse through the directories to locate the folder.

6. If necessary, click the **Preferences** button and update the required information.

7. Click the **OK** button to complete the registration process.

## Main menu

Click any of the four keyboarding buttons shown in the center of the Main menu to proceed directly to the corresponding *Keyboarding Pro* module. (See Figure 3.)

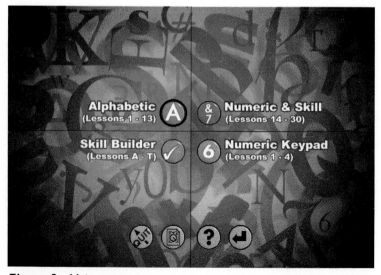

**Figure 3:** Main menu

**Alphabetic:** You will learn the alphabetic keys in this module.

**Numeric & Skill:** Activities focus on building skill as well as learning the top-row and symbol keys. Diagnostic Writings are available to analyze your progress.

**Skill Builder:** After you know the alphabetic keys, use these 20 lessons to boost your keyboarding speed and control. Each lesson can focus on either speed or accuracy, so you really have 40 lessons.

**Numeric Keypad:** You will learn the numeric keypad operation by completing four lessons in this module. See Appendix C for additional practice.

**Module activities**

**Alphabetic/numeric and skill**

A variety of exercises are included in each lesson. In *Textbook keying*, the software directs you to key an exercise from the textbook. Space is available to key 20 lines. If you complete the exercise more than once, only the most recent exercise is stored and displayed in the Lesson report. Click the **Print** button to print the current exercise before repeating the exercise.

**Timed writing:** This exercise occurs in each review lesson. Indicate the length of your timing in the Timed Writing dialog box (see Figure 4). You will key from the textbook. The software highlights the errors along with providing the gross words a minute (*gwam*). If you complete the exercise more than once, only the most recent writing is stored and displayed in the Lesson Report. Click the **Print** button at the bottom of the screen to print the current timed writing before repeating the timing.

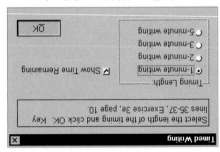

Select the length of the timing and click OK. Key lines 35-37, Exercise 3e, page 10.

Timing Length:
- ● 1-minute writing
- ○ 2-minute writing
- ○ 3-minute writing
- ○ 5-minute writing

☑ Show Time Remaining

OK

**Figure 4:** Timed Writing dialog box

**Additional features**

**Game:** The Commander Key game challenges you to meet a speed goal as you key drill lines from the screen. A score area shows your progress.

**Lesson Report:** After the last exercise in a lesson, a Lesson Report appears showing which lessons and lesson parts were completed and, if applicable, your speed scores and keying lines for *Build skill, Textbook keying,* and *Timed writing.*

**Open Screen:** The Open Screen is a word processor that includes many formatting options, a spell checker, and a built-in timer. You can practice your keyboarding skills, key letters and reports, and take a speed timed writing. These features can be accessed from the menu bar, and many of them are available on the toolbar. When you take a timed writing in the Open Screen, click the Timer button and save each timing with its own name. For example, *8e-t1* (exercise 8e, timing 1) and *8e-t2* (exercise 8e, timing 2).

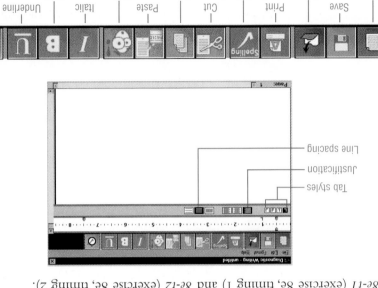

Tab styles

Justification

Line spacing

New
Save
Open
Print   Spell Check   Cut   Copy   Paste   Undo   Italic   Bold   Underline   Timer

**Diagnostic writings:** Timed writings can also be taken using the Diagnostic Writings option, which provides extensive error analysis. The Diagnostic Writings feature measures both speed and accuracy. Writings are keyed from the textbook. You may do a 1', 3', or 5' writing. Diagnostic Writings are available from the lesson menus of Numeric & Skill and Skill Builder.

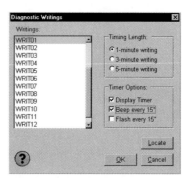

**Diagnostic Writing Selection**

**Quick review:** This feature of the Skill Builder module presents drill lines for you to practice various keys.

**Games:** Each of the keyboarding modules (Alphabetic, Numeric & Skill, Skill Builder, and Numeric Keypad) incorporates a game into various lessons. These games are a fun way to focus on improving your keyboarding skills. Top-ten lists that show student performance will challenge you to improve your speed and accuracy.

## Student reports

The *Keyboarding Pro* software provides numerous reports: Lesson Report, Summary Report, Keypad Data Sets, Top-Ten Lists, Certificate of Completion, and Performance Graphs. All of these reports, except the Lesson Report, are accessed by using the Reports menu.

The Lesson Report shows your performance data for each lesson. Performance Graphs are accessed by clicking the *Graph* button on Lesson Report. The Alphabetic keyboarding module performance graph represents your average/fastest speed for Build Skill sections. The Numeric & Skill keyboarding module also has a performance graph for the Commander Key game.

## Quitting *Keyboarding Pro*

To quit *Keyboarding Pro:*

1. Click the **Quit** button on the Main menu.

2. Or, choose *Exit* from the File menu.

## Quitting *Windows*

After you quit *Keyboarding Pro*, your instructor may want you to leave the computer running, or you may be instructed to shut down the computer. You need to shut down *Windows* before you turn off or restart your computer. To avoid damaging files, always shut down *Windows* before turning off your computer.

1. Click the **Start** button on the taskbar.

2. Click **Shut Down** from the drop-down list.

3. From the Shut Down dialog box, click **Yes**. A screen message lets you know when you can safely turn off your computer.

**Step 1**

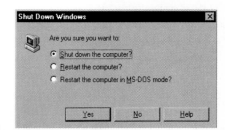

**Step 2**

# Keyboarding Pro Multimedia

*Keyboarding Pro Multimedia* is the CD-ROM version of *Keyboarding Pro*. The new features are high-lighted in the Main menu shown below. *Keyboarding Pro Multimedia* also gives classes the option of using one or two spaces after a period, and audio instruction is available for using the exercises. The other features of *Keyboarding Pro Multimedia* are exactly the same as *Keyboarding Pro*. Refer to the discussion of *Keyboarding Pro* (pages xii–xv) for information on starting the software, the Open Screen, student reports, and more.

**Main menu**

Click any of the four keyboarding titles to proceed directly to the corresponding module. The buttons on the Main menu help you access various features quickly and manipulate the software easily.

**Games:** The four games provide fun ways for improving your skills.

**Movies:** The movies discuss keyboarding issues and demonstrate correct techniques.

**3-D Animations:** See precisely and clearly a view of the correct body posture and the proper slant of your arms, curvature of your fingers, and position of your wrists and fingers. You can manipulate them and view them from any angle.

**Open screen:** *Windows* word processor with a timer button.

**Help:** Help is also available from nearly every screen throughout the program.

**Exit:** Click the **Exit** button to exit the program.

**Send file:** Send the electronic file containing your lesson report to your instructor using the *Send File* button. *Send File* can also be accessed from the Lesson Report screen.

**Quick review:** Use it to practice alphabetic keys, numeric keys, or specific reaches.

**Back:** Returns you to the previous menu.

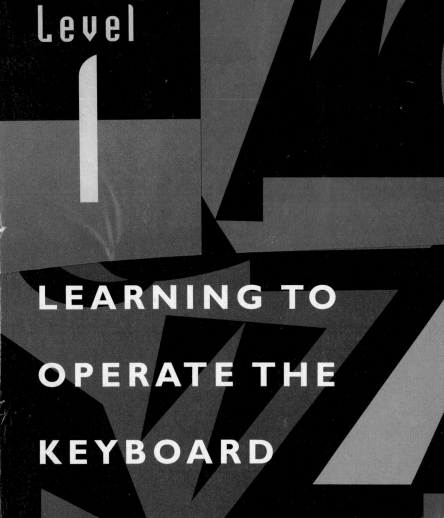

# Level 1

# LEARNING TO OPERATE THE KEYBOARD

# Activity
## twenty-two

Research recent developments in voice recognition technology and

**Setting:** You plan to invest time learning how to use voice recognition software. Before you do so, you would like to update the information you gained by reading the paper on Speech Recognition Software (pp. 562–564).

**Problem:** With an evolving technology, information is outdated very quickly. To make sure that your information is current, search the Internet to find the most current information on the major topics covered in the paper.

### Web sites to consider:
www.lhsl.com
www.dragonsys.com
www.naturalspeech.com
www.zdnet.com
www.corel.com
www.ibm.com/software/speech
www.speech.be.philips.com

**Outcomes:** As a minimum, you should have updated information about the following topics:

- New versions of speech recognition software available

- Results of new tests or studies showing accuracy of dictation

- Development of applications for specialized groups, such as medical or legal

- Ergonomics, as it pertains to speech recognition

# ALPHABETIC KEYREACHES

## OBJECTIVES

1. Key the alphabetic keys by touch.

2. Key using proper techniques.

3. Key at a rate of 14 *gwam* or more.

---

**LESSON**

## Home Row, Space Bar, ENTER, I

### 1a ●

### **G**ETTING
### started

**Open *Keyboarding Pro* software**

As you learn and practice the alphabetic keys, you will use *Keyboarding Pro* software. Many lessons introduce new keys, while others review what you have learned. Some lessons contain a challenging keyboarding game. You will key from the screen and from your textbook. The software tracks your performance and provides feedback. The first time you use *Keyboarding Pro* you must complete the registration process. Turn to p. 7.

From the Main menu, you can click any of the four buttons to go directly to the corresponding *Keyboarding Pro* lessons. The Main menu also includes the following buttons that appear at the bottom of the screen—Quit, Open Screen, Help, and Back.

Click Quit to exit *Keyboarding Pro*. The Quit button appears only on the Main menu.

Click the Open Screen button to access the built-in word processor, to practice your keyboarding skills, or to take a timed writing.

Click the Help button to display help for the feature you are currently using. The context-sensitive Help button appears on almost every screen throughout the program.

From the Main menu, clicking Back returns you to the Log In dialog box. On other screens, Back takes you to the previous menu. Click the large A button to go directly to *Alphabetic*, which you will use in Lessons 1-13.

---

# APPLICATION

**H8**

Dictate the material at the right:

- Say all text that is shown in bold.
- Commands are shown in bold and placed in brackets.
- Remember to pause before and after but not while you say each command.
- Punctuation is shown in italic.
- Divider marks are shown to help you dictate in phrases.
- Correct and train the system on any misrecognized words.

**Statement of Conditional Approval** | [select previous four words] [format that initial caps] | [bold] | [center line] | [new paragraph] |

**This statement provides you with conditional authorization** | **to proceed with the development of the training centers** | **based on the commitment made by the [cap] Coordinating [cap] Council** *period* | **As you know** *comma* | **this authorization is conditional until the [cap] Coordinating [cap] Council** | **meets and officially reviews the grant application** *period* | **You may submit expenses for any costs incurred** | **on or after the date stamped on this approval statement** *period* | **Any expenditures prior to the official review of the grant application** *comma* | **however** *comma* | **are made at your own risk** *period* | [new paragraph]

**The only decision the [cap] Coordinating [cap] Council makes during the formal application review process** | **is either to approve or to disapprove the grant** *period* | **If the grant is approved** *comma* | **the amount of the commitment made will remain the same** *period* | **Please call if you have any questions** *period* |

# APPLICATION

**H9**

The list at the right directs you to dictate paragraphs on pp. 562–564 of your text. Read each paragraph carefully before dictating it and determine the types of commands you will need to dictate. Remember that you must dictate punctuation. Correct and train the system on all recognition errors.

1. From p. 562, (first page of the white paper), dictate both paragraphs under the heading *Speaker Dependent Systems*. Then dictate the paragraph with the heading *Software Considerations*. Be sure to dictate the heading for each of the segments of text that you dictate.

2. From p. 563, dictate the paragraph under the heading *Continuous Speech Input*. Include the heading.

3. From p. 564, dictate the paragraph under the heading *The Future of Speech Recognition*. Include the heading.

**Optional Challenge**

Dictate the entire white paper (pp. 562–564). Format it as an unbound report using one column.

To select a lesson from *Alphabetic*, click the number next to the desired lesson with the left mouse button. Any time you want to practice your keyboarding skills, you can simply click the Open Screen button to access the built-in word processor.

Once you select a lesson, the first activity is displayed. In the illustration below, *Learn home row* is in yellow because this activity is active. You can move to a selected exercise by clicking one of the tabs. Follow the directions on screen and press ENTER. Key directly from the screen unless directed otherwise by the software or your instructor.

**Figure 1-1** Alphabetic Keyboarding Lesson Menu

**Figure 1-2** Alphabetic Keyboarding (Lesson 1: Learn Home Row and i)

## Ib ●

### Locate home keys

Examine the naming/numbering system for finger positions in the illustration at the right. Then, practice several times the steps below for placing fingers in home row position and for reaching to ENTER and the Space Bar.

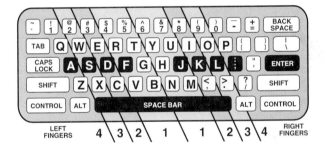

Drop hands to the side; allow fingers to curve naturally.

Lightly place the left fingertips over **a s d f**.

Lightly place right fingertips over **j k l** ; . Repeat.

**ENTER:** Reach with the 4th (little) finger of the right hand to ENTER and press it. Quickly return the finger to its home position (over ;).

**Space Bar:** Strike the Space Bar with a down-and-in motion of the right thumb.

# Apply What You Have Learned

**Quick Tour**

In the first lesson you viewed the Quick Tour for an overview and to help you get started. In this lesson, you will view the Quick Tour with a different purpose. Pay particular attention to the way the material is dictated on each slide. Note the differences in dictating text and dictating commands. This application takes approximately 15 minutes. To access the Quick Tour, click **Help** and then click **Quick Tour**.

**Using Help**

Click several topics in each category to review the type of information provided.

**Use Help to review what you have learned**

Help has four main categories of information. Each of these categories provides a wealth of helpful information as you continue to learn to dictate.

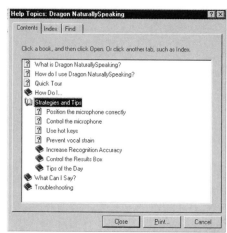

**How Do I** provides step-by-step instructions on how to dictate, edit, and format documents.

**Strategies and Tips** provide help on improving recognition and accuracy.

**What Can I Say?** provides a list of valid commands that can be used to accomplish formatting, editing, navigation, and other functions.

**Troubleshooting** provides information to help you solve problems.

## lc

**Learn home row keys**

Select *Learn Home Row* from Lesson 1 menu. Follow on-screen instructions.

**Optional:**

In Open Screen, key each line once single spaced (SS); press ENTER twice to double-space (DS) between 2-line groups. Do not key the numbers.

LEFT FINGERS  4 \ 3 \ 2   1 \   1   2 / 3 / 4  RIGHT FINGERS

Press Space Bar once.

```
1 fff   jjj   fjf   fff   jjj   fjf   fjf   jfj   jfj   fjf
2 ddd   kkk   dkd   ddd   kkk   dkd   dkd   kdk   kdk   dkd
```
Press ENTER twice to **DS**.

```
3 sss   lll   sls   sss   lll   sls   sls   lsl   lsl   sls
4 aaa   ;;;   a;a   aaa   ;;;   a;s   a;a   ;a;   ;a;   a;a
```
**DS**

```
5 ff  jj  ff  jj  fj  fj  fj  dd  kk  dd  kk  dk  dk  dk
6 ss  ll  ss  ll  sl  sl  sl  aa  ;;  aa  ;;  a;  a;  a;
```

```
7 fj  fj  dk  dk  sl  sl  a;  a;  fjdksla;  jfkdls;a
8 fj  fj  dk  dk  sl  sl  a;  a;  fjdksla;  jfkdls;a
```

## ld

**Learn ENTER**

Key each line once; double-space (DS) between lines.

```
 9 f j d k s l a ;
```
**DS**
```
10 ff jj dd kk ss ll aa ;;
```

```
11 fff jjj ddd kkk sss lll aaa
```

```
12 ff jj dd kk ss ll aa ;; fjdksla; fjdksla;
```

## le

**Practice reaches**

each line once; repeat if time permits

```
13 a a; al ak aj s s; sl sk sj d d; dl dk dj
```
**DS**
```
14 j ja js jd jf k ka ks kd kf l la ls ld lf
```

```
15 a; sl a;sl dkfj a;sl dkfj a;sldkfj asdf jk
```

```
16 a; sl a;sl dk fj dkfj a;sl dkfj fkds;a; fj
```

```
17 f ff j jj d dd k kk s ss l ll a aa ; ;; fj
```

```
18 afj; a s d f j k l ; asdf jkl; fdsa jkl; f
```

## APPLICATION

**H6**

Dictate the material shown at the right. Say all text that is shown in bold. Commands are shown in bold and placed in brackets. Remember to pause before and after but not during each command. Punctuation is shown in bold italic. Divider marks are included to help you dictate in phrases. Correct and train the system on any misrecognized words.

**The next [cap] Board of [cap] Directors meeting** | **will be held on May 15** *period* | **Our forestry consultants offered** | **to host the meeting** | **at the [cap] Lodge** | **on [caps on] Prince George Plantation [caps off]** *period* | **The business meeting begins at ten o'clock** *comma* | **and it should last about two hours** *period* | **Your packet of materials for the meeting contains** *colon* **[new line]** |

**Agenda [new line]** |

**Financial Report [new line]** |

**President's Report** | **[move up two lines]** | **[Format that bulleted style]** | **[Move down one line]** | **[Format that bulleted style]** | **Move down one line]** | **[Format that bulleted style]** | **[new paragraph]**

**After the meeting** *comma* | **our hosts will provide lunch** | **and a tour of Prince George** *period* | **We think you will find the tour** | **to be both beneficial and enjoyable** *period* | **Some of the property management techniques** | **that are proposed for our property** | **are in effect at Prince George** *period* |

## APPLICATION

**H7**

*Be creative*

Print and close the document when you have finished.

Dictate two paragraphs completing the following statement. Be sure to include punctuation and appropriate commands.

**If I inherited $50,000 today, I would ....**

**Save speech files**

Each time you exit *Dragon NaturallySpeaking*, the system asks if you want to save your speech files. Click **Yes** if you have trained the system to recognize words you say. Your speech files are automatically backed up every fifth time you save them. If you want to back them up each time you save them, click **User** on the Menu bar, and then click **Backup**.

## 1f •

### Learn i

1. Find i on the illustrated keyboard; find it on your keyboard.
2. Reach up with the *right second* finger.
3. Watch your finger make the reach to i and back to k a few times without striking the keys. Keep fingers curved and wrists low.
4. Try to keep your eyes on the copy as you key.

## 1g •

### Review

each line once; DS between 2-line groups; repeat as time permits

## 1h •

### End the lesson

1. Review and print your Lesson Report.
2. To exit the software:
   - From the Lesson menu, click the **Back** button.
   - Click the **Quit** button on the Main menu.
   - Remove your storage disk. Store materials as directed.

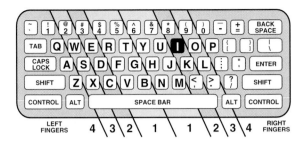

i Reach up with *right second* finger.

```
19  i ik ik ik is is id id if if ill i ail did kid lid
20  i ik aid ail did kid lid lids kids ill aid did ilk

21  id aid aids laid said ids lid skids kiss disk dial
22  id aid ail fail sail jail ails slid dill sill fill


23  as as ask ask ad ad lad lad all all fall fall asks
24  as asks did disk ail fail sail ails jail sill silk
                                                        DS
25  ask dad; dads said; is disk; kiss a lad; salad lid
26  fill a sail; aid a lad; is silk; if a dial; a jail

27  is a disk; dads said; did fall ill; if a lass did;
28  aid lads; if a kid is; a salad lid; kiss a sad dad

29  as ad all ask jak lad fad said ill kill fall disks
30  is all sad lass a lid; is silk; silk disk; dad is;
```

The figure below shows the Lesson Report for Lesson 1. A check mark opposite an exercise indicates that the exercise has been completed. At the bottom of the screen are various buttons. Click the **Print** button to print your Lesson Report. Click the **Graph** button to view the Performance Graph. To get help concerning the Lesson Report, click the **Help** button. If you click the **Back** button here, you return to the Lesson menu.

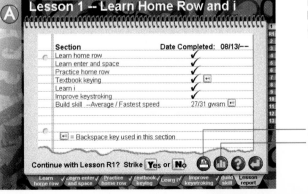

**Figure 1-3** Alphabetic Keyboarding (Lesson Report)

5. Note that after you spell **error**, the system lists numbered alternatives in the Correction box. Say **Select <number>**—in this case, **Select 9**. When you click **OK**, the system will change *era* to *error*. However, it is better to train the system to recognize *error*.

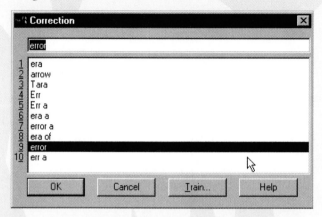

6. With *error* selected, click the **Train** button in the Correction box. The Train Words dialog box appears.

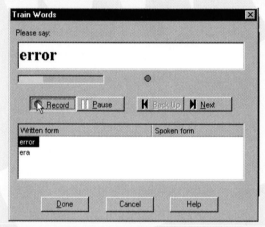

7. Click the **Record** button; then say **error**.
8. Click the **Done** button.
9. The Correction box displays again. Click **OK**.

**Drill 1**

Dictate the list of words or phrases shown at the right.

| | |
|---|---|
| **is this mine** | **find** |
| **is the sky blue** | **clean the grate** |
| **my dog buddy** | **have a great day** |
| **when I tried to dictate** | **surround** |
| **thank you** | **think** |

If the system misrecognizes any of the words or phrases you say, correct and train the system to recognize the words. After you have trained the system on all of the words that were not recognized correctly, dictate the list a second time to see if the system learned and recognized the words correctly. If it missed any, train the system again on the incorrect words.

# Review

## 1Ra

### GETTING started

**Review home row**

1. Open *Keyboarding Pro* software.
2. Click the ↓ next to *Class ID* and select your section. Click your name.
3. Key your password and click **OK**.
4. Click **A** for *Alphabetic* and then select *Lesson R1*.

Key each line once; DS between groups. Repeat if time permits.

Fingers curved and upright

LEFT FINGERS  4 3 2 1   1 2 3 4  RIGHT FINGERS

```
1  f j fjf jj fj fj jf dd kk dd kk dk dk dk

2  s ; s;s ;; s; s; s; aa ;; aa ;; a; a; a;
                                              DS
3  fj dk sl a; fjdksla; jfkdls;a ;a ;s kd j

4  f j fjf d k dkd s l sls a ; fj dk sl a;a

5  a; al ak aj s s; sl sk sj d d; dl dk djd

6  ja js jd jf k ka ks kd kf l la ls ld lfl

7  f fa fad s sa sad f fa fall fall l la lad s sa sad

8  a as ask a ad add j ja jak f fa fall; ask; add jak
```

## 1Rb

**Review i**

each line once; repeat as time permits

```
9   ik ki ki ik is if id il ij ia ij ik is if ji id ia

10  is il ill sill dill fill sid lid ail lid slid jail

11  if is il kid kids ill kid if kids; if a kid is ill

12  is id if ai aid jaks lid sid sis did ail; if lids;
```

## 1Rc

**Review all reaches**

each line once; DS between groups; repeat

```
13  a lass; ask dad; lads ask dad; a fall; fall salads

14  as a fad; ask a lad; a lass; all add; a kid; skids

15  as asks did disk ail fail sail ails jail sill silk

16  ask dad; dads said; is disk; kiss a lad; salad lid

17  aid a lad; if a kid is; a salad lid; kiss sad dads

18  as ad all ask jak lad fad kids ill kill fall disks
```

# Correct Text and Train the System

Errors occur when you dictate text. In some cases, they occur because you did not say what you intended to say. Therefore, you edit the text and revise it to convey the meaning you intended. In Lesson H1, you learned to correct errors by immediately saying **scratch that** and then saying the words that you intended to say. Another way of correcting errors that you make in speaking is to select the incorrect text (say **select** and specify the text to be selected or actually select the text with the keyboard or the mouse), and then supply the correct text (by dictating or keying it).

In other cases, you said the words you intended to say, but errors occurred because the system did not recognize those words and substituted incorrect ones. You can use the **scratch that** command to remove the incorrect words and then repeat the correct ones. However, if the system does not recognize what you are saying, it is likely to substitute incorrect words again. In this case, you not only have to correct the errors, you also have to train the system to recognize the words you are saying so it will not continue to make the same errors the next time you say those words. Note the following examples of recognition errors.

**Distinguish between editing errors and recognition errors.**

| What was dictated | What the system thought was dictated |
|---|---|
| did I make an error | did I make an era |
| is the sky blue | is this guy blue |
| my dog buddy | by dog bloody |
| when I tried to dictate | when I tried a bit take |
| thank you | think |

**NEW FUNCTION**

**To correct recognition errors and train the system:**

1. Say **select** and the misrecognized words as soon as the error occurs. Then repeat the correct words.

2. If the error is not corrected, say **correct** and the misrecognized words. For example, say **correct era** or say **correct this guy blue**.

3. The Correction window appears with the misrecognized text shown.

4. In the first example, no options show for correcting the text (see below). Spell **error**. (Note that you could also key **error** in the Correction box.)

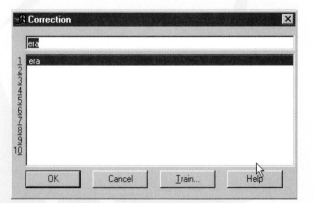

# E and N

## 2a ●

### GETTING started

1. Open *Keyboarding Pro* software.
2. Insert your student data disk into Drive A.
3. From the Log In dialog box, select your section and then your name.
4. Key your password and click **OK**.
5. Click **A** for *Alphabetic* and then select *Lesson 2*.

### SKILLBUILDING WARMUP

Home position

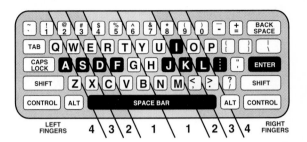

1 ff dd ss aa ff dd ss aa jj kk ll ;; fj dk sl a; a;

2 fj dk sl a; fjdksla; a;sldkfj fj dk sl a; fjdksla;

3 aa ss dd ff jj kk ll ;; aa ss dd ff jj kk ll ;; a;

4 ki ik ki ik di si li ia is if ji id ia il ik li id

## 2b ●

**Review home keys and i**
each line once; DS between groups

5 ff ss kk dd fs ks ds sk lf as fa ll kk ff lk fl kl

6 as as ad ad fad fad al all fall fall lass jak jaks

7 a lass; ask dad; all lads; add all; all fall; dads

8 a lad; a lad asks; lads ask dad; adds all; ask all

9 as as ask ask ad ad add dad a ja jak jak ad ad add

10 ki ik ki ik di si li ia is if ji id ia il ik li id

11 as is; if ad; aid jak lid fad sad jak ail if a lad

12 aid laid said did jak flak is id if dial disk jaks

13 if a lad; a jail; is silk; is ill; a dais; did aid

14 aid jak lid fad sad jak ail if a lad; as if; if ad

Additional commands that you will use frequently are navigation, formatting, and editing commands.

| | |
|---|---|
| **Select** | **Move** |
| **Go** | **Cap** |
| **Delete** | **Caps on** |
| **Bold** | **Caps off** |
| **Underline** | **Numeral + number** |

The commands that you will be giving the system in the following exercises will be placed in brackets [**Wake up**] to distinguish commands from text to be dictated. The brackets serve as a reminder to you to pause before and after—but not during—a command. Punctuation will be italicized so that you will remember to dictate the punctuation marks.

**Drill 2**

Dictate the material at the right. You will give some commands during the dictation. Then you will go back and give additional commands after the text has been entered.

Remember that you can say [**scratch that**] if you want to remove words you have just said and dictate them again.

Repeat Drill 2 to see if you can improve your accuracy.

[Wake up]

The new wellness and fitness center will be located | on the south side of the campus *period* | The [cap] Foundation is currently in the process of buying | a significant amount of property for this facility *period* | A new [caps on] Greek Village [caps off] will be located | adjacent to the wellness and fitness center *period* [new paragraph] |

Three major problems have been encountered *colon* [new line]

Much of the property in that area | has environmental contamination *period* [new line] |

Property values have escalated | since the project was announced *period* [new line] |

Acquiring property has taken more time | than we originally expected it to take *period* |

[move up two lines] *numeral* 1 *period* [Move down one line] *numeral* 2 *period* [Move down one line] *numeral* 3 *period*

[Go to sleep]

**APPLICATION**

**H5**

*Be creative*

Turn your microphone on. Complete each of the statements at the right. Add additional sentences if you wish.

After you complete Application H5, turn your microphone off and exit the system.

My favorite things to do during the summer are …

The things I like to do least are …

My idea of a great vacation is …

## Learn e and n

Read carefully the "Standard procedures for learning new keyreaches" at the right. Use them to learn new keyreaches in this lesson and in lessons that follow.

### Standard procedures for learning new keyreaches

1. Find the new key on the illustrated keyboard; then find it on your keyboard.
2. Study the illustrated keyreach.
3. Watch your finger make the reach to the new key a few times. Keep other fingers curved in home position. For an upward reach, straighten the finger slightly; for a downward reach, curve it a bit more.
4. Key each line twice (slowly, then faster).
5. Repeat if time permits. Work to eliminate pauses.

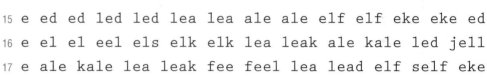

**e** Reach *up* with *left second* finger.

**n** Reach *down* with *right first* finger.

e

15 e ed ed led led lea lea ale ale elf elf eke eke ed

16 e el el eel els elk elk lea leak ale kale led jell

17 e ale kale lea leak fee feel lea lead elf self eke

n

18 n nj nj an an and and fan fan and kin din fin land

19 n an fan in fin and land sand din fans sank an sin

20 n in ink sink inn kin skin an and land in din dink

**all reaches learned**

21 den end fen ken dean dens ales fend fens keen knee

22 if in need; feel ill; as an end; a lad and a lass;

23 and sand; a keen idea; as a sail sank; is in jail;

## Improve keystroking

each line once; repeat the drill

### End the lesson

1. Print the Lesson Report.
2. Exit *Alphabetic*; remove the disk and store.
3. Follow these procedures for the remaining lessons.

24 de de ed ed led fed ade lea lead ale fale eke deal

25 de jell sake lake led self sea fled sled jell feel

26 jn jn nj nj in fan fin an; ink sin and inn an skin

27 jn din sand land nail sank and dank skin sans sink

28 if fin in end is den fen as ink lee fed an jak and

29 in nine inns; if an end; need an idea; seek a fee;

30 add a line; and safe; asks a lass; sail in a lake;

31 dine in an inn; fake jade; lend fans; as sand sank

## Understanding the results box

Commands are also shown in the results box, but they are executed rather than entered in the document. If the system is taking extended time to analyze text in the results box, you can click the red button in the box to stop the processing.

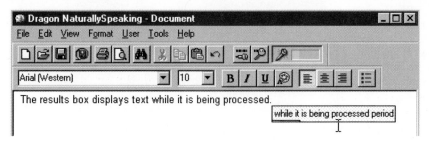

### Guides for giving commands:

- Pause slightly before giving a command so that the system will not mistake the command for dictation. Give the entire command without any pauses.
- Watch the results box on the toolbar to see if the command was recognized.
- Say **scratch that** if the command was not recognized and you want to change the action the system took.
- Pause slightly after a command before resuming dictation.

Commands must be valid. If you are not sure that a command you are giving the system is valid, refer to the *What Can I Say?* section of Help. Each section will give you a long list of valid commands.

If you have trouble getting the system to recognize your commands as commands rather than as dictation, use the Command hotkey. Hold down the CTRL key as you say the command. This hotkey disables dictation and forces the system to recognize the words you said as a command. ■

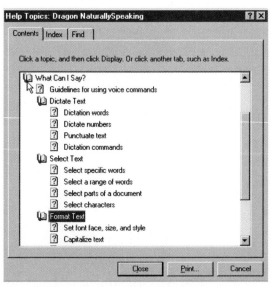

In this brief module, you will learn to use a few of the most common commands. So far, you have been introduced to several dictation commands.

|                |              |
|----------------|--------------|
| New line       | Wake up      |
| New paragraph  | Go to sleep  |
| Scratch that   |              |

# LESSON 3

## Review

### 3a ●

**GETTING started**

Follow the steps on p. 7 to open *Keyboarding Pro.*

Key each line at a slow, steady pace; strike and release each key quickly. Key each line again at a faster pace.

### 3b ●

**Master keys learned**

key the lines once SS; DS between groups

**Technique goals**

- fingers curved
- wrists low, but not resting
- eyes on copy

### 3c ●

**Review stroking techniques**

each 2-line group twice SS

```
home 1 ad ads lad fad dad as ask fa la lass jak jaks alas
   n 2 an fan and land fan flan sans sand sank flank dank
   i 3 is id ill dill if aid ail fail did kid ski lid ilk
 all 4 ade alas nine else fife ken; jell ink jak inns if;
```

Eyes on copy; feet flat on floor

```
home  5 a s d f j k l ; as df jk l; asdf jkl; a; sl dk fj;
      6 a as ask ad add fad dad all fall jaks lass sad sak

   i  7 i ik ik ik is is id id il il if if ail kid did lid
      8 i ik aid did lid kids aid ail sill fill ails fails

   e  9 e ed ed el el led led els els elk elk lea lea leak
     10 e ale lea fee lea elf eke lead feel leaf deal kale

   n 11 jn jn nj nj in fan fin an; din ink sin and inn an;
     12 n de den end fen an an and and ken keen fens deans
```

**home row:** fingers curved and upright

```
13 jak lad as lass dad sad lads fad fall la ask ad as
14 asks add jaks dads a lass ads flak adds sad as lad
```

**upward reaches:** straighten fingers slightly; return quickly to home position

```
15 fed die led ail kea lei did ale fife silk leak lie
16 sea lid deal sine desk lie ale like life idea jail
```

**double letters:** don't hurry when stroking double letters

```
17 fee jell less add inn seek fall alee lass keel all
18 dill dell see fell eel less all add kiss seen sell
```

# Dictation, Punctuation, and Commands

Dictation consists of the words that you speak in the microphone and that the system will print in your document. Remember that the system has to recognize what you are saying in order to enter it correctly in your document. The system will enter punctuation if you dictate the punctuation marks as words. The system will also execute standard commands if it can distinguish the commands from your dictation. Commands are used both in dictating and in controlling the operating system and applications of your computer.

> **Guides for dictating (speaking):**
> - Position the microphone at the corner of your mouth about a thumb's width from your mouth so that your breathing is not picked up as words.
> - Try to dictate the way you speak normally—use your normal pace, volume, and manner of speaking.
> - Dictate phrases or sentences rather than isolated words with pauses between them.
> - Enunciate each word clearly, but don't distort the way you say words.
> - Dictate punctuation as words.

**Drill 1**

1. Open *Dragon NaturallySpeaking* and turn your microphone on.

2. Read the material in bold in thought phrases. The phrases are separated by a dividing mark (|) to help you learn to talk in continuous phrases. Read all of the words between the dividers without pausing.

**The accuracy of my dictation will improve** | **if I say phrases rather than isolated words** *period* | **The system can use** | **the phrases that I say** | **to help determine exactly what I am saying** *period* | **If I make a mistake** *comma* | **I can use simple commands** | **to correct the mistake during dictation** *period* | **Another option is to correct the errors** | **during the editing process** | **after I complete the dictation** *period*

Pause the microphone [**Go to sleep**] and look at the paragraph that is keyed on the screen. If you have errors, try dictating the paragraph again to see if you will have fewer recognition errors. You can expect to have a large number of errors until you get accustomed to the system, and the system learns to recognize your speech.

### The results box

*Dragon NaturallySpeaking* displays dictated text while it analyzes the text in a small window. After the text is processed, *Dragon NaturallySpeaking* enters the text in the document. You may notice that during the processing, *Dragon NaturallySpeaking* may change some of the words before entering them in the document. You can adjust the length of time the results box is displayed on the screen (on the Tools menu, click **Options**). For now, just use the defaults.

## 3d

3d ●

### Practice easy words and phrases

Key each line at an easy speed; do not key the vertical rules separating phrases.

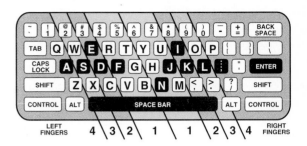

LEFT FINGERS    4 \ 3 \ 2 \ 1   1 \ 2 \ 3 \ 4    RIGHT FINGERS

**easy words**

19 if is as an ad el and did die eel fin fan elf lens
20 as ask id lid kid and ade aid el eel feel ilk skis

21 ail fail aid did ken ale led an flan inn inns alas
22 le le led led ad ad fad fad al al all all fall ale

23 as as ask ask ad ad lad lad id id lid lid kid kids
24 and and land land el el elf elf self self ail nail

**easy phrases**

25 ask a lass;|as a dad|a fall fad|as all ask;|sad ad
26 as a jak;|as a lass|ask dad|as a lad;|as a fall ad

27 is as if;|is a disk|aid all kids|did ski|is a silk
28 skis skid|is a kid|aid did fail|if a dial|laid lid

29 as kale|sees a lake|elf fled|as a deal|sell a sled
30 sell a lead|seal a deal|feel a leaf|as a jade sale

3e ●

### Practice common reaches

each line once
The reach is identified in the first two letters of each line.

31 ea sea lea seas deal leaf leak lead leas flea keas
32 as ask lass ease as asks ask ask sass as alas seas
33 sa sad sane sake sail sale sans safe sad said sand
34 le sled lead flee fled ale flea lei dale kale leaf
35 el eel eld elf sell self el dell fell elk els jell
36 in fin inn inks dine sink fine fins kind kine lain
37 an and fan dean elan flan land lane lean sand sane

**Drill 1,** *continued*

San Francisco **comma California** pause **new line** pause

Sacramento **comma California** pause **new line** pause

Flagstaff **comma Arizona** pause **new line** pause

Phoenix **comma Arizona** pause **new line** pause

Minneapolis **comma Minnesota** pause **new line** pause

St. Paul **comma Minnesota** pause **new line** pause

Seattle **comma Washington** pause **new line** pause

Spokane **comma Washington** pause **new line** pause

Use the same procedures to add two cities of your choice in Texas. Then for fun, say one or two sentences about one of the cities listed.

**[Go to sleep]**

## APPLICATION

Dictate the paragraph at the right. For now, ignore the errors in your document.

Text that you read is shown in bold. Punctuation is in bold and italic. Commands are in brackets; pause before and after but not during each command.

Try to read the copy in thought phrases. Say all of the material up to the divider line without pausing. This will help to improve your dictation accuracy.

**[Wake up]**

**Learning to dictate can be both fun and frustrating** *period* | **The fun part is experimenting with a new system** *period* | **The frustrating part is seeing** | **the number of errors that appear in the copy** | **when the system is learning to recognize the words you say** *period* | **Practice and training the system** | **are the keys to success in speech recognition** *period* | **[new paragraph]**

**[Go to sleep]**

Close your file. Do not save it.

Turn your microphone off and exit *Dragon NaturallySpeaking* (**File**; **Exit**).

# Left Shift, H, T, Period

## 4a ●

### GETTING started

each line twice SS; keep eyes on copy

home row 1 al as ads lad dad fad jak fall lass asks fads all;

e/i/n 2 ed ik jn in knee end nine line sine lien dies leis

all reaches 3 see a ski; add ink; fed a jak; is an inn; as a lad

easy 4 an dial id is an la lake did el ale fake is land a

## 4b ●

### Learn left SHIFT and h

each line twice SS

Follow the "Standard procedures for learning new keyreaches" on p. 8 for all remaining reaches.

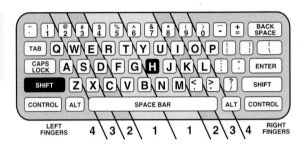

LEFT FINGERS   4  3  2  1     1  2  3  4   RIGHT FINGERS

**left shift** Reach *down* with *left fourth* (little) finger; shift, strike, release.

**h** Reach to *left* with *right first* finger.

### left shift

5 J Ja Ja Jan Jan Jane Jana Ken Kass Lee Len Nan Ned

6 and Ken and Lena and Jake and Lida and Nan and Ida

7 Ina Kale; Jill Lask; Nels Insa; Ken Jalk; Lin Nial

### h

8 h hj hj he he she she hen aha ash had has hid shed

9 h hj ha hie his half hand hike dash head sash shad

10 aha hi hash heal hill hind lash hash hake dish ash

### all reaches learned

11 Nels Kane and Jake Jenn; she asked Hi and Ina Linn

12 Lend Lana and Jed a dish; I fed Lane and Jess Kane

13 I see Jake Kish and Lash Hess; Isla and Helen hike

## 4c ●

### Practice ENTER

Key the drill once; DS and repeat. Use fluid, unhurried movements.

**enter**: return without looking up

14 Nan had a sale;

15 He did see Hal;

16 Lee has a desk;

17 Ina hid a dish;

**Drill 1,** *continued*

6. The following lines contain words, phrases, punctuation, and commands that you will dictate. The system will recognize some of the words and get them correct. Some of the words may be incorrect. As you practice using *Dragon NaturallySpeaking* and train the system to recognize your unique speech patterns, you will get more and more of your words correct. Do not worry about the incorrect words at this point. However, if you would like to change something you just said, you may do so by saying **scratch that**. The Scratch That command works the same way as the **Undo** command does in *WordPerfect*. Now, try saying in a natural conversational tone *only* the words shown in bold.

**I have the following books** pause **colon** pause **new line** pause

**History** pause **new line** pause

**Algebra** pause **new line** pause

**English** pause **new line** pause

**Biology** pause **scratch that** pause

**Science** pause **new line** pause

**Accounting** pause **new line** pause

**Go to sleep**

*Go to sleep* is the command used to pause the microphone. To activate it, say **wake up**. In this short exercise, you used three features: continuous dictation, punctuation, and commands. Notice that you paused before and after giving system commands, but not during the command—**new line** should be said as though the two words were one word. You may have errors in your document just as you made many errors when you were learning to key. Soon, you will learn to correct errors and train your system. Now try dictating more text using the same procedures you just followed.

**Wake up**   Check to see that your microphone is now on.

**We visited five states** pause **colon** pause **new line**   Remember to pause and say *new line* after each state.

**California**

**Arizona**

**Minnesota**

**Washington**

**Texas** pause **new paragraph** Note the double space between lines.

**We visited two cities in each state colon** pause **new paragraph**

> Note that some states may display as 2-letter abbreviations rather than words. ■

*(continued on next page)*

## Learn t and . (period)
each line twice SS

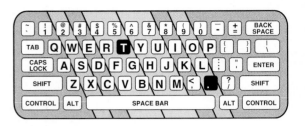

**Period:** Space once after a period that follows an initial or an abbreviation. To increase readability, space twice after a period that ends a sentence.

**t** Reach *up* with *left first* finger.

**. (period)** Reach *down* with *right third* finger.

t

18 t tf tf aft aft left fit fat fete tiff tie the tin
19 tf at at aft lit hit tide tilt tint sits skit this
20 hat kit let lit ate sit flat tilt thin tale tan at

. (period)

21 .l .l l.l fl. fl. L. L. Neal and J. N. List hiked.
22 Hand J. H. Kass a fan.  Jess did.  I need an idea.
23 Jane said she has a tan dish; Jae and Lee need it.

**all reaches learned**

24 I did tell J. K. that Lt. Li had left.  He is ill.
25 Lee and Ken left at ten; the jet had left at nine.
26 I see Lila and Ilene at tea.  Jae Kane ate at ten.

## Practice new reaches
each line once; DS between 2-line groups

reach review

27 tf .l hj ft ki de jh tf ik ed hj de ft ki l. tf ik
28 elf eel left is sis fit till dens ink has delt ink

DS

i/t

29 it if id fit sit let hat at tie let lit hit id lid
30 if it|if it|it has|it has|if it is|if it is|it has

h/e

31 he he she she held held shed shed ash ash has hash
32 she had; held sale; has jade; had jade; he had ash

shift

33 Hal and Nel; Jade dishes; Kale has half; Jed hides
34 Hi Ken; Helen and Jen hike; Jan has a jade; Ken is

all

35 Ina lies in the sand at ten; she needs a fast tan.
36 Jan asks if I had all the tea that Len said I had.

After you have viewed all 16 items, close the window. A new document window will be available for you to begin using *Dragon NaturallySpeaking*. Close *Dragon NaturallySpeaking* by clicking the Close button ⊠ in the top right corner of the window so that you can review how to start the system.

**Drill I**

1. Click **Programs** on the Start menu; then click **Dragon NaturallySpeaking for WordPerfect Office 2000**, and then **Dragon NaturallySpeaking**.

2. Select your name and click **Open** when the Open User dialog box displays. (If you are the only user, *Dragon NaturallySpeaking* skips this step.)

3. A Tip of the Day displays unless this feature has been discontinued. Read the tip; then close it.

4. The *Dragon NaturallySpeaking* document window displays.

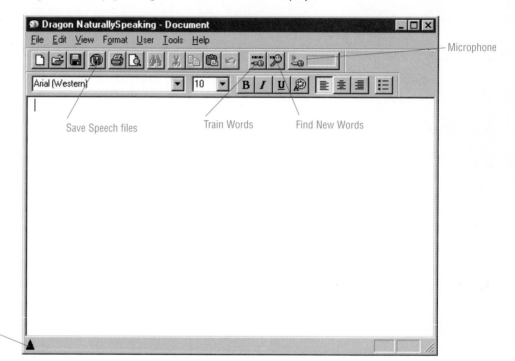

Note that the *Dragon NaturallySpeaking* word processor is very similar to any *Windows*-based word processor that you may have used. Click each command on the menu bar to become familiar with the options available on the drop-down menus. You will recognize most of the icons on the toolbar. The *Dragon NaturallySpeaking* icons are labeled on the illustration above.

5. Click the **Microphone** icon to turn it on. The status window turns yellow. You can pause the microphone temporarily by saying **go to sleep**; to turn it back on, say **wake up**.

# R, Right Shift, C, O

## 5a
### GETTING started
each line twice SS; keep eyes on copy

| | | |
|---|---|---|
| home keys | 1 | a; ad add al all lad fad jak ask lass fall jak lad |
| t/h/i/n | 2 | the hit tin nit then this kith dint tine hint thin |
| left shift/. | 3 | I need ink.  Li has an idea.  Hit it.  I see Kate. |
| all reaches | 4 | Jeff ate at ten; he left a salad dish in the sink. |

## 5b

### Learn r and right SHIFT
each line twice SS

**r** Reach *up* with *left first* finger.

**right shift** Reach *down* with *right fourth* finger; shift, strike, release.

## 5c

### Practice techniques
each line once, striving for the goals listed below:

Lines 14-15: smoothly, without pauses

Lines 16-17: without looking at hands or keyboard

Lines 18-20: without pausing or looking up from the copy

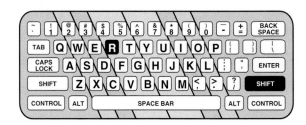

r

5 r rf rf riff riff fir fir rid ire jar air sir lair

6 rf rid ark ran rat are hare art rant tire dirt jar

7 rare dirk ajar lark rain kirk share hart rail tart

right shift

8 D D Dan Dan Dale Ti Sal Ted Ann Ed Alf Ada Sid Fan

9 and Sid and Dina and Allen and Eli and Dean and Ed

10 Ed Dana; Dee Falk; Tina Finn; Sal Alan; Anna Deeds

all reaches learned

11 Jake and Ann hiked in the sand; Asa set the tents.

12 Fred Derr and Rae Tira dined at the Tree Art Fair.

13 Alan asked Dina if Neil and Reed had left at nine.


14 Kent said that half the field is idle in the fall.

15 Lana said she did sail her skiff in the dark lake.

16 All is still as Sarah and I fish here in the rain.

17 I still see a red ash tree that fell in the field.

18 I had a kale salad;

19 Elia ate his steak;

20 and Dina drank tea.

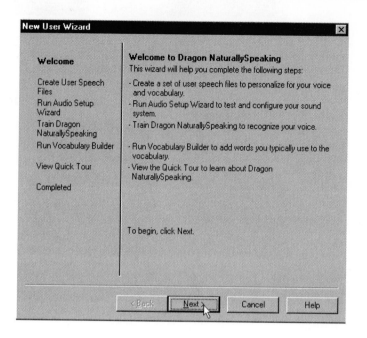

1. *Create User Speech Files.* You will key your name and the system will set up files for your use.

2. *Run Audio Setup Wizard.* This wizard tests your system sound and your microphone to adjust the input volume and the quality of your sound.

3. *Train Dragon NaturallySpeaking.* This step takes at least 45 minutes and must be completed at one sitting. Training is in two stages. The first stage requires you to read a few paragraphs while the system makes some adjustments to your voice. The second stage requires you to read aloud for at least 30 minutes from copy presented on the screen while *Dragon NaturallySpeaking* adjusts to your voice. Then the system processes your input to prepare itself to recognize your words as you speak them.

4. *Run Vocabulary Builder (can be delayed).* Vocabulary Builder increases your accuracy by personalizing your vocabulary to words you normally use, including words related to the subject area in which you dictate, such as law, medicine, construction, or any other field. Vocabulary Builder processes documents that you have authored and stored on the system to personalize your vocabulary.

5. *View the Quick Tour.* This step requires about 15 minutes. Read the information in the left column; then click the **Play** button at the bottom of the picture. When the clip has completed playing, click the arrow button next to Menu at the top of the left column to move to the next topic.

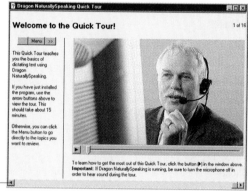

Play button

## 5d ●

**Learn c and o**
each line twice SS

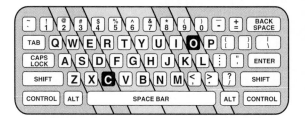

**c** Reach *down* with *left second* finger.

**o** Reach *up* with right *third* finger.

c

21 c c cd cd cad cad can can tic ice sac cake cat sic
22 clad chic cite cheek clef sick lick kick dice rice
23 call acid hack jack lack lick cask crack clan cane

o

24 o ol ol old old of off odd ode or ore oar soar one
25 ol sol sold told dole do doe lo doll sol solo odor
26 onto door toil lotto soak fort hods foal roan load

**all reaches learned**

27 Carlo Rand can call Rocco; Cole can call Doc Cost.
28 Trina can ask Dina if Nick Corl has left; Joe did.
29 Case sent Carole a nice skirt; it fits Lorna Rich.

## 5e ●

**Practice new reaches**
each line once SS; key at a steady pace

o/r
30 or or for for nor nor ore ore oar oar roe roe sore
31 a rose|her or|he or|he rode|or for|a door|her doll

i/t
32 is is tis tis it it fit fit tie tie this this lits
33 it is|it is|it is this|it is this|it sits|tie fits

e/n
34 en en end end ne ne need need ken ken kneel kneels
35 lend the|lend the|at the end|at the end|need their

c/o
36 ch ch check check ck ck hack lack jack co co cones
37 the cot|the cot|a dock|a dock|a jack|a jack|a cone

all reaches
38 Jack and Rona did frost nine of the cakes at last.
39 Jo can ice her drink if Tess can find her a flask.
40 Ask Jean to call Fisk at noon; he needs her notes.

**Getting started**

# Introduction to Dragon NaturallySpeaking

*Dragon NaturallySpeaking* is a continuous speech recognition program that will enable you to operate your computer system by using voice commands and to dictate documents to your computer. Just as you had to learn and practice how to use the keyboard to input information into your computer, you will have to learn and practice how to use your voice and a microphone to input information into your computer with speech recognition. Learning *Dragon NaturallySpeaking* will be easy and fun, but it takes much practice before you will be accurate and productive using it. The following lessons are designed to introduce you to basic concepts and applications of *Dragon NaturallySpeaking*.

The document "Speech Recognition Software—An Evolving Input Technology" provides you with an overview of different types of speech recognition programs and how they can be used effectively. Having read this white paper, you should have a better understanding of why you have to prepare the system to recognize your voice and how you can improve the accuracy of the system's recognition of the words you speak.

**Prepare Dragon NaturallySpeaking to recognize your voice**

1. Check to see that you have a microphone plugged into your system.

2. Start *Dragon NaturallySpeaking*. (Click **Start**, then **Programs**, then **Dragon NaturallySpeaking for WordPerfect Office 2000**, and then **Dragon NaturallySpeaking**.)

3. Use the New User Wizard to set up *Dragon NaturallySpeaking* to recognize your voice.

    • If you get a Welcome to *Dragon NaturallySpeaking* screen, you are the first user. Follow the onscreen directions to prepare *Dragon NaturallySpeaking* to recognize your voice.

    • If you get a blank screen or an Open User dialog box, someone else has used the system. Select *User* and then *New* to access the New User Wizard.

**Train the system**

The New User Wizard will lead you through five steps to prepare *Dragon NaturallySpeaking* for your use. You should follow the directions on the screen carefully.

# W, Comma, B, P

## 6a ● 8'

### GETTING started

each line twice; avoid pauses

Note suggested minutes for practices shown in headings.

## 6b ● 12'

**Learn w and , (comma)**
each line twice

**w** Reach *up* with *left third* finger.

**, (comma)** Reach *down* with *right second* finger.

## 6c ● 5'

**Improve techniques**
each line once; DS between groups; repeat

### SKILLBUILDING WARMUP

| | | |
|---|---|---|
| home row | 1 | a ad as lad las fad sad; jak flask fall jaks salad |
| n/i/t | 2 | in tin nit nil its tan din tie ten tine fins stein |
| c/h/r/o | 3 | code herd rode cold hock hark roll rock ache chore |
| all reaches | 4 | Holt can see Dane at ten; Jill sees Frank at nine. |

**Comma:** Space once after a comma.

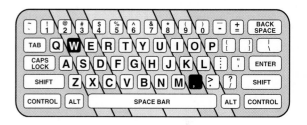

**w**

5 w ws ws was was wan wit low win jaw wilt wink wolf

6 ow wow how owl howl owe owed row cow cowl new knew

7 wide sown wild town went jowl wait white down walk

**, (comma)**

8 k, k, k, irk, ilk, ask, oak, ark, lark, jak, rock,

9 skis, a dock, a fork, a lock, a fee, a tie, a fan,

10 Jan, Lee, Ed, and Dan saw Nan, Kate, Len, and Ted.

**all reaches learned**

11 Win, Lew, Drew, and Walt will walk to West Willow.

12 Ask Ho, Al, and Jared to read the code; it is new.

13 The window, we think, was closed; we felt no wind.

**shift keys:** shift; strike key; release both quickly

14 Fiji, Don, Cara, and Ron will see East Creek soon.

15 Kane Losh and Janet Hart will join Nan in Rio Ono.

**double letters**

16 Renee took a class at noon; call her at Lann Hall.

17 Ed and Anne saw three deer flee across Wood Creek.

### Editing and Formatting Documents

Documents can be edited and formatted during the dictation process or after the dictation has been completed. Using a combination of voice, keystrokes, and mouse clicks produces the most efficient editing results. Editing is a critical skill that often requires more time than dictation.

### Efficiency and Effectiveness

A tremendous amount of hype exists about the productivity and accuracy of speech recognition software. Users—particularly those associated with the vendors or trainers—frequently brag about input at 160 words per minute with accuracy rates above 95 percent. Generally, they have trained the system extensively and are experienced dictators. They rarely talk about the input source material or about the total productivity time.

Most of the accuracy rate information comes from reading from written copy. The accuracy rate produced from reading is dramatically higher than the accuracy rate produced from composing and dictating to the system. The real test of accuracy is the rate achieved by composing and dictating directly to the system. Reading is an excellent technique for initial learning, but the most crucial skills that need to be learned to use speech recognition software effectively are composition and dictation skills.

Reports are available from a number of studies conducted to determine the efficiency and effectiveness of speech recognition programs. However, many of these studies used limited samples and were not conducted under stringent testing conditions.

Results from independent laboratory tests indicate average accuracy rates of 87 to 91 percent, which is not acceptable for general usage. The process of editing a document with a high percentage of errors is painstaking and time-consuming. Some users, however, are able to achieve 98 percent accuracy consistently. Some laboratory tests compared keyboard input with speech recognition input. If the typist had average keying skill, the time required to produce 100 percent accurate documents was less than the time required to accomplish the same task with voice recognition. The time that matters in the business world is the time that it takes to complete a document with 100 percent accuracy. Some of the laboratory tests reported differences in accuracy rates based on gender in all of the speech recognition programs tested. The average accuracy rate was higher for females than for males.[4]

Several recent studies indicate somewhat higher rates of accuracy for the latest software versions depending on system capabilities and microphone quality. However, vendors released these reports.

## Successful Applications

Some applications of speech recognition technology are more advanced than other applications. Professionals in the medical field have extensive experience with dictation systems and with speech recognition systems. Large dictionaries have been built and incorporated in speech recognition programs for many medical specialties—radiology, pathology, orthopedics, internal medicine, and emergency medicine. Special editions have also been developed for the legal profession.

## Ergonomic Considerations

Speech recognition software offers tremendous potential for individuals who are keyboard impaired. Many people think speech recognition is the answer to carpal tunnel problems. However, extensive, repetitive dictation may be even more harmful to the voice than repetitive motion is to the wrists. Care needs to be taken to avoid these harmful effects. Another key concern is the noise pollution that is likely to occur now that most employees work in an open office environment.

### The Future of Speech Recognition

The technology will continue to evolve and mature. Productivity and accuracy will increase and so will general acceptance of the technology. While it is unlikely that voice recognition will replace keyboarding in the near future, it is likely that it will complement the use of the keyboard and the mouse.

Learning to use speech recognition software effectively is a very good investment of time. Learning to compose and dictate effectively may be an even better investment of time. Oral communication skills are skills for the future.

---

[4]Greg Alwang and Craig Stinson, "Speech Recognition: Finding Its Voice," *PC Magazine* (October 20, 1998).

## 6d ● 12'

**Learn b and p**
each line twice

**b** Reach *down* with *left first* finger.

**p** Reach *up* with *right fourth* (little) finger.

## 6e ● 13'

**Build technique**
each line once; keep hand movement to a minimum

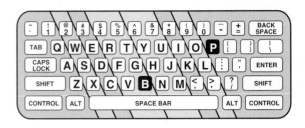

**b**

18  b bf bf biff boff bit bid bib bird boa ban bon bow
19  be rib fib sob dob cob bob crib lab slab fobs blob
20  born oboe blab bribe able bode belt bath bide both

**p**

21  p p; p; pa pa; pal pal pan pad par pen pep pap per
22  pa pa; lap lap; nap nap; hep ape spa asp leap clap
23  span park paper pelt tips soap pane pops rope ripe

**all reaches learned**

24  Barb and Bob wrapped a pepper in paper and ribbon.
25  Rip, Joann, and Dick were all closer to the flash.
26  Bo will be pleased to see Japan; he works in Oslo.

all reaches
27  ws ws ,k ,k bf bf p; p; ol ol cd cd rf rf nj nj ed
28  ah was kid fab fab pal for tic poll cod row jak to

s/w
29  ws ws lows now we shown win cow wow wire jowl when
30  Wes saw an owl in the willow tree in the old lane.

b/p
31  bf bf fib rob bid ;p p; pal pen pot nap hop cap bp
32  Rob has both pans in a bin at the back of the pen.

33  Dick owns a dock at this lake; he paid Ken for it.
34  Jane also kept a pair of owls, a hen, and a snake.

all reaches
35  Blair soaks a bit of the corn, as he did in Japan.
36  I blend the cocoa in the bowl when I work for Leo.

37  Albert, Lisa Planke, and I saw a few hidden flaws.
38  Karla has the first slot; she wants to win for Jo.

Four vendors of speech-recognition software currently lead the market:

*L&H Voice Xpress*™
*Dragon NaturallySpeaking*™
*IBM ViaVoice*™
*Phillips FreeSpeech*™

This white paper focuses on

- *L&H Voice Xpress* because it is supported by Microsoft and is completely integrated into *Microsoft Word*

- *Dragon NaturallySpeaking* because it is bundled with the *Corel WordPerfect Office 2000* suite

## Common Features

Both software programs share common features. Although slightly different terminology may be used to describe them, the features really are very similar. Installing the software is only the beginning of the startup process.

### Audio and Microphone Setup

Both programs are speaker dependent; therefore, the microphone and speakers have to be adjusted and tuned for each speaker. Correct tuning and positioning of the microphone are just as important to speech recognition as correct posture and keying techniques are to keyboarding.

### Enrollment

Training the software is part of the startup process. This process consists of developing and storing a speech profile or voiceprint for each speaker. The initial enrollment requires the speaker to read into the microphone from text provided on the screen by the system. The amount of time varies from 30 minutes to more than an hour. When the reading has been completed, the system then processes and stores the individual's speech files. This profile is then used each time the speaker dictates text into the system. Depending on how clearly the speaker enunciates and how easily the system recognizes the words the user says, enrollment or training may have to be repeated several times. Training is an important way to increase accuracy.

### Multimedia Tours and Tutorials

Both programs offer video tours of the software to introduce the new user to the features of the system including how to position the microphone. Online help including demonstrations of what to do and what not to do also makes it easier to learn how to use the software.

### System Training Features

When saying new words that the system does not recognize, the speaker has to stop and train the system to recognize those words. Training consists of keying or selecting a word and then pronouncing it for the system. Both software packages also have features to increase the system's vocabulary. Virtually all users agree that the more you use and train the system and build the vocabulary, the more accurate your dictation will be. In his review of *ViaVoice Gold* and *Dragon NaturallySpeaking Preferred*, Gregg Keizer recommended not to even think about using speech recognition software unless you are ready to spend time training, working with, and retraining the application. He indicated it takes a month or more of daily use to see accuracy rates rise.[3]

### Continuous Speech Input

Users speak in a normal fashion without pauses between words. In fact, accuracy increases when the speaker uses long phrases or whole sentences because the context helps the system to recognize and select the correct word. All systems require the speaker to use words to indicate punctuation marks.

### Commands

The speaker has to help the system distinguish between words that are dictated and words that are commands used to tell the system what to do. This is accomplished by pausing before a command, then dictating the entire command without a pause, and pausing after the command has been given. A variety of commands exist. Some commands are designed to control application software. For example, *L&H Voice Xpress* is completely integrated into *Microsoft Word* and can be used to give any command on the menu system, such as Close File or Print.

Many global commands are used for editing, formatting, and navigating through a document. They are accomplished in much the same way that they would be executed from the keyboard or the mouse. For example, words are selected before a formatting characteristic such as bold, italics, or underline is applied. The same is true with dictating a command. The user tells the system to go to and select a word or words and apply bold to the selected text.

---

[3]Gregg Keizer, *CNET Reviews*, <www.cnet.com/Contents/Reviews/Compare/speech/ss01.html> (April 14, 1998).

# Review

## 7a ● 8'

### GETTING started

each line twice; begin new lines promptly

### SKILLBUILDING WARMUP

| | | |
|---|---|---|
| home row | 1 | fa la la; a sad lad; jaks fall; a lass had a salad |
| 1st row | 2 | Ann Bascan and Cabal Naban nabbed a cab in Canada. |
| 3d row | 3 | Rip went to a water show with either Pippa or Pia. |
| all letters | 4 | Dick will see Job at nine if Rach sees Pat at one. |

## 7b ● 8'

### Review new reaches

each line once; keep hands quiet

5 ws ws was was wan wan wit wit pew paw nap pop bawl
6 bf bf fb fb fob fob rib rib be be job job bat back
7 p; p; asp asp pan pan ap ap ca cap pa nap pop prow

8 Barb and Bret took an old black robe and the boot.
9 Walt saw a wisp of white water renew ripe peppers.
10 Pat picked a black pepper for the picnic at Parks.

## 7c ● 10'

### Build speed

1. Key each line once; DS between groups.
2. Key a 1' writing on each of lines 17-19.

*Think*, *say*, and *key* words and phrases.

concentrate on words

11 a an pan so sot la lap ah aha do doe el elf to tot
12 bow bowl pin pint for fork forks hen hens jak jaks
13 chap chaps flak flake flakes prow prowl work works

concentrate on phrases

14 is in a|as it is|or if|as a|is on a|to do it|is so
15 is for|did it|is the|we did a|and so|to see|or not
16 as for the|as for the|and to the|to see it|and did

concentrate on words and phrases

17 Jess ate all of the peas in the salad in the bowl.
18 I hid the ace in a jar as a joke; I do not see it.
19 As far as I know, he did not read all of the book.

| 1 | 2 | 3 | 4 | 5 | 6 | 7 | 8 | 9 | 10 |

# SPEECH RECOGNITION SOFTWARE— AN EVOLVING INPUT TECHNOLOGY

## Introduction

The idea of talking to computers seems like something out of a science fiction movie. However, speech and voice recognition technologies are not new; they have been around for more than fifty years. Voice recognition (sometimes called *voiceprint*) is used most frequently for security identification purposes. Speech recognition is being used for transaction systems and as input complementing the use of the keyboard and mouse. A common example of using a transaction system is speaking commands into the telephone to access voice mail or in responding to automated telephone answering systems. Commands—such as *Say or press 1*—are frequently used. What is really evolving now is speaking into a microphone to input text rather than keying the text. These two types of systems are very different.

### Speaker-Independent Systems

With the telephone illustration, the system has to recognize the words spoken by any person who uses it; that is, it is speaker independent. Therefore, the vocabulary that the system recognizes is very limited and usually relates to a very specific field or topic. These systems tend to be *discrete* systems; that is, each word spoken is a separate unit, which is preceded and followed by a pause. The vocabulary limitations and the requirement of a slight pause before and after words generally result in a high accuracy rate.

### Speaker-Dependent Systems

Dictating into a microphone and having the software automatically enter the text dictated is a far more complex operation because speech patterns vary dramatically among individuals.

Therefore, the system has to learn how to recognize the words spoken by each speaker. Continuous speech is generally used for dictation.

In continuous speech (often called *natural language*), words are spoken as phrases or sentences without pauses before or after them.

## Hardware and Software

Wise users carefully analyze both hardware and software needs prior to selecting and installing a continuous speech recognition system.

### Hardware Requirements

When asked about the resources needed to run continuous speech recognition software, users often respond, "More resources and faster resources are always better." Although the minimum requirements specified by vendors vary somewhat, most knowledgeable users recommend a personal computer with a Pentium MMX/200 or higher processor, 48–64 MB of RAM and 2 or more GB of hard disk space. If a system has more than 98 MB of memory, additional features can be installed that reduce training time and improve accuracy.[1] A good sound system and a good noise-canceling headset are also essential. Studies show that the quality of the microphone affects dictation accuracy.[2]

Currently, most continuous speech recognition software users operate on stand-alone personal computers. If multiple users share a computer and store speech files, such as in a classroom setting, the resource requirements may be even greater. While the software runs on networked systems, large corporate networks present tremendous challenges. Bandwidth and layers of servers become critical issues. Supporting the systems and training users are issues not easily resolved.

### Software Considerations

Software components include:

- A continuous speech recognition engine
- Dictionaries or vocabularies
- Interfaces with application software
- Algorithms for processing natural language

---

[1]Stan Miastkowski, "Voice Xpress 4 Eases Training," *PC World*, <www.pcworld.com/pcwtoday/article/0,1510, 11179,00.html> (May 28, 1999).

[2]Martin J. Furey, III, "Andrea's Active Noise Cancellation," *CMP Net*, <www.byte.com/feature/ BYT1990720S0007> (July 23, 1999).

**Check spacing/shifting technique**

each set of lines once SS; DS between 3-line groups

▼ Space once after a period following an abbreviation.

spacing:  space *immediately* after each word

20 ad la as in if it lo no of oh he or so ok pi be we
21 an ace ads ale aha a fit oil a jak nor a bit a pew
22 ice ades born is fake to jail than it and the cows

spacing/shifting        ▼                              ▼

23 Ask Jed.  Dr. Han left at ten; Dr. Crowe, at nine.
24 I asked Jin if she had ice in a bowl; it can help.
25 Freda, not Jack, went to Spain.  Joan likes Spain.

Enter:  reach for ENTER without looking up

26 Blake owns a pen for the foal.
27 Jan lent the bowl to the pros.
28 He fit the panel to the shelf.
29 This rock is half of the pair.
30 I held the title for the land.

**Build skill**

Key each line twice, trying to increase your speed the second time.

31 Jake held a bit of cocoa and an apricot for Diane.
32 Jan is to chant in the still air in an idle field.
33 Dick and I fish for cod on the docks at Fish Lake.
34 Kent still held the dish and the cork in his hand.
    |  1  |  2  |  3  |  4  |  5  |  6  |  7  |  8  |  9  | 10  |

**Check speed**

Take two 1' writings. Determine *gwam*.

**Goal:** 12 *gwam*

It is hard to fake a confident spirit.  We will do
better work if we approach and finish a job and
know that we will do the best work we can and then
not fret.
    |  1  |  2  |  3  |  4  |  5  |  6  |  7  |  8  |  9  | 10  |

# Introduction to Speech Recognition

## Basic concepts

Pay careful attention as you read the white paper entitled "Speech Recognition Software—An Evolving Input Technology," which begins on p. 562. If you have *Dragon NaturallySpeaking* software, turn to Lesson H1 on p. 565 after you have finished reading the white paper. If you do not have *Dragon NaturallySpeaking* software, continue with the activities on this page when you finish reading the white paper.

### Understanding basic concepts

The following six topics were featured in the white paper (pp. 562–564). Be prepared to discuss each of them:

- Types of speech recognition systems and uses of each
- What is meant by enrollment and why it is important
- Understanding the differences between continuous speech input and dictating system commands
- The input (or dictation) part of using speech recognition software and the editing of documents after the text has been input
- Ergonomic issues
- Future of speech recognition

## APPLICATION H1

*Concepts*

**Key the white paper (pp. 562–564) using unbound report format.**

Format the paper using headings styles so that you can generate a table of contents that includes all headings. Design an effective title page. You are preparing the white paper for your instructor. Key the references as footnotes, and add a Reference page with the entries in proper format.

## APPLICATION H2

*Concepts*

**Reformat the paper following the directions at the right.**

Format the paper as a two-column document. Use TextArt for the banner that spans the two columns. Find appropriate clipart, and insert it in the document. Update the table of contents, and use decorative features on the title page.

## APPLICATION H3

*Concepts—challenge*

Complete the Internet activity on p. 578. Use the information you obtained from it to modify the content of this paper to reflect the updated information.

# LESSON 8

# G, Question Mark, X, U

## 8a ● 8'

### GETTING started

each line twice SS; eyes on copy

all letters 1 We often can take the older jet to Paris and back.
w/b 2 As the wind blew, Bob Webber saw the window break.
p/, 3 Pat, Pippa, or Cap has prepared the proper papers.
all reaches 4 Bo, Jose, and Will fed Lin; Jack had not paid her.

## 8b ● 12'

### Learn g and ?

each line twice SS; DS between 2-line groups; eyes on copy

**g** Reach to *right* with *left first* finger.

**?** Left SHIFT; reach *down* with *right fourth* finger.

**Question mark:** The question mark is usually followed by two spaces.

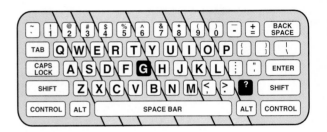

g

5 g g gf gaff gag grog fog frog drag cog dig fig gig
6 gf go gall flag gels slag gala gale glad glee gals
7 golf flog gorge glen high logs gore ogle page grow

?

8 ? ?; ?; ? ? Who?  When?  Where?  Who is?  Who was?
9 Who is here?  Was it he?  Was it she?  Did she go?
10 Did Geena?  Did he?  What is that?  Was Jose here?

**all reaches learned**

11 Has Ginger lost her job?  Was her April bill here?
12 Phil did not want the boats to get here this soon.
13 Loris Shin has been ill; Frank, a doctor, saw her.

## 8c ● 5'

### Practice new reaches

each line once; DS between groups

concentrate on correct reaches; repeat

14 gf nj ng gin gin rig ring go gone no nog sign hung
15 to go|to go|go on|go in|go in|to go in|in the sign
16 I said to enter Ga. for Georgia and Id. for Idaho.

17 ?; ?;? who? when? where? how? what? who?  Is it I?
18 Did Reno jog to the new sign at the lake?  Did Jo?
19 Did Ti look for a sharp thorn, a cobweb, or a saw?

# SPEECH RECOGNITION SOFTWARE

H

module

## OVERVIEW

### Option 1:  Concepts of speech recognition

Even though you do not have *Dragon NaturallySpeaking* software, you can still learn the basic concepts of speech recognition. Speech recognition is an evolving technology that has not yet been perfected; however, it is becoming a useful tool that is both fun and worthwhile to learn. The guides on the next page direct you to the activities that are specially designed for students who want to learn about this exciting new technology but do not have access to voice recognition software.

### Option 2:  Using Dragon NaturallySpeaking software

These lessons (H1-H4) introduce you to the basics of using *Dragon NaturallySpeaking* software. As a new user, you may be amazed at the discrepancies between what you say and what the system understands and prints on the screen. Effective microphone use and tuning, enrollment, and system training will decrease the number of errors you make. You made many errors when you first learned to key by touch. Effective practice helped to minimize those errors. The same is true with speech recognition. Effective practice and training will improve your accuracy significantly.

## 8d ● 12'

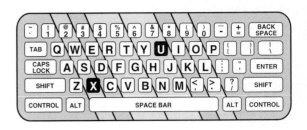

### Learn x and u
each line twice SS

**x** Reach *down* with *left third* finger.

**u** Reach *up* with *right first* finger.

## 8e ● 13'

### Check speed
Take a 1' writing on each paragraph (¶). Follow the directions at the right.

**x**

20  x x xs xs ox ox lox sox fox box ex hex lax hex fax
21  sx six sax sox ax fix cox wax hex box pox sex text
22  flax next flex axel pixel exit oxen taxi axis next

**u**

23  u uj uj jug jut just dust dud due sue use due duel
24  uj us cud but bun out sun nut gun hut hue put fuel
25  dual laud dusk suds fuss full tuna tutus duds full

**all reaches learned**

26  Paige Power liked the book; Josh can read it next.
27  Next we picked a bag for Jan; then she, Jan, left.
28  Is her June account due?  Has Lou ruined her unit?

---

**Timed writing in the Open Screen**

1. From the Lesson menu, click the **Open Screen** button.
2. Click the **Timer** button on the toolbar. In the Timer dialog box, check **Count-Down Timer** and time; click **OK**.
3. Key until the Timer reaches zero.
4. In the File menu, save the timing, using the exercise and number of the timing as the filename.
   Example: **8e-t1** (exercise 8e, timing 1)
5. Click the **Timer** button to start a new timing.
6. Each new timing must be saved with its own name, such as **8e-t2** (8e, timing 2).

---

              .        4        .       8        .

How a finished job will look often depends on how
      12       .      16      .      20

we feel about our work as we do it.  Attitude has
   .      24      .      28      .

a definite effect on the end result of work we do.

           .        4        .       8        .

When we are eager to begin a job, we relax and do
      12       .      16      .      20

better work than if we start the job with an idea
   .      24      .      28      .

that there is just nothing we can do to escape it.

## Document 13
### Merge and embed spreadsheet

1. Review the addresses below right. Then create the data file.
2. Create a form document for the letter at the right. Using Paste Special, embed the *Quattro Pro* file **figure4** where indicated.
3. Sign the letter from **Roger Thompson, Account Executive**. Save the form document as **p6-d13-form**.
4. Merge the form document with the data file. Verify the accuracy of the merge. Then save the letters as **p6-d13-letters** and print.

## Document 14
### Insert spreadsheet as icon

1. Open *p6-d13-form*. Delete the merge fields and the embedded spreadsheet. Save the document as **p6-d14**.
2. Insert the *Quattro Pro* file **figure4** as an icon. Click **Insert, Object**. From the Insert Object dialog box, click **Create From File**. Browse to select **figure4**, and click **Insert**. Then click **Display As Icon** and click **OK**.
3. Double-click the spreadsheet icon in the document to display the spreadsheet. Click the **Close** button on the *Quattro Pro* screen to close it.

---

Palmer and Associates is a commercial corporation that specializes in marketing major office, industrial, and investment properties. We currently are working with a client who is seeking commercial office space in your area. Are you considering selling or leasing your facility? Would you like to expand to a larger facility? Is it time to relocate to another area?

Palmer and Associates is headquartered in Lexington with branch offices in Fayette and Clark Counties. For two decades, our firm has excelled in marketing major office, industrial, and investment properties throughout the East.

Our sales staff consists of trained career professionals who possess extensive market knowledge, outstanding negotiating skills, and a commitment to timely performance. At Palmer and Associates, our project-focused approach enables us to meet the goals of our clients. Our diligent work ethic, active leadership, and professional reputation have produced incomparable market results.

Palmer and Associates consistently closes multimillion-dollar transactions with broadly recognized principals. Our professionalism and strong industry relationships have positioned us as Kentucky's leading commercial brokerage firm.

I have provided you with the average lease rates in the Lexington area to give you an idea of what your property could lease for, and what the cost would be for you to secure another lease.

*Insert figure4 here.*

I will call you within the next few weeks to answer any questions you may have.

### Data file:
### Record 1
Hayashi and Associates
5297 Ashton Blvd.
Lexington, KY 50511-1278

### Record 2
Mr. Lew Baker
Baker Brothers Inc.
8621 Blue Ridge Road
Lexington, KY 50516-9843

### Record 3
Just-Rite Paints
110 Alexander Blvd.
Lexington, KY 50517-6498

**LESSON 9**

# Q, M, V, Apostrophe

## 9a ● 8'

### GETTING started

each line twice SS

## 9b ● 12'

### Learn q and m
each line twice SS

**q** Reach *up* with *left fourth* finger.

**m** Reach *down* with *right first* finger.

## 9c ● 8'

### Practice reaches
each pair of lines once; repeat

eyes on copy; arms and hands quiet; finger-action keystroke ■

### SKILLBUILDING WARMUP

all letters 1 Lex gripes about cold weather; Fred is not joking.

space bar 2 Is it Di, Jo, or Al?  Ask Lt. Coe, Bill; he knows.

easy 3 I did rush a bushel of cut corn to the sick ducks.

easy 4 He is to go to the Tudor Isle of England on a bus.

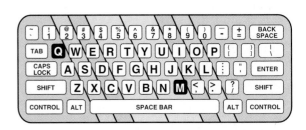

**q**

5 q qa qa quad quad quaff quant queen quo quit quick

6 qa qu qa quo quit quod quid quip quads quote quiet

7 quite quilts quart quill quakes quail quack quaint

**m**

8 m mj mj jam man malt mar max maw me mew men hem me

9 m mj ma am make male mane melt meat mist amen lame

10 malt meld hemp mimic tomb foam rams mama mire mind

**all reaches learned**

11 Quin had some quiet qualms about taming a macaque.

12 Jake Coxe had questions about a new floor program.

13 Max was quick to join the big reception for Lidia.

g 14 fg gn gun gun dig dig nag snag snag sign grab grab

n 15 Georgia hung a sign in front of the union for Gib.

u 16 ju uj cu cue cut cut cute cute tuck tucks cuts

c 17 Chuck and Jo can check accurate accident accounts.

n 18 nj nj nu nun mint mint mend mend man union minimum

m 19 Emma Max expressed an aim to make a mammoth model.

## Document 12
### Web page

Create a Web page for the survey results of the Fayette and Clark Counties market survey.

1. In *WordPerfect*, click **File**, **Internet Publisher**, **New Web Document**, and choose *Create a blank web document.*

2. Key the headings shown at the right (top). Use Heading 1 and Heading 2 styles. DS.

3. Insert the *WordPerfect* file **webpage** from the Formatting Template.

4. Re-create the table using the HTML table feature (*Extras, Add a Table*).

5. Format the document attractively for the Web. Use creativity, but do include each of the following items:
   a. Horizontal line(s)
   b. Change colors and background
   c. Last date modified

6. Open the *Quattro Pro* file **chart** and embed it in the space above the heading **Conclusions**. (Hint: Use *Edit, Paste Special, Paste.*)

7. Save as **Fayette and Clark Counties Results**.

8. View the Web page in *Internet Explorer*.

---

# Survey Results for Fayette and Clark Counties

## Industrial Manufacturing, Warehouse, and Distribution Space

### Purpose and Methods

The purpose of the study was to determine the key real estate attributes, such as size, location, rental rate, availability, and construction of all industrial sties located in Fayette and Clark Counties. The following information was desired: (1) property location data, (2) owner and contact data, (3) availability data, and (4) property description data

Consultants divided Fayette and Clark Counties into three zones for reporting real estate information. The three zones were Downtown Lexington, South Lexington, and Winchester.

| INDUSTRIAL REAL ESTATE ZONES | |
|---|---|
| **Zone** | **Description** |
| 1 | Downtown Lexington |
| 2 | South Lexington |
| 3 | Winchester |

The data seem to indicate that little change is expected in the next ten years for expanding space for industrial manufacturing, warehouse, or distribution use. As shown in the chart, below, over 75% of the respondents indicated no change. Over 20% of the respondents in Zone 3 did respond that an increase was expected in the next ten years. Only 2 to 4% responded a decrease in space requirements in the next ten years.

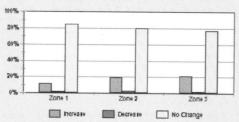

### Conclusions

☐ Owner-occupied companies seem to be the preferred occupancy of industrial manufacturing, warehouse, and distribution space.

## Learn v and '
## (apostrophe)

each line twice SS (slowly, then faster)

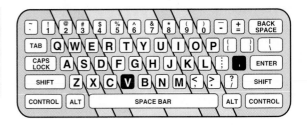

**Apostrophe:** The apostrophe shows (1) omission (as Rob't for Robert or it's for it is) or (2) possession when used with nouns (as Joe's hat).

v Reach *down* with *left first* finger.

' Reach to ' with *right fourth* finger.

**v**

20 v vf vf vie vie via via vim vat vow vile vale vote

21 vf vf ave vet ova eve vie dive five live have lave

22 cove dove over aver vivas hive volt five java jive

**' (apostrophe)**

23 '; '; it's it's Rod's; it's Bo's hat; we'll do it.

24 We don't know if it's Lee's pen or Norma's pencil.

25 It's ten o'clock; I won't tell him that he's late.

**all reaches learned**

26 It's Viv's turn to drive Iva's van to Ava's house.

27 Qua, not Vi, took the jet; so did Cal.  Didn't he?

28 Wasn't Fae Baxter a judge at the post garden show?

29 I'd wear gloves to pack those boxes of quince jam.

30 Jacques Poll might fix the seven wrecked tugboats.

31 Two judges found ropes and fixed the broken limbs.

32 Quade quit squirting Quarla after quite a quarrel.

33 Most of them jammed the museum to see the mummies.

34 We walked to the window to watch as the wind blew.

## Build skill

Key ¶ at an easy pace.
Repeat; try to increase speed.

```
              •           4           •           8           •
We must be able to express our thoughts with ease
        12        •           16          •           20
if we desire to find success in the business world.
        •         24          •           28
It is there that sound ideas earn cash.
|  1  |  2  |  3  |  4  |  5  |  6  |  7  |  8  |  9  |  10  |
```

**Document 11**
*Presentations* **slide show**

1. Prepare the 8 slides below using a background of your choice.
2. In Slide 4, insert the Figure 2 pie chart and link it to the *Quattro Pro* spreadsheet.
3. Add transitions to Slides 2-8.
4. Add appropriate clipart to Slides 2, 5, and 7. Animate the clipart in Slide 2, and display bulleted items one at a time.
5. Save as **kisner**.
6. Print audience handouts as thumbnails in the format 2 × 4.

Slide 1

> ### Industrial Manufacturing, Warehouse, and Distribution Space
> Fayette County and
> Clark County

Slide 2

> ### Goals of Study
> Determine space available for
>    Industrial manufacturing
>    Warehouse
>    Distribution
> Create database to include
>    Contact information
>    Property description

Slide 3

> ### Industrial Zones
> Zone 1  Downtown Lexington
> Zone 2  South Lexington
> Zone 3  Winchester

Slide 4

> ### Figure 2
> **Total Industrial Space per Zone**
> (Insert pie chart)

Slide 5

> ### Rental Rate
> Highest rate $6.83      Zone 1
> Lowest rate $2.40       Zone 2
> Average rate $3.84
> Range $.50 to $10

Slide 6

> ### Property Size
> 43%  between 10,001-50,000 sq. ft
> 40%  between  5,000-10,000 sq. ft
> 17%  less than 5,000 sq. ft or
>        greater than 50,000 sq. ft.

Slide 7

> ### Projections
> 75% expected no change in space
>    requirements
> 20% expected an increase
> 2-4% expected a decrease

Slide 8

> ### Final Analysis
> Conclusions
>    Owner-occupied seems to be
>    preferred occupancy
>    Space shortage may be future
>    challenge
> Recommendations
>    Purchase property in South
>    Lexington

# Z, Y, Quotation Mark, Tab

## 10a ● 8'

### GETTING started

each line twice SS

## 10b ● 12'

**Learn z and y**
each line twice SS

**z** Reach *down* with *left fourth* finger.

**y** Reach *up* with *right first* finger.

## 10c ● 10'

**Practice specific keyreaches**
each line twice SS; repeat troublesome lines

### SKILLBUILDING WARMUP

| | | |
|---|---|---|
| all letters | 1 | Quill owed those back taxes after moving to Japan. |
| spacing | 2 | Didn't Vi, Sue, and Paul go?  Someone did; I know. |
| q/v/m | 3 | Marv was quite quick to remove that mauve lacquer. |
| easy | 4 | Lana is a neighbor; she owns a lake and an island. |

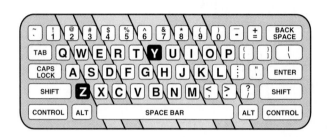

z

5 za za zap zap zing zig zag zoo zed zip zap zig zed

6 doze zeal zero haze jazz zone zinc zing size ozone

7 ooze maze doze zoom zarf zebus daze gaze faze adze

y

8 y yj yj jay jay hay hay lay nay say days eyes ayes

9 yj ye yet yen yes cry dry you rye sty your fry wry

10 ye yen bye yea coy yew dye yaw lye yap yak yon any

**all reaches learned**

11 Did you say Liz saw any yaks or zebus at your zoo?

12 Relax; Jake wouldn't acquire any favorable rights.

13 Has Mazie departed?  Tex, Lu, and I will go alone.

g 14 Is Gregg urging Gage to ship eggs to Ragged Gorge?

x 15 Dixi expects Bix to fix her tax bill on the sixth.

u 16 It is unusual to house unused units in the bunker.

b 17 Barb Robbes is the barber who bobbed her own hair.

p 18 Pepe prepared a pepper salad for a special supper.

**Document 9**
**E-mail**

1. Prepare the memo as an e-mail message to your instructor. (Assume your instructor is the **Market Research Analyst** and you are **Melanie Winters, Project Coordinator**.)
2. Attach the *WordPerfect* file *p6-d8* and the *Quattro Pro* file *projections*.

If e-mail is not available, key as a memo using the memo template.

August 8, 200-

The draft of the market study report for the Kisner Industrial Co. project is now complete. Anne and Donna should have the first draft of the electronic presentation ready for review on August 15. In the meantime, would you review the enclosed report draft? Specifically, compare the conclusions with the findings presented on pages 2-5.

Based on these findings, we have recommended South Lexington as the best area for industrial expansion. I would appreciate your reviewing the attached Quattro Pro spreadsheet (projections.qpw) showing ten-year projections for expansion. Do you agree that South Lexington is the preferred zone for future expansion?

I appreciate your sharing your research skills and knowledge of industrial real estate trends.

**Document 10**
**Letter**

Compose an overnight letter to the president of Kisner from **Melanie Winters, Project Coordinator.** Follow the outline at the right. Date the letter **August 15, 200-.**

Send a copy of the letter to **Phillip Day** and **Kent Bass**.

1. Inform the president that the market study authorized by Kisner Industrial Co. has been completed. Also tell him that the formal presentation will be:
   a. August 20 (provide weekday)
   b. at MarketAnalysis, Inc.
   c. 10 a.m., Fultz Conference Room
2. Tell him that Phillip Day (president of MarketAnalysis, Inc.) and Kent Bass (market analyst) will attend the presentation.
3. Close with a goodwill paragraph that shows your enthusiasm for this project and for sharing the results of the study with him on August 20.

**Learn " (quotation mark) and TAB**
each line once

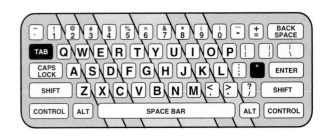

" Shift; then reach to "
with *right fourth* finger.

**TAB** Reach up with *left fourth* finger.

**" (quotation mark)**

19 "; "; " " "lingo" "bugs" "tennies" I like "malts."
20 "I am not," she said, "going." I just said, "Oh?"

**tab key**

21     The tab key is used for indenting paragraphs and aligning columns.
22     Tabs that are set by the software are called default tabs, which are usually a half inch.

**all reaches learned**

23     The expression "I give you my word," or put
24 another way, "Take my word for it," is just a way I
25 can say, "I prize my name; it clearly stands in back
26 of my words."  I offer "honor" as collateral.

**Check speed**
Take two 1' writings on ¶ 1.
**Suggested goal:** 15 *gwam*

**Optional**:
Take two 1' writings in the Open Screen. See 8e, p. 20, for instructions if necessary.

```
         .        4          .        8
    All of us work for progress, but it is not
     .      12        .        16        .
always easy to analyze "progress."  We work hard
    20        .        24        .        28
for it; but, in spite of some really good efforts,
    .      32        .        36        .
we may fail to receive just exactly the response we
     40
want.

         .        4          .        8
    When this happens, as it does to all of us,
     .      12        .        16        .
it is time to cease whatever we are doing, have
    20        .        24        .        28
a quiet talk with ourselves, and face up to the
    .      32        .        36        .
questions about our limited progress.  How can we
     40
do better?
```

**Document 8,** *continued*

**Appendixes**

Prepare a divider page for each appendix. Use the sample at the right as a guide. Obtain the names of the appendixes from the Contents.

**Table of contents**

1. Position insertion point on a new page following the transmittal letter.
2. On the Ruler, set a left tab at 1.5", a dot right tab at 7.25", and a right tab at 7.4".
3. Create a table of contents—part of it is shown at the right. Insert appropriate page numbers.

**List of figures**

1. Insert a hard page break after the contents.
2. Set a left tab at 1.5", a dot right tab at 7.25", and a right tab at 7.4".
3. Key the list of figures at the right, inserting appropriate page numbers.

**Paginate**

1. Number the preliminary pages using Roman numerals. Suppress page number on the title page.
2. Insert the following header for the body:
   a. Key at the left: **Market Study for Kisner Industrial Co**.
   b. Key **Page** and insert the page number flush right (**F7**).
   c. Add a bottom border line to create an impressive header.
3. Insert a hard page break after the body of the report (between last page and Appendix A).
4. Suppress the header on Appendix pages.

---

**APPENDIX A**

**SURVEY FORM AND COVER LETTER**

**(Begin about 1.5".)**

## CONTENTS

**(Complete the contents from the report.)**

**(Begin about 1.5".)**

## LIST OF FIGURES

**(Complete the list of figures from the report.)**

---

**Optional:** You may use the Table of Contents feature to generate the contents page, but do so *after* you create the list of figures. Review marking heading levels before you begin. **Caution:** Save before you begin.

# Keyboarding Mastery

**11a ● 8'**

**GETTING started**

each line twice SS
(slowly, then faster)

| alphabet | 1 | Max Jewel picked up five history quizzes to begin. |
| " (quote) | 2 | Can you spell "chaos," "bias," "bye," and "their"? |
| y | 3 | Ty Clay may envy you for any zany plays you write. |
| easy | 4 | She kept the fox, owls, and fowl down by the lake. |

| 1 | 2 | 3 | 4 | 5 | 6 | 7 | 8 | 9 | 10 |

**11b ● 6'**

**Improve keying techniques**
each line once

**first row:** keep hand movement to a minimum; pull fingers under

5 Can my cook, Mrs. Zackman, carve the big ox roast?

6 Did Cam, the cabby, have extra puzzles?  Yes, one.

**home row:** use fingertips; keep fingers curved

7 Jack was sad; he had just lost his gold golf ball.

8 Sal was glad she had a flashlight; Al was as glad.

**third row:** straighten fingers slightly; do not move hands forward

9 Did Troy write to Terry Reppe?  Did he quote Ruth?

10 Powers quit their outfit to try out for our troop.

**11c ● 10'**

**Practice new reaches**
each line once; repeat if you
do not key the lines fluently

11 za za zap az az maze zoo zip razz zed zax zoa zone

12 Liz Zahl saw Zoe feed the zebra in an Arizona zoo.

13 yj yj jy jy joy lay yaw say yes any yet my try you

14 Why do you say that today, Thursday, is my payday?

15 xs xs sax ox box fix hex ax lax fox taxi lox sixes

16 Roxy, you may ask Jay to fix any tax sets for you.

17 qa qa aqua quail quit quake quid equal quiet quart

18 Did Enrique quietly but quickly quell the quarrel?

19 fv fv five lives vow ova van eve avid vex vim void

20 Have Vivi, Vada, or Eva visited Vista Valley Farm?

Work for smoothness, not for speed. ■

**Document 8,** *continued*

4. Follow these steps to link the rotated 2-D bar chart to the report:
   a. Open *Quattro Pro* file *figure3*.
   b. Use Copy and Paste Special method used in Step 3 to link this chart.
   c. Size object appropriately.
5. Link the column chart to the report:
   a. Open *Quattro Pro* file *figure4*.
   b. Use Copy and Paste Special.
   c. Size object appropriately.
6. Two project analysts have prepared the remainder of the report. Insert their two files from the Formatting Template:
   a. Insert *insrtrpt* a DS below Figure 4.
   b. Insert *conclusion* a DS below *insrtrpt*.
   c. Key the handwritten recommendations.

---

Insert file:
- Position insertion point.
- Choose *Insert*, *File*, and then the filename.

---

owned by occupants, while 23% reported their properties were leased by the occupants. Vacancy rates for the area were reported to be about 5%. Eight percent of survey respondents did not know or would not report whether their property was owner-occupied or leased.

*Link bar chart.*

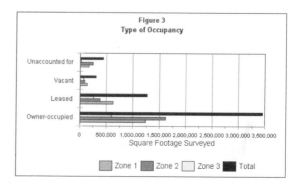

Figure 3
Type of Occupancy

## Lease Rate by Property Size

The average rental rate per square foot is presented by zone in Figure 4. The highest average rental rate was $6.83 in Zone 1. The lowest average rental rate was $2.40 in Zone 2. The overall average rental rate was $3.84 for all leased properties. The rental rate ranged from a low of $.50 per square foot from a property in Zone 2 to a high of $10 from a property in Zone 3.

*Link column chart.*

Figure 4
Average Rental Rate by Zone

**(Insert file *insrtrpt* here.)**

**(Insert file *conclusion* here.)**

*Recommendations*

*Kisner Industrial Co. should estimate space requirements for the next ten years. If additional space is indicated in these projections, management should pursue purchase of property in South Lexington (Zone 2) for the following reasons:*

- *South Lexington is highly populated with organizations using properties for industrial, warehouse, or distribution purposes.*
- *South Lexington has the lowest average rental rates, ranging from $2.40 to $4.57.*
- *South Lexington is second only to Zone 1 in vacant space available at present.*

**Control service keys**
each line once; DS between groups

enter: key smoothly without looking at fingers

21 Make the return snappily
22 and with assurance; keep
23 your eyes on your source
24 data; maintain a smooth,
25 constant pace as you key.

space bar: use down-and-in motion

26 us me it of he an by do go to us if or so am ah el
27 Have you a pen?  If so, print "Free to any guest."

shift keys: use smooth shift-key-release motions

28 Juan Colon will see Lyle Branch in Oak Creek Park.
29 Mo, Lucy, and Sky left for New Orleans, Louisiana.

**Check speed**
Take two 1' writings.

**Goal:** 16 *gwam*

**Optional:**

1. Click the **Open Screen** button.
2. Key all ¶s once SS using wordwrap. Work for smooth, continuous stroking (not speed).
3. Save as 11e.
4. Take a 1' timing on each ¶. Note your *gwam*.
5. **Optional:** Take a 2' writing on all ¶s. (To set the Timer, click **Variable** and enter **2** in the Minutes box.)

**Copy difficulty**
What factors determine whether copy is difficult or easy?  Research shows that difficulty is influenced by syllables per word, characters per word, and percent of familiar words. Carefully controlling these three factors ensures that speed and accuracy scores are reliable—that is, increased scores reflect increased skill.

In Level 1, all timings are easy.  Note "E" inside the triangle above the timing. Easy timings contain an average of 1.2 syllables per word, 5.1 characters per word, and 90 percent familiar words.  Easy copy is suitable for the beginner who is mastering the keyboard.

all letters                                                                 *gwam*  2'

Have we thought of communication as a kind          4  31

of war that we wage through each day?               8  35

When we think of it that way, good language         12  39

would seem to become our major line of attack.      17  44

Words become muscle; in a normal exchange or in     22  49

a quarrel, we do well to realize the power of words. 27  54

**Document 8,** *continued*

3. Link the *Quattro Pro* pie chart showing total industrial space by zone. You saved this as *figure2*.
   a. Open *Quattro Pro* file *figure2*.
   b. Select pie chart; click **Copy**.
   c. Switch back to the report in *WordPerfect*.
   d. Choose *Edit, Paste Special, Paste Link, Quattro Pro 9 Chart;* click **OK**.
   e. Size object appropriately.

location, and descriptive information, such as fair market value, building classification, and building quality. Fayette County reported 194 sites, and Clark County reported 128 sites. Information concerning manufacturing space was obtained from the Kentucky Department of Revenue; 150 properties were identified. Fifty-two properties were identified as duplicate sites, thus resulting in a total of 420 distinct industrial sites for the market study.

After comparing the publicly available information to the desired information, a survey form was developed to verify information gained from the county agencies and to obtain the remaining desired data. The survey targeted the following information: property street address, square footage, usage, occupancy, rental rates, plans for expansion, and appropriate contact person regarding the property. Surveys were mailed to the 420 property owners. Copies of the survey and cover letter are found in Appendix A.

A follow-up plan was designed to obtain information from survey recipients not returning their survey forms. Phone numbers for the properties were obtained from the City of Lexington phone book and the *Cross Reference Directory*. These phone interviews were conducted with the owner or occupant of the properties. The interviews followed guidelines provided by Kisner Industrial Co. as documented in Appendix B, based on previous phone surveys conducted by MarketAnalysis, Inc. The phone survey began with a brief introduction of the interviewer and the purpose of the project. The questions followed the exact format of the mail survey. The findings are based on results of the combined mail and phone surveys.

### Findings

Of the 420 surveys mailed, 114 (27%) were returned; 8 (2%) were returned by the postal service because of incorrect owner addresses. A total of 127 phone surveys were conducted with complete information reported, resulting in a 57% return rate.

A total of 5,025,101 square feet were surveyed in Fayette and Clark Counties. Figure 2 below illustrates the distribution of industrial space by zone. The industrial properties seem to be concentrated in two zones: Downtown Lexington and South Lexington.

**Figure 2**
**Total Industrial Space per Zone**

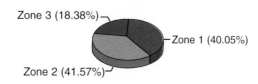

Zone 3 (18.38%)
Zone 1 (40.05%)
Zone 2 (41.57%)

Findings of the market study have been presented in four areas: (1) type of occupancy, (2) average lease rate by property size, (3) property size, and (4) ten-year projections concerning expansion.

### Occupancy

The vast majority of industrial properties surveyed were owner-occupied. Figure 3 shows that 64% of the respondents reported that properties were

# Review

## 12a ● 8'

### GETTING started

each line twice SS
(slowly, then faster)

alphabet 1 Which big market for quality jazz has Vi expanded?
q 2 Quin Racq quickly and quietly quelled the quarrel.
z 3 Zaret zipped along sizzling, zigzag Arizona roads.
easy 4 Can they handle the auditory problems of the city?
| 1 | 2 | 3 | 4 | 5 | 6 | 7 | 8 | 9 | 10 |

## 12b ● 12'

### Practice new reaches

each line once; DS between groups; work for smoothness, not for speed

b/f 5 bf bf fab fab ball bib rf rf rib rib fibs bums bee
6 Did Buffy remember that he is a brass band member?

z/y 7 za za zag zig zip yj yj jay eye day lazy hazy zest
8 Liz amazed us with the zesty pizza on a lazy trip.

q/u 9 qa qa quo qt. quit quay quam quarm que uj jug quay
10 Where is Quito? Qatar? Boqueirao? Quebec? Quilmes?

v/m 11 vf vf valve five value mj mj ham mad mull mass vim
12 Vito, enter the words vim, vivace, and avar; save.

all 13 I faced defeat; only reserves saved my best crews.
14 In my opinion, I need to rest in my reserved seat.

all 15 Holly created a red poppy and deserves art awards.
16 My pump averages a faster rate; we get better oil.

## 12c ● 7'

### Control service keys

each line once

**enter:** do not pause or look up to return

17 Successful keying is not just
18 a matter of speed; rather, it
19 is a combination of rapid and
20 slow, but constant, movements.

**space bar:** use correct spacing after each punctuation mark

21 Was it there?  I saw it; Jan saw it, too.  We did.

**shift keys:** depress shift key firmly; avoid pauses

22 Pam was in Spain in May; Bo Roy met her in Madrid.

**Report**
1. Insert a page break below the letter.
2. Use QuickCorrect entries prepared in Document 1. The entries are highlighted to remind you to use this feature.
3. Prepare Figure 1 as a 2-column table.
   • Add a double border at the top of the table.
   • Add a single border above and below the column headings and at the bottom of the table. (Use your creativity.)
   • Center table horizontally.

# INDUSTRIAL MANUFACTURING, WAREHOUSE, AND DISTRIBUTION SPACE IN FAYETTE AND CLARK COUNTIES

## Introduction

In long-term planning, the management of Kisner Industrial Co. identified the immediate need to determine current space being used in Fayette and Clark Counties for (1) industrial manufacturing, (2) warehouse space, and (3) distribution space. Two internal studies of industrial distribution and warehouse space had been conducted. The study completed in 1999 focused on properties over 10,000 square feet, while the 2000 study examined properties ranging from 2,000 to 10,000 square feet.

Kisner Industrial Co. authorized MarketAnalysis, Inc. to conduct an expanded market study to include manufacturing sites, in addition to distribution and warehouse space. Because long-term plans of Kisner Industrial Co. include expanding into Clark County, the study also included Clark County as well as Fayette County.

## Purpose of the Study

The purpose of the study was to determine the key real estate attributes, such as size, location, rental rate, availability, and construction of all industrial sites located in Fayette and Clark Counties. The following information was desired:

• **Property location data:** Tax map number, real estate zone (based on ZIP Code), full street address, and county.

• **Owner and contact data:** Owner's name, address, and telephone number; contact person's name, address, and telephone number.

• **Availability data:** Whether the property was available for sale or lease; whether property was owner-occupied or leased; and lease expiration date.

• **Property description data:** Total square footage of property, subdivided by warehouse, manufacturing, and office space; rent per square foot per year; and building quality. Building quality included such factors as year built, type of construction (metal, concrete, etc.), roof height, and utilities present.

## Methods and Procedures Used

Consultants divided Fayette and Clark Counties into three zones for reporting real estate information. Figure 1 shows the three zones.

**Figure 1**

### INDUSTRIAL REAL ESTATE ZONES

| Zone | Description |
|------|-------------|
| 1 | Downtown Lexington |
| 2 | South Lexington |
| 3 | Winchester |

The two county assessors' offices provided information regarding warehouse and distribution space in their respective counties. Information provided in both print form and in tape format included owner's name and address, property

## 12d ● 9'

**Improve keystroking**
each line once; work for smooth, unhurried keying

de/ed
23 ed fed led deed dell dead deal sled desk need seed
24 Dell dealt with the deed before the dire deadline.

ol/lo
25 old tolls doll solo look sole lost love cold stole
26 Old Ole looked for the long lost olive oil lotion.

as/sa
27 as say sad ask pass lass case said vase past salsa
28 Ask the lass to pass the glass, saucers, and vase.

op/po
29 pop top post rope pout port stop opal opera report
30 Stop to read the top opera opinion report to Opal.

we/ew
31 we few wet were went wears weather skews stew blew
32 Working women wear sweaters when weather dictates.

## 12e ● 14'

**Check speed**
Take two 1' writings on ¶ 1.

**Goal:** 16 *gwam*

**Optional:**
1. Click the **Open Screen** button.
2. Key ¶s once SS using word-wrap. Work for smooth, continuous stroking (not speed).
3. Save as **12e**.
4. Take a 1' timing on ¶ 1. Save as **12e-t1**.
5. Take a 1' timing on ¶ 2. Save as **12e-t2**. Print the better 1' writing.
6. Set the Timer for 2'. Take a 2' writing on both ¶s. Print.

**To determine gross-words-a-minute (*gwam*) rate for 2'**
Follow these steps if you are *not* using the Timer in the Open Screen.
1. Note the figure at the end of the last line completed.
2. For a partial line, note the figure on the scale directly below the point at which you stopped keying.
3. Add these two figures to determine the total gross words a minute (*gwam*) you keyed.

 all letters                                            *gwam*   2'

```
        •            4         •            8
    There  should  be  no  questions,  no  doubt,  about       5  35
   •            12        •            16        •
the  value  of  being  able  to  key;  it's  just  a  matter   10  40
   20         •            24        •            28        •
of  common  sense  that  today  a  pencil  is  much  too  slow.  15  45

            •            4         •            8
    Let  me  explain.   Work  is  done  on  a  keyboard        19  49
   •            12        •            16        •
three  to  six  times  faster  than  other  writing  and       24  54
   20         •            24        •            28
with  a  product  that  is  a  prize  to  read.   Don't  you    29  59
   •
agree?                                                          30  60
```

2' |    1    |    2    |    3    |    4    |    5    |

## Document 8
## Long report

This multipage report consists of preliminary pages (title page, transmittal letter, contents, list of figures), the body of the report, and appendix pages. You will prepare the entire report as one document. Number the pages after the entire report is keyed.

### Title page

Use the information at the right above. Insert a page break after the title page.

For **title page:** Center vertically; bold; increase font size for title; remaining parts larger than 12 point. Use your imagination for borders, artwork, etc. ▣

### Transmittal letter

1. Position the insertion point on p. 2.
2. Prepare the transmittal letter in block letter style. Address it to the president of Kisner Industrial Co. **Melanie Winters** is the project coordinator.
3. Insert the letterhead prepared in Document 2.

Mr. Jerry Chitturi,
President
Kisner Industrial Co.
1783 Portland Dr.
Lexington, KY 40503-1783

**Functions applied:**
Footers
Link
Insert File
Borders

Use the following information to design an impressive title page:

Title: Use title of report. Key using three lines in the preferred inverted pyramid style.

Prepared for: Mr. Jerry Chitturi, President, Kisner Industrial Co. | Lexington, Kentucky

Prepared by: MarketAnalysis, Inc. | (Include full address.)

Date: Use date of presentation.

INDUSTRIAL MANUFACTURING, WAREHOUSE, AND DISTRIBUTION SPACE IN FAYETTE AND CLARK COUNTIES

Prepared for
Mr. Jerry Chitturi, President
Kisner Industrial Co.
Lexington, Kentucky

Prepared by
MarketAnalysis, Inc.
P.O. Box 5643
Lexington, KY 40515-5643
www.marketanalysis.com

August 23, 200-

**Sample**

The market study authorized by Kisner Industrial Co. is now complete.

The report presents data for 249 properties in Fayette and Clark Counties. The market information was collected through an initial mail survey and finally a phone survey. The rate of return was rather high at 59 percent. Data were then analyzed to determine trends in industrial real estate.

After careful consideration of the data, MarketAnalysis, Inc. recommends expansion to the South Lexington area. This area is a prime area for industrial use, has the lowest average rental rate, and was second only to the downtown area in terms of vacant space available at the present time.

Thank you for allowing our organization the opportunity to conduct this market study. Our project staff will be happy to discuss any part of this report and wish you the best in making long-term plans for Kisner Industrial Co.

# Review

## 13a ● 8'

**G**ETTING
**started**

each line twice SS
(slowly, then faster)

alphabet 1 Bev quickly hid two Japanese frogs in Mitzi's box.
shift 2 Jay Nadler, a Rotary Club member, wrote Mr. Coles.
, (comma) 3 Jay, Ed, and I paid for plates, knives, and forks.
easy 4 Did the amendment name a city auditor to the firm?

| 1 | 2 | 3 | 4 | 5 | 6 | 7 | 8 | 9 | 10 |

## 13b ● 10'

**Practice response patterns**

each line once SS

**word-level response:** key short, familiar words as units

5 is to for do an may work so it but an with them am
6 Did they mend the torn right half of their ensign?
7 Hand me the ivory tusk on the mantle by the bugle.

**letter-level response:** key more difficult words letter by letter

8 only state jolly zest oil verve join rate mop card
9 After defeat, look up; gaze in joy at a few stars.
10 We gazed at a plump beaver as it waded in my pool.

**combination response:** use variable speed; your fingers will let you feel the difference

11 it up so at for you may was but him work were they
12 It is up to you to get the best rate; do it right.
13 This is Lyn's only date to visit their great city.

| 1 | 2 | 3 | 4 | 5 | 6 | 7 | 8 | 9 | 10 |

## 13c ● 8'

**Practice keyreaches**

each line once; fingers well curved, wrists low; avoid punching keys with 3d and 4th fingers

p 14 Pat appears happy to pay for any supper I prepare.
x 15 Knox can relax; Alex gets a box of flax next week.
v 16 Vi, Ava, and Viv move ivy vines, leaves, or stems.
' 17 It's a question of whether they can't or won't go.
? 18 Did Jan go?  Did she see Ray?  Who paid?  Did she?
. 19 Ms. E. K. Nu and Lt. B. A. Walz had the a.m. duty.
" 20 "Who are you?" he asked.  "I am," I said, "Marie."
; 21 Find a car; try it; like it; work a price; buy it.

| 1 | 2 | 3 | 4 | 5 | 6 | 7 | 8 | 9 | 10 |

**Document 7**
*Quattro Pro* **spreadsheets**

Prepare the three spreadsheets shown at the right. Create the accompanying charts and embed them on the appropriate spreadsheet. Save files as **figure2**, **figure3**, and **figure4**.

**Figure 2**
1. Key Spreadsheet 1.
2. Select A3..B5; create a 3-D pie chart.
3. Embed at Cell A8; drag to fill the range A8..E22.

**Figure 3**
1. Key Spreadsheet 2.
2. Select A3..E7 and create a rotated 2-D bar chart.
3. Embed at Cell A10; drag to fill the range A10..F28.

**Figure 4**
1. Key Spreadsheet 3.
2. Hold down the CTRL key and select the Averages (B8-D8).
3. With the CTRL key still held down, select B2-D2 (column heads).
4. Create a column chart.
5. Embed at Cell A11; drag to fill the range A11..D23.

**Spreadsheet 1**

| Industrial Space by Zone | |
|---|---|
| | **Square Feet** |
| Zone 1 | 2,012,686 |
| Zone 2 | 2,088,901 |
| Zone 3 | 923,514 |

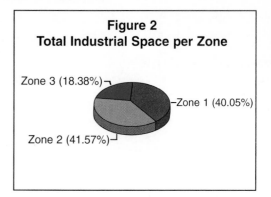

**Figure 2**
**Total Industrial Space per Zone**

**Spreadsheet 2**

| Type of Occupancy | | | | |
|---|---|---|---|---|
| | **Square Footage Surveyed** | | | |
| | **Zone 1** | **Zone 2** | **Zone 3** | **Total** |
| Owner-occupied | 1,241,720 | 1,614,847 | 600,161 | 3,456,728 |
| Leased | 628,272 | 387,628 | 253,339 | 1,269,239 |
| Vacant | 142,694 | 86,426 | 70,014 | 299,134 |
| Unaccounted for | 173,837 | 243,986 | 24,566 | 442,389 |

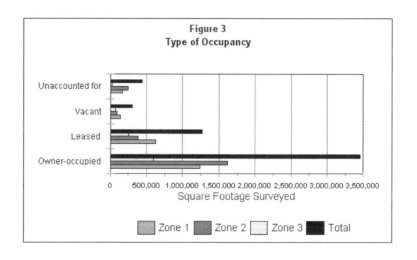

**Spreadsheet 3**

| Average Lease Rate by Property Size | | | |
|---|---|---|---|
| | **Zone 1** | **Zone 2** | **Zone 3** |
| Less than 5,000 | 6.83 | n/a | 2.74 |
| 5,000-10,000 | 3.22 | 4.57 | 5.41 |
| 10,001-50,000 | 3.17 | 2.4 | 4.73 |
| 50,001-100,000 | 3.25 | 2.47 | n/a |
| Over 100,000 | n/a | 3 | n/a |
| **Average** | $ 4.12 | $ 3.11 | $ 4.29 |

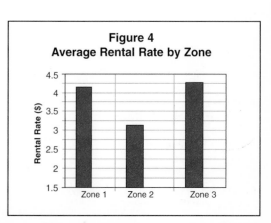

## 13d ● 12'

**Practice troublesome pairs**

each line once; repeat if time permits

> Keep hands and arms still as you reach up to the third row and down to the first row.

```
 t 22  at fat hat sat to tip the that they fast last slat
 r 23  or red try ran run air era fair rid ride trip trap
t/r 24  A trainer sprained an arm trying to tame the bear.

 m 25  am me my mine jam man more most dome month minimum
 n 26  no an now nine once net knee name ninth know never
m/n 27  Many men and women are important company managers.

 o 28  on or to not now one oil toil over only solo today
 i 29  it is in tie did fix his sit like with insist will
o/i 30  Joni will consider obtaining options to buy coins.

 a 31  at an as art has and any case data haze tart smart
 s 32  us as so say sat slap lass class just sassy simple
a/s 33  Disaster was averted as the steamer sailed to sea.

 e 34  we he ear the key her hear chef desire where there
 i 35  it is in tie did fix his sit like with insist will
e/i 36  An expression of gratitude for service is desired.
        |  1  |  2  |  3  |  4  |  5  |  6  |  7  |  8  |  9  |  10  |
```

## 13e ● 12'

**Check speed**

Take two 1' writings on ¶ 1.

**Goal:** 16 *gwam*

**Optional:**
1. In the Open Screen, key the ¶s once SS.
2. Save as **13e**.
3. Take a 1' timing on ¶ 1. Save as **13e-t1**.
4. Take a 1' timing on ¶ 2. Save as **13e-t2**.
5. Print the better 1' writing.
6. Take a 2' writing on both ¶s. Start over if time permits.

all letters                                              *gwam*  2"

```
         •               4          •              8
    The  questions  of  time  use  are  vital  ones;  we      5
      •               12         •              16
miss  so  much  just  because  we  don't  plan.               9

           •               4          •              8
    When  we  organize  our  days,  we  save  time  for       13
      •               12         •              16
those  extra  premium  things  we  long  to  do.             17
2'|    1    |    2    |    3    |    4    |    5    |
```

## Document 6
### Merge form letter with *Paradox* table

Review Merge in the Software Training Manual.

The letter at the right will be the form document for a mail merge. You will select a database table from the Formatting Template as the data file. Other than selecting a *Paradox* table as the data file, the merge process is the same as if you were using a *WordPerfect* data file.

1. In *WordPerfect*, click **Tools**, **Merge**, **Create Document**. Select *Use file in active window*.
2. In the Associate Form and Data dialog box, click **Associate a data file**.
3. Click the folder icon and locate **Kisner Industrial Co.db** from the Formatting Template. Change the File type to *All files*. Select the table and click **OK**.
4. Key the letter, inserting the appropriate fields for the letter address and salutation. Insert the letterhead.
5. Merge the document. Save the merged letters as **p6-d6**.
6. Print the first and last letters from the file.

**Functions applied:**
Merge
QuickCorrect

---

(Insert Date Code.)


(Insert address.)

Dear

MarketAnalysis, Inc. is conducting a survey of industrial manufacturing, ware-house, and distribution space in Fayette and Clark Counties. The goal of this market study is to provide information on trends in the industrial real estate market. This information is not currently available in Lexington, Kentucky, through any other source.

Your property has been identified as an industrial property by your county assessor's office. To assist us in making this study as complete as possible, please take a few minutes to fill out the survey in one of the following ways:

1. Return the enclosed survey in the preaddressed, postage-paid envelope.
2. Fax the completed survey to (606) 555-1029.
3. Complete the survey form online at www.marketanalysis.com.

While the specific information you provide in the survey will not be published, the aggregate results of this study will be available to you through various reports such as the *Thoroughbred Real Estate Report.*

Since our time is relatively short, please respond as quickly as possible so that we can include your property in our survey.

Sincerely

*Kent Bass, Analyst*

*Attachment*

*In addition, you may view an abstract of this study at the Web site www.marketanalysis.com/ market_surveys.htm.*

# SKILLBUILDING WORKSHOP

Use the Open Screen for Workshop 1. Save each drill as a separate file.

## Drill 1

**Goal:** reinforce key locations

Key each line at a comfortable, constant rate; check lines that need more practice; repeat those lines.

Keep
- your eyes on source copy
- your fingers curved, upright
- your wrists low, but not touching
- your elbows hanging loosely
- your feet flat on the floor

A We saw that Alan had an alabaster vase in Alabama.
B My rubber boat bobbed about in the bubbling brook.
C Ceci gave cups of cold cocoa to Rebecca and Rocco.
D Don's dad added a second deck to his old building.
E Even as Ellen edited her document, she ate dinner.
F Our firm in Buffalo has a staff of forty or fifty.
G Ginger is giving Greg the eggs she got from Helga.
H Hugh has eighty high, harsh lights he might flash.
I Irik's lack of initiative is irritating his coach.
J Judge J. J. Jore rejected Jeane and Jack's jargon.
K As a lark, Kirk kicked back a rock at Kim's kayak.
L Lucille is silly; she still likes lemon lollipops.
M Milt Mumm hammered a homer in the Miami home game.
N Ken Linn has gone hunting; Stan can begin canning.
O Jon Soto rode off to Otsego in an old Morgan auto.
P Philip helped pay the prize as my puppy hopped up.
Q Quiet Raquel quit quoting at an exquisite marquee.
R As Mrs. Kerr's motor roared, her red horse reared.
S Sissie lives in Mississippi; Lissa lives in Tulsa.
T Nat told Betty not to tattle on her little sister.
U Ula has a unique but prudish idea on unused units.
V Eva visited every vivid event for twelve evenings.
W We watched as wayworn wasps swarmed by the willow.
X Tex Cox waxed the next box for Xenia and Rex Knox.
Y Ty says you may stay with Fay for only sixty days.
Z Hazel is puzzled about the azure haze; Zack dozes.
alphabet Jacky and Max quickly fought over a sizable prawn.
alphabet Just by maximizing liquids, Chick Prew avoids flu.
| 1 | 2 | 3 | 4 | 5 | 6 | 7 | 8 | 9 | 10 |

SKILLBUILDING WORKSHOP 1

31

**Document 5**
**Survey form**
Create the survey form shown. Use the handwritten notes on the form to guide you.

**Functions applied:**
Columns
Borders
QuickCorrect

*.5" margins all around*

# Industrial Distribution, Warehouse, and Manufacturing Space
## Fayette and Clark Counties

*use TextArt for title.*

*cityscape*

*heavy line*

**Property address**

*12-pt. Arial*

Street: _____ *9-pt. Times Roman* City: _____
ZIP Code: _____ County: _____ Industrial Real Estate Zone: _____

*Text box*

**Building**

Square footage: _____ _____ % Owner-occupied _____ % Leased _____ % Vacant

**Occupants**  □ Single occupant in building  □ Multiple occupants in building

**Space requirements next 12 months**  □ Increase expected  □ Decrease expected  □ No change expected

**Rental rate per square foot per year**  $ _____  □ Net  □ Gross

**Lease expiration date**  Month/Year _____ / _____  Square footage that becomes available _____

*2 equal columns*

**Future rental needs:** *12-pt. bold 1.5 line spacing*

_____
_____
_____
_____
_____
_____
_____
_____

□ Please send me a copy of the completed study results.

**Property contact:** *8-pt. Times Roman double spacing*

Name: _____
Title: _____
Organization: _____
Telephone: _____
FAX: _____
E-mail: _____
Street: _____
City: _____
State: _____ ZIP Code: _____

Thank you for completing this survey.  Send completed forms to:

*small caps*

**MarketAnalysis, Inc.**
**P.O. Box 5643**          **OR**
**Lexington, KY 40515-5643**          **FAX:**  **(606) 555-1029**

## Drill 2

**Goal:** strengthen up and down reaches

Keep hands and wrists quiet; fingers well curved in home position; stretch fingers up from home or pull them palmward as needed.

### home position

1 Hall left for Dallas; he is glad Jake fed his dog.
2 Ada had a glass flask; Jake had a sad jello salad.
3 Lana Hask had a sale; Gala shall add half a glass.

### down reaches

4 Did my banker, Mr. Mavann, analyze my tax account?
5 Do they, Mr. Zack, expect a number of brave women?
6 Zach, check the menu; next, beckon the lazy valet.

### up reaches

7 Prue truly lost the quote we wrote for our report.
8 Teresa quietly put her whole heart into her words.
9 There were two hilarious jokes in your quiet talk.

## Drill 3

**Goal:** strengthen individual finger reaches

Rekey troublesome lines.

### first finger

1 Bob Mugho hunted for five minutes for your number.
2 Juan hit the bright green turf with his five iron.
3 The frigates and gunboats fought mightily in Java.

### second finger

4 Dick said the ice on the creek had surely cracked.
5 Even as we picnicked, I decided we needed to diet.
6 Kim, not Mickey, had rice with chicken for dinner.

### third/fourth finger

7 Pam saw Roz wax an aqua auto as Lex sipped a cola.
8 Wally will quickly spell Zeus, Apollo, and Xerxes.
9 Who saw Polly?  Zoe Pax saw her; she is quiet now.

## Drill 4

**Goal:** strengthen special reaches

Emphasize smooth stroking. Avoid pauses, but do not reach for speed.

### adjacent reaches

1 Falk knew well that her opinions of art were good.
2 Theresa answered her question; order was restored.
3 We join there and walk north to the western point.

### direct reaches

4 Barb Nunn must hunt for my checks; she is in debt.
5 In June and December, Irvin hunts in Bryce Canyon.
6 We decided to carve a number of funny human faces.

### double letters

7 Anne stopped off at school to see Bill Wiggs cook.
8 Edd has planned a small cookout for all the troop.
9 Keep adding to my assets all fees that will apply.

| 1 | 2 | 3 | 4 | 5 | 6 | 7 | 8 | 9 | 10 |

## Document 4
## Memo

1. Key the memo at the right, using the Memo template.
2. The memo is being sent to **Kisner Industrial Co. Project Staff** from **Melanie Winters, Project Coordinator**. Use **June 15** date and supply a reference line.
3. Format the table as follows:
   a. Size columns.
   b. Column headings: bold, shade, and center.
   c. Center table horizontally.
4. Create header for second page:
   Left margin: **Kisner Industrial Co. Project Staff**
   Right margin: **June 15, 200-**
5. Save as **p7-d4**; print. Place calendars behind memo.

**Note:** Refer to Document 3 for weekdays for July/August.

**Functions applied:**
Template
Table
QuickCorrect

Thank you for your ideas, energy, and enthusiasm this morning as we planned the Kisner Industrial Co. project. I am very pleased with our team and look forward to working with each one of you. I have summarized our tasks and timelines in the table below.

*(Please key table here. See notes from this morning's meeting. Arrange in chronological order and insert the days of the week before the completion dates.)*

Please note that the survey form and form letters must be created and mailed by July 3. One week will be adequate for completing a phone survey if needed. Calvin, please begin developing a sample script for the phone survey scheduled July 24-28. Kent Bass will head the analysis of data. Because of the short deadlines, it's very important that we be ready to analyze data by July 31.

By August 11 we should have completed a draft of the report with the final copy being ready for printing on the 15th. Anne Smith and Donna Irvin will have primary responsibility for preparing the electronic presentation for presenting the results of the project on August 23. I would like to review the draft of the slides on the 18th.

The enclosed calendars for July and August will be useful to us. Please post them in an easy-to-see location. Our important dates are highlighted—red for drafts and preliminary work and green for actual work or final copy. Thanks for joining this team and committing to completing our work on schedule.

6/15/-- Project Staff Meeting Notes    *Arrange in order. Spell out dates.*

| Task | Completion Date |
|---|---|
| Present project | August 23 |
| Complete revision of survey form and form letter | 7/3 |
| Mail survey form with cover letters | 7/5 |
| Complete draft of report | 8/11 |
| Conduct phone survey follow-up | Week of July 24-28 |
| Finalize script for phone survey | July 18 |
| Print final copy of report | 8/15 |
| Complete draft of presentation | 8/18 |

**Drill 5**

**Goal:** improve troublesome pairs

Use a controlled rate without pauses.

1 ad add did does dish down body dear dread dabs bad
d/k 2 kid ok kiss tuck wick risk rocks kayaks corks buck
3 Dirk asked Dick to kid Drake about the baked duck.

4 deed deal den led heed made needs delay he she her
e/i 5 kit kiss kiln kiwi kick kilt kind six ribs kill it
6 Abie had neither ice cream nor fried rice in Erie.

7 fib fob fab rib beg bug rob bad bar bed born table
b/v 8 vat vet gave five ever envy never visit weave ever
9 Did Harv key jibe or jive, TV or TB, robe or rove?

10 aft after lift gift sit tot the them tax tutu tyro
t/r 11 for far ere era risk rich rock rosy work were roof
12 In Toronto, Ruth told the truth about her artwork.

13 jug just jury judge juice unit hunt bonus quiz bug
u/y 14 jay joy lay you your only envy quay oily whey body
15 Willy usually does not buy your Yukon art in July.

**Drill 6**

**Goal:** build speed

Set the Timer for 1'.
Key each sentence for 1'. Try to complete each sentence twice (20 *gwam* or more). Ignore errors for now.

1 Dian may make cocoa for the girls when they visit.
2 Focus the lens for the right angle; fix the prism.
3 She may suspend work when she signs the torn form.
4 Augment their auto fuel in the keg by the autobus.
5 As usual, their robot did half turns to the right.
6 Pamela laughs as she signals to the big hairy dog.
7 Pay Vivian to fix the island for the eighty ducks.

| 1 | 2 | 3 | 4 | 5 | 6 | 7 | 8 | 9 | 10 |

| | words | 30" | 20" |
|---|---|---|---|

**Drill 7**

**Goal:** build speed

From the columns at the right, choose a *gwam* goal that is 2-3 words higher than your best rate. Set the Timer for **Variable** and then either **20"** or **30"**. Try to reach your goal.

| | | 30" | 20" |
|---|---|---|---|
| 1 | Did she make this turkey dish? | 12 | 18 |
| 2 | Blake and Laurie may go to Dubuque. | 14 | 21 |
| 3 | Signal for the oak sleigh to turn right. | 16 | 24 |
| 4 | I blame Susie; did she quench the only flame? | 18 | 27 |
| 5 | She turns the panel dials to make this robot work. | 20 | 30 |

| 1 | 2 | 3 | 4 | 5 | 6 | 7 | 8 | 9 | 10 |

## Use Calendar template

1. Use the Calendar template to prepare the calendar for the project. Click **File**, **New from Project**. On the Create New tab, choose *Calendar*, *Monthly*. Click **Create**.
2. Start the calendar in July (of the current year) for 2 months (to end in August of the current year). Click **Finished** to create the calendar.

## Key annotations and add graphics

1. Position insertion point in July 3 box and key **Complete revision of survey form and form letter**.
2. Select *3* and the text and change font color to red to show work in progress.
3. Repeat Steps 1–2 for remaining project dates shown in the table in Document 4 on the next page.
4. Click **Add Graphics** from the left window and choose *Add Clipart from Scrapbook*. Insert **constitu.wpg** on July 4. Size the graphic small enough so that **Holiday** can be keyed at the bottom of the date box.
5. Add the graphic **BILLS037.wpg** to the last square on the July calendar. Add a graphic of your choice to the last square on the August calendar.
6. Change the Table Look to *Lines All*.
7. Save as **p7-d3** and print.

**Note:** Green denotes a "Go" or completion; red denotes "Work in Progress" or preliminary deadline. ■

**Functions applied:**
Template
Clipart

See your instructor if the Calendar template is not available.

### July 2000

| Sunday | Monday | Tuesday | Wednesday | Thursday | Friday | Saturday |
|---|---|---|---|---|---|---|
| | | | | | | 1 |
| 2 | 3 Complete revision of survey form and form letter | 4 Holiday | 5 Mail survey form with cover letters | 6 | 7 | 8 |
| 9 | 10 | 11 | 12 | 13 | 14 | 15 |
| 16 | 17 | 18 Finalize script for phone survey | 19 | 20 | 21 | 22 |
| 23 | 24 Conduct phone survey follow-up | 25 Conduct phone survey follow-up | 26 Conduct phone survey follow-up | 27 Conduct phone survey follow-up | 28 Conduct phone survey follow-up | 29 |
| 30 | 31 | | | | | |

### August 2000

| Sunday | Monday | Tuesday | Wednesday | Thursday | Friday | Saturday |
|---|---|---|---|---|---|---|
| | | 1 | 2 | 3 | 4 | 5 |
| 6 | 7 | 8 | 9 | 10 | 11 Complete draft of report | 12 |
| 13 | 14 | 15 Print final copy of report | 16 | 17 | 18 Complete draft of presentation | 19 |
| 20 | 21 | 22 | 23 Present project | 24 | 25 | 26 |
| 27 | 28 | 29 | 30 | 31 | | |

**Drill 8**

**Goal:** build staying power
1. Key each ¶ as a 1' timing.
2. Key a 2' timing on both ¶s.

all letters

These writings may be used as Diagnostic Writings.

Writing 1: **18 gwam**

gwam 2'

```
      •         4         •         8         •
Why spend weeks with some problem when just a few        5
      12        •        16        •
quiet minutes can help us to resolve it.                 9

      •         4         •         8         •
If we don't take time to think through a problem,       15
      12        •        16        •
it will swiftly begin to expand in size.                18
```

Writing 2: **20 gwam**

```
      •         4         •         8         •
We push very hard in our quest for growth, and we        5
      12        •        16        •        20
all think that only excellent growth will pay off.      10

      •         4         •         8         •
Believe it or not, one can actually work much too       15
      12        •        16        •        20
hard, be much too zealous, and just miss the mark.      20
```

Writing 3: **22 gwam**

```
      •         4         •         8         •
A business friend once explained to me why he was        5
      12        •        16        •        20
often quite eager to be given some new project to       10
      •
work with.                                              11

      •         4         •         8         •
My friend said that each new project means he has       16
      12        •        16        •        20
to organize and use the best of his knowledge and       21
      •
his skill.                                              22
```

Writing 4: **24 gwam**

```
      •         4         •         8         •
Don't let new words get away from you.  Learn how        5
      12        •        16        •        20
to spell and pronounce new words and when and how       10
      •        24
finally to use them.                                    12

      •         4         •         8         •
A new word is a friend, but frequently more.  New       17
      12        •        16        •        20
words must be used lavishly to extend the size of       22
      •        24
your own word power.                                    24
```

```
2' |    1    |    2    |    3    |    4    |    5    |
```

Follow these general guidelines for completing the project. The functions applied in each document are listed.

| Letters | One of your first tasks will be to design a letterhead for this project. You will print other letters that you create on this letterhead. Letters should be formatted in block letter style with open punctuation. Be sure all notations are included and formatted correctly. Refer to the Reference Guide as necessary. |
|---|---|
| Memos | Use the memo template: **File**, **New from Project**, **Create New** tab, **Memo**, **Create**. |
| Spreadsheets | Prepare spreadsheets and graphs in *Quattro Pro,* and then link them as directed to the report and to the *Presentations* electronic slide presentation. |
| Long report | Key the long report SS using 10 point for the body and 12 point for main headings; bold all headings. MarketAnalysis prepares all summary reports as formal leftbound reports with title page, transmittal letter, table of contents, list of figures, report, and an appendix with supporting documentation. The report is bound in an attractive binder before presentation to the client. |
| Database merge | Use a *Paradox* database file to merge the form letter mailed to properties identified for the survey. |
| Slide presentation | Use *Presentations* to prepare a slide presentation that will be used in the formal meeting with Mr. Jerry Chitturi, the president of Kisner Industrial Co. |
| Web page | Use Internet Publisher to design a Web page to distribute market study results. |

**Document 1**
**QuickCorrect**

1. Choose *QuickCorrect* from the Tools menu; key the abbreviation (Column A at right) in the Replace text box.
2. Key the word or phrase (Column B) in the With text box. Click **Add Entry**.
3. Repeat for each entry in Column A.

QuickCorrect entries will be highlighted in later documents to remind you to use this feature.

**Document 2**
**Letterhead**

1. Design a letterhead for MarketAnalysis. Use the sample at right as a guide; however, use your creativity in your design.
2. Key the footer **"Member of National Federation of Consultants, Inc."**
3. Print and save as **letterhead-ma** for the letters you key later.

**Functions applied:**
Footer
Graphic line
Fonts

| Column A | Column B |
|---|---|
| ma | MarketAnalysis, Inc. |
| kic | Kisner Industrial Co. |
| fac | Fayette and Clark Counties |
| lex | Lexington |

# MarketAnalysis, Inc.

P.O. Box 5643, Lexington, KY 40515-5643    (606) 555-0168    FAX (606) 555-1029
Internet: www.marketanalysis.com

*"Member of National Federation of Consultants, Inc."*

Writing 5: **26 *gwam***                                                    *gwam*   2'

```
     •                4          •                8          •
We usually get best results when we know where we          5
     12         •               16         •               20
are going.  Just setting a few goals will help us          10
     •               24          •
quietly see what we are doing.                             13

     •                4          •                8          •
Goals can help measure whether we are moving at a          18
     12         •               16         •               20
good rate or dozing along.  You can expect a goal          23
     •               24          •
to help you find good results.                             26
```

Writing 6: **28 *gwam***

```
     •                4          •                8          •
To win whatever prizes we want from life, we must          5
     12         •               16         •               20
plan to move carefully from this goal to the next          10
     •               24          •               28
to get the maximum result from our work.                   14

     •                4          •                8          •
If we really want to become skilled in keying, we          19
     12         •               16         •               20
must come to see that this desire will require of          24
     •               24          •               28
us just a little patience and hard work.                   28
```

Writing 7: **30 *gwam***

```
     •                4          •                8          •
Am I an individual person?  I'm sure I am; still,          5
     12         •               16         •               20
in a much, much bigger sense, other people have a          10
     •               24          •               28          •
major voice in thoughts I think and actions I take.        15

     •                4          •                8          •
Although we are each a unique person, we all work          20
     12         •               16         •               20
and play in organized groups of people who do not          25
     •               24          •               28          •
expect us to dismiss their rules of law and order.         30
```

2'  |     1     |     2     |     3     |     4     |     5     |

# MARKETANALYSIS, INC., INTEGRATED APPLICATIONS

## OBJECTIVES

Prepare compound documents that integrate spreadsheet, database, or presentation files.

Use language effectively, make decisions, and work without direct supervision.

Design documents that communicate a strong message.

Use the tools on your desktop effectively.

## OVERVIEW

MarketAnalysis, Inc., located in Lexington, Kentucky, is a consulting organization that has gained a statewide reputation in market analysis. You are working under the supervision of Melanie Winters, project coordinator, for a market study authorized by President Jerry Chitturi, Kisner Industrial Co., Lexington. This study is to determine the trends in industrial real estate in Fayette and Clark Counties.

Project 6 applies many of the skills you have learned in this course, including:

- Designing a letterhead
- Formatting sophisticated tables
- Merging a word processing document with a database file
- Entering frequently used terms as QuickCorrect entries
- Creating a spreadsheet
- Creating charts from the spreadsheet
- Inserting clipart
- Linking and embedding *Quattro Pro* spreadsheets with *WordPerfect* documents
- Preparing a *Presentations* slide show
- Designing a Web page

Good luck to you as you join the Kisner project. Your knowledge of formatting principles, creative design abilities, and expertise in embedding and linking objects make you a valuable member of this team.

# FIGURE AND SYMBOL KEYS

## OBJECTIVES

1. Key the numeric keys by touch.

2. Master selected symbol keys.

3. Develop a relaxed, confident attitude.

4. Apply correct number expression.

**module**

LESSON **14**

# 1 and 8

**14a ● 7'**

**GETTING started**

each line twice SS

| | | |
|---|---|---|
| alphabet | 1 | Jessie Quick believed the campaign frenzy would be exciting. |
| shift keys | 2 | L. K. Coe, M.D., hopes Dr. Lopez can leave for Maine in May. |
| 3d row | 3 | We were quietly prepped to write two letters to Portia York. |
| easy | 4 | Kale's neighbor works with a tutor when they visit downtown. |

| 1 | 2 | 3 | 4 | 5 | 6 | 7 | 8 | 9 | 10 | 11 | 12 |

**14b ● 10'**

**SKILLBUILDING**

**Review high-frequency words**

The words at the right are from the 100 most used words. Key each line once; work for fluency.

Top 100

5 a an it been copy for his this more no office please service

6 our service than the they up was work all any many thank had

7 business from I know made more not me new of some to program

8 such these two with your about and have like department year

9 by at on but do had in letter most now one please you should

10 their order like also appreciate that there gentlemen letter

11 be can each had information letter may make now only so that

12 them time use which am other been send to enclosed have will

## Using the Web Publishing Wizard

Web Publishing Wizard provides you with an easy way to transfer your personal Web pages to your ISP's Web server or to a Web server on your local area network (LAN). To get started, make sure you have the following:

- A connection to your ISP—you must connect prior to using the Wizard.
- The connection method your ISP uses, such as FTP, HTTP Post, or SS CD.
- The Uniform Resource Locator (URL) for the Web server you will use.
- The name of the folder on the server where you will publish the files.

If you do not have this information, contact your ISP or system administrator.

## Adding a Web server

You'll need to provide Web Publishing Wizard with information about your Web server before posting for the first time. The Wizard saves the location of your Web server using the name you provide, so you can easily post to the same location in the future.

1. Click **File**, **Send To**, and then **Web Publishing Wizard**.

2. When the Welcome dialog box appears, click **Next**. Select a folder or file you want to publish and then click **Next**.

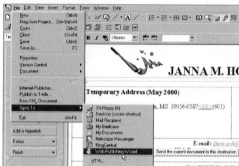

3. In the Descriptive name box, key a friendly name for your Web server, such as **My Web Server**. The descriptive name can be anything you want to use to identify your server in the drop-down list.

4. If you use a particular connection method to publish to your Web server, click **Advanced** to select that connection method from the list. If you do not know which connection method to use, click **Next**.

5. In the URL or Internet address box, key the Internet address you use to access the Web server.

6. In the Local directory box, key the path to the files on your computer that you want to publish.

7. Click **Next** and then **Finish**.

8. If you have any problems, it is best to contact the technical support staff for your ISP and request their help.

**To publish multiple files:**

1. Open *Windows Explorer* and select the files you want to publish.

2. Right-click the selected files and choose *Send To*, then *Web Publishing Wizard*.

3. Follow Steps 2–7 above.

## Learn 1 and 8

each line once SS

**Note:** The digit "1" and the letter "l" have separate values on a computer keyboard. Do not interchange these characters.

1 Reach *up* with *left fourth* finger.

8 Reach *up* with *right second* finger.

### SKILLBUILDING

**Improve figure keyreaches**

Control your reading speed; read only slightly ahead of what you are keying. Key each line once DS; repeat lines 23, 25, and 27.

### SKILLBUILDING

**Build skill**

each sentence twice

**Goals for 1':**
14-15 *gwam*, acceptable
16-17 *gwam*, good
18-21 *gwam*, very good
22+ *gwam*, excellent

**Abbreviations**
Do not space after a period within an abbreviation, as in Ph.D., U.S., C.O.D., a.m.

**1**

13  1 la a1 1 1; 1 and a 1; 1 add 1; 1 aunt; 1 ace; 1 arm; 1 aye
14  1 and 11 and 111; 11 eggs; 11 vats; Set 11A; May 11; Item 11
15  The 11 aces of the 111th Corps each rated a salute at 1 p.m.

**8**

16  8 8k k8 8 8; 8 kits; ask 8; 8 kites; kick 8; 8 keys; spark 8
17  OK 88; 8 bags; 8 or 88; the 88th; 88 kegs; ask 88; order 888
18  Eight of the 88 cars score 8 or better on our Form 8 rating.

**all figures learned**

19  She did live at 818 Park, not 181 Park; or was it 181 Clark?
20  Put 1 with 8 to form 18; put 8 with 1 to form 81.  Use 1881.
21  On May 1 at 8 a.m., 18 men and 18 women left Gate 8 for Rio.

22  The 188 men in 8 boats left Docks 1 and 18 at 1 p.m., May 1.
23  *On August 18, I saw 81 mares and 18 foals in fields 1 and 8.*
24  The 8 boxes on Pier 1 left on Ship 18 at 8 p.m. on March 11.
25  *Jane and Paul are 18; Sean and Harry are 81; Jake is now 18.*
26  Our 188 trucks moved 1881 tons on August 18 and December 18.
27  *Send Mary 181 No. 188 panes for her home at 8118 Oak Street.*

28  Did  their  form  entitle  them  to  the  land?
29  Did  the  men  in  the  field  signal  for  us  to  go?
30  I may pay for the antique bowls when I go to town.
31  The auditor did the work right, so he risks no penalty.
32  The man by the big bush did signal us to turn down the lane.

| 1 | 2 | 3 | 4 | 5 | 6 | 7 | 8 | 9 | 10 | 11 | 12 |

2. Many ISPs are beginning to provide users with FTP (File Transfer Protocol) access for sending files to their server. The ISP will provide you with the following:
   - Host name—something similar to ftp://www.netdoor.com
   - User ID—a unique user identification
   - Password—a unique password; it may or may not be the same one used to log onto the Internet
   - Remote directory path—where your files will be stored
   - URL—how the URLs for your Web pages will be displayed

3. If your ISP does not provide FTP access, you can download software such as WS-FTP LE, an easy-to-use program that can be obtained as freeware from several sites. Two suggested sites are www.download.com or www.tucows.com.

4. Once the software is installed, you are ready to send your files to the remote server. First, connect to the Internet. Then open the FTP program. Key the host name, your user id, and your password in the appropriate text boxes and click **OK**.

5. When you have connected with the remote server, the screen will display your local (hard) drive on one side and the remote (ISP) server on the other side (see below).

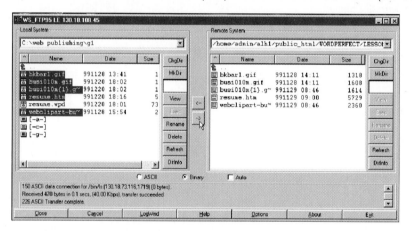

6. To send files to the server, select the file(s) on the local side (hard drive) and click the arrow pointing to the right (ISP server). (With some FTP programs, you would click an Up arrow to send files to the server.)

7. For Lessons G1 and G2, transfer all files in each folder except the original .wpd file.

**Final testing**

View your Web pages once you have made the transfer and make sure all links are working properly. It is a good idea to test your pages on different size/resolution monitors and on different browsers. The Web pages created in these lessons are best viewed in Internet Explorer.

The Uniform Resource Locator (URL) for each of your Web pages and sites may vary depending on your ISP, but it will be similar to the following format:

Lesson 1: www.domain.server/directory/resume.htm

Lesson 2: www.domain.server/directory/newslett.htm

Your ISP would provide the domain name and the directory, but the filename in the URL would be the same.

# 5 and 0

## 15a ● 7'

### GETTING started

For a series of capital letters press CAPS LOCK with the left little finger. Press again to release.

alphabet 1 John Quigley packed the zinnias in twelve large, firm boxes.

1/8 2 Idle Motor 18 at 8 mph and Motor 81 at 8 mph; avoid Motor 1.

caps lock 3 Lily read BLITHE SPIRIT by Noel Coward.  I read VANITY FAIR.

easy 4 Did they fix the problem of the torn panel and worn element?

| 1 | 2 | 3 | 4 | 5 | 6 | 7 | 8 | 9 | 10 | 11 | 12 |

## 15b ● 7'

### SKILLBUILDING

**Improve response patterns**

each line once SS; repeat if time permits

**word response:** read word by word

5 el id la or by doe so am is go us it an me ox he of to if ah
6 Did the air corps hang a map of the glens on the big island?

**stroke response:** read stroke by stroke

7 up you be was in at on as oh are no ad pop fad pun cad hi ax
8 Face bare facts, we beg you; read a free tract on star wars.

**combination response:** vary speed but maintain rhythm

9 be a duty|as junk|to form|at rest|of corn|do work|he read it
10 Doria paid the taxes on six acres of rich lake land in Ohio.

## 15c ● 12'

**Learn 5 and 0**

each line twice SS

5 Reach *up* with *left first* finger.

0 Reach *up* with *right fourth* finger.

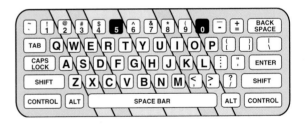

**5**

11 5 5f f5 5 5; 5 fans; 5 feet; 5 figs; 5 fobs; 5 furs; 5 flaws
12 5 o'clock; 5 a.m.; 5 p.m.; is 55 or less; buy 55; 5 and 5 is
13 Call Line 555 if 5 fans or 5 bins arrive at Pier 5 by 5 p.m.

**0**

14 0 0; ;0 0 0; skip 0; plan 0; left 0; is below 0; I scored 0;
15 0 degrees; key 0 and 0; write 00 here; the total is 0 or 00;
16 She laughed at their 0 to 0 score; but ours was 0 to 0 also.

**all figures learned**

17 I keyed 550 pages for Invoice 05, or 50 more than we needed.
18 Pages 15 and 18 of the program listed 150, not 180, members.
19 On May 10, Rick drove 500 miles to New Mexico in car No. 08.

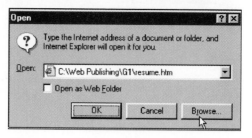

**Figure 1   Microsoft Internet Explorer**

**Figure 2   Netscape Navigator**

2. If you find anything that needs to be changed, close your browser, and open the appropriate document in *WordPerfect*. Avoid editing the *.htm* file that Internet Publisher creates when you publish to HTML. It is always best to make any changes to the original *.wpd* file, and then republish to HTML.

3. Make changes, save the document, and republish it to HTML.

**Editing hyperlinks**

When you have finished testing the Web documents, edit each hyperlink created. Remove the full path name of the files to be linked, replacing with only the filename and the extension.

1. There are no hyperlinks in Lesson 1 files. In Lesson 2, change the following:

| **newslett.wpd** | **From:** | **To:** |
|---|---|---|
| 2nd bullet in TOC | C:\Web Publishing\G2\alumni.wpd | alumni.htm |
| 3rd bullet in TOC | C:\Web Publishing\G2\alumni.wpd#Middle | alumni.htm#Middle |
| 4th bullet in TOC | C:\Web Publishing\G2\tour.wpd | tour.htm |

| **alumni.wpd** | **From:** | **To:** |
|---|---|---|
| lefarrow.gif | C:\Web Publishing\G2\newslett.wpd | newslett.htm |
| rigarrow.gif | C:\Web Publishing\G2\tour.wpd | tour.htm |

| **tour.wpd** | **From:** | **To:** |
|---|---|---|
| lefarrow.gif | C:\Web Publishing\G2\alumni.wpd | alumni.htm |
| rigarrow.gif | C:\Web Publishing\G2\newslett.wpd | newslett.htm |

2. Republish each of these three files.

**Sending the Web documents to your ISP**

1. To post pages on the Web, an Internet Service Provider (ISP) is needed. The provider can be a local ISP or a commercial one such as America Online (AOL). Some ISPs provide Web space with no cost other than a regular monthly service fee, and others charge more based on the amount of disk space you need to host the page(s). Check with your ISP to see what services are provided.

**SKILLBUILDING**

**Improve figure keyreaches**

Work to avoid pauses; each line once DS; repeat lines 21 and 23.

20 After May 18, French 050 meets in Room 185 at 10 a.m. daily.

21 *Read pages 5 and 8; duplicate page 18; omit pages 50 and 51.*

22 We have Model 80 with 10 meters or Model 180 with 15 meters.

23 *Between 8 and 10 that night, 5 of us drove to 580 Park Lane.*

24 Flight 508 left Reno at 1 on May 10; it landed in Lima at 8.

15e ● 9'

**SKILLBUILDING**

**Improve technique**

Reach up or down without moving your hands; each line once; repeat drill.

**direct reaches**

25 fr ki aq lo sw ;p de ju bg ,k xs mj za .l cd njy cde mju xsw

26 za mj cd .l xs ,k vf jp xs jy bg ,ki zaq .lo xsw mjy cde juj

27 Decide before long the freedom needed to justify the switch.

**adjacent reaches**

28 as oil red ask wet opt mop try tree open shred operas treaty

29 were pore dirt stew ruin faster onion alumni dreary mnemonic

30 The opened red hydrants were powerful, fast, and very dirty.

**outside reaches**

31 pop zap cap zag wasp equip lazy zippers queue opinion quartz

32 zest waste paper exist parquet azalea acquaint apollo apathy

33 The lazy wasp passed the potted azalea on the parquet floor.

15f ● 10'

**SKILLBUILDING**

**Build skill**

Key ¶ 2 twice for 1'. Try to increase speed by 2 words the second time.

**Optional:**

1. Click the **Open Screen** button.
2. Take two 1' writings on ¶ 2. Note your *gwam*.
3. Take two 1' writings on ¶ 1. Try to equal ¶ 2 rate.
4. Take one 2' writing on both ¶s.

all letters/figures                                              *gwam*  2' | 3'

•            4            •            8            •
I thought about Harry and how he had worked for me for          6 | 4
12            •            16            •            20           •
10 years; how daily at 8 he parked his worn car in the lot;     12 | 8
24            •            28            •            32           •
then, he left at 5.   Every day was almost identical for him.   18 | 12

•            4            •            8            •
In a quiet way, he did his job well, asking for little          23 | 15
12            •            16            •            20           •
attention.  So I never recognized his thirst for travel. I      29 | 19
24            •            28            •            32           •
didn't expect to find all of those maps near his workplace.     35 | 23

2' |  1  |  2  |  3  |  4  |  5  |  6
3' |    1    |    2    |    3    |    4

7. Click **Close**.

8. Open Windows Explorer and look at the *G1* directory to see the files associated with the *resume* file. You will see the following files:
   **LESSON 1:**

   > webclipart.gif
   > resume.wpd
   > busi010m.gif
   > busi010{1}.gif
   > resume.htm

9. Repeat Steps 2–8 for each of the files in Lesson G2: *newslett*, *alumni*, and *tour*. You will see the following files in Windows Explorer after completing these steps:
   **LESSON 2:**

   > alumni.gif
   > alumni.htm
   > alumni.wpd
   > bar.gif
   > bar{1}.gif     (You will see this file if you adjusted the bar.gif banner.)
   > graduate.gif
   > lefarrow.gif
   > logo.gif
   > masthead.gif
   > newlett.htm
   > newlett.wpd
   > paw.gif
   > rigarrow.gif
   > spacer.gif
   > stripe.gif
   > tour.gif
   > tour.wpd
   > yelball.gif

## Testing and editing the Web document

Prior to sending your documents to your ISP's Web server, it is a good idea to test your Web documents and their respective hyperlinks on the Web and make sure they are all working properly. You should test them in several browsers and on several different monitors.

1. Close the *.wpd* file and *WordPerfect*. Launch your Web browser and open each Web page. (**File**, **Open** in *Internet Explorer* or **File**, **Open Page** in *Netscape*)
   Lesson 1: *resume.htm*
   Lesson 2: *newslett.htm*

# 2 and 7

## 16a ● 7'

### GETTING started

each line twice SS

## 16b ● 14'

### Learn 2 and 7

each line twice SS

2 Reach *up* with *left third* finger.

7 Reach *up* with *right first* finger.

## 16c ● 5'

### SKILLBUILDING

**Improve keying techniques**

fingers curved, wrists low; each line once; repeat as time permits

alphabet 1 Perry might know I feel jinxed because I have missed a quiz.

figures 2 Channels 5 and 8, on from 10 to 11, said Luisa's IQ was 150.

caps lock 3 Ella Hill will see Chekhov's THE CHERRY ORCHARD on Czech TV.

easy 4 The big dog by the bush kept the ducks and hen in the field.

| 1 | 2 | 3 | 4 | 5 | 6 | 7 | 8 | 9 | 10 | 11 | 12 |

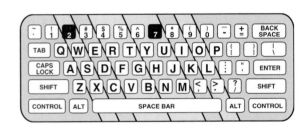

**2**

5 2 2s s2 2 2; has 2 sons; is 2 sizes; was 2 sites; has 2 skis

6 add 2 and 2; 2 sets of 2; catch 22; as 2 of the 22; 222 Main

7 Exactly at 2 on August 22, the 22d Company left from Pier 2.

**7**

8 7 7j j7 7 7; 7 jets; 7 jeans; 7 jays; 7 jobs; 7 jars; 7 jaws

9 ask for 7; buy 7; 77 years; June 7; take any 7; deny 77 boys

10 From May 7 on, all 77 men will live at 777 East 77th Street.

**all figures learned**

11 I read 2 of the 72 books, Ellis read 7, and Han read all 72.

12 Tract 27 cites the date as 1850; Tract 170 says it was 1852.

13 You can take Flight 850 on January 12; I'll take Flight 705.

**caps lock**

14 Our OPERATOR'S HANDBOOK says to use either AC or DC current.

**adjacent reaches**

15 He said that poised talk has triumphed over violent actions.

**direct reaches**

16 Murvyn must not make any decisions until Brad has his lunch.

**double letters**

17 He will tell all three cooks to add a little whipped butter.

**combination**

18 Kris started to blend a cocoa beverage for a shaken cowhand.

# Publish Files to the Web

Now that you have a basic understanding of creating a Web document using *WordPerfect's* Internet Publisher, and have created several documents, you are ready to post your documents on the Web. So far you have been viewing temporary copies of your Web documents in your browser, which is a quick way to check your documents as you work. To post information on the World Wide Web, Web pages must be stored on a Web server. Most Internet Service Providers (ISPs) offer Web hosting services for customers' Web pages. However, before you send documents to your ISP, you must convert the files to Hypertext Markup Language (HTML), which is a process called "publishing" in Internet Publisher.

**Publishing the Web document**

1. Open a new Web document using Internet Publisher. Open the PerfectExpert panel.

2. Open *resume.htm*. Click the **Finish** button on the PerfectExpert panel and select *Publish to HTML*. In the Publish to HTML dialog box, the name of the current document with an *.htm* extension appears in the HTML Source File Name text box.

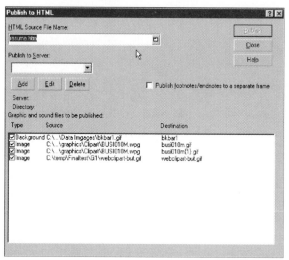

3. You must specify a location to publish to, either your hard drive or the location on a Web server for a specific ISP. You will publish to your hard drive first. Click the **Add** button to display the Server Information dialog box.

4. Key **Hard Drive** in the Label text field as the name of your server.

5. To specify a directory on your hard drive, click the appropriate directory or key the directory path in the Directory text box. The paths are:

   **Lesson 1:** c:\Web Publishing\G1\
   **Lesson 2:** c:\Web Publishing\G2\

6. Click **OK**; then click **Publish** in the Publish to HTML dialog box. You may see a quick flicker of this dialog box.

**Improve figure reaches**
each line twice; DS between
2-line groups

19 Both towns bid for six bushels of produce down by the docks.

20 *The cowl of the formal gown is held down by a bow.*

21 I work 18 visual signals with 2 turns of the lens.

22 Did he fix the shape of the hand and elbow of the clay form?

23 *The ivy bowl is a memento of their visit to Japan.*

24 Did 7 of them fix the signals for the 50 bicycles?

16e ● 10'

SKILLBUILDING

**Review high-frequency words**
The words at the right are from the 200 most used words. Key each line once; work for fluency.

Top 200

25 above again before call cost day feel further good how get

26 line meet opportunity per possible report since take today

27 account amount before check could sure hope cost used give

28 days find future help however its mail might every because

29 percent present request see special then through necessary

30 under well additional area being city could due get number

31 help insurance just mail month need plan interested return

32 state those upon what after complete present wish same its

33 available best course during form hope interest let matter

34 materials much next people policy prices receives possible

35 school want forward above into information letters however

16f ● 5'

SKILLBUILDING

**Reach for new goals**
Key each line twice. Work to increase your speed by 2 words the second time.

| | 30" | 20" |
|---|---|---|
| 36 If they wish, she may make the form for the disks. | 20 | 30 |
| 37 Did the chap focus the lens on the airy downtown signs? | 22 | 33 |
| 38 The formal gowns worn by the girls hang in the civic chapel. | 24 | 36 |
| 39 Di paid us to go to town to bid for an authentic enamel owl. | 26 | 39 |
| 40 Busy firms burn coal; odor is a key problem in the city air. | 28 | 42 |

## Inserting hyperlinks and bookmarks

Now you are ready to insert the hyperlinks and bookmarks that will connect the 3 pages. A visitor could then navigate with ease through all 3 pages of the newsletter. Make sure all 3 files you have just created are in the *G2* subfolder.

1. Open *newslett*. The first item in the table of contents does not need a hyperlink. Highlight the second item, **Cother Alumnus Of the Year**, and select *Add a Hyperlink* from the PerfectExpert panel.

2. Click the folder icon and select *alumni* from the *G2* subfolder. Click **OK**.

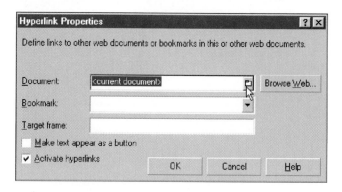

3. Highlight the third bulleted item, **Two Alumni Honored with Awards**. Click **Add a Hyperlink** and select the file *alumni*. Key **Middle** in the Bookmark textbox. You will create this bookmark in the next steps. Click **OK**.

4. Set a bookmark on the *alumni* file. Open *alumni* and place the insertion point in the blank Row 2 of the table, above the graphic. (See illustration below.)

blank row

5. Click **Tools**, **Bookmark**. Click **Create**. Key **Middle** in the Bookmark name box and click **OK**.

6. Next, add a hyperlink from the fourth item on the table of contents to the *tour* file.

7. Save both documents and view the *newslett* file on the Web. Test the links.

8. Now, make the arrow graphics on both the *alumni* and *tour* pages hyperlinks.

   • In the *alumni* file, link the Left arrow to the *newslett* file. Link the Right arrow to the *tour* file.

   • In the *tour* file, link the Left arrow to the *alumni* file. Link the Right arrow to the *newslett* file.

9. Save all of the files. View *newslett* on the Web and test all of the links.

Congratulations! You have successfully created an online newsletter!

# LESSON 17    4 and 9

## 17a ● 7'

### GETTING started

each line twice

## SKILLBUILDING WARMUP

alphabet 1 Bob realized very quickly that jumping was excellent for us.

figures 2 Has each of the 18 clerks now corrected Item 501 on page 27?

space bar 3 Was it Mary? Helen? Pam?  It was a woman; I saw one of them.

easy 4 The men paid their own firms for the eight big enamel signs.

| 1 | 2 | 3 | 4 | 5 | 6 | 7 | 8 | 9 | 10 | 11 | 12 |

## 17b ● 14'

### Learn 4 and 9

each line twice SS

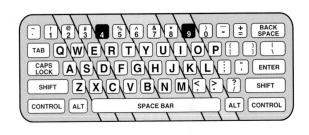

4 Reach *up* with *left first* finger.

9 Reach *up* with *right third* finger.

**4**

5  4 4f f4 4 4 4; if 4 furs; off 4 floors; gaff 4 fish; 4 flags

6  44th floor; half of 44; 4 walked 44 flights; 4 girls; 4 boys

7  I order exactly 44 bagels, 4 cakes, and 4 pies before 4 a.m.

**9**

8  9 9l l9 9 9 9; fill 9 lugs; call 9 lads; Bill 9 lost; dial 9

9  also 9 oaks; roll 9 loaves; 9.9 degrees; sell 9 oaks; Hall 9

10  Just 9 couples, 9 men and 9 women, left at 9 on our Tour 99.

**all figures learned**

11  Memo 94 says 9 pads, 4 pens, and 4 ribbons were sent July 9.

12  Study Item 17 and Item 28 on page 40 and Item 59 on page 49.

13  Within 17 months he drove 85 miles, walked 29, and flew 490.

## 17c ● 5'

### SKILLBUILDING

**Improve figure keyreaches**

each line twice; DS between 2-line groups

14  My staff of *18* worked *11* hours a day from May *27* to June *12*.

15  There were *5* items tested by Inspector *7* at *4* p.m. on May *8*.

16  Please send her File *10* today at *8*; her access number is *97*.

17  Car *47* had its trial run.  The qualifying speed was *198* mph.

18  The estimated score? *485*. Actual? *190*. Difference? *295*.

## Creating Page 3,
*continued*

6. Press ENTER and key the following text using Numbered List style:

   **Name:** _____
   **Title:** _____
   **Class Year:** _____
   **Card #:** _____
   **Signature:** _____

7. Press ENTER and key the following text using Normal style:

   **Reservations to be paid in full 45 days prior to departure.**

8. In Row 3, click center justification and insert the graphic *stripe.gif*.

9. In Row 4, insert and left-align the graphic *rigarrow.gif*.

10. Click **Change Colors**, **Custom**. Select the *Text/Background Colors* tab and select a background color of white.

Congratulations! You have completed the final page of your online newsletter. It should look similar to the figure below. Save the document and view it on the Web.

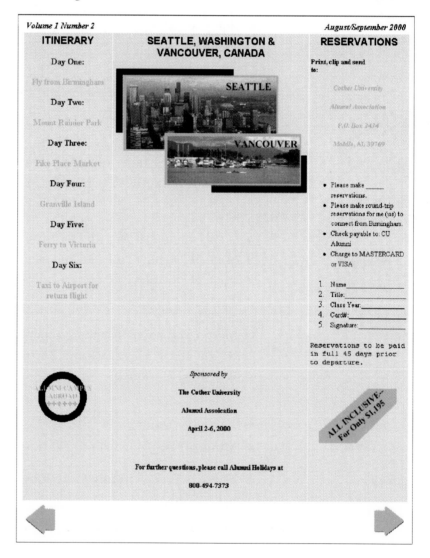

## SKILLBUILDING

**Improve keying technique**

key smoothly; strike the keys at a brisk, steady pace

**first finger**

19 buy them gray vent guy brunt buy brunch much give huge vying
20 Hagen, after her July triumph at tennis, may try volleyball.
21 Verna urges us to buy yet another of her beautiful rag rugs.

**second finger**

22 keen idea; kick it back; ice breaker; decide the issue; cite
23 Did Dick ask Cecelia, his sister, if she decided to like me?
24 Suddenly, Micki's bike skidded on the Cedar Street ice rink.

**third/fourth finger**

25 low slow lax solo wax zip zap quips quiz zipper prior icicle
26 Paula has always allowed us to relax at La Paz and at Quito.
27 Please ask Zale to explain who explores most aquatic slopes.

17e ● 14'

## SKILLBUILDING

**Reach for new goals**

1. Key each ¶ in the Open Screen for a 1' writing. Save the timings; print the best one.
2. Set the Timer for **2'**. Take two 2' writings on all ¶s. Reach for a speed within 2 words of 1' *gwam*. Save both timings; print the best one.
3. Take a 3' writing on all ¶s. Reach for a speed within 4 words of 1' *gwam*. Print.

**C** all letters                                                                    *gwam*   2' | 3'

|  |  |  |  |  | 2' | 3' |
|---|---|---|---|---|---|---|

We consider nature to be limited to those things, such    6 | 4
as air or trees, that we humans do not or cannot make.    11 | 7

For most of us, nature just exists, just is. We don't    17 | 11
question it or, perhaps, realize how vital it is to us.    22 | 15

Do I need nature, and does nature need me? I'm really    28 | 19
part of nature; thus, what happens to it happens to me.    33 | 22

2' | 1 | 2 | 3 | 4 | 5 | 6
3' | 1 | 2 | 3 | 4

**Creating Page 3,**
*continued*

### To format Column B:

1. Leave Row 1 blank.

2. In Row 2, center the title below using Arial, 14 point, bold:

   **Seattle, Washington & Vancouver, Canada**

3. Press ENTER. Select *Heading 5* from the Font Properties dialog box. Key the following in Arial, 12 point, Normal style:

   **An Exclusive Alumni**
   **Education and Travel Program**

4. Press ENTER. Insert and center the graphic *tour.gif*.

5. In Row 3, key the following information:

   *Sponsored by* ——————— (11 pt., Arial, italic)
   **The Cother University** ——— (Heading 5, bold, 10 pt.)
   **Alumni Association**
   **April 2-6, 2000**

6. Press ENTER. Click **Insert, Horizontal Line**. DS below the line and key:

   *For further questions, please call Alumni Holidays at* —— (8 pt., Arial)
   *800-555-0173* ————————————— (12 pt., Arial, italic)

7. Leave Row 4 blank.

### To format Column C:

1. In Row 1, key the date in bold, italic, 12 point Times New Roman, right-aligned.

   ***August/September 2000.***

2. In Row 2, center the title below in Arial, 14 point, bold.

   **RESERVATIONS**

3. Press ENTER. Select *Heading 5* style. Key the following in Arial, 12 point.

4. Press ENTER and key the following text in 12 pt. Bold the last 4 lines.

   Print, clip and send:
   **Cother University**
   **Alumni Association**       (Change font color for
   **P.O. Box 2434**            these 4 lines to gold.)
   **Mobile, AL 39769**

5. Press ENTER and key the following text in 10 point Arial, left-aligned, using the Bulleted List style in the Font Properties dialog box.

   - Please make _____ reservations.
   - Please make round-trip reservations for me (us) to connect from Birmingham.
   - Check payable to: CU Alumni
   - Charge to MASTERCARD or VISA

## 18a ● 7'

**G ETTING**
**started**

each line twice SS

**SKILLBUILDING WARMUP**

alphabet 1 Jim Kable won a second prize for his very quixotic drawings.
figures 2 If 57 of the 105 boys go on July 29, 48 of them will remain.
caps lock 3 Captain Jay took HMS James and HMS Down on a Pacific cruise.
easy 4 With the usual bid, I paid for a quantity of big world maps.
| 1 | 2 | 3 | 4 | 5 | 6 | 7 | 8 | 9 | 10 | 11 | 12 |

## 18b ● 14'

**Learn 3 and 6**
each line twice SS

**3** Reach *up* with *left second* finger.

**6** Reach *up* with *right first* finger.

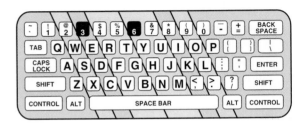

**3**

5 3 3d d3 3 3; had 3 days; did 3 dives; led 3 dogs; add 3 dips
6 we 3 ride 3 cars; take 33 dials; read 3 copies; save 33 days
7 On July 3, 33 lights lit 33 stands holding 33 prize winners.

**6**

8 6 6j 6j 6 6; 6 jays; 6 jams; 6 jigs; 6 jibs; 6 jots; 6 jokes
9 only 6 high; on 66 units; reach 66 numbers; 6 yams or 6 jams
10 On May 6, Car 66 delivered 66 tons of No. 6 shale to Pier 6.

**all figures learned**

11 At 6 p.m., Channel 3 reported the August 6 score was 6 to 3.
12 Jean, do Items 28 and 6; Mika, 59 and 10; Kyle, 3, 4, and 7.
13 Cars 56 and 34 used Aisle 9; Cars 2 and 87 can use Aisle 10.

## 18c ● 7'

**SKILLBUILDING**

**Improve keying techniques**
each line once; repeat drill

**caps lock**
14 The USS San Simon sent an SOS; the USS McVey heard it early.

**adjacent reaches**
15 Ersa Polk sang three hymns before we lads could talk to her.

**direct reaches**
16 Brace Oxware hunted for a number of marble pieces in Greece.

**double letters**
17 Tell the cook to add eggs and cheese to Ann's dinner entree.

**combination**
18 Jimmy's drab garage crew tests gears fastest, in my opinion.

## Creating Page 3

Follow the steps below to create Page 3 of the Web site.

1. Open another blank Web document. Save the file as **tour** in the *G2* folder created earlier. Key the title **Cother University Alumni Education**.

2. Follow the instructions at the right for Column A. The final Page 3 is illustrated on page 537.

When inserting a graphic, you should select the appropriate justification first. In HTML format, you cannot drag and drop the graphics to move them after they are inserted. ■

1. Insert a table with 3 columns and 4 rows with the following specifications:

   | | | | |
   |---|---|---|---|
   | a. | Table Width | Pixels | 750 |
   | b. | Table Border | | 0 |
   | c. | Cell spacing | | 1 |
   | d. | Inside cell margin | | 3 |
   | e. | Click inside Column A | Percent | 25 |
   | f. | Click inside Column B | Percent | 50 |
   | g. | Click inside Column B | Percent | 25 |

### To format Column A:

2. In Row 1, key the volume and number in bold, italic, 12 point Times New Roman, left-aligned.

   ***Volume 1 Number 2***

3. In Row 2, center the title below in Arial, 14 point, bold.

   **ITINERARY**

4. DS and click the **Change Font Attributes** button. Select *Heading 4*. Key the following text, pressing ENTER after each line. Use the Heading 4 style for the first row of each two rows.

   **Day One:**
   Fly from Birmingham
   **Day Two:**
   Mount Rainier Park
   **Day Three**
   Pike Place Market
   **Day Four:**
   Granville Island
   **Day Five:**
   Ferry to Victoria
   **Day Six:**
   Taxi to airport for return flight

5. In Row 3, click center justification. Insert the graphic *logo.gif*.

6. In Row 4, insert and left-align the graphic *lefarrow.gif*.

7. Select the activity for each day and change the font color to gold: R=233, G=173, B=16.

8. Select the cells in Rows 2 and 3 of Columns A, B, and C. Click the **Change Properties** button and select the *Cell* tab. Click **Cell Background Color** and choose light gold: R=250, G=232, B=188.

**Improve response patterns**

each line once SS; DS between 2-line groups; repeat

**word response:** *think* and *key* words

19 he el id is go us it an me of he of to if ah or bye do so am
20 Did she enamel emblems on a big panel for the downtown sign?

**stroke response:** *think* and *key* each stroke

21 kin are hip read lymph was pop saw ink art oil gas up as mop
22 Barbara started the union wage earners tax in Texas in July.

**combination response:** vary speed but maintain rhythm

23 upon than eve lion when burley with they only them loin were
24 It was the opinion of my neighbor that we may work as usual.

### 18e ● 14'

**SKILLBUILDING**

**Build staying power**

1. Key the ¶ as directed in Step 2. Remember to save each timing with its own name (**18e-t1, 18e-t2,** etc.). If you finish the ¶ before time is up, repeat the ¶ until the Timer stops. Print a timing at each speed.
2. Key two 1' writings, then a 2' writing, and a 3' writing. Work for good rhythm.

**Goals:**

1', 17-23 *gwam*
2', 15-21 *gwam*
3', 14-20 *gwam*

**Optional:**

Return to the Numeric Lesson menu. Click the **Diagnostic Writings** button. Key the ¶ as a 3' *Diagnostic Writing.*

**A** all letters                                                           *gwam*  2'  3'

|  |  |  | 4 |  | 8 |  |  | 2' | 3' |
|---|---|---|---|---|---|---|---|---|---|

I am something quite precious.  Though millions of people    6  4

in other countries might not have me, you likely do.  I have   12  8

a lot of power.  For it is I who names a new president every   18  12

four years.  It is I who decides if a tax shall be levied.   24  16

I even decide questions of war or peace.  I was acquired at   30  20

a great cost; however, I am free to all citizens.  And yet,   36  24

sadly, I am often ignored; or, still worse, I am just taken   42  28

for granted.  I can be lost, and in certain circumstances I   48  32

can even be taken away.  What, you may ask, am I?  I am your   54  36

right to vote.  Don't take me lightly.   58  39

| 2' | 1 | 2 | 3 | 4 | 5 | 6 |
| 3' | 1 | 2 | 3 | 4 |

## Creating Page 2,
*continued*

1. Save your document. View it on the Web. It should look similar to the figure below right.
2. If there is a visible border around your table (not gridlines), remove it by using the **Turn Border On/Off** button.
3. Congratulations! You have completed Page 2 of your online newsletter. Close your document for now as you work on the final page of the Web site.

**To format Column B,** *continued*

6. Key the following paragraphs:

Two young alumni from the School of Business were honored recently with the Stanberry Foundation National Accountants Awards. With these recent awards, Cother University graduates have garnered 15 of the 37 Stanberry awards given in Alabama since 1987. Rose Cook of Huntsville and Thomas Miller of Montgomery received their awards last fall at a dinner sponsored by the Alabama Society of Certified Accountants.

Cook, a certified accountant for Hicks, Collier, and Smith Accounting Firm since 1998, received her bachelor's degree in finance and management from Cother University in 1997. She has received several statewide awards in her field.

Miller, an auditor with C. E. Lott & Company, received his bachelor's degree in accounting in 1996. He received his master's degree from Cother University in 1997. Miller is president of the Alabama Society for Certified Public Accountants.

With more than 35 percent of the Alabama awards given to Cother University graduates, President William Russell said he thinks the university has been well represented.

7. Press ENTER. Insert and center the graphic *paw.gif*.
8. Leave Row 5 blank.
9. In Row 6, insert and right-align the graphic *rigarrow.gif*.

# $ and -, Number Expression

## 19a ● 7'

### GETTING started

each line twice SS

| | |
|---|---|
| alphabet | 1 Why did the judge quiz poor Victor about his blank tax form? |
| figures | 2 J. Boyd, Ph.D., changed Items 10, 57, 36, and 48 on page 92. |
| 3d row | 3 To try the tea, we hope to tour the port prior to the party. |
| easy | 4 Did he signal the authentic robot to do a turn to the right? |

| 1 | 2 | 3 | 4 | 5 | 6 | 7 | 8 | 9 | 10 | 11 | 12 |

## 19b ● 14'

**Learn $ and - (hyphen)**
each line twice SS; DS
between 2-line groups

**$** Shift; then reach *up* with *left first* finger.

**- (hyphen)** Reach *up* with *right fourth* finger.

- = hyphen
-- = dash
Do not space before or
after a hyphen or a dash.

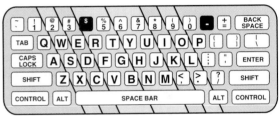

$

5 $ $f f$ $ $; if $4; half $4; off $4; of $4; $4 fur; $4 flats
6 for $8; cost $9; log $3; grab $10; give Rolf $2; give Viv $4
7 Since she paid $45 for the item priced at $54, she saved $9.

- (hyphen)

8 - -; ;- - - -; up-to-date; co-op; father-in-law; four-square
9 pop-up foul; big-time job; snap-on bit; one- or two-hour ski
10 You need 6 signatures--half of the members--on the petition.

all symbols learned

11 I paid $10 for the low-cost disk; high-priced ones cost $40.
12 Le-An spent $20 for travel, $95 for books, and $38 for food.
13 Mr. Loft-Smit sold his boat for $467; he bought it for $176.

## 19c ● 5'

### SKILLBUILDING

**Practice troublesome pairs**
Key at a controlled rate without pauses.

| | |
|---|---|
| e/d | 14 Edie discreetly decided to deduct expenses in making a deed. |
| w/e | 15 Working women wear warm wool sweaters when weather dictates. |
| r/e | 16 We heard very rude remarks regarding her recent termination. |
| s/d | 17 This seal's sudden misdeeds destroyed several goods on land. |
| v/b | 18 Beverley voted by giving a bold beverage to every brave boy. |

**Creating Page 2,**
*continued*

**To format Column A:**

1. In Row 1, key the volume and number in bold, italic, 12 point Times New Roman, left-aligned.

   ***Volume 1 Number 2***

2. In Row 2, center the title below in Arial, 14 point, bold.

   **1985 Science Education Graduate Cother
   Alumnus of the Year**

3. Press ENTER. Insert and center the graphic *bar.gif.* Adjust width of the bar, if necessary.

4. Press ENTER again. Key the following paragraphs:

   Mobile native and 1985 Science Education graduate from Cother University Elizabeth Anne Davis is the Department of Secondary Education's Alumnus of the Year for 1999. Davis holds the Pendleton Endowed Professorship of Science Education at the University of Arkansas at Little Rock. She received her master's degree in secondary education with an emphasis in science education from Cother University in 1977 and later received her doctorate from the University of Florida. She taught junior and senior high school for several years before turning to college teaching at the University of Arkansas at Little Rock.

   Davis is a seven-time recipient of the coveted American Society of Science Educators award. She is the author of several science education textbooks. She is married to Kent Davis, who is a 1983 graduate of Cother University, and they have three children.

5. Press ENTER. Insert and center the graphic *paw.gif.*

6. Leave Row 3 blank.

7. In Row 4, insert the graphic *alumni.gif* and center it.

8. Leave Row 5 blank.

9. In Row 6, insert and left-align the graphic *lefarrow.gif.*

**To format Column B:**

1. In Row 1, right-align the date in bold, italic, 12 point Times New Roman:

   ***August/September 2000***

2. In Row 2, insert the graphic *graduate.gif.*

3. Leave Row 3 blank.

4. In Row 4, center the heading below in Arial, 14 point, bold.

   **Two Alumni Honored with Awards**

5. Press ENTER. Insert and center the graphic *bar.gif.* Adjust the width of the bar if needed. Press ENTER again.

**19d ● 10'**

## SKILLBUILDING

**Build fluency**
Key each line once, working for fluid, consistent stroking. Repeat at a faster speed.

- Key the easy words as "words" rather than stroke by stroke.
- Key each phrase (marked by a vertical line) without pauses between words. ▪

**easy words**

19 am it go bus dye jam irk six sod tic yam ugh spa vow aid dug
20 he or by air big elf dog end fit and lay sue toe wit own got
21 six foe pen firm also body auto form down city kept make fog

**easy phrases**

22 it is|if the|and also|to me|the end|to us|it it|it is|to the
23 if it is|to the end|do you wish|to go to|for the end|to make
24 lay down|he or she|make me|by air|end of |by me|kept it|of me

**easy sentences**

25 Did the chap work to mend the torn right half of the ensign?
26 Blame me for their penchant for the antique chair and panel.
27 She bid by proxy for eighty bushels of a corn and rye blend.

**19e ● 14'**

## COMMUNICATION

**Learn number-usage rules**
1. Study the rules at right.
2. Key the sample sentences 28-33.
3. Change figures to words as needed in sentences 34-36.

**Numbers expressed as words**
Good writers know how to use numbers in their writing. The following rules illustrate when numbers should be expressed as words. Key as words:
- a number that begins a sentence.
- numbers ten and lower, unless they are part of a series of numbers any of which is over ten.
- the smaller of two adjacent numbers.

- isolated fractions and approximate numbers.
- round numbers that can be expressed as one or two words.
- numbers that precede "o'clock."

**Note:** Hyphenate spelled-out numbers between 21 and 99 inclusive. Also, hyphenate fractions expressed as words.

28 **Six** or **seven** older players were cut from the **37**-member team.
29 I have **2** of **14** coins I need to start my set.   Kristen has **9**.
30 Of **nine 24**-ton engines ordered, we shipped **six** last Tuesday.
31 Shelly has read just **one-half** of about **forty-five** documents.
32 The **six** boys sent well over **two hundred** printed invitations.
33 **One** or **two** of us will be on duty from **two** until **six** o'clock.
34 The meeting begins promptly at 9.   We plan 4 sessions.
35 The 3-person crew cleaned 6 stands, 12 tables, and 13 desks.
36 The 3d meeting is at 3 o'clock on Friday, February 2.

## Creating Page 1,
*continued*

1. In Column B, center the title in Arial, 14 point bold.
2. DS and insert the graphic *bar.gif*. Center it, if necessary.
3. DS and key the text left-aligned in Times New Roman, 12 point.
4. If there is a border around your table (not gridlines), remove it (click the **Turn Border On/Off** button and choose **Off**).
5. Save the document and view it on the Web.
6. Close the document.

## Column B

### Alumni Receive National Certification

Four alumni from the College of Education received National Board of Professional Teaching Standards certification last fall after participating in the World Class Teaching Program and passing the national certification exam.

Susan Jones and Bill Smith of Mobile, Alabama, Mary Ford of Jackson, Mississippi, and Betty Franks of Pensacola, Florida, are now 4 of 911 teachers from 40 states who have earned the designation.

Jones, who teaches in the Mobile Public School System, received her bachelor's degree in elementary education from Cother University in 1991. Smith, who teaches in the Mobile County School System, received his bachelor's degree in elementary education from Cother University in 1989 and his master's degree in 1992. Because of his contributions to education, Smith was inducted into the Alabama Teacher Hall of Fame and was named Alabama Teacher of the Year.

Ford, who teaches mathematics at Birmingham High School, received her bachelor's degree in mathematics education from Cother University in 1991. Franks, who teaches science at Birmingham High School, received her bachelor's degree in secondary education with an emphasis in science from Cother University in 1986 and her master's in 1988.

President Russell said that "these educators are at the very top of their profession, and Cother University is proud to call them our own. These are the kind of educators school systems nationwide are searching for and these are the ones who will make a difference in the lives of our youth."

**Insert the graphic *paw.gif*. Center it.**

## Creating Page 2

1. Follow steps on p. 529 to open another blank Web document. Save the file as **alumni** in the **G2** folder. Add this title for the title bar: **Cother University Alumni Awards.**
2. Insert a table using the specifications shown at the right.
3. Enter the text and graphics in Column A and then in Column B. Directions are provided for each row on the next page. The graphic files are found on the Formatting Template.

Insert a table with 2 columns and 6 rows with the following specifications:

| | | |
|---|---|---|
| a. Table Width | Pixels | 700 |
| b. Column A | Pixels | 350 |
| c. Column B | Pixels | 350 |
| d. Table Border | | 0 |
| e. Cell spacing | | 1 |
| f. Inside cell margin | | 3 |

# # and /

## 20a • 7'

### GETTING started

each line twice SS

alphabet 1 Freda Jencks will have money to buy six quite large topazes.

symbols 2 I bought 10 ribbons and 45 disks from Cable-Han Co. for $78.

home row 3 Dallas sold jade flasks; Sal has a glass flask full of salt.

easy 4 He may cycle down to the field by the giant oak and cut hay.

| 1 | 2 | 3 | 4 | 5 | 6 | 7 | 8 | 9 | 10 | 11 | 12 |

## 20b • 14'

### Learn # and /

each line twice SS

# = number sign, pounds
/ = diagonal, slash

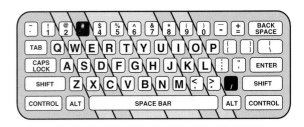

# Shift; then reach *up* with *left second* finger.

/ Reach *down* with *right fourth* finger.

#

5 # #e e# # # #; had #3 dial; did #3 drop; set #3 down; Bid #3
6 leave #82; sold #20; Lyric #16; bale #34; load #53; Optic #7
7 Notice #333 says to load Car #33 with 33# of #3 grade shale.

/

8 / /; :/ / / /; 1/2; 1/3; Mr./Mrs.; 1/5/94; 22 11/12; and/or;
9 to/from; /s/ William Smit; 2/10, n/30; his/her towels; 6 1/2
10 The numerals 1 5/8, 3 1/4, and 60 7/9 are "mixed fractions."

**all symbols learned**

11 Invoice #737 cites 15 2/3# of rye was shipped C.O.D. 4/6/95.
12 B-O-A Company's Check #50/5 for $87 paid for 15# of #3 wire.
13 Our Co-op List #20 states $40 for 16 1/2 crates of tomatoes.

## 20c • 7'

### SKILLBUILDING

**Reach for new goals**
Key 30" writings on both lines of a pair. Try to key as many words on the second line of each pair. Work to avoid pauses.

*gwam* 30"

14 She did the key work at the height of the problem. 20
15 Form #726 is the title to the island; she owns it. 20

16 The rock is a form of fuel; he did enrich it with coal. 22
17 The corn-and-turkey dish is a blend of turkey and corn. 22

18 It is right to work to end the social problems of the world. 24
19 If I sign it on 3/19, the form can aid us to pay the 40 men. 24

## Creating an e-mail link

Make Janna's name an e-mail hyperlink so visitors to this page can submit an e-mail message or an article for the next issue of this newsletter to her.

1. Highlight Janna's name and click **Add a Hyperlink** from the PerfectExpert panel.

2. Key **mailto:jhoward@netdoor.com** in the Document text box and click **OK**. The term **mailto:** in front of the e-mail address is part of the behind-the-scenes HTML (HyperText Markup Language) coding that makes this link work properly for submitting e-mail through the browser. When a visitor clicks this link, it will bring up his or her default mail program. *Internet Explorer* will launch *Microsoft Outlook* by default.

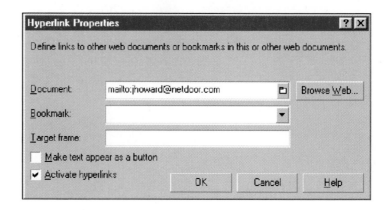

## Customizing color

1. Press ENTER 4 times and key the text below. Apply the Normal style, centered, bold, and italic. To change the color, click **Change Colors**, **Custom**. Select *regular text*, then *More*, and set the font color to gold (Red: 233; Green: 173; and Blue: 16).

   ### COTHER UNIVERSITY
   ### Home of the Fighting Bulldogs

2. Notice the color of the link for JANNA M. HOWARD. It is blue, by default, and referred to as a Hypertext link in *WordPerfect* (*unvisited link* in HTML). When it is clicked, it becomes purple by default, and is referred to as a Visited hypertext link in *WordPerfect* (*visited link* in HTML). To make the links more visually pleasing with the color scheme for the rest of the Web site, you can change the colors by modifying the color for Hypertext link, Visited hypertext link, and Active Hypertext link.

3. Click **Change Colors**, **Custom**. Set the colors listed below by clicking the paint bucket button, then **More** for each:
   Hypertext link (R 255, G 255, B 255=white), Visited hypertext link (R 250, G 232, B 188=light gold) Active hypertext link (R 255, G 0, B 0=red)

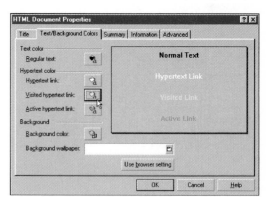

4. To change the background color:
   - Click **Format**, **Text Colors/ Wallpaper**; select the *Text Colors* tab.
   - Click once anywhere on the background in the lower frame, and choose *white* on the color palette. Close the lower frame.

## 20d ● 8'

### COMMUNICATION

**Review number usage**
DS; decide whether the circled numbers should be keyed as figures or as words and make needed changes. Check your finished work with 19e, p. 47.

20 Six or ⑦ older players were cut from the �37-member team.

21 I have ② of 14 coins I need to start my set.   Kristen has ⑨.

22 Of ⑨ 24-ton engines ordered, we shipped ⑥ last Tuesday.

23 Shelly has read just ① half of about ㊺ documents.

24 The ⑥ boys sent well over ⑳⓪⓪ printed invitations.

25 ① or ② of us will be on duty from ② until ⑥ o'clock.

## 20e ● 14'

### SKILLBUILDING

**Improve speed**
1. From the Lesson menu, click the **Open Screen** button.
2. Follow the procedures at the right for increasing your speed by taking guided writings.
3. Take a 3' writing without the guide on the complete writing.

**Guided writing procedures**
1. In the Open Screen, take a 1' writing on ¶ 1. Note your *gwam*.
2. Add 4 words to your 1' *gwam* to determine your goal rate.
3. Set the Timer for 1'. Set the Timer option to beep every 15".
4. From the table below, select from Column

4 the speed nearest your goal rate. Note the 1/4' point at the left of that speed. Place a light check mark within the ¶s at the 1/4' points.
5. Take two 1' guided writings on ¶s 1 and 2. Do not save.
6. Turn the beeper off.

|  |  |  | *gwam* |
|---|---|---|---|
| 1/4' | 1/2' | 3/4' | 1' |
| 4 | 8 | 12 | 16 |
| 5 | 10 | 15 | 20 |
| 6 | 12 | 18 | 24 |
| 7 | 14 | 21 | 28 |
| 8 | 16 | 24 | 32 |
| 9 | 18 | 27 | 36 |
| 10 | 20 | 30 | 40 |

Ⓔ all letters                                                                         *gwam*   2'   3'

Some of us think that the best way to get attention is    6   4  35

to try a new style, or to look quixotic, or to be different   12   8  39

somehow.   Perhaps we are looking for nothing much more than   18  12  43

acceptance from others of ourselves just the way we now are.   24  16  47

There is no question about it; we all want to look our   29  19  50

best to impress other people.   How we achieve this may mean   35  23  54

trying some of this and that; but our basic objective is to   41  27  58

take our raw materials, you and me, and build up from there.   47  31  62

2' | 1 | 2 | 3 | 4 | 5 | 6 |
3' | 1 | 2 | 3 | 4 |

**Creating Page 1**

1. In the PerfectExpert panel, click **Extras**, **Add a Table**. Create a 2-column, 2-row table.

2. Select *Column A*. Click the **Change Properties** button. On the Column tab, click **column width**. Select *Pixels* in the drop-down box and key **200**. Select the *Table* tab and choose *Pixels* and *650* for table width. Make the following choices: Table borders=0; Cell spacing=1; Inside cell margin=3. Click **Apply**, then **OK**.

3. Select *Column B*. Click the **Change Properties** button; on the Column tab, click **column width**, select *Pixels*, and key **440**. Click **OK**.

4. In Cell A1, key the volume and number in bold, italic, left-aligned. Key the date in bold, italic, right-aligned in Cell B1.

   ***Volume 1 Number 2***                    ***August/September 2000***

**To format Column A:**

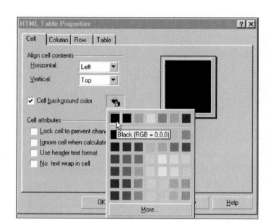

1. With the insertion point in Cell A2 (1st cell in Row 2), click **Change Properties**. Click the **Cell** tab and click the check box beside Cell background color. Select the *Color* button (paint bucket) to display the color palette; select *Black*. Click **OK**. Column A turns black.

2. Press ENTER once. Click the **Change Font Attributes** button, then the **Font** tab, and choose Arial, bold, 12 point, white. Click **OK**. Click **Justification** on the toolbar and select *Center*. Key **TABLE OF CONTENTS**. DS.

3. Select left justification, and insert the graphic *yellball.gif*. Space once and key in bold **Alumni Receive National Certification**. DS.

4. Insert 3 more large bullets (graphic *yellball.gif*) and key the following text:
   - Cother Alumnus of the Year
   - Two Alumni Honored with Awards
   - Alumni Tour Set for Seattle/Vancouver

5. Click **View in Web Browser** and notice that the text for these bulleted items wraps to two lines due to the width of the column. They do not align in a visually pleasing manner. Close the browser.

6. Place the insertion point at the beginning of the 2nd row of text for each item (3rd row in *WordPerfect* document) and insert the graphic *spacer.gif*. This graphic is a small black rectangle used as a spacer. Since tabs cannot be used in the HTML table in *WordPerfect 9*, the graphic is inserted to make lines of text align like a hanging indent. See the Table of Contents figure at right.

7. DS after the last bulleted item and key the text below. Apply the Normal style, Times New Roman, and bold.

   For information about this online newsletter or to submit articles for future newsletters, please contact
   **JANNA M. HOWARD** —— (centered, bold)

8. Click **OK** and then save.

# 21

## % and !

### 21a ● 7'

## Ⓖ ETTING started

each line twice SS

alphabet 1 Merry will have picked out a dozen quarts of jam for boxing.

fig/sym 2 Jane-Ann bought 16 7/8 yards of #240 cotton at $3.59 a yard.

1st row 3 Can't brave, zany Cave Club men/women next climb Mt. Zamban?

easy 4 Did she rush to cut six bushels of corn for the civic corps?

| 1 | 2 | 3 | 4 | 5 | 6 | 7 | 8 | 9 | 10 | 11 | 12 |

### 21b ● 14'

**Learn % and !**

each line twice SS

% = percent sign
Use % with business forms or where space is restricted; otherwise, use the word "percent."
Space twice after the exclamation point!

% Shift; then reach *up* with *left first* finger.

%

5 % %f f% % %; off 5%; if 5%; of 5% fund; half 5%; taxes of 5%

6 7% rent; 3% tariff; 9% F.O.B.; 15% greater; 28% base; up 46%

7 Give discounts of 5% on rods, 50% on lures, and 75% on line.

!: reach *up* with the *left fourth* finger

8 ! !a a! ! ! !; Eureka! Ha! No! Pull 10! Extra! America!

9 Listen to the call! Now! Ready! Get set! Go! Good show!

10 I want it now, not next week! I am sure to lose 50% or $19.

**all symbols**

11 The ad offers a 10% discount, but this notice says 15% less!

12 He got the job! With Clark's Supermarket! Please call Mom!

13 Bill #92-44 arrived very late from Zyclone; it was paid 7/4.

### 21c ● 5'

**Improve response patterns**

each line once; repeat

**words:** *think, say,* and *key* words

14 may big end pay and bid six fit own bus sit air due map lays

15 also firm they work make lend disk when rush held name spend

16 city busy visit both town title usual half fight blame audit

**phrases:** *think, say,* and *key* phrases

17 is the|to do|it is|but so|she did|own me|may go|by the|or me

18 it may|he did|but if|to end|she may|do so|it is|to do|is the

19 the firm|all six|they paid|held tight|bid with|and for|do it

G2

# Create a Web Site with Multiple Documents

Now that you have a basic understanding of many of the features of creating a Web page using *WordPerfect 9's* Internet Publisher, you are ready to create a Web site with multiple pages. You will connect the pages using hyperlinks and bookmarks.

In this lesson, you will create an online newsletter that will consist of three Web pages for the Cother University Alumni Association. Page 1, the main page of the newsletter, is shown below. It consists of a masthead (banner) in the upper-left corner, the publication information, a table of contents, and the first article. The table of contents and first article are formatted as a two-column table.

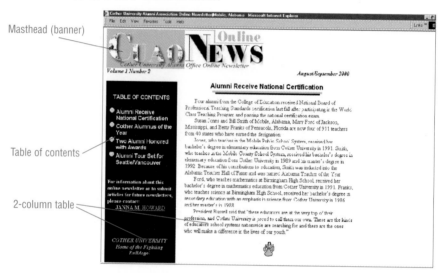

Masthead (banner)

Table of contents

2-column table

## Opening a blank Web document and adding a title

1. Open a blank Web document (**File**, **Internet Publisher**, **New Web Document**, **Create a blank web document** template). Click **Help**, **PerfectExpert** to open the PerfectExpert panel.

2. Save the document as **newslett** in a new folder named *G2* within the Web Publishing folder.

3. Click the **Add a Title** button in the PerfectExpert panel and select *For the Title Bar.* Click **Custom Title** and key the following title: **Cother University Alumni Association Online Newsletter—Mobile, Alabama**

## Inserting a graphic

1. Insert the graphic *masthead.gif* from the Formatting Template in the upper-left corner of the page. DS below the banner. *Note:* All graphic files are saved on the Formatting Template.

2. Click the **View in Web Browser** button to see how the document will look on the WWW.

> **Function review**
>
> **To insert a graphic**
> Click **Insert**, **Graphics**, and **From File**. Select the graphic to be inserted and click **Insert**. ■

**Improve finger reaches**
Key each set of lines SS; DS
between each group; fingers
curved, hands quiet. Repeat if
time permits.

**1st finger**

20 by bar get fun van for inn art from gray hymn July true verb
21 brag human bring unfold hominy mighty report verify puny joy
22 You are brave to try bringing home the van in the bad storm.

**2d finger**

23 ace ink did cad keyed deep seed kind Dick died kink like kid
24 cease decease decades kick secret check decide kidney evaded
25 Dedre likes the idea of ending dinner with cake for dessert.

**3d finger**

26 oil sow six vex wax axe low old lox pool west loss wool slow
27 swallow swamp saw sew wood sax sexes loom stew excess school
28 Wes waxes floors and washes windows at low costs to schools.

**4th finger**

29 zap zip craze pop pup pan daze quote queen quiz pizza puzzle
30 zoo graze zipper panzer zebra quip partizan patronize appear
31 Czar Zane appears to be dazzled by the apple pizza and jazz.

21e ● 4'

**Practice speed runs
with numbers**
Take 1' writings; the last number you key when you stop is
your approximate *gwam*.

1 and 2 and 3 and 4 and 5 and 6 and 7 and 8 and 9 and 10 and

11 and 12 and 13 and 14 and 15 and 16 and 17 and 18 and 19

and 20 and 21 and 22 and 23 and 24 and 25 and 26 and 27 and

# *on...* One Space or Two?

VIEWS

Traditionally, two spaces follow end-of-sentence punctuation in documents. In desktop publishing, one space
generally follows end-of-sentence punctuation. As a
result of desktop publishing and the proportional fonts of
today's word processing programs, some users have suggested change.

With proportional fonts, characters use a varied amount
of space depending upon their width. Monospace fonts
such as Courier (also used by typewriters) use the same
amount of space for each character; thus, two spaces are
required after end-of-sentence punctuation for readability.

We believe the critical factors are readability and ease of retention, and not all fonts provide a distinct end-of-sentence look.
End-of-sentence punctuation decisions will continue to be
reevaluated with changing technologies. In this textbook, you
will use two spaces after end-of-sentence punctuation for typical document production. In the Desktop Publishing module,
however, you will use one.

## The final product

Save your document and view your completed resume using **View in Web Browser**. It should look similar to the figure below.

### JANNA M. HOWARD

| Temporary Address (May 2000) | Permanent Address |
|---|---|
| 587 Birch Circle | 328 Fondren Street |
| Clinton, MS 39056-0587 | Orlando, FL 32801-0328 |
| (601) 555-4977 | (407) 555-3838 |

E-mail: jhoward@netdoor.com
Web Page: www.netdoor.com/~jhoward

#### CAREER OBJECTIVES

To obtain a graphic design position with an opportunity to advance to a management position.

#### SUMMARY OF ACHIEVEMENTS

Bachelor's degree with double major in office systems technology and graphics design; proficient in computer environments and major software applications. Related work experiences in three organizations including internship in foreign country. Speak Japanese and enjoy photography.

#### EDUCATION

**B.S. Office Systems Technology and Graphics Design**

- College/University: Cother University, Mobile, Alabama
- Graduation Date: May 2000
- Grade point average: 3.8/4.0
- Honors: Served as president of Graphic Designers' Society

#### SPECIAL SKILLS

| | |
|---|---|
| Environments: | *Microsoft Windows® and Macintosh OS®* |
| Software: | *Office 2000®, Netscape®, CorelDraw®, PageMaker®, HyperStudio®, Photoshop®, Illustrator®, and FreeHand®* |
| Language: | BASIC and HTML |
| Keyboarding: | 70 words per minute |
| Foreign language: | Japanese |
| Travel: | Japan (two summers working as graphic design intern) |

#### EXPERIENCE

Cother University Alumni Office, Mobile Alabama
Assistant editor and producer of the Cother Alumni News, 1998 to present.

- Designed layout and production of six editions; met every publishing deadline
- Received the "Cother Design Award"
- Assisted editor in design of Alumni Office Web page (www.cu.edu/alumni/)

Cother Library, Mobile, Alabama
Student assistant in Audiovisual Library, 1997-1998.

- Created Audiovisual Catalog using computerized database
- Prepared monthly and yearly report using database
- Designed brochure to promote library services (www.cu.edu/~jhoward/samples/brochure)

#### REFERENCES

Request portfolio from Cother University Placement Office.

*Last Modified: January 28, 2000 (2:28pm)*
This page was created in WordPerfect Office 2000 and is best viewed in Microsoft Internet Explorer.
Free graphics taken from:

---

*Additional Practice:* Using the skills learned in Lesson G1, create a Web page that might be provided by the Placement Office with your references, their contact information, and their comments about you. Name this file **reference**.

*Bonus:* Create a hyperlink from the word *portfolio* in the sentence under the *REFERENCE* section of your resume to link to your new *reference* file.

# LESSON 22

# ( and )

## 22a ● 7'

### GETTING started

each line twice SS

| | | |
|---|---|---|
| alphabet | 1 | Avoid lazy punches; expert fighters jab with a quick motion. |
| fig/sym | 2 | Be-Low's Bill #483/7 was $96.90, not $102--they took 5% off. |
| caps lock | 3 | Report titles may be shown in ALL CAPS; as, BOLD WORD POWER. |
| easy | 4 | Do they blame me for their dismal social and civic problems? |

| 1 | 2 | 3 | 4 | 5 | 6 | 7 | 8 | 9 | 10 | 11 | 12 |

## 22b ● 14'

### Learn ( and )
### (parentheses)

each line twice SS

( ) = parentheses
Parentheses indicate off-hand, aside, or explanatory messages.

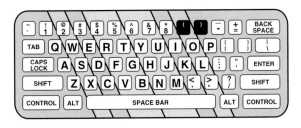

( Shift; then reach *up* with the *right third* finger.

) Shift; then reach *up* with the *right fourth* finger.

5 ( (l l( (; (; Reach from l for the left parenthesis; as, ( (.
6 ) ); ;) ) ); Reach from ; for the right parenthesis; as, ) ).

( )

7 Learn to use parentheses (plural) or parenthesis (singular).
8 The red (No. 34) and blue (No. 78) cars both won here (Rio).
9 We (Galen and I) dined (bagels) in our penthouse (the dorm).

**all symbols learned**

10 The jacket was $35 (thirty-five dollars)--the tie was extra.
11 Starting 10/29, you can sell Model #49 at a discount of 25%.
12 My size 8 1/2 shoe--a blue pump--was soiled (but not badly).

## 22c ● 6'

### SKILLBUILDING

### Review numbers and symbols

Key each line twice, keeping eyes on copy. DS between pairs.

13 Jana has one hard-to-get copy of her hot-off-the-press book.
14 An invoice said that "We give discounts of 10%, 5%, and 3%."
15 The company paid Bill 3/18 on 5/2/97 and Bill 3/1 on 3/6/97.
16 The catalog lists as out of stock Items #230, #710, and #13.
17 Elyn had $8; Sean, $9; and Cal, $7. The cash total was $24.

4. Notice the Graphics toolbar that appears when the images are selected. Select the image on the left and use the **Flip Top/Bottom** button. Select the image on the right and repeat the top/bottom flip but also **Flip Left/Right**. Compare your images to those on page 528.

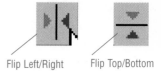

Flip Left/Right    Flip Top/Bottom

5. Position the insertion point after the last row of text in your document. Click **Insert**, **Line Break**. Click **Insert**, **Graphics**, and then click **From File**. Select *webclipart.gif* from the Formatting Template.

6. Right-click the graphic; then click **HTML Properties**. Click the **Image** tab. In the Alternate Text box, key **Web Clipart** for users who have disabled graphics display in their browser.

7. Click the radio button beside **Link**. Click the **Link** tab and key **www.webclipart.about.com**. Click **OK**. This link will take users to the site on the World Wide Web where the free graphics used on your page are located.

8. Save your document.

## Publishing your Web document

1. To publish to HTML, click **File**, **Send To**, **HTML**. The filename *resume.htm* should appear in the HTML Source File Name box. If you do not have an Internet Service Provider (ISP), publish to the hard drive or to a disk.

2. Click the **Add** button under Publish to Server. Key a name such as **Hard Drive** or **Disk** in the Label text box. Browse in the lower box and locate the folder and sub-folder you created earlier: **C:\Web Publishing\G1**.

3. Click **OK** and then **Publish**.

## 22d ● 14'

COMMUNICATION

**Learn number-usage rules**

Study the rules at the right; then key lines 18-23.

### Numbers expressed as figures

In most business communications, some numbers are expressed in figures, while others are expressed in words. The following guidelines indicate instances when writing numbers as figures is preferred practice. Key as figures:

- numbers coupled with nouns
- house numbers (except house number One) and street names (except ten and under); if street name is a number, separate it from the house number with a dash (--)
- time when expressed with a.m. or p.m.
- a date following a month; a date preceding the month (or standing alone) is expressed in figures followed by "d" or "th"

- money amounts and percents, even when approximate (use the $ symbol and/or the words "cents" or "percent")
- round numbers in the millions or higher with their word modifiers (with or without a dollar sign)

**Note:** When speaking or writing numbers (as in writing numbers on a check), the word "and" should be used only to signify a decimal point. Thus, 850 is spoken or written as "eight hundred fifty," not "eight hundred and fifty."

18 Ask **Group 1** to read **Chapter 6** of **Book 11** (**Shelf 19, Room 5**).

19 All **six** of us live at **One Bay Road**, not at **126--56th Street**.

20 At **9 a.m.** the owners decided to close from **12 noon** to **1 p.m.**

21 Ms. Vik leaves **June 9**; she returns the **14th or 15th of July**.

22 The **16 percent** discount saves **$115**. A stamp costs **35 cents**.

23 Elin gave **$3 million** to charity; our gift was only **75 cents**.

## 22e ● 9'

SKILLBUILDING

**Build staying power**

1. Take two 1' timings on each ¶.
2. Take a 3' timing on all ¶s. Determine *gwam*.

**Goal:** 17 *gwam*

Ⓔ all letters                                                                    *gwam*    3"

|  |  |
|---|---|
| Most people will agree that we owe it to our children | 4 \| 28 |
| to pass the planet on to them in better condition than we | 7 \| 32 |
| found it. We must take extra steps just to make the quality | 12 \| 36 |
| of living better. | 13 \| 37 |
| If we do not change our ways quickly and stop damaging | 16 \| 41 |
| our world, it will not be a good place to live. We can save | 21 \| 45 |
| the ozone and wildlife and stop polluting the air and water. | 25 \| 49 |

3'   1          2          3          4

6. Remove any background wallpaper and set colors to the default before proceeding.

7. Click **Change Background**, **Custom** and click the folder icon. Select the graphic *bkbar.gif* from your Formatting Template. Click **OK**. Preview your document on the Web.

8. Change the color scheme of all text in your document to match the new background: Click **Format** menu, **Text Colors/Wallpaper**. Click the **Text Colors** tab. Each of the phrases listed below is a button. Click each of the buttons, select *More*, and make the following changes in the Color values using the default RGB Color Model.

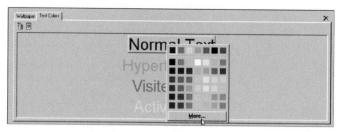

| | | | |
|---|---|---|---|
| Normal Text | Red=0 | Green=0 | Blue=90 |
| Hypertext Link | Red=214 | Green=165 | Blue=0 |
| Visited Link | Red=231 | Green=0 | Blue=0 |
| Active Link | Red=255 | Green=239 | Blue=0 |

9. Save your document and preview it on the Web.

## Working with graphics

Using Internet Publisher, you can insert an image in any format *WordPerfect* supports. When you **Publish to HTML** or **View in Web Browser**, the graphics are converted to *.gif* or *.jpg* files.

1. Position the insertion point to the left of Janna's name in the title line of your document. Insert two spaces; then move the insertion point in front of the two spaces, using Reveal Codes if necessary.

2. Click **Insert**, **Graphics**, and then click **Clipart**. Select *BUSI010M.wpg* from the Scrapbook dialog box. Click **Insert** to place it on your document page. Position the insertion point at the end of Janna's name, insert two spaces, and insert this same graphic again.

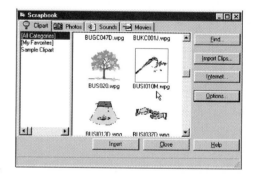

3. Right-click each graphic; then click **HTML Properties**. In the Alternate Text box, key **Paint Brush** for users who have disabled the graphics display in their browsers. Click **OK**. Do this for both images.

# & and :, Proofreaders' Marks

**LESSON 23**

## 23a • 7'

### GETTING started

each line twice SS

## 23b • 14'

### Learn & and : (colon)

each line twice SS

**&** Shift, then reach *up* with *right first* finger.

**: (colon)** Left Shift, then press key with *right fourth* finger.

## 23c • 9'

### SKILLBUILDING

### Improve response patterns

each line once; repeat

---

### SKILLBUILDING WARMUP

alphabet 1 Roxy waved as she did quick flying jumps on the trapeze bar.

symbols 2 Ryan's--with an A-1 rating--sold Item #146 (for $10) on 2/7.

space bar 3 Mr. Fyn may go to Cape Cod on the bus, or he may go by auto.

easy 4 Susie is busy; may she halt the social work for the auditor?

| 1 | 2 | 3 | 4 | 5 | 6 | 7 | 8 | 9 | 10 | 11 | 12 |

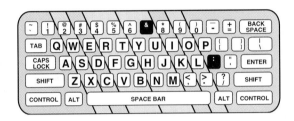

& = ampersand, "and" sign
The ampersand is used only as part of company names.
Space twice after a colon.

### & (ampersand)

5 & &j j& & & &; J & J; Haraj & Jay; Moroj & Jax; Torj & Jones

6 Nehru & Unger; Mumm & Just; Mann & Hart; Arch & Jones; M & J

7 Rhye & Knox represent us; Steb & Doy, Firm A; R & J, Firm B.

### : (colon)

8 : :; :; : : :; as:   for example:   notice:   To:   From:   Date:

9 in stock:   8:30; 7:45; Age:   Experience:   Read:   Send:   See:

10 Space twice after a colon, thus:   To:   No.:   Time:   Carload:

### all symbols learned

11 Consider these companies:   J & R, Brand & Kay, Uper & Davis.

12 Memo #88-89 reads as follows:   "Deduct 15% of $300, or $45."

13 Bill 32(5)--it got here quite late--from M & N was paid 7/3.

### word response

14 Did the busy girl also fix the torn cowl of the formal gown?

15 Clement works with proficiency to make the worn bicycle run.

16 They may pay the auditor the duty on eighty bushels of corn.

### stroke response

17 Lou served a sweet dessert after a caterer carved oily beef.

18 After noon, a battered red streetcar veers up a graded hill.

19 Jim gave up a great seat; give him a few cases of free soap.

| 1 | 2 | 3 | 4 | 5 | 6 | 7 | 8 | 9 | 10 | 11 | 12 |

## Inserting background images and color

Now you will apply background colors, background images, and text colors to give your document some pizzazz! Experiment with the various color schemes by applying them and then viewing the document on the Web. Do not save your document during this exercise.

1. Position the insertion point outside the table and click the **Change Colors** button in the PerfectExpert panel. Choose a color. Notice when you select a different color scheme, not only does the background color change but the text and hyperlink colors are changed also to compliment each other and the background color. Various parts of each scheme may be customized.

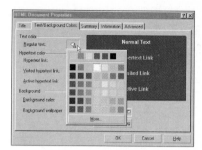

2. Select the color scheme *Maroon*. Click **Change Colors** again and click **Custom** at the bottom of the list. You can see that for the Maroon scheme, normal text is white, hypertext is gold, visited hypertext links are yellow, and active links are pink. Click one of the paint bucket buttons to customize these text colors.

3. After you have experimented with the color schemes, click the **Change Colors** button and choose *<Default>*.

4. Next, experiment with background options. Position the insertion point outside the table and select the *Change Background* button in the PerfectExpert panel. Choose one of the 20 backgrounds. To remove a background, click **Change Background**, **Custom**. Highlight and delete the path in the **Background wallpaper** text box. Click **OK**.

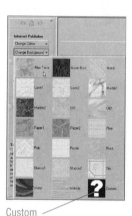

Custom

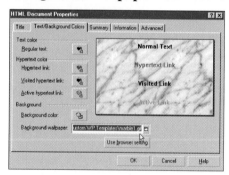

Note that you have the option to choose a picture or texture that you have stored on your hard drive. You could also use an image that you created in a graphics-editing program. Experiment with the options.

5. An alternate way to delete the background wallpaper is to select *Format* menu, *Text Colors/Wallpaper*. The screen will split. In the bottom frame, select the *Wallpaper* tab. Click the garbage can icon to remove the wallpaper selection. Close the bottom screen.

## COMMUNICATION

### Edit as you key

Read the information about proofreaders' marks. Key each line, making the revisions as you key.

Errors are often circled in copy that is to be rekeyed. More frequently, perhaps, the copy is marked with special symbols called "proofreaders' marks" that indicate desired changes.

Some commonly used proofreaders' marks are shown below. Study them. Read carefully. Concentrate on content of the copy as you key.

| Symbol | Meaning | Symbol | Meaning |
|---|---|---|---|
| *Cap* or ≡ | Capitalize | # | Add horizontal space |
| ∧ | Insert | / or *lc* | Lowercase letters |
| ∂ | Delete | ⌒ | Close up space |
| ⊏ | Move to left | ∼ | Transpose |
| ⊐ | Move to right | *stet* | Leave as originally written |
| ¶ | Paragraph | | |

20  We miss 50% of life's rewards by refusing to new try things.

21  do it now--today--then tomorrow's load will be 100%% lighter.

22  Satisfying work--whether it pays $40 or $400--is the pay off.

23     Avoid mistakes:  confusing a #3 has cost thousands. for a #5

24  Pleased most with a first-rate job is the person who did it.

25  My wife and/or me mother will except the certificate for me.

26  When changes for success are 1 in 10, try a new approach.

## SKILLBUILDING

### Build staying power

Key two 1' writings on each ¶; then two 3' writings on both ¶s; compute *gwams*.

**Goals:**  1', 20-27 *gwam*
  3', 17-24 *gwam*

all letters

*gwam*  3'

Is how you judge my work important?  It is, of course;  4 | 26

I hope you recognize some basic merit in it.  We all expect  8 | 30

to get credit for good work that we conclude.  11 | 33

I want approval for stands I take, things I write, and  14 | 36

work I complete.  My efforts, by my work, show a picture of  18 | 41

me; thus, through my work, I am my own unique creation.  22 | 44

3'  |  1  |  2  |  3  |  4  |

text in each of the two subsections and press ENTER after each of the other lines of text.  Use bold and bullets where shown:

**Cother University Alumni Office,** Mobile Alabama
Assistant editor and producer of the Cother Alumni News, 1998 to present.
- Designed layout and production of six editions; met every publishing deadline
- Received the "Cother Design Award"
- Assisted editor in design of Alumni Office Web page (www.cu.edu/alumni/)

**Cother Library,** Mobile, Alabama
Student assistant in Audiovisual Library, 1997-1998.
- Created Audiovisual Catalog using computerized database
- Prepared monthly and yearly report using database
- Designed brochure to promote library services (www.cu.edu/~jhoward/samples/brochure)

5.  DS after this section.
6.  Place the insertion point after **REFERENCES** and press ENTER.  Key the following text.  Use bold and center.

**Request portfolio from Cother University Placement Office.**

7.  Insert another horizontal line directly below this sentence.
8.  Save your document and preview it on the Web.

**Inserting date and time**

1.  With the insertion point in the last row, 2nd cell, click **Change Font Attributes**.  Select Heading 6, and select italic and bold from the *Font* tab.  Key the following text:

**Last Modified:**

2.  Click **Insert**, **Date/Time**.  Choose a format that displays both the date and the time.  Place a check mark in the *Keep the inserted date current* checkbox.  Now viewers can see when the online resume was last updated.

3.  Although you are using a *Corel* product to create your Web page, it looks best when viewed in *Microsoft Internet Explorer*.  To let the viewers know this, insert a line break and key the following sentence in the same font and size (but not italic), immediately below the date and time:

**This page was created with Corel WordPerfect 9 and is best viewed with Microsoft Internet Explorer.**

4.  Save your document and preview it on the Web.

# LESSON 24

## Other Symbols

**24a ● 7'**

**G**ETTING
**started**

each line twice SS

### SKILLBUILDING WARMUP

alphabet 1 Pfc. Jim Kings covered each of the lazy boxers with a quilt.

figures 2 Do Problems 6 to 29 on page 175 before class at 8:30, May 4.

" 3 They read the poems "September Rain" and "The Lower Branch."

easy 4 When did the busy girls fix the tight cowl of the ruby gown?

| 1 | 2 | 3 | 4 | 5 | 6 | 7 | 8 | 9 | 10 | 11 | 12 |

---

**24b ● 14'**

**Note location of <, >, [, ], @, *, +, and =**

each pair of lines once SS; DS between 2-line groups

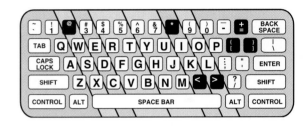

These keys are less commonly used, but they are needed in special circumstances. Unless your instructor tells you otherwise, you may key these reaches with visual help.

* = asterisk, star
+ = "plus sign" (use a hyphen for "minus"; x for "times")
@ = "at sign"
= = "equals sign"
< = "less than"
> = "more than"
[ = "left bracket"
] = "right bracket"

*: shift; reach *up* with *right second* finger to *

5 * *k k8* * *; aurelis*; May 7*; both sides*; 250 km.**; aka*
6 Note each *; one * refers to page 29; ** refers to page 307.

+: shift; reach *up* with *right fourth* finger to +

7 + ;+ +; + + +; 2 + 2; A+ or B+; 70+ F. degrees; +xy over +y;
8 The question was 8 + 7 + 51; it should have been 8 + 7 + 15.

@: shift; reach *up* with *left third* finger to @

9 @ @s s@ @ @; 24 @ .15; 22 @ .35; sold 2 @ .87; were 12 @ .95
10 Ship 560 lbs. @ .36, 93 lbs. @ .14, and 3 lbs. @ .07 per lb.

=: reach *up* with *right fourth* finger to =

11 = =; = = =; = 4; If 14x = 28, x = 2; if 8x = 16, then x = 2.
12 Change this solution (where it says "= by") to = bx or = BX.

<: shift; reach *down* with *right second* finger to <; >: shift; reach *down* with *right third* finger to >

13 Can you prove "a > b"? If 28 > 5, then 5a < x. Is a < > b?
14 Is your answer < > .05? Computer programs use < and > keys.

[ ]: reach *up* with *right fourth* finger to [ and ]

15 Mr. Wing was named. [That's John J. Wing, ex-senator. Ed.]
16 Mr. Lanz said in his note, "I am moving to Filly [sic] now."

| 1 | 2 | 3 | 4 | 5 | 6 | 7 | 8 | 9 | 10 | 11 | 12 |

7. Save your document and preview it on the Web. It should look similar to the figure below.

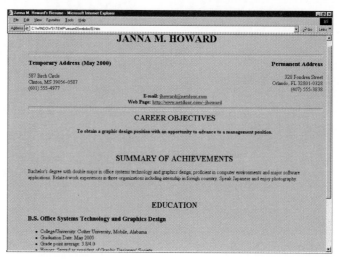

## Adding additional information

Now you will add some text to the **SPECIAL SKILLS** section of the resume. Because HTML does not support the use of tabs, you will add 6 more rows to the table for this information.

1. Position the insertion point after **SPECIAL SKILLS** and click **Table**, **Insert**. Add **6** rows and select *After* under *Placement*. Click **OK**.

2. Key the text below. Use italic and symbols as shown. This section of your resume should look like the figure below when you have finished this step.

| 1st Column | 2nd Column |
|---|---|
| Environments: | *Microsoft Windows*® and *Macintosh OS*® |
| Software: | *Office 2000*®, *Netscape*®, *CorelDraw*®, *PageMaker*®, *HyperStudio*®, *PhotoShop*®, *Illustrator*®, and *FreeHand*® |
| Language: | BASIC and HTML |
| Keyboarding: | 70 words per minute |
| Foreign language: | Japanese |
| Travel: | Japan (two summers working as graphic design intern) |

3. DS at the end of this section.

4. Position the insertion point after **EXPERIENCE** and press ENTER. Left-align if necessary and key the information below. Insert a line break after the first lines of

## SKILLBUILDING

**Review high-frequency words**

The words at the right are from the 300 most used words. Key each line once; work for fluency.

Top 300

17 able attention bill card less concerning employees following
18 given him invoice list members note long recent until within
19 position provide several advise back board case free without
20 contract enclosing home items loan money offer payment where
21 public card regarding soon therefore making with application
22 basis book charge copies equipment free happy price hospital
23 job lock months period prices rate pay reply stock think own
24 where write association important both supply federal having
25 come credit full believe name paid personal products receipt
26 please increase past total attached better building customer
27 committee few general high increase life week while national
28 tax type property receive set system life able employees own

## COMMUNICATION

**Edit as you key**

Read carefully and key each line twice at a controlled pace; edit as indicated by proofreaders' marks; compare your completed lines with those of 22d, p. 53.

29 Ask Group 1 to read Chater 6 of Book 11 (Shelf 19, Room 5).
30 All 6 of us live at One Bay road, not at 126-56th Street.
31 AT 9 a.m. the owners decided to close form 12 noon to 1 p.m.
32 Ms. Vik leaves June 9; she returns the 14 or 15 of July.
33 The 16 per cent discount saves $115.  A stamp costs 35 cents.
34 Elin gave $300,000,000; our gift was only 75 cents.

## SKILLBUILDING

**Build staying power**

Keep eyes on copy, wrists low. Key a 1' writing on each ¶; then key two 3' writings on both ¶s.

all letters

*gwam* 3'

Why don't we like change very much?  Do you think that — 4 | 26

just maybe we want to be lazy; to dodge new things; and, as — 8 | 30

much as possible, not to make hard decisions? — 11 | 33

We know change can and does extend new areas for us to — 14 | 36

enjoy, areas we might never have known existed; and to stay — 18 | 40

away from all change could curtail our quality of life. — 22 | 44

3' | 1 | 2 | 3 | 4

## Adding and editing horizontal lines

You will insert two horizontal lines to separate the address information from the rest of the resume.

1. Position the insertion point in Row 1, Column 2. Click the **Horizontal Line** button on the toolbar to insert a line. Then insert another horizontal line at the end of the Web Page address (~jhoward).

2. Right-click the first line, then click **Edit Horizontal Line**. Click the button next to **Thickness**. For each horizontal line, select the line thickness shown at right and click **OK**.

3. Save your document. Preview it on the Web.

## Adding additional information and bullets

1. Add the additional information under each of the other main headings. Place the insertion point after **CAREER OBJECTIVES** and press ENTER. Change Font Attributes to **Normal** and key the following in 12 point, center-aligned:

   **To obtain a graphic design position with an opportunity to advance to a management position.**

2. DS after this section.

3. Press ENTER after **SUMMARY OF ACHIEVEMENTS**. Change Font Attributes to **Normal** and key the following text in 12 point, left-aligned:

   **Bachelor's degree with double major in office systems technology and graphics design; proficient in computer environments and major software applications. Related work experiences in three organizations including internship in foreign country. Speak Japanese and enjoy photography.**

4. DS after this section.

5. Press ENTER after **EDUCATION**. Change Font Attributes to **Normal**, and in 12 point, left-aligned, key the following, pressing ENTER after each line of text as shown below:

   **B.S. Office Systems Technology and Graphics Design**
   **College/University: Cother University, Mobile, Alabama**
   **Graduation Date: May 2000**
   **Grade point average: 3.8/4.0**
   **Honors: Served as president of Graphic Designers' Society**

6. Change the first line under **EDUCATION** to 14 point bold. Select the next four lines under **EDUCATION** and click the **Bullets** button.

# Assessment

## 25a ● 7'

### GETTING started

each line twice SS

## 25b ● 10'

### SKILLBUILDING

**Assess straight copy**
Key two 3' writings with controlled speed.

**Goal:** 3', 19-27 *gwam*

alphabet 1 My wife helped fix a frozen lock on Jacque's vegetable bins.

figures 2 Sherm moved from 823 West 150th Street to 9472--67th Street.

double letters 3 Will Scott attempt to sell his bookkeeping books to Elliott?

easy 4 It is a shame he used the endowment for a visit to the city.

| 1 | 2 | 3 | 4 | 5 | 6 | 7 | 8 | 9 | 10 | 11 | 12 |

all letters                                                                      *gwam*   3'

The term careers can mean many different things to          3 | 51

different people.   As you know, a career is much more than a          8 | 55

job.   It is the kind of work that a person has through life.          12 | 59

It includes the jobs a person has over time.   It also involves          16 | 63

how the work life affects the other parts of our life.   There          20 | 67

are as many types of careers as there are people.          23 | 71

Almost all people have a career of some kind.   A career          27 | 74

can help us to reach unique goals, such as to make a living          31 | 79

or to help others.   The kind of career you have will affect          35 | 83

your life in many ways.   For example, it can determine where          39 | 87

you live, the money you make, and how you feel about yourself.          44 | 91

A good choice can thus help you realize the life you want.          47 | 95

3' | 1 | 2 | 3 | 4 |

## Changing Font Attributes

You can use a variety of text and heading styles and effects in Internet Publisher. For example, you can choose preformatted or monospaced text, which results in a uniformly spaced font, such as Courier. You can also create blinking text and choose the text color for your Web document.

1. Leave the row after the addresses blank. Highlight all of the remaining cells in the 2nd column. Select *Change Font Attributes* in the HTML Tables PerfectExpert panel.

2. In the Font Properties dialog box, select *Heading 2*. Then click the **Font** tab, click bold, and click **OK**. Center the following text in Rows 3–8:

> ***CAREER OBJECTIVE***
> ***SUMMARY OF ACHIEVEMENT***
> ***EDUCATION***
> ***SPECIAL SKILLS***
> ***EXPERIENCE***
> ***REFERENCES***

3. Save your document. Click **View in Web Browser**. Your document should look similar to the figure below.

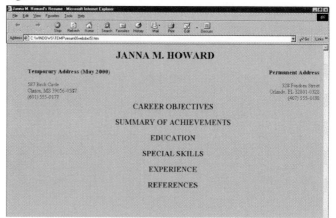

## Adding automatic hyperlinks

1. Place the insertion point in Row 3, Column 2 (Janna's e-mail and Web page addresses). Click the **Change Font Attributes** button and select *Normal*.

2. *WordPerfect* allows you to create automatic hyperlinks with the **SpeedLinks** feature. Choose *Tools, QuickCorrect* and click the **SpeedLinks** tab. Select the *Format words as hyperlinks when you type them* checkbox.

3. Using 12 point, bold, and center justification, key in the following text:

> **E-mail: jhoward@netdoor.com**
> **Web Page: www.netdoor.com/~jhoward**

You must press ENTER after each line of text to complete the link, although doing so adds extra space after each line. Remove the [HRt] codes using Reveal Codes. Click **Insert, Line Break** after the e-mail address to adjust the spacing.

4. Save your document and view it.

## 25c ● 10'

### SKILLBUILDING

**Review reaches**
Key smoothly, avoid pauses, and allow your fingers to work. Repeat if time permits.

**symbols**

5 He spent $25 for gifts, $31 for dinner, and $7 for cab fare.
6 As of 6/28, my code number is 1/k; Mona's, 2/k; John's, 3/k.

**symbols**

7 Bill #773 charged for us 4# of #33 brads and 6# of #8 nails.
8 He deducted 12% instead of 6%, a clear saving of 6%, not 7%.

**outside reaches**

9 When did Marq Quin go?   Did Quentin or Quincy Quin go?   Why?
10 We were quick to squirt a quantity of water at Quin and Wes.

**long reaches**

11 Barb Abver saw a vibrant version of her brave venture on TV.
12 Call a woman or a man who will manage Minerva Manor in Nome.

**figures**

13 On July 5, 54 of us had only 45 horses; 4 of them were lame.
14 Back in '90, Car 009 traveled 90 miles, getting 9 to 10 mpg.

| 1 | 2 | 3 | 4 | 5 | 6 | 7 | 8 | 9 | 10 | 11 | 12 |

## 25d ● 13'

### SKILLBUILDING

**Assess figure skill**
In the Open Screen, key two 1' writings and two 3' writings at a controlled speed.

**Goal:** 3', 16-24 *gwam*

**E** all letters/figures                                                           *gwam*   3'

|  |  |  |  |  |  |  |  |  |
|---|---|---|---|---|---|---|---|---|

Do I read the stock market pages in the news?   Yes; and     4 | 35
at about 9 or 10 a.m. each morning, I know lots of excited     8 | 39
people are quick to join me.   In fact, many of us zip right     12 | 43
to the 3d or 4th part of the paper to see if the prices of     16 | 47
our stocks have gone up or down.   Now, those of us who are     19 | 51
"speculators" like to "buy at 52 and sell at 60"; while the     23 | 55
"investors" among us are more interested in a dividend we     27 | 59
may get, say 7 or 8 percent, than in the price of a stock.     31 | 62

3' | 1 | 2 | 3 | 4 |

the lines in the HTML coding for the street, city, and phone number. This tag was inserted when you pressed ENTER in *WordPerfect*, and it automatically inserts additional space between the lines. Close the text editor window and your browser window to return to the *WordPerfect* document.

2. There are 2 ways to adjust the spacing. Click **View**, **Reveal Codes** in the *WordPerfect* document. Delete the hard return [HRt] at the end of the word *Circle* on the second line of the Temporary Address. Click **Format**, **Custom HTML**. Key in a break tag, **<BR>**. The

<BR> forces a line to break with no extra space between the lines and is often better for short lines of text. Delete the hard return [HRt] after the ZIP codes, turn on **Custom HTML**, and insert another break tag **<BR>**. Save the document. Click **View in Web Browser** to see how it will appear on the Web.

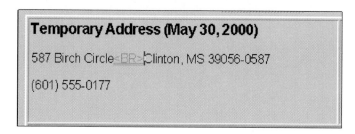

3. The second way to adjust the spacing is to insert a line break, which places the <BR> tag in the coding automatically but is not visible in the *WordPerfect* document. To format the **Permanent Address**, place the insertion point after *Street* and delete the hard return. Select *Insert, Line Break*. Repeat this step after the ZIP code. Save and view the document as it will appear on the Web.

**Editing table properties**

You can edit the appearance of a table in HTML format much as you would a table in *WordPerfect*. You will adjust the width of cells in this table.

1. With the insertion point in the cell with the Temporary Address, click **Change Properties** in the HTML Tables PerfectExpert panel. On the Column tab, check the box beside **Column width** and change the number to **50**.

2. Repeat for the cell with the **Permanent Address**.

3. Save your document. Click **View in Web Browser** to see the changes made.

By default, the table border is turned on. Turn the table border off by clicking **Turn Border On/Off** in the HTML Tables PerfectExpert panel and choosing **Off**. When you turn the table border off, the gridlines will be visible in your *WordPerfect* document, but the border will not show up when you view the document in your Web browser.

# EXTENDED SKILLBUILDING

## OBJECTIVES

1. Improve speed and accuracy.

2. Key from rough-draft copy.

3. Key a 3' writing at 25 *wam* or higher.

LESSON 26

# Skillbuilding

### 26a ● 7'

## GETTING started

The Skillbuilding Warmup is recorded on your software but not in the book. Key it and then progress to 26b in the usual manner.

### 26b ● 13'

## SKILLBUILDING

**Practice reaches**
each line at the right once; avoid pauses

**outside reaches**

1 zap papaw was zipper quale paper axle zag aquas azure ataxia
2 apex wasp assay zip axial sassy pappy sassafras exit pallial
3 Was Polly acquainted with the equipped jazz player in Texas?

**long reaches**

4 ce cede cedar wreck nu nu nut punt nuisance my my amy mystic
5 ny ny any many company mu mu mull lumber mulch br br furbish
6 The absence of receiving my umbrella disturbed the musician.

**figure reaches**

7 Memo 461 dated May 20 was filed in drawer 85 and folder 397.
8 The November revenue of 836, 940, 271, and 573 averaged 655.
9 She purchased 62 pens, 139 stamps, 48 rulers, and 507 disks.

**adjacent reaches**

10 as we opt try web sad buy rest hurt tree join suit open trip
11 perk true union energy weave poster seeds backlog ergonomics
12 The opponent heard the treasurer read her opinion on unions.

| 1 | 2 | 3 | 4 | 5 | 6 | 7 | 8 | 9 | 10 | 11 | 12 |

## Viewing the file on the Web

*WordPerfect 9* saves a copy of your file and opens it in your default Web browser. If your browser is not open, *WordPerfect* will automatically open it for you when you click the **View in Web Browser** button on the Internet Publisher toolbar. Click the icon now to view your page as it will appear on the Web. After viewing, close your browser and you will return to your *WordPerfect* document.

## Working with tables

Tables are an effective way to display information on the Web. Follow these steps to add a table to your Web page:

1. Click **Extras** in the PerfectExpert panel and select *Add a Table*. In the HTML Table Properties dialog box, key 2 Columns, 10 Rows. Click **OK**.

Notice the PerfectExpert has changed to **HTML Tables**. If you click outside the table, the PerfectExpert toggles back to **Internet Publisher**.

2. Highlight the cells in the first column. Select *Change Properties* in the HTML PerfectExpert panel. On the Column tab, select *Column width*. Change to **Pixels** and set the value to **50**. Click **OK**. (This setup will center the text of the resume in the right column.)

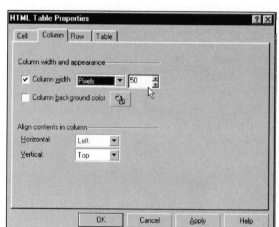

3. Highlight Cell B2 (2nd column, 2nd row). Click **Table**, **Split**, **Cell** and click **OK** to split into 2 cells.

4. In Cell B2 (new left cell), key

   **Temporary Address (May 30, 2000)**
   587 Birch Circle
   Clinton, MS 39056-0587
   (601) 555-0177

5. In Cell B3 (right cell), key the following and justify at the right.

   **Permanent Address**
   328 Fondren Street
   Orlando, FL 32801-0328
   (407) 555-0138

6. Change the first line of each address to bold. Save your document and view it on the Web.

## Inserting custom HTML and line breaks

Notice that there is an undesirable amount of space between the lines in the addresses. This is caused by HTML coding, called *tags*, that were automatically inserted. While still in the browser, you can view the HTML tags and determine which tags are causing the extra spacing.

1. Click **View in Web Browser** to open your browser. Click **View**, **Source** from your browser's menu. (The name and location of this command may vary slightly depending upon the browser you are using.) The source is automatically opened in the default text editor, usually *Notepad*. Notice the <P> or Paragraph tag in front of

## 26c • 5'
### COMMUNICATION

**Edit as you key**
Read carefully; each line contains 2 errors, but only 1 is circled. Correct both errors as you key.

13 (i) asked Ty for a loan of $40; his interest rate is two high.
14 Please advice me how I can (spent) $18 for a second-hand book.
15 I'm sorry I lost (you) first-balcony tickers for the concert.
16 Linda saws 3659 Riley (rode) is her daughter-in-law's address.

## 26d • 8'
### SKILLBUILDING

**Practice opposite-hand reaches**
each group once; repeat Concentrate on the proper reach.

g/h

17 gag go gee god rig gun log gong cog gig agog gage going gang
18 huh oh hen the hex ash her hash ah hush shah hutch hand ache
19 ugh high ghoul rough ghosts cough night laugh ghee bough ghi
20 Hush; Greg hears rough sounds. Has Hugh laughed or coughed?

r/u

21 row or rid air rap par rye rear ark jar rip nor are right or
22 cut us auk out tutu sun husk but fun cub gun nut mud tug hug
23 rut aura run your rub cure rum our rue cur rug urn true pure
24 Ryan is sure you should pour your food from an urn or cruet.

| 1 | 2 | 3 | 4 | 5 | 6 | 7 | 8 | 9 | 10 | 11 | 12 |

## 26e • 17'
### SKILLBUILDING

**Check speed**
Key two 3' writings.

**Optional:**
*Diagnostic Writing*
1. Return to the Lesson menu and click the **Diagnostic Writings** button.
2. From the list of writings, select *26e*. Set the Timer for **3'**.
3. Key the timing from the textbook.
4. Review your results on the Summary Report, Diagnostic Writings Summary.

all letters                                      *gwam* 1' | 3'

I have a story or two or three that will carry you away     11 | 4
to foreign places, to meet people you have never known, to  23 | 8
see things you have never seen, to feast on foods available 35 | 12
only to a few. I will help you to learn new skills you want 47 | 16
and need; I will inspire you, excite you, instruct you, and 59 | 20
interest you. I am able, you understand, to make time fly.  71 | 24

I answer difficult questions for you. I work with you       11 | 27
to realize a talent, to express a thought, and to determine 23 | 31
just who and what you are and want to be. I help you to     35 | 35
know words, to write, and to read. I help you to comprehend 47 | 40
the mysteries of the past and the secrets of the future. I  59 | 44
am your local library. We ought to get together often.      70 | 47

1' | 1 | 2 | 3 | 4 | 5 | 6 | 7 | 8 | 9 | 10 | 11 | 12 |
3' |     1     |       2       |       3       |      4      |

# Create a Web Page Using Internet Publisher

Creating a Web page is made simple by using *WordPerfect's* Internet Publisher. In this lesson, you will create an online resume for Janna M. Howard.

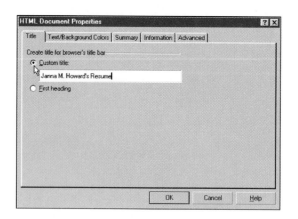

1. To start a new Web document, select **File**, **Internet Publisher**.

2. Click **New Web Document**. Click **Select** to choose *Create a blank web document* (it is the only template shown). A new blank Web document opens, and the Internet Publisher toolbar displays.

3. Select **PerfectExpert** from the Help menu. The Internet Publisher PerfectExpert panel opens at the left of the screen.

4. Click **Add a Title** and select *At the Top* to automatically format your title. Key **JANNA M. HOWARD**.

5. Select *Add a Title* again and choose *For the Title Bar*. The HTML Document Properties dialog box appears with the *Title* tab selected by default.

6. Click the radio button beside **Custom title** and key **Janna M. Howard's Resume**. Click **OK**. This title will appear in the title bar of the reader's Web browser and is also used by search engines when searching Web pages by keywords. It is the text that is saved as a Bookmark in Netscape or a Favorite in Internet Explorer when finding URLs (Uniform Resource Locators) on the Web.

**Saving your document—Create a new folder for Web page files**

1. Save your document. From the Save As dialog box, create a new folder on your hard drive or floppy disk (**File**, **New**, **Folder**) to store your files. Name the folder **Web Publishing**.

2. Create a subfolder inside **Web Publishing**; name it **G1**. All files associated with this lesson will be stored in this subfolder.

3. Name your file **resume** and click **Save**.

# LESSON 27

# Skillbuilding

## 27a • 7'

### GETTING started

each line twice SS;
(slowly, then faster)

SKILLBUILDING WARMUP

alphabet 1 Hose Wevs and Bruce Fox kept Zaney Quigly in Mexico in June.
figures 2 Do Problems 7 to 18 on page 264 before class at 9:30, May 5.
quotes 3 "I know the book is ready," she said, "to be shipped today."
easy 4 If she is not going with us, why don't we plan to leave now?
| 1 | 2 | 3 | 4 | 5 | 6 | 7 | 8 | 9 | 10 | 11 | 12 |

## 27b • 10'

### SKILLBUILDING

**Practice opposite-hand reaches**
Key at a controlled rate; concentrate on the reaches.

i/e
5 ik is fit it sit laid site like insist still wise coil light
6 ed he ear the fed egg led elf lake jade heat feet hear where
7 lie kite item five aide either quite linear imagine brighter
8 Imagine the aide eating the pears before the grieving tiger.

u/r
9 uj use jut jug dust sue duel fuel just sun tuna usual vacuum
10 rf red jar ear for rag over czar rose yarn real friend broom
11 fur urn run user turn pure utter under bursar course furnace
12 The younger bursar turned the ruined urns under the furnace.

w/o
13 ws we way was few went wit law with weed were week gnaw when
14 ol on go hot old lot joy odd comb open tool upon money union
15 bow owl word wood worm worse tower brown toward wrote weapon
16 The workers lowered the brown swords toward the wood weapon.

y/t
17 yj my say may yes rye yarn eye lye yap any relay young berry
18 tf at it let the vat tap item town toast right little attire
19 yet toy yogurt typical youth tycoon yacht tympani typewriter
20 Yesterday a young youth typed a cat story on the typewriter.

b/n
21 bf but job fibs orb bow able bear habit boast rabbit brother
22 nj not and one now fun next pony month notice runner quicken
23 bin bran knob born cabin number botany nibble blank neighbor
24 A number of neighbors banked on bunking in the brown cabins.
| 1 | 2 | 3 | 4 | 5 | 6 | 7 | 8 | 9 | 10 | 11 | 12 |

# WEB PUBLISHING

G

*module*

## OVERVIEW

### Creating effective Web pages

The World Wide Web (WWW), an extension of the Internet, is a collection of online documents or pages formatted in HyperText Markup Language (HTML). Since 1991, when Tim Berners-Lee, of the European Particle Physics Laboratory (CERN) in Switzerland, developed the WWW, one has had to know how to use HTML language to create Web pages. Now with HTML editors, creating a Web page is much like creating a letter on your favorite word processor. *WordPerfect 9* has built-in HTML support and provides an easy way to save your documents to the Web. Web pages can be created with *WordPerfect* by:

- using Internet Publisher to format a page as a Web page
- saving an existing *WordPerfect* document as an HTML document

The activities in this module will focus on creating simple Web pages with *WordPerfect 9* using these techniques.

**Lesson G1** will use Internet Publisher to create an online resume.

**Lesson G2** will assist you in creating an online newsletter. The newsletter will consist of three Web pages linked together to form a Web site.

**Lesson G3** will show you how to post the files you created to the WWW.

## 27c ● 8'

### SKILLBUILDING

**Build skill**
Key the easy, balanced-hand copy without hesitation. Repeat at a faster pace.

25 is if he do rub ant go and am pan do rut us aid ox ape by is
26 it is|an end|it may|to pay|and so|aid us|he got|or own|to go
27 Did the girl make the ornament with fur, duck down, or hair?

28 us owl rug box bob to man so bit or big pen of jay me age it
29 it|it is|time to go|show them how|plan to go|one of the aims
30 It is a shame they use the autobus for a visit to the field.
| 1 | 2 | 3 | 4 | 5 | 6 | 7 | 8 | 9 | 10 | 11 | 12 |

## 27d ● 5'

### COMMUNICATION

**Key edited copy**
Make corrections as indicated by proofreaders' marks.

*, but unhappy,*                                                                  *ss*

There was once a rich man, ~~who was not very happy~~; He had
                                        *money*              *lovely*
spend large sums of for fancy clothes, a ~~beautiful~~ home,

luxurious cars --even his own plane --but none of it brought

him happiness.  his psychiatrist, after weeks of therapy,
finally explained that happiness can't be bought; it must
be found.  And--you guessed it--the unhappy man paid for
these words of wisdom with ~~another~~ large sum.
                                *stet*

## 27e ● 14'

### SKILLBUILDING

**Check speed**
Key two 3' writings.

**Optional:**

*Diagnostic Writing*
1. Return to the Lesson menu and click the **Diagnostic Writings** button.
2. From the list of writings, select *27e.* Set Timer for **3'.**
3. Key the timing from the textbook.

  all letters                                          *gwam*  1'  3'

    The computer is the basic teaching tool to use in distance   12   4  43
education.  You quickly learn to work in the class as though   24   8  47
you were in the same room in a school house.                   33  11  50

    In distance education, you can take the class at a local     44  15  53
school.  Class times are not so rigid.  The class does not     56  19  57
have a certain time to stop.  All of the communication can be  68  23  62
kept in the computer.                                          73  24  63

    This type of education does not have face-to-face instruc-   84  28  67
tion.  The machines may not be known to those on the job.      96  32  71
Too much data may be realized.  The cost can be high.  As     108  36  75
networks grow, so will distance education.                    116  39  77

1' | 1 | 2 | 3 | 4 | 5 | 6 | 7 | 8 | 9 | 10 | 11 | 12 |
3' |     1     |      2      |      3      |      4      |

## Application F8,
*continued*

1. Key the document shown at the right.
2. Format the document using the same format you have used for other sections of the PRVH Enterprises report.
3. Use Heading 1 style for the main heading, *Recommendations*, and Heading 2 for all other headings.
4. Use 1.5 spacing between ¶s.
5. Save the document as **appf8rec**.

## Recommendations

Specific recommendations have been included in each section of the report. This section provides a general summary of all recommendations relative to PRVH Enterprises' benefits package.

### Benefits Plan Effectiveness

Overall PRVH offers excellent benefits to its employees. The comprehensive benefits package meets the needs of most employees and exceeds the benefits offered by many companies. Medical and disability benefits are excellent. Death benefits are very satisfactory for employees in the mid-to-lower salary levels. Although the retirement plan is a reasonable one, employee utilization of the plan is quite low. Better education may be the best way to increase the utilization rate. Increasing company contribution to the retirement plan would have a major cost impact.

PRVH Enterprises does not currently offer a wellness program to its employees. Wellness programs tend to help lower medical costs; therefore, a detailed study will be commissioned to determine the most effective type of program, the costs of running the program, and the benefits expected from the program.

### Cost of Benefits Plan

Cost of benefits compared to national averages varies significantly. Health and dental costs exceed the national average; insurance and disability are comparable, whereas retirement costs are significantly lower than the national average. Costs can be contained by incorporating an employee contribution for spouses and dependent children and by moving to a self-funded plan. These two options need board approval before they can be implemented.

### Communication

Overall communication about benefits is effective. The variety of media used for communication, the communication frequency, and the individualized statements are the strengths of the program. The most significant communication problem relates to the readability of documents including the *Benefits Update*. This issue needs to be addressed immediately.

---

**Text for title page**

Report title:    An Assessment of the Benefits Package Offered by PRVH Enterprises

Prepared for:    The Executive Committee

Prepared by:    Benefits Team 1

Date:    Current

# Skillbuilding

## 28a ● 7'

### GETTING started

each line twice (slowly, then faster)

SKILLBUILDING WARMUP

| | |
|---|---|
| alphabet | 1 A quaint report was given that amazed Felix, Jack, and Boyd. |
| figures | 2 Do read Section 4, pages 60-74 and Section 9, pages 198-235. |
| fig/sym | 3 Invoice #384 for $672.91, plus $4.38 tax, was due on 5/20/97. |
| easy | 4 Do you desire to continue working on the memo in the future? |

| 1 | 2 | 3 | 4 | 5 | 6 | 7 | 8 | 9 | 10 | 11 | 12 |

## 28b ● 8'

### SKILLBUILDING

**Practice specific rows**

each line once; repeat
Work for smooth, continuous stroking.

5 Sarah Hall had a half dish of hash as she asked for a glass.
6 The lass had to wash half of the tall glasses in the washer.

7 Calvin named the excited zebra Zabic as the men boxed it in.
8 Can Nancy Cox be amazed by winning six dozen boxes of cocoa?

9 You are trying to type every top row key with a quick touch.
10 Put your power to rest if you are not trying to win the bet.

11 On May 19-23, the 72 employees worked from 6:30 to 8:45 a.m.
12 His social security number is 247513086; it arrived on 7/27.

## 28c ● 12'

### SKILLBUILDING

**Improve rhythm**

each line twice; do not pause at the end of the lines

**words**: *think, say,* and *key* words
13 is do am lay cut pen dub may fob ale rap cot hay pay hem box
14 box wit man sir fish also hair giant rigor civic virus ivory
15 laugh sight flame audit formal social turkey bicycle problem

**phrases**: *think, say,* and *key* phrases
16 is it|is it|if it is|if it is|or by|or by|or me|or me|for us
17 and all|for pay|pay dues and|the pen|the pen box|the pen box
18 such forms|held both|work form|then wish|sign name|with them

**easy sentences**
19 The man is to do the work right; he then pays the neighbors.
20 Sign the forms to pay the eight men for the turkey and hams.
21 The antique ivory bicycle is a social problem for the chair.

| 1 | 2 | 3 | 4 | 5 | 6 | 7 | 8 | 9 | 10 | 11 | 12 |

Earlier in Module F, you worked on a part of a team report on Benefits for PRVH Enterprises. In this application, you will use the master document feature to combine several documents prepared by different team members into the final document.

1. Open *f8report* from the Formatting Template. Save it as **appf8md**.
2. Key the document on the next page and save it as **appf8rec**. Use Heading 1 style for the main heading, *Recommendations*, and Heading 2 style for all other headings. Use 1.5 spacing between ¶s.
3. Insert **f8cost** from the Formatting Template as a subdocument at the end of the master document (*appf8md*).
4. Insert **f8com** as a subdocument after *f8cost*.
5. Insert **appf8rec** as a subdocument after *f8com*.
6. Expand the master document and check that no headings are left alone at the bottom of a page. Apply Block Protect if necessary.
7. Insert a page break at the beginning of the master document for the table of contents; adjust the page number on the first page of the master document to 1; suppress the page number on the first page.
8. Define the table of contents on the blank page.
9. Generate the table of contents for the entire master document, including all subdocuments.
10. Key **TABLE OF CONTENTS** in Heading 1 style at the top of the first page.
11. Use the information on the next page to develop an attractive cover for the report. Use clipart, borders, shading, or other decoration of your choice.

## VIEWS

### *on...*Team Effectiveness

Many companies today organize their employees as teams rather than as departments. Teams go through a variety of stages before they develop into effective, cohesive units. An effective team is far more than just a group of people in a work environment who get along well while they are doing their jobs. An effective team is one that achieves synergy; that is, the results produced by the group are greater than the sum of the results that could be produced by the individuals working separately.

Defining what makes a team effective is difficult, but recognizing a team that is functioning effectively is obvious. Each member of an effective team has a clear understanding of the team's goals and the procedures for attaining those goals. Team members respect and trust each other and are open and honest in their communication with each other. They recognize that each individual has unique knowledge and skills to contribute to the success of the team's projects. They understand and respect the value of each person's time and recognize when additional expertise is needed to solve a problem.

Once the team reaches a consensus on the solution of a problem, the entire team accepts the solution and focuses on effective implementation. Making a decision is of limited value if the decision is not implemented effectively. A truly effective team is self-managed; that is, the team is empowered to control its work and the way that it is done. Learning to be an effective team member is preparing for lifetime employability.

## COMMUNICATION

**Key edited copy**
Make corrections as indicated
by proofreaders' marks.

take time to evaluate your completed work. Look

caefully at what you havee done. Would be you impressed

with it if you wre a reader? Is it attractive in form and

accurate in content? Does it look like something you would

pick up because it looks interesting? Does the title

attract you? Do the first couple of lines catch your atten-

tion? Personal appraisal of your own work is very

important. For If it does not impress you, it

will not impress any one else.

28e ● 13'

## SKILLBUILDING

**Check speed**
Key two 1' writings on ¶ 1.

**Optional:**

1. Set the Timer in the Open
   Screen for **2'**.
2. Take a 2' writing on ¶ 1.
   Note your *gwam*.
3. Take two 2' writings on ¶ 2.
   Try to equal your *gwam* on
   ¶ 1.
4. Take a 3' writing on both
   ¶s.

**C** all letters                                                    *gwam* 1' | 2' | 3'

|  | 1' | 2' | 3' |
|---|---|---|---|
| Good health is a matter not so much for its contribution | 11 | 6 | 4 |
| to a longer life but for a better life. Good health is attain- | 24 | 12 | 8 |
| able now to all. A few can measure up better than those who | 36 | 18 | 12 |
| are whole and sound in body but lacking in mind and spirit. | 48 | 24 | 16 |
| Learning to live and to live well is the highest concept. | 60 | 30 | 20 |
| How can we affect our future health? It is quite obvious | 12 | 36 | 24 |
| quite once at that there are some limit that we must accept. We | 24 | 42 | 28 |
| must learn to make the most of what we have. We can take | 35 | 48 | 32 |
| steps to hazards from with out and to control dangers | 47 | 53 | 36 |
| from within. WITH good health, we expect to live a just | 59 | 59 | 39 |
| life. | 60 | 60 | 40 |

| 1 | 2 | 3 | 4 | 5 | 6 | 7 | 8 | 9 | 10 | 11 | 12 |

## Drill 2

1. Open a new document.

2. Key the heading **Sample Subdocument 1** and apply Heading 2 style.

3. Key the following text:

   This text shows how to create a subdocument. In a new blank document screen, key and format the text for the subdocument. Save the document with an appropriate name and close it. Open the master document and place the insertion point where you want to add the subdocument. Click File, Document, Subdocument. Select the subdocument filename and click Include. Notice the icon that appears in the left margin of the master document.

4. Save the document as **f5-d2sd1** and close it.

5. Use the steps above to create a second subdocument. Key the following text:

   **Sample Subdocument 2**
   The same procedures apply to creating any number of subdocuments. You can link as many subdocuments to the master document as you wish.

6. Save the document as **f5-d2sd2** and close it.

7. Open the master document and place the insertion point a DS below the text.

8. Click **File** menu, **Document**, then **Subdocument**.

9. Select *f5-d2sd1*; click **Include** to link the file as a subdocument.

10. Repeat steps 8 and 9 to add *f5-d2sd2*.

11. Click **File** menu, **Document**, **Expand Master**. Print the document.

12. Click **File** menu, **Document**, **Condense Master**. Click **OK** to condense and save both subdocuments. Close the master document.

## APPLICATION

Always check the expanded document to make sure that headings are not left alone at the bottom of a page and that the Widow/Orphan feature is turned on.

1. Open *appf7* from the Formatting Template; save it as **appf7md**. Do not close.

2. Position the insertion point on a blank line at the end of the document.

3. Open *appf7undexp* from the Formatting Template. Review it as the author and accept all of the revisions noted. Save the document as **appf7sd1** and close it.

4. Open *appf7shapex* from the Formatting Template; save it as **appf7sd2** and close it.

5. Open *appf7percep* from the Formatting Template; save it as **appf7sd3** and close it.

6. Select *Document* from the File menu; click **Subdocument** and link the 3 subdocuments to the master document.

7. Expand the master document and print it.

8. Condense the master document; close and save all subdocuments. Close the master document.

LESSON 29

# Skillbuilding

## 29a • 7'

### GETTING started

each line twice SS

### SKILLBUILDING WARMUP

| | | |
|---|---|---|
| alphabet | 1 | Juni, Vec, and Zeb had perfect grades on weekly query exams. |
| shift | 2 | Give a monetary prize to J. W. Fuqua and B. K. Charles next. |
| figures | 3 | Her grades are 93, 87, and 100; his included 82, 96, and 54. |
| combination | 4 | You should be interested in the special items on sale today. |

| 1 | 2 | 3 | 4 | 5 | 6 | 7 | 8 | 9 | 10 | 11 | 12 |

## 29b • 8'

### SKILLBUILDING

**Practice figures**
each line once; repeat

| | | |
|---|---|---|
| 8/1 | 5 | line 8; Book 1; No. 88; Seat 11; June 18; Cart 81; date 1881 |
| 2/7 | 6 | take 2; July 7; buy 22; sell 77; mark 27; adds 72; Memo 2772 |
| 3/9 | 7 | feed 3; bats 9; age 33; Ext. 99; File 39; 93 bags; band 3993 |
| 4/0 | 8 | set 0; push 4; Car 00; score 44; jot 04; age 40; Billet 4004 |
| 6/5 | 9 | April 6; lock 5; set 66; fill 55; hit 65; pick 56; adds 5665 |
| all | 10 | Do Problems 6 to 29 on p. 175 before class at 8:30 on May 4. |

## 29c • 10'

### SKILLBUILDING

**Improve reaches**
each line once; fingers curved
and relaxed; wrists low

| | | |
|---|---|---|
| 3d/1st | 11 | cry tube wine quit very curb exit crime ebony mention excite |
| | 12 | Remember to be invited to petition the men in the hot tower. |
| 1st/2d | 13 | bad fun nut kick dried night brick civic thick hutch believe |
| | 14 | The huge knight began to certify everything in the gem tray. |
| 3d/4th | 15 | pop was lap pass slaw wool solo swap apollo wasp load plaque |
| | 16 | Sally saw the son-in-law pass the wool and plaque proposals. |
| top | 17 | 1 1a 11; 8 8k 88; 5 5f 55; 0 0; 00; 2 2s 22; 7 7j 77; 9 9l 9 |
| | 18 | 3 3d 33; 6 6j 66; 4 4f 44; 777 East 747 West; 3:40 on 3/5/97 |

| 1 | 2 | 3 | 4 | 5 | 6 | 7 | 8 | 9 | 10 | 11 | 12 |

3. Click **File** menu, **Document**, and then **Subdocument**.

4. Select the file you wish to link as a subdocument.

5. Click **Include**.

6. Repeat the 5 steps above for each subdocument you wish to add.

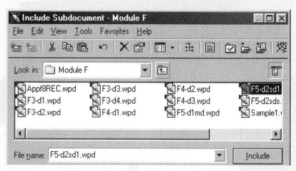

### To open subdocuments in a master document:

1. Open the master document.

2. Select *Document* from the File menu; then click **Expand Master**.

3. A check mark will appear in the box for each subdocument that you can open in the master document. Click the check boxes to add or remove a check mark.

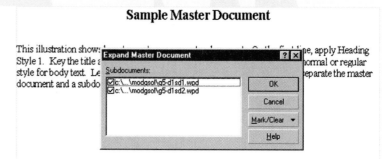

### To remove a subdocument from a master document:

Turn on Reveal Codes and delete the subdocument code [Subdoc] from the Reveal Codes window.

### To close subdocuments in a master document:

1. Open the master document.

2. From the File menu, click **Document**, then **Condense Master**.

3. Leave the check mark in the box of each document that you want to close or save; remove the check mark if you do not want to close or save a subdocument.

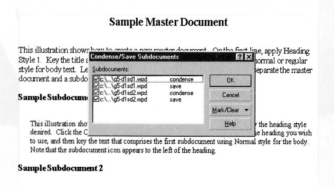

## 29d ● 8'

### SKILLBUILDING

**Improve figures/symbols**
Key the paragraph once; keep wrists low and hands quiet.

**Optional:**
Take a 3' writing in the Open Screen.

 all letters/figures/symbols                                    *gwam* 3'

| | | |
|---|---|---|
| At your request, you just sold on 2/18/97 125 shares | 4 | 34 |
| of stock for $34.96 a share. The stock was purchased on | 7 | 38 |
| 7/08/93 for $26.43 a share and that during the current year | 11 | 42 |
| you realized $1.95 a share in cash dividends. You have a | 15 | 46 |
| capital gain of $1,066.25 ($34.96/share - $26.43/share x 125 | 19 | 50 |
| shares) and $243.75 in dividend income ($1.95 x 125 shares). | 23 | 54 |
| If you were in a 31% group, your dividends would be subject | 27 | 58 |
| to a 31% tax rate ($243.75 x .31 = $75.56 in taxes). | 31 | 62 |

3' | 1 | 2 | 3 | 4 |

## 29e ● 12'

### SKILLBUILDING

**Check speed**
Key two 3' writings.

**Optional:**
1. In the Open Screen, take two 1' guided writings on ¶ 1.
2. Take a 2' writing; try to maintain 1' rate.
3. Take a 3' writing; try to maintain 1' rate.

(See p. 49 for instructions on taking a guided writing.)

 all letters                                    *gwam* 2' 3'

| | 2' | 3' |
|---|---|---|
| A wise man once said that we have two ears and one | 5 | 3 33 |
| tongue so that we may hear more and talk less. Therefore, | 11 | 7 37 |
| we should be prepared to talk less quickly and exert more | 17 | 11 41 |
| effort to listen carefully to what others have to offer. | 22 | 15 45 |
| Most people do not realize that when we listen, we use | 28 | 19 48 |
| not just our ears, but our eyes and mind as well. To form | 34 | 23 52 |
| the art of listening well, show interest in what is said, | 40 | 26 56 |
| pay attention, ask questions, and keep an open mind. | 45 | 30 60 |

2' | 1 | 2 | 3 | 4 | 5 | 6 |
3' | 1 | 2 | 3 | 4 |

## 29f ● 5'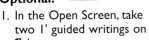

### SKILLBUILDING

**Improve number speed**
Take 1' writings; the last number you key when you stop is your approximate *gwam*.

1 and 2 and 3 and 4 and 5 and 6 and 7 and 8 and 9 and 10 and 11 and 12 and 13 and 14 and 15 and 16 and 17 and 18 and 19 and 20 and 21 and 22 and 23 and 24 and 25 and 26 and 27 and

# Use Master Documents

## Master Document

A **master** document is one that contains links to other documents called **subdocuments**. The master document feature makes it easy for you to manage a long document that has subparts or for individual members of a team to work on different sections (subdocuments) of a long document at the same time. For example, if you were writing a textbook, the module could be the master document, and each lesson could be a subdocument. Styles set in the master document apply to all subdocuments. This simplifies formatting, page numbering, and producing a table of contents for the master document.

In this lesson, you will learn how to create a new master document with subdocuments.

**To create a new master document:**

1. Create a new document.
2. Apply formatting styles (font, margins, other formatting features) that you wish to use for the entire document. Create needed headers or footers.
3. Key the introductory text, if any, that you wish to include in the master document.
4. Position the insertion point on a blank line below the introductory text where you want the subdocument to begin.

**Drill 1**

1. Read and then key the following text in a new document window:

### Sample Master Document

This text explains how to create a new master document. On the first line, apply Heading 1 style. Key the title as shown above. Then key this introductory text using regular style for body text. DS after the text so that a blank line separates the master document from a subdocument that will be added.

2. DS; the insertion point should be on a new line.
3. Print and save the document as **f5-d1md**. Keep the document open.

## Subdocuments

A **subdocument** is a regular document that is linked to a master document. Once subdocuments have been added to a master document, they can be opened or closed in the master document. They can also be removed from the master document.

**To create a subdocument:**

1. Key a document and save it with an appropriate name.
2. Open the master document and place the insertion point where you wish to add a subdocument.

# Skillbuilding

**30a ● 7'**

## GETTING
## started

each line twice SS

**SKILLBUILDING WARMUP**

| | | |
|---|---|---|
| alphabet | 1 | Jewel quickly explained to me the big fire hazards involved. |
| – (hyphen) | 2 | Pam has an up-to-the-minute plan to lower out-of-town costs. |
| fig/sym | 3 | Pay Invoice #378 and #9605 by 6/21 to receive a 4% discount. |
| easy | 4 | Susie is busy; may she halt the social work for the auditor? |

| 1 | 2 | 3 | 4 | 5 | 6 | 7 | 8 | 9 | 10 | 11 | 12 |

---

**30b ● 8'**

**SKILLBUILDING**

**Practice long reaches**
each line once; repeat;
keep hands quiet

| | | |
|---|---|---|
| n/y | 5 | deny many canny tiny nymph puny any puny zany penny pony yen |
| | 6 | Jenny Nyles saw many, many tiny nymphs flying near her pony. |
| b/r | 7 | bran barb brim curb brat garb bray verb brag garb bribe herb |
| | 8 | Barb Barber can bring a bit of bran and herbs for her bread. |
| c/e | 9 | cede neck nice deck dice heck rice peck vice erect mice echo |
| | 10 | Can Cecil erect a decent cedar deck?   He erects nice condos. |
| n/u | 11 | nun gnu bun nut pun numb sun nude tuna nub fun null unit gun |
| | 12 | Eunice had enough ground nuts at lunch; Uncle Launce is fun. |

---

**30c ● 9'**

**SKILLBUILDING**

**Improve rhythm**
work for even, continuous
stroking

| | | |
|---|---|---|
| double letters | 13 | feel pass mill good miss seem moons cliffs pools green spell |
| | 14 | Assets are being offered in a stuffy room to two associates. |
| balanced hand | 15 | is if of to it go do to is do so if to to the it sign vie to |
| | 16 | Pamela Fox may wish to go to town with Blanche if she works. |
| one hand | 17 | date face ere bat lip sew lion rear brag fact join eggs ever |
| | 18 | get fewer on; after we look; as we agree; add debt; act fast |
| combination | 19 | was for\|in the case of\|they were\|to down\|mend it\|but pony is |
| | 20 | They were to be down in the fastest sleigh if you are right. |
| combination | 21 | I need to rest for an hour in my reserve seat in my opinion. |
| | 22 | Look at my dismal grade in English; but I guess I earned it. |

| 1 | 2 | 3 | 4 | 5 | 6 | 7 | 8 | 9 | 10 | 11 | 12 |

## APPLICATION

### F6

You have drafted the "Communications" section of the benefits study for PRVH and circulated it to all the members of the benefits team. The team members made several revisions and made suggestions that are included in the document as annotations. The document with those changes is *appf6* on the Formatting Template.

1. Open *appf6*.
2. Click the **Author** button to view the suggestions made by team members.
3. Accept all of the revisions—grammar corrections, insertions, and deletions.
4. Incorporate the comments, using the resource materials shown at right.
5. Italicize *PRVH News and Benefits Update* throughout the document.
6. Proofread the document carefully to be sure revisions have all been entered.
7. Format as an unbound report. Number pages.
5. Save as **app-f6**.

Always check a document that has been revised to ensure that spacing is correct and that headings are not left alone at the bottom of a page. ■

**[JP1] Revise the sentence as suggested.**

**[AR]** Resource Material:

*Corporate Philosophy* (Use Heading 2)

The benefits program should be linked directly to PRVH's corporate philosophy and culture, ensuring effective communication. PRVH's philosophy regarding its employee benefits program is:

PRVH strives to provide for all employees, hourly and salaried, catastrophic coverage while maintaining "fairness" by offering the same benefits and options to all. PRVH also wants to provide long-term economic security by offering a 401(k) plan. These corporate goals must be achieved in the most cost-effective manner.

**[CF4]** Resource Material:

*Brochures* (Use Heading 3)

A series of brochures, some developed by PRVH and some furnished by the providers of various benefits, is available for employees. These brochures are available in the benefits offices, at group meetings, and are mailed upon request of an employee.

**[SV5]**

Revise the sentence to read: Both *PRVH News* and the *Benefits Update* should...

**[SV6]** Resource Material:

**Evaluation of Communication Plan** (Use Heading 1)

Overall PRVH has a good system designed for communicating to its employees. The quantity and frequency of information are adequate to meet the needs of most employees. However, the quality of information provided is not as good as the quantity. Two areas were noted in particular.

*Readability of Materials* (Use Heading 2)

The readability level of many of the brochures and of some articles is above the reading level of many employees. Six brochures were analyzed to determine the reading level, and the test results for all six brochures showed that the average reading level required is the equivalent of two years of college. The education level of many employees is well below the two-year college standard.

*Interest Level of Newsletters* (Use Heading 2)

Focus groups of employees were used to determine the effectiveness of the *PRVH News* and the *Benefits Update* in providing information about the benefits package. The results indicated that the *PRVH News* was more interesting than the *Benefits Update*. The articles were written in a lively style that attracted attention. The problem with the *Benefits Update* appeared to relate to its technical nature and the level of readability.

## 30d ● 10'

COMMUNICATION

**Check number usage**
Change words to figures or figures to words as needed.

23 32 of the graduates gave $9,431 to the charity.
24 Luis lives at 23 West 57 Street, not 23 West 58 Street.
25 5 players were cut from our 21-player soccer roster.
26 We invited 6 girls and 5 boys to the dinner party.
27 Only 5 of 35 people who were invited actually attended.
28 2 of us will be working here until after six o'clock.

## 30e ● 6'

SKILLBUILDING

**Check speed**
Key a 1' and 2' writing.

 all letters                                          *gwam*  1' | 2'

Teams are the basic unit of performance for a firm.   11 | 5 | 42
They are not the solution to all of the organizational needs.   23 | 12 | 48
They will not solve all of the problems, but it is known   35 | 17 | 54
that a team can perform at a higher rate than other groups.   47 | 23 | 60
It is one of the best ways to support the changes needed for   59 | 30 | 66
a firm. The team must have time in order to make   71 | 36 | 72
a quality working plan.   74 | 37 | 74

1' | 1 | 2 | 3 | 4 | 5 | 6 | 7 | 8 | 9 | 10 | 11 | 12
2' | 1 | 2 | 3 | 4 | 5 | 6

## 30f ● 10'

SKILLBUILDING

**Assess skill**
Key two 3' writings.

 all letters                                          *gwam*  1' | 3'

Do you know how to use time wisely? If you do, then its   11 | 4 | 51
proper use can help you organize and run a business better.   24 | 8 | 55
If you find that your daily problems tend to keep you from   35 | 12 | 59
planning properly, then perhaps you are not using time well.   48 | 16 | 63
You may find that you spend too much time on tasks that are   60 | 20 | 67
not important. Plan your work to save valuable time.   70 | 24 | 70

A firm that does not plan is liable to run into trouble.   12 | 27 | 74
A small firm may have trouble planning. It is important   23 | 31 | 78
to know just where the firm is headed. A firm may have a   35 | 35 | 82
fear of learning things it would rather not know. To say   46 | 39 | 86
that planning is easy would be absurd. It requires lots of   58 | 43 | 90
thinking and planning to meet the expected needs of the firm.   70 | 47 | 94

1' | 1 | 2 | 3 | 4 | 5 | 6 | 7 | 8 | 9 | 10 | 11 | 12
3' | 1 | 2 | 3 | 4

**Drill 3**

1. Open *f4dr3* from the Formatting Template.  Click the **Author** button.

2. Click the button to insert the first annotation; the suggested correction is made in the document. *WordPerfect* automatically moves to the second annotation; click the button to insert it.

3. Click the **Insert all annotations** button to accept the rest of the corrections.

4. Save the document as **f4-d3**.

## APPLICATION

**F5**

To remove highlighting:
- Click in the word containing the highlighting.
- Click the **Highlight** button on the Power bar to turn off highlighting.

1. Open *athletes* from the Formatting Template.  Save it as **app-f5**.

2. Review the document as the author.  Make the following changes:
   - Change the second sentence of the paragraph under the heading **Schedule** to read: A detailed interview guide (*see attached guide*) provides . . .
   - Change the third sentence under the heading **File Repository** to read: A general summary of information (*not comments attributed to specific athletes*) is used . . .
   - In the last sentence under the heading **Contingency Plan**, delete *existence of a* so that the sentence reads:  . . .*in this process, the plan ensures* . . .

3. Click each Comment icon in the left margin and read the comments.

4. Make the changes recommended in Comments 1 and 2.  Then delete all 3 comments.

5. Review all of the revisions marked in the document.  Accept and insert all revisions except the one made by Al Roane under the heading **Schedule**.

6. Remove the turquoise highlighting that was added for emphasis.

7. Create a table of contents.

8. Prepare an appropriate title page—use your name as the author and the current date.

9. Save and print the document.

# Level 2

# FORMATTING BASIC BUSINESS DOCUMENTS

## OBJECTIVES

### Keyboarding

To key about 40 *wam* with good accuracy.

### Formatting Skills

To format business letters, memos, reports, and tables.

### Word Processing

To use the basic word processing functions with skill.

### Communication Skills

To proofread and apply language art skills.

## Revisions

Documents can be sent to others for review. The person who writes the document is the **author**; others who review the document and suggest changes are called **reviewers**. The Review feature enables the reviewer to **redline** or strike out text, and to insert text in a color. The author can accept or reject the revisions.

If you open a document that someone else has already reviewed, the Review Document dialog box displays when the document opens. ▨

### To review a document as a reviewer:

1. Make sure you have keyed your name and initials and selected a color in the Environment Settings dialog box (see p. 507) so that your revisions will be identified.

2. Select *File* menu, *Document*, *Review*; then click the **Reviewer** button.

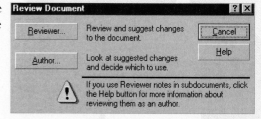

3. While you are in review mode, the copy you delete will display with a line through it, and text you insert will display in the color you selected. You can change the color you use by clicking the **Set color** button and choosing another color.

 **Drill 2**

1. Open *f4dr2* from the Formatting Template.

2. Click **Reviewer** in the Review Document dialog box.

3. Look at the changes that have already been made in the document by other reviewers.

4. Revise the last sentence in the copy so that it reads: *Inserted text is shown in the color selected by the reviewer.*

5. Print the document and save as **f4-d2**.

### To review a document as an author:

1. Click **File** menu, **Document**, **Review**. Click the **Author** button.

2. Use the buttons on the Property bar to move through the annotations and to accept (insert) or reject (delete) annotations.

Next annotation    Insert all annotations        Delete all annotations

Other user colors: ▨ Karen Schmohe    ▨ Al Roane    ▨ Jane Phelan      Close    Help

This document will illustrates the way that revisions can beare indicated when multiple peoplereviewers work on the same document. Note that text shown with a line drawn through it is text that was deleted. Text iInserted text ins shown in the color selected by the userreviewer.

Previous annotation    Insert current annotation    Delete current annotation

# ENTERING AND EDITING TEXT

**4**

*module*

## OBJECTIVES

1. Enter, save, open, and print a document.

2. Learn simple character and paragraph formats.

3. Improve speed and accuracy.

LESSON **31**

## Getting Started

**31a • 5'**

**GETTING started**

You are about to learn one of the leading word processing packages available today. You will learn to create and format documents that are professional in appearance. At the same time, you will continue to increase your keyboarding skill. You will use *WordPerfect 9* to create professional-looking documents. *WordPerfect* will make keying documents such as letters, tables, and reports easy and fun. Follow the steps to create a new document in *WordPerfect*.

**Drill**

1. Turn on the computer and monitor.

2. The Welcome to Windows 98 screen displays.

3. Click the **Start** button at the bottom of the screen.

4. Click **WordPerfect Office 2000**, then **WordPerfect 9**.

5. The *WordPerfect* document screen displays as shown on the next page.

**To insert comments:**

1. Place the insertion point where you want to insert a comment.
2. Select *Insert* menu, *Comment, Create.* Key the comment text.
3. Click the **Close** button on the Property bar to return to the document. *WordPerfect* places the reference mark in the left margin.

**To display comments:**

1. Click the reference mark to display the comment.
2. Right-click the displayed comment, and click **Information** to display information about the author and the date the comment was inserted.
3. If 2 or more comments are inserted in the same line, 2 overlapping bubbles display in the margin (see second paragraph of illustration below). Click the overlapping bubbles to display the reviewers' initials.

 **Drill 1**

1. Open *f4dr1* from the Formatting Template.
2. Click the first reference mark in the left margin.
3. Right-click the comment that displays, and select *Information* to see author and date information.
4. Click the second reference mark to display the comment and then display author and date information.
5. Click the overlapping bubbles in the margin next to ¶ 2, and view the information for each comment.

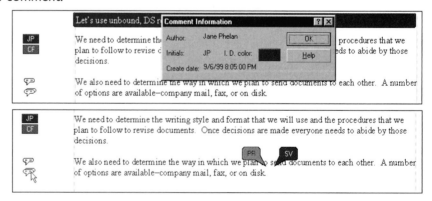

6. Position the insertion point at the end of the first paragraph, and insert the following comments (**Insert, Comment, Create**):

    Comment 1: *Wouldn't SS, leftbound format be better for a long report?*

    Comment 2: *Let's involve the whole team in decision making.*

7. Check to see that your reference mark displays along with the original comments. Save the document as **f4-d1**.

Review the screen shown at the right. Complete Drills 1 and 2.

## WordPerfect document screen

The *WordPerfect* document screen contains many of the elements that you reviewed in the Welcome to Windows 98 section.

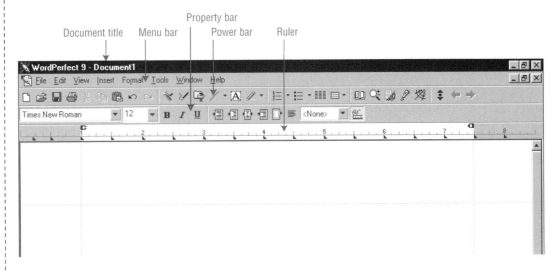

**Drill 1**

1. Point to each button on the Power bar. Notice the name of each button as it displays.

2. Repeat Step 1 on the Property bar.

**Drill 2**

1. Key ¶ 1 using wordwrap.

2. Press ENTER twice after keying ¶ 1 to DS between paragraphs. Ignore the red and green wavy lines that may appear under text as you key.

3. Keep the document on the screen for the next exercise.

**Title bar:**  Name of the application that is currently open.

**Menu bar:**  Menus from which commands can be selected.

**Power bar and Property bar:**  Buttons provide access to common commands. The name of each button displays when you point to it. The Property bar displays different buttons depending upon what you are doing in the document. For example, the Table button only appears after you have created a table.

**Ruler:**  Use the Ruler to set tabs within a document. To change the display of the Ruler, choose **Ruler** from the View menu.

**Insertion point:**  Shows where the text you key will appear.

The wordwrap feature automatically moves (wraps) text to the next line when a line has been filled.  The Enter key is pressed to end a line before it reaches the right margin.

(Strike ENTER twice.)

Note that pressing the Enter key once moves the insertion point to the next line. To leave a blank line between paragraphs, press the Enter key again.

# Team Reviewing and Revising Documents

Teams or workgroups often work on the same document. *WordPerfect* provides tools to facilitate multiple writers and reviewers working on the same document. Earlier you learned to insert files, to drag and drop or copy text from other documents, and to use automated formatting features to ensure consistency in the final document. In this lesson, you will learn to use the comments, revisions, text highlighting, and review document features.

## Comments

**Comments** are notes or annotations that are included in a document without changing the document text. *WordPerfect* stores each comment in a separate pane and places a reference mark in the left margin to indicate that a comment exists. The reference mark generally contains the user's initials and an identifying color. You must enter user information in order for *WordPerfect* to display your initials and color.

### To enable the Comments feature:

1. Click **Tools** menu, **Settings**; then select *Display*.
2. On the Document tab, click to check the **Margin icons** box.
3. Click **OK** to return to the Settings dialog box.

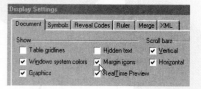

### To enter user information:

1. Click **Environment** to display the Environment Settings dialog box.
2. On the General tab, key your name and initials in the User information text boxes. Select the color you wish to use for your comments.
3. Click **OK**. Close the Settings dialog box.

> If an author has not included a name or initials and a color in the Environment Settings dialog box, the comment bubble will not include identifying initials. ■

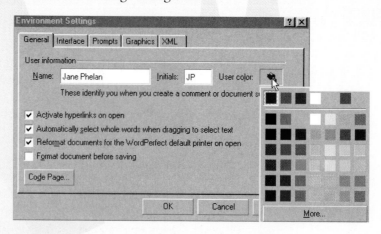

1. Review the commands on the Menu bar.
2. Complete the drill.

## Menu bar

The Menu bar contains eight menus of commands that are useful in formatting and editing documents. When a name on the Menu bar is clicked, a menu cascades or pulls down and displays the functions that are available. The File menu shown below illustrates many characteristics of pull-down menus.

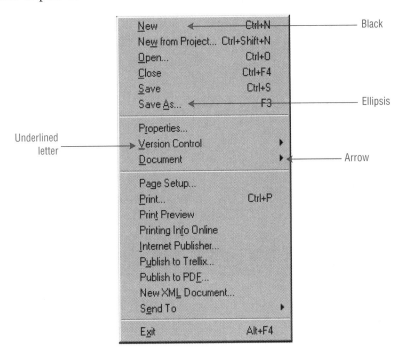

**Ellipsis (...)** following a command: A dialog box will display.

**Arrow:** Additional commands are available.

**Black:** Command is available for use.

**Dimmed command:** Command is unavailable for use.

**Underlined letter:** Keying the underlined letter activates a command (rather than clicking the command with the mouse).

### Drill

1. Use the mouse to point to *File* on the Menu bar; click the left mouse button.
2. Use the mouse to point to the arrow next to the word "Document." Note that additional commands display.
3. Click **Edit** on the Menu bar. Note that *Cut* is dimmed. Click **Cut**. Note that nothing happens because a dimmed command is not available.
4. Click the **File** menu. Note that the *Save As* command is followed by an ellipsis (...). Click **Save As** to display the Save As dialog box. Click **Close** to close the Save As dialog box.
5. Click the **File** menu. Note that the *O* of the *Open* command is underlined. Press **O** on the keyboard. The Open File dialog box displays. Close the dialog box.
6. From the File menu illustrated, note that *Crtl + P* is the keyboard command for *Print*. Hold down the CTRL key and press **P**. The Print dialog box displays. Close the dialog box.

## Work with multiple documents

Collaborative work often involves combining documents or segments of documents from several individuals. Earlier you learned to insert files in a document. In this lesson, you will learn to drag and drop segments from one document to another document.

### To move text from one document to another:

1. Open both documents.
2. Click the **Window** menu, and select *Tile Top to Bottom* (shown below) or *Tile Side by Side*. Both documents will appear on the screen. There are separate scroll bars for each document.
3. Select the text you wish to move from one document to another; then drag it to the other document and drop it. The text will be moved, not copied.

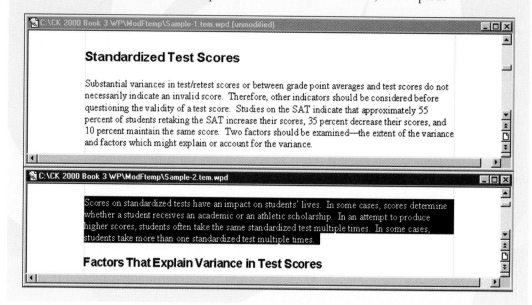

1. Open *sample1* and *sample2* from the Formatting Template. Save the documents as **sample1a** and **sample2b**.
2. Click the **Window** menu; then click **Tile Top to Bottom** to display both documents on the screen.
3. Select the first paragraph from *sample2b*. Drag and drop it below the heading *Standardized Test Scores* in *sample1a*.
4. Select all text under the heading *Factors That Explain Variance in Test Scores*. Drag and drop it at the end of *sample1a*.
5. Insert a page break at the top of *sample1a*; insert page numbers to begin at 1 on the first page of the body. Create a table of contents.
6. Save *sample1a* as **f3-d4**. Print.

31d ● 10'

**NEW FUNCTION**

1. Review the Save As information at the right.
2. Complete the drill.

## Save As

Saving a document preserves it so that it can be used again. If a document is not saved, it will be lost once the computer is shut off. The **Save As** command is used to save and name a new document or to rename an existing document. In this course, name documents with the exercise number and letter, such as **31d**.

The Save As dialog box contains a *Save in* list box, a *File name* text box, and a *File type* list box. The text area may either be blank or have a list of files if previous documents have been saved on your disk.

**To save a new document:**

1. From the File menu, click **Save As**. The Save As dialog box displays.

2. Click the arrow in the *Save in* list box to display the list of drives available. Point to the drive where you want to save your file and highlight it. Click the left mouse button to select it.

3. In the *File name* box, key the filename.

4. Click **Save**.

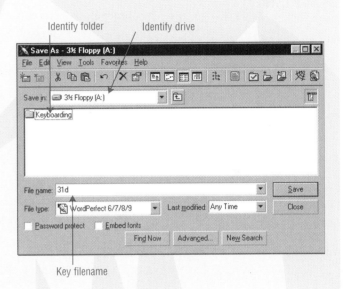

Identify folder    Identify drive

Key filename

### Drill

1. Insert your storage disk in Drive A. A storage disk is a blank formatted disk. You will use this disk to save your files.

2. Select the *File* menu and click **Save As**.

3. Click the arrow in the *Save in* list box to display the list of drives available. Point to Drive A to highlight it; click the left mouse button to select it.

4. Use the mouse and point to the *File name* text box. Click the left mouse button to place the insertion point in the *File name* text box.

5. Key **31d** as the filename.

6. Note that the default, *WordPerfect 6/7/8/9,* is displayed in the *File type* list box.

● 7. Click **Save**.

4. Select following headings and use the Mark **2** button to mark them: *Introduction, Purpose, Methodology, Design of the Benefits Plan, Insurable Risks, Cost of Benefits Plan, Communication, and Recommendations.* Select the other headings and use the Mark **3** button to mark them.

5. Define and generate the table of contents.

6. Print and save the document.

## Table of contents— hyperlinks

Each table of contents entry can be set up as a hyperlink to that topic in the document. To create hyperlinks, check the **Build hyperlinks** box when you generate the table of contents; then click **OK**. The page number for each heading is displayed as a hyperlink; you can go directly to a heading in the document by clicking that heading's page number in the table of contents.

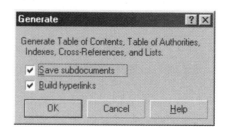

1. Open *f3dr3* from the Formatting Template. Save as **f3-d3**.

2. Click **Tools**, **Reference**, **Table of Contents** to display the Table of Contents toolbar.

3. Position the insertion point after the **<< Table of Contents will generate here >>** message and click **Generate**.

4. Click to check the **Build hyperlinks** box; then click **OK**. Note that the page numbers appear as hyperlinks when the table of contents is generated.

5. Click on the link (page number) for Recommendations to go to that topic in the document.

6. Save the document again. Print only the first page.

## Updating a table of contents

If you make changes in a document after a table of contents has been created, you may need to update the headings and page numbers in the table of contents. You can update them manually, or you can delete the table of contents and generate a new one after the changes have been made.

## Print

The Print button on the Power bar is an efficient way to print an entire document.

### Close and Exit

**Close** clears the screen of the document and frees it from memory. You will be prompted to save the document before closing if you have not saved it or if you have made changes to the document since the previous save.

To close a document, click **File** on the Menu bar; then click **Close**.

**Exit** saves all documents that are on the screen and then exits the software. You will be prompted to save before exiting if you have not already saved the document or if you have made changes to it since last saving.

To exit *WordPerfect*, click **Exit** from the File menu.

### Close and Exit Option 🗙

Close and Exit can also be accomplished using the buttons in the upper right corner. The Close button is on the right side of the Menu bar. Exit is located at the top right of the document title bar. Click the Close button at the top right side of the document window to exit *WordPerfect*.

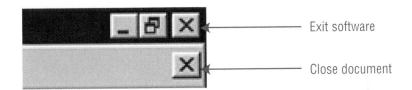

Exit software

Close document

**Drill 1**
1. Locate the Print button on the Power bar.
2. With Document **31d** displayed on the screen, click the **Print** button.
3. Review the Print dialog box. Note you will print *1* copy of the *full* document. Click **Print**.
4. Close **31d**.
5. Exit *WordPerfect*.

**Drill 2**
1. Start *WordPerfect*.
2. Key the paragraph.
3. Insert a storage disk into Drive A and save the document as **31e**.
4. Close the document.
5. Exit *WordPerfect*.

In Lesson 31, I have learned the basic operations of my word processing software. Today I opened the word processor, created a new document, saved the document, printed the document, closed the document, and exited the software. This new document that I am creating will be named 31e. I will save it so that I can use it in the next lesson to open an existing document.

**Drill 1**

1. Open *f3dr1* from the Formatting Template. Save the file as **f3-d1**. Note that the headings have been created using heading styles.

2. Position the insertion point at the top of the document before all codes, and insert a page break.

3. Set the page number of the first page of the body to 1. Leave the position in the Page Numbering dialog box set to Top Right. Use Suppress to position the page number at the bottom of the page.

4. At the top of the blank page, press ENTER for approximately 1.5" top margin and key **TABLE OF CONTENTS** in bold, 14-point type, center-aligned.

5. DS and position insertion point at left margin.

6. From the Tools menu, select *Reference*, then *Table of Contents*.

7. Click the **Define** button on the Table of Contents toolbar. Change the number of levels to 5 and click **OK**.

8. Click **Generate**. Ignore the subdocuments box in the Generate dialog box, and click **OK**. You will use subdocuments in a later lesson.

9. Save the document again and print.

Remember to turn on Reveal Codes to work with the table of contents. ▪

## Mark headings

**To mark the headings in a document:**

1. Display the Table of Contents toolbar (**Tools, Reference, Table of Contents**).

2. Select each heading; then click the **Mark** button with the appropriate heading level, such as Mark 2 or Mark 3. (Generally, you won't use Mark 1, because the main heading is not included in the table of contents.)

3. After all headings are marked, click **Define**. Select the number of levels (5) and click **OK**.

4. Generate the table of contents.

**Drill 2**

1. Open *f3dr2* from the Formatting Template. Save it as **f3-d2**.

2. Insert a page break before all codes. Set the page number of the body to 1. Key **TABLE OF CONTENTS** on the first page in bold, 14-point type, center-aligned, leaving a 1.5" top margin.

3. Display the Table of Contents toolbar (**Tools, Reference, Table of Contents**).

# Create a Document

Serendipity, a new homework research tool from Information Technology Company, is available to subscribers of the major online services via the World Wide Web.

Offered as a subscription service aimed at college students, Serendipity is a collection of tens of thousands of articles from major encyclopedias, reference books, magazines, pamphlets, and Internet sources combined into a single searchable database.

Serendipity puts an electronic library right at students' fingertips. The program offers two browse-and-search capabilities. Users can find articles by entering questions in simple question format or browse the database by pointing and clicking on key words that identify related articles. For more information, call 800-555-0174 or address e-mail to <<lab@serendipity.com>>.

32a ● 12'

### GETTING started

**Reinforcement**
1. Open *WordPerfect*.
2. Key the ¶s. Press ENTER twice between ¶s. Disregard keying errors.
3. Save the document with the name **32a**.
   • Click **File** menu, then **Save As**.
   • In the *Save in* list box, click **Drive A**.
   • Key **32a** in the *File name* text box.
   • Click **Save**.
4. Close the document.

## 32b ● 10'

### NEW FUNCTION

1. Read the procedures for opening an existing document.
2. Complete the drill on page 77.

## Open

Documents that have been saved can be opened and used again. Choose Open from the File menu or click the Open button on the Power bar. The Open dialog box displays the name of the files within a folder.

**To open a document:**
1. From the File menu, click **Open**. The Open File dialog box displays.
2. In the *Look in* box, select the drive where your files are stored (Drive A).
3. Click the desired filename and click **Open**.

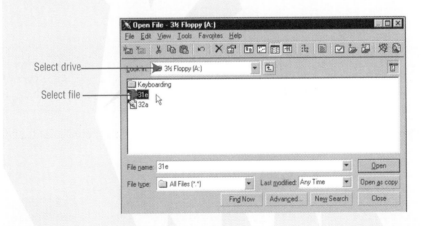

LESSON 32     CREATE A DOCUMENT     76

# Table of Contents and Multiple Documents

A **table of contents** contains the headings in a document and the page numbers on which the headings appear. It is prepared after the document has been completed. A table of contents with up to five heading levels can be generated automatically in *WordPerfect*.

It is very easy to generate a table of contents from a document that uses *WordPerfect* heading styles. The heading styles determine the level of indent in the table of contents. When heading styles are not used, you must mark the headings before the table of contents can be defined and generated.

### To create a table of contents in a document using heading styles:

1. Insert a page break (CTRL+ENTER) at the beginning of the document to provide a blank page for the table of contents. **Tip:** Use Reveal Codes to ensure that the page break is positioned *before* any formatting codes.
2. Set the page numbering to begin at 1 on the first page of the body (**Format**, **Page**, **Numbering**, **Set Value**, **1**, **Apply**, **OK**).
3. If the page is numbered at the top right, click **Format**, **Page**, **Suppress**, and check the *Print page number at bottom center on current page* box. Do not change the position in the Page Numbering dialog box, because you want the number at the bottom center on the first page only.
4. Position the insertion point at the top of the blank page and press ENTER for a 1.5" margin. Key **TABLE OF CONTENTS** in bold 14-point, center-aligned.
5. DS and position the insertion point at the left margin. If necessary, turn off bold and return the font to 12 point.
6. Click **Tools** menu, **Reference,** and then select *Table of Contents* to display the Table of Contents toolbar.

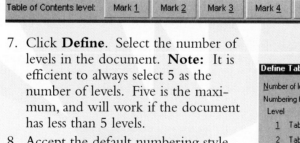

**Table of Contents toolbar**

7. Click **Define**. Select the number of levels in the document. **Note:** It is efficient to always select 5 as the number of levels. Five is the maximum, and will work if the document has less than 5 levels.
8. Accept the default numbering style (text with leaders and the page number). Click **OK**.
9. The text **<< Table of Contents will generate here >>** displays in the document.
10. Click the **Generate** button on the toolbar to generate the table of contents.

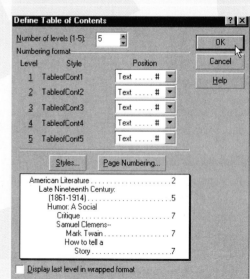

**32b,** *continued*

In Lesson 31, you created a document, named it **31e**, and saved it on your storage disk. Follow the steps at the right to open that document and add a paragraph.

To rename and save an existing file, click **File** and then **Save As** instead of clicking the Save button on the Power bar. ▓

**Drill**

1. Place your storage disk in Drive A.
2. From the File menu, click **Open**.
3. If file *31e* does not show in the Open File dialog box, click the arrow in the *Look in* box and click **Drive A**. Click the document named **31e** and then click **Open** (or double-click the document named **31e**).
4. Place your insertion point at the end of the paragraph by moving the I-beam there and clicking. Press ENTER twice and then key the following paragraph:

This paragraph modifies the document created for 31e in the last lesson. Documents that have been saved may be reused without any changes, or they may be modified.

5. Save the document as **32b**. Close the document.
6. Click **Open** on the File menu to display the Open File dialog box. Check to see that both files *31e* and *32b* are stored on your disk, as shown in the illustration below.

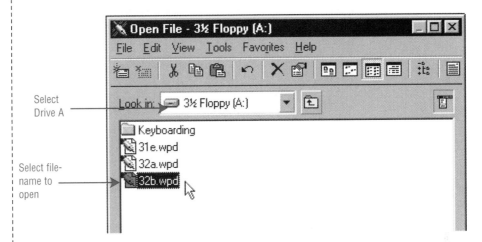

Select Drive A

Select file-name to open

7. Open *32b*; check to see that the document contains the second paragraph that you just keyed. Close the document.
8. Open *31e*. Note that this is the original file you opened. It should contain only one paragraph.
9. Close the document.

**32c ● 3'**

**NEW FUNCTION**

1. Open *32b*.
2. Key your name a DS below ¶ 2. Click the **Save** button on the Power bar.
3. Close the document.

## Save an existing file with the same name 💾

Whenever you want to save an existing document on screen with the same name, click the Save button on the Power bar. Since you are not renaming the file, the Save As dialog box does not appear.

## Project Templates

Earlier you learned to use a memo template. *WordPerfect* provides a number of project templates to simplify the formatting of documents. Some of the templates contain several designs from which you can choose. Follow the steps in Drill 2 to experiment with project templates.

**Drill 2** **Use a Project Template**

1. Click **File** menu, **New from Project**.

2. Select the *Fax Cover Sheet* template.

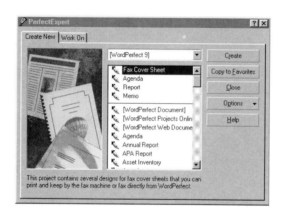

3. Click **Create**. Do not enter your personal information. Click **OK** and close CorelCENTRAL Address Book.

4. Note the options that are shown at the left side of the screen. Click **Choose a Look**, then **Traditional**.

5. Click **Fill in Heading Info** to display the Fax Cover Sheet Heading dialog box.

6. Fill in the information: The fax is to **your instructor** from **you**. Use **your school** as the organization and fill in the fax and phone numbers and the current date. The subject is **Using Templates**. It will be 3 pages long including the cover.

7. Click **Finish**, then **Print/Fax**. Print the cover sheet, then close without saving.

## Print using Print dialog box

In Lesson 31, you learned to print an entire document by clicking the Print button on the Power bar. Additional options for printing a document are available in the Print dialog box.

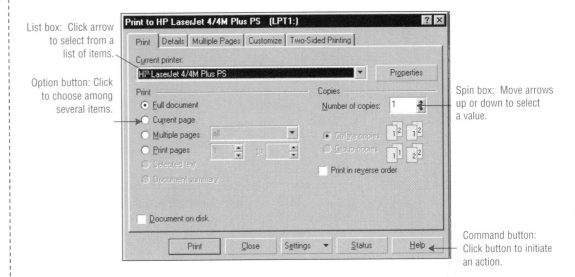

List box: Click arrow to select from a list of items.

Option button: Click to choose among several items.

Spin box: Move arrows up or down to select a value.

Command button: Click button to initiate an action.

### Drill

1. Open *32a.* Click the **Print** button on the Power bar.
2. Click the option button for *Current page* under Print.
3. Click the spin arrow to increase the number of copies to 2. Click **Print**.
4. Check to see that two copies of the page print.
5. Keep the document open.

**Insertion point movement**
1. Read the information at the right.
2. Complete the drill.

## Moving within a document

Changes often need to be made to text after it has been keyed. To change or edit the text, you must move the insertion point around in the document. The insertion point, or the blinking vertical bar, is where the text will appear when you begin to key. You can move to different parts of the document by using the mouse, the keyboard, or the scroll bars. In this lesson, you will learn to move by pointing the mouse and clicking the left mouse button.

### Drill

1. Using the mouse, point to the beginning of the last sentence of *32a.*
2. Click the left mouse button to move the insertion point before the words *For more information;* then key the following sentence:

**Articles can be printed in full.**

3. Point the mouse at the beginning of the word *students* in the second sentence; click the left mouse button, then key **and high school**.
4. Close the document; do not save it.

## QuickStyle

The **QuickStyle** feature allows you to name and describe an existing style that you like. QuickStyles are saved with the document, so you will need to re-create them to use them in other documents. To create your own style, click the Select Style down arrow and choose **QuickStyle**. In the Style name box, key a meaningful name. In the Description box, key the attributes that you used in the style. Then click OK. To use the style that you just created, click the style from the Styles list available on the Power bar.

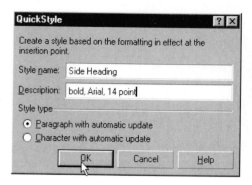

## APPLICATION F4

*Create and apply styles*

Key the document as shown at the right. The side and paragraph headings are circled; disregard the circles at this point. Follow the steps to create QuickStyles and apply them in the document.

(Purpose of the Study)

The purpose of the study was to determine the key real estate attributes, such as size, location, rental rate, availability, and construction of all industrial sites located in Hamilton and Green counties. The following information was desired:

(Property location data:) tax map number, real estate zone (based on ZIP Code), full street address, and county.

(Owner and contact data:) owner's name, address, and telephone number; contact person's name, address, and telephone number.

(Availability data:) whether the property was available for sale or lease; whether property was owner-occupied or leased; and lease expiration date.

(Methods and Procedures Used)

Consultants divided Hamilton and Green counties into three zones for reporting real estate information.

1. Select the first side heading and format it with bold, Arial, 14 point.
2. Deselect the side heading and click the insertion point in the side heading.
3. Click the Select Style down arrow; choose *QuickStyle*.
4. In the QuickStyle dialog box, key **side heading** as the name. In the Description box, key **bold, Arial, 14 point**. Click **OK**.
5. Move to the first paragraph heading (property location data). Select it and format it with bold, italic, 12 point.
6. Follow Steps 2-4 above to create a style called **paragraph heading**. However, click the **Character** radio button in the QuickStyle dialog box. Then when you apply the style, it will not affect the entire paragraph.
7. Select the second paragraph heading (Owner and contact data). Click the **Select Style** down arrow. Click **paragraph heading**. (The format should only be applied to the paragraph heading.)
8. Repeat Step 7 for the third paragraph heading.
9. Position the insertion point somewhere in the second side heading. Choose *side heading* from the Select Style drop-down list.
10. Save the document as **app-f4**; print.
11. Select the first side heading. Change the font to Times New Roman. Note that the second side heading changed automatically. Do not save or print.

## 32f ● 10'

**Review**

1. Key your name and press ENTER 4 times.
2. Key the ¶s SS, pressing ENTER twice between ¶s.
3. Practice moving the mouse:
   - Beginning of document
   - Down 2 lines
   - End of document
4. Save the document as **32f**.
5. Print the document.
6. Exit the software.

The World Wide Web and Internet Usenet News groups are electronic fan clubs that offer users a way to exchange views and information on just about any topic imaginable with people around the world.

World Wide Web screens contain text, graphics, pictures, and, on some sites, real-time audio and video. Simple pointing and clicking on the pictures and links (underlined words) bring users to new pages or sites of information.

## 32g ● 5'

# S E L F ✔
# c h e c k

Answer the True/False questions at the right to see whether you have mastered the material presented in this lesson.

T  F

1. The quickest way to print a document is to click the Print button on the Power bar.

2. When you save an existing document using the Save As command and a new name, both the original and the new document are saved.

3. The insertion point does not move to the position of the mouse pointer until the left mouse button is clicked.

4. Commands such as printing the current page and printing multiple copies cannot be accessed by clicking the Print button on the Power bar.

## NEWS

# on... **Netiquette**

With the growth of the Internet, it is becoming increasingly important for people to be aware of good online etiquette. Netiquette (Net etiquette) is the unwritten code of behavior for the Net, news groups, chat rooms, the World Wide Web, e-mail, and other networks. The basic premise of netiquette is to treat people with courtesy and consideration. Apply these basic rules of netiquette:

**Stick to the subject**, whether chatting in a theme room, posting to a news group, or answering e-mail. Posting an irrelevant message is considered rude and exposes you to being "flamed" or electronically abused by others. Also, don't send irrelevant e-mail messages; people don't have time for frivolous mail.

**Use shortcuts with care.** Emoticons, such as :-( for a sad face, :-) for a happy face, or ;-) for a wink for a joke or sarcasm, are sometimes fun to use. Some people believe, however, that emoticons are becoming obsolete. Acronyms such as IMO (in my opinion) are effective only if both parties know the meaning.

**Write clearly and concisely.** State exactly what you mean to reduce time and need for clarification. And remember to use proper grammar. Avoid using ALL CAPS for emphasis, particularly in a chat room or news group; it is considered SHOUTING.

As the Internet evolves, so will its protocols, including netiquette. So stay "plugged in."

Heading 1 ⟶ **STYLES** (18 pt., centered)

An overall document format can be applied to one document or to different documents.
A document is usually formatted manually if the style is applied to a single document. However, many documents produced in offices are formatted using the same style.

Heading 2 ⟶ **Built-in Styles** (14.4 pt.)

Consistency is very important if documents are to have a professional appearance. One way to ensure consistency is to use one of the built-in styles contained in *WordPerfect* software. Many organizations, however, prefer to use customized formats. The way they can ensure consistency is to create the specific style that they want to use in their documents, name the style, and apply it to all documents that they wish to format with that particular style. Various styles are used for automatic formatting of text.

Heading 3 ⟶ Paragraph Style (12 pt.)

A number of formats and attributes may comprise the total style of a paragraph. These formats and attributes include font, size, spacing, tab stops, alignment, bullets, and any other features that affect the appearance of the paragraph.

Heading 3 ⟶ Character Style

The Font command contains a number of formats that can be applied to characters. The various attributes contained on the Font Properties dialog box (such as font style, size, underline, color, and effects) make up character style.

Heading 3 ⟶ Document Style

Document styles affect all text from the insertion point to the end of the document. Once you turn on a document style, it stays in effect to the end of the document. The exception is heading styles, which stay in effect until you press ENTER.

Heading 2 ⟶ **Style Usage**

Historically, organizations ensured consistency of style by preparing a procedures manual that contained style guides and model documents. Today, they often rely on the built-in styles or on customized styles they create and store in the word processing software. These customized styles can then be applied to their documents in the same manner as the built-in styles.

HEADING STYLES

# LESSON 33

# Enter and Edit Text

## 33a ● 5'

### GETTING started

**Reinforcement**

1. Key both ¶s SS; press ENTER twice between ¶s.
2. Practice moving the insertion point with the mouse.
3. Save the document on your storage disk as **33a**.
4. Print the document; close.

A wise man once said that we have two ears and one tongue so that we may hear more and talk less. Therefore, we should be prepared to talk less quickly and exert more effort to listen carefully to what others have to offer.

Most people do not realize that when we listen, we use not just our ears, but our eyes and mind as well. To form the art of listening well, show interest in what is said, pay attention, ask questions, and keep an open mind.

## 33b ● 20'

### NEW FUNCTION

Read about the features, then complete Drills 1–4. Follow these procedures for the remainder of textbook.

### Insert, Delete, Typeover

The Insert, Delete, and Typeover features are often used when revising documents.

#### Insert

*WordPerfect* is set for the Insert mode by default. To insert text, simply position the insertion point where the new text is to appear and key the text. Existing text moves to the right.

#### Delete

The DELETE key can be used to erase text that is no longer wanted.

> **To delete a character:** Position the insertion point to the left of the character to delete and press DELETE, or position the insertion point to the right of the character to delete and press BACKSPACE. Be careful not to hold down the DELETE or BACK-SPACE keys as they will continue to erase characters.

> **To delete a word:** Double-click the word to be deleted and press DELETE.

#### Typeover

The Typeover mode replaces text with new text as you key it. Press the INSERT key at the right of your keyboard to turn on Typeover mode. "Typeover" displays on the status bar as long as you are in Typeover mode. Return to the Insert mode by pressing INSERT again.

### Drill 1

1. Open *32a*.
2. Click **File**, then **Save As** to save the file with a new name, **33b-d1**.
3. Make the corrections shown at right to ¶ 3. (Your text will be single-spaced.)
4. Click the **Save** button.
5. Print the document.

```
        Serendipity puts an electronic library right at students'
fingertips  The program offers two browse-and-search capabili-
                        on just about any subject
ties. Users can find articles by entering questions in simple
question format or browse the database by pointing and clicking on
key words that identify related articles.  For more information,
call 800-555-0174 or address e-mail to <lab@serendipity.com>.
            with just a computer and a
            modem.
```

# Styles

The **Styles** feature provides an easy way to format similar types of text such as headings in the same way. Using Styles ensures that your document has a consistent format. Should you change your mind about the look of your text, you can edit the style, and all your headings will be updated at once. Styles are saved with the documents they format. Styles can also be associated with a template. *WordPerfect* has created styles in the standard template; these can be accessed from the Select Styles down arrow on the Power bar. You can also access them from the Format menu.

**To apply Styles:**

1. Select the text to which you wish to apply a style.
2. Click the **Select Styles** down arrow, and select the style you wish to apply.

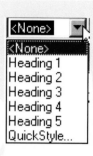

**Drill 1** **Apply Styles**

1. Key your name. Click the Down arrow on the Select Styles box. Select Heading 1.
2. Note that Heading 1 is centered, bold, and 18-point font.
3. Apply Heading 2, then Headings 3, 4, and 5.

## APPLICATION
 **F2**

*Report with Styles*

Format the leftbound report on the next page with full justification. Apply Heading 1, 2, and 3 from the drop-down Styles list where indicated. Read the report carefully as you key it. The report presents information that you will need to know to use styles effectively. Save the report as **app-f2**.

## APPLICATION
 **F3**

*Edit report*
1. Open *app-f2*.
2. Reformat the document DS; indent ¶s.
3. Number the pages.
4. Add the two ¶s at the right to the bottom of the document. Save as **app-f3**.

Styles can be modified or copied very easily. For example, the Heading 1 style applies Times New Roman. The heading could be changed by using a different font, such as Arial. This change would affect all other Heading 1s in the document.

Using the Styles feature has benefits that extend beyond helping to format documents. It helps to simplify other document processing tasks, such as a table of contents with headings, leaders, and page numbers. The table of contents can be generated automatically.

## Drill 2

1. Open *33b-d1* if needed.
2. Delete the text in ¶s 1 and 2 as shown at the right.
3. Save as **33b-d2**.
4. Print, then close the document.

Serendipity, a ~~new homework~~ research tool from Information Technology Company, is available to subscribers of ~~the major~~ on-line services via the World Wide Web.

Offered as a subscription service aimed at ~~college~~ students, Serendipity is a collection of tens of thousands of articles from ~~major~~ encyclopedias, reference books, magazines, pamphlets, and Internet sources combined into a single searchable database.

## Drill 3

Key the words in the first column, and then use the Typeover feature to replace the words with the words in the second column. Close without saving.

| can | may |
|-----|-----|
| November | December |
| decide on | determine |

## Drill 4

Follow the directions at the right.

1. Open *33a*.
2. Delete each occurrence of the word "talk" and insert "speak" in its place.
3. Use the Typeover feature to replace "may" with "can."
4. Correct any additional errors that you may have made in your document.
5. Save as **33b-d4**. Print. Close the document.

## 33c ● 10'

### Review

1. Key the document, correcting errors as you key. Errors may be identified with red wavy lines.
2. Proofread and correct any errors that you made.
3. Save as **33c**.
4. Click the **Save** button to save the file with the same name.
5. Print.

As the man says, I have some good news and some good news. Let me give you first the bad news. Due to a badly pulled muscle, I have had to withdraw from the Eastern Racquet Ball tournament. As you know, I have been looking forward to the tournament for a long time and I had begun to hope that I might even win it. I've been working hard.

That's the bad news. The good news is that I have been picked to help officiating, so I'll be coming to Newport News any way. In fact, I'll arrive there a day earlier than I had planned originally.

So, put the racquet away; but get out the backgammon board. I'm determined to win something on this trip!

**Drill 4**    **Create QuickWord entries**

1. Key the letterhead and save it as a QuickWord entry named *asa*.

   - Center-align the address in 14-point Arial. Add a horizontal line a DS below the letterhead name. Press ENTER after the line and choose left justification.

American Studies Association
Liberty Bell University
2385 Chestnut Street
Philadelphia, PA 19174-0802

---

   - Select the entire letterhead. **Tip:** To be sure you include the formatting codes, choose *Edit* menu, *Select*, *All*.
   - Choose *QuickWords* from the Tools menu.
   - Key **asa** in the Abbreviated form box, and click **Add Entry**.
   - In a new document, key the abbreviation *asa* at the top of the document. As soon as you press the Space Bar after *asa*, the abbreviated form expands to the full letterhead.

2. Create a QuickWord entry for **Murphy, Gillick, Wicht & Prachthauser**. Use 14-point bold italic and center-align. Name the abbreviated form **mg**. Close the document; in a new screen, enter the **mg** entry.

3. Use the information below to create a QuickWord entry for the closing of a letter. Use block format and 12-point type. Name the entry **closing**.

Cordially | Susan B. Archual | Director of Human Relations

## APPLICATION

 F1

Key the letter, using the automated features you have learned.

1. Insert the letterhead using QuickWord **asa**.
2. Insert the date.
3. Key the body of the letter shown at the right.
4. Insert QuickWord **closing**.
5. Save as **app-f1**. Print.

(Insert *mg*.  Then format correctly.)
113 E. Wisconsin Ave.
Milwaukee, WI 53223-3578

Ladies and Gentlemen

Thank you for completing our Family Status Survey.  We will be using the information to determine composite statistics concerning the psychological welfare of today's American family. The **(Insert QuickCorrect deoc.)** has also been extremely helpful with providing statistics for this survey.

In appreciation for your help, the American Studies Association invites you to attend our convention here in Philadelphia June 7-10 at the Hickory Suites. The **(Insert QuickCorrect deoc.)** will be presenting a workshop on cultural diversity, which is open to all participants.

## Using Help

The Help Topics dialog box allows you to access every form of help that is available with *WordPerfect 9*. Learning to rely on the Help feature rather than your instructor will enable you to learn new software independently. Always try online Help before asking your instructor to assist you.

You can print a Help topic or keep it displayed on the screen for easy reference. ■

**To access Help Topics:**

1. Click **Help** on the Menu bar; then click **Help Topics**. The Help Topics dialog box displays.

2. Note the four tabs that indicate ways to access Help:

   • Contents—lets you browse through topics by category.

   • Index—provides a list of index entries.

   • Find—lets you search for a particular word or phrase in online Help.

   • Ask the PerfectExpert—lets you ask for help in your own words.

3. Click the **Index** tab.

4. Key a word pertaining to the topic on which you need help.

5. Click the desired topic; then click **Display**.

6. Click the **Close** (**X**) button to close Help.

**Drill 1**

1. From the Help menu, click Help Topics, then the **Index** tab.

2. Key **help** in the text box.

3. Select *Help Topics* from the list by clicking on it; then click **Display**. Read the information.

4. Click the **Close** (**X**) button to close Help.

## SpeedLinks

The **Speedlinks** feature converts text to a hyperlink automatically. To activate SpeedLinks, click the SpeedLinks tab in the QuickCorrect dialog box and check the *Format words as hyperlinks when you type them* box.

SpeedLinks automatically converts text beginning with "www," "http," "ftp," or "mailto." You can also cross-reference sections of an online document with SpeedLinks.

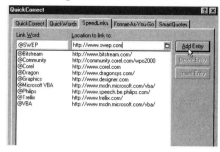

### Drill 3

Create a SpeedLink to the South-Western Educational Publishing Web site.

1. Click **Tools**, **QuickCorrect**, and click the **SpeedLinks** tab.

2. Key **swep** in the Link Word box. (*WordPerfect* adds the @.)

3. Key www.swep.com in the Location to link to box.

4. Click **Add Entry**, then **OK**.

5. In a new document, key **@swep**, then press the Space Bar. Note that the text appears in blue and underlined.

6. If you have Internet access, click the hyperlink swep to go to the Web site.

## QuickWords

**QuickWords** can be used to enter text or graphics automatically. A QuickWord is an abbreviation for a longer text entry or graphic. It is very similar to the shortcut in QuickCorrect. QuickWords are commonly used for entering letterhead, logos, closing lines of a letter, or other repetitive sections of text.

**To use QuickWords:**

1. Select the text for which you wish to create a QuickWord entry.

2. Select *Tools* menu, *QuickWords*.

3. In the Abbreviated form box, key the shortcut you want *WordPerfect* to replace automatically.

4. Check the *Expand QuickWords when you type them* box.

5. Click **Add Entry**.

**33d,** *continued*

## Drill 2

1. From Help, click **Ask the PerfectExpert**.
2. Key **How do I access help topics?**
3. Click **Search**.
4. Select *Accessing Help Topics*.
5. Click **Display** and read the information.
6. Click the **X** button to close Help.

## Using PerfectExpert

1. From the Help menu, click **Ask the PerfectExpert**.
2. In the text box, key the question you wish to ask.
3. Click **Search** to display topics.
4. Select the desired topic and click **Display**.

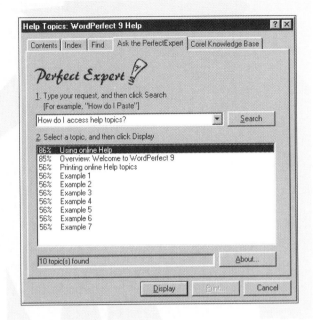

**33e** •

## SKILLBUILDING

Use the remaining class time to build your skills using *Keyboarding Pro,* Skill Builder Module. Follow the directions at the right.

### Keyboarding Skill Builder

1. Open *Keyboarding Pro* or *Keyboarding Pro Multimedia*.
2. Open the Skill Builder module.
3. Insert your storage disk for *Keyboarding Pro* into Drive A.
4. Select *Lesson A* for speed practice.

5. Beginning with Keyboard Mastery, complete as much of the lesson as time permits.
6. Exit the software. Remove your storage disk. Store your materials as directed.

# *on...* Ergonomic Keyboards

**NEWS**

Concerned about repetitive strain injuries (RSI) resulting from extensive keying, keyboard manufacturers now offer keyboards designed to improve hand posture and make keying more comfortable.

Ergonomic keyboards come in many different designs. Most of them, however, have several features in common: the standard QWERTY key layout, a split design with left and right banks of keys, and the ability to tilt or rotate the keyboard for comfort.

Ergonomic keyboards are curved and have either added keys, such as a *Windows* function key, or moved keys to a different location, such as the BACKSPACE key in the center of the keyboard between the right and left banks of keys.

Many people believe ergonomic keyboards are more comfortable than conventional keyboards. More research is needed to determine just how effective they are in preventing RSI and carpal tunnel syndrome.

### Drill 1 — Apply QuickCorrect and SmartQuotes

1. Scroll through the QuickCorrect list to see the kinds of entries that *WordPerfect* revises automatically.

2. Key the lines below exactly as shown. Notice how *WordPerfect* revises the text when you press the Space Bar after each incorrect word.

   the technician can acomodate us on the first monday of february.
   I recieve alot of requests from disatisfied comittee members.

3. Key these lines and note how the quotation marks differ.

   "I'm learning WordPerfect."
   I stand 5' 10" tall.

### Drill 2 — Create QuickCorrect Entries

1. Create a QuickCorrect entry so that *WordPerfect* replaces *wp*. Key **wp** in the Replace box. In the With box, key **WordPerfect**. Click **Add Entry**, then **OK**.

2. Key this sentence: **It is fun to learn new applications found in wp software.**

3. Create a QuickCorrect entry for **Diverse Employment Opportunities Commission**. Name it **deoc**.

4. Key this sentence: **The deoc is a federally funded organization to protect the employee against discrimination.**

## Format-As-You-Go

Format-As-You-Go lets you specify settings for automatic capitalization, spacing between words, and other options. Click the Format-As-You-Go tab of the QuickCorrect dialog box. Note the corrections that are made automatically. Click the **Exceptions** button to add exceptions to the capitalization rules shown. For example, if you key *Venus de Milo* and do not want *WordPerfect* to capitalize *de*, you can add *Venus* to the Exception list.

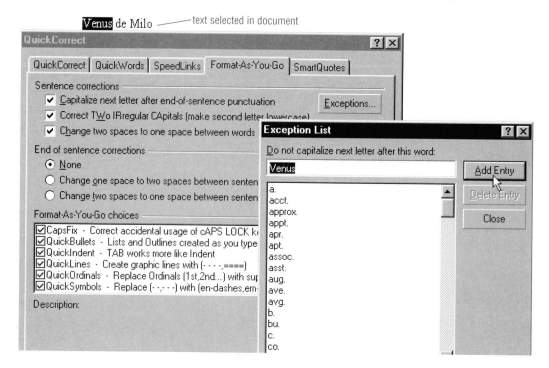

# Text Appearance

## 34a ● 7'

### GETTING started

**Reinforcement**

1. Open *33c*.
2. Insert and delete text as marked in the first 2 paragraphs. Save as **34a**. Print and close.

As the man says, I have some good news and some ~~good~~ *bad* news. Let me give you (first) the bad news. Due to a badly ~~pulled~~ *strained* muscle, I have had to withdraw from the Eastern Racquet Ball *lc* tournament. As you know, I have been looking forward to the tournament for a long time, and I had begun to hope that I might even win it. I've been working hard *and it might have paid off.*

That's the bad news. The good news is that I have been *Chosen* ~~picked~~ to help *with the* officiating, so I'll be coming to Newport News any way. In fact, I'll arrive ~~there~~ a day earlier than I had planned originally.

## 34b ● 8'

### NEW FUNCTION

## Select

**Select** identifies text to be modified. Selected text appears black on the screen. Text may be selected by using the mouse or the keyboard.

**To select text with the keyboard:**

1. Position the I-beam on the first character. Press SHIFT + CTRL and → or ←.
2. To select large portions of text, press SHIFT + CTRL and ↑ or ↓ .
3. Cancel Select by pressing an arrow key.

**To select text with the mouse:**

1. Position the I-beam on the first character to be selected.
2. Click on the left mouse button and drag the mouse over the text to be selected. Or, instead of dragging, you can use these shortcuts to select:

   A word: Double-click.
   A sentence: Triple-click.
   A paragraph: Quadruple-click.

3. To cancel a selection, click the mouse button again or press any arrow key.

### Drill

1. Open *33b-d4*.
2. Use the mouse to select each item; cancel Select after each item:
   - The first sentence
   - The word "wise" in ¶ 1
   - The first line
   - The first ¶
3. Use the keyboard to select:
   - The word "attention" in the last sentence
   - ¶ 1
   - Both ¶s
4. Move the insertion point to the top of the document. Key your name; press ENTER twice.
5. Save as **34b**; print; close the document.

# Automated Formatting Features

In this lesson, you will learn some easy and timesaving features of *WordPerfect*. The QuickCorrect dialog box has five tabs that provide useful options to automate your work. Each tab is illustrated in this lesson.

## QuickCorrect

**QuickCorrect** corrects typos and substitutes words for abbreviations as you key. If you key *adn*, *WordPerfect* automatically corrects the spelling to *and*. You can expand the capability of QuickCorrect by adding entries. For example, you could create a QuickCorrect entry to enter your full name when you key your initials.

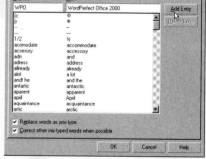

**To create a QuickCorrect entry:**

1. Select *Tools*, then *QuickCorrect*.
2. In the Replace box, key the shortcut or the error you want *WordPerfect* to replace automatically.
3. In the With box, key the correct word or words.
4. Click **Add Entry**, then **OK**.

**To delete a QuickCorrect entry:**

Because other students will be using your computer, you will need to delete any QuickCorrect entries you create. Select *Tools* menu, then *QuickCorrect*. Select the entry and click **Delete Entry**.

## SmartQuotes

**To use the Smart Quotes option:**

The SmartQuotes feature automatically converts straight quotes to the curved quotes normally used in desktop publishing. Straight quotes are used after numbers. To activate these options, click the SmartQuotes tab in the QuickCorrect dialog box and place a check in each of the three option boxes.

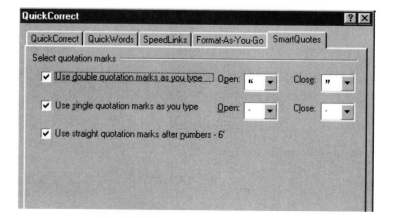

**N E W**
**F U N C T I O N**

1. Read the information at the right.
2. Complete Drills 1–3.

## Format text

The **toolbars** provide an efficient way to apply formats such as bold, underline, italic and justification. These formatting options can be applied while you are keying, or they can be applied to existing text.

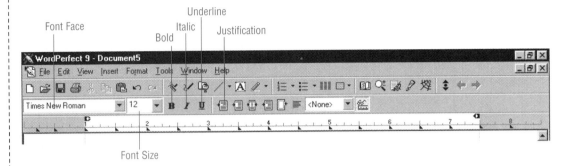

### To apply formats as you key:

1. Click the appropriate format button and key the text. When the formatting feature has been turned on, the button appears lighter and depressed.
2. Click the same button again to turn off the format.

### To apply character formats to existing text:

1. Select the text.
2. Click the appropriate format button.

## Font size

The size of the font is measured in points. One vertical inch is equal to 72 points. Most text is keyed in a 10-, 11-, or 12-point font, although a larger font may be used to emphasize headings. To change the size of the font, select the text to be changed and then click the Font Size down arrow. A list of available font sizes displays; select the desired one.

**Drill 1**

Key each of the sentences, applying the formats as you key. Save as **34c-d1**.

**These words are keyed in bold.**

*These words are keyed in italic.*

<u>These words are underlined.</u>

This line is keyed in 14 point.

**Drill 2**

Select the text and click the appropriate format button.

1. Open *34a*; save as **34c-d2**.
2. Bold the words "good," "win," and "day earlier."
3. Italicize the words "bad" and "badly."
4. Underline the last sentence in the third paragraph. Select the line and change it to 14 point.
5. Key your name and **34c-d2 Keyboarding** at the top of the document. Press ENTER 4 times. Save and print.

# WORKING COLLABORATIVELY

F

*module*

## OVERVIEW

In this module, you will learn how to use word processing features that are designed to facilitate collaborative writing and to improve your productivity. *Collaborative writing* refers to using a team rather than an individual to produce a document or complete a project. In today's office, most projects are the work of a team rather than an individual. To be productive, a team must work in the right way—using the tools that produce the best results in the least amount of time.

*WordPerfect* has very effective tools—automated formatting features, styles, comments, master document/subdocument feature—for creating and managing team writing and for managing long documents effectively.

**34c,** *continued*

**Drill 3**

Follow the steps at the right.

1. Open *34a*.
2. Key your name on the first line in 14 point.
3. Underline the last sentence of the document.
4. Italicize all occurrences of the words "bad news."
5. Bold all occurrences of the words "good news."
6. Print and save as **34c-d3**.

**34d ● 10'**

**NEW FUNCTION**

## Justification

**Justification** refers to the way in which text aligns. Options for justifying text include Left, Right, Center, Full, and All. Click Format; then point to Justification to access the options. Or click the Justification button on the Property bar.

As you point to each option, the text aligns to let you preview how it will look before you click the option to select it. ▪

**To justify as you key:**

1. Click the **Justification** button and select the justification you want.
2. Key the paragraph. This alignment will remain in effect until you change it.

**To justify existing text:**

1. Select the text to be justified; or position the insertion point in the paragraph.
2. Click the **Justification** button and choose the justification you want.

**Drill**

1. Select *Left justify*; key ¶ 1.
2. Select *Center justify*; key ¶ 2.
3. Select *Right justify*; key ¶ 3.
4. Select *Full justify*; key ¶ 4.
5. Select *All justify*; key ¶ 5.
6. Center the page.
7. Save as **34d**; print.

Text is generally **left justified** because it is easy to read. The first letter of each line begins at the left margin, making an even left margin and a ragged right margin.

*Center Justified*
*WordPerfect* automatically centers
each line between the left and right margins.
Center alignment is often used in keying announcements.

*Right Justified*
All text lines up with the right margin.
This produces a ragged left margin.

***Full justification*** produces even left and right margins. Full justification is achieved by placing extra spaces between words in the line. Note that the last line of the paragraph does not have extra spaces inserted and may not end at the right margin.

***All justification*** also produces even left and right margins. All justification is achieved by placing extra spaces between words and letters in the line. Note that the last line of the paragraph is stretched to end at the right margin.

# Activity

*twenty-one*

## Creating Web pages using Quattro Pro

*Quattro Pro 9* has the capability of saving a spreadsheet as a Web page. This allows the user to display the spreadsheet using a browser. Storing the spreadsheet as a Web page allows a larger number of people to view the spreadsheet through the Internet using their browsers. They do not need to have the *Quattro Pro* software, nor do they need to know how to use *Quattro Pro.*

### Create a Web page using a Quattro Pro spreadsheet

1. Open the *Quattro Pro* file *p5-d1* you created in Project 5. If you do not have this file, follow the steps on page 487 to create it.
2. Click **File**, then **Publish to Internet**. The **HTML** radio button in the *Publish as* section should be enabled.
3. Select a range of cells using the Pointer button under *Ranges and charts to convert.* Click the dialog box to bring it to the foreground. Click **Add**.
4. Key a path and filename in the Save file text box. Click **OK**.

### View the Web page using your browser

1. Access the Internet.
2. Key the path and filename of your document in the Address or Location bar of your browser. Press ENTER.
3. Use the scroll bar to view the spreadsheet.
4. Close your browser. Close the *Quattro Pro* file.

# Spelling and Reveal Codes

### GETTING started

**Reinforcement**
1. Key the paragraph. Disregarding keying errors for now.
2. Save as **35a**.
3. Print and close.

35b ● 20'

## NEW FUNCTION

Accidents on the job can often be avoided if each employee is aware of the hazards involved in his or her duties.  Employees should be informed of things that they may inadvertently do or leave undone that may jeopardize others.  It is always better to play it safe when working with others.  Remember, accidents don't just happen; they are caused.

## Writing Tools

Spelling and grammar checking and correcting features *assist* you in proofreading and editing documents—they do not *replace* editing and proofreading. *WordPerfect* provides several options for checking spelling and grammar. In this lesson, you will use features to check spelling.

### Spell-As-You-Go

Common keying errors are corrected automatically as you key. For example, if you key *hte*, the Spell-As-You-Go feature automatically corrects the spelling to *the*. If Spell-As-You-Go is not enabled, you can access it by choosing *Proofread* from the *Tools* menu.

### Spelling automatic check

*WordPerfect* automatically checks the spelling of text as you key, placing a red wavy line under misspelled words. This feature is called QuickCorrect. You can customize Quick-Correct by choosing *QuickCorrect* from the *Tools* menu.

By reviewing the document, you can quickly see where corrections are needed. To correct a misspelled word underlined in red, right-click the word, and then choose the correct spelling from the pop-up menu that displays.

**Drill 1**
1. Key the sentences as shown, including errors.
   **Note:** Errors in Sentences 1 and 2 are corrected automatically (Spell-As-You-Go). Possible errors in Sentences 3 and 4 are marked.
2. Right-click the marked words and correct the errors.
3. Can you locate the error that is not marked?

Spelling errors will be marked with a red line.
Right click to correct the error.

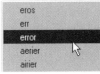

i beleive alot of dissatisfied customers will not return.

a seperate comittee was formed to deal with the new issues.

(please) (includ) a self-addressed, (stampted) envelope with your letter.

if you don't receive a (repsonse) to your e-mail (messige,) call Robbins and (Assocaites) at 555-9870

## Document 5
### Create *Paradox* table

Open the *telecom* database. Create a new table named **Commission**. Name the 1st field **ID** and specify it as *autoincrement*.

## Document 6
### Create query

1. Create a query to select salespeople with a commission greater than $500. Include all fields except ID in the query. Save as **Top Achievers Query**.
2. Assign the Answer table the name **Top Achievers Table**. (Refer to E6, p. 481.)

## Document 7
### Mail merge

1. Merge the letter at the right with **Top Achievers Table**. Start the merge in *Paradox* using the Expert option.
2. Enter the date to update automatically. Add missing letter parts and merge fields. Key the $ before the Commission variable in the third column of the table. Send the letter from **Valerie Schnieder, Executive Vice President**. Save the form letter as **commission.frm**.
3. Saved the merged documents as **p5-d7merge**. Print the first two letters.

## Document 8
### Update linked file

1. Update the spreadsheet **p5-d1** with the data at the right. Save changes.
2. Open **p5-d2** in *WordPerfect*. Click **Yes** to update the links.
3. Change the date on the memo to 1 week later. Update the body to reflect the changes.
4. Save as **p5-d8**; print.

| Title | First | Last | Address | City | State | ZIP | Commission |
|---|---|---|---|---|---|---|---|
| Mr. | Justin | Henderson | 2346 Ashley, #17 | Los Alamitos | CA | 92345 | 885.00 |
| Mr. | Russ | Toby | 840 Primrose Circle | Seal Beach | CA | 92848 | 740.00 |
| Ms. | Joan | Padilla | 22 Crescent Lane | Anaheim | CA | 92503 | 399.00 |
| Ms. | Judy | Chen | 541 Garden Ave. | Brea | CA | 92166 | 653.00 |
| Mr. | Robert | Hutton | 77 Mulberry Lane | Lake Forest | CA | 94655 | 585.00 |
| Ms. | Lisa | Ayala | 93 Dale St. | Anaheim | CA | 92503 | 466.00 |
| Mr. | James | Clarkston | 54 Ocean Blvd. | Dana Point | CA | 95788 | 610.00 |
| Ms. | Ann | Troung | 103 Prince Circle | Lake Forest | CA | 94655 | 457.00 |
| Ms. | Sarah | Nelson | 1225 Stevens Lane | Lake Forest | CA | 94655 | 525.00 |
| Mr. | Harvey | Cross | 3561 Birchwood | Seal Beach | CA | 92848 | 611.00 |

---

Dear «Title» «Last»

Congratulations on your outstanding sales record this month! Your diligence and hard work have placed you among the top achievers for the Western Region. Visit our Web site at **www.wwtelecom.com** and see your name posted as a Western Region outstanding sales representative.

Below is a copy of your sales record for August 1, 200- to August 31, 200-. Your commission check is also enclosed.

| Last Name | First Name | Commission |
|---|---|---|
| <<Last>> | <<First>> | $<<Commission>> |

Keep up the good work! See you at Sales Conference next month.

---

| Company | Long Distance | Internet |
|---|---|---|
| American Communications | 13,900,000 | 52,500 |
| SouthWest Utilities, Inc. | 9,750,000 | 27,000 |
| Seattle Telecommunications | 12,200,000 | 41,000 |
| WorldWide Telecom | 19,200,000 | 87,000 |
| Others | 8,200,000 | 82,000 |

**35b,** *continued*

## Spell Checker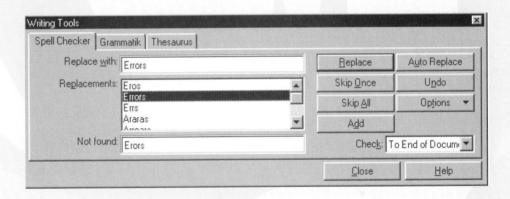

Spell Checker can be used at any time to correct misspelled or duplicate words and improper capitalization.

### To use Spell Checker:

From the *Tools* menu, choose *Spell Checker.* **Option:** Click the **Spell Checker** button on the toolbar.

### To make a correction, use one of the following methods:

- Replace a word by choosing the correct word from the suggested list and clicking the **Replace** button.
- Edit words manually by keying the replacement word in the *Replace with text* box.
- Skip the word once by clicking **Skip Once**, or skip it each time it occurs in the document by clicking **Skip All**.
- Add the correct word to the dictionary by clicking **Add**.

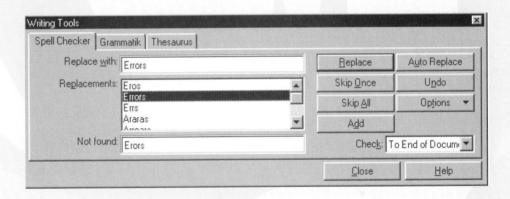

**Drill 2**

1. Open *35a.*

2. Click the **Spell Checker** button on the Power bar to check the document.

3. Proofread and make additional corrections as needed.

4. Save as **35b-d2** and print.

**Drill 3**

1. Key the document; SS the paragraphs and apply other spacing as marked. Center and bold the headings.

2. Correct number expression errors as you key. (See page RG1 to review Number Expression guidelines.)

3. Check spelling and correct errors.

4. Save as **35b-d3**.

5. Print. Proofread the printout. If you find additional errors, correct and reprint.

### JOINT VENTURE ANNOUNCED ⎯14 pt ⎯ DS

Commtec Corp. notified the CCI today that its Board of Directors aproved the proposal for a communications research joint venture. Under the contract signed, Commtec has agreed to provide hardware, software, and services worth over one million dollars to the CCI. The CCI, in turn, has agreed to provide staff and suport resources to conduct the research.

### The Project ⎯ DS

The research is focused on two primary areas: Using the computer as a tool to enhance the communications process and as a tool for teeching communication skills. These 2 areas were selected on the basis of both need and opportunity.

### Project Management ⎯ DS

The project team consists of twenty staff members; a list of members was included with the copy of the proposol sent to all employees a couple of weeks ago. The project team is responsible for the direction and success of the project. The membership of the Project Steering Comittee will be announced this week.

## Perform a mail merge with a *Quattro Pro* file

Data stored in *Quattro Pro* can be mail merged with *WordPerfect* form documents. When creating a *Quattro Pro* file to be merged, it is best not to have main and secondary headings in the file. *Quattro Pro* will automatically use the first row for field names. After the *Quattro Pro* file is saved, it must be imported into *WordPerfect* to be used as a merge data file.

1. In *WordPerfect*, click **Insert** menu, **Spreadsheet/Database**, **Import**. Check that the Data type is *Spreadsheet*. Click the *Import as* drop arrow and choose *Merge Data File*.

2. Click the folder icon to the right of the Filename box and change to the Formatting Template folder. Select the file *contacts.qpw*. Click **Select**, then click **OK** twice. Save as **contacts.dat**. The spreadsheet has been imported.

3. Click the **Go to Form** button on the Mail Merge toolbar. The Associate dialog box displays telling you no form document is currently associated with this data file.

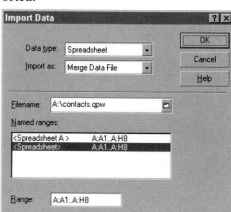

4. Click **Create**. Key the form document shown below and insert the merge fields. Insert the WWTelecom letterhead, *letterhd-wwt* (Project 3, Document 2, p. 365). Use the Date function to update the date automatically.

5. Supply a complimentary closing and your name as the writer. Save as **p5-d4-form**.

6. Click the **Merge** button to merge the letters; print. Save the merged letters as **p5-d4**. (The fonts may vary within the document.)

Current date (Enter 4 times)

«Title» «First» «Last»
«Address»
«City» «State» «Zip»

Dear «Title» «Last»

A mutual friend of ours, «Recommendation», gave me permission to invite you to participate in a business opportunity in the growing field of telecommunications. WorldWide Telecom is the sixth-largest long-distance company in the United States; we are the fastest-growing carrier.

A special meeting will be held at the Anaheim Convention Center on Saturday, October 16, 200-, at which James McFry, Executive Director of WorldWide Telecom, will speak. Mr. McFry will relay his experience starting as a part-time representative to building his multimillion-dollar business. Mr. McFry will discuss the many services that WorldWide Telecom has to offer.

Visit our Web site at **www.wwtelecom.com** to learn more about the exciting things we are doing. Now is the time to join this booming industry!

Come on Saturday, October 16, to learn more about starting a new career. I will call you next week to make arrangements to meet with you at the convention center.

# Reveal Codes

Most of the commands that you enter, such as bold, underline, and italic, are represented by a code in *WordPerfect*. These codes can be seen in the Reveal Codes screen. Identifying them is essential for editing documents.

The shaded portion at the bottom of the screen shows the document with the embedded codes (see the illustration below). In Reveal Codes, the insertion point is shown as a red block. The insertion point in Reveal Codes corresponds to the insertion point in the document. Spaces are displayed as diamonds and formatting codes as buttons. If you move the insertion point left of the margin code, it displays the margin settings.

Some codes are paired, which means that you will see the code twice—once where the feature is turned on and again where it is turned off. (See Bold or Underline code.) Click before or after a code to delete it. In a pair code, you only need to delete one.

| Command | Code |
|---|---|
| **bold** | Bold |
| **italic** | Italc |
| **underline** | Und |
| **9-point font** | Font Size: 9pt |
| **hard return** | HRt |
| **soft return** | SRt |

**To use Reveal Codes:**

• Click **View**, then **Reveal Codes**.

The *Internet* is a web of wide-area networks that allows you to connect with computers all over the world. Most major universities, science research centers, government agencies, and technology-oriented businesses have linked their networks to the *Internet* to exchange electronic information.

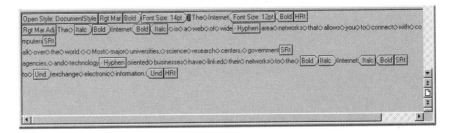

## Drill 1
### Identify the codes and edit.
1. Open *34c-d2*. Click on **View, Reveal Codes**.
2. Find the insertion point in the Reveal Codes screen.
3. Find a space.
4. Find a SRt code (soft return), indicating that wordwrap returned the insertion point to the next line.

5. Find a HRt code (hard return). This code indicates that you pressed ENTER.
6. Find the 14-point font code; delete it.
7. Find the underline codes; delete them.
8. Find the italic codes; delete them.
9. Find the bold codes; delete them.
10. Delete the HRt code between ¶s 1 and 2 to form one paragraph. Insert spaces between sentences.
11. Save as **35c-d1**. Print and close.

## Drill 2
1. Open *34c-d1*.
2. Delete all bold, underline, and italic codes.
3. Save as **35c-d2**; print.

## Drill 3
1. Open *35b-d3*. Save as **35c-d3**.
2. Reveal codes:
   • Delete the DS [HRt] above and below the three headings.
   • Delete the justify code before the last two headings. Text will be left-aligned.
   • Close Reveal Codes.
3. Change the spacing of the entire document to DS. Indent ¶s.
4. Save and print.

Use the remaining time to improve your speed using *Keyboarding Pro*.

**Document 3,** *continued*
## Slide 8
### Insert Microsoft Clipart
1. Open *WordPerfect.*
2. Click **Insert,** then **Object.**
3. Choose *Microsoft ClipArt Gallery.* Click **OK.**
4. Search for a **light bulb.** Insert the light bulb on the *WordPerfect* page. Select and copy it.
5. Go to *Presentations* and click **Paste** on Slide 8. Size and position graphic.

## Part 2
### Transition, animation, and timing
1. Apply transitions to all slides.
2. Apply animation so that each bullet appears separately.
3. Animate the graphic in Slide 8:
   a. Click the picture.
   b. Click **Object Animation** on the toolbar.
   c. Select *Animate object in place.*
   d. Choose *Burst Out* effect, medium speed.
4. Set the slide show to run automatically with a 15-second delay between slides.
5. Save as **p5-d3.**

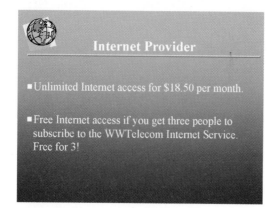

**Slide 5**

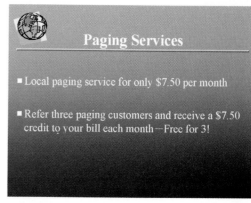

**Slide 6**

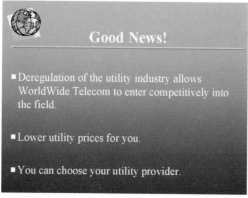

**Slide 7**

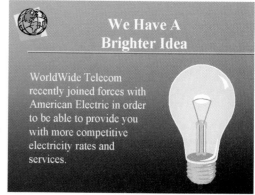

**Slide 8**

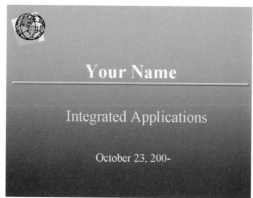

**Slide 9**

# Formatting

**36a • 5'**

# Getting
started

**Formatting a document**
**Formatting** refers to the arrangement of the document on the page. Word processing not only involves keying a document, but also arranging it attractively on the page.

Click the Format menu to see the many different ways that you can format a document. Point to Page; the Page submenu displays more options.

**36b • 10'**

**NEW
FUNCTION**

## Center Page

The **Center Page** command centers a document vertically on the page. Should extra hard returns [HRt] appear in a document, these are also considered to be part of the document. Be careful to delete extra hard returns before centering the document.

The Center Page command is shown in Reveal Codes as [Cntr Cur Pg]. This code appears at the top of the document. To cancel Center Page, delete the code in the Reveal Codes screen.

**To center text vertically on a page:**
1. Position the insertion point on the page to be centered.
2. From the Format menu, select *Page*.
3. Click **Center**. The Center Page(s) dialog box displays.
4. Click the **Current Page** button. Click **OK**.

**Drill 1**
1. Key the ¶s below and indent ¶s.
2. Bold each occurrence of "stress."
3. Center the page.
4. Save as **36b-d1**; print.
5. Delete the Center Page code and the bold code.
6. Print and close without saving.

**Drill 2**
1. Open *35a*; save as **36b-d2**.
2. Italicize "avoided" and "accidents."
3. Underline "aware" and "inadvertently."
4. Insert ¶ at the beginning of Sentence 3.
5. Center the page. Save again; print.
6. Delete the Center Page code. Print and close without saving.

The topic of stress has received considerable attention over the past few years. Everyone experiences some stress during his or her lifetime.

People are affected by stress in many different ways. A situation that causes stress may upset some people but may not have an effect on others. Coping with stress and knowing the difference between productive and nonproductive stress will help you to live a full and happy life.

**Document 3**
*Presentations* **slide show**

**Part 1**
**Background layer**
1. From the Start-up Master Gallery, choose the category Color and the design Ice.
2. Follow the steps at the right to add the WorldWide Telecom logo to the background of the slides.
3. Create the slides shown. Follow specific directions for slides 3 and 8.

The graphic image from the WorldWide Telecom logo is to appear on all the slides. The most efficient way of placing the image on all the slides is to add it to the background layer. An image placed on the background layer will automatically appear on each new slide.

**To add the logo to the background layer:**
1. Right-click the first slide. Select *Background Layer*.
2. Click **Insert** menu, **File**. Change the File type to *All Files*.
3. Select *world* from the Formatting Template and click **Insert**.
4. Size the graphic and place it in the upper-left corner of the slide.
5. Click the Slide Layer tab at the right to switch back to the slide layer.
6. Click the Slide Sorter tab to view the placement of the logo on the slides. Adjust the logo placement on each slide as needed.

**Slide 3**
1. Choose the Data Chart layout.
2. Key the title as shown. Delete the box for Subtitle.
3. Open *Quattro Pro*. Open the file **p5-d1**.
4. Select the chart. Click **Copy**.
5. Switch to *Corel Presentations*. Double-click the Data Chart area and paste the chart. Adjust the size and position of the chart.

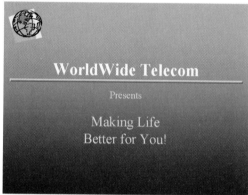

**Slide 1**

**Slide 2**

**Slide 3**

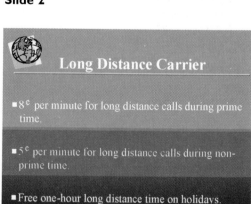

**Slide 4**

## Line spacing

**Line spacing** controls the spacing between lines of text. The default is single spacing. When you change the line spacing, it takes effect beginning in the paragraph where the insertion point is positioned. The line spacing change affects the remainder of the document. If you select paragraphs and change the line spacing, the change will affect the selected paragraphs.

**To change line spacing:**

1. Place the insertion point at the beginning of the line where the new line spacing is to take effect.

2. Click the **Format** menu, **Line**, then **Spacing**. Increase or decrease the spacing. The values most commonly used are 1, 1.5, or 2.

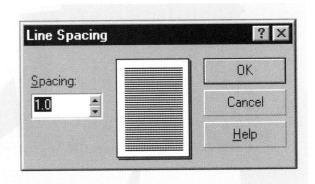

**Drill 1**

1. SS the paragraph. Indent the first line.

2. With the insertion point in the paragraph, click **Format**; then **Line, Spacing**.

3. Change line spacing to 2 (double spacing).

Indenting paragraphs properly helps to enhance the appearance of the text and to make it more readable. Remember to indent paragraphs when double spacing is used. Do not indent single-spaced paragraphs.

**Drill 2**

1. Key the paragraphs at the right SS; do not indent them. Leave a blank line between paragraphs.

2. At the beginning of ¶ 1, change the spacing to DS; indent paragraphs. Delete the HRt code between ¶s 1 and 2.

3. Print the document.

4. Change the spacing to 1.5 lines.

5. Print and close.

Commitment is an important concept that helps to build credibility. Commitment simply means following up on promises and doing what you said you would do. Many people think that commitments should be put in writing. Others feel that a verbal commitment is just as valid. DS

If circumstances make it impossible for you to keep a commitment, notify the individual to whom the commitment was made as quickly as possible so that other arrangements can be made for someone else to assume your commitment. Letting people down at the last minute puts them in an awkward position.

## Document 2
### Link *Quattro Pro* chart to a memo

1. Key the memo. Insert the WorldWide Telecom logo. If you have not created the logo, complete Document 1 on p. 365 in Project 3.
2. Use Paste Special to link the *Quattro Pro* chart created in Document 1 to the *WordPerfect* memo.
3. Change the wrap on the chart to In front of text. (Right-click, choose **Wrap**, then choose *In front of text*.)
4. Save the memo as **p5-d2**.
5. Print the memo.

### Technology Review

Paste Special is found in the Edit menu. In the Paste Special dialog box, click the **Paste Link** button.

*WorldWide* **Telecom**

**TO:**  Jonathan Smith

**FROM:**  Your Name

**DATE:**  Current Date

**SUBJECT:**  WorldWide Telecom—The Leader!

Good News!  WorldWide Telecom is gaining a greater share of the telecommunications market each day!  As you can see from the graph below, we now have 26% of the market.  Our closest competitor, American Communications, has 23% of the market.

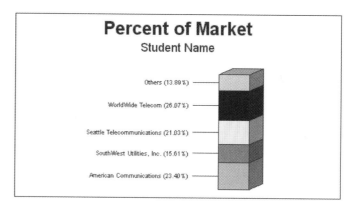

WorldWide Telecom's market share will increase tremendously when we begin offering utility services.

xx

**FORMATTING**

# THE INTERNET

**Document 1**

1. Key the text; apply formats as shown.
2. Center the page vertically.
3. Save as **36d-d1**. Do not close the document.

Full justify → The Internet is the greatest entertainment medium since television and the greatest business tool since the computer.   Don't be left wondering; cruise the Internet and find out for yourself.

DS — strike ENTER twice

Left justify → Each time you browse, you will find different places and different information.   Here are a few of the benefits the Internet offers you:

DS

Center justify →
Interactive entertainment
A chance to meet people on the Net
Research sites
Business opportunities

DS

Left justify → <u>Even if you don't like computers, the Internet will be the catalyst that brings you into the computer age</u>.

DS

For more information or help, contact:

Right justify →
*THE INTERNET HELP DESK*
301 Web Avenue
Seattle, WA 98543-3276

Left justify → (Your Name)

**Document 2**

The document *36d-d1* should be displayed. Follow the steps at the right to change the formatting.

1. Click **Reveal Codes**.
2. Change the heading to 14-pt. bold font.
3. Select ¶ 1. Change line spacing to **1.5**. Note that ¶ 2 is not affected.
4. Italicize *Internet* in the first line of the first ¶.
5. Select ¶ 2.  Change line spacing to **1.5**.
6. Select the 4 center-justified lines and change the justification to left. Use single spacing for these 4 lines. With the 4 lines still selected, click the **Bullets** button on the Formatting toolbar.
7. Select the ¶ that is underlined; change line spacing to **1.5**.  Change the format from underline to bold.  (With the ¶ selected, click the **Underline** button to remove underlining; then apply bold format.)
8. Add a blank line before the line *THE INTERNET HELP DESK*.
9. Insert 3 blank lines before *your name*.
10. Compare your document to the illustration on the next page.
11. Save the document as **36d-d2** and close it.

## Document 1

### Quattro Pro spreadsheet with chart

1. Create the spreadsheet. Key the main heading in Row 1 and the column heads in Row 3.
2. Adjust column width so that all text is visible.
3. Key the column heading **Total Dollars** in Cell E3 and **Percentage of Market** in F3.
4. Enter a formula in Column E that totals Long Distance, Paging, and Internet for each company.
5. In E9, add the total dollars of all the companies.
6. Enter a formula in F4 that calculates each company's share of the market. (Divide each company total by the grand total in E9.) Save as **p5-d1**.
7. Select *B4..E9* and change the numeric format to Currency: **Format**, **Selection**, **Numeric Format** tab, **Currency**. Enter **0** for the number of decimal places.

| COMPETITOR'S SHARE OF TELECOMMUNICATIONS MARKET | | | |
|---|---|---|---|
| Company | Long Distance | Paging | Internet |
| American Communications | 13,500,000 | 87,000 | 47,000 |
| SouthWest Utilities, Inc. | 9,020,000 | 53,000 | 24,000 |
| Seattle Telecommunications | 12,150,000 | 62,000 | 39,000 |
| WorldWide Telecom | 15,043,000 | 93,000 | 57,000 |
| Others | 7,995,000 | 19,500 | 78,000 |

### Create a 3-D column chart

8. Create the chart on the same sheet as the spreadsheet. Select Cells F4-F8. Hold down the CTRL key and select Cells A4–A8.
9. Click **Insert**, **Chart** and select a *Regular 3-D* column chart from the Pie category. Key **Percent of Market** as the title and your name as the subtitle.
10. Place the chart below the spreadsheet.

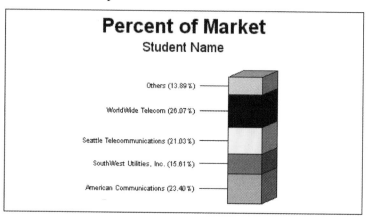

11. Right-click the chart and choose *Type/Layout*. In the Chart Types dialog box, choose *3-D Column*. Click **OK**.
12. Click one of the boxes in the column to select it, then right-click. Choose *Column Chart Properties*.
13. Click the **Label Options** tab. In the Label Series box, key **A4..A8**.
14. Click the **Text Font** tab. Change the size of the font to 12 point. Click **OK**.
15. Adjust the size and position of the chart box so that all the labels are visible.

### Format the spreadsheet

16. Format cells B4-E9 in currency format with no decimal places. Format F4-F8 in general format.
17. Format the spreadsheet using the Conservative I style (SpeedFormat).
18. Center, bold, and apply 14 point font to the main heading.
19. Format the spreadsheet with a 1.5" top margin.
20. Save as **p5-d1**. Print the spreadsheet and the chart.

**36d,** *continued*

How does your
document compare
to this solution?

**THE INTERNET**

The *Internet* is the greatest entertainment medium since television and the greatest business tool since the computer. Don't be left wondering; cruise the Internet and find out for yourself.

Each time you browse, you will find different places and different information. Here are a few of the benefits the Internet offers you:

- Interactive entertainment
- A chance to meet people on the Net
- Research sites
- Business opportunities

**Even if you don't like computers, the Internet will be the catalyst that brings you into the computer age.**

For more information or help, contact:

DS

*THE INTERNET HELP DESK*
301 Web Avenue
Seattle, WA 98543-3276

QS

Your Name

**Document 3**
1. Key the text.
2. Format the document as shown at the right. Use 14-pt. bold for title.
3. Center page vertically.
4. Save as **36d-d3**. Print.

**36e** ●

SKILLBUILDING

Use remaining time to improve your speed using *Keyboarding Pro,* Skill Builder Module.

# NEW MISSION FOR EDUCATION

In a time of increasing emphasis on diversity, schools must find a way to focus on conveying common human and democratic values and to validate their expressions in a multicultural context.

As reflected in our mission statement, the fundamental expectations of our schools are to develop:

*Well-Informed Citizens*

*A Professional, Adaptive, World-Class Workforce*

# WORLDWIDE TELECOM INTEGRATED APPLICATIONS

## OBJECTIVES

Create a worksheet with a chart.

Create a memo with a linked *Quattro Pro* chart; update linked files.

Produce a *Presentations* slide show.

Perform a mail merge with a *Quattro Pro* file.

Create a query and merge with a letter.

## OVERVIEW

Your business with WorldWide Telecom has taken off to a good start. You look for additional ways to enhance the promotion of your business and decide that you will prepare a *Presentations* slide show. The slide show, set up to run automatically on a computer, will be a handy marketing tool for you to take with you to trade shows.

As your business is rapidly growing, you have decided to keep your contact list in *Quattro Pro* and to create a data-base in *Paradox* that will keep track of all your providers and clients. This allows you to use mail merge to send announcements and letters to contacts and clients. Since you decided to use all *WordPerfect Office 2000* products for your automated office, you will have the advantage of being able to integrate and link your word processing, spreadsheet, database, and presentation packages.

## Objective Assessment

Answer the questions below to see whether you have mastered the content of this module.

1. An ellipsis following a command on a pull-down menu indicates that a _____ will display.

2. A(n) _____ command on a menu indicates that it is not available for use.

3. To modify a document and save both the original version and the modified version, use the _____ command.

4. The insertion point is on page 2. To print only that page, click _____ in the Print dialog box.

5. The _____ command replaces existing characters with text that is keyed.

6. The _____ command is used to bring a previously stored document onto the screen.

7. _____ refers to the way in which the characters or text lines up.

8. In Reveal Codes, the insertion point appears as a(n) _____.

9. To use the DELETE key to delete a character, place the insertion point to the _____ of the character to be deleted.

10. The Center Page command is accessed from the Page command on the _____ menu.

## Performance Assessment

1. Key the document at the right.
2. DS the ¶s. SS the list.
3. Center justify the two headings. Use 14 point for GROUPWARE heading line.
4. Right justify your name and date a DS below the list.
5. Center the document vertically on the page.
6. Save as **ckpt4**.

GROUPWARE
What Is It?

The term *Groupware* has received a lot of publicity over the past few months. But ironically enough, a recent survey showed that the majority of the people could not define Groupware. *ital*

*Groupware* is software that allows people to work together; "it supports collaboration and the collaborative process by enhancing the productivity and effectiveness of a group of people." Groupware *ital* software gives the traveling executive the capability of being able to access their corporate databases, communicate with his employees, and schedule meetings while on the road.

The six categories of groupware *ital* include the following:

SS
center
justify
E-mail and communications
Calendaring and scheduling
Information sharing and conferencing
Meeting support and group decision making
Shared document and image management
Word-flow management
DS

right
justify
Your Name
Current Date

**Document 3**
**Create a report**
Use the Report Expert to create a report based on the Savings Balance Query. Follow the directions at the right.

1. Include all the fields in the report.
2. Do not add any grouping levels.
3. Select multiple records and the default style.
4. Assign a centered title of **Savings Balance Report**.
5. Add page numbering.

**Document 4**
**Merge with a table**
Create and merge the memo at the right with the Savings Balance Answer Table.

1. Use the Merge Expert to define the data source. Assign the name **Bank Balance Form** for the new form letter.
2. Use *WordPerfect* to enter the form memo in proper memo format. Insert merge fields for the fields in quotes and insert the current date code.
3. Merge the form document and the data source to a new document.
4. Save the merged files as **E6-d4** and print.

| **TO:** | <First Name> <Last Name> |
| | Account Number: <Account #> |
| **FROM:** | Richard Goldstein |
| **DATE:** | Current date |
| **SUBJECT:** | Welcome VIP Customer |

Welcome to the National Bank VIP Customer Club. You are eligible for membership in the VIP Customer Club since you have maintained a balance of $<Savings> in your account. The VIP membership entitles you to the following banking privileges:

- Credit limit extended up to $20,000.
- Free checking as long as a minimum of a $5,000 balance is maintained in the combined checking and savings accounts.
- No monthly charge for using National Bank Online Banking Services.

Thank you for choosing National Bank; we look forward to serving you again soon.

**Document 5**
**Labels**

1. Use the Label Expert to create labels based on the Savings Balance Query.
2. Select the *Avery 5162* label or a 2-column label appropriate for file folders.
3. Use Times New Roman, 14 point, bold.
4. Select an order of left to right.
5. Include the customer's first name and last name on the first line and the account number on the second line.
6. Name the report **Savings Balance Labels**.
7. Print labels on plain paper.

# BUSINESS CORRESPONDENCE

## OBJECTIVES

1. Learn block and modified block letter formats.

2. Learn standard memorandum format.

3. Change the format of existing documents.

4. Improve speed and accuracy.

**5**

*module*

---

## LESSON 37 — Interoffice Memorandum

### 37a • 7'
**GETTING started**

each line twice SS; DS
between 2-line groups

| | | |
|---|---|---|
| alphabet | 1 | The explorer questioned Jack's amazing story about the lava flow. |
| fig/sym | 2 | I cashed Cartek & Bunter's $2,679 check (Check #3480) on June 15. |
| adjacent reaches | 3 | As Louis said, few questioned the points asserted by the porters. |
| easy | 4 | The eighty firms may pay for a formal audit of their field works. |

| 1 | 2 | 3 | 4 | 5 | 6 | 7 | 8 | 9 | 10 | 11 | 12 | 13 |

### 37b • 5'
**SKILLBUILDING**

**Build staying power**
Take a 1' writing on each ¶.

all letters

*gwam* 1' 3'

All of us can be impressed by stacks of completed work; yet, we should recognize that quality is worth just as much praise, or maybe even more, than the quantity of work done.

Logically, people expect a fair amount of work will be finished in a fair amount of time; still, common sense tells us a bucket of right is better than two wagonloads of wrong.

The logic of the situation seems lucid enough:  Do the job once and do it right.  If we plan with care and execute with confidence, our work will have the quality it deserves.

| 12 | 4 | 39 |
| 25 | 8 | 44 |
| 35 | 12 | 47 |
| 12 | 16 | 51 |
| 24 | 20 | 55 |
| 35 | 24 | 59 |
| 12 | 27 | 63 |
| 24 | 32 | 67 |
| 35 | 35 | 70 |

1' | 1 | 2 | 3 | 4 | 5 | 6 | 7 | 8 | 9 | 10 | 11 | 12 | 13 |
3' | 1 | 2 | 3 | 4 |

## Assessment

**Document 1**
**Create database**

1. Set the working directory to the Bank database found on the Formatting Template (*Module E\Bank*).
2. Design and enter a new table named **Account List**. Include the field names shown in the table below.
3. Determine the data type and size of each field.
4. Set these validity checks:
   • Last name, First name, Address, City, State, and ZIP as required fields.
   • State as a picture so that the two-letter abbreviation must be capitalized.
5. Set Account # as the key field.
6. Enter the records from the information in the table.

| Account # | Title | Last Name | First Name | Address | City | State | ZIP | Checking | Savings |
|-----------|-------|-----------|------------|---------|------|-------|-----|----------|---------|
| 101 | Mr. | Ristine | Lawrence | 169 King St. | Portland | ME | 04101 | $3,588 | $3,900 |
| 102 | Mr. | Leung | Roy | 229 Bretton Dr. | Billings | MT | 59101 | $2,085 | $1,500 |
| 104 | Ms. | Reynolds | Debra | 50 Chittenden Ave. | Omaha | NE | 68108 | $1,650 | $6,255 |
| 105 | Ms. | Wimmer | Alison | 440 Bluejay Dr. | Sun Valley | NV | 89433 | $ 955 | $2,650 |
| 106 | Mr. | Beem | Joseph | 691 Lodge Ln. | Rochester | NH | 03867 | $ 360 | $1,500 |
| 107 | Ms. | Marselli | Marla | 6323 Cannon Dr. | Fargo | ND | 58102 | $8568 | $5,450 |
| 108 | Mr. | Patel | Rajah | 281 Winter Ln. | Sioux City | IA | 51115 | $2,089 | $8,305 |
| 109 | Mrs. | Smith | Mary | 1253 Northfield Dr. | Pocatello | ID | 83201 | $4,445 | $4,005 |

**Document 2**
**Create query**

Create a query to list each customer's account #, title, complete name and address, and the balance in the savings account. Follow specific steps at the right.

1. Add criteria to the Savings field so that only customers who have a balance greater than $5,000 are reported.
2. Sort the balances in ascending order.
3. Click the **Properties** icon on the Property toolbar. From the Answer tab, assign **Savings**
 **Balance Answer Table** as the Answer Table name.
4. Save the query as Savings Balance.
5. Run the query; then key an answer to the questions below.

a. On what field will *Paradox* automatically sort first?

b. What other sort order has been specified and on what field?

c. How many records are included in the query after it is run?

d. What field type was Savings assigned?

e. Which criteria formula did you include? Which field was the criteria applied to?

f. What is unique about the records that are in the query?

## COMMUNICATION

### Proofreading

Read the information at the right. Follow these steps for each document you key from now on.

### Proofreading

Before documents are complete, they must be proofread and errors must be corrected. Error-free documents send the message that you are detail-oriented and capable. Apply these procedures for all exercises in this textbook:

### Proofreading procedures

1. Use the Spell Checker when you have completed the document.
2. Proofread the document on screen to be sure that it makes sense. Errors of omission or repeated copy are easy to miss.
3. Verify the vertical position and overall appearance of the document using Print Preview or Zoom. (See Lesson 39, p. 104.)
4. Save the document again and print.
5. Proofread the printed document by comparing it to the source copy (textbook).
6. If errors are found on the printed copy, revise the document, save, and print.
7. Verify the corrections and placement of the second printed copy.

## FORMATTING

### Interoffice memos

Read the information. Then key the two documents on p. 97.

### Interoffice memorandums

Messages sent to persons within an organization are called **memorandums** (memos for short). Memos include a heading, a body, and one or more notations. Addresses are not required; and the use of default margins and tabs makes memos a streamlined, efficient means of communication. An increasingly popular form of internal communication is electronic mail, or **e-mail**. Users create and send the message on their computer.

Memos may be printed on plain paper or memohead. They are sent in plain envelopes or interoffice envelopes, which can be reused several times.

### Memo format

**Headings:** Double-space (DS), bold, and ALL CAPS. Job titles and department names of the sender and receiver are optional. Depending on formality or writer's preference, courtesy titles (Mr., Ms.) of the receiver may be included. Generally courtesy titles are not used for the sender.

**Body:** Single-space (SS) the body and DS between paragraphs. Do not indent ¶s.

**Reference initials:** When the memo is keyed by someone other than the sender, the keyboard operator's initials are keyed in lowercase letters a DS below the body. Initials are not included when keying your own memo.

**Notations:** Items clipped or stapled to the memo are noted as *attachments*; items included in an envelope are *enclosures*. Key notations a DS below the reference initials.

**Side and bottom margins:** Default or 1".

**Top margin:** Approximately 1.5". To position the first line of the heading, insert 3 hard returns from the default top margin.

**Font size:** Use 12 point for readability.

✦✦✦ Interoffice Memo ✦✦✦

TO: Loretta Howerton, Office Manager

FROM: Lawrence Schmidt, OA/CIS Consultant

DATE: March 16, 200–

SUBJECT: Memorandums for Internal Correspondence

A memorandum is an internal communication that is sent within the organization. It is often the means by which managers correspond with employees and vice versa. Memos provide written records of announcements, requests for action, and policies and procedures.

*Templates*, or preformatted forms, are often used for keying memos. Templates provide a uniform look for company correspondence and save the employee the time of having to design and format each memo. Word processing software also has memo templates that can be customized. An example of a template is attached.

xx

Attachment

*Merge with query*

1. Create a query of employees celebrating a December birthday. Save the query as a table for use in the merge.
2. Run the Merge Expert.
3. Create the form file.
4. Merge the form and data files.

**Document 1  Query**

1. Create a query to list employees who will be celebrating a birthday in December. Include these fields in the query:
   *Team table:* Team name.
   *Employee table:* Last name, First Name, Birthdate.
2. Add the criteria **12/../....** to the birthdate field so that only December birthdates are included. The string ../.... acts like a wildcard, returning December birthdates on any day and in any year.
3. Assign the Answer table a name: Click the **Properties** button on the Property toolbar. From the Answer tab, assign **December Birthdays Table**. Click **OK**.
4. Save the query as **December Birthdays Query**.

**Document 2  Merge announcement and query**

1. Run the Merge Expert following the steps listed for Application E14.
   • Choose *December Birthdays* as the table for the form letter.
   • Assign December birthdays as the filename of the form letter.
2. Create a form file inserting the fields for the variables. Save as **December birthdays**.
3. Format the announcement as a one-page document. Change the font to 20 point.
4. Merge the form document and data.
5. Scroll through the merged announcements and delete the year from the birthdates. Verify the accuracy of the merge. Save as **App-E14**; print.

Congratulations, <First Name> < Last Name>

*Insert a clipart suitable for December birthdays. Size attractively.*

You've got a special day coming up this month!
Celebrate your special day, <date>, with two passes to the Clearwater Cinema. The passes are valid for six months from <date>.

Thank you for working with us.
Happy Birthday from all of us on the <Team>.

**APPLICATION**

*Report from Query*

1. Create a report based on the Equipment Service Query. Include all the fields.
2. Group by equipment category.
3. Select a style of your choice.
4. Assign a title of **Equipment Service Report**. Assign page numbering.
5. Name the report **Equipment Service Report**. Print the report.

**APPLICATION**

*Labels from Query*

1. Create labels based on the Equipment Service Query.
2. Select *Avery 5262* labels. Use Times New Roman, 14 point, bold.
3. Select an order of left to right. Include Last Name on the first line of the label. Include Model and Category on the second line.
4. Assign **E16** as the label report name. Select the *print the labels now* box. Print in portrait view.

**37d,** *continued*

**Document 1
Memo**

1. Press ENTER 3 times to position the insertion point for a 1.5" top margin.
2. Key the memo.
3. Follow "Proofreading procedures" in 37c, p. 96.

 **Interoffice Memo**

1.5"

**TO:** TAB TAB Loretta Howerton, Office Manager

**FROM:** TAB Lawrence Schmidt, OA/CIS Consultant

**DATE:** TAB March 16, 200-

**SUBJECT:** TAB Memorandums for Internal Correspondence

1"  A memorandum is an internal communication that is sent within the organization. It is often the  1" means by which managers correspond with employees and vice versa. Memos provide written records of announcements, requests for action, and policies and procedures.

*Templates,* or preformatted forms, are often used for keying memos. Templates provide a uniform look for company correspondence and save the employee the time of having to design and format each memo. Word processing software also has memo templates that can be customized. An example of a template is attached.

xx

Attachment

words

**Document 2**

Key the document at the right. Save as **37d-d2**.

| | | words |
|---|---|---|
| **TO:** | Lonny Ashmyer DS | 4 |
| **FROM:** | Breton S.  Vreede DS | 9 |
| **DATE:** | January 11, 200- | 13 |
| **SUBJECT:** | Wheelchair Access | 19 |

Recently, I explained to you my efforts on a variety of projects to facilitate  35
wheelchair entry into public buildings.  I may have found a solution to one  50
problem, Lonny;  that is, how does someone open a large public door from  64
a wheelchair?  67

The answer may lie in the installation of an electrical signal similar to a  83
garage door opener that can be activated from the chair.  All signals would  98
be identical, of course, permitting universal application.  110

Please provide me with a rough estimate of the costs for conducting the  125
necessary preliminary search, equipping a wheelchair, and tooling our fac-  139
tory to manufacture this item.  146

xx  146

## Merge process,
*continued*

### Step 2: Create form file

9. Key the text of the form document.

10. When a variable needs to be added, click the **Insert Fields** button from the Merge toolbar. A dialog box appears listing the fields in the table. Select the field you need and click **Insert**.

11. Close the dialog box when all variables are inserted.

### Step 3: Merge the form document and data

12. Click **Merge** from the Merge toolbar. The Perform Merge dialog box indicates that the Form document is the current document; the Data Source is the *Paradox* data file created in Step 1; and the Output should print to a new document.

13. Verify that the data is accurate and is positioned correctly in the first record. Scroll through the rest of the memos to verify the accuracy of each record.

14. Save the merged letters with a new filename. Print.

## APPLICATION

*Merge with Database Query*

### Document 1  Save query as table
1. Open the Telecom database.
2. Using the Employee and Equipment tables, create a query to list each employee who has equipment. Include the fields *Last Name, First Name, Category, Model, Date Serviced.*
3. Sort by Equipment Category, then by the Date Last Serviced.
4. Assign the table a name: **Equipment Service Query**. Click **OK**.
5. Save the query as **Equipment Service**.

### Document 2
1. Run the Merge Expert following the steps listed above.
   - Choose *Equipment Service Query* as the table the merge will be based on.
   - Assign **Equipment Service Form** as the filename of the form letter.
2. Create a form memo by keying the text of the memo and inserting the fields for the variables. Save the memo as **Equipment Service**.
3. Merge the form document and data.

| | |
|---|---|
| **TO:** | \<First Name> \<Last Name> |
| **FROM:** | Student's name |
| **DATE:** | Date field |
| **SUBJECT:** | Equipment Service |

Our records indicate that you have a \<Model> \<Category>.

Your \<Category> will be serviced on a regular basis every six months. Your last date of service was \<Date Serviced>. When your next service date arrives, please be prepared to be without your \<Category> for as much as one-half day to allow sufficient time for necessary repairs or software updates to be made.

Thanks for your cooperation in keeping your equipment up to date.

## 37e ● 10'

**NEW FUNCTION**

1. Read the information at the right.
2. Complete the drill.

## Open a document as a copy

When you open a document as a copy, a new copy of the document is created in the folder that contains the original document. The original document is not changed.

When you use the formatting template, open each document as a copy so that you will always have the original document in case something happens to the document while you are working on it.

**To open a document as a copy:**

1. Click **File**, then **Open**. The Open File dialog box displays.
2. Choose the appropriate drive in the *Look in* box.
3. Select the file you want to open by clicking the filename.
4. Click **Open as copy**.

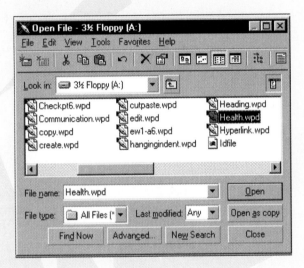

**Drill**

The disk in the back of your textbook contains Formatting Template files. It has extra documents you will use in this course. Insert the Formatting Template disk into Drive A and proceed.

1. Open the template file *health* as a copy.
2. Prepare the message as a memo, using the heading information below.
3. Insert a ¶ after *4 p.m.*
4. Add your reference initials.
5. Save as **37e**, proofread, and print.

| | |
|---|---|
| **TO:** | All Employees |
| **FROM:** | T. R. McRaimond |
| **DATE:** | (Current) |
| **SUBJECT:** | Gym Benefits |

# Database Merge

A *WordPerfect* document and a *Paradox* query file can be merged using a similar process as merging with a *WordPerfect* data file. When addresses and other data exist in the database, it makes sense to use the *Paradox* file rather than re-creating it in *WordPerfect*.

The *Paradox* file is the *data* file, which contains the *variables* that will be merged into the *WordPerfect* document. The *source document* contains text and merge fields showing where other variable information such as names and amounts will be added. The source document is prepared in *WordPerfect*. You may want to review the merge process in the Software Training Manual (pages TM1-4 of Integrated Applications) or in Lesson 111.

## Assigning a table name to a query

*Paradox* merges data from a table into a form document. When the information is available in the form of a query, you must assign the answer to the query a *table* name. By assigning a name, the Answer table from the query becomes a permanent table. If the information is being merged directly from a table, this step is not necessary before starting the merge process.

### To assign a table name to a query:

1. Open the query if it is already created. If not, create the query in the usual manner.
2. Click the **Properties** button on the Property toolbar. From the Answer tab, assign the table a name. Click **OK** to exit the dialog box.
3. Save the query if it has not been saved.

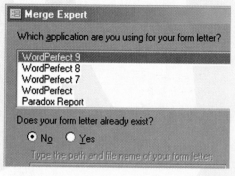

**Equipment Service Answer table**

## Merging with Paradox table

### Step 1:  Run the Merge Expert

1. From the Tools menu of *Paradox*, select the *Expert* option. Select *Merge* and click **Run Expert**.
2. Click **Create New Merge Settings**. Click **Next**.
3. Select *WordPerfect 9* as the application you will use for your form letter. When asked if your form letter already exists, click **No**. (If the letter did exist, then you would click **Yes** and enter the filename.) Click **Next**.
4. Select the table the merge will be based on, such as *Equipment Service Query*. Click **Next**.
5. Click **Next** again without selecting a sort order.
6. Click **Next** without changing the format of a field.
7. Do not save the merge settings. Assign a form filename such as *Equipment Service Form*. *Paradox* will automatically open a *WordPerfect 9* file with this name. Click **Finish**.

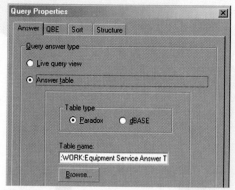

# Review Memo

## 38a ● 12'

### GETTING started

fingers curved, hands quiet;
each line twice as shown

1st
1 My 456 heavy brown jugs have nothing in them; fill them by May 7.
2 The 57 bins are numbered 1 to 57; Bins 5, 6, 45, and 57 are full.

2d
3 Ed decided to crate 38 pieces of cedar decking from the old dock.
4 Mike, who was 38 in December, likes a piece of ice in cold cider.

3d/4th
5 Polly made 29 points on the quiz; Wex, 10 points.  Did they pass?
6 Sally saw Ezra pass 200 pizza pans to Sean, who fixed 10 of them.

alphabet
7 Which oval jet-black onyx ring blazed on the queen's prim finger?
8 When Jorg moves away, quickly place five dozen gloves in the box.

| 1 | 2 | 3 | 4 | 5 | 6 | 7 | 8 | 9 | 10 | 11 | 12 | 13 |

## 38b ● 38'

### FORMATTING

**Interoffice memos**

**Distribution lists**

When memos are sent to more than one person, list their names after **TO:**.  Generally the names are listed in alphabetical order; some organizations, however, list the names in order of rank.  For readability, key the names on separate lines. When sending the memo to many people, refer to a distribution list at the end of the memo. *Example:*  **TO:** Task Force Members--Distribution Below.

words

**Document 1**

1. Key the memo.
2. Add your reference initials.
3. Include the following names for distribution.  Indent names to the first tab.
   **Distribution:**
   **Allen Bejahan**
   **Janet James**
   **Terry Johnson**
   **Ray Lightfoot**
4. Use Spell Checker. Proofread carefully.  Save as **38b-d1**.

| | | words |
|---|---|---|
| **TO:** | Team Leaders -- Distribution Below | 8 |
| | DS | |
| **FROM:** | J. Mac Chandler, Office Manager | 15 |
| **DATE:** | May 14, 200- | 19 |
| **SUBJECT:** | New Multimedia Lab Available June 12 | 29 |
| | DS | |

We are pleased to announce the opening of our new Multimedia Lab effec-   43
tive June 12.  The lab is in the front office just beyond the Advertising   58
Department.  The lab has four new computers with full multimedia capa-   72
bility, two laser disc players, a VCR, two presentation projection devices,   87
two scanners, and various color and laser printers.   97

Use this lab if your computer is too small for your job, too slow, or too   112
limited to handle a specific job.  Just complete the sign-up sheet located   127
adjacent to the equipment.  Projection equipment and two laptop com-   141
puters may be checked out for presentations.  Please reserve this equipment   156
twenty-four hours in advance.   162

Please share any feedback on the usefulness of the lab and suggestions for   176
improvements.   180

closing   194

*Report from query*

You will create a query based on the Employee and Team tables and then use the Report Expert to generate a report based on the query.

### Create a query

1. Open the Telecom database. Set the working directory to the Telecom database (File menu, Working Directory; select *Module E\Telecom*). Use the WORK alias.
2. Using the Employee and Team tables, create a query to list the employees' names, team, and phone numbers. Sort in ascending order on Team Name. Save as **Team List**.

### Create report with expert

3. Use the Report Expert to create a report based on the Team List query.
4. Include all fields in the report.
5. Select *Team Name* as the Grouping Level. Do not specify any summaries.
6. Select the multiple records option. Select the style of your choice.
7. Assign **Employee Team List** as the title, positioned top left. Include page numbering at the top right.
8. Assign *Employee Team List* as the report name. Notice how the report is grouped by team name. Close the report without printing.

### Modify report

9. Open the report in Design view.
10. Modify the report following the steps below; then print it.
    - *Report Title:* Click the title box; then drag it to center it over the fields.
    - *Column Heading:* Widen the Home Phone box to display the full column heading.
    - *Record:* Widen the Home Phone box to display the phone numbers on one line.
11. Close the report. From the Project Viewer, print the report.

# APPLICATION

*Create mailing labels*

Mailing labels are a type of report. You will use an expert.

### Create and save query

1. Create a query to include the employees' complete names and complete addresses.
2. Sort in ascending order by Last Name.
3. Save the query as **E12–Employee List**. Close the query.

### Create labels with expert

4. From Types, right-click **Reports**, then **New**. Select *Label Expert*. Click **Next**.
5. Select the *Avery 5262* label. Click **Next**.
6. Select the query *E12-Employee List*. Click **Next**.
7. Use Times New Roman, 12 point, bold. Click **Next**.
8. Choose *Left to Right* as the order to print the labels. Click **Next**.
9. Position the fields as shown in the example. Insert a space between the First and Last Names, City and State, and State and ZIP. Include a comma after City.

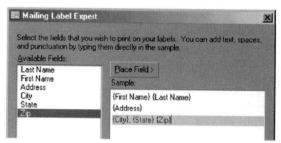

10. Use **Employee Mailing Labels** as the name for the report.
11. Select *Print the Labels Now*. Click **Finish**. The labels are alphabetized by Last Name.

Use the ↓ to move to the next row.

**38b,** *continued*

## Document 2

1. Key the memo.
2. DS before keying the last 4 lines. Then select them, center, bold, and apply font size.
3. Add your reference initials.
4. Follow the "Proofreading procedures," p. 96. Save and print.

| | | |
|---|---|---|
| **TO:** | Manufacturing Team | 5 |
| **FROM:** | Mei-Ling Yee, Administrative Assistant | 14 |
| **DATE:** | April 14, 200- | 18 |
| **SUBJECT:** | Enrichment Seminar | 24 |

As was stated by Robert Beloz in the January newsletter, *Focus for the*   38
*New Year*, Foscari & Associates will be offering a series of enrichment semi-   54
nars for its employees in the year ahead. If you have suggestions for semi-   69
nars that would be beneficial to your team, please let me know.   82

We are proud to announce our first seminar offering, *First Aid and CPR.*   96
Participants will be awarded CPR Certificates from the American Heart   110
Association upon successful completion of this eight-hour course. If you   125
are interested in taking this seminar, please call me at ext. 702 or send   140
me an e-mail message by *April 25.*   147

Mark your calendar for this important seminar.   156

**First Aid and CPR Enrichment Seminar** –18 pt.   164
**May 16 and 17**   167
**1:00-5:00 p.m.** } 14 pt.   170
**Staff Lounge**   172

## Document 3

Key the memo; make changes as shown. Use your reference initials.

```
TO:  J. Ezra Bayh                                    4
FROM: Greta Sangtree                          ) DS   8
DATE: August 14, 200-                                13
SUBJECT: Letter-Mailing Standards /                  20
```
ck sp
, because of the delay.

Recently the post office delivered late a letter that   35
caused us some (embarassment). To avoid recurrence, please   47
ensure that all administrative assistants and mail person-   58
nel follow postal service guidelines.   67
U.S.

Perhaps a refresher seminar on correspondence guidelines is   79
~~in~~ in order. Thanks ~~or you~~ help. (for your   86

## Document 4
## Challenge activity

1. Open *38b.* Save as **38b-d4** on your disk. The file contains the body of the memo in double-spaced format.
2. Prepare the memo to **All Staff** from **D. Howard, MIS**.
3. Change the line spacing to single.
4. Format the memo correctly; use the current date, provide an appropriate subject line, and use your initials as reference initials.
5. Follow "Proofreading procedures," p. 96.

## Modifying or formatting the report

After the report is closed, its name is listed in the Project Viewer. To modify the report, right-click the report and select *Design*. The Design view shows the structure of the report, similar to the way it shows the structure of a query.

The report is divided into three bands: report bands, page bands, and record bands.

**Report band**     Defines the report header and report footer areas. *Paradox* prints the report header once at the beginning of the report and the report footer once at the end of the report. The report title is listed in the report band.

**Page band**     Defines the header and footer areas of each page. *Paradox* places three objects in the page header band: date of the report, default title of the report, and page number.

**Record band**     Contains the body of the report—the records of the table being reported.

To format the report, you can select part of the report, such as the title, and drag it to the left or right. Space can be added between report bands by grabbing the bands and moving them up or down. Check your formatting edits by toggling between the Design Report and Run Report on the View menu (or click those buttons on the Property bar).

Run Report

Design Report

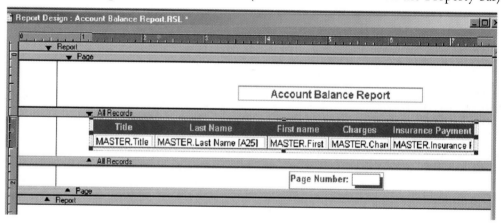

**Report shown in Design Report view**

### Drill 3  Modify report

1. Open the Account Balance Report in Design view. (From Project Viewer, click **Reports**, right-click the filename, and select *Design*.)

2. Center the report title by clicking the title box and dragging it so that it is centered over the fields.

3. Toggle between Design Report and Run Report on the View menu. Make adjustments until you are satisfied with the format.

3. Close the report. A dialog box will display asking if you want to save the changes to the design of the report. Click **Yes**.

4. The Project Viewer screen is now displayed. Right-click the **Account Balance Report**, and select *Print*. Your report should look similar to the one shown on page 477.

# Block Letter Format, Zoom

## 39a ● 8'

### GETTING started

**Reinforcement**

1. Open *communication*. Save as **39a**.
2. Edit the ¶ as marked. DS.
3. Save and print.

---

Delete word: Double-click on the word; press DELETE.

Delete line: Click in area left of line; press DELETE. ▨

---

Writing ~~concise~~ responses, formulating ~~competitive~~ bids, creating ~~effective~~ business plans, answering ~~customer~~ feedback, composing messages ~~and letters~~ to clients, resp~~o~~nding to customers and staff, maintaining relations with coworkers and supervisors, interpreting messages, and persuading customer﹀ these are just a few examples of ~~written and oral~~ communication that ~~is~~ *are* handled ~~by~~ *every day* by competent business people. ~~Communicating skills and a keen knowledge of business are valuable assets for anyone seeking success in business.~~

## 39b ● 12'

### FORMATTING

**Block letters**
Study carefully the information about business letter parts and placement at the right and on the next page.

### Parts of a business letter
Business letters contain a variety of parts that serve very specific purposes. Listed below are basic parts of a typical business letter:

**Dateline:** The letter is dated the day it is mailed.

**Letter address:** The address of the person who will receive the letter begins a quadruple space (QS) below the dateline. Include a personal title (for example, Mr. or Ms.) unless a professional title (Dr.) is appropriate.

**Salutation:** Key the salutation, or greeting, a double space (DS) below the letter address. The salutation should correspond to the first line of the letter address. Use *Ladies and Gentlemen* when the first line of the address is a company name.

**Body:** The body is the message of the letter. Begin the body a double space (DS) below the salutation. Single-space (SS) the body and double-space between paragraphs.

**Complimentary close:** The complimentary close, which is the formal closing of the letter, begins a double space (DS) below the body.

**Writer's name and title:** Leave three blank lines (QS) for the writer's signature, keying the name on the fourth line. If the writer's title is short, it may follow the name; if the title is long, key it on the next line.

### Reference initials:
When business letters are keyed by someone other than the writer, the operator's initials are keyed in lowercase a double space (DS) below the writer's keyed name and/or title. Initials are not included when the writer keys the letter.

---

*Colbran's Market, Inc.*
*Consumer Affairs Department*
*P. O. Box 3058*
*Natchez, MS 39120-8476*
*1-800-555-9473     1-800-555-9990 (FAX)*

March 6, 200–

Ms. Brenda A. O'Flynn
468 Heumann Dr.
Lincoln, NE 68504-5046

Dear Ms. O'Flynn

Let me introduce myself. My name is Jorge Lund; and since last August I have served as marketing manager for Colbran's Market, a Midwest chain of retail grocery stores.

Since its advent, the purpose and philosophy of "grocery store" operation has rested on providing for the needs, particularly in the kitchen, of the American home. Part of my "mission," as it has evolved here in Colbran's, encompasses exploring new concepts in the field of food retailing.

History shows that the grocery store has progressed through a number of stages, from the small corner shop to the modern supermarket. Colbran's is now ready to take the next step; to extend store services beyond simply selling food items. We are gearing up now to be a total food center, introducing nutritional and cooking services. We intend to become your local headquarters for food selection, preparation, and consumption.

Edward Kinlo, of our Lincoln office, tells me that you might be interested in serving as one of our planning consultants for this new endeavor. Hours would not be demanding, and remuneration and privileges accompany the appointment. If, as we hope, you have interest in working with a progressive group dedicated to improving consumer service, please contact me for details.

Sincerely yours

Jorge L. Lund
Marketing Manager

pd

**Long Letter**

## Select report fields

Select the fields you want to include in the report. Click the **>** button to move the fields from the Available fields list to the Display these fields list. The **>>** button moves all fields. To remove a field from the Selected Fields, click the **<** button.

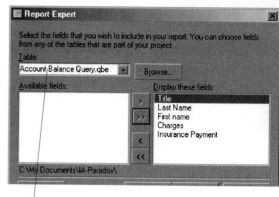

Select table or query and fields

3. Select the *Account Balance Query* as the table (query) on which to build this report.

4. Move all of the fields to the Display These Fields column.

5. Click the **Next** button when complete.

## Group and sort report

The Grouping feature allows you to group records based on any field. For example, you may decide to group the patients by city and subtotal the balance field based on each city. You will learn more about grouping later.

6. Do not specify any grouping for this report.

7. Click the **Next** button when complete.

## Report layout and style

A layout or style is automatically applied to the report based on your choice.

8. Click the button for **Multiple records**; then choose the *Primary objects* style.

## Assign report title

Select a descriptive name.

9. *Title:* Check in the title box, set position at Top Center, and key **Account Balance Report** as the title.

10. *Page Numbering:* Add a check mark for page numbering positioned at bottom center. Click the **Next** button when complete.

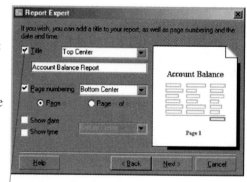

Assign report title and style

## Assign report name

11. *Report Name:* Key the report name, **Account Balance Report**.

12. Check the print box to print a copy of the report.

13. Click **Finish**. Close the report.

### Block letter format

All lines begin at the left margin in **block format**, making this an efficient letter style. **Open punctuation** requires no punctuation following the salutation or the complimentary close.

### Letter placement

Business letters are prepared on letterhead stationary, which has the company name, address, telephone number, and logo. The letterhead often includes the fax and/or e-mail address and company slogan. Most letterheads are between 1" and 2" deep. If a letter is printed on plain stationary, the sender's return address is keyed immediately above the date.

To be attractive, letters are positioned on the page according to their length (short, average, long). As the Letter Placement Table shows, the length of letters is determined by estimating the number of words in the letter or by the number of paragraphs. For example, short letters have only one or two paragraphs and fewer than 100 words.

Default margins are used regardless of the letter's length. Short or average letters may be positioned vertically by using the Center Page command. To avoid interfering with the letterhead, Center Page should not be used in long letters or average-length letters containing many extra letter parts. Instead, position the dateline on the appropriate line. Preview the letter before printing to check vertical placement.

| Letter Placement Table | | |
|---|---|---|
| **Length** | **Dateline Position** | **Margins** |
| Short: 1–2 ¶s | Center page or 3" | Default |
| Average: 3–4 ¶s | Center page or 2.7"* | Default |
| Long: 4 or more ¶s | 2.3" (default + 7 hard returns) | Default |

**\*Decrease for extra lines; position based on 12-point font.**

**Short Letter**

**Average Letter**

**39c • 25'**

FORMATTING

**Block letters**
Document 1

1. Key the letter on p. 103.
2. Center the letter vertically.
3. Study "Zoom" on p. 104.

4. Follow "Proofreading procedures" listed in 37c on p. 96. Use Zoom to verify vertical placement.
5. Save as **39c-d1** and print.

# Database Reports

Reports are designed for printing information contained in a table or query in an attractive and easy-to-read format. Reports are used to create mailing labels, invoices, and form letters. The report in Figure 1 looks like a sophisticated table. *Paradox* refers to this format as a report.

## Accounts Balance Report

| Title | Last Name | First name | Charges | Insurance Payment |
|---|---|---|---|---|
| Mr. | Pham | Chinh | 60 | 0 |
| Mr. | Smith | Jacob | 60 | 0 |
| Ms. | Nelson | Laura | 60 | 0 |
| Ms. | Lopez | Alicia | 75 | 68 |
| Mr. | Thompson | Joel | 95 | 75 |
| Mrs. | Reynoza | Maria | 145 | 125 |
| Ms. | Johnson | Sally | 190 | 190 |
| Mr. | Woo | Willie | 215 | 190 |
| Mr. | Nguyen | Than | 250 | 185 |
| Mr. | Richardson | Michael | 380 | 300 |

**Figure 1 Database report**

## Creating Reports

Reports can be created using an expert or they can be based on a blank report. A blank report includes little if any formatting. In this lesson, you will use an expert. The Report Expert guides you through the report creation process by allowing you to select the layout based on a variety of templates. You might compare a report created with an expert to a table created with SpeedFormat.

  **Create a query**

In this drill, you will create a query. In Drill 2, you will create a report based on the query.

1. Open Paradox; close the Welcome Window. Change the working directory to *Module E\Patients* (click **File** menu, **Working Directory**). Under Types, click **Tables**. Two tables are saved in the Patient database: Billing Table and Names and Addresses. (Use the WORK alias.) Use the Patient database for Drills 1 and 2.

2. Create a query using the Names/Addresses table and the Billing table that have been saved on the Formatting Template.

3. Select the fields:
   • Names/Addresses table: *Title, Last Name*, and *First Name*.
   • Billing table: *Charges* and *Insurance Payment*.

4. Join the two tables on the common field.

5. Save the query as **Account Balance Query**.

6. Exit the Query screen, but do not exit the Patients database.

**Drill 2 Use Report Expert**

Follow each of the steps to create a report using the Report Expert.

### Start the Expert

1. From the Types window, right-click **Reports**. Click the **New** button. Select the *Expert* option.

2. The Report Expert dialog box displays. Choose to build the report based on one table. Click the **Next** button when complete.

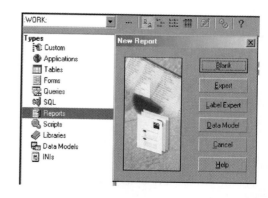

# Professional Office Consultants, Inc.

584 Castro St.
San Francisco, CA 94114-2201
415-555-8725
415-555-8775 (FAX)

Dateline

January 17, 200-
QS

Letter
address

Ms. Armanda Castillo, Office Manager
TeleNet Corporation
24 Technology Dr.
Irvine, CA 92865-9845
DS

Salutation

Dear Ms. Castillo
DS

Thank you for selecting Professional Office Consultants, Inc. to assist with the setup of your new corporate office. You asked us for a recommendation for formatting business letters. We highly recommend the block letter style because it is easy to read, economical to produce, and efficient. DS

Body

This letter is keyed in block format. As you can see, all lines begin at the left margin. Most letters can be keyed using default side margins and then centered vertically on the page for attractive placement. The block letter format is easy to key because tabs are not required.

We think that you will be happy using the block letter format. Over 80 percent of businesses today are using this same style. DS

Complimentary
close

Sincerely
QS

Writer's name
Title

Anderson Cline
OA & CIS Consultant
DS

Reference
initials

xx

BLOCK LETTER

**Application E8,**
*continued*

2. Create a query that lists the complete name of all employees on the Solutions and JPEG Pike teams.

   a. Select the table: *Employee.*

   b. Select the appropriate fields: *Last Name, First Name, Team Name.*

   c. Apply the criteria *Solutions OR JPEG Pike* to the Team Name field.

   d. Run the query; print but do not save. Label the printout **AppE8-Query2**.

3. Create a query that lists all employees' first and last names whose Employee ID is greater than 5000.

   a. Select the table: *Employee.*

   b. Select the fields: *Employee ID, First Name, Last Name.*

   c. Apply the criteria *> 5000* to the Employee ID field.

   d. Run the query.

   e. How many names were listed? What was the first employee's name?

   f. Print but do not save the query. Label the printout **AppE8-Query3**.

## APPLICATION

*Create a query and memo*

1. Bill Towney, Operations Manager for Telecom, has requested that two queries be created. Create a query to answer each request. Print the results from both queries. Do not save them.

   a. Create a query to list all records in the Equipment table. Include every field.

   b. Create a query to list all employees' first and last names and team name. Sort the employees by Last Name in ascending order

2. Create a short memo to Bill from you. Attach the two printouts to the memo. In your message, explain what you are attaching.

## APPLICATION

*Create query and memo*

1. Create a query to list all of the employees who have a computer. Include the employee's Last Name, Equipment ID, and Model, in this order. Save this query as **Computer Users**.

2. Lisa Blair, Training Director, has requested a list of employees who have computers. Create a short memo to Lisa explaining the results of the Computer Users query. Attach the query to it.

**39c,** *continued*

**Document 2**

Key the letter at right in block letter format. Center the letter vertically on the page. Save but do not close.

Current date  <sub>QS</sub>

Ms. Alice Ottoman
Premiere Properties Inc.
52 Ocean Dr.
Newport Beach, CA 92747 <sub>DS</sub>

Dear Ms. Ottoman <sub>DS</sub>

Internet Solutions has developed a new technique for you to market your properties on the World Wide Web.  We can now create 360-degree panoramic pictures for your Web site.  You can give your clients a virtual spin of the living room, kitchen, and every room in the house.  <sub>DS</sub>

Call today for a demonstration of this remarkable technology.  Give your clients a better visual understanding of the property layout--something your competition doesn't have.  <sub>DS</sub>

Sincerely <sub>QS</sub>

Lee Rodgers
Marketing Manager <sub>DS</sub>

xx

---

**39d ● 5'**

**NEW
FUNCTION**

**Viewing a document**

The View menu provides various options for viewing a document; the choices include:

- **Page:** Displays document with margins and all formats.
- **Draft:** Displays side margins but not the top margin or other features such as headers.
- **Two page:** Displays a miniature of two pages of a document.
- **Zoom:** Provides numerous options for enlarging or decreasing the view of a document. Zoom is useful for checking the placement of a document before printing.  A Zoom button is available on the toolbar.

**To use Zoom:**

1. Open the **View** menu and choose *Page*. Page view is the best view for previewing a document.
2. Click the **Zoom** button on the toolbar. The drop-down menu appears. The view percentages change as you point to each option.
3. Click **Full Page** to check document placement.
4. To return to normal view, click the **Zoom** button and choose *100%*.

| Margin Width |
| Page Width |
| Full Page |
| 50% |
| 75% |
| 100% |
| 150% |
| 200% |
| Other... |

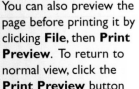

You can also preview the page before printing it by clicking **File**, then **Print Preview**. To return to normal view, click the **Print Preview** button on the property bar that is displayed.

**Conditions** further limit the number of records that will be returned from a query. Use AND and OR to find records that meet more than one condition. The AND condition returns data that meets all the specified conditions; for example, employees who live in OH and who were hired after 1998. The OR condition returns data that meets either of the specified conditions; for example, employees who live in OH or in KY. The query below would return all employees who live in OH or KY.

**Drill 5** **Run query with criteria**

1. Create a query based on the Employees table to list the employees who live in OH or KY. After selecting the fields, key **OH OR KY** in the gray area of the State field.

2. Sort the fields by State and then by Last Name (click the **Sort** button and then move the fields to the Sort order box).

3. Run the query. How many employees' names were returned?

**Drill 6** **Query with more than one condition**

1. Create a query based on the Employee table to list the employees who live in OH or KY and who were hired after 12/31/1997. The expression *>12/31/1997* instructs *Paradox* to return only fields that are greater than December 31, 1997.

2. Compare your query window with the portion of the window shown below; the illustration only shows the 2 fields with conditions.

3. Run the query and print it. Do not save.

| State | Zip | Home Phon | Birthday | Date Hired |
|-------|-----|-----------|----------|------------|
| ☑ OH OR KY | ☐ | ☐ | ☐ | ☑ >12/31/1997 |

# APPLICATION

*Query using criteria*

**Query multiple tables and sort**

1. List employees by Team Name and by State. Sort by Team Name.

   a. Create a new query.

   b. Choose tables: *Employee* and *Team*.

   c. Select fields: *Team Name, Last Name, First Name, State*.

   d. Sort the Team Name field in ascending order.

   e. Run the query; print but do not save.

   f. Label the printout with your name and **AppE8–Query 1**.

# LESSON 40

# Review Block Letters

## 40a ● 7'

### GETTING started

each line twice SS; DS
between 2-line groups

## SKILLBUILDING WARMUP

| | | |
|---|---|---|
| alphabet | 1 | Jim Daley gave us in that box the prize he won for his quick car. |
| figures | 2 | Send 345 of the 789 sets now; send the others on April 10 and 26. |
| one hand | 3 | I deserve, in my opinion, a reward after I started a faster race. |
| easy | 4 | Enrique may fish for cod by the dock; he also may risk a penalty. |

| 1 | 2 | 3 | 4 | 5 | 6 | 7 | 8 | 9 | 10 | 11 | 12 | 13 |

## 40b ● 8'

### SKILLBUILDING

Key two 1' timings on each ¶. The second and third ¶s each contain 2 more words than the previous ¶. Try to complete each ¶ within 1'.

all letters                                           *gwam*   1' │ 3'

Have you thought about time?  Time is a perplexing commod-   12  4 40
ity.  Frequently we don't have adequate time to do the things we   25  8 45
must; yet we all have just the same amount of time.   35 12 48

We seldom refer to the quantity of time; to a great extent,   12 16 52
we cannot control it.  We can try to set time aside, to plan,   24 20 56
and therefore, to control portions of this valuable asset.   37 24 60

We should make an extra effort to fill each minute and hour   12 28 64
with as much quality activity as possible. Time, the most pre-   25 32 68
cious thing a person can spend, can never be realized once it   37 36 72
is lost.   39 36 73

1' | 1 | 2 | 3 | 4 | 5 | 6 | 7 | 8 | 9 | 10 | 11 | 12 | 13 |
3' |    1    |    2    |    3    |    4    |

## 40c ● 12'

### COMMUNICATION

**Compose at the keyboard**

1. Compose an answer to each question in 1 or 2 sentences. Join the sentences into 3 ¶s (as shown).  Center the title **MY CAREER** over the ¶s.
2. Save as **40c** and print.
3. Edit the printed document, using proofreaders' marks to make corrections.
4. Revise, save, and print.

¶ 1 What is your present career goal?
¶ 2 Why do you think you will enjoy this career?

¶ 3 Where do you think you would most like to pursue your career?
¶ 4 Why do you think you would enjoy living and working in that area?

¶ 5 What civic, political, or volunteer activities might you enjoy?
¶ 6 What other careers may lie ahead for you?

## Criteria

Applying **criteria** to a query limits the information the query returns. By restricting the search, the user has more specific information. For example, if you want to find only employees who live in Ohio, you would key OH in the gray area next to the check box in the State field. To show this field in the Answer table, click the check box. To apply the criteria without the field actually showing in the Answer table, do not click the check box. In the example below, the query will return only names of employees who live in Ohio.

### Drill 3  Create query with conditions

1. Create a query based on the Employee table that lists the first and last names of employees living in OH. Key **OH** in the gray area next to the State checkbox. Your Query window should look like the example shown.

2. Run the query. How many employees' names were returned?

### Drill 4  Run query with conditions

1. Open and run the query **E3-Query5** from the Formatting Template. Print the query results.

2. Review your printout. No sort order was specified, but *Paradox* automatically sorted on what field? In fact, *Paradox* automatically sorts the Answer table on the fields from left to right.

3. Compare the E3-Query5 printout to the E3-Query4 printout. What is different?

4. What *criteria* was applied to the State field in E3-Query 5? Note that the Answer table only listed employees from Ohio.

5. Close the Answer window; the query window displays. Note that **OH** has been entered as a criteria in the State field and that both Team ID fields have been joined.

6. Click the **Sort** button. Notice that no fields appear in the Sort Order window. Review your answer to #2 above.

**Comparison Operators** can also be used to refine a search. For example, you might want to find only employees who were hired after 1999, or only accounts that were more than 60 days overdue, or only employees whose salary is greater than $40,000. Use the operators below to set criteria.

| Operator | Description | Operator | Description |
|---|---|---|---|
| = | Equal to | <= | Less than or equal to |
| > | Greater than | >= | Greater than or equal to |
| < | Less than | <> | Not equal |

## 40d ● 3'

Read and apply the information on "Salutations" in the letters that you format.

### Salutations

The **salutation** greets the person receiving the letter. A proper salutation consists of the title of the person and his/her last name. Do not greet someone on a first-name basis unless you have a personal relationship with the receiver.

Personal titles (such as Mr. or Ms.) should be included in the letter address and the salutation unless a professional title (Dr.) is appropriate. Use Ms. when the recipient's first name is obviously feminine and no other title (Mrs., Miss) is indicated. Use salutations as recommended below:

| | Receiver | Salutation |
|---|---|---|
| To an individual: | Mr. Alexander Gray | Dear Mr. Gray |
| | Dr. and Mrs. Thompson | Dear Dr. and Mrs. Thompson |
| | Ms. Mara Rena | Dear Mara (personal relationship) |
| To a corporation: | Esquire Electronics, Inc. | Ladies and Gentlemen |
| To the title of a person: | Advertising Manager | Dear Advertising Manager |

## 40e ● 20'

### Block letter review
### Document 1

1. Key the letter in block format. Use the current date. Proofread and check spelling.
2. Center the letter vertically on the page.
3. Preview the letter before printing; make additional changes if needed.
4. Save as **40e-d1** and print.

### Document 2

Follow the same directions as in Document 1. Save as **40e-d2**.

words

Current date|Mr. Trace L. Brecken|4487 Ingram St.|Corpus Christi, TX 78409-8907|Dear Mr. Brecken 13 / 19

We have received the package you sent us in which you returned goods from a recent order you gave us. Your refund check, plus return postage, will be mailed to you in a few days. 33 / 48 / 55

We are sorry, of course, that you did not find this merchandise personally satisfactory. It is our goal to please all of our customers, and we are always disappointed if we fail. 70 / 85 / 92

Please give us an opportunity to try again. We stand behind our merchandise, and that is our guarantee of good service. 105 / 116

Cordially yours|Mrs. Margret Bredewig|Customer Service Department|xx 130

Current date|Mrs. Rose Shikamuru|55 Lawrence St.|Topeka, KS 66607-6657|Dear Mrs. Shikamuru 14 / 19

Thank you for your recent letter asking about employment opportunities with our company. We are happy to inform you that Mr. Edward Ybarra, our recruiting representative, will be on your campus on April 23, 24, 25, and 26 to interview students who are interested in our company. 33 / 47 / 62 / 75

We suggest you talk soon with your student placement office, as all appointments with Mr. Ybarra will be made through that office. Please bring with you the application questionnaire the office provides. 89 / 103 / 115

Within a few days, we will send you a company brochure and more information about our offices; plant; salary, bonus, and retirement plans; and the beautiful community in which we are located. We believe a close study of this information will convince you, as it has many others, that our company builds futures as well as small motors. 128 / 143 / 158 / 172 / 183

If there is any other way we can help you, please write to me again. 197

Yours very truly|Miss Myrle K. Bragg|Human Services Director|xx 209

5. Move Team Name to the right by clicking the Right arrow.

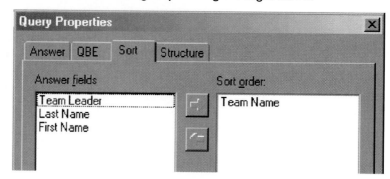

6. Run the query. Your Answer table should display as shown below. Note that the fields are sorted first by Team; then individuals within each team are sorted in ascending order by Last Name. The status bar shows the name of the query the Answer table is based on.

| | Team Name | Team Leader | Last Name | First Name |
|---|---|---|---|---|
| 1 | Disk Drive | Wong | Barkley | Scott |
| 2 | Disk Drive | Wong | Hall | Earl |
| 3 | Disk Drive | Wong | Perez | Margaret |
| 4 | Disk Drive | Wong | Rowe | Michelle |
| 5 | Disk Drive | Wong | Skirvin | Al |
| 6 | Disk Drive | Wong | Wong | Chris |
| 7 | JPEG Pike | Goldstein | Goldstein | Mike |
| 8 | JPEG Pike | Goldstein | Judd | Nancy |
| 9 | JPEG Pike | Goldstein | Jung | Betty |
| 10 | JPEG Pike | Goldstein | Morad | David |
| 11 | JPEG Pike | Goldstein | Moretz | Carlos |
| 12 | Solutions | Coates | Ball | Paul |
| 13 | Solutions | Coates | Coates | Sue |
| 14 | Solutions | Coates | Kleene | Joe |
| 15 | Solutions | Coates | Mart | Tomas |
| 16 | Solutions | Coates | Morales | Alfredo |

**Drill 2**  Analyze saved query

1. Open the query *E3-Query 4* from the Formatting Template (click **Query** in the Types window and double-click the filename.)  Print the query results.  Save the printout for the next drill.

2. From the Answer table, identify which field has been sorted in ascending order.

3. Close the Answer table.  From the Query window, answer the following questions:

   a. Which tables is E3-Query 4 based on?

   b. Which fields are included?

   c. Which fields do the two tables have in common?

   d. What command indicates that the tables are "joined"?

**Field Order**

To change the order in which your fields display in the Answer table, click the **Query Properties** button on the Property toolbar and then the **Structure** tab.  Use the Up and Down arrows to change the order of the fields in the Answer table.

# Tabs

4la • 7'

**G**ETTING
started

**Reinforcement**
1. Edit as you key; DS.
2. Check spelling; save, print.
3. Proofread printed document; revise if necessary.

Someone has said, "you are what you eat". The speaker did not mean to imply that fast food make fast people, or that a hearty meal makes a person heart, or even that good food makes a person good. On the other hand, though, a healthfull diet does indeed make person healthier; and good health is one of the most often over looked treasures within human existence.

## Tabs

**Tabs** are useful for aligning text. Tabs move one line of text to the next tab stop. Default tabs are set every half inch; however, you can reset or change the tab stops. If you change tab settings within a document, the changes take effect from the insertion point through the rest of the document.

### Measuring tabs

Tabs may be measured from the left margin (relative) or from the left edge of the paper (absolute). Default tab settings are relative (measured from the left margin). If you change the left margins, the tabs shift to new positions, but they remain the same distance from the left margin. In this course, you will set relative tabs.

**To set tabs:**

1. Choose *Format, Line,* then *Tab Set.* The Tab Set dialog box displays.

2. Click **Clear All** to delete all tabs. To delete a specific tab, key the tab position and click **Clear**.

3. Choose a tab type from the Tab type drop-down list; left tab is the default.

4. Click the *Tab position* box, enter the tab setting, and click **Set**. Delete the tab setting in the entry box before entering the second tab position.

5. After you set the last tab, click **Set and Close**. Or click the **Close (X)** button.

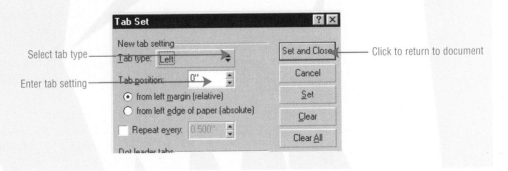

## Select special conditions

Various features are available that will display the information in a more desirable format or that will restrict the information that is returned from the query.

### Sort

Sort is a query property. Instructions for the sort apply only to that query and are saved with the query. By default, *Paradox* sorts first under the left-most field in the Answer table. The sort order of the Answer table can be changed before you run the query without affecting the order in which fields are displayed in the answer.

**To change the sort order of the Answer table:**

1. Click the **Sort** button on the Property toolbar.

2. Use the Right Arrow button to move the fields from the Answer Fields list to the Sort Order list. Add the fields in the order you want the Answer table sorted.

The default sort order is ascending. To change to descending, right-click the check box beneath the field that is being sorted. Click the Descending arrow. A descending arrow now appears next to the check box.

**Drill 1**

Create a query of Employees' First and Last Names and Team Names and Team Leaders. Sort the Answer table first by Team Names and then by Last Names.

1. Set up the query.

2. Select the fields (*Employee table*: Last Name, First Name; *Team table*: Team Name, Team Leader).

3. Join the related fields—Team ID (click the **Join** button in the gray area next to Team ID in each table).

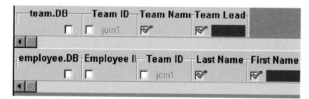

4. Click **Sort**. The field names are displayed as shown.

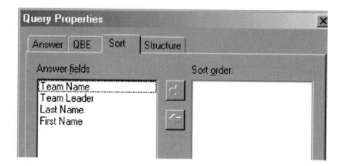

## FORMATTING

**Document 1**
**Memo**

1. Key the memo through ¶ 2, using default tabs.
2. After keying ¶ 2, press ENTER twice.
3. Clear all tabs; set a tab at 2.5".
4. Tab and key the last 4 lines.
5. Save as **41b-d1**; print. Do not close the document.

**Document 2**
**Tabs and Reveal Codes**

1. With Document 1 open, position the insertion point on *Eric* in the 4th line from the bottom.
2. Reveal codes. Read the information at the right.
3. Delete the [Tab Set] code. Text is now indented to the first default tab.

**Document 3**

1. Bold, center, and key the title in 14-point font.
2. Press ENTER twice after keying ¶ 2. Clear all tabs and set tabs at 1.5" and 3" for the columns.
3. Tab and key the text, going across the columns.
4. Preview, save, and print.

| | | words |
|---|---|---|
| **TO:** | All Sunwood Employees | 5 |
| **FROM**: | Julie Patel, Human Relations | 13 |
| **DATE**: | Current | 17 |
| **SUBJECT:** | Eric Kershaw Hospitalized | 24 |

We were notified by Eric Kershaw's family that he was admitted into the 38
hospital this past weekend.  They expect that he will be hospitalized for 53
another ten days.  Visitations and phone calls are limited, but cards and 68
notes are welcome. 72

A plant is being sent to Eric from the Sunwood staff.  Stop by our office 87
before Wednesday if you wish to sign the card.  If you would like to send 101
your own "Get Well Wishes" to Eric, send them to: 111

| | words |
|---|---|
| Eric Kershaw | 114 |
| County General Hospital | 119 |
| Room 401 | 121 |
| Atlanta, GA 38209-4751 | 125 |

When you reveal codes, a [Tab Set] code displays. Press the left arrow key to move the insertion point left of the [Tab Set] code. The code now displays [Tab Set {Rel} + 2.5"L], indicating a left code is set at 2.5". If the tab is no longer needed, it can be deleted by deleting the code in Reveal Codes.

### INTERNET NEWS GROUPS                                   4

The Internet has electronic discussion groups, called *news groups*, 18
where people with similar interests can post or send in their opinions 32
regarding specific topics.  These articles that accumulate on a specific 46
topic are called a *thread*. 52

A news group name may begin with a category name, which identi- 65
fies the main topic of the group.  For example, the news group 77
comp.lang.c++ is a computer group formed to discuss use of the C++ com- 91
puter language.  Below is a list of some of the news group prefixes. 105

| **Name** | **Description** | |
|---|---|---|
| | | 109 |
| comp | Computer topics | 113 |
| biz | Business groups | 117 |
| ieee | Electrical engineering groups | 124 |
| rec | Recreational topics | 129 |
| sci | Scientific topics | 133 |

5. Join the related fields: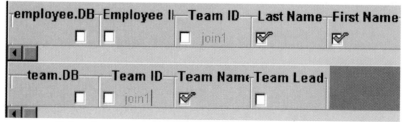

   a. Click the **Join** button on the Property toolbar. The pointer changes shape to allow you to establish a relationship between the two tables based on the common field, Employee ID.

   b. Click the pointer in the gray area to the right of the check box in the Employee ID field in the Employee table. The words *join1* appear.

   c. Click in the gray area to the right of the check box in the Employee ID field in the Equipment table. The words *join 1* appear. Your query should look like the one shown on page 470.

6. Save the query as *Employee Equipment* (**File** menu, **Save As**).

7. Run the query. Compare the printout to the illustration below.

| | Category | Model | Employee ID | Last Name |
|---|---|---|---|---|
| 1 | Computer | Compel | 24671 | Morad |
| 2 | Computer | Compel | 53251 | Jung |
| 3 | Computer | Compel | 56789 | Perez |
| 4 | Computer | Pierce | 42631 | Wong |
| 5 | Computer | Wilber | 46782 | Tipton |
| 6 | Monitor | Champion | 43215 | Moretz |
| 7 | Monitor | Prescott | 54102 | Sneed |
| 8 | Monitor | Prescott | 54303 | Barkley |
| 9 | Printer | Peale | 35789 | Morales |
| 10 | Printer | Peale | 54214 | Phan |
| 11 | Scanner | Olympia | 45689 | Skirvin |

Table : :PRIV:ANSWER.DB

## Query 2:  Query multiple tables

Create a query to list all employees' first and last names and their team names.

1. Determine which tables and which fields are needed.

2. Start the query.

3. Select the tables (*Employee* and *Team*).

4. Select the fields names. From the Employee table, select *Last Name* and *First Name*. From the Team table, select *Team Name*.

5. Join the related fields:

   a. Click the **Join** button once in the gray area to the right of the Team ID field name in the Employee table.

   b. Click once in the gray area to the right of Team ID field in the Team table. The command *join1* will appear in both locations, indicating that the two tables are now joined on the Team ID field.

6. Run the query. Print the query. On the printout, write the name of the tables that each field was taken from. Do not save the query.

**Tab types**

## Working with tab types

The tabs that you have been working with thus far have all been left tabs. Left tabs align text at the left. You can select from three other main types of tabs: center, right, and decimal. When you press TAB, the type of tab inserted is determined by the current tab setting. To change the tab type, click the Tab type drop-down list in the Tab Set dialog box.

**Drill 1**

1. From the Tab Set dialog box, clear all tabs.

2. Set a center tab at 1":
- Click the **Tab type** button to display the types of tabs. Select *Center*.
- Click in the *Tab position* box. Delete what is in the box and enter **1**; then click the **Set** button.

3. Use Step 2 as a guide to set a decimal tab at 3.5" and a right tab at 5.5". Then click **Set and Close**.

4. Press **TAB** before keying the first column. Tab to key each column across the page.

5. Save as **41d-d1**.

**Drill 2**

1. Clear all tabs.

2. Set tabs: left 0.5", right 2.5", center 3.5", decimal 5.0". Key the drill.

| Tab Type | Result |
|---|---|
| Left | Aligns text on the left at the tab stop. |
| Center | Centers text around the tab stop. |
| Right | Aligns text on the right at the tab stop. |
| Decimal | Aligns numbers at the decimal. |

| | | |
|---|---|---|
| Chicago | $1,112.00 | 100,000 |
| Dallas | 872.50 | 3,000 |
| San Francisco | 43.00 | 250 |
| Center 1" | Decimal 3.5" | Right 5.5" |

| | | | |
|---|---|---|---|
| Almich | West | San Francisco | 400.00 |
| Cambridge | Midwest | Chicago | 20.20 |
| Langfield | Southeast | Miami | 1,000.00 |
| Left 0.5" | Right 2.5" | Center 3.5" | Decimal 5.0" |

**Tab ruler**

**Drill**

1. Open *41d-d1*; save as **41e**.

2. Display the Ruler.

3. Observe that the tabs in 41c now measure 2", 4.5", and 6.5" (these are absolute tabs).

4. Drag the tab from 4.5" to 4".

Tabs can also be set, cleared, moved, or deleted directly on the Ruler using the mouse. Tabs set on the Ruler are measured from the edge of the paper (absolute). In contrast, the tabs you set in the Tab Set dialog box are positioned from the left margin (relative).

**To display the Ruler:** From the View menu, click Ruler.

**To set a tab:** Click anywhere on the Ruler to set a new tab.

**To set a different type of tab or to clear tabs:** Double-click a tab marker on the Ruler; change the tab type. **Option:** Click the right mouse button and choose a tab type or choose Clear All Tabs.

**To delete a tab setting:** Drag it down and off the Ruler.

**To move a tab:** Press the left mouse button on a tab marker and drag the tab to the new location.

## Create query from multiple tables

Queries based on two or more tables give users access to a wider range of information. To query multiple tables, however, the tables must share a common field, which must be the key field in one of the tables. One additional step is required: The tables must be joined or linked before the query is run.

**To create a query with two tables:**

1. Start the query in the usual manner and select the first table.
2. Select the additional table by holding down the CTRL key and clicking the other table name. Once you are in the Query window, add additional tables by selecting the *Add Table* button on the Property toolbar.
3. Maximize the Query window.
4. Create a link between the common fields by clicking the **Join** button in the gray area to the right of the check box in each table; *join1* displays in the fields.

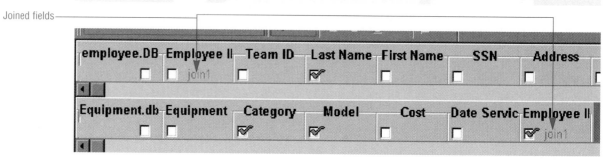

Joined fields

**Figure 4    The two tables are joined by their common field.**

## APPLICATION

**E7**

*Query multiple tables*

### Query 1:  Query multiple tables

List the employee's ID, last name, and the equipment assigned to each employee by category and model.

1. Identify the tables and fields needed:
   a. Determine which tables contain the needed information: (Employee and Equipment).
   b. Determine which fields are required:
      *Employee table:*  Last name
      *Equipment table:*  Employee ID, Category, Model
   c. Determine which field is common to both tables: Employee ID.
2. Start the query (**Queries, New**).
3. Select the tables *Employee* and *Equipment*: Press CTRL and click the table names. Both tables should appear in the Query window. Maximize the window.
4. Select the fields required for the query:
   *Equipment table:*  Employee ID, Model, Category (*Note:* Employee ID may be selected in either table, but not both.)
   *Employee table:*  Last name

# Modified Block Letter Format

## Getting started

### Review

1. Bold and center the title at about 1.5" from the top margin.
2. Set line spacing to DS.
3. After keying the ¶, clear all tabs.
4. From the Tab Set dialog box, set a left tab at 2.75".
5. SS the last 4 lines.
6. Save as **42a**. Print and close.

## FORMATTING

### Determine tab setting

Read "Set tab at center"; then do the drill below.

**THRIVING IN A MULTICULTURAL WORKPLACE**

To avoid conflict and misunderstanding in the workplace, we must be aware of the cultural differences that exist among peoples from other cultures. Become more sophisticated in your relationships by knowing some American customs that often prove confusing to persons from other countries.

2.75" → Love of individualism
Informality of workers
Hierarchy and protocol
Directness

### Set tab at center

When formatting documents such as a modified block letter, you will need to set a tab at the center of the page. The center point of a standard sheet of 8.5"-wide paper is 4.2". Tabs are measured in inches from the left margin.

To determine the tab setting for keying text at center, subtract the left margin setting from 4.2". For example, if the left margin is set at 1", set a tab at 3.2" to key text at center. See example.

```
   4.2"   Center (or desired tab setting)
 − 1.0"   Margin
   3.2"   Tab setting
```

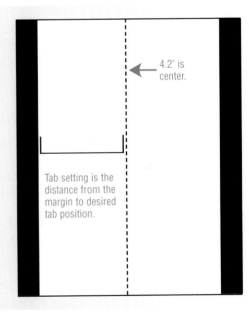

4.2" is center.

Tab setting is the distance from the margin to desired tab position.

### Drill

Key the drill at the right using default margins. Set a tab at center for the closing lines.

We shall hold your merchandise for 30 days. After that time, it will be transferred to our main warehouse at 291 Harvard Ave., East; unfortunately, we must charge a rental fee for each day the goods are stored.

Sincerely yours
QS

Elizabeth A. LeMoyne
Dispatcher

*Create and run simple queries*

Follow the 5 steps outlined on the previous page to create and run the first 2 queries. The third and fourth queries have already been created on the Formatting Template. You will open and run them.

## Query all fields

Create a query to list information about all fields in the Employee table.

1. From the Types window, right-click **Queries**. Select *New*.
2. Select *Employee* from the Open File dialog box. Click **Open**.
3. Click the check box under the table name to select all the fields.
4. Run the query by clicking the **Run Query** button on the Property toolbar.
5. Review the results. Notice that all fields are listed. Do not save or print this query.

Click table check box to select all fields.

## Query specific fields

Create a query to list employees' first and last names and states in the Employee table.

1. Start the query. (Types window, right-click **Queries**; then **New**.)
2. Select the Employee table. Click **Open**.
3. Select *Last Name*, *First Name*, and *State* by clicking the check box under each field name.
4. Run the query by clicking the **Run Query** button on the Property toolbar.
5. Review the results. Notice that all employees are listed by name and state. No other fields were included in the query. Do not save or print this query.

## Open and run a saved query

1. From the Project Viewer, select *Queries*. Double-click the **E3-Query 2** icon. Both the query and Answer table are open.
2. Which fields are included in the query?
3. Print E3-Query 2, and close both the Answer table and the query.
4. Run **E3-Query** again by right-clicking the query name and selecting *Run* (an alternate way to run a query).
5. Close both the Answer table and the query.

## Open and analyze a query

1. Double-click **E3-Query 3** to run it. Print the results.
2. Close the Answer table.
3. From the Query window, answer these questions. Write your answers on your printout.
   a. Which table is this query based on?
   b. Which fields are included in this table?
4. Close the Query window.

## FORMATTING

## Modified block letters

Study the information at the right and then key Documents 1 and 2.

### Document 1

1. Study the modified block letter on the next page.
2. Clear all tabs. Set a tab at 3.2". Key the letter; press **TAB** before keying the dateline and closing lines.
3. Because of the many single lines, key the date at approximately 2.1" from the top of the paper.
4. Proofread, save, and print.

### Document 2

Key Document 2 according to the directions in Document 1. Key the current date at 2.1" and supply an appropriate salutation. Preview before printing.

### Modified block format

The **modified block format** is a variation of the block format. It is "modified" by moving the dateline and the closing lines from the left margin to the center point of the page. Set a tab so that the date and closing are keyed at center. Paragraphs may be indented, but it is more efficient not to indent them. Do not indent paragraphs in this module.

**Reference initials:** If the writer's initials are included with those of the keyboard operator, the writer's initials are listed first in ALL CAPS followed by a colon:

**BB:xx**

**Enclosure notation:** If an item is included with a letter, an enclosure notation is keyed a DS below the reference initials. Acceptable variations include:

**Enclosure**
**Enclosures: Check #8331**
                        **Order form**
**Enc. 2**

**Copy notation:** A copy notation, c, indicates that a copy of the document has been sent to the person(s) named. Key it a DS below reference initials (or enclosure notation):

**c Andrew Wilkes**

---

**Express Rapid Delivery**

1400 Broadway * Denver, CO 80203-2137
(303) 865-2405 * FAX: (303) 865-5839

October 19, 200–

Miss Latanya Denny
208 Humboldt St.
Denver, CO 80218-8828

Dear Miss Denny

Today our delivery service tried unsuccessfully a second time to deliver at the above address the merchandise you ordered. The merchandise is now at our general warehouse at 8000 Iliff Ave.

We regret that no further attempts at delivery can be made. You may claim your merchandise at the warehouse if you will show a copy of your order (a duplicate is enclosed) to John Kimbrough at the warehouse.

We shall hold your merchandise for 30 days. After that time, it will be transferred to our main warehouse at 218 Harvard Ave., East; unfortunately, we must charge a rental fee for each day the goods are stored there.

Yours truly

Elizabeth A. LeMoyne
Dispatcher

BB:xx

Enclosure

c John Kimbrough

---

|  | words |
|---|---|
| opening | 3 |

Mr. Jose E. Morales, Director│Flint Business Association│584 Brabyn — 15
Ave.│Flint, MI 48508-5548 — 22

The Octagon Club is concerned about Baker House. — 35

As you know, Baker House was built on Calumet Rd. in 1797 by Zaccaria — 49
Baker; he and his family lived there for many years. It was home for vari- — 64
ous other families until 1938, when it became an attractive law and real — 79
estate office. Flint residents somehow assumed that Baker House was a — 93
permanent part of Flint. It wasn't. — 101

Baker House was torn down last week to make room for a new mall. It's — 115
too late to save Baker House. But what about other Flint landmarks? — 129
Shall we lose them too? Shopping malls may indicate that a community — 143
is growing, but need growth destroy our heritage? — 153

We ask for your help. Will you and Mr. Wilkes include 20 minutes on your — 168
January meeting agenda for Myrna Targlif, president of the Flint Octagon — 182
Club, to present our views on this problem? She has information that you — 197
will find interesting; a brief outline is enclosed. — 208

Sincerely yours│Barbara Brahms│Secretary, Octagon Club│BB:xx│ — 220
Enclosure│c Andrew Wilkes — 225

**Figure 2   Fields checked are included in the query**

### Step 4:  Set special options.

Other options include sorting and setting criteria. These options are applied to fields when appropriate. You'll learn more about them later.

### Step 5:  Run the query.

To run a query is to execute it. Similar to clicking OK on a dialog box or pressing ENTER after a command, the Run command carries out the query.

To run a query, click the Run Query button on the toolbar. *Paradox* displays the results in an Answer table called *answer.db* and stores the query in a directory called *Priv*. The Answer table is only temporary. Each time you run the query, a new Answer table is created that overwrites the previous one. The Answer table can be printed. The illustration below shows a portion of the Answer table from a query. Note that the title bar displays the directory *Priv:* name and a temporary filename.

*Note:* A query that has been saved can be opened and run from the Project Viewer. To run a saved query, select *Queries* from the Project Viewer and double-click the desired query file icon. Both the query and Answer table open.

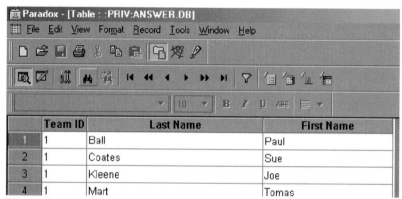

**Figure 3   Query Answer table**

### Step 6:  If desired, save the query in the working directory.

### Step 7:  Close the Answer table to return to the Query window.

To return to the Query window from the Answer window, click the **Window** menu and select the name of the query. Changes can be made to the query; it can be run again and saved as a new query.

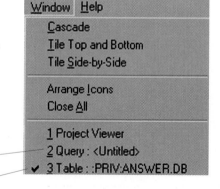

Query (unsaved)

Answer to query

All Business Communication

18950 Bonanza Way
Gaithersburg, MD 20879-1211
301-555-1256
301-555-1268 (FAX)

Left tab 3.2"

December 14, 200-
QS

Ms. Mukta Bhakta
9845 Buckingham Rd.
Annapolis, MD 21403-0314 DS

Dear Ms. Bhakta DS

Thank you for your recent inquiry on our electronic bulletin service. The ABC BBS is an interactive online service developed by All Business Communication to assist the online community in receiving documents via the Internet.

All Business Communication also provides a *Customer Support Service* and a *Technical Support Team* to assist bulletin board users. The Systems Administrators will perform various procedures needed to help you take full advantage of this new software.

For additional information call: DS

Customer and Technical Support        Center-justify
Telephone: 1-900-555-1212
9:00 a.m.-5:00 p.m., Monday-Friday, Eastern Time

Please look over the enclosed ABC BBS brochure. I will call you within the next two weeks to discuss any additional questions you may have.

Sincerely QS

Alex  Zampich
Marketing Manager DS

xx DS

Enclosure DS

c Laura Aimes, Sales Representative

MODIFIED BLOCK LETTER

## LESSON E3-E4 Database Queries

**Query a database**

Information in itself is not valuable unless you can get to it quickly and easily. Queries help you locate specific information within a database. A query finds the answer to a question based on information that is contained in one or more tables.

Queries can be based on a single table or two or more tables. In this lesson, you will learn to run, change, and create **select queries**, the most common type of query. A select query retrieves information from one or more tables and displays it in the order that you specify. Queries can be saved. If data are added to the database, the queries are automatically updated each time you run them.

**Create query based on one table**

Before creating a query, you must clearly define what information you are trying to retrieve. You must then define or specify which fields contain the desired information.

**Step 1: Start the query.**

In the Types window of the Project Viewer, right-click **Queries**. Select *New*.

**Step 2: Select the table to be included.**

From the Select File dialog box, click the filename of the table to be queried. The table filename appears in the File name text box. Click **Open**.

The Query window appears with *Untitled* in the title bar. The table name you selected is listed in the left-most column followed by the field names. Below each field name is a check box with a blank area to the right of it. Maximize the Query window.

Table being queried          Fields      Field check box

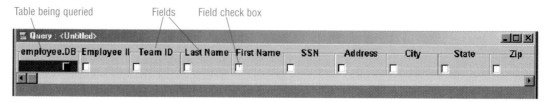

**Figure 1    Query window of the Employee table**

**Step 3: Select the fields.**

Only fields that are relevant to the information you need are included in a query. For example, if you want to print a list of all employees and their Team ID, you would select the fields for the employees' first name, last name, and Team ID. See Figure 2, p. 468.

*To select specific fields*: Click the check box under each field name to be included in the query.

*To select all fields*: Click the check box under the table name.

# Review Modified Block Letters

## 43a ● 7'

### GETTING started

each line 2 times SS; DS between 2-line groups

alphabet 1 Melva Bragg required exactly a dozen jackets for the winter trip.

figures 2 The 1903 copy of my book had 5 parts, 48 chapters, and 672 pages.

shift 3 THE LAKES TODAY, published in Akron, Ohio, comes in June or July.

easy 4 Did he vow to fight for the right to work as the Orlando auditor?

| 1 | 2 | 3 | 4 | 5 | 6 | 7 | 8 | 9 | 10 | 11 | 12 | 13 |

## 43b ● 10'

### SKILLBUILDING

**Build production skill**

1. Arrange each drill line in correct modified block letter format.
2. Use default top and side margins; return 5 times between drills. Use your reference initials.
3. Repeat the drill using block format.

**Optional:** Key a 1' writing on each line.

gwam 1'

5 May 28, 200-    3

QS

Ms. Dora Lynn    6
128 Avon Ln.    9
Macon, GA 31228-1421    12

DS

Dear Ms. Lynn    15

gwam 1'

6 Sincerely    2

QS

Rebecca Dexter    5
Engineer    7

DS

xx    8

DS

Enclosures:    Draft 251    13
               Area maps    15

7 February 4, 200-|Ms. Lilly Bargas|3945 Park Ave.|Racine, WI 53404-3822    14

8 Sincerely yours|Manuel Garcia|Council President|MG:xx|c Ron N. Nesbit    14

9 Yours truly|Ms. Loren Lakes|Secretary General|xx|Enclosure|c Libby Uhl    14

## 43c ● 33'

### FORMATTING

**Business letters: modified block**

**Document 1**

Key the letter in modified block format; center vertically. Save, preview before printing, and print.

words

Current date | Dr. Burtram M. Decker | 800 Barbour Ave. |    10

Birmingham, AL 35208-5333 | Dear Dr. Decker    19

The Community Growth Committee offers you its sincere    30
thanks for taking an active part in the sixth annual Youth    41
Fair. We especially appreciate your help in judging the    53
Youth of Birmingham Speaks portion of the fair and for    64
contributing to the prize bank.    70

Participation of community leaders such as you makes this    81
event the annual success it has become. We sincerely hope    93
we can seek your help again next year.    101

Cordially | Grace Beebe Hunt | Secretary | HNJ:xx    110

*Analyze field data*

**Part 1  Employee table**

1. Open the *Employee* table.
2. From the View menu, choose *Table Structure*.
3. Answer the questions below.
   a. Why are Employee ID, Team ID, SSN, and Home Phone listed as alpha fields rather than as number fields?
   b. Which field is the key field?  Why was this field selected?
   c. For Social Security Number: What does SSN in the Picture column mean?
   d. For ZIP code: Why is this an alpha field?
   e. For Home Phone: How will the numbers appear when they are entered?

**Part 2  Team Table**

Open the *Team* table.  Follow Steps 2 and 3 above.

1. What type of field is Team ID and why?
2. Why was the field length of Team ID changed from the default of 30 characters to 1 character?
3. Why was the first field named Team ID instead of Team Identification Number?
4. Which field is the key field?
5. What field is common to both the Team and Employee tables?

## 43c, continued

### Document 2

Key the letter at the right in modified block format. Make corrections as marked. Save as **43c-d2** and print.

### Document 3

1. Open *43c-d2* and save as **43c-d3**.
2. Select the letter address and then delete it.
3. Address the letter to:
   **Mr. Charles B. Onehawk**
   **139 Via Cordoniz**
   **Santa Barbara, CA**
   **93015-0319**
4. Delete the final paragraph and the enclosure notation.
5. Save and print.

### Document 4
### Challenge document

**Changing a letter from block to modified block format**

1. Open *39c-d1*.
2. Clear all tabs; set a tab at 3.2".
3. Click the insertion point at the beginning of each line that should begin at center. Press **TAB**.
4. Save as **43c-d4**.

*Current date*                                                                  3

Mr. Herbert *Brackmun*                                                          7
747 Myrtle Street                                                               10
Evansville, IN 47710 -3277                                                      15

Dear Mr. *Brackmun*                                                            19

Your recent letter has us more than a little entrigued.                         30

In it, you describe a back yard squirrel feeder you                             40
have built, one that keeps out birds.  This is certainly                        52
the turnaround from the usual winter animal feeding                             61
situation, and we believe it may have some apeal for    *bird-*                 72
many of our customers.  We are interested.                                      81

We are interested enough, in matter of fact, to                                 88
invite you to send or bring to our office plans for your                       100
new feeder.  If it can be built at a reasonable cost, we                       111
want to talk with you about representation in the market                       123
place.                                                                        124

We have several agency plans that we used have with                            135
success in representing clients like you for a number of                       146
years.  We shall be happy to explain them to you.                             156

A copy of our recent catalog is enclosed.                                      165
                                                *sincerely*
                                          very truly yours                     169


                             Miss Debra Stewert                               173
                             Sales manager                                    176
                             xx — *use your initials*                         176
                             Enclosured                                       178

## Add validity checks

The remaining fields on the Field Roster tab are **validity checks**, which establish rules or guidelines for entering data. Validity checks prohibit data from being entered inconsistently.

**Minimum**    Specifies a minimum value for the selected field. The values entered in the field must be greater than or equal to the minimum specified.

**Maximum**    Values entered must be less than or equal to the maximum specified.

**Default**    Specifies a default value. *Paradox* enters the value you specify here if you do not enter another value when you edit this field.

**Picture**    Restricts the types of information that can be entered in a field. Pictures specify a character string as a template for the values that can be entered into this field.

    *Picture Assist:*   Opens the Picture Assistance dialog box, where you can select or modify a predefined string to use as a picture.

**Required Field**    Specifies that a value must be entered in the field for each record.

## APPLICATION

*Part 2: Add validity checks and enter records*

1. Add the validity checks to the Equipment table.
2. Save the changes to the structure of the table. The structure of your table should look similar to the one shown on the previous page.
3. Switch to Edit mode.
4. Enter the records at the right in the Equipment table.
5. Proofread your work carefully. Your data will be saved automatically upon exiting.

### Validity checks

| | |
|---|---|
| Equipment ID | Required: **Yes** |
| Category | Required: **Yes** |
| Model | Required: **Yes** |
| Cost | Required: **Yes** |
| Date Serviced | Required: **Yes** |
| Employee ID | Required: **Yes** |

### New records

| Equipment ID | Category | Model | Cost | Date Serviced | Employee ID |
|---|---|---|---|---|---|
| 1 | Computer | Compel | 3500 | 1/15/00 | 56789 |
| 2 | Computer | Prescott | 2800 | 1/15/00 | 54303 |
| 3 | Scanner | Olympia | 1800 | 6/15/00 | 45689 |
| 4 | Computer | Compel | 3700 | 6/15/00 | 53251 |
| 5 | Computer | Prescott | 2800 | 6/15/00 | 54102 |
| 6 | Computer | Compel | 3200 | 6/15/00 | 24671 |
| 7 | Computer | Compel | 3200 | 6/15/00 | 43215 |
| 8 | Printer | Peale | 450 | 1/15/00 | 35789 |
| 9 | Printer | Peale | 550 | 1/15/00 | 54214 |
| 10 | Computer | Pierce | 4500 | 1/15/00 | 35789 |
| 11 | Computer | Pierce | 2950 | 1/15/00 | 46782 |

# 44

# Assessment

## LESSON

### 44a ● 7'

**G** **ETTING**
**started**

each line 2 times SS; DS
between 2-line groups

alphabet 1 Two exit signs jut quietly above the beams of a razed skyscraper.
figures 2 At 7 a.m., I open Rooms 18, 29, and 30; I lock Rooms 4, 5, and 6.
direct
reaches 3 I obtain many junk pieces dumped by Marvyn at my service centers.
easy 4 The town may blame Keith for the auditory problems in the chapel.

| 1 | 2 | 3 | 4 | 5 | 6 | 7 | 8 | 9 | 10 | 11 | 12 | 13 |

### 44b ● 10'

## SKILLBUILDING

**Assess straight-copy
skill**

Take two 3' writings; key
fluently, confidently; determine
*gwam*; proofread; count errors.

all letters

*gwam* 3'

Whether or not a new company will be a success will depend    4 | 62
on how well it fits into our economic system. Due to the demands    8 | 66
of competition, only a company that is organized to survive will    13 | 71
likely ever get to be among the best. Financial success, the    17 | 75
reason why most companies exist, rests on some unique ideas that    21 | 79
are put in place by a management team that has stated goals in    25 | 83
mind and the good judgment to recognize how those goals can best    30 | 88
be reached.    31 | 89

It is in this way that our business system tries to assure    34 | 92
us that, if a business is to survive, it must serve people in the    39 | 97
way they want to be served. Such a company will have managed to    43 | 101
combine some admirable product with a low price and the best ser-    47 | 106
vice--all in a place that is convenient for buyers. With no    52 | 110
intrusion from outside forces, the buyer and the seller benefit    56 | 114
both themselves and the economy.    58 | 116

3' | 1 | 2 | 3 | 4 |

### 44c ● 33'

## FORMATTING

**Assess basic business
correspondence**
**Time schedule:**
Planning time . . . . . . . . . 3'
Timed production . . . . . . 25'
Final check; proofread;
   determine *g-pram* . . . . . 5'

1. On the signal to begin, key Documents 1, 2,
   3, and 4 in sequence; use the current date
   and your reference initials.
2. Repeat Document 1 if time allows.

3. Proofread all documents; count errors;
   determine *g-pram*.

$$g\text{-}pram = \frac{\text{total words keyed}}{25'}$$

**Time:** Times should be defined with the Time type.

**Autoincrement:** Consecutive numbers that are assigned by *Paradox*.

**Size:** Specifies the size of the field; the default is 30 characters. Set the size a little larger than you anticipate will be required.

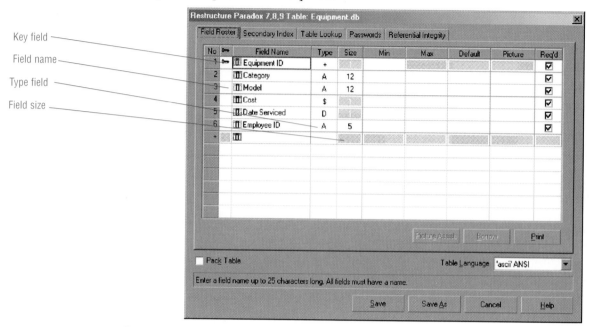

Key field
Field name
Type field
Field size

**Paradox 7, 8, 9 Table: dialog box with fields entered**

## APPLICATION
### E4

*Part 1: Create a table*

1. Select *Tables* from the Types window, right-click, and click **New**.
2. From the New Table dialog box, select *Blank*, and then *Paradox 7,8,9*.
3. On the Field Roster tab, enter the first field name, type, and size.
   a. Key **Equipment ID** under Field Name. Press TAB.
   b. From the list of field types, scroll down to select *Autoincrement*. Press TAB.
   c. Size is automatically assigned because the field type is Autoincrement.
   d. Set *Equipment ID* as the key field by clicking in the Key column.
4. Enter the remaining field names, types, and sizes from the information listed below.

| Field Names | Types | Size |
|---|---|---|
| Equipment ID | Autoincrement | automatically assigned |
| Category | Alpha | Length: 12 |
| Model | Alpha | Length: 12 |
| Cost | Money | automatically assigned |
| Date Serviced | Alpha | Length: 10 |
| Employee ID | Alpha | Length: 5 |

5. Click the **Create** button. In the Table Save As dialog box, save the table as **Equipment**. Keep the Equipment table open; you will use it in the next document.

**44c,** continued

**Document 1**
**Memorandum**
Save as **44c-d1**.

TO: Brenda Hull | FROM: Bruna Wertz | DATE: Current | SUBJECT:   13

Current Promotion   17

We have a problem, Brenda. I have learned that some of our distributors   31

are using older stock with our latest promotion. As you know, our older   46

boxes have no logos; but our refund plan asks for them.   57

I hope you will agree, however, that we must honor the coupons that arrive   72

without logos--hopefully there will not be too many of them. Please alert   87

your staff. | xx   90

**Document 2**
**Business letter in block format**
Supply an appropriate salutation. Save as **44c-d2**.

Current date | AMASTA Company, Inc. | 902 Greenridge Dr. | Reno,   12
NV 69505-5552   15

We sell your videocassettes and have since you introduced them. Follow-   33
ing instructions in your recent flyer, we tell customers who buy your   47
Super D videocassettes to return to you the coupon we give them; and you   62
will refund $1 for each cassette.   69

Several of our customers now tell us they are unable to follow the direc-   83
tions on the coupon. They explain, and we further corroborate, that there   98
is no company logo on the box to return to you as requested. We are not   113
sure how to handle our unhappy customers.   122

What steps should we take? A copy of the coupon is enclosed, as is a   136
Super D container. Please read the coupon, examine the box, and then   150
let me know your plans for extricating us from this problem.   162

Sincerely | John J. Long | Sales Manager | xx | Enc. 2   171

**Document 3**
**Business letter in modified block format**
Supply an appropriate salutation. Save as **44c-d3**.

**Document 4**

1. Open *44c-d3*. Save as **44c-d4**.
2. Replace the letter address with the following:
   **Viadex Corporation**
   **3945 Alexandria Blvd.**
   **Detroit, MI 48230-9732**
3. Supply the salutation.
4. Change to block format.
5. Save and print.

Current date | Mr. John J. Long, Sales Manager | The Record Store |   12
9822 Trevor Ave. | Anaheim, CA 92805-5885   20

With your letter came our turn to be perplexed, and we apologize. When we   38
had our refund coupons printed, we had just completed a total   50
redesign program for our product boxes. We had detachable logos put on   65
the outside of the boxes, which could be peeled off and placed on a   80
coupon.   81

We had not anticipated that our distributors would use back inventories   96
with our promotion. The cassettes you sold were not packaged in our   110
new boxes; therefore, there were no logos on them.   120

I'm sorry you or your customers were inconvenienced. In the future,   134
simply ask your customers to send us their sales slips, and we will honor   149
them with refunds until your supply of older containers is depleted.   163

Sincerely yours | Bruna Wertz | Sales and Promotions Dept. | xx   174

**Creating tables**

# Create and Design Tables

Tables are the basis of all other parts of the database. Learning to work with tables is an important step in becoming familiar with database software. In Lesson E1, you opened a table, added records, and edited records. In this lesson, you will create a new table.

Tables can be created using the Table Expert or from a blank grid. Using the blank database grid gives you the most control over the way information is entered. It allows fields to be defined and precautions included that will help ensure the accuracy of data entered later. When creating a table, you must specify the type of table. Various *Paradox* versions are available as well as other database programs. Choose *Paradox 7,8,9*.

### To create a table:

1. From the File menu, choose *Table*, then *New*. (*Option*: Select *Tables* from the Types window, right-click, and click **New**.)
2. From the New Table dialog box, click **Blank**.
3. From the Table type dialog box, choose *Paradox 7,8,9*. Click **OK**.

The next two steps, defining fields and creating validity check, require more explanation.

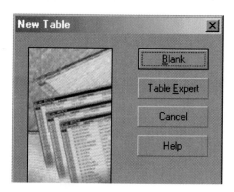

### Define fields

The quality of a database starts with defining quality fields in the table. On the Field Roster tab of the Create Paradox 7,8,9 Table dialog box, you will enter and define the fields to be included in the table. (See next page.) The four main field properties are key, name, type, and size.

**Key** Specifies whether the field is a key field. One field in each table should be designated as the **key field**. The key field must be the first field listed. A key field uniquely identifies a field and prevents a second record being added with the same key value. To designate the key field, click in the key column next to the key field name.

**Field Name** Specifies the name of the field. Name is a required field (all fields must have a name). Field names should be clear and descriptive.

**Type:** Specifies the type of field. Click in the Type field to display a list of data types. Following is a brief description of the most common data types.

> **Alpha:** Alphabetic or numeric characters that do not require calculations. Examples of numeric characters that are entered as alpha include social security numbers, telephone numbers, serial numbers, or invoice numbers.
>
> **Number:** Numbers are used in calculations.
>
> **Money:** Numbers that include the dollar symbol; like numbers, currency can be used in calculations.
>
> **Logical:** Requires a Yes/No, True/False value. Yes/No would be appropriate to indicate memberships or dues paid.

## Objective Assessment

Answer the questions below to see whether you have mastered the content of this module.

1. A _____ is a form of written communication that is used primarily for internal communication.

2. _____ is a method of transmitting documents and messages via the computer system.

3. A(n) _____ is keyed at the end of the document when something is included with the correspondence.

4. If several people are to receive a copy of a memo, key a _____ list at the end of the memo.

5. The _____ contains the name and address of the person who will receive the letter.

6. The formal closing of the letter is called the _____ .

7. _____ allows you to check the layout of the document before it is printed.

8. The proper salutation for a letter addressed to Human Resources Director is _____ .

9. The proper salutation for a letter addressed to Computer-Tech Industries is _____ .

10. A _____ aligns copy at the decimal point.

11. The center point for a standard 8.5" x 11" paper is _____ .

12. A _____ indicates that a copy of the document has been sent to the person(s) named.

## Performance Assessment

### Document 1
### Modified block letter

1. Estimate the letter length.
2. Include the letter address below. Use current date; add an appropriate salutation and closing. The letter is from **Alberto Valenzuela**.

**Ms. Shawna Olson**
**Western Regional Manager**
**Acune, Inc.**
**5450 Signal Hill Rd.**
**Springfield, OH 45504-5440**

3. Save as **ckpt5-d1**. Print.

### Document 2
### Interoffice memo

1. Key the same message as a memo to **Ms. Sandra Habek** from **Alberto Valenzuela**. Use the current date and **May Seminar** as the subject line.
2. Add a copy notation to **Mark Roane**.

I have invited Lynda A. Brewer, P h.D., Earlham College, Richmond, Indiana, to be our seminar leader on Friday afternoon, May 10.

Dr. Brewer, a well-known psychologist who has spent a lot of time researching and writing in the field of ergonomics, will address "Stress Management."

Please make arrangements for rooms, speaker accommodations, staff notification, and refreshments. I will send you Dr. Brewer's vita for use in preparing news releases.

## Using a form to add records

A form provides a structure for entering or editing data found in a table. *Paradox* automatically links a form to the related table. If you enter or change data in a form, the same changes are reflected in the table.

### To enter records in a form:

1. Click **Forms** under Types, and then double-click to open the form.
2. Choose *Edit* from the View menu or click the **Edit** button.
3. Click the **Last Record** navigation button to go to the last record. Then click the **Next Record** button to get a blank form.
4. Use the TAB key to move across the form or use the Down arrow.

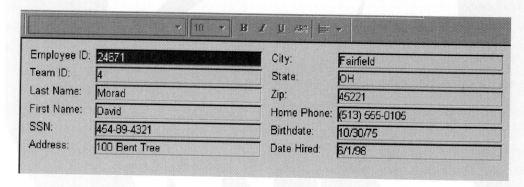

## APPLICATION

*Enter records using a form*

1. Enter records in the Employee Data Form to update the Employee table. Add a zero to put the month or day in a double-digit form (e.g., key **06** for June).
2. Close the form when finished. Open the Employee table; it should have 22 records.
3. Print the table and compare the results to the printout in Application E2.
4. Verify the accuracy of your printout.
5. Close the database and exit *Paradox*.

| Field names | Record 1 | Record 2 | Record 3 |
|---|---|---|---|
| Employee ID | 25678 | 74569 | 77412 |
| Team ID | 2 | 1 | 3 |
| Last Name | Hall | Ball | Jones |
| First Name | Earl | Paul | Tony |
| SSN | 312-25-8963 | 253-55-4189 | 175-82-6741 |
| Address | 901 Adams Dr. | 80 King Ave. | 101 Roman Ct. |
| City | Florence | Dayton | Cincinnati |
| State | KY | KY | OH |
| Zip | 41042 | 41201 | 45251 |
| Home Phone | (606) 555-0122 | (606) 555-0123 | (513) 555-0124 |
| Birthdate | 03/15/1972 | 06/04/1975 | 08/31/1950 |
| Date Hired | 05/23/1999 | 06/15/1999 | 10/01/1999 |

# Activity

*one*   ## Open a Web browser

*WordPerfect 9* users can access the Internet while in *WordPerfect*: Select Internet Publisher from the File menu. The Internet Publisher dialog box displays.

Open your Web browser (e.g., Netscape or Internet Explorer) by clicking Browse the Web. The Web page you have designated as your Home or Start page displays.

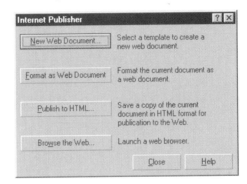

**Practice**

1. Open *WordPerfect*.
2. Click **File**, then **Internet Publisher**.
3. Choose *Browse the Web* to launch the Internet browser.

**Note:** You may also open your Web browser from the *Windows* desktop.

# Activity

*two*   ## Understand Web addressing

A **Web address**—commonly called the *URL or Uniform Resource Locator*—is composed of one or more domains separated by periods, e.g., http://www.house.gov or http://www.li.suu.edu. A *domain name* is the name given to a network or site that is connected to the Internet. As you move from left to right in the address, each domain is larger than the previous one. For example, in the Web address http://www.house.gov, *gov* (United States government) is larger than *house* (House of Representatives). The table below identifies types of high-level domains.

| | |
|---|---|
| .gov | Non-military government sites |
| .com | Commercial organizations |
| .edu | Educational institutions |
| .org | Other organizations |
| .mil | Military sites |

## Selecting and editing records

Once a field is selected, it can be edited in the same way text or data is edited in a spreadsheet or a word processing table. If the entire field must be edited, simply select the field and rekey it. If just a couple of characters are affected, click in the field and edit it.

| To select | Action |
|---|---|
| A field | Click in the field. |
| Column | Double-click a field name or several field names. |
| Record | Double-click the record number (extreme left side). |

| To edit data | |
|---|---|
| Delete a record | Select the record and press CTRL+DELETE. |
| Delete a field | Click field and press DELETE. |
| Insert a record | Generally, new records are added below the last existing record. However, to insert a record at a specific point, click any field in the record below where you want to insert the new record. Click the **Record** menu and select *Insert*. |

### Locate records

The Locate feature will help you find a field quickly. Locate is especially helpful when the table is large.

### To locate a field:

1. Click the **Locate** button on the Property toolbar.
2. Select the field you will search by from the drop-down list on the Locate Value dialog box.
3. Key the name of the field you are looking for in the Value box.

## APPLICATION

*Edit records*

1. The Employee table should be open. Switch to Edit mode.
2. The employee named Margaret Balli just got married. Change her last name to **Perez**. (Select *Balli* and key her new name.)
3. Margaret will also be relocating, so change the city to **Alexandria**; ZIP, **41032**.
4. Employee ID #35801 has moved. Change his mailing address to **101 Park Dr**.
5. Employee ID #54291 is no longer with the company. Double-click the record number (**13**) and press CTRL+DELETE. You should now have 19 records in the Employee table.
6. Use the Locate button to find the person with the social security number of **325-00-9897**.
7. Change the name for employee Carlos Moretz to **Carl Moretz**.
8. Using the Locate button to find the record for Anna Tipton. Change her home phone number to **(606) 555-0101**.
9. Print the table in landscape orientation (**Print** menu, **Properties** button, **Landscape**). Change the Overflow Handling option to *Create horizontal overflow pages as needed*. Do not exit the database.

A Web address may also include a directory path and filenames separated by a slash, e.g., http://msstate.edu/athletics/. The Web document named *athletics* resides at this site.

**Practice**
1. Identify the high-level domain for the following Web sites:
   a. http://www.senate.gov
   b. http://www.fbla-pbl.org
   c. http://www.army.mil
   d. http://www.ibm.com
2. Identify the filenames for the following Web sites:
   a. http://www.reebok.com/soccer/
   b. http://www.espn.com/golf/
   c. http://www.cnn.com/QUICKNEWS/
   d. http://www.nike.com/participate

## Activity three

### Open a Web site

To open a Web site from your browser, click Open or Open Page from the File menu (or click the Open button if it is available on your browser's toolbar). Key the URL http://www.weather.com as shown below and click Open. The home page for The Weather Channel displays.

**Shortcut:** Click inside the Netsite, Location, or Address entry box, key the URL, and press ENTER.

**Practice**
Open the following Web sites:
1. http://weather.com
2. http://www.abc.com
3. http://www.cnn.com/QUICKNEWS/
4. http://www.espn.com/golf/
5. http://www.usps.gov/ctc/welcome.htm

## Activity four

### Explore the browser's toolbar

The browser's toolbar is very valuable when surfing the Internet. Become familiar with your browser's toolbar by studying the toolbar below and the items on p. 120. Toolbars may vary slightly.

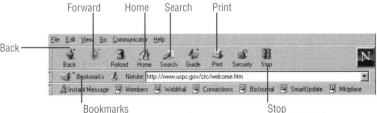

The navigation buttons on the Property toolbar are useful for moving around in large databases. You can move to the next record, the previous record, the first or last record, or to the previous or next record set. A **set** is what you can see on the screen at one time.

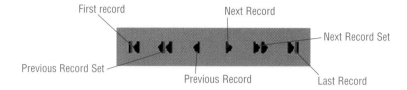

First record
Next Record
Next Record Set
Previous Record Set
Previous Record
Last Record

*Add records*

The Employee table should be open. Your table should look similar to the illustration on p. 458.

1. Use the navigation buttons to move the insertion point to: (a) the last record; (b) the first record; (c) the next record; (d) the previous record.
2. Use the arrow keys to move (a) to the end of Record 1; (b) to the beginning of Record 1; (c) down two rows; (d) up one row.
3. Switch to Edit mode by clicking the **Edit** button on the toolbar.
4. Click the **Last Record** navigation button. Press the Down arrow key to move to Record 16 (Row 16). Enter the first record:

   a. Key **55687** as the Employee ID; press TAB to move to the next field.

   b. Key **4** as the Team ID; press TAB to move to the next field. After keying the data for the last field, press TAB to start a new record. When keying dates, add a zero if a single digit represents the month or day; thus, key **06** and **05** for June 5.

5. Add the next 4 records in the same manner.

| Fields | Record 1 | Record 2 | Record 3 | Record 4 | Record 5 |
|---|---|---|---|---|---|
| Employee ID | 55687 | 28544 | 33987 | 44123 | 33214 |
| Team ID | 4 | 3 | 2 | 1 | 1 |
| Last Name | Judd | Barkley | Rowe | Kleene | Mart |
| First Name | Nancy | Liz | Michelle | Joe | Tomas |
| SSN | 444-89-9987 | 228-89-3366 | 332-15-9874 | 114-56-8523 | 441-58-7993 |
| Address | 10 Holly Ave. | 8 Mark Ct. | 77 Hibiscus | 241 Grand Rd. | 5 Scenic Dr. |
| City | Florence | Dayton | Cincinnati | Alexandria | Dayton |
| State | KY | OH | OH | KY | OH |
| Zip | 41042 | 45410 | 45251 | 41032 | 45410 |
| Home Phone | (606) 555-0199 | (513) 555-0118 | (513) 555-0019 | (606) 555-0130 | (513) 555-0113 |
| Birthdate | 10/15/1978 | 06/12/1961 | 09/21/1960 | 11/04/1957 | 09/22/1935 |
| Date Hired | 01/01/1999 | 05/12/1999 | 09/01/1999 | 06/05/1999 | 07/14/1999 |

6. Proofread your work. *It is not necessary to save your work. Paradox* will automatically save the table with the new records. Your table should have 20 records.

| | |
|---|---|
| **Netsite or Address entry box:** | Displays the active URL or Web site address. |
| **Back:** | Moves back to Web sites or pages visited since opening the browser. |
| **Forward:** | Moves forward to Web sites or pages visited prior to using the Back button. (The Forward button is ghosted if the Back button has not been used.) |
| **Print:** | Prints a Web page. |
| **Home:** | Returns to the Web page designated as the Home or Start page. |
| **Stop:** | Stops the computer's search for a Web site. |
| **Search:** | Opens one of the Internet search engines. |
| **Bookmarks or Favorites:** | Moves to a list of Web sites marked for easy access. |

### Practice

1. Open the following Web sites:
   a. http://www.nike.com
   b. http://www.adidas.com
   c. http://www.reebok.com
   d. a site of your choice
2. Click the **Back** button twice. The _____ Web site displays.
3. Click the **Forward** button once. The _____ Web site displays.
4. Print the active Web page.
5. Key **http://www.msstate.edu** in the Netsite or Address entry box. Stop the search before the Web site is located.

**Activity five**

## Bookmark a favorite Web site

When readers put a book aside, they insert a bookmark to mark their place. Internet users also add bookmarks to mark their favorite Web sites or sites of interest for later browsing. Often bookmarks are added to and accessed from a folder called *Favorites*.

> **To add a bookmark:**
> 1. Open the desired Web site.
> 2. Click **Bookmarks** and then **Add Bookmark**. (Browsers may vary on location and name of Bookmark button.)
>
> **To use a bookmark:**
> 1. Click **Bookmarks** (or **Favorites, Communicator,** or **Window Bookmarks**).
> 2. Select the desired bookmark. Click or double-click, depending on your browser. The desired Web site displays.

### Practice

1. Open these favorite Web sites and bookmark them on your browser:
   a. http://www.weather.com
   b. http://www.cnn.com
   c. http://www.usps.gov
   d. add one of your choice
2. Use the bookmark to go to the following Web sites:
   a. The Weather Channel
   b. CNN
   c. The United States Postal Service
   d. The Web site you bookmarked

a. The numbers at the far left of the screen indicate how many records (rows) are in the table. Note the message in the status bar that reads Record 1 of 15. Use the scroll bar at the right to scroll through the 15 records.

b. How many fields (columns) are in this table?

c. Where does the name of this table appear on your screen?

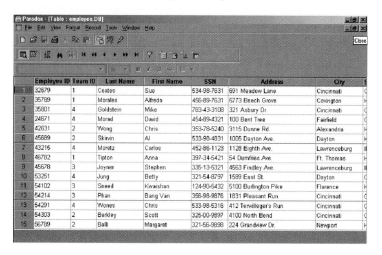

3. Close the table by clicking Close (**X**) on the document title bar. Notice the Project Viewer is still displayed even though you closed the table.

4. Click **Queries** in the Types window. The filenames of all queries saved in your working directory display. Note that queries have the file extension *.qbe*.

5. Open the Employee table again; click **Table** under Types and then double-click the filename **Employee** on the right side of the screen. Leave the table open for the next drill.

**Entering records in a table**

When you open a table, it opens in *view mode*. View mode allows you to view the data but not add records or edit the table in any way. *Edit mode* allows you to enter or edit data in the table. To switch between modes, click either the Edit mode button or the View mode button on the Property toolbar.

Edit mode button ———           View mode button ———

To move around in a table, use these keys:

| Key | Result |
| --- | --- |
| TAB, ENTER, or right arrow | Next field |
| Left arrow or SHIFT+TAB | Previous field |
| END | Last field in the current record |
| HOME | First field in the current record |
| Up and Down arrows | Up or down one record |

# Activity

### six

## Surf the Net with hyperlinks

A **hyperlink** is used to link one Web document to another Web document. The hyperlink inserted in the Web site may be a link to another page in the Web site or to another Web site. For example, the Web page for a university may include hyperlinks to the various academic departments within the university (pages within the Web site) and a hyperlink to the local visitors' and convention center (another Web site).

A hyperlink may be applied to either text or images. Hyperlinked text displays in a different color and is underlined. When the mouse is pointed at hyperlinked text or images, the mouse pointer changes to a pointing hand. Click the hyperlink, and the new Web document displays. Remember to click the Back button to return to the original Web site.

### Practice

1. At http://www.army.mil, click the following hyperlinked text: Installations.
2. From that page, click the database hyperlinked text.
3. Click the **Back** button twice to return to the original Web page.
4. At http://www.yahoo.com, click the following hyperlinked text and images:
   a. Email
   b. People Search
   c. Image for What's New
5. Open a Web site for a university or college of your choice.
   a. List two hyperlinked images.
   b. List two examples of hyperlinked text.
   c. Which text or image is linked to another Web document within the Web site?
   d. Which text or image is linked to another Web site?

# Activity

### seven

## Electronic mail

**Electronic mail** or **e-mail** refers to electronic messages sent by one computer user to another computer user. To be able to send or receive e-mail, you must have an e-mail address, an e-mail program, and access to the Internet or to an Intranet (in-house network).

### Set up e-mail address

Many search engines such as Yahoo!, Excite, Lycos, AltaVista, and others are now providing free e-mail via their Web sites. These e-mail programs enable users to set up an e-mail address and then send and retrieve e-mail messages. To set up an account and obtain an e-mail address, the user must (1) agree to the terms of agreement, (2) complete an online registration form, and (3) compose an e-mail name and password.

### Practice

1. Click the **Search** button on the browser's toolbar. Click a search engine that offers free e-mail.
2. Click **Free Email** or **Email** or **Get Email**. (Terms will vary.)
3. Read the Terms of Agreement and accept.
4. Enter an e-mail name. This name will be the login-name portion of your e-mail address.
5. Enter a password for your e-mail account. For security reasons, do not share your password, do not leave it where others can use it, and avoid choosing pet names or birth dates. Use number and letter combinations that make no sense.

Database files are stored in the *working directory*, which is the default data directory. Paradox assigns the working directory the temporary alias WORK, even if it has another alias name. Various databases have been stored on the Formatting Template. Each database was saved in its own folder within Module E. To access these files, you will set the working directory to the specific database you are working with. To change directories, click the Select Directory button (…) on the toolbar or choose File menu, Working Directory.

**Drill 1  Start Paradox and set working directory**

1. Open *Paradox*: Click **Start**, **Programs**, *WordPerfect Office 2000*, and *Paradox 9*.

2. The Welcome Screen appears. Click **X** to close it. The Project Viewer displays.

3. Set the working directory:

   a. Click the **File** menu and choose *Working Directory*.

   b. In the Set Working Directory dialog box, select the directory for the Telecom database (See the directory where the Formatting Template files are located: *Module E\Telecom*.

   c. Leave WORK as the alias. Click **OK**.

4. Click the Maximize button to enlarge the window.

5. Close *Paradox*. Then open *Paradox* again. From the Welcome screen, choose *Open Database*. Select WORK from the list of alias names. Leave *Paradox* open.

## Learning about tables

Data in *Paradox* is organized into tables. A **table** stores data about a single subject; a database consists of one or many tables. Each table contains records. A **record** stores all the information relating to a single person or item and can contain one or more fields. Each row is a record. A **field** is a piece of information, such as a person's last name. Each column represents a field. *Paradox* assigns the extension *.db* to tables.

**To open a table:**

- Double-click the filename.
- Select the filename, right-click, and choose **Open**.
- Click the **Open Table** button on the Property toolbar.

Field name        Field (column)

| Employee ID | Team ID | Last Name | First Name | SSN | Address |
|---|---|---|---|---|---|
| 24671 | 4 | Morad | David | 454-89-4321 | 100 Bent Tree |
| 32679 | 1 | Coates | Sue | 534-98-7631 | 691 Meadow Lane |
| 35789 | 1 | Morales | Alfredo | 456-89-9864 | 5773 Beech Grove |
| 35801 | 4 | Goldstein | Mike | 783-43-3108 | 321 Asbury Dr. |

Record

**Figure 4   Parts of a database table**

**Drill 2  View database**

1. In the first column of the Project Viewer, click **Tables**. The filenames of all tables stored in your working directory display in the column at the right. Notice that all table objects are represented with a common icon and have the extension *.db*.

2. Open the Employee table by double-clicking the filename.

6. Review the entire registration form and submit it. You will be notified immediately that your e-mail account has been established. (If your e-mail name is already in use by someone else, you may be instructed to choose a different name before your account can be established.)

### Send e-mail message

To send an e-mail message, you must have the address of the computer user you wish to write to. Business cards, letterheads, directories, etc., now include e-mail addresses. Sometimes you may need to call the person by telephone and ask for his or her e-mail address. An e-mail address includes the user's login name followed by @ and the domain name(s); e.g., sthomas@yahoo.com or sdt3@jn.ndu.edu.

Creating an e-mail message is quite similar to preparing a memo. The e-mail header includes TO, FROM, and SUBJECT. Key the e-mail address of the recipient on the TO line, and compose a subject line that concisely describes your message. Your e-mail address will automatically display on the FROM line.

### Practice

1. Open the search engine used to set up your email account. Click **Email**, **Free Email**, or **Get Email**. (Terms will vary.)
2. Enter your e-mail name and password when prompted.
3. Enter the e-mail address of your instructor or another student.
4. Compose a brief message. Be sure to include a descriptive subject line.
5. Send the message.

### Read e-mail messages

Reading one's e-mail messages and responding promptly are considered important rules of *netiquette* (etiquette for the Internet). However, avoid responding too quickly to sensitive situations.

### Practice

1. Open your e-mail account if it is not open.
2. Read your messages and respond immediately. Click **Reply** to answer the message. (E-mail programs may vary.)

### Forward e-mail messages

Received e-mail messages are often shared or forwarded to other e-mail users. Be considerate of others as you make decisions about forwarding messages.

### Practice

1. Open your e-mail account if it is not open.
2. Forward a message received from a student to your teacher or another student.
3. Delete all read messages.

### Attach a document to an e-mail message

Electronic files can be attached to an e-mail message and sent to another computer electronically. Recipients of attached documents can transfer these documents to their computers and then open for use.

### Practice

1. Open your e-mail account if it is not open.
2. Create an e-mail message to your teacher that states that your homework is attached. The subject line should include the specific homework assignment (44b-d1, for example).
3. Attach the file by clicking **Attach**. Use the browser to locate the homework file. (E-mail programs may vary.)
4. Send the e-mail message.

# Database Basics

## Starting Paradox

To start *Paradox*, click the **Start** button, select *Programs*, *WordPerfect Office 2000*, and click **Paradox 9**. The Paradox Welcome screen displays six icons. From the Welcome screen, you can create a new database or open an existing one. You can bypass this opening screen by clicking Close (**X**).

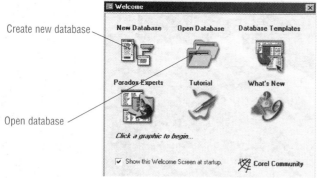

Create new database

Open database

**Figure 1   Paradox Welcome Screen**

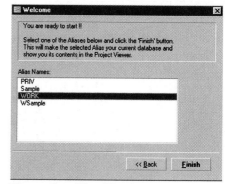

**Figure 2   Alias Names**

If you choose to open an existing database, the Welcome screen displays a list of alias names (Figure 2). An **alias** is a name the user assigns when the database is created. Selecting an alias name from the list (Figure 2) automatically makes it the current database.

The contents of the default database or alias shows in the Project Viewer. The Project Viewer is split into two sections. The left section is entitled **Types** and lists the parts of a database. The right section lists the actual contents of the database. In this module, you will work with four types: Tables, Queries, Forms, and Reports. In the top left corner of the Project Viewer is a drop-down box that lists directories or aliases. If the database is given an alias name when it is created, you can select the alias name from this list. In this module, select WORK, which is the default alias.

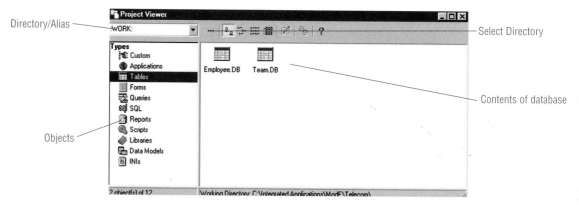

Directory/Alias

Objects

Select Directory

Contents of database

**Figure 3   Project Viewer**

# SIMPLE REPORTS

**6**

*module*

## OBJECTIVES

1. Format two-page unbound and leftbound reports.

2. Format long references and title pages.

3. Learn additional word processing functions.

4. Change the format of existing documents.

5. Improve speed and accuracy.

---

**LESSON 45**

## Skillbuilding/Formatting Text

### 45a ● 8'

## GETTING started

Key each line twice at a slow but steady pace. DS between 2-line groups. Rekey twice lines having more than one error.

### SKILLBUILDING WARMUP

one-hand sentences

1 Few beavers, as far as I'm aware, feast on cedar trees in Kokomo.
2 A plump, aged monk served a few million beggars a milky beverage.
3 Johnny, after a few stewed eggs, ate a plump, pink onion at noon.
4 In regard to desert oil wastes, Jill referred only minimum cases.
5 Link agrees you'll get a reward only as you join nonunion racers.
| 1 | 2 | 3 | 4 | 5 | 6 | 7 | 8 | 9 | 10 | 11 | 12 | 13 |

### 45b ● 12'

## SKILLBUILDING

**Reach for new goals**

1. Key 1' guided writings; determine *gwam*.
2. Take two 2' writings; try to maintain your best 1' rate.
3. Take a 3' writing. Use your *gwam* in Step 1 as your goal.

 all letters

*gwam* 2' | 3'

|   |   |
|---|---|

If you believe that office management is a viable objective — 6 | 4
on your horizon, maybe you envision how essential it is that you — 13 | 8
learn to work with others. As a leader, for example, you should — 19 | 13
quickly become part of the company team. You will learn much by — 26 | 17
working closely with your fellow workers; at first, you actually — 32 | 21
depend on them to give you a better idea of how everyone fits in — 39 | 26
the overall picture and how best to improve on office efficiency. — 45 | 30

2' | 1 | 2 | 3 | 4 | 5 | 6 |
3' | 1 | 2 | 3 | 4 |

# PARADOX

**E**

*module*

## OVERVIEW

Information or data is valuable only if it is readily available. For instance, if you call the airlines and ask for the next available flight to Hawaii, you expect to get an answer immediately. If you call your bank and request the balance on your account, you expect an answer immediately. This information can be provided for you quickly because the data is stored in a database.

Using a database involves three main activities:
Entering data (ensuring accuracy and validity)
Editing data (editing, updating, deleting)
Retrieving data (querying, reporting, merging)

In this module, you will work with a company that you are already familiar with, Telecom. You will learn about a database by using Telecom's database that is already set up. You will enter records directly in the table using a form; retrieve information by running queries and creating queries on your own, and present information in attractive reports. You will use the information in the database to create labels, complete mail merges, and link data from the database to a word processing document. By the time you complete this unit, you will understand the power of a database and have confidence with the basics.

## Indent

**Indent** moves all lines of a paragraph to the right one tab stop. (Tabs, on the other hand, move only the first line of a paragraph to the next tab stop.) The width of the indent depends on the current tab setting. Insert the Indent command at the beginning of each paragraph to be indented. Indent can be applied before or after the text is keyed. Various indent options are available. You will use Indent and Hanging Indent in this course.

| Indent | Moves entire paragraph to the right one tab stop. |
|---|---|
| Hanging Indent | Moves all but the first line to the right one tab stop. |
| Double Indent | Indents paragraph equally from both left and right margins. |
| Back Tab | Moves first line of ¶ left of the left margin one tab stop. |

### To indent text:

1. Place the insertion point at the beginning of the paragraph to be indented.
2. Click **Format**, **Paragraph** and then choose the indent style.

Note the quick keystrokes to execute indents.

| Indent | F7 |
|---|---|
| Hanging Indent | Ctrl+F7 |
| Double Indent | Ctrl+Shift+F7 |
| Back Tab | |

**Document 1**
1. DS ¶ 1.
2. Indent ¶ 2 and SS.
3. DS ¶ 3 in the normal manner.
4. Save as **45c-d1** and print.

However, the thrust to use e-mail almost exclusively is causing a tremendous challenge for both e-mail recipients and companies.

Indent → With the convenience of electronic mail resulting in its widespread use, many users are forsaking other forms of communication—face-to-face, telephone (including voice mail), and printed documents. Now companies are challenged to create clear e-mail policies and to implement employee training on effective use of e-mail (Ashford, 1998, 2).

Communication experts have identified problems that may occur as a result of misusing e-mail: information overload (too many messages) and inappropriate forms of communication.

**Document 2**
Key the document; insert the proper Indent commands.

**Document 3**
1. Open *hangingindent* from the template disk.
2. Select the two bibliographic entries; apply Hanging Indent.
3. Select the three glossary entries; apply Hanging Indent.

TAB ——→ Use the TAB key to move only the first line of text to the right. The TAB key is used to indent paragraphs of a document.

Hanging Indent — Hanging Indent places the first line of a paragraph at the left margin and indents all other lines to the first tab. Common uses of Hanging Indent are bibliography entries, glossaries, and lists.

Double Indent — *WordPerfect* can also double-indent text. When text is double-indented, it is indented from both the left and right margins.

## Document 4

**Embed screen capture**

1. Key the document at right; set 1.5" top margin.
2. Capture the *Paragraph* dialog box and embed it a DS below the last ¶.
3. Size the object appropriately and center.
4. Save as **d5-d4**; print.

## Widow/Orphan

Widow/Orphan prevents a single line of a paragraph from being left at the bottom of a page or a single line from being carried to the top of a page. Widow/Orphan does not prevent side headings from being left at the bottom of a page.

1. Position the insertion point at the beginning of the document.
2. Click **Format**, then **Keep Text Together**.
3. Click the **Widow/Orphan** box and **OK**.

## Document 5

**Link *Quattro Pro* spreadsheet and update**

1. Key the memo at right.
2. Open the *Quattro Pro* file *bakery*.
3. Sort by delivery date in ascending order; resave as **d5-d5**.
4. Select rows that contain orders for 11-24; shade (**Format**, **Selection**, **Fill/Pattern** tab, **Background color**).
5. Select *A3..G13*; use **Paste Special** to link in the memo.
6. Save as **d5-d5**; print.
7. Orders have changed. **Edit the object:**
   • Carol Fortune: Add 2 carrot cakes (11-25)
   • Anna Tibbett: Delete 1 chess pie; add 1 pound cake (11-24): shade row.
   **Add new order:** Tracy Nash: 1 carrot cake (11-24). Copy formula for total due. Shade row.
8. Save as **d5-d5a**; print.

| TO: | Members, Alpha Honor Society |
|---|---|
| **FROM:** | Audrey Sullivan, President |
| **DATE:** | November 23, 200- |
| **SUBJECT:** | Bakery Orders for November 24 |

A special thanks is extended to all of our members who baked and delivered the two orders due today. Also, we appreciate Cindy Watson's efforts in obtaining the bakery boxes as a donation. This special packaging along with the beautiful thank-you card that Charlene Holmes and her committee designed have enhanced the attractiveness of our baked products. In fact, we have already had calls for new orders and reorders. You have done an excellent job!

The spreadsheet below shows all orders received at this time. Most importantly, please note the highlighted orders due tomorrow (11-24). Please bring your pie or cake to Room 253 by 8 a.m. Designated deliverers are to report no later than 8:15 a.m. to receive delivery assignments. Remember we guaranteed that all orders would be delivered by 9 a.m.

*Link spreadsheet here.*

**Setting margins**

## Drill I

1. Set 1.5" side margins. Key the ¶ below right. Press ENTER twice.

2. Set 2" side margins. Key the ¶ again. Press ENTER twice.

3. Print and save as **45d-d1**.

## Drill 2

1. Open *45d-d1*.

2. Click **View, Reveal Codes**.

3. Find the codes for 1.5" left and right margins.

4. Find the codes for 2" left and right margins.

5. Delete the codes for 2" left and right margins. Notice that the second ¶ now has the same margins as the first.

6. Delete the codes for the 1.5" side margins. The ¶s are now at default (1") margins.

7. Print and save as **45d-d2**.

## Margins

Margins are the distance between the edge of the paper and the text. The default settings are 1" side margins and 1" top and bottom margins. Default margins stay in effect until you change them.

Margins can be changed on the Ruler by dragging the margin marker to a new location, or they can be changed from the Format menu.

### To change the margins from the Format menu:

1. Click **Format**, then **Margins**.

2. Enter the new settings on the Margins/Layout tab.

3. Click **OK**.

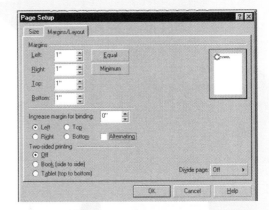

Reveal Codes shows changes in margin settings as [Lft Mar], [Rgt Mar], [Top Mar], [Bot Mar]. To see the margin setting, place the insertion point immediately to the left of the margin change code. When a new margin is set, all text that follows the new setting takes on the new margins. Margin sets stay in effect until they are changed. If a margin code is deleted, then the copy will take on the margins of the previous setting.

### Drills I and 2

Documents are more attractive when the margins are set an equal distance from the left and right edges of the paper. This gives the document the appearance of being balanced. How the copy looks is just as important as what you key.

## *on...* **WordPerfect 9**

Margins can also be changed directly on the screen using the margin guidelines.

1. Display the margin guidelines and the Ruler (View, Guidelines, Margins and View, Ruler).

2. To change the margins for the entire document, click the insertion point at the top of the document.

3. Drag the dotted margin guidelines to the new location.

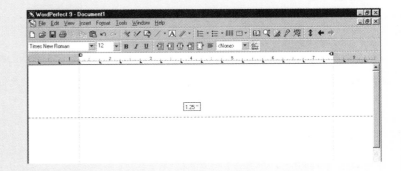

# Assessment

**Document 1**
**Create TextArt object**

1. Open the *WordPerfect* file *seed collection* from the Formatting Template.
2. Position the insertion point at the top of the page.
3. Create the title **SEED COLLECTION** as TextArt. Use your creativity in this design.
4. Save as **d5–d1**; print.

**Document 2**
**Memo with inserted**
***Quattro Pro* notebook**

1. Key the memo shown at right.
2. Insert a *Quattro Pro* spreadsheet below ¶ 1. Enlarge to 5 rows.
3. Key the data shown. Sort Column B in descending order.
4. Compute **Total** in *B6*.
5. Format using *Conservative 2* SpeedFormat style.
6. Format B4 and B8 as Currency, B5..B7 as Comma.
7. Save as **d5-d2**; print.

| TO: | Hugh T. Barton, Vice President of Marketing |
|---|---|
| **FROM:** | John Watson, Advertising Specialist |
| **DATE:** | Current |
| **SUBJECT:** | Report of Advertising Medium Used in 2000 |

As requested for the annual report, I am providing the advertising medium used by Felton Enterprises this year. The spreadsheet shown below reflects the dollar amounts spent for radio, television, Internet, and newspaper advertising. It is important to point out that 2000 marked the third year for advertising on the Internet. Dollars spent in this new arena were second among our four avenues for advertising.

| | A | B |
|---|---|---|
| 1 | **FELTON ENTERPRISES** | |
| 2 | Advertising Medium Used 200- | |
| 3 | | |
| 4 | Internet | $8,000 |
| 5 | Newspapers | 4,500 |
| 6 | Radio | 10,000 |
| 7 | Television | 7,500 |
| 8 | Total | $30,000 |

**Document 3**
**Link photo in**
***Presentations***

1. Create the slide at right using a slide show master of your choice.
2. Insert *computer.jpg* from the Formatting Template as a linked object to save disk space.
3. Format attractively.
4. Save as **d5-d3**; print.

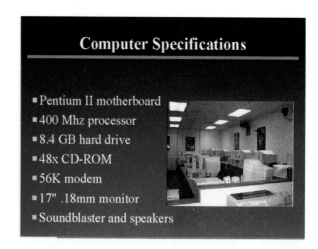

**Computer Specifications**

- Pentium II motherboard
- 400 Mhz processor
- 8.4 GB hard drive
- 48x CD-ROM
- 56K modem
- 17" .18mm monitor
- Soundblaster and speakers

# Editing Text

## FORMATTING

### Review

1. Set 1.5" side margins. DS ¶ 1.
2. Indent and single-space the last 2 ¶s.
3. Save as **46a** and print.
4. Click **Reveal Codes**.
   • Delete the DS code.
   • Delete the 1.5" margins.
   • Delete the Indent codes.
5. Print and exit without saving.

Software is at its best when it saves you time. One timesaving feature that you may want to learn about is QuickMenus. They are pop-up menus that appear when you use the right mouse button. Right-click in the text area of a document and up comes a menu that offers you some timesaving features. You can use the QuickMenus for copying and pasting text.

> Select the text to be copied. Then click the right mouse button. You are provided these options, among others: Cut, Copy, Paste, and Delete.

> To paste the text that you've cut or copied, move the insertion point to the new location; right-click again. Choose Paste from the Quick-Menu.

## NEW FUNCTION

Read about "Cut," "Paste," and "Copy," and then do Drill 1 below and Drills 2 and 3 on p. 127.

## Cut

**Cut** is used to delete blocks of text not needed. The Cut feature is preferred over using the DELETE key because the cut text remains on the Clipboard (temporary storage location) and can be retrieved once deleted. To use the Cut feature, select the text and then click the Cut button.

## Paste

**Paste** is often used with Cut to move selected text in the document. First, cut the selected text; then move the insertion point to the new location for the text; then click the Paste button. The text has now moved to the new location.

## Copy

Text can be copied from one location to another within a document using the Copy feature. The software will "copy" the text and "paste" the copy in a new location. The original copy remains in its place. If another copy is needed, click Paste again. The same text is pasted because the copied text remains on the Clipboard until new text is copied.

### Drill 1   Cut and Paste

1. Open *cutpaste*. Save as **46b-d1**.
2. Select the text beginning with the side heading "Cut and Paste" to the end of the file (two paragraphs). Click **Cut**.

3. Move the insertion point to the top of the document.
4. Click **Paste**. Press ENTER as needed to insert blank lines.

# APPLICATION

 **D16**

 *Insert screen capture on Presentations slide*

1. Open *Presentations* file *training* from the Formatting Template.
2. Animate the bulleted list to Fly In Left to Right and to display one at a time.
3. Capture the Bulleted List Properties dialog box using ALT+PRINT SCREEN. Paste it on Slide 1 to the right of the animated list.
4. Size the object and position it appropriately.
5. Save as **app–d16**. Print the slide.

# APPLICATION

**D17**

 *Create Presentations slides with objects*

1. Create the slides at the right using a slide show master of your choice.
2. Replace the text with your personal information.
3. Insert the objects as follows:
   - *Slide 3*: Embed *wpmchart* using Paste Special.
   - *Slide 4*: Embed the file *sampleflyer* or scan one of your desktop publishing projects to embed. Format attractively.

   **Optional:** For *Slide 2*: Scan your most recent diploma and insert as an object. Add additional slides as time permits.
4. Save as **app–d17**; print handout as 2x3 thumbnails.

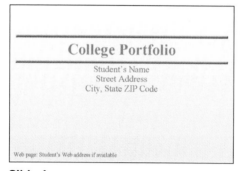

**Slide 1**

**Slide 2**

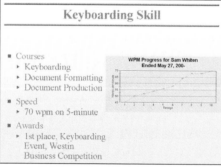

**Slide 3**

**Slide 4**

**Slide 5**

**46b,** *continued*

### Drill 2  Copy and Paste

1. Open *select.* Save as **46b-d2**.
2. Select ¶ 1 and click **Copy**.
3. Move the insertion point to the blank line below the last ¶. Click **Paste**.
4. Save and print.

### Drill 3  Copy and Paste

1. Open *copy.* Save as **46b-d3**.
2. Select the entire form. Choose **Edit** menu, **Select,** then **All**. Click **Copy**.
3. Move the insertion point below the form. Press ENTER 3 times. Click **Paste**.
4. Save and print.

---

**46c ● 10'**

**NEW FUNCTION**

### Undo and Redo

Clicking the Undo button reverses the most recent action you have taken (e.g., inserting or deleting text, bolding, changing margins). Each time the Undo button is clicked, Undo reverses the previous action.

To reverse several actions, first display a list of recent actions by choosing Undo/Redo History from the Edit menu. Then click the action you wish to reverse. However, remember that all actions above the action selected will be reversed also. Commands such as Save and Print cannot be undone.

Redo reverses the last Undo. What may have been accidentally "undone" can be reinstated. To use Redo for several actions, display the actions from the Undo/Redo History dialog box (choose Edit, Undo/Redo History).

CELLULAR PHONES

A car or cellular phone is essential in today's high-tech, fast-paced society. Secretaries, administrative support personnel, and managers are finding themselves dealing with critical, last-minute telecommunications.

Cellular phones provide safety as well as convenience. A person experiencing car trouble can solicit assistance without leaving the car. If medical assistance is needed, 911 can be called immediately.

### Drill 1

1. Key the text SS.
2. After the document is keyed, center and bold the title.
3. Save as **46c-d1**.

### Drills 2 and 3
With Drill 1 on your screen, complete Drills 2 and 3.

### Drill 2

1. Change side margins to 2".
2. Click **Undo**:
   • twice to restore default margins.
   • again to return title to left margin.
   • again to remove bold.
3. Click **Redo** 4 times; watch as it restores each function.

### Drill 3

1. Select and bold *911*. Click **Undo** to remove bold; restore the bold.
2. Select and italicize *solicit assistance.* Use Undo to remove italic; restore the italic.
3. Delete the first sentence. Use Undo to restore the sentence.

## Embed screen capture

Screen captures are easy to embed and are very useful as we develop thorough training materials or as we capture an important Web site for an electronic presentation. Consider other useful ways to use screen captures.

### To embed a screen capture:

1. Display screen or dialog box to be captured.
2. Press the PRINT SCREEN key to capture the entire screen; press ALT+PRINT SCREEN to capture a dialog box.
3. Position the insertion point where object is to be embedded. Click the **Paste** icon.

### To crop unneeded parts of the screen capture:

4. Right-click the image and click **Image Tools**.
5. Click the **Zoom** flyout, and then the **Crop Image** button.
6. Point to the image; the insertion point becomes a magnifying glass. Drag a selection frame around the portion of the image that you want to keep.

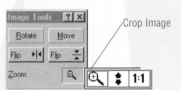
Crop Image

**APPLICATION**

*Capture dialog boxes*

1. Key the document at right; set 1.5" top margin.
2. Embed the two screen captures shown, using ALT + PRINT SCREEN.
   **Hint:** Close the dialog box before pasting the screen capture in the *WordPerfect* file.
3. Size appropriately; center.
4. Save as **app-d15**; print.

### Page Numbers

The Page Numbering command inserts the page number 1" from the top of each page. Insert the Page Numbering command on the first page of the document before any text. You may print the page number in a variety of positions. For this class, select Top Right. To avoid printing the page number on page 1, enter the Suppress command immediately following the Page Numbering command.

### To insert page numbering:

1. Position the insertion point at the beginning of the document.
2. Click **Format**, **Page**, and **Numbering**.
3. From the Position drop-down box, select *Top Right*.
4. From the Page numbering format box, click **1**. Click **OK**.

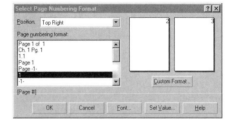

### To suppress page numbers on the first page:

1. Choose *Format*, *Page*, and *Suppress*.
2. Click the Page Numbering box to place a ✓ in the box.

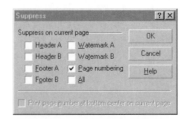

**46d ● 10'**

**N E W**

**F U N C T I O N**

**Drills 1–3**

Repeat Drills 1–3 in 46b using drag-and-drop editing.

### Drag-and-drop editing

**Drag-and-drop editing** allows selected text to be moved (same as cutting and pasting) simply by (1) selecting the desired text and (2) dragging and dropping to the new location. The mouse pointer will display a rectangle to indicate drag-and-drop editing.

To copy (or duplicate) the selected text, (1) select the text, (2) hold down the CTRL key, and (3) drag and drop using the mouse. The mouse pointer will display a rectangle with a plus sign (+) when copying.

If you should drop the text in the wrong location, click the Undo button and try again.

**46e ● 8'**

**N E W**

**F U N C T I O N**

### Window

More than one document can be open at a single time. Each document is displayed in its own window. To move from document to document, click the Window menu. The file-name of each document that is open will display. A check mark appears next to the active window. Text can be copied and pasted between documents.

#### Drill

1. Open the three drills completed in *46b*.
2. Use the Window menu to go to each document.
3. Go to *46b-d2*. Copy the document.
4. Go to the bottom of document *46b-d1*. Click **Paste**.
5. Go to the bottom of document *46b-d3*. Click **Paste**.
6. Close all documents without saving.

## VIEWS *on...* **Dress**

Appropriate dress plays an important role in the impression an employee creates with clients, customers, and other employees. To help employees judge what is *appropriate*, many companies define (in written or unwritten fashion) attire for business and for special events or days. Often companies classify attire as *business*, *business casual*, or *casual attire*.

**Business attire** is the traditional, conservative clothing worn by professional employees. For men, business attire refers to a suit or a sports coat with coordinated slacks, a tie, and dress shoes. For women, business attire refers to a suit or tailored dress with dress shoes. Often a coordinated pants suit is acceptable.

**Business casual** connotes more relaxed and less formal attire. For men, business casual refers to slacks, a shirt with a collar, and shoes with socks. Jeans, shorts, T-shirts, and sandals are not appropriate. For women, business casual usually refers to a comfortable dress, skirt and blouse, or a slacks set. "City shorts" (longer length with hose) are considered acceptable in most cases. Jeans, shorts, and T-shirts are not.

**Casual attire** refers to slacks, jeans, shorts, and other comfortable apparel worn to picnics and similar events. Good taste and a conservative approach are recommended, however.

# More Embedded and Linked Objects

 *Embed TextArt*

Review Desktop
Publishing, Module A

1. Create the announcement at the right. Use your own design or follow the one shown.
2. Using TextArt, create the band name **The Jazz Trios**.
3. Add borders and clipart. **Optional:** Search the Web for borders and clipart.
4. Save as **app-d13**; print.

**Magnolia Café**

*at the beach in Gulfport*

presents

**The Jazz Trios**

in concert on
June 11-14
9 p.m. – midnight

playing all your favorites
from the 70s, 80s, and 90s

*Thursday night only*
*Guest appearances by Randy Webber and Rich Smith*

 *Link photograph in Presentations*

1. From the Formatting Template, open the *Presentations* file *gridley*. Key the slide title and bulleted text.
2. Link object:
   a. Click **Insert**, **Object**, **Create from file**.
   b. Browse to locate *copper.jpg*. Click **Link**.
3. Size object appropriately.
4. Save as **app-d14**; print slide.

**Note:** Linking this photo saves valuable disk space.

**Adoption Agreement**

- Take animal to veterinarian within five days of adoption
- Provide food, fresh water, and shelter
- Exercise daily
- Spay or neuter within six months
- Do not sell

Gridley Humane Society

## 46f • (optional)

**Build staying power**
Take two 3' writings on all ¶s.

all letters

| | gwam | 1' | 3' |
|---|---|---|---|

In a recent show, a young skater gave a great performance.    12 | 4 | 69

Her leaps were beautiful, her spins were impossible to believe,    25 | 8 | 74

and she was a study in grace itself.   But she had slipped during    38 | 13 | 78

a jump and had gone down briefly on the ice.   Because of the high    51 | 17 | 82

quality of her act, however, she was given a third-place medal.    <u>64</u> | 21 | 87

Her coach, talking later to a reporter, stated his pleasure    12 | 25 | 91

with her part of the show.   When asked about the fall, he said    25 | 30 | 95

that emphasis should be placed on the good qualities of the per-    37 | 34 | 99

formance and not on one single blemish.   He ended by saying that    50 | 38 | 104

as long as his students did the best they could, he would be    63 | 42 | 108

satisfied.    <u>65</u> | 43 | 108

What is "best"?   When asked, the young skater explained she    12 | 47 | 112

was pleased to have won the bronze medal.   In fact, this perfor-    25 | 51 | 117

mance was a personal best for her; she was confident the gold    37 | 55 | 121

would come later if she worked hard enough.   It appears she knew    50 | 60 | 125

the way to a better medal lay in beating not other people, but her    64 | 64 | 130

own personal best.    <u>67</u> | 65 | 131

| 1' | 1 | 2 | 3 | 4 | 5 | 6 | 7 | 8 | 9 | 10 | 11 | 12 | 13 | |
|---|---|---|---|---|---|---|---|---|---|---|---|---|---|---|
| 3' | | 1 | | | 2 | | | | 3 | | | 4 | | |

## 46g • (optional)

**Practice paragraph**
1. Key the paragraph once at a comfortable speed.
2. Key one or two 1' writings at a slightly higher speed.
3. Key one or two 1' writings at a slightly lower speed for control.

              2      4      6      8      10      12
To build your skill, force your speed to higher levels.   To
   14      16      18      20      22      24
reduce errors, lower your speed and work with greater control.
   26      28      30      32      34      36
When you are being timed to measure the level of your skill,
   38      40      42      44      46      48      50
however, work at an in-between rate--somewhere between top speed
   52      54      56      58
and low-error speed.   This is the right speed.

# APPLICATION

## D10

*Embed Quattro Pro chart on Presentations slide*

Previously you embedded and linked *Quattro Pro* notebooks and charts in *WordPerfect* documents. In Application D10, you will embed a *Quattro Pro* chart on a *Presentations* slide.

1. From the Formatting Template, open:
    a. *Quattro Pro* file *message* (source).
    b. *Presentations* file *message* (client).
2. Go to the *Quattro Pro* document. Select the bar chart and click **Copy**.
3. Go to Slide 1 in *Presentations*. Embed the column chart using **Paste Special**.
4. Format the object attractively:
    a. Select the bar chart. Point to a corner handle; hold down the ALT key and drag out to enlarge it.
    b. Move the chart to center on the slide.
5. Click the **QuickPlay** view button to preview the slide. Save as **app-d10**; print the slide.

# APPLICATION

## D11

*Embed Quattro Pro file in WordPerfect document*

1. Key memo at right.
2. Embed the entire *Quattro Pro* file *videorqt* using Insert, Object.
3. Save as **app-d11**; print.

**TO:** Jim Stone

**FROM:** Mark S. Singleton

**DATE:** Current date

**SUBJECT:** Update on Image Editing Software Training Video Requests

Your predictions were certainly on target last year in the area of image editing software. Adobe Illustrator led in software training video requests. Approximately 200 requests were recorded this year in comparison to 158 in 1999. The second-highest software was QuarkXPress with 150 in 2000—that was an increase of 60 percent over 1999. The full report of image editing software training video requests is shown below.

*Embed videorqt here.*

# APPLICATION

## D12

*Link chart to Presentations slide*

1. Open *Quattro Pro* file *videorqt* and *Presentations* file *video*.
2. Link the bar chart to Slide 1.
3. Save as **app-d12a**.
4. Double-click the chart to edit it. Change C5 from 190 to **201**.
5. Save as **app-d12b** and print.

# Unbound Reports

## 47a ● 10'

### GETTING started

**Functions applied:**
- Margins
- Line spacing
- Preview (Zoom)
- Spell Check

1. Open *report* from the template. Save as **47a**.
2. Use default side margins. Position the main heading with a 1.5" top margin.
3. Change line spacing to DS.
4. Check spelling and save.
5. Preview the document before printing. It should fit on one page.

## 47b ● 40'

### FORMATTING

### Unbound report format

Read "Unbound reports" carefully and study the illustration at the right; then key Documents 1–4 as directed.

### Document 1

1. Key the model educational report on the next page.
2. Use default side margins. Position insertion point for a 1.5" top margin.
3. Set DS.
4. Key the main heading. Then select the heading and change the font size to 14 point. Bold the heading.
5. Bold side and paragraph headings.
6. Save as **47b-d1**.

### Unbound reports

Reports prepared without covers or binders are called **unbound reports**. Pages may be attached with a staple or paper clip in the upper left corner.

**Top margins:** About 1.5" for the first page; 1" for second and succeeding pages.

**Side margins:** 1" or default margins.

**Bottom margins:** Approximately 1"; last page bottom margin may be deeper.

**Font size and spacing:** Use 12-point size for readability. Double-space educational reports and indent paragraphs 0.5". Business reports are usually single-spaced; paragraphs begin at the left margin; DS between paragraphs.

**Page numbers:** The first page of a report is not numbered. The second and succeeding pages are numbered in the upper right corner.

**Headings:** Headings break a lengthy report into smaller, easy-to-understand parts. Reports will generally include side headings that are often further divided with paragraph headings. Format headings as follows:

- **Main headings:** Center title in uppercase and bold. Use 14-point size.
- **Side headings:** Begin at left margin; bold heading. Capitalize first letters of main words; DS above and below headings. Use 12-point type.
- **Paragraph headings:** Begin at the paragraph point. Use 12-point type. Bold the heading. Capitalize the first word only and follow heading with a period.

---

1.5"

**DOCUMENT FORMAT**

Effective page layout begins with the knowledge of basic document formatting guidelines. The format should enhance communication and create a consistent image.

**Page Design**

Two simple formatting features related to page layout are the use of white space and appropriate use of attributes.

**White space.** The first rule of page design is to provide adequate white space to avoid a cluttered page and to enhance reading. Formatting guides include (1) using side margins of 1" or more, (2) beginning the first page of the report 1.5" from the top edge of the paper, and (3) using appropriate line spacing.

**Attributes.** Applying various attributes such as bold, font size, and italic to text affects the physical appearance of a document. Bold adds emphasis to headings or selected words. Increasing the font size draws attention to parts of the document. Italic also adds emphasis as well as allowing the writer to follow established English rules. For example, titles of complete works can easily be italicized rather than underlined.

**Typestyle**

Another important decision of the page designer is choosing appropriate typestyles. A basic rule is to select typestyles that are appropriate to the type of communication and the audience to whom the communication is intended. A second rule is to limit typestyle changes within a document. Experts recommend using no more than two typestyles in one document.

---

# Review Embedding and Linking Objects

## APPLICATION

D9

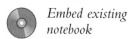

*Embed existing notebook*

1. Open the *Quattro Pro* notebook *order* from the Formatting Template. Save as **app-d9**.

2. Enter the following formulas:

    a. E4—Compute total price (qty * price). Copy the formula to *E5..E8*.

    b. E9—Click **QuickSum** for subtotal.

    c. E10—Compute 25% discount (subtotal * 25%).

    d. E11—Compute total due after discount (subtotal – discount).

3. Format as follows:

    e. *A1..E2* bold and centered across columns A-D.

    f. Center and bold column headings in Row 3.

    g. Center items in Column A.

    h. Right-align *D9:D11*.

    i. Format *D4..E4, E9,* and *E11* as Currency.

    j. Format *D5:E8* and *E10* as Comma.

4. In *WordPerfect*, key the memo shown below.

5. Position the insertion point a DS below ¶ 2.

6. Embed the notebook **app-d9**.

7. Move the embedded notebook to center in the line of writing. Save as **app-d9**; print.

| | A | B | C | D | E |
|---|---|---|---|---|---|
| 1 | ALL-SPORT COMPANY | | | | |
| 2 | Individual Order Form | | | | |
| 3 | Item | Qty | Description | Price | Total |
| 4 | 105 | 12 | Soccer lapel pin | 1.5 | |
| 5 | 110 | 12 | Poster | 3 | |
| 6 | 115 | 50 | Bumper stickers | 2 | |
| 7 | 118 | 10 | Insulated mug | 7.5 | |
| 8 | 120 | 2 | Soccer promotion video | 17.95 | |
| 9 | | | | Subtotal | |
| 10 | | | | 25% Discount | |
| 11 | | | | Total | |
| 12 | | | | | |

**Function Review**

Embed existing notebook:
**Insert, Object, Create from File**, choose file.

---

**TO:** Susan Owens, Office Manager | **FROM:** Brian Barton, Soccer Coach
**DATE:** Current date | **SUBJECT:** Request for Soccer Promotional Materials

As we discussed last week, the soccer program needs materials to promote the new team. I have reviewed the budget and determined we have approximately $200 that can be used in this area.

After contacting all local sporting goods companies, I found that the All-Sports Company is offering a 25 percent discount on sports promotional materials during June only. Please process the following order by the June 30 deadline. Details on ordering are located at www.allsports.com.

# DOCUMENT FORMAT
DS

Effective page layout begins with the knowledge of basic document formatting guidelines. The format should enhance communication and create a consistent image.
DS

Side heading → **Page Design**
DS

Two simple formatting features related to page layout are the use of white space and appropriate use of attributes.
DS

Paragraph heading → **White space**. The first rule of page design is to provide adequate white space to avoid a cluttered page and to enhance reading. Formatting guides include (1) using side margins of 1" or more, (2) beginning the first page of the report 1.5" from the top edge of the paper, and (3) using appropriate line spacing.

1"

**Attributes**. Applying various attributes such as bold, font size, and italic to text affects the physical appearance of a document. Bold adds emphasis to headings or selected words. Increasing the font size draws attention to parts of the document. Italic also adds emphasis as well as allowing the writer to follow established English rules. For example, titles of complete works can easily be italicized rather than underlined.

1"

**Typestyle**

Another important decision of the page designer is choosing appropriate typestyles. A basic rule is to select typestyles that are appropriate to the type of communication and the audience to whom the communication is intended. A second rule is to limit typestyle changes within a document. Experts recommend using no more than two typestyles in one document.

UNBOUND REPORT

*Link Quattro Pro and WordPerfect files*

In this exercise, you will open a *Quattro Pro* file with a chart and a *WordPerfect* document. You will copy and then link the chart to the word processing document. Your document will be similar to the one shown below at the right.

1. From the Formatting Template, open:
   - *WordPerfect* file *destin*.
   - *Quattro Pro* file *destin*.
2. In the *WordPerfect* document, position the insertion point a DS below ¶ 1.
3. Switch to the notebook; select the pie chart. Click **Copy**.
4. In the *WordPerfect* document, link the chart:
   - Choose *Edit, Paste Special*; then *Paste Link*.
   - Choose the *Quattro Pro 9 Chart*. Click **OK**.
5. Select, move, and size chart appropriately to center in the line of writing. Add extra hard returns to move ¶ 2 below the chart.
6. Save the *WordPerfect* document as **app-d7**. Do not save the notebook.

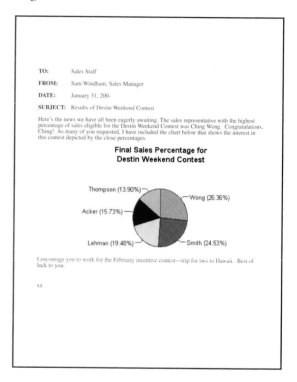

*Edit a linked file*

1. Open *app-d7*.
2. Make the following edits to the pie chart:
   - Double-click the pie chart.
   - Make B8 the active cell. Key **27000** as a change.
   - Sort by Total to sequence the sales representatives by percentage. Refer to Application D6 to review the steps.
3. Save the *WordPerfect* document as **app-d8**; save the *Quattro Pro* notebook.

| When to Embed or Link | |
|---|---|
| **Embed when** | The source document may not be available to the user. Information in one document becomes part of another document. |
| **Link when** | Data are dynamic (will change frequently), and they can be stored in a source document. |
| | Updates to the client document occur automatically. |
| | The source file is a large file, such as a video and sound clip. |

## 47b, continued

**Document 2**
1. Open *report*.
2. Position main heading at approximately 1.5".
3. Set proper line spacing.
4. Format headings correctly.
5. Edit as marked.
6. Save as **47b-d2**.

Did you check...
Paragraph alignment?
Capitalization?
Heading format?

**Document 3**
1. Open template file *heading*.
2. Edit main, side, and paragraph headings.
3. Save as **47b-d3**. Print a copy and compare it to the model on the previous page.

**Document 4**
1. Open *47b-d2*.
2. Move the section "Choosing a Typeface" above "Working with Blocks." (Use either Cut and Paste or drag-and-drop editing.)
3. Save as **47b-d4**.

WHO CAN DESIGN A BETTER BROCHURE?    7

Producing a brochure with a professional appearance    17
requires careful creativity and planning.  Not every one is    29
an accomplished paste-up artist who is capable of creating    41
a complex piece of printed art, but most skilled computer    50
users can create an attractive layout for a basic brochure.    62

Working with blocks    66

Work with copy and illustrations in blocks.  Type body    76
or text copy, leaving plenty of space for illustrations and    87
headlines.  The blocks should then be arranged in an orderly    99
and eye-appealing manner.    101

Using a small a small size type (or font) is not recommended.    112
In most cases, use a font that is 12 point or larger to    122
make the document easy to read.  Copy that is arranged in    133
more than one column is also more attractive.  Try not to key    143
copy across the full width of a page.  Preferably break the    147
page into smaller columns of copy and intersperse with photos or    160
illustrations.    163

Choosing a typeface    167

Typeface refers to the style of printing on the page.    178
Matching the style or "feeling" of the type with the purpose    190
of the finished product is very important.  For example,    202
a layout  include  of    215
you would not want to use a gothic or "old style" typeface    227
to promote a modern, high/tech product. Consider the bold-    233
ness or lightness of the style, and the readability factor, and    251
the decorativeness or simplicity. Mixing more than three    271
different typefaces on a page should also be avoided. Vary    275
the type sizes to give the effect of different type styles.    286
ital.  Bold and italics can also be added for emphasis and vari-    297
ety, especially when only one type style is being used.

## APPLICATION D5

 *Link object*

1. From the Formatting Template, open:
   - *WordPerfect* file *ranked* (client).
   - *Quattro Pro* file *gradebook* (source). Resave as **Spring 2000 gradebook**.
2. Go to the *Quattro Pro* document. Change F6 to **97**. (The change in Application D2 affected only the client document since the object was embedded.)
3. Go to the *WordPerfect* document. Position the insertion point a DS below ¶ 1.
4. Switch to the *Quattro Pro* notebook.
5. Select *A4..H10*. Click **Copy**.
6. Switch back to the *WordPerfect* document.
7. Link the object:
   - Click **Edit**, **Paste Special**.
   - Click **Paste Link**.
   - Choose *Quattro Pro 9 Notebook*. Click **OK.**
8. Select the object and drag it to the horizontal center.
9. Edit ¶ 1 with Wayne's updated average and **President's List** honor. Save the *WordPerfect* document as **app-d5**. Save the *Quattro Pro* file. How many bytes does *app-d5* contain?

## APPLICATION D6

*Edit linked document*

1. Open *app-d5*. Double-click the notebook. Note that you are automatically switched to *Quattro Pro,* the source application.

**To edit a *Quattro Pro* notebook:**

2. Make F10 the active cell. Key **92** to replace 0 and press ENTER. You have edited the *Quattro Pro* notebook in *Quattro Pro.*

**To sort a *Quattro Pro* notebook:**

> When editing a linked object, you are editing in the source document. Also, updates are made automatically in the client document. ▓

3. To move Donna's score in correct order, select *A5..H10*. Click **Tools**, **Sort**. The Sort dialog box displays.
4. In the Cells box, the block *A:A5..H10* displays. In the *Top to bottom* area, key **G5** for 1st column. Click the **Ascending** box, removing the check to place in descending order. Click **OK.**

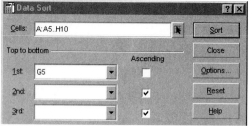

**To update a *WordPerfect* document:**

5. Switch back to the *WordPerfect* memo. Because Paste Link was used, the notebook linked in the *WordPerfect* memo has been automatically updated.
6. Edit ¶ 1 to include Donna Hoop's name and average as a Dean's List student.
7. Save memo as **app-d6**.

# Report with References

**G**ETTING
**started**

**Review hanging indent**

> Hanging Indent:
> **Format, Paragraph,
> Hanging Indent.** ▨

### SKILLBUILDING WARMUP

Dehlinger, Joyce E. "Policies to Monitor Internet Use." *Computer Weekly*, April 1998, p. 34.

DePriest, J. Shannon. "WWW Citations." *Graduate Education Journal.* Spring 1998. <http://www.gej.edu/citations/wwwcitations.htm> (23 July 1998).

Shaffer, Helen. *Guidelines for Effective Use of Electronic Mail.* New York: Concord International Press, Inc., 1999.

**48b • 12'**

**NEW
FUNCTION**

## Hard page break

When a page is filled with copy, the software automatically inserts a *soft page break*, which is indicated by a solid gray line across the screen. The status line will indicate that the insertion point is on the next page. Reveal Codes shows a soft page break as [SPg].

You may need to begin a new page, however, before the page is filled. To insert a **hard page break**, press CTRL + ENTER. *WordPerfect* inserts a black line across the screen and moves the insertion point to the next page; the status line at the bottom of the screen indicates this change. Reveal Codes shows a hard page break as [HPg]. A hard page break will not move as text is inserted or deleted.

To remove a hard page break, delete the code from the Reveal Codes screen.

**Drill**

1. Key the text for Goal 1 at right, using the Indent command.

2. Insert a hard page break between 1st and 2d goal.

3. Continue keying page 2.

4. Save and print.

> Indent: **Format,
> Paragraph, Indent.** ▨

### GOAL 1: MEMBERSHIP DEVELOPMENT

**Objective: To increase membership.**

Indent ⟶ **Plan**

    A. ᵀᵃᵇ Review and evaluate membership benefits.
    B.    Study avenues for additional membership benefits.
    C.    Develop new membership markets.

*Insert page break.*

### GOAL 2: STAFF DEVELOPMENT

**Objective: To enhance performance and motivation of staff.**

Indent ⟶ **Plan**

    A. ᵀᵃᵇ Review and evaluate previous staff development programs.
    B.    Survey staff to determine needs.
    C.    Implement relevant staff development program.

**Note:** Pressing Tab after keying **A.** will turn on the QuickNumbers feature and cause the next letter to appear when you press ENTER. Backspace to delete unwanted letters.

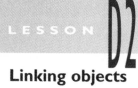

LESSON D2

**Linking objects**

# Link Objects

**Linked objects** are stored as a field code in the client application. For example, when a *Quattro Pro* notebook is linked to a *WordPerfect* document, the notebook is stored only as a code in the *WordPerfect* document. A display of the *Quattro Pro* notebook is seen in *WordPerfect;* however, the *notebook is linked—not stored* in the *WordPerfect* document. A file that is linked requires less disk space than a file that is embedded.

Linking is very useful when data are dynamic or change frequently. By linking the notebook in this example, the *WordPerfect* document is updated automatically when a change is made in the *Quattro Pro* notebook. The chart within the memo below is linked to the notebook.

**Notebook file**

**Compound document**

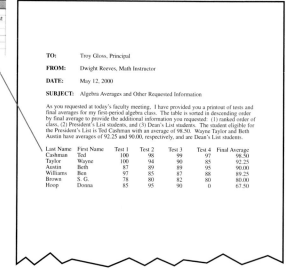

When a file is linked, a change to either the source document or the compound document updates the other file.

**To link an object:**

1. Open the source document and its application and the client document and its application. Position the insertion point in the client document where you want to link the object.

2. In the source document, select and copy the information to be linked.

3. In the client document, link the object:

   • Click **Edit**, **Paste Special**.

   • From the Paste Special dialog box, click **Paste Link**.

   • In the As box, select the appropriate object. Click **OK.**

4. Select the object for moving and sizing.

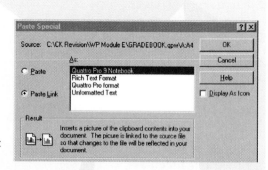

## Unbound report with references

Read "Report documentation." Key and format the document on the next page.

### Report documentation

Reports must include the sources of all information included in the report. Within the report, the writer uses footnotes, endnotes, or internal citations to cite sources. A complete list of references is included at the end of the report.

### Internal citations

Internal citations are an easy and practical method of documentation. The last name of the author(s), the publication date, and the page number(s) of the cited material are shown in parentheses within the body of the report (Gholston, 1999, 134). This information cues a reader to the name Gholston in the references listed at the end of the report.

Short direct quotations of three lines or fewer are enclosed within quotation marks. Long quotations of four lines or more are indented from the left margin and single-spaced. If a portion of the text referenced is omitted, use an ellipsis (…) to show the omission.

### List of references

References cited in the report are listed at the end of the report in alphabetical order by authors' last names. The reference list may be titled REFERENCES or BIBLIOGRAPHY.

Become familiar with the three types of references listed below:
- A book reference includes the name of the author (inverted), book title (italicized), city of publication, publisher, and copyright date.
- A magazine reference shows the name of the author (inverted), article (in quotation marks), magazine title (italicized), date of publication, and page references.
- A reference retrieved electronically includes the name of the author (inverted), article (in quotation marks), publication (italicized), publication information, Internet address (in brackets), and date the document was retrieved or accessed.

If the entire reference section does not fit at the bottom of the last page, insert a hard page break and position the entire reference section on the next page. Use the same margins as the first page of the report, and number the page at the top right. Single-space references in hanging indent format. DS between references.

If references are keyed on the last page of the report, separate them from the body of the report with a DS.

---

1.5"

### THE REFERENCE LIST

When a report has been prepared, a list of references is often provided to clarify and/or support statements made in the report, to cite sources, and to give the reader an opportunity to read more on the topic. Conventions for references vary somewhat depending on the reference manual that is used. Two popular style manuals are *A Manual for Writers of Term Papers, Theses, and Dissertations* and the *Publication Manual of the American Psychological Association*. A valuable Website for referencing formats is http://www.utexas.edu/depts/uwc/.html/citation.html.

The sample reference format shown at the end of this report illustrates various types of references, including books, magazines, and electronic citations. Note that references are (1) arranged alphabetically, usually by last name of author, (2) formatted in hanging indent style, and (3) single-spaced with a double space between each reference item.

To format references for documents retrieved electronically, Lehman, Dufrene, Himstreet, and Baty (1999, B-9) offer the following guidelines:

The various referencing styles are fairly standardized as to the elements included when citing documents retrieved electronically. . . . Include the following items: author (if given), date of publication, title of article and/or name of publication, electronic medium (such as on-line or CD-ROM), volume, series, page, and path (Uniform Resource Locator or Internet address) and date you retrieved or accessed the resource.

If the entire list of references does not fit at the bottom of the last page of the report, position them on the following page. However, if all references fit on the last page of the report, separate the body of the report from the references with a DS.

---

1.5"

### REFERENCES

Altese, Rachel M. "Referencing Electronic Documents." *Multimedia Quarterly*. April 1999, pp. 45–51.

DePriest, J. Shannon. "WWW Citations." *Graduate Education Journal*. (Spring, 1998): <http://www.gej.edu/citations/wwwcitations.htm> (23 July 1998).

Lehman, C. M., D. D. Dufrene, W. C. Himstreet, and W. M. Baty. *Business Communication*. 12th ed. Cincinnati, OH: South-Western Educatinoal Publishing, 1999.

Thompson, John D. <jdt3@.umt.edu>. "Electronic Citations Update." E-mail to Matthew P. Crowson (mpcrowson@umt.edu) (23 January 1999).

## Embed new Quattro Pro worksheet

You can embed a new *Quattro Pro* spreadsheet into a *WordPerfect* document. Application D4 provides practice inserting a spreadsheet. It is important to note that the spreadsheet is embedded automatically.

**APPLICATION**

*Insert Quattro Pro spreadsheet*

1. Open the *WordPerfect* file *slsrmemo* from the Formatting Template.
2. Position insertion point a DS below ¶ 1.
3. Click **Insert, Object Create New**. Close *Quattro Pro 9 Notebook*. Click **OK**. A *Quattro Pro* spreadsheet displays in the *WordPerfect* document. Toolbars change to *Quattro Pro* toolbars.
4. Enlarge the spreadsheet as needed by dragging down the bottom center handle on the spreadsheet.

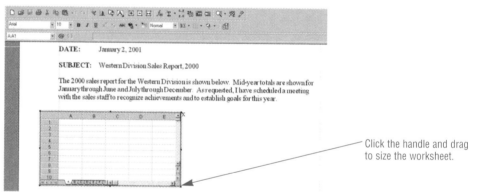

Click the handle and drag to size the worksheet.

5. Key the information in the table below. Leave Row 2 blank. Key **Total** in D3.
6. Compute totals: Select *D4:D7*. Click **QuickSum**. Select *B8:D8*. Click **QuickSum**.
7. Select *A3:D8;* click **Format, SpeedFormat**. Choose *Basic 4*; click **OK**.
8. Point mouse outside spreadsheet and click *WordPerfect* document. Select spreadsheet. Drag spreadsheet to center horizontally on page.
9. Deselect the worksheet; save as **app-d4** and print.

Should you need to edit the spreadsheet after de-selecting it, double-click the spreadsheet. *Quattro Pro* toolbars will display.

### WESTERN DIVISION SALES REPORT, 2000

| Sales Staff | Jan-Jun | Jul-Dec |
|---|---|---|
| Anthony, Sam | 78564 | 75003 |
| Fowler, Julie | 96541 | 95544 |
| Lee, Wanda | 85647 | 84551 |
| Smith, Steve | 99871 | 98752 |
| Total | | |

## THE REFERENCE LIST
DS

1. DS the unbound report.
2. SS the quote, indenting from the left margin.
3. Insert a hard page break before the reference section since the references will not all fit on the first page. At this point, you have not learned to number pages, so do not number the second page.
4. Use Spell Checker.
5. Save as **48c.**
6. View the document and check format before printing.

When a report has been prepared, a list of references is often pro-    17
vided to clarify and/or support statements made in the report, to cite    31
sources, and to give the reader an opportunity to read more on the topic.    46
Conventions for references vary somewhat depending on the reference    60
manual that is used. Two popular style manuals are *A Manual for Writers*    75
*of Term Papers, Theses, and Dissertations* and the *Publication Manual of the*    89
*American Psychological Association.* A valuable Web site for referencing    103
formats is http://www.utexas.edu/depts/uwc/.html/citation.html.    117

The sample reference format shown at the end of this report illustrates    131
various types of references, including books, magazines, and electronic    145
citations. Note that references are (1) arranged alphabetically, usually by    161
last name of author, (2) formatted in hanging indent style, and (3) single-    176
spaced with a double space between each reference item.    187

To format references for documents retrieved electronically, Lehman,    201
Dufrene, Himstreet, and Baty (1999, B-9) offer the following guidelines:    216

The various referencing styles are fairly standardized as to the    229
elements included when citing documents retrieved electronically. . . .    241
Include the following items: author (if given), date of publication, title    258
of article and/or name of publication, electronic medium (such as on-    273
line or CD-ROM), volume, series, page, and path (Uniform Resource    286
Locator or Internet address) and date you retrieved or accessed the    300
resource.    302

If the entire list of references does not fit at the bottom of the last page    317
of the report, position them on the following page. However, if all references    333
fit on the last page of the report, separate the body of the report from the    348
references with a DS.    353

## REFERENCES    355
DS

Altese, Rachel M. "Referencing Electronic Documents." *Multimedia*    368
*Quarterly,* April 1999, pp. 45–51.    375
Journal →
DS

DePriest, J. Shanon. "WWW Citations." *Graduate Education Journal.*    390
Spring 1998. <http://www.gej.edu/citations/wwwcitations.htm>    402
(23 July 1998).    406
Online Journal →
DS

Lehman, C. M., D. D. Dufrene, W. C. Himstreet, and W. M. Baty.    419
*Business Communication.* 12th ed. Cincinnati, OH: South-Western    432
Educational Publishing, 1999.    438
Book →
DS

Thompson, John D. <jdt3@umt.edu>. "Electronic Citations Update."    452
E-mail to Matthew P. Crowson <mpcrowson@umt.edu> (23 January    464
1999).    465
E-mail →

*Edit embedded objects*

To edit the *Quattro Pro* notebook embedded in a *WordPerfect* document, double-click the embedded notebook. The *Quattro Pro* toolbars replace the *WordPerfect* toolbars for your use in editing the notebook.

1. Open *app-d1*.

2. Double-click the embedded notebook. Note the *WordPerfect* toolbars are replaced with the *Quattro Pro* toolbars.

3. Make F6 the active cell. Key **97** and press ENTER. You have changed the 85 to 97 in the *Quattro Pro* notebook while in the *WordPerfect* document.

4. Deselect the notebook by clicking off to the right of the notebook. Note the *WordPerfect* toolbars are now displayed.

5. Edit ¶ 1 with Wayne's updated average and President's List honor. Save as **app-d2**.

*Editing can be done only for the three students' grades that had been embedded in the WordPerfect memo. The edits you made in the client document do not affect the source document.*

6. Open *gradebook* from the Formatting Template. Note that the score for Test 4 is still 85.

## Embed existing object

Another way to embed objects is to create an object from an existing file. You will choose Object from the Insert menu. The Create from file tab will allow you to browse for the appropriate file to be embedded. Because often the object (or file) already exists, it is very simple to embed the object created from another application, e.g., *Quattro Pro* spreadsheet embedded in *WordPerfect* document or on *Presentations* slide.

 *Embed existing Quattro pro spreadsheet*

1. Open the *WordPerfect* file *cellular* from the Formatting Template.

2. Position insertion point a DS below ¶ 2.

3. Click **Insert**, then **Object**. Select *Create from File*.

4. In the File name entry box, enter the filename **newcomer.qpw** or click **Browse** to locate the file. Click **OK**.

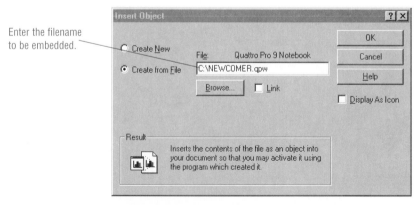

Enter the filename to be embedded.

5. Save as **app-d3** (*WordPerfect* document).

# Two-Page Reports

## GETTING started

Use the drill lines in 45a, p. 123, to get started.

### 49b ● 5'

## FORMATTING

### Two-page reports

Read "Two-page reports." Use the steps for formatting a two-page report after you learn to insert page numbers and use Widow/Orphan and Block protect in 49c and 49d.

### Two-page reports

The report format is widely used in various environments. Some basic considerations are:

- **Side margins**: Set according to binding.
- **Top margin**: 1.5" for first page of report, preliminary pages, reference page; 1" on other pages.
- **Page numbers**: Include page numbers for the second and succeeding pages of a report. Page numbers should be positioned in the right top margin.
- **Single lines:** Avoid single lines at the top or bottom of a report (called *widow/orphan lines*). Do not separate between pages a side heading from the paragraph that follows.

### Formatting a report

1. Turn on Widow/Orphan protection.
2. Insert *Page Numbering* command.
3. Suppress the page number on page 1.
4. Position the insertion point for an approximate 1.5" top margin.
5. Change line spacing to DS.
6. Key and center the main heading. Select the heading and apply 14-point font, bold.
7. Key the entire report, including Reference section. Bold headings.
8. Protect side headings that may get separated from the related paragraph with the Block protect feature.
9. If the references must be formatted on a separate page, insert a hard page break. Position the heading REFERENCES at 1.5".
10. Use Zoom to preview the report before printing.

---

1.5" ▼

**THE PROFESSIONAL TOUCH**

Although its contents are of ultimate importance, a finished report's looks are of almost equal importance. If it is to achieve the goal for which it was written, every report, whether it serves a business or academic purpose, should be acceptable from every point of view.

**Citations, for Example**

No matter which format is used for citations, a good writer knows citations are inserted for the reader's benefit; therefore, anything the writer does to ease their use will be appreciated and will work on the writer's behalf. Standard procedures, such as those stated below, make readers comfortable.

Italicize titles of complete publications; use quotation marks with parts of publications. Thus, the name of a magazine is italicized, but the title of an article within the magazine is placed in quotation marks. Months and certain locational words used in the citations may be abbreviated if necessary (Mayr, 2000, 13).

**And the Final Report**

The final report should have an attractive, easy-to-read look.

The report should meet the criteria for spacing, citations, and binding that have been established for its preparation. "Such criteria are set up by institutional decree, by generally accepted standards, or by subject demands" (Chung, 1999, 27). A writer should discover limits within which he or she must write and should observe those limits with care.

---

2

**In Conclusion**

Giving the report a professional appearance calls for skill and patience from a writer. First impressions count when preparing reports. Poorly presented materials are not read, or at least not read with an agreeable attitude.

**REFERENCES**

Chung, Olin. *Reports and Formats.* Cedar Rapids: Gar Press, Inc., 1999.

Hull, Brenda, and Muriel Myers. *Writing Reports and Dissertations.* 5th ed. New York: Benjamin Lakey Press, 1999.

Mayr, Polly. "Styles/Formats/Computers." *Business Weekly,* June 2000, p. 13.

## Embed objects using Paste Special

One of the easiest ways to embed an object is to use the **Paste Special** feature from the **Edit** menu. This method requires that both the source and client documents be open. The object is copied from the source document and pasted into the client document using Paste Special. The object becomes part of the client document and can be edited using the tool-bars of the source application.

### To embed an object:

Switch between documents: Click the application tab on the Status bar.

1. Open the two software application programs of the source document and the client document (such as *Quattro Pro* and *WordPerfect*). Open both the client document and the source document. Position the insertion point where you want to embed the object in the client document.

2. In the source document, select and copy the information to be embedded.

3. In the client document, embed the object:
   - On the Edit menu, click **Paste Special**.
   - In the Paste Special dialog box, click **Paste**.
   - In the As box, select the appropriate object being embedded. Click **OK.**

4. Select the object and then move and size the object appropriately.

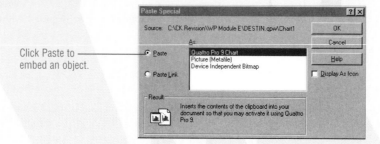

Click Paste to embed an object.

## APPLICATION

*Embed a Quattro Pro notebook in a WordPerfect document*

1. From the Formatting Template, open:
   - *WordPerfect* file *list* (client).
   - *Quattro Pro* file *gradebook* (source).

2. Position the insertion point a DS below ¶ 1 in the *WordPerfect* document.

3. Switch to the *Quattro Pro* notebook.

4. Select range *A4..H7* and copy it.

5. Switch back to the *WordPerfect* document.

6. Embed the object:
   - Paste special the object (**Edit, Paste Special**).
   - From the dialog box, click **Paste.**
   - Choose *Quattro Pro 9 Notebook*. Click **OK.**

|   | A | B | C | D | E | F | G | H |
|---|---|---|---|---|---|---|---|---|
| 5 | Last Name | First Name | Test 1 | Test 2 | Test 3 | Test 4 | Average | Honors |
| 6 | Cashman | Ted | 100 | 98 | 99 | 97 | 98.50 | President's List |
| 7 | Taylor | Wayne | 100 | 94 | 90 | 85 | 92.25 | Dean's List |
| 8 | Austin | Beth | 87 | 89 | 89 | 95 | 90.00 | Dean's List |
| 9 | Williams | Ben | 97 | 85 | 87 | 88 | 89.25 | |
| 10 | Brown | S. G. | 78 | 80 | 82 | 80 | 80.00 | |
| 11 | Hoop | Donna | 85 | 95 | 90 | 0 | 67.50 | |
| 12 | | | | | | | | |
| 13 | Average for each test | | 91.17 | 90.17 | 89.50 | 74.17 | | |
| 14 | No. taking test | | 6 | 6 | 6 | 6 | | |
| 15 | Minimum test score | | 78 | 80 | 82 | 0 | | |
| 16 | Maximum test score | | 100 | 98 | 99 | 97 | | |
| 17 | | | | | | | | |

DATE: May 12, 200-

SUBJECT: Algebra Students Eligible for President's and Dean's Lists

As you requested at today's faculty meeting, I have listed below the students in my algebra class who are eligible for the President's and Dean's lists. Ted Cashman has a 98.50 average and qualifies for the President's List. Wayne Taylor and Beth Austin have averages of 92.25 and 90.00 respectively, and both qualify for the Dean's List.

Embed the spreadsheet file here.

7. Select the object and move it to center it in the line of writing.

8. Save the *WordPerfect* document as **app-d1.** Do not save the *Quattro Pro* file again.

**49c ● 7'**

NEW
FUNCTION

**Drill**

1. Open *48c* from your storage disk.

2. Insert *Page Numbering*.

3. Suppress the page number on page 1.

4. Preview the document to verify page numbers.

5. Save as **49c** and print.

## Page Numbering and Suppress

The **Page Numbering** command inserts the page number on each page. Insert Page Numbering on the first page of the document. You may print the page number in a variety of positions. For this class, select Top Right to print the page number 1" from the top. To avoid printing the page number on page 1, enter the Suppress command immediately following the Page Numbering command.

### To insert Page Numbering:

1. Position the insertion point at the beginning of the document.

2. Click **Format** menu, **Page,** then **Numbering.**

3. Choose position and format preferences; click **Top Right,** then **OK.**

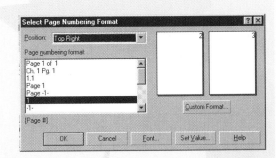

### To use Suppress:

1. Choose **Format** menu, **Page,** and **Suppress**.

2. Click **Page Numbering**, then **OK**.

**49d ● 8'**

NEW
FUNCTION

Read the information at the right and on p. 138.

**Drill**

1. Open *proftch*. Save as **49d**.

2. Apply *Widow/Orphan*.

3. Insert page numbers. Suppress the page number on the first page.

4. Select the heading "In Conclusion" and the ¶ that follows. Apply *Block protect*.

5. Correctly format headings.

6. Use Zoom to verify page numbers and margins.

7. Save and print. Compare your document to the model on p. 136.

## Keep Text Together

Pagination (breaking pages at appropriate locations) can be controlled easily using two features: Widow/Orphan and Block protect.

- **Widow/Orphan** prevents a single line of a paragraph from printing at the bottom or top of a page. Always apply this control at the top of a multipage document.
- **Block protect** prevents selected text from being divided across two pages. Use this function when a side heading approaches the bottom of a page to prevent the heading from being left alone.

### To use Widow/Orphan:

1. Position the insertion point at the start of the document.

2. Click **Format** menu, then **Keep Text Together**.

3. Click the *Widow/Orphan* box and **OK**.

### To use Block protect:

1. Select the side heading and the paragraph that follows.

2. Click the *Block protect* box and **OK**. The side heading moves to the next page along with the paragraph.

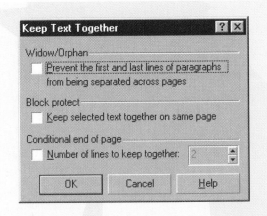

# Embed Objects

A **compound document** is a document composed of text or data from one application along with text, data, graphics, or sound from another application. The information created in the other application is called an **object**. The compound document shown below illustrates a *Quattro Pro* spreadsheet as an embedded object in a *WordPerfect* document.

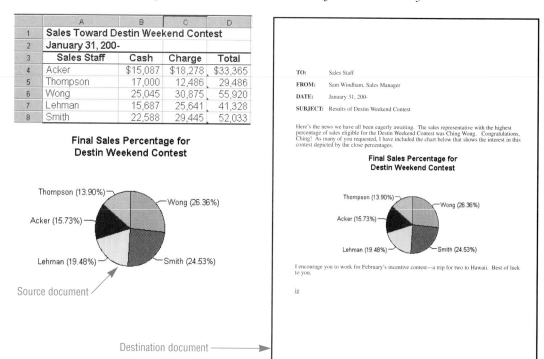

Source document

Destination document

A **compound document** includes an object from another application.

The application in which the object is created is called the source application, and the document is the **source document**. The object is placed in a **client document**, which is located in another application. In the illustration, the source document is the *Quattro Pro* spreadsheet, and the client document is the memo created in *WordPerfect*. The compound document includes the memo with the embedded spreadsheet object.

Embedded objects become part of the client document. The size of the client document does increase because the object (*Quattro Pro* spreadsheet) is stored in the client document (*WordPerfect* memo). If the object in the client document is edited, the edit only affects the client document, not the source document. (The original file does not change.)

This lesson presents three easy ways to embed a *Quattro Pro* spreadsheet in a *WordPerfect* document.

- Use the Paste Special feature from the Edit menu.
- Embed an existing worksheet.
- Insert a new *Quattro Pro* spreadsheet.

In future lessons in this module, you will share objects among other applications, including *WordPerfect*, *Quattro Pro*, and *Presentations*.

## FORMATTING

**Two-page report with references**

1. Place the insertion point at the beginning of the document.
2. Apply *Widow/Orphan.*
3. Insert *Page Numbering.*
4. Suppress the page number on the first page.
5. Key the report DS.
6. Use Zoom to verify page numbers.
7. Save as **49e** and print.

Are references keyed on the second or third page?

## SOME PEOPLE YOU CAN'T LIVE WITHOUT

Are you looking for a career that will challenge you to use your mind and skills and one that will give you rich and varied rewards? Some people we absolutely cannot live without today are health care professionals. As a health care professional, you're part of something needed, something special, something exciting, and something respected.

### Shortage of Health Care Workers

Rumors regarding a surplus of nurses have periodically circulated. A study of the employment market shows that in the last 20 years three periods of time have occurred when we have experienced a shortage of nurses! The surplus that some speak of occurs because of hiring freezes and cutbacks. Each time the economy picked up and employers began hiring, the surplus quickly became a shortage.

The underlying demand for allied health practitioners is greater now than ever before. Increasing numbers of people are living longer, and as the population grows older, the need and demand for quality health care grows (Elliott, 1999, 64). Political leaders are talking about national health insurance and making health care available for all Americans. Due to the fact that health care is a national priority, it is a growth industry.

### Skills Required

Health care workers must possess skills in the following areas: command of the English language, including written and oral communication skills; computer skills; conflict resolution; supervision/delegation of tasks; and knowledge of cultural diversity (Sabella, 1999, 42). Fluency in more than one language is a valuable asset. Medical professionals must be willing to continually improve their knowledge and skills and stay current of the latest technological developments in the field.

### REFERENCES

Elliott, Thomas A. "A Career in Allied Health." *National Occupational Projection Handbook.* Chicago: Chicago-Versaille Press, 1999.

Sabella, Irene C. "Make a Difference with Your Life." *Health Professionals in the Year 2000.* Ann Arbor: Alexandria Press, 1999.

20
34
48
63
76

83

95
108
122
136
149
162
175
189
203
217
231
245
250

254

267
280
293
308
322
336
350
353

355

369
382

394
408

# COMPOUND DOCUMENTS

**D**

*module*

## OVERVIEW

Your diligent work through the earlier modules in this book has prepared you now for the integrated activities presented in Module D. Remember that productivity is a key factor for the user who truly desires to utilize the capabilities of his/her computer system.

In Module D, you will understand how organizations benefit by sharing information among applications and users. You will also produce compound documents that combine various software applications. For example,

- A *Quattro Pro* pie chart created by the financial department is linked by another user to a *Corel Presentations* slide show.

- A *Quattro Pro* spreadsheet is embedded in a report created in *WordPerfect*.

- A TextArt design is embedded in a *WordPerfect* table.

- A screen capture is embedded and cropped attractively in a *Presentations* slide or training manual created in *WordPerfect*.

- A photograph is linked to a *Presentations* slide to save disk space.

Enjoy the activities in this module. Focus on the effectiveness of creating compound documents that utilize the capabilities of the entire *WordPerfect Office* suite and more.

# Two-Page Report with Title Page

## 50a • 7'

### GETTING started

each line twice; DS between groups

alphabet 1 Dave Cagney alphabetized items for next week's quarterly journal.

figures 2 Close Rooms 4, 18, and 20 from 3 until 9 on July 7; open Room 56.

up reaches 3 Toy & Wurt's note for $635 (see our page 78) was paid October 29.

easy 4 The auditor is due by eight, and he may lend a hand to the panel.

| 1 | 2 | 3 | 4 | 5 | 6 | 7 | 8 | 9 | 10 | 11 | 12 | 13 |

## 50b • (optional)

### SKILLBUILDING

**Build staying power**
Take a 3' writing.

all letters

gwam 1' | 3'

When you write, how does the result portray you? Some of us    12  4  38

seem to take on some unique personality when we write. We forget    25  8  42

writing is just another way of talking, and what we write may    38  13  47

project an image that is not natural. Some writers, on the other    51  17  51

hand, try to humanize what they write so that it extends genuine    64  22  56

warmth and makes one want to read it. Apparently, correct format    77  26  60

and language, common sense, and some idea that a writer is still    90  30  64

among the living can add up to be very fine writing.    101  34  68

1' | 1 | 2 | 3 | 4 | 5 | 6 | 7 | 8 | 9 | 10 | 11 | 12 | 13 |
3' |   1   |     2     |     3     |     4     |

## 50c • 5'

**Review**
Key the first two lines of the report DS. Change to SS. Indent. Press TAB to indent the first line of the ¶ an additional 0.5".

Review Indent:
**Format, Paragraph, Indent.**

attention be paid to the application, implementation, and administration of communication within a business venture.

Indent    Effective communication results when information is transmitted from a sender to a receiver, and the message is understood. It is not necessary that the message result in any specific outcome, only that it be sent, received, and understood (Higgason, 1999, 39).

# Activity
## twenty

### Scholarship for exchange student

**Setting:** Your school offers one-semester exchange programs in the following international cities: Budapest, Hungary; Florence, Italy; and Seville, Spain. You have been selected to receive a scholarship to participate in one of the programs. The scholarship provides transportation to and from the city, tuition, dormitory-type housing, and a meal ticket for breakfast and lunch.

**Problem:** The exchange program requires you to research the city and country you plan to visit and present an *acceptable* three- to five-page paper, which includes the following topics:

**Overview**—General information about the country, the city, the type of government, and the people.

**Culture**—General information about the customs, traditions, and behavioral expectations.

**Environment**—General information about the weather, type of clothing required, food, transportation, and other related information that would influence living conditions.

**Educational enhancement**—General information about things and places you should visit while you are in the city to enhance your educational experience.

**Budget**—Use a spreadsheet to prepare a budget for expenses that you expect to incur beyond those provided by the scholarship. Insert a hyperlink in the paper to the budget you prepared.

**Sources of information**—Prepare a list of at least ten Web sites from which you obtained information.

**Outcomes:** Complete the research required above and prepare the paper. Remember that the quality of the paper is the final criteria for obtaining the scholarship. Be sure to edit the paper carefully and to format it in appropriate style. You want it to have an especially good appearance. Use clipart and other graphic enhancements to present a good image.

**50d ● 23'**

FORMATTING    **Two-page report with direct quotations**    Review steps for "Formatting a report" in
Apply the skills you have learned so far.    49b, p. 136, if necessary.

words

## COMMUNICATION: KEY TO BUSINESS SUCCESS

5
8

Probably no successful enterprise exists that does not rely for its success upon the ability of its members to communicate with each other and with third parties. The role that effective communication plays in business success cannot be stressed too strongly; it is essential that strict attention be paid to the application, implementation, and administration of communication within a business venture.

15
24
33
39
48
56
65
74
81
90

Effective communication results when information is transmitted from a sender to a receiver, and the message is understood. It is not necessary that the message result in any specific outcome, only that it be sent, received, and understood (Higgason, 1999, 39).

96
103
110
117
125
133
140
143

Business communication falls into two main categories: written and verbal. More time is spent by most business firms studying and perfecting their written communications. It is verbal communication, however, that makes up a major portion of all communication and deserves more attention than is typically the case. "Successful businesses have long known the importance of good verbal communication, yet many of them still give written communication greater emphasis" (Catlette, 1999, 29).

150
159
166
175
183
191
199
207
215
223
231
239
242

Written communication confirms facts and intentions, and any important verbal conversation should be confirmed in writing. Written communication also constitutes proof; a letter signature can have the same effect as a contract signature. Further, written communications can be retained

249
257
265
272
281
291
300

words

for later reference, affirmation being as close as a hard copy in a file folder or an electronic file on a computer server. Written communication avoids some of the natural barriers of verbal communication. Shyness, speech problems, and other distractions are not found in a written document.

310
320
329
339
347
356
359

Since verbal communication often involves encounters on a one-on-one basis, it can bring quicker results. Misunderstandings are avoided; questions are answered. It is usually less formal and friendlier; moods, attitudes, and emotions are more easily handled. Verbal communication is augmented with facial expressions and gestures, assuring greater clarity of the message. Words and phrases can be given special emphasis not possible in a written message, where emphasis is given by the receiver, not the sender.

368
377
387
396
405
414
424
433
442
451
461
463

Schaefer points out the importance of communication:

470
474

Make no mistake; both written and verbal communication are the stuff upon which success is built. . . . Both forms deserve careful study by any business that wants to grow. Successful businesspeople must read, write, speak, and listen with skill (Schaefer, 1998, 28).

480
488
496
504
512
521
528

## REFERENCES

530

Catlette, Darby. *Communicating Effectively in the Next Millennium.* San Francisco: Thomas Publishers, Inc., 1999.

540
547
554

Higgason, Carol. "The Art of Communicating in Business." *New Age Magazine*, July 1999, pp. 39-43.

563
572
574

Schaefer, Adam. "Tools for Executive Success." *Executive Minutes.* 1998. <http://www.en. edu/executivenews/ToolsforExecutive Success.htm> (19 May 1998).

584
592
600
605

# APPLICATION

Key the invoice at right. Fit cells appropriately. Follow specific directions provided below.

1. In A2, enter Date function and format as MM-DD-YY.
2. Center titles over Columns A–D.
3. In D5, enter the formula to compute total costs. Copy down to other items.
4. Use QuickSum to compute subtotal.
5. In D10, enter the formula to compute 7% sales tax. Format as number with 2 decimal places.
6. In D11, enter the formula to compute total. Format D11 as $.
7. Save as **app-c13**.

|  | A | B | C | D |
|---|---|---|---|---|
| 1 | Invoice for Weston Construction Company | | | |
| 2 | | | | |
| 3 | | | | |
| 4 | Quantity | Description | Unit Price | Total |
| 5 | 1 | Fax machine 930-23 | 525.00 | |
| 6 | 2 | Color inkjet printer | 249.99 | |
| 7 | 2 | Laser printer | 499.00 | |
| 8 | 3 | Color scanner | 199.99 | |
| 9 | Subtotal | | | |
| 10 | 7% tax | | | |
| 11 | Total | | | |

# APPLICATION

*Bar chart embedded on spreadsheet*

1. Open the spreadsheet *computer* shown at right. Save as **app-c14**.
2. Select cells to create the chart.
3. Create a bar chart and embed it on the spreadsheet.
   a. Main title: **New Computer Installations**
   b. Chart subtitle: **by Quarter 2000**
   c. X-axis title: **Sales Representative**
   d. Y-axis title: **Number**
4. Edit chart title attractively.

### New Computer Installations by Quarter, 2000

|  | Qtr 1 | Qtr 2 | Qtr 3 | Qtr 4 | Legend |
|---|---|---|---|---|---|
| Campbell | 25 | 30 | 32 | 35 | |
| Mylroie | 20 | 25 | 18 | 21 | |
| Neely | 22 | 20 | 21 | 25 | |
| Koehn | 10 | 12 | 15 | 12 | |
| Zismann | 15 | 18 | 20 | 17 | |

# APPLICATION

*Insert data labels and edit pie chart*

1. Open the spreadsheet *installations* from the Formatting Template. Save as **app-c15**. Activate the pie chart.
2. Change data labels to 14 point.
3. Add the chart titles:
   Main title: **Percentages of New Computer**
   Subtitle: **Installations by Sales Reps, 2000**
4. Format chart title using a custom border, colored background, and white text.
5. **Challenge:** Format chart area by selecting a color.

## 50e ● 12'

FORMATTING

### Title page/center
#### Document 1
1. Format the title page shown for an unbound report; use bold and key in 14 point.
2. Center the page vertically.
3. Preview before printing.

#### Document 2
Prepare a title page for the unbound report completed in 50d. Prepared for **National Commerce Bank**. Prepared by: **Teresa DuChaine, Manager**. Save as **50e-d2**.

---

**Function review**

Center Align:
Center Page: **Format, Page, Center, Current Page.** ■

---

#### Document 3
#### Challenge activity
1. Enhance the appearance of the title page prepared in Document 2 by adding a border with shading. Follow the directions at right.
2. Choose single line border (3rd option).
3. Choose 10% fill (3rd option).

### Title page/center
The title page should convey to the reader a concise title that identifies the report. A **title page** includes the title of the report, the name and title of the individual or organization for whom the report was prepared, the name and title of the writer, and the date the report was completed.

Center items on a title page horizontally. Vertical placement depends on the amount of copy contained on the title page. The information should be positioned so that it is attractive and easy to read.

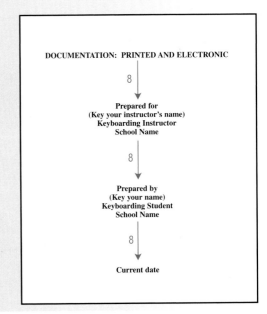

**To use Page Border/Fill:**
1. Click **Format** menu, **Page, Border/Fill.**
2. On the **Border** tab, choose the style and type of border desired. Click **Apply.**
3. Click the **Fill** tab. Choose the desired style.
4. Click **Apply,** then **OK.**

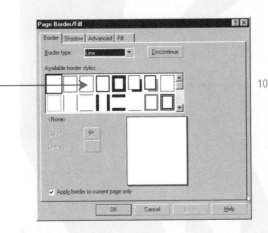 Single line border

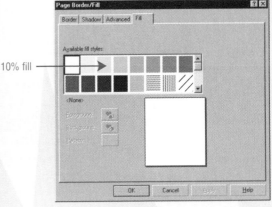 10% fill

## 50f ● 3'

# SELF ✓
# check

Answer the True/False questions at the right to see whether you have mastered the material presented in this lesson.

**T  F**

1. A direct quotation that is two or more lines is single-spaced and indented .5" from the left margin.
2. To indent a direct quotation, click Format, Paragraph, Indent.
3. An ellipsis (. . .) means text has been omitted.
4. The bibliography or reference list is keyed using hanging indent format.

# LESSON C4

# Assessment

## Screen parts

Study the lettered screen part or icon. Write the correct name on the corresponding line below the screen.

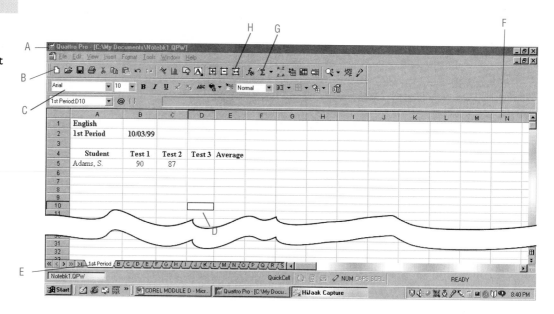

A _____     E _____

B _____     F _____

C _____     G _____

D _____     H _____

## APPLICATION

*Spreadsheet assessment*

1. Key the spreadsheet at the right. Fit the column to the longest entry.
2. Use QuickSum to compute the total number of lipsticks on hand.
3. Enter formula in Cell D6 to compute cost of inventory on hand.
4. Copy formula down to Cells, D7..D10.
5. Use QuickSum to compute a total cost of all inventory on hand in D11.
6. Format using SpeedFormat; choose *Basic 4*.
7. Save as **app-c12**.

| | A | B | C | D |
|---|---|---|---|---|
| 1 | **Jan Phillips Cosmetic, Inc.** | | | |
| 2 | 2000 End-of-Year Inventory | | | |
| 3 | | | | |
| 4 | | Quantity | | |
| 5 | Lipsticks | On Hand | Price | **Total** |
| 6 | Fuchsia | 4 | 9 | |
| 7 | Grape | 2 | 6 | |
| 8 | Copper | 3 | 7 | |
| 9 | Really Red | 7 | 7 | |
| 10 | Antique Rose | 2 | 9 | |
| 11 | Totals | | | |

# Leftbound Reports and Hyperlinks

## 51a ● 3'

### GETTING started

each line once

SKILLBUILDING WARMUP

**SKILLBUILDING WARMUP**

alphabet 1 Jayne Cox puzzled over workbooks that were required for geometry.

figures 2 Edit pages 308 and 415 in Book A; pages 17, 29, and 60 in Book B.

one hand 3 Plum trees on a hilly acre, in my opinion, create no vast estate.

easy 4 Did the foal buck? And did it cut the right elbow of the cowhand?

| 1 | 2 | 3 | 4 | 5 | 6 | 7 | 8 | 9 | 10 | 11 | 12 | 13 |

## 51b ● 7'

### SKILLBUILDING

**Reach for new goals**
1. Take two 1' writings.
2. Take a 2' writing. Try to maintain your 1' rate.

**A** all letters

*gwam* 1' | 2'

The value of an education has been a topic discussed many    12 | 6 | 48

times with a great deal of zest. The value is often measured in    25 | 12 | 54

terms of costs and benefits to the taxpayer. It is also judged    37 | 19 | 61

in terms of changes in the individuals taking part in the    49 | 24 | 67

educational process. Gains in the level of knowledge, the    61 | 30 | 72

development and refinement of attitudes, and the acquiring of    73 | 36 | 79

skills are believed to be crucial parts of an education.    84 | 42 | 84

1' | 1 | 2 | 3 | 4 | 5 | 6 | 7 | 8 | 9 | 10 | 11 | 12 | 13 |
2' |    1 |    2 |    3 |    4 |    5 |    6 |

## 51c ● 15'

### FORMATTING

**Leftbound reports**
Read the information at right.

**Document**
Key the leftbound report on p. 143.

### Formatting leftbound reports

The binding on a report usually takes about one-half inch of space; therefore, on a leftbound report, a 1.5" left margin should be used on all pages.

The same right side, top, and bottom margins are used for both unbound and leftbound reports. Reports may be either single-spaced or double-spaced. Paragraphs must be indented when double spacing is used.

1.5"

**PROFESSIONAL AFFILIATIONS**

A survey of our employees indicated that approximately 20 percent are members of professional associations. However, technical employees were more likely to belong to these organizations than were individuals in other occupational groups.

Senior managers expressed a strong desire to have a high percentage of all employees affiliate with professional organizations. This study focused on ways to encourage employees to join professional associations.

**Reasons for Not Joining Associations**

The primary reasons cited for not joining organizations were lack of time, cost, unawareness of associations for field, and never giving organizations much thought.

**Reasons for Joining Associations**

The major reasons cited for belonging to professional associations were the opportunity to network with other professionals, availability of literature addressing current issues in the field, and commitment to the profession.

**Company Incentives**

Employees indicated that with more company incentives they would join professional associations. Incentives desired were dues paid by company, recognition of employees who participate, and establishment of company chapters.

1.5"        1"

*Memo and chart sheet*

1. Key the memo at right.
2. At bottom of memo, insert a new page command. Change page layout to landscape.
3. Open *app-c6* and copy the chart.
4. Paste the chart on the page after the memo.
5. Save as **app-c10** and print.

**Optional:** Prepare this memo as an e-mail message to your instructor. Attach the *Quattro Pro* spreadsheet *app-c6*.

**TO:**        Jason W. Riley
**FROM:**    Your Name
**DATE:**     Current date
**SUBJECT:** Update on Selected Training Video Requests

In your latest e-mail, you requested a comparison of training video requests of the following three software training videos: Adobe Illustrator, Microsoft PowerPoint, and QuarkXpress. The attached chart clearly illustrates the strong interest in QuarkXpress (60 percent increase) and Illustrator (20 percent increase) training videos. The trend in the first quarter of the current year still shows a large number of requests for both training videos.

Our statistics also show that PowerPoint video requests have held steady with a slight decline last year of 14 percent. A review of request records for the past five years showed a steady increase of 20 percent for each of the past five years.

*Block letter with embedded chart*

1. Key the letter at right in block letter style with open punctuation.
2. Open *advertising* from the Formatting Template and copy the embedded chart.
3. Paste the chart as shown at right. Center the chart by dragging to the right.
4. Insert an appropriate header for the second page.
5. Save as **app-c11** and print.

Mr. Alan B. Swann|Swann Advertising Agency|298 North Johnson Street| Wenatchee, WA 98801-1016|Dear Mr. Swann

The analysis of our advertising expenditures conducted by your agency has been very helpful in our planning expenditures for the current year. The chart below illustrates the new allocation of advertising expenditures for this fiscal year.

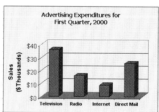

As you recommended, 10 percent of advertising expenditures were allocated to Internet advertising. Sales figures show approximately 25 percent was earned from Internet sales. The change in television and radio advertising expenditures is also showing a benefit in terms of sales.

Thank you for your recommendations. Our accountants will update these figures at the end of the second quarter and will schedule the interim meeting with you and your consultants.

Sincerely|J. Thomas Bouchard|Advertising Manager

# PROFESSIONAL AFFILIATIONS
DS

A survey of our employees indicated that approximately 20 percent are members of professional associations. However, technical employees were more likely to belong to these organizations than were individuals in other occupational groups.

Default margin

Senior managers expressed a strong desire to have a high percentage of all employees affiliate with professional organizations. This study focused on ways to encourage employees to join professional associations.

Side heading

## Reasons for Not Joining Associations

The primary reasons cited for not joining organizations were lack of time, cost, unawareness of associations for field, and never giving organizations much thought.

## Reasons for Joining Associations

The major reasons cited for belonging to professional associations were the opportunity to network with other professionals, availability of literature addressing current issues in the field, and commitment to the profession.

## Company Incentives

Employees indicated that with more company incentives they would join professional associations. Incentives desired were dues paid by company, recognition of employees who participate, and establishment of company chapters.

**Note:** When reports are double-spaced, ¶s are indented. Extra space is not added between ¶s.

LEFTBOUND REPORT—DOUBLE-SPACED

## APPLICATION

**C8**

*Edit pie chart*

You will create a pie chart and then edit various parts of the chart.

1. Open *videos* from the Formatting Template. Save as **app-c9**.
2. Create a new chart: Select *A5..C7*; then click the **QuickChart** button. Drag the crosshair to the desired position and drop the chart.

### Activate the chart
3. Click the chart to select it. Right-click inside the chart. Select *Type/Layout*; then *Pie*.

### Edit data labels
Data labels are the titles of the pie slices printed adjacent to each slice.
4. a. Point to a data label; right-click.
   b. Select *Pie Chart Properties*; click **Text Font** tab and make the following selections: Font: *Century Gothic*; appearance: *Bold*; Size: *16*. Click **OK**.

### Insert chart title and subtitle
5. Right-click inside the chart; select *Titles*. Key the main title: **Software Training Video Requests**, and subtitle: **1999-2000**. Click **OK**.

### Edit chart title and subtitle
6. Click the main chart title to select it; then right-click and select *Chart Title Properties*.
7. From the Box Settings tab, choose: Border: *Column 2, Row 2*; Fill Color: *Red*.
8. From the Fill Settings tab, choose: Fill Style: *Pattern*; Pattern Color: *Yellow*; Background Color: *Yellow*.
9. From the Text Font tab, choose: Font: *Century Gothic, Bold, 30 point*.
10. From the Text Settings tab, choose: Fill Style: *Solid*; Color: *Red*. Click **OK**.
11. Repeat Steps 6, 9, and 10 for the subtitle.

### Edit data points
12. Click the **Adobe Illustrator** pie slice; then right-click and select *Pie Chart Properties*.
13. From the Fill Settings tab, choose: Fill Style: *Pattern*; Pattern Color: *Light Blue*.
14. Follow Steps 12-13 to change all pie slices to the color of your choice. Click **OK**.

### Explode slice
15. Select the *Adobe Illustrator* pie slice; then right-click and select *Pie Chart Properties*.
16. Click the **Explode slice** tab; drag the scroll bar to a distance of 25%. Click **OK**. Save.

**Note:** When finished with Step 16, click outside the chart to exit Edit mode. Now you can select the chart and size it attractively.

## APPLICATION

**C9**

*Create chart window*

1. Open *videos* and save as **app-c9**. Select *A5..C7*.
2. Click **Insert** menu, **Chart**.
3. Make the following selections to create a line chart. Click **Next** at each step.
   Step 1: Chart data—A:A5..C7
   Step 2: Choose *Line or Area* chart type.
   Step 3: Choose Regular.
   Step 4: Key the title: **Software Training Video Requests**, and subtitle: **1999-2000**. Click **Chart Window** to create a chart window.
   Step 5: Choose the color scheme *Bright and Bold*. Click **Finish**.
4. Right-click and choose Series; key in the Legend cell area **A:B4..C4**.
5. Change title and subtitle font to 24 point; X-axis, 12 point. Save.

## Hyperlinks

**Hyperlinks** enable the online computer user to view the contents of another file or a Web page without leaving the *WordPerfect* document. It is easy to recognize a hyperlink because hyperlinked text is displayed in another color and is underlined. Images such as clipart, charts, etc., may also be hyperlinked to another document. When the mouse is pointed at a hyperlink, a pointing hand displays. To go to the hyperlinked document, just click the hyperlinked text or object.

Some advantages of creating hyperlinks are (1) disk space is conserved as the hyperlinked document is not saved with the *WordPerfect* document, (2) the reader does not have to know the filename or Web address of the hyperlink, and (3) the reader has quick access to this new document.

**To create a hyperlink:**

1. Select the text or graphic to be displayed as a hyperlink.

2. Click the **Hyperlink** button, then **Create Link**. Or, if the Hyperlink Tools toolbar is displayed, click the **Hyperlink Create** button. (To display the toolbar, click **View**, **Toolbars**, **Hyperlink Tools**.)

3. The Hyperlink Properties dialog box displays.

4. Select a file or Web page to be linked by using one of the following methods:

   a. Key the filename or Web address in the Document/Macro entry box.

   b. Click the folder icon to locate the desired filename.

   c. Click the **Browse Web** button if the Web address is not known. When you locate the desired file or Web page, click **Select.**

5. Click **OK.**

**Hyperlink Properties**

Define links to other documents or bookmarks in this or other documents. Or, define a macro to be executed when the user clicks on the link.

Document/Macro: http://www.swep.com/keyboarding/index    Browse Web...

Bookmark:

☐ Make text appear as a button
☑ Activate hyperlinks

OK    Cancel    Help

---

# *on...* **Trackballs**

A traditional mouse works by moving the mouse casing, which contains a ball, across the desk on a mouse pad. A trackball is a type of pointing device that is similar to a mouse without a casing covering the ball. With a trackball, the thumb or finger is used to move the ball directly. Using a finger-activated trackball places less strain on the hand than using a traditional mouse repetitively. The ergonomic design of the trackball generally features buttons contoured to the shape of the hand. A trackball enables the user to control the pointer without hand or wrist movement. Trackballs range in price from less than $20 to more than $100, depending on the sophistication of the device.

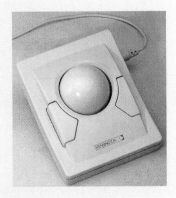

## Creating embedded chart

To create a chart, the spreadsheet must be displayed on the screen. Begin by selecting the data from the spreadsheet that you want to include in the chart and clicking the QuickChart icon. The complete steps are explained as you work through Application C6.

**A P P L I C A T I O N**

**C6**

 *Create chart from worksheet*

1. Open the *Quattro Pro* spreadsheet *videos* from the Formatting Template.
2. Select the data to be included in the chart: Cells A5..C7. **Note:** B4..C4 will be used later as legend data.
3. Click the **QuickChart** button on the toolbar.
   The mouse pointer changes to a crosshair with a chart icon.
4. Move the crosshair to A9 (below the spreadsheet data). Click and drag the chart to stretch from A9 to D22; release the mouse button.
5. Click in the chart background to edit (slashed border appears in edit mode).

*Quattro Pro 9* plots each column as a single **data series** (group of related information). If the first column (the first series) contains labels, the labels are placed along the X-axis (horizontal). If the first row contains labels, these labels are used in the graph legend. **Legend text** labels the data series and identifies comparisons. Refer to p. 434. **Note:** If the first column or row contains labels that are numbers (i.e., 1999, 2000, etc.), these numbers will be included in the chart as values.

6. Right-click in the chart background; a pop-up menu displays.
   a. Click **Type/Layout**. With *Bar* as the category, click the top left icon. Click **OK**.
   b. Right-click again. From the pop-up menu, click **Series**; then key **A:B4..C4** in the *Legend* text box or click the pointer icon to the right of *Legend*, highlight cells B4..C4, and press ENTER. Click **OK**.
   c. Right-click and select *Titles*. Key **Software Training Video Requests** (Main Title), **1999-2000** (Subtitle), **Software** (X-axis), and **Number** (Y1-axis). Click **OK**.
7. Click the main title; a border displays around it. Right-click and choose *Chart Title Properties*. Click the **Text Font** tab and change the typeface to Times New Roman and point size to 30.
8. Select the subtitle. Right-click and choose *Chart Subtitle Properties*. Click the **Subtitle Font** tab and choose Times New Roman, 30 point, and bold.
9. Format the spreadsheet. Size the chart attractively. **Note:** If in Edit mode (slashed border), click outside the chart box, then select the border before attempting to resize.
10. Save as **app-c6**.

**A P P L I C A T I O N**

**C7**

 *3-D bar chart*

1. Use spreadsheet *app-c6*. Select *A5..C7*; click the **QuickChart** button.
2. Drag and drop the chart below the chart created in *app-c6*.
3. Create a 3-D bar chart, repeating the chart created in *app-c6*, except:
   a. On the pop-up menu under *Type/Layout*, choose *Bar*, then select the *3-D bar chart* (Row 3, item 1).
   b. Under *Series*, click **Row/Column Swap** to use the rows as the data series. For *X-axis*, key **A:B4..C4**.
   c. Under *Titles*, key **Year** as the X-axis title.
4. Save as **app-c7** and print.

**Drill 1**

1. Open *Hyperlink* from the Formatting Template. Save as **51d.**
2. Create a hyperlink to a file:
   a. Select the text *50d* in the left column of the table; click the **Hyperlink Create** button.
   b. Click the folder icon and browse for the file named *50d.* Click **Select**, then **OK.**
3. Create a hyperlink to a Web page:
   a. Select the text *South-Western's College Keyboarding;* click the **Hyperlink Create** button.
   b. Key **http://www.swep.com/keyboarding/index.html** in the Document/Macro entry box. Click **OK.**
4. Link an object to the Weather Channel Web site:
   a. Select the image of the sun; click the **Hyperlink Create** button.
   b. Key **http://www.weather.com** in the entry box. Click **OK.**
5. Create a hyperlink to your favorite Web site:
   a. Select the text *My Favorite Web Site;* click the **Hyperlink Create** button.
   b. Click the **Browse Web** button to launch your Internet browser.
   c. Locate your favorite Web site.
   d. Minimize the browser window, or click your *WordPerfect* document on the taskbar. The URL address should display in the Document/Macro entry box. Click **OK.**

## HYPERLINK ACTIVITY

Hyperlinks are an easy way to send online readers to other files and to Web pages. Create the following hyperlinks in the table below.

| Files/Web Pages | Hyperlink |
|---|---|
| 50d *(Step 2 Document link)* | This hyperlink is to the *WordPerfect* file (50d) that you created in Lesson 50. Click the folder icon next to the Document/Macro textbox to locate this file. |
| South-Western's College Keyboarding *(Step 3 Web link)* | Hyperlink to Web page. Key http://www.swep.com/keyboarding/index.html. |
| Weather *(Step 4 Object link)* | Hyperlink to Web Page. Select image. Key http://www.weather.com. |
| My Favorite Web Site *(Step 5)* | Hyperlink to Web Page. Use *Browse Web* to launch your browser. Find your favorite Web page. When the Web site is located, use taskbar to return to this document; the Web address you selected will display. |

**Drill 2**

1. Open *51c* and save it as **51d-d2.**
2. Add the sentence shown below as the last sentence of Paragraph 4; key the name of your student organization and create a hyperlink to its Web page.

Visit the Web page of Student Organization (insert hyperlink) to review its benefits.

LESSON C3

# Create Charts

## Overview of charts

Information from a spreadsheet can be illustrated in a more meaningful way by displaying the data as a chart. Charts make it much easier for the reader to understand, to make comparisons, and to remember the information. Charts may be created in many different styles; the common ones include bar charts, column charts, line charts, and pie charts.

Charts are created in two ways: A **floating chart** appears next to the spreadsheet data. Because floating charts are displayed on the same page as the spreadsheet, the reader has the advantage of seeing both the chart and the data from which it was derived. **Chart pages** are displayed on a separate page of the spreadsheet. A chart page is automatically labeled Chart 1. Chart pages appear before Page A on the Page tabs at the bottom of the screen.

The parts of a chart are labeled on the chart shown below. Learn these parts. You will use this information as you create charts.

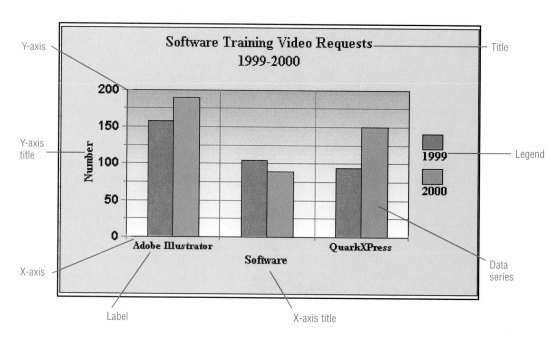

## Working with charts

Open *Quattro Pro* spreadsheet *requests* from the Formatting Template. Follow the steps at right.

Once a chart has been created, you will likely want to resize it, move it, or perhaps delete it. To work on a chart, you must first select it, much like you do when working with a graphic.

1. **Select chart:** Click the chart border to select it. Eight black handles display around the chart.
2. **Move chart:** With chart selected, drag it to Cell A11 and drop.
3. **Edit chart:** Click the chart while pointing to the title. A slashed border displays around the chart. In the title text box, change the subtitle to **1999-2000**.
4. **Size chart:** Point to one of the handles; click when the pointer changes to a double arrow. To size horizontally or vertically, drag a middle handle. To size proportionally, hold down the ALT key and drag a corner handle. Size the chart proportionally to stretch over to Column H. Save as **c3-d1** and print.
5. **Delete chart:** After selecting the chart, press the DELETE key. **Note:** To undo the deletion, click the **Undo** button.

## 51e ● 15'

**Leftbound report with references**

**Document 1**
**Challenge activity**

1. Insert *Widow/Orphan*, *Page Numbering*, and *Suppress* commands.
2. Open *reference* and format it as a leftbound report; DS. Make the revisions as shown.
3. Insert the following side headings:
   **The First Step**
   after ¶ 1
   **The Correct Style**
   after ¶ 2
   **The Finished Product**
   after ¶ 3
4. Format references using hanging indent, and italicize book titles.
5. Create a hyperlink to the American Psychological Association (http://www. apa.org/publications/).
6. Be sure to check for widow/orphan lines.

**Document 2**
1. Prepare a title page for:
   **Dr. Mary E. Compton, Business Communication Instructor, Holcombe Community College**
2. Assume the paper was prepared by **Skyler Atencio**. Use current date.

**Optional:** Add border with shading on title page.

---

Basic Steps in Report Writing     6

the effective writer makes certain that reports that    17

leave her or his desk are technically usable in content,    24

correct in style, and attractive in format.    37

Information is gathered about the subject; the effective    51

writer takes time to outline the data to be used in the report.    64

This approach allows the writer to establish the organization of    77

the report. When a topic outline is used, order of presenta-    90

tion, important points, and even various headings can be deter-    102

mined and followed easily when writing begins.    112

The purpose of the report often determines its style.    126

Most academic reports (term papers, for example) are double-    138

spaced with indented paragraphs. Most business reports, how-    151

ever, are single-spaced, and paragraphs are blocked.    161

When a style is not stipulated, general usage may be    172

followed. The most capable writer will refrain from making    188

a report deliberately *impressive*, especially if doing so    200

makes it less *expressive*.    205

follow the outline. The writer does, how ever follow    216

the outline carefully as a first draft is written. Obvious    228

errors are ignored momentarily.    234

edit the draft. Refinement comes later, after all the    245

preliminary work is done. The finished product will then be    257

read and reread to ensure it is clear, concise correct, and    270

complete. Effective writers use the on line thesaurus, *printed and references, including a*    300

spelling tool of the software. *desk references,* and manuscript style manuals In addition, they will keep   

in easy reach an up-to-date desk reference and manuscript

style manual. Examples of these resources *are* listed in the    309

reference section below.    315

References    317

*Alphabetize references, please*

Publication Manual of the American Psychological    328
Association. 4th ed. Washington, D.C.: American    336
Psychological Association, 1999.    343

"APA-Style Helper." Version 1.0. <http://www.apa.org/    354
apa-style/> (22 Dec. 1998). *December*    360

Fowler, H. Ramsey. The Little, Brown Handbook. 2nd ed.    372
Boston, MA: Little, Brown and Company, 1998.    380

**Application C5,**
*continued*

5. Copy this formula down to the other students.

    a. Make G5 the active cell.

    b. Click **Copy** on the Notebook toolbar.

    c. Select the range *G6..G9.*

    d. Click **Paste** on the Notebook toolbar.

6. Make C11 the active cell. Enter the function to average scores for Test 1: **@avg(C5..C9)**. Copy across to Columns D through F.

7. Make C12 the active cell. Enter function to count number of students taking Test 1: **@count(C5..C9)**. Copy to D-F.

8. Make C13 the active cell. Enter function to find the minimum score made on Test 1: **@min(C5..C9)**. Copy to D-F.

9. Make C14 the active cell. Enter function to find the maximum score made on Test 1: **@max(C5..C9)**. Copy to D-F.

| A:C11 | | @ {} | @AVG(C5..C9) | | | | |
|---|---|---|---|---|---|---|---|
| | A | B | C | D | E | F | G |
| 1 | Algebra I | | 01/21/00 | | | | |
| 2 | 1st Period | | | | | | |
| 3 | | | | | | | |
| 4 | Last Name | First Name | Test 1 | Test 2 | Test 3 | Test 4 | Student's Average |
| 5 | Austin | Beth | 86 | 88 | 89 | 95 | 89.5 |
| 6 | Brown | S. G. | 78 | 80 | 82 | 80 | 80.00 |
| 7 | Hoop | Donna | | 56 | 78 | 20 | 51.33 |
| 8 | Taylor | Wayne | 100 | 94 | 90 | | 94.67 |
| 9 | Williams | Ben | 97 | 85 | 88 | 88 | 89.5 |
| 10 | | | | | | | |
| 11 | Average for each test | | 90.25 | 80.6 | 85.4 | 70.75 | |
| 12 | No. taking test | | 4 | 5 | 5 | 4 | |
| 13 | Minimum test score | | 78 | 56 | 78 | 20 | |
| 14 | Maximum test score | | 100 | 94 | 90 | 95 | |
| 15 | | | | | | | |

**Format cells**

10. Select *G5..G9.* Click **Format, Selection, Numeric Format** tab, **Number, 2.** Click **OK.** This formats values to two decimal places.

11. Save as **app-c5.**

12. Select the entire worksheet (*A1..G14*). Then click **Format, SpeedFormat.** Choose *Computer Paper* and click **OK.**

13. Reformat G5..G9 to two decimal places.

14. Enter **0** for each of the two students who did not take Tests 1 and 4.

15. Save as **app-c5r.**

# Assessment

**52a • 7'**

## GETTING started

each line 3 times SS (work for fewer than 3 errors per group); DS between 3-line groups

alphabet 1 Jacki might analyze the data by answering five complex questions.

figures 2 Memo 67 asks if the report on Bill 35-48 is due the 19th or 20th.

double letters 3 Aaron took accounting lessons at a community college last summer.

easy 4 Hand Bob a bit of cocoa, a pan of cod, an apricot, and six clams.

| 1 | 2 | 3 | 4 | 5 | 6 | 7 | 8 | 9 | 10 | 11 | 12 | 13 |

**52b • 10'**

## SKILLBUILDING

**Assess straight-copy skill**

1. Key one 3' writing.
2. Key one 5' writing.

  all letters                                                                  *gwam*  3' | 5'

Subtle differences exist among role models, mentors, and       4   2 32
sponsors.   A role model is a person you can emulate, or one who   8   5 35
provides a good example to follow.   A mentor is one who will    12   7 37
advise, coach, or guide you when you need information about your  16  10 40
job or your organization.   A sponsor is a person who will support  21  12 42
you or recommend you for a position or a new responsibility.     25  15 45

One person may fill all three roles, or several people may      30  18 48
serve as role models, mentors, or sponsors.   These individuals  34  20 50
usually have higher ranks than you do, which means they will be  38  23 53
able to get information that you and your peers may not have.    42  25 55
Frequently, a mentor will share information with you that will   46  28 58
enable you to make good decisions about your career.            50  30 60

3' |      1      |      2      |      3      |      4      |
5' |         1         |         2         |         3         |

**52c • 33'**

**Assessment: Unbound and leftbound reports and title page**

**Time schedule:**
Planning time . . . . . . . . 3'
Timed production . . . . . 25'
Final check; proofread;
    determine *g-pram* . . . . . 5'

1. Organize your desktop.
2. On the signal to begin, key the documents in sequence. Check spelling after keying each document. Preview before printing.

3. Proofread all documents; count errors; determine *g-pram*.

$$g\text{-}pram = \frac{\text{total words keyed}}{25'}$$

## Functions

### Date, average, count, mini, maxi

**Functions** are shortcuts that have formulas already entered. *Quattro Pro 9* has more than 200 functions built into the software. Click the @ button on the input line to view the Functions dialog box (shown below). Listed are the various categories of functions. Generally, functions are entered as either a range or a union. A **range** refers to consecutive cells; a **union**, to individual cells.

Range uses two dots: @sum(A5..A9) adds all cells from A5 through A9.

Union uses a comma: @sum(A5,A9) adds only A5 and A9.

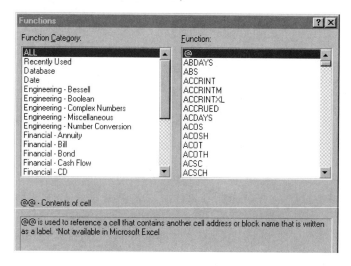

---

## APPLICATION

### C5

The steps of this application are broken into major parts.

1. Open *algebra* from the Formatting Template. Save as **app-c5**.

**QuickFill**

2. Make C4 the active cell. Select *C4..F4*. Click **QuickFill**.

**Date function**

3. Make C1 the active cell. Enter a Date function to show the current date each time the spreadsheet is opened:
   a. Key **@TODAY** and press ENTER.
   b. Click in C1 and click **Format**, **Selection**. From the Numeric Format tab, choose *Date* and the *Long Date Intl* format. Click **OK**. You may need to make the column wider to see the date.

**Functions**

4. Make G5 the active cell. Enter the formula to compute Austin's test average.
   a. Key **@avg(**
   b. Click **C5** and drag through F5. Press ENTER. The average is 89.5.

*(continued on the next page)*

## Document 1
## Leftbound report with references

1. Format the report DS.
2. Number the pages correctly.
3. On the text *Americans with Disabilities Act* (¶4), insert a hyperlink to http://www. civilrights.com/disability. html/.
4. Save as **52c-d1**.

## Document 2
## Unbound report

1. Open *present*. Save as **52c-d2**.
2. Insert *Widow/Orphan*, *Page Numbering*, and *Suppress* commands.
3. Convert this leftbound report to an unbound report; DS.
4. Format main, side, and paragraph headings correctly.

## Document 3
## Title page for leftbound report

Prepare a title page for Document 1.

1. Assume the report was prepared for **Ms. Leslie Chafee** by **Julian Houser, Project Director**.
2. Use the current date.

**UNTAPPED RESOURCES**

Directors of company personnel have important responsibilities, among the most important being the acquisition of dedicated, conscientious workers to carry out the daily functions of our businesses.

### Staff Resources

Generally, we each have developed our own sources, which range from local educational institutions, through employment offices, newspapers, and on down to walk-ins, from which we find new employees. But we always welcome new sources.

One supply often overlooked--though not by the more ingenious of us--is the pool of available workers who have one or more noticeable or definable "disabilities" or "handicaps." Occasionally, a supply of these potential workers will go untapped in an area for a long period of time; when discovered, they become a genuine treasure trove for a wide variety of jobs.

### Performance Level

Since the passage of the Americans with Disabilities Act in 1990, studies have shown that disabled workers, while perhaps restricted to the exact jobs they can do, perform well above the minimum requirements on jobs not beyond their capabilities. Limitations vary with individuals; but once reasonable accommodations are made, these workers become uniquely qualified employees.

Abrahms, writing of the reluctance of some employers to hire handicapped workers, says that "workers with handicaps have high rates of production, often higher than those achieved by other workers" (Abrahms, 1998, 61). Munoz goes one step further by reminding us that disabled workers "have high work-safety histories with low job-changing and absentee records" (Munoz, 1999, 37).

From a practical as well as a personal point of view, then, hiring workers who are physically or mentally handicapped can provide a positive occupational impact for a company as well as a very rewarding experience for its human resource director. One such director says:

Recently, I told a potential employee who was sitting in my office in her wheelchair of our success with handicapped workers. "That's great," she said. "You know, most of us rarely think about things we can't do. There are too many things we can do and can do well." I hired her (Belli, 1999, 78).

And so say all of us who sit in the employer's chair.

**REFERENCES**

Abrahms, Hollin C. "Searching for Employees." *The Human Services Monthly*, January 1998, pp. 61-68.

Belli, L. R. "An Investment in Social Action." *Human Resources Quarterly*. 1999. <http://www.sainc.org/article/> (20 April 1999).

Munoz, Hector. "Changing Aspects of the American Workforce at the Close of the Twentieth Century." *National Vo-Tech News*, May 1999, pp. 15-37.

| words |
|---|
| 4 |
| 17 |
| 31 |
| 44 |
| 47 |
| 60 |
| 74 |
| 87 |
| 95 |
| 108 |
| 122 |
| 137 |
| 151 |
| 166 |
| 168 |
| 172 |
| 185 |
| 198 |
| 212 |
| 226 |
| 240 |
| 248 |
| 260 |
| 273 |
| 288 |
| 302 |
| 316 |
| 325 |
| 338 |
| 351 |
| 365 |
| 379 |
| 391 |
| 405 |
| 418 |
| 431 |
| 440 |
| 451 |
| 453 |
| 467 |
| 474 |
| 489 |
| 500 |
| 515 |
| 529 |

## Zoom, QuickFill

Frequently a spreadsheet is too wide to view it all on the screen. **Zoom** allows you to change the size of the spreadsheet to various percentages.

**QuickFill** is a *Quattro Pro* shortcut command that enables you to copy data into the cells immediately adjacent to the original cell. QuickFill gives you the same result as Copy and Paste with only one operation. To use QuickFill, the destination cells must be touching the original cell; select the cells to be filled and click QuickFill on the Notebook toolbar. (This procedure gives consecutive data, such as 1, 2, 3, etc.) To use QuickFill as a Copy and Paste feature to fill several cells with the same data, two adjacent cells must contain the same number, such as 80, 80. Select the first two cells as well as any other cells that need to contain like data, click the right mouse button, and select QuickFill.

**A P P L I C A T I O N**

-------- **C4** ------------

1. Open *mcmullan* from the Formatting Template. Save as **app-c4**.
2. Center spreadsheet titles (Rows 1-2) over spreadsheet (Columns A-H).
3. Select *F4..G4*. Center **Deductions** over Columns F-G.
4. Fit the column widths with longest entry.

### Zoom

5. Click the down arrow on the Zoom button on the Power bar.
6. Choose *75%*. Now you can see Columns A-H.

### QuickFill

7. Make B6 the active cell.
8. Copy B6 to B7; select *B6, B7*, and all other cells needing the same number; then click **QuickFill**. (To use QuickFill, a number must be in two adjacent cells in order to fill other selected cells with like numbers.)

### Enter formulas

9. In E6, enter formula for gross earnings (overtime pay is 1.5 times regular pay):
   **+(B6\*D6)+(C6\*D6\*1.5)**.
10. In F6, enter the formula that computes a 7.65% deduction based on gross earnings:
    **+E6\*7.65%**.
11. Copy the formula entered in E6 down to other employees.
12. Copy the formula entered in F6 down to other employees.
13. In H6, enter the formula for net pay: **+E6-(F6+G6)**.
14. Copy the formula entered in H6 down to other employees.
15. Use QuickSum to compute totals for all columns except hourly rate.

### Format

16. Select *D6..H12*; click **Format, Selection.** From the Numeric Format tab sheet, click **Currency**. Then verify that a **2** shows in the spin box and click **OK**.

### Print landscape and Header/Footer

17. Click **File, Page Setup, Paper Type** tab, and then **Landscape**. Then click the **Header/Footer** tab and verify that *Page #* appears in the Footer box. Click **Print**, then **Print**. Save as **app-c4**.

# MODULE 6 checkpoint

**Objective Assessment**

Answer the questions below to see whether you have mastered the content of this module.

1. The _____ command is used to delete blocks of text that are no longer needed. To place the deleted text in another location, simply click the _____ button.

2. The _____ command is used to repeat text from one location to another. To place the repeated text in the new location, simply click the _____ button.

3. To set margins, choose _____ from the _____ menu.

4. You have just added bold to text; now you have decided to delete the bold. You could delete the bold code in Reveal Codes or you could click the _____ button to reverse this recent action.

5. When copying selected text using drag-and-drop editing, press the _____ key; then drag and drop the text in the desired location.

6. Use _____ point for main headings, _____ point for side headings, and _____ point for paragraph headings.

7. Margins for unbound reports are _____ side margins, _____ top margin (first page), _____ top margin (second page), and _____ bottom margin.

8. Margins for leftbound reports are _____ side margins, _____ top margin (first page), _____ top margin (second page), and _____ bottom margin.

9. The _____ format displays the first line of text at the left margin and all other lines indented to the first tab.

10. To number pages of a multipage report, choose _____ from the _____ menu.

11. Insert a hard page break by pressing _____ + _____.

12. Delete a hard page break by deleting the code in the _____ _____ screen.

13. Quotations of _____ or more lines should be _____ -spaced and indented _____ inch(es).

14. The _____ command is inserted to prevent a single line of text from being left at the bottom of the page or carried to the top of the next page.

15. When formatting the title page for a leftbound report, use _____ left margin and _____ right margin.

## Performance Assessment
### Unbound report

1. Open *checkpt6*.
2. Make the necessary changes to convert it to a DS, unbound report.
3. Insert the ¶ at the right between ¶ 1 and ¶ 2.
4. Create a title page for **Altman Corporation** prepared by **Jason T. Forrest**.

*A complete proposal is attached. The proposal includes the cost justification, the procurement alternatives, and the specifications of the system recommended. A brochure describing the system recommended is also attached.*

Follow the steps for entering a simple spreadsheet that contains a formula and a function and a centered title.

## Key the spreadsheet

1. Key the following spreadsheet; then save as **app-c2**.

|   | A | B | C | D |
|---|---|---|---|---|
| 1 | Invoice | | | |
| 2 | | | | |
| 3 | Quantity | Description | Unit Price | Total |
| 4 | 2 | WX-1098 color copier | 725.99 | |
| 5 | 10 | 279 TX internal modem | 59.59 | |
| 6 | 1 | FX-19 laser printer | 999.99 | |
| 7 | Totals | | | |

## Enter and copy a formula

2. In D4, key the formula **+a4*c4** to multiply quantity and unit price.
3. Copy the formula down to the next two items:
   a. Make D4 the active cell.
   b. Click **Copy** on the toolbar or click the right mouse button and **Copy**. The formula is stored on the Clipboard.
   c. Select the range *D5..D6*.
   d. Click **Paste**.

## QuickSum

4. Make D7 the active cell. To total Column D, click the **QuickSum** button (Σ) on the Notebook toolbar. The sum displays.

## Center over columns

5. Select *A1..D1*.
6. Click the **Alignment Menu** button on the Power bar; select *Center Across Block*.
7. Save again as **app-c2** and print.

1. Open the spreadsheet *c2-d2*.
2. Key **Totals** in A10; key **Total Sales** in D4.
3. Select *B5..D10*. Use the QuickSum feature to compute all of these totals at one time.
4. Center titles in A1..D2 over Columns A-D.
5. Format Row 1 in Arial Black, 14 point; Row 2 in Arial Black, 12 point.
6. Save as **app-c3** and print.

# internet activities

## Activity eight

### Explore search engines

The World Wide Web contains millions of pages of information and is growing rapidly. Search engines are used to locate specific information on the Web. Just a few examples of search engines are AltaVista, Excite, Infoseek, Dogpile, Metacrawler, LookSmart, Lycos, and Yahoo!.

To go to a search engine, click the Search or Net Search button on your Web browser. (**Note:** *Web browsers will vary.*)

Search —

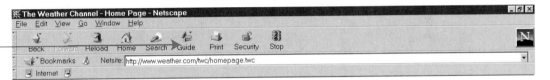

#### Practice

1. Click the **Search** button in your Web browser. This will bring up a screen that shows several different search engines. Click the first search engine. Browse the hyperlinks available (Maps, People Finder, News, Weather, Stock Quotes, Sports, Games, etc.).
2. Click each search engine and explore the hyperlinks.
3. Conduct the following search using Dogpile, a multithreaded search engine that searches multiple databases:
    a. Open the Web site for Dogpile (http://www.dogpile.com).
    b. In the Search entry box, key the keywords **American Psychological Association publications**; click **Fetch**.

## Activity nine

### Search Yellow Pages

Searching the Yellow Pages for information on businesses and services is a common task both in business and at home. Let your computer do the searching for you next time. Several search engines provide a convenient hyperlink to the online Yellow Pages.

#### Practice

1. Click the **Search** button in your Web browser. Browse the search engines to locate the hyperlink for the Yellow Pages; click to open this valuable site.
2. Determine a city that you would like to visit. Use the Yellow Pages to find a listing of hotels in this city.
3. Your best friend lives in (*you provide the city*); you want to send him/her flowers. Find a listing of florists in this city.
4. Write a third scenario and find the appropriate listing.

## Drill 3

1. Open a new notebook. Rename Page A **Text**.
2. Enter the following as label cells:

    **Column A**
    Sales Staff
    206 Pinebrook Rd.
    239TXY

3. Click on **Page B**. Rename Page B **Numbers**.
4. Enter the following as value cells:

| Column A | Column B |
|---|---|
| 25 | 10 |
| 4.25 | +428-02-5321 |
| 2,454 | +(a3*a2)–(a2-a4) |
| +a1+a2 | 105555555555 |

5. Save as **c2-d3**. Both pages are saved each time the Save command is issued.

**Entering formulas**

**Formula**: A set of instructions to perform calculations in a cell. All formulas keyed begin with a plus sign (+) or equals sign (=). A formula consists of a number or cell reference and an *operator* (mathematical symbol) that indicates what to do. The cell reference may be a cell address such as D4 or a range of cells (D4..D8). A range is indicated by two dots.

Formulas may also include **functions**, which are prestored formulas that perform specific calculations. SUM is a common function that totals a range of numeric values. Because SUM is such a common function, it has a special button on the toolbar called QuickSum ($\Sigma$). All such predefined formulas begin with the @ sign.

| Operation | Operator | Example | Meaning |
|---|---|---|---|
| Addition | + | =B4+D4 | Adds the values in Cells B4 and D4. |
| Subtraction | – | =B4–D4 | Subtracts the value in D4 from the value in B4. |
| Division | / | =B4/D4 | Divides the value in B4 by the value in D4. |
| Multiplication | * | =A4*C4 | Multiplies the values in A4 and C4. |
| Percent | % | =E6*8% | Calculates 8% of the value of E6. |
| Exponentiation | ^ | =B4^3 | Increases the value of B4 to the third power. |

**Copying data**

When you copy cell data, you are making a duplicate of the data, similar to when you copy text in *WordPerfect*. Cells that have been copied can be pasted into other cells.

**To copy data:**

1. Select the cell or range containing the data to be copied.
2. Click the **Copy** button on the toolbar.
3. Select the cell or range into which you want to put the data.
4. Click **Paste**.

# TABLE BASICS

## OBJECTIVES

1. Create tables using the Table function.

2. Format and edit tables.

3. Improve speed and accuracy.

# Create Tables

## 53a • 6'

### GETTING started

each line 3 times SS; DS
between 3-line groups

### SKILLBUILDING WARMUP

| | | |
|---|---|---|
| alphabet | 1 | Jim Ryan was able to liquefy frozen oxygen; he kept it very cold. |
| figures | 2 | Flight 483 left Troy at 9:57 a.m., arriving in Reno at 12:06 p.m. |
| direct reaches | 3 | My brother served as an umpire on that bright June day, no doubt. |
| easy | 4 | Ana's sorority works with vigor for the goals of the civic corps. |

| 1 | 2 | 3 | 4 | 5 | 6 | 7 | 8 | 9 | 10 | 11 | 12 | 13 |

## 53b • 6'

### NEW FUNCTION

### Tables

Tables consist of columns and rows of data—either alphabetic, numeric, or a combination of both. Use correct terminology for the components of a table.

**Column:** Vertical list of information. Columns are labeled alphabetically from left to right.

**Row:** Information arranged horizontally. Rows are labeled numerically from top to bottom.

**Cell:** An intersection of a column and a row. Each cell has its own address consisting of the column letter and the row number.

| | Column A | Column B | Column C |
|---|---|---|---|
| Row 1 | Cell A1 | | |
| Row 2 | | | Cell C2 |

# Manipulate Spreadsheet Data

**Fitting column width**

Often the contents of the columns of a spreadsheet exceed the width of the columns. When the contents are too wide, the copy is not lost; it just does not display. The text reappears when you increase the width of the column. You can change the width of a column to fit the longest entry in two ways:

1. Drag the column border to the desired width.

2. With the column selected or the insertion point positioned in the column, click the **QuickFit** button (↔) on the Notebook toolbar.

QuickFit

| | A | B | C | D | E | F | G | H | I |
|---|---|---|---|---|---|---|---|---|---|
| 1 | Software, Inc. Sales | | | | | | | | |
| 2 | January 1-31, 200- | | | | | | | | |
| 3 | | | | | | | | | |
| 4 | Sales Staff | Cash | Charge | | | | | | |
| 5 | Acker, Wanda | 12786 | 18278 | | | | | | |
| 6 | Thompson, Steve | 9478 | 12486 | | | | | | |
| 7 | Wong, Joan | 22555 | 30875 | | | | | | |
| 8 | Lehman, R. P. | 14589 | 25641 | | | | | | |
| 9 | Smith, Terry | 17891 | 29445 | | | | | | |
| 10 | | | | | | | | | |
| 11 | | | | | | | | | |
| 12 | | | | | | | | | |

**Drill 1**

1. Open *app-c1*.

2. Point to the right border of Column A in the column heading row (a double black arrow will replace the arrow pointer).

3. Click and drag to the right until the longest entry fits. Release the mouse button.

4. Save as **c2-d1** and close.

**Drill 2**

1. Open *app-c1* again.

2. Select Column A by clicking the column heading.

3. Click the **QuickFit** button on the Notebook toolbar.

4. Save as **c2-d2**.

**Entering text and values**

You can enter three types of data in a spreadsheet: labels, values (or numbers), and formulas. In this section, you'll learn to enter labels and values.

**Label**: Any combination of numbers, spaces, and nonnumeric characters. For example, Sales Staff, 206 Pinebrook Rd., 206-555-2222, or 239TXY are all examples of labels.

**Number**: A constant value that can include numeric characters as well as +, -, ( ), /, S, %, .. If the cell is not large enough to display a number, a row of asterisks (*****) will appear. The data will reappear on screen when you increase the column width. A very large number will be displayed in scientific notation (4.57E+17). Numbers align at the right. Press ENTER after keying the data, and the cell directly below becomes the active cell. **Fit-As-You-Go (Tools, Settings, General** tab, **Fit-As-You-Go)** automatically increases the column width as you key so the number values are always visible.

**53b,** *continued*

You can create and format tables automatically using word processing, spreadsheet, or database software. Word processing software offers advantages for creating tables with complex formatting, whereas spreadsheet software works better for complex calculations. Database software provides powerful sorting and searching capabilities.

## Create a table

The table you create in *WordPerfect 9* will include the number of columns and rows that you specify and will spread from the left to the right margin, with each column being of equal width.

When the insertion point is clicked in the table, a table toolbar displays at the top of the screen. The Table button provides easy access to options related to tables.

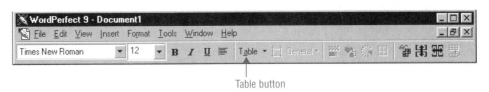

Table button

**Drill**

1. Create a 2-column, 5-row table.
2. With the insertion point in the table, click the **Table** button on the toolbar.
3. Highlight each option on the drop-down menu to see what it does.
4. Close the document without saving.

**To create a table:**

1. Click the **Insert** menu, then **Table**.
2. Enter the number of columns and rows and click **Create**.
3. To display the column letters and row numbers, click the **Table** button on the toolbar and then click **Row/Col Indicators**.

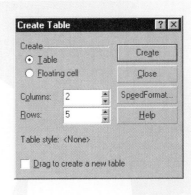

**53c • 5'**

## Move within a table

To move in a table, use the mouse or the keystrokes listed below. The status line reports the cell address of the insertion point.

| Press | Movement |
|---|---|
| TAB | To move to the next cell. |
| SHIFT + TAB | To move to a previous cell. |
| ENTER | To add another line to a cell. If you press ENTER by mistake, press BACKSPACE to delete the line. |
| TAB | To add a row; insertion point must be in the last cell. |

**Drill**

1. Create a 4-column, 4-row table.
2. Click the **Table** button, then **Row/Column Indicators**.
3. Move the insertion point to various cells; note the status line position each time you move to a new cell.
4. Close the document without saving.

## Entering information

Information is entered in a spreadsheet as either a label (words), values (numbers), or formulas. **Formulas** are sets of instructions for calculating values in cells. You will learn about entering formulas in the next lesson.

When a label is keyed in a cell, it appears both in the cell and in the input line. If there are more characters than space allows, the excess characters spill over into the next cell. Data are entered by keying the data and then either pressing ENTER or clicking the check mark button on the input line.

## APPLICATION

*Create spreadsheet*

1. Click the **New** button on the Notebook toolbar.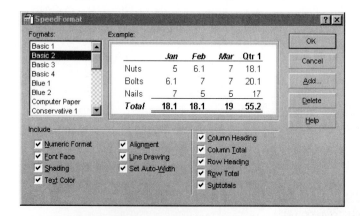
2. In A1, key the spreadsheet title: **Software, Inc. Sales**.
3. In A2, key the spreadsheet subtitle: **January 2000**.
4. Enter data as shown in the table below. Do not worry about fitting the long entries in Column A. You will use SpeedFormat in Step 7 to format the spreadsheet.

| Sales Staff | Cash | Charge |
|---|---|---|
| Acker, Wanda | 12786 | 18278 |
| Thompson, Steve | 9478 | 12486 |
| Wong, Joan | 22555 | 30875 |
| Lehman, R. P. | 14589 | 25641 |
| Smith, Terry | 17891 | 29445 |

| | A | B | C |
|---|---|---|---|
| 1 | Software, Inc. Sales | | |
| 2 | January 1-31, 200- | | |
| 3 | | | |
| 4 | Sales Sta | Cash | Charge |
| 5 | Acker, Wa | 12786 | 18278 |
| 6 | Thompson | 9478 | 12486 |
| 7 | Wong, Joa | 22555 | 30875 |
| 8 | Lehman, F | 14589 | 25641 |
| 9 | Smith, Ter | 17891 | 29445 |

5. Save the spreadsheet as **app-c1** (*File, Save As*) and print. All *Quattro Pro* files are automatically saved with the extension *.qpw*. These extensions will help you recognize *Quattro Pro* files.
6. Select the range *A1* through *C9*.
7. Click **Format**, **Speed Format**. Select *Basic 2*, and then click **OK**.
8. Save as **app-c1r** and print. **Note:** The purpose of Step 7 is to apply a format. Realistically this spreadsheet does not have a "Total" row.

FORMATTING

## Create tables
1.5" top margin for each table

### Document 1
1. Center and bold the main heading; press ENTER twice. Turn off bold and change justification to left below the heading.
2. Create a 2-column, 5-row table.
3. Key the table.

**QUOTATION ON TIMBER PRICES** DS

| | | |
|---|---|---|
| Pine poles | $50.00 per ton | 11 |
| Pine saw timber | $36.50 per ton | 17 |
| Pine pulpwood | $8.50 per ton | 22 |
| Hardwood saw timber | $20.00 per ton | 29 |
| Hardwood pulpwood | $7.00 per ton | 36 |

5

### Document 2
1. Center and bold the main heading; press ENTER twice.
2. Create a 3-column, 6-row table.
3. Key the table.

**KEY CONTACTS FOR BUILDING PROJECT**

| | | | |
|---|---|---|---|
| Lara G. Elkins | Architect | (555) 134-5867 | 15 |
| James C. Weatherwax | Contractor | (555) 156-3190 | 24 |
| Peggy R. Lancaster | Engineer | (555) 176-2480 | 33 |
| Joanna B. Breckenridge | Site Supervisor | (555) 183-2164 | 43 |
| Marshall C. Dinkins | Interior Designer | (555) 156-0937 | 54 |
| Patrick R. Hinson | Kitchen Consultant | (555) 183-0926 | 64 |

7

### Document 3
1. Open *Pommery*; save as **53d-d3**.
2. Edit the table as marked.
3. Add a row at the bottom of the table.

Position insertion point in last cell and press TAB to add a row. ▓

POMMERY SPRINGS PROJECT STATUS  *Center and Bold*

| Job | Description | Date Completed | |
|---|---|---|---|
| Road work | Building and grading | February 10, 2000 | 22 |
| Drain | Adding french drain | February 25, 2000 | 31 |
| Lot prep ^*aration* | Clearing and leveling | March 12, 2000 | 42 |
| *Pond* | *Adding silt fence* | *March 15, 2000*  (add row) | 49 |

6

12

## Selecting cells

To work with a spreadsheet, you must be able to select a single cell or a group of cells called a **range**. In a range, all cells touch each other and form a rectangle. A range could also be an entire column or row. After a range is selected, you can perform one operation on all cells within that range. To select a range of cells, click the mouse in the first cell and drag diagonally from the first cell to the last cell. To select all cells on the sheet, click the Select All button.

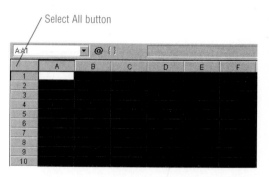

To select a range of cells, click and drag diagonally from the first to last cell.

To select all cells on the sheet, click the Select All button.

The table below summarizes selecting ranges.

| To Select: | Move: |
|---|---|
| Single cell | Click the cell. |
| Range of cells | Drag diagonally from the first cell to the last cell. |
| Nonadjacent cells or ranges | • Select the first range; then release mouse button. <br> • Hold down **CTRL** and drag to select the next range. |
| Entire row | Click row heading. |
| Entire column | Click column heading. |
| Entire spreadsheet | Click **Select All** button (see illustration above). |

### Drill 6    Ranges

This drill applies selecting ranges of various sizes. The 2000 spreadsheet should still be displayed.

**Select range**

1. Select the range *A4 through B8*: click **A4** and drag diagonally to B8.

**Select nonadjacent ranges**

2. Select the range *A4 through B8*; then release the mouse button.
3. With the first range still selected, press CTRL and select *A13 through B15*.

**Select rows, columns, and all**

4. Click the row heading **3** to select all of Row 3.
5. Click the column heading **C** to select all of Column C.
6. Click the rectangle above Row 1 to select the entire spreadsheet.

**53d,** *continued*

**Document 4**

Create the table as shown.

**KEY PROJECT DATES**

| | | |
|---|---|---|
| Architectural plans completed | November 15, 1999 | 13 |
| Site engineering and preparation | December 12, 1999 | 23 |
| Foundation and framing completed | January 18, 2000 | 33 |
| Phase I construction completed | March 15, 2000 | 43 |
| Phase II construction completed | May 6, 2000 | 51 |
| Final construction completed | August 30, 2000 | 60 |

**Document 5**

Key the table in standard format.

**OFFICIAL BIRDS AND FLOWERS**

**For Selected States**

| State | Official Bird | Official Flower | |
|---|---|---|---|
| Alaska | willow ptarmigan | forget-me-not | 24 |
| Arkansas | mockingbird | apple blossom | 31 |
| California | California valley quail | golden poppy | 41 |
| Connecticut | American robin | mountain laurel | 49 |
| Delaware | blue hen chicken | peach blossom | 57 |
| Georgia | brown thrasher | Cherokee rose | 65 |
| Idaho | mountain bluebird | syringa | 71 |
| Illinois | cardinal | native violet | 78 |
| Louisiana | eastern brown pelican | magnolia | 86 |
| Maryland | Baltimore oriole | black-eyed Susan | 94 |
| Massachusetts | chickadee | mayflower | 101 |

Header word counts: OFFICIAL BIRDS AND FLOWERS = 5, For Selected States = 9, State/Official Bird/Official Flower = 17

**53e ● 3'**

**S E L F ✔**

**c h e c k**

Answer the True/False questions at the right to see whether you have mastered the material presented in this lesson.

**T   F**

☐ ☐  **1.** Rows are labeled alphabetically from top to bottom.

☐ ☐  **2.** To move to a previous cell in a table, press BACKSPACE.

☐ ☐  **3.** The Insert menu is used to insert a table in a document.

☐ ☐  **4.** A cell is an intersection of a row and a column.

### Using keystrokes

Keystrokes also help you move quickly in a spreadsheet. Refer to the table below as you learn to move quickly in a spreadsheet. When keystrokes are used, the active cell moves.

| To move: | Press: |
|---|---|
| Up, down, left, or right one cell | ↑, ↓, ←, → |
| Up or down one window | PgUp or PgDn |
| One window to left or right | CTRL ← or → |
| Move to Cell A1 | HOME |
| Move to lower right corner of data | END, HOME |

### Using Go To

Just as you used Go To in *WordPerfect* to move to a specific part of a document, the Go To command in *Quattro Pro 9* takes you to a specific cell location. Go To is located on the Edit menu. Go To can also be accessed by keying the command CTRL+G or F5. In the Go To dialog box, enter the cell reference, such as G8.

**Drill 1** **Rename spreadsheet**

1. Open the spreadsheet *budget* from the Formatting Template.
2. Rename the spreadsheet **2000**:
   a. Double-click **Page A**.
   b. Enter **2000** in the Page A tab space.
3. Double-click **Page B**. Rename it **1999**.
4. Click the page named **2000**. You will use it for Drills 2–6. Do not close it after each drill.

**Drill 2** **Scroll**

1. Click the Down arrow on the vertical scroll bar to move down one row.
2. Click in the scroll bar below the vertical scroll box to move down one screen.
3. Click the Right arrow on the horizontal scroll bar to move right one column.
4. Scroll left one column.
5. Click and drag the vertical scroll box down any distance.
6. Drag the horizontal scroll box right 1 screen.

**Drill 3** **Keystrokes**

1. Click in **C10** to make it the active cell.
2. Press HOME to move to the beginning of the page.
3. Press END, then HOME to move to the last cell with data.
4. Press HOME to move to the beginning of the page.

**Drill 4** **Scroll and keystrokes**

1. Make **C10** the active cell.
2. Click to the right of the horizontal scroll box to move to the right one screen.
3. Press END, HOME to return to the last cell with data.
4. Click **Page 1999** to make it the active page.
5. Make **Page 2000** the active page.

**Drill 5** **Go To**

1. Use Go To to make **C10** the active cell.
   a. Press CTRL+G, or F5.
   b. Enter **C10** and click **OK**.
2. Go to cell D40.

**LESSON 54**

# Format Tables

**54a • 6'**

**G**ETTING
s t a r t e d

## SKILLBUILDING WARMUP

adjacent key

1 her err ire are cash said riot lion soil join went wean news
2 art try pew sort tree post upon copy opera maker waste three
3 sat coil riot were renew forth trade power grope owner score

one hand

4 him bear joy age kiln casts noun loop facet moon deter edges
5 ad null bar poll car upon deed jump ever look feed hill noon
6 get hilly are imply save phony taste union versa yummy wedge

balanced hand

7 aid go bid dish elan glen fury idle half jamb lend make name
8 oak pay hen quay rush such urus vial works yamen amble blame
9 cot duty goal envy focus handy ivory lapel oriel prowl queue

| 1 | 2 | 3 | 4 | 5 | 6 | 7 | 8 | 9 | 10 | 11 | 12 |

**54b • 9'**

**Format cells**

Key Drills 1 and 2 on the same screen. Save as **54b** but do not close. Continue to the next page.

Generally, tables are created, keyed, and then formatted. Formatting may include applying bold, italic, underline, or a different font size. Align columns at the left, right, or center using the Justification button.

**To format cells:**

1. Select the cell (column or row) to be formatted.
2. Click the appropriate button on the toolbar: **Bold**, **Italic**, **Underline**, or **Font Size**.
3. To align copy, click the **Justification** button; drag the highlighting down to the appropriate alignment.

**Drill 1**

1. Create and key the 3-column, 3-row table.
2. Select *Row 1,* then bold column headings.
3. Select *Column B* and center-align column.
4. Select *Column C* and right-align column.
5. QS before keying Drill 2.

| **Employee** | **Position** | **Identification** |
|---|---|---|
| Ralph Marshall | Associate | 486028476 |
| Janice Goodman | Manager | 3495075 |

↑ Left-align      ↑ Center      ↑ Right-align

**Drill 2**

1. Create and key the 2-column, 2-row table.
2. Save again. Leave the document on the screen and continue with 54c.

| May | $53,764 |
|---|---|
| June | $80,291 |

**Page tabs:** Tabs are located at the bottom of the spreadsheet for the various pages in this one *Quattro Pro* spreadsheet. Pages can be related to each other. For example, sales for each month could be captured in separate pages, and all monthly pages can be related to one summary page. Each page has 256 columns and 1,000,000 rows. To make a page active, click on the Page tab. The active page is displayed in bold. Use the Tab Scroll buttons to move from page to page.

Pages can be named to make the tabs more meaningful. To rename a page, double-click the Page tab. Then key a name and press ENTER. The name will appear on the Page tab.

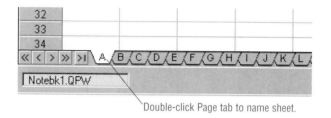

Double-click Page tab to name sheet.

## Moving within a spreadsheet

If a spreadsheet is large, you will not be able to view all of it on the screen at one time. To move within a spreadsheet, you can use the scroll bar, keystrokes, or the Go To command. As you use spreadsheets, you will find the methods that work best for you.

### Using the mouse

With the mouse, you can scroll through a spreadsheet using the vertical and horizontal scroll bars. To scroll, click the scroll box and drag it. You can also click the Up and Down arrows on the scroll bar or click the area above or below the scroll box. The active cell does not move to the area displayed when the scroll bars are used. To activate a cell, you must click the cell. Refer to the table below as you learn to move in a spreadsheet.

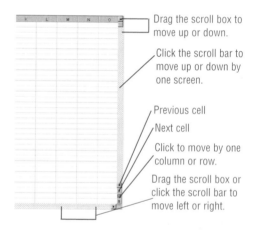

Drag the scroll box to move up or down.

Click the scroll bar to move up or down by one screen.

Previous cell

Next cell

Click to move by one column or row.

Drag the scroll box or click the scroll bar to move left or right.

| To scroll: | Action: |
|---|---|
| Up or down one row | Click Up or Down arrow buttons in the vertical scroll bar. |
| Up or down one window | Click area above or below the scroll box. |
| Any distance up or down | Drag the scroll box on the vertical scroll bar up or down. |
| Left or right by one column | Click the Left or Right arrow buttons on the horizontal scroll bar. |
| Left or right by one window | Click the scroll bar area to the left or right of the scroll box on the horizontal scroll bar. |
| Any distance left or right | Drag the scroll box on the horizontal scroll bar left or right. |

**54c • 8'**

## NEW FUNCTION

Read the information at right. Then complete the drill.

### Adjust column widths

The tables you have created thus far extend the full width of the margins. Often tables are more attractive if the columns are narrower. Column widths can be changed manually using the mouse.

**Using the mouse**

1. Point to the column border between the first and second column in the table.

2. When the point changes to ←|→, drag the border to the left to make the first column narrower or to the right to make the column wider.

3. Adjust the column width to leave approximately the same amount of space between the text and the border in each column (about .5").

When in position to drag a column boundary, the mouse pointer changes.

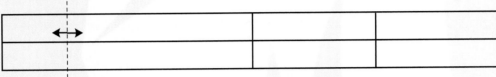

**Centering the adjusted table horizontally**

After the columns have been sized, the table should be centered horizontally to make it more attractive. Do this by changing the table position to Center.

1. With the insertion point in the table, click the **Table** button (see Table menu at left). Then click **Format**. (see Format menu below.)

2. Click the **Table** tab. Select **Center** in the *Table position on page* box.

3. Click **Apply**, then **OK**.

**Table menu**

**Drill**

1. Change the width of both columns of Drill 2 in 54b, using the mouse. Leave about .5" of space to the right of each column.

2. Center the table horizontally.

3. Save as **54c**. Print.

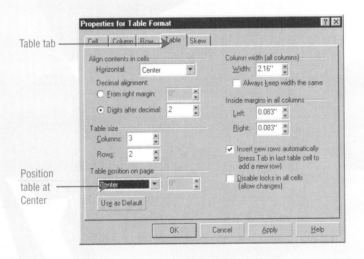

Table tab

Position table at Center

# Create a Spreadsheet

Start *Quattro Pro* by clicking the **Start** button, then selecting **Programs**, **WordPerfect Office 2000**, then **Quattro Pro 9**. When you start *Quattro Pro*, a spreadsheet will be displayed on the screen. The **spreadsheet** is where you enter your information. The *Quattro Pro* term for spreadsheet is "notebook." This module will use the generic term "spreadsheet" throughout.

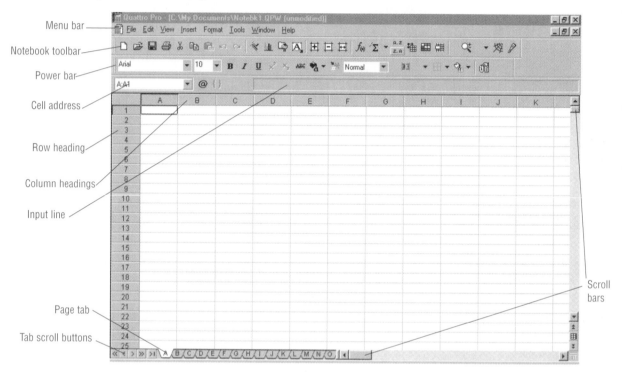

*Quattro Pro* includes many of the basic features that you have already learned while using *WordPerfect*. The **Menu bar**, common to all *Windows* software, provides access to all commands. The **Notebook toolbar** and the **Power bar** contain command buttons that are common to *WordPerfect* and others that are specific to the spreadsheet application. Further, spreadsheets include these specific components:

**Column:** Vertical list of information. Columns are labeled alphabetically from left to right; columns A–ZZZ are contained on one spreadsheet.

**Row:** Information arranged horizontally. Rows are numbered from top to bottom; Rows 1–1,000,000 are available on one spreadsheet.

**Cell:** An intersection of a column and row. Each cell has its own address consisting of the column letter and the row number such as A1 or AB36. A1 refers to Column A, Row 1; AB36 refers to Column AB, Row 36. The cell address displays the address of the **active cell**, which is the one that is ready for information to be entered. The active cell is surrounded by a dark border.

**Cell pointer:** An arrow-shaped pointer that appears when the mouse is over a cell. Similar to the arrow in *WordPerfect*, the cell pointer does not indicate the active cell. The cell that is highlighted with the dark border is the active cell. To select a specific cell, click inside that cell.

**FORMATTING**

**Table Format**

**Table format guides**

Effective use of character formats and appropriate justification improve the readability and appearance of tables. Character formats (e.g., bold, italic) provide emphasis. Justification positions text within a cell for easy reading.

**Main heading:** Center; ALL CAPS; bold.

**Secondary heading:** Center; bold; DS below main heading; capitalize main words.

**Column headings:** Bold; capitalize main words; shade row (optional). Justification: Generally center; however, headings may be left-, right-, or center-justified.

**Type size:** Generally use 12 point. Use 10 or 11 point when necessary to fit text in the column.

**Vertical placement:** Use a top margin of 1.5" or center vertically on the page.

**General:** Use italic for publication titles. Use underlining only in tables without borders. Right-justify whole numbers. Align decimal numbers at the decimal.

**Tables within documents:** DS above and below.

words

**Adjust column widths and center table**

1.5" top margin for each table

**Document 1**

1. Key the table.
2. Select the column heads in Row 1; bold and center.
3. Use the mouse to adjust column widths to have about .5" of space between the text and border.
4. Center the table horizontally.

**COLLEGE SPORTS PROGRAM**

| Fall Events | Winter Events | Spring Events |
|-------------|---------------|---------------|
| Football | Basketball | Golf |
| Soccer | Gymnastics | Baseball |
| Volleyball | Swimming | Softball |

5
13
18
23
29

**Document 2**

1. Key the table.
2. Bold and center headings.
3. Adjust column widths to have about .5" of space between text and border.
4. Right-align Column C entries.
5. Center the table horizontally.

MAJOR METROPOLITAN AREAS OF CANADA

| City | Province | Population |
|------|----------|-----------|
| Toronto | Ontario | 3,427,250 |
| Montreal | Quebec | 2,921,375 |
| Vancouver | British Columbia | 1,380,750 |
| Ottawa | Ontario | 819,275 |
| Winnipeg | Manitoba | 625,325 |
| Quebec | Quebec | 603,275 |
| Hamilton | Ontario | 557,250 |

7
12
17
22
30
34
40
44
49

# SPREADSHEET BASICS

**C**

*module*

## OVERVIEW

*Quattro Pro 9* is a sophisticated application that assists its users in managing numeric information, creating charts, and maintaining databases. A **spreadsheet** consists of rows and columns containing text, data, and formulas. The purpose of a spreadsheet is to solve numerical problems. Spreadsheets are used to calculate expenses, track sales, and prepare budgets. With spreadsheets you can do repetitive or complex calculations quickly and accurately. You can then format the information attractively or create charts that are easy to read.

In this module, you will learn to create a simple spreadsheet by entering text, values (numbers), and formulas. Then you will learn to adjust the column widths and format the information attractively. In the third lesson, you will create charts from spreadsheets as well as edit existing charts. The final lesson integrates these skills as an assessment.

**54d,** *continued*

**Document 3**

The Table feature provides an easy way to organize columnar data.

1. Key the short resume as a two-column table. Use a 1.5" top margin.
2. Format Column 1 in bold and adjust column widths. You will use this document in a later lesson.

**Kathleen O'Connor**
**1203 Grand Junction Ave.**
**Rupert, Idaho 83350-4321**
**208-555-8844**

| Objective | To work as an Accountant Assistant |
|---|---|
| Employment | Customer Service Representative<br>Anderson Hills Sports Shop, May 2000-September 2000<br>Quality Control--Freelancer for *Reflections* publication |
| Education | Midland Community College<br>Boise, Idaho<br>Associate Degree in Applied Technology<br>September 1999—June 2001<br>GPA 3.5 |
| Achievements | Barker English Scholarship Recipient, 6/99<br>Business Student of the Year, 5/2001<br>President of PBLA Chapter |
| References | Available upon request |

## 54e ● (optional)

### SKILLBUILDING

1. Key three 1' guided writings; determine *gwam*.
2. Key two 2' writings; try to maintain your best 1' rate.

**A** all letters                                                                *gwam*  1'  2'

Good plans typically are required to execute most tasks        11  6  50
successfully.   If a task is worth doing, it is worth investing   24  12  56
the time that is necessary to plan it effectively.   Many people  37  18  62
are anxious to get started on a task and just begin before they   49  25  69
have thought about the best way to organize it.   In the long run,  63  31  75
they frequently end up wasting time that could be spent more    75  37  81
profitably on important projects that they might prefer to tackle.  88  44  88

1' | 1 | 2 | 3 | 4 | 5 | 6 | 7 | 8 | 9 | 10 | 11 | 12 | 13 |
2' | 1 | 2 | 3 | 4 | 5 | 6 |

## 54f ● 3'

### SELF ✓ check

Answer the True/False questions at the right to see whether you have mastered the material presented in this lesson.

T  F

1. Column widths can be changed by using the mouse to drag the borders.
2. Copy can be aligned in cells using the Justification button.
3. Formatting applied to Cell A1 will affect all the cells in the table.
4. Each time you make changes to the table width, you must recenter the table horizontally.
5. Use the Center Page feature to center a table horizontally on the page.

**Document 3**
**Search for telecommunications organizations**

Technology and the telecommunications industry are impacting our work habits, how we solve problems, and national and state policies in numerous ways. Visit at least two telecommunications organizations on the Web. Explore the sites to learn about their purpose, who they serve, and how. Look for current press releases on topics such as cyber-cities, employment opportunities, training, and educational requirements.

Create a three- or four-paragraph article that focuses on employment and educational opportunities that appeal to you. Add at least one graphic element to your document. Suggested sites:

www.itaa.org, Information Technology Association of America

www.ccianet.org, Computer & Communications Industry Association

www.atis.org, Alliance for Telecommunications Industry Solutions

---

**Document 4**
**Job search announcement**
**Part 1**

Create a job search announcement that can be posted on the Web. Add a picture from the Internet. Make *searching* (¶ 1) a hyperlink. Apply color to the heading and eye-catching bullets. Use Help to learn to save a document in HTML format.

**Part 2**

Modify the announcement so it will be appropriate as a bulletin board posting for WW-HTV employees. Add at least 2 graphic elements.

**Optional:** Add a chart or table that provides meaningful data to job candidates. (Include information you've gained from your Internet search.)

### Careers and Internships in Telecommunications

Windows of opportunity. That's right—and the opportunity is here for you. Create your own opportunity by searching WW-HTV's online job bank with some of the industry's most dynamic and lucrative high-tech positions. WW-HTV is looking for bright and highly motivated people. If you are interested in cutting-edge technology, we are interested in you.

Are you a self-starter who likes to seize new opportunities?

Can you manage multiple demands and change priorities midstream without losing your cool?

Do you expect the best from yourself most of the time?

Do you enjoy brainstorming and strategizing?

Are you Internet-savvy?

Do you have outstanding communication skills—both verbal and written?

Are you a team player who can also work independently without losing focus?

If you can answer yes to three of the questions above, we're interested in you. Whether you're changing careers or just getting started, we have a position for you. E-mail chambers@wwhtv.xxx with your questions or call 1-800-555-0111, ext. 6289.

---

**Document 5**
**Create presentation**

Create a short presentation to be viewed by potential employees. Include the title of the joint venture, mission, location, and position opportunities. Include at least one slide that briefly defines or explains a joint venture. Apply what you have learned from Application 3.

# Tables with Decimals

## 55a ● 6'

### GETTING started

Key each pair of lines 3 times at a controlled rate. DS between 4-line groups.

## SKILLBUILDING WARMUP

2d finger
1 Dick Cen said he did kick Ike, but he did not intend to kick him.
2 Kami, Cedric, and Dick decided to check Dudley's new cedar cabin.

3d/4th fingers
3 Paul saw six-year-old Polly swallow a pepper plant last Saturday.
4 Zam said that Wallace will wash and wax all his old autos weekly.

| 1 | 2 | 3 | 4 | 5 | 6 | 7 | 8 | 9 | 10 | 11 | 12 | 13 |

## 55b ● 11'

### SKILLBUILDING

Key a 3' and a 5' writing.
**Goal:** maintain good control

all letters                                                            *gwam*   3'   5'

| | | | |
|---|---|---|---|
| Something that you can never escape is your attitude.  It | | 4 | 2 | 44 |

Something that you can never escape is your attitude.  It    4  2 44
will be with you forever.  However, you decide whether your    8  5 47
attitude is an asset or a liability for you.  Your attitude   12  7 49
reflects the way you feel about the world you abide in and   16  9 52
everything that is a part of that world.  It reflects the way you   20 12 54
feel about yourself, about your environment, and about other peo-   25 15 57
ple who are a part of your environment.  Oftentimes, people with   29 17 59
a positive attitude are people who are extremely successful.   33 20 62

At times we all have experiences that cause us to be   36 22 64
negative.  The difference between a positive and a negative per-   41 24 66
son is that the positive person rebounds very quickly from a bad   45 27 69
experience; the negative person does not.  The positive person is   49 30 72
a person who usually looks on the bright side of things and   53 32 74
recognizes the world as a place of promise, hope, joy, excite-   58 35 77
ment, and purpose.  A negative person generally has just the   62 37 79
opposite view of the world.  Remember, others want to be around   66 40 82
those who are positive but tend to avoid those who are negative.   70 42 84

| 1 | 2 | 3 | 4 |
|---|---|---|---|
| 1 | 2 | 3 | |

## Document 2

1. Use the information at the right for the presentation. Select the design Parchment from the Theme category.
2. Choose an appropriate clipart image (world map, satellite, etc.) and insert the image on each slide. Size the art and drag it to the upper-left corner of the slide. Click the title place-holder and drag it to the right to provide space for the clipart. See illustration.
3. Use Left to Right Sweep transition. Animate the bulleted items, using Fly In Left to Right; display one at a time.
4. Print a handout with 6 slides per page to attach to the newsletter.

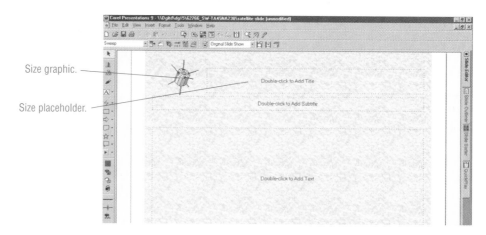

Size graphic.

Size placeholder.

**WW–HTV**
A Telecommunications Venture
Designed to Turn Dreams into
    Reality

**WW–HTV Components**
Satellite
Internet
Digital cable
Telephone

**WW–HTV Components**
CD-ROM
Broadband network
Programming
Video

**Satellite**
Digitally compressed direct broadcast
    satellite service
Current satellite—medium power
New launch—high power
Significantly expanded channel capacity

**Internet**
High-speed services
Secure data transmission
Real-time video
Multimedia animation

**Digital Cable**
Digital compression
Expanded channel capacity
Video and audio quality enhancement
Multiplexed movie service
Interactive navigator

**Telephone**
Wired cable/telephone service
Wireless cable/telephone service
Hybrid fiber/coaxial cable
Unified architectural platform

**CD-ROM**
Video games
Interactive software
Upgradeable media box

**Broadband Network**
Distribute voice, video, and data
Unique packaging and integrated
    product delivery
Integrated delivery of advanced
    communication services

**Programming**
Expand distribution of current
    products globally
Equity interest in over 100
    programming services
Content creation—new products

**Video**
Vivid multimedia animation
Digital video
Video display headset
Virtual reality

**WW–HTV**
Presented by
(Insert your name)

## Decimal align

*WordPerfect* can align copy within a table at the decimal point. The default is set for two decimal places. If the copy you are aligning contains more than two decimal places, you will need to increase the number of digits after the decimal.

**To format decimal places:**

1. Click the insertion point in the column where decimal align will be added or select the columns that will be decimal-aligned.
2. Click the **Table** button, then **Format**, then the **Column** tab.
3. Change the horizontal alignment to **Decimal Align**.
4. Click the *Digits after decimal* box and indicate the number of digits after the decimal. To make the text appear centered within the column, increase the number of places to the right of the decimal point. Click **Apply**, then **OK**.

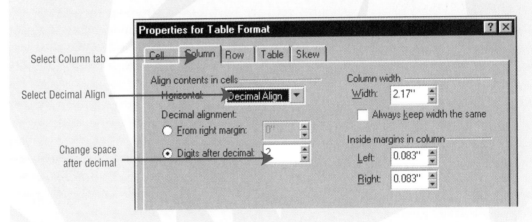

1. Format the table shown at the right.
2. Change the number of digits after the decimal to 4 in Column D.
3. Now increase digits after decimal to 8. Notice data appears centered in column.

55d • 25'

**FORMATTING**

**Document I**
1.5" top margin

1. Adjust column widths and center table horizontally.
2. Decimal-align the numbers in Column D. Increase digits after the decimal so the numbers appear centered.

| Employee | Position | Identification | Rating |
|----------|----------|----------------|--------|
| Ralph Marshall | Associate | 486028476 | 564.3333 |
| Janice Goodman | Manager | 3495075 | 87654.01 |

↑ Left-align    ↑ Center-align    ↑ Right-align    ↑ Decimal-align

### SALES OF BOOKS BY LEE RICE

words

| Book Title | Publication | Total Sales | Unit Price | |
|------------|-------------|-------------|------------|---|
| *Horrel Hill Adventures* | 1995 | $138,769 | $16.25 | 5 |
| *Tales of Tom's Creek* | 1998 | 92,761 | 8.95 | 15 |
| *Pommery Springs* | 1999 | 561,039 | 14.50 | 25 |

↑ Left-align    ↑ Center-align    ↑ Right-align    ↑ Decimal-align

**Second-column text**

The official launch of WW-HTV (WorldWide–Home Technology Ventures) opens a world of opportunity for all of our key stakeholders—our customers, employees, stockholders, joint venture partners, suppliers, and regulators—as well as the many other constituents with whom we interact on a daily basis. The six joint venture partners who created WW-HTV bring together an array of products and services in an integrated delivery system that is destined to turn our most futuristic dreams into reality very quickly. As you know from previous newsletters, all of the joint venture partners offer very successful state-of-the-art technology, products, and services that made them leading-edge competitors. While each partner excelled in its own core competency area, no one had the technology, the expertise, the resources, or the strategic focus to put the products and services together in an integrated delivery system and take it worldwide.

## Global perspective

All joint venture partners in the past focused primarily on the domestic market and then only secondarily in trying to bring the product or service to other parts of the world. WW-HTV totally reorders the priorities of everyone involved. Today, every component of WW-HTV begins with a global focus. Currently, the joint venture partners operate in 18 nations on four continents. With the synergies WW-HTV creates, representation on all continents and in at least 50 nations within five years is a very feasible target.

## Entrepreneurial perspective

The common thread binding all joint venture partners is a passion for being entrepreneurial that is so strong that it is best described as an entrepreneurial culture. The commitment to being an incubator for creativity and innovation drives every aspect of WW-HTV.

The job description for every new position to be filled clearly specifies that WW-HTV seeks an entrepreneurial leader who is both willing and capable of taking ownership of the operation involved. The incentive compensation system for current as well as new employees involved with WW-HTV is designed to reward innovation and creativity and to remove the fear from being a reasonable risk-taker. Employees who add value to WW-HTV not only are appreciated—they are compensated for the value they add to this exciting venture.

WW-HTV components consist of leading-edge products, services, and an integrated distribution system.

Create a diagram using text boxes for the components shown at the right. Refer to the illustration on the previous page.

| Satellite | Internet | Digital Cable |
|-----------|----------|---------------|
| Video | WW-HTV | Telephone |
| Programming | Broadband Network | CD-ROM |

Successful integration of all components in a global distribution network revolutionizes the telecommunications industry. WW-HTV currently has the capability to distribute data, voice, and video globally. Hybrid fiber networks, digital compression, direct broadcast satellite transmission, and the widespread home use of personal computers capable of handling extensive multimedia games and programs have created opportunities that heretofore did not exist.

**Insert file *WW-HTV Part 2*.**

## 55d, continued

**Document 2**

1. Key the table at right.
2. 1.5" top margin; center and bold headings.
3. Apply 20% fill to Row 1.
4. Decimal-align the numbers.
5. Key the source note a DS below the table.
6. Save as **55d-d2** and print.

### UNITED STATES DOLLAR TABLE
### Rates from January 27, 1999

| Foreign Currency | To United States Dollar | In United States Dollar |
|---|---|---|
| Australian Dollars | 1.5941 | 0.6273 |
| Austrian Schillings | 11.9853 | 0.834 |
| Belgian Francs | 35.1362 | 0.0285 |
| British Pounds | 0.6066 | 1.6485 |
| Greek Drachmas | 280. | 0.0036 |
| Italian Lira | 1686.4994 | 0.0006 |
| Japanese Yen | 115.62 | 0.0086 |
| Malaysian Ringgit | 3.8 | 0.2632 |
| Portuguese Escudo | 174.6207 | 0.0057 |
| Singapore Dollars | 1.689 | 0.5921 |
| South Korean Won | 1176. | 0.0009 |
| Taiwan Dollars | 32.36 | 0.0309 |

Source: Exchange Rates <http://www.x-rates.com>

**Document 3**

**Memo with table**

1. Key the memo in proper format.
2. Center and bold column heads in table.
3. Center Columns A and C.

TO:        Eugene Fernando
FROM:      Lori Smith
DATE:      Current
SUBJECT:   Purchase Order 1522

The items that you requested on Purchase Order 1522 will be shipped to you today. However, item #702 is currently backordered and is not expected to be available for shipping for another six weeks.

We have the following similar cabinets currently in stock. Please let us know if one of these cabinets would be a suitable replacement. We will ship the cabinet to you the same day we receive your order.

| Item Number | Description | Unit Price |
|---|---|---|
| 329 | Lordusky locking cabinet | 212.00 |
| 331 | Anchorage heavy-duty locking cabinet | 265.00 |
| 387 | Lordusky locking cabinet (unassembled) | 175.00 |

xx

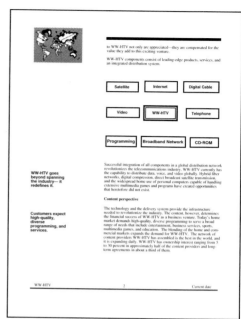

Position the first-column text across from the topic being discussed in the newsletter. See illustration above.

**First-column text—page 1**

**WW-HTV has a mission of turning dreams into reality.**

**WW-HTV shifts the focus from a domestic market to a global market.**

**An entrepreneurial culture with a commitment to being an incubator for creativity and innovation drives WW-HTV.**

**First-column text—page 2**

**WW-HTV goes beyond spanning the industry—it redefines it.**

**Customers expect high-quality, diverse programming and services.**

**First-column text—page 3**

**WW-HTV is dedicated to building long-term shareholder value.**

**WW-HTV strives to meet customer needs and to exceed customer expectations.**

**WW-HTV takes great pride in contributing to the communities it serves.**

# Tables with Shading

## 56a • 6'

## GETTING started

each line 3 times SS; DS
between 3-line groups

alphabet 1 Frank expected to solve a jigsaw puzzle more quickly than before.

figures 2 I moved from 1892 Main Street, Apt. 3, to 7065 Main Street, Apt. 4.

adjacent reaches 3 We walked to the hilltop when we were here last autumn with Guy.

easy 4 If I burn the signs, the odor of enamel may make a toxic problem.

| 1 | 2 | 3 | 4 | 5 | 6 | 7 | 8 | 9 | 10 | 11 | 12 | 13 |

## 56b • 20'

## NEW FUNCTION

You can click the **Cell Fill** button on the Tables toolbar to quickly choose a fill pattern. ▒

### Shading cells

For emphasis, shading can be applied to cells. Normally, shading is used to emphasize headings, totals, or divisions or sections of a table.

**To shade cells:**

1. Place insertion point in the cell to be shaded, or select the cells if more than one.
2. Click the **Table** button and choose *Borders/Fill*.
3. Click the **Cell** tab.
4. Under *Cell fill*, click the box next to *Fill*.
5. Point to a fill or pattern and click the drop-list arrow.
6. Click **Apply**, then **OK**.

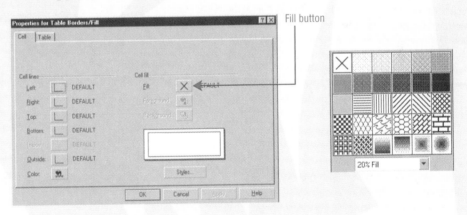

Fill button

## Drill

Key table as illustrated at the right. Use 20% Fill in Row I.

| Committee Member | Telephone Number |
|---|---|
| Christopher H. McMaster | (803) 555-3928 |
| Eric W. Blankenship | (604) 555-1749 |

**Document 1
Newsletter**

Read the information at the right; then format the newsletter on the next page according to the specifications provided at the right. Note that you will need to insert the file *WW-HTV Part 2*, which is saved on the formatting template.

Use a nonbreaking hyphen with WW-HTV to keep the name from breaking at the end of lines.

**Functions applied:**
Columns
Clipart
Drawing
TextArt

## Newsletter Specifications

### Page setup

**Margins:** Use 1".

**Footer:** Insert horizontal line.

**Footer text:** Position **WW-HTV** at the left margin; the page number at the center; and *current date* at the right margin.

**Columns:** First column—1.5" wide; gutter spacing—.5" wide; second column—4.5" wide.

**Spacing:** Single-space the document; use 9-pt. space between paragraphs.

### Text specifications

**Columns:** First-column heads—Arial, 12 pt., bold; second-column body—Times New Roman, 11 pt.

**Headings:** Side—Arial, 12 pt., bold; paragraph—Times New Roman, 11 pt., bold.

**Spacing:** Use 1 space after period at the end of sentences.

### Graphic elements

**Clipart:** Insert a world map at the top left corner of each page. If you do not have the map illustrated on the next page, use an appropriate substitute that depicts the world or the communications industry. Scale the image to about 2" wide and maintain proportions.

**Banner:** Use TextArt for the first-page banner. Select a shape that inflates the top. On pages 2 and 3, use a thick line as a top border over the right column.

**Illustration:** Use text boxes to position the components in the illustration on page 2. Place a heavy line and thin line border around the center text box containing WW-HTV so that it will stand out from the components.

**56b,** *continued*

**Document I**

1. Key the table. Apply bold and shading (20%) as shown.
2. Adjust column widths.
3. Decimal-align Columns B and C. Increase Digits after decimal to 8 to make the columns appear centered.
4. Center the table vertically and horizontally.

The dollar sign is included with the first figure of a column and with totals. To align the dollar sign left of the numbers, you may need to insert blank spaces between the figure and the $ sign.

Use Center Page to center the table vertically. Choose *Format, Page, Center.* ▪

**FALL DRY CLEANING SPECIALS**

| Garment | Regular Price | Special Price | |
|---|---|---|---|
| Wool sweater | $ 6.00 | $ 4.75 | 13 |
| Men's two-piece suit | 6.00 | 4.75 | 24 |
| Men's three-piece suit | 7.25 | 5.50 | 31 |
| Women's two-piece suit | 5.50 | 4.25 | 37 |
| Leather jacket | 12.50 | 10.00 | 43 |
| Slacks | 2.25 | 1.75 | 46 |
| Skirt | 2.00 | 1.50 | 49 |
| Blazer | 3.50 | 2.00 | 53 |
| Silk blouse | 4.75 | 4.25 | 57 |

(5, 18 appear at top right of header/first row)

**Document 2**

1. Key the table at the right. Apply bold to the column heads and shade the bottom row (20%).
2. Decimal-align Column C.
3. Adjust column widths.
4. Center the table horizontally and vertically.

**MILE-HIGH PASTRIES, INC.**

| Item | Quantity | Price | |
|---|---|---|---|
| Blueberry muffins | 3 dozen | $18.75 | 16 |
| Dinner rolls | 2 dozen | 8.00 | 21 |
| Whole wheat breadsticks | 2 dozen | 10.50 | 28 |
| Brownies | 1 dozen | 7.50 | 33 |
| Pastries | 2 dozen | 9.75 | 37 |
| Total | | $54.50 | 40 |

(5, 9 appear at top right of title/header)

# WW-HTV, NEWSLETTER AND PRESENTATION

## OBJECTIVES

Create a two-column newsletter with clipart and text boxes.

Create *Corel Presentations* slide show.

Create a job search announcement for posting to the Web.

Search the Web for telecommunications organizations.

## OVERVIEW

**WW-HTV** In this project, you will utilize your desktop publishing, *Presentations*, and Web skills. You will prepare a newsletter announcing a new business—WW-HTV (WorldWide-Home Technology Ventures)—that puts together current products and services of six companies that have formed a joint venture. The newsletter will serve as a public relations document; therefore, it is important that it be desktop published following principles of good design. You will also prepare a *Presentations* slide show that will be used in describing the new venture to various groups of people. You will update your knowledge of the telecommunications industry by visiting various telecommunications organizations and creating a document that addresses job skills and education. You will prepare a job search announcement that can be posted to the Web, and create a presentation for new employees from what you have learned.

## Tables without lines (SpeedFormat)

SpeedFormat contains preformatted table styles. In some cases, you may want to apply one of these attractive formats rather than using the default format. For example, to create a table without the printed gridlines, you would select the *No Lines No Border* style. When the No Lines No Border style is selected, dotted gray lines will display in place of the gridlines. The dotted lines will not print; they simply indicate the cell borders.

### To format a table without lines:

1. Key the table; adjust column width if necessary.
2. With the insertion point in the table, click the **Table** menu; then select *SpeedFormat*. The Table SpeedFormat dialog box displays.
3. Select *No Lines No Border* from the *Available styles* box.
4. Click **Apply.**

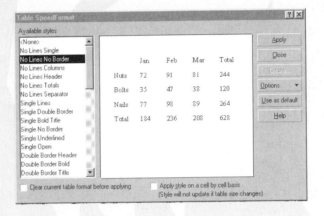

### Drill

1. Open *54d-d2*.
2. Experiment applying different styles.
3. Apply the *No Lines No Border* style.
4. Save as **56c** and print.

56d ● 19'

### Document 1

1. Open *54d-d3*. Save as **56d-d1**.
2. Using SpeedFormat, experiment applying different styles to the table.
3. Apply *No Lines No Border* style, save, and print. Now this table has an attractive format that is appropriate for a resume.

### Document 2

1. Format the table, applying a style that displays the information attractively. Use the same style for documents 2 and 3.
2. Key the source note a DS below the table.

## Annual Salary Ranges by Job Title

## (Rounded to the Nearest Dollar)

| Title/Position | Quoted Salary Range | Average Salary Range |
|---|---|---|
| Office Manager | $15,500-$85,900 | $36,200-$38,464 |
| Executive Assistant | $23,600-$46,000 | $35,000-$35,807 |
| Administrative Assistant | $20,700-$43,700 | $32,377-$33,742 |
| Secretary | $16,500-$57,500 | $31,436-$32,075 |

Source: Office Institute, 2000.

**A**ctivity

*nineteen*

### Prepare a Presentation for the Great Outdoors Club

**Setting:** You have just joined the Great Outdoors Club—a group of relatively inexperienced campers who enjoy being outside and have decided to learn how to make camping more enjoyable and to take camping trips together.

**Problem:** You are one of six club members who have been asked to be responsible for putting together a presentation recommending a specific site for the next camping trip. The Club will select one of the six sites recommended. In the discussion, members made it clear that they did not want to visit the routine tourist-type places. The Club recommended that you recruit a team of three or four other members to help you prepare the presentation. If your recommendation is selected, you (and the members of your team) will receive a special travel pack for the trip.

#### Web sites to consider:

www.fs.fed.us (USDA Forest Service)
www.gorp.com (Great Outdoor Recreation Pages)
www.sierraclub.org (Sierra Club)
www.sportsafield.com (Sports Afield)
www.rei.com (Recreational Equipment Incorporated)
www.lnt.org (Leave No Trace)
www.Packlitefoods.com (Pack Lite Foods)
www.GreatOutdoors.com (Outdoors Web site)

#### Outcomes

Your team should plan the process you will use to put together your presentation. Each team member should be responsible for finding several sites and deciding on the site you will recommend. Once a site has been determined, divide the responsibilities for researching and preparing the presentation among your team. Select a design template so that the slides can be merged. Include the following topics:

* The site selected, why you chose it, and what is unique about it

* Realistic estimate of cost—use a spreadsheet or table to break down major cost items

* What each member should bring on the trip, including items that can be shared so that everybody will not be bringing the same items

* Hints for packing effectively and lightly

* Hints on food and cooking on a camping trip

* Safety tips for the type of trip chosen

* List of at least five Web sites used in addition to the ones suggested

**56d,** *continued*

**Document 3**

1. Format the table using the same style as Document 2.
2. Adjust column widths and center the table horizontally. Set a tab for the source note to align it under Column A entries.

| Skills Mentioned in Want Ads | |
| --- | --- |
| Skill/Ability | Percentage Requested |
| Computer | 87.2 |
| Office Suite | 60 |
| Organization | 47.6 |
| Telephone | 25.2 |

Source: Office Institute, 2000.

**(optional)**

**Document 4**
**Memo with table**
Key the data at the right as a memo from **Elizabeth Barkley** to **Team Members**. Add a subject line and current date. Then copy the tables (Documents 2 and 3) and paste them after the memo body. Delete the source lines. Adjust the vertical space of the document if necessary so that both tables and the memo fit on one page.

The Office Institute collected data from more than 2,000 want ads to track skills, requirements, and salary ranges for different positions. Listed below are some of the findings. They also found that:

Indent →The "secretary" classification has diminished dramatically in the past five years. "Executive assistant" and "administrative assistant" have increased significantly.

Indent →Internet skills and knowledge of software application suites are being requested far more frequently than in past years.

**56e** ● **(optional)**

**SKILLBUILDING**

**Improve accuracy**
Key a 2' writing; count errors. Key two more 2' writings. Try to reduce errors with each writing.

 all letters                                                                 *gwam*  2'

| | | |
| --- | --- | --- |
| Little things do contribute a lot to success in keying. | 6 | 53 |
| Take our work attitude, for example. It's a little thing; yet, | 12 | 59 |
| it can make quite a lot of difference. Demonstrating patience | 18 | 66 |
| with a job or a problem, rather than pressing much too hard for a | 25 | 72 |
| desired payoff, often brings better results than we expected. | 31 | 79 |
| Other "little things," such as wrist and finger position, how we | 38 | 85 |
| sit, size and location of copy, and lights, have meaning for | 44 | 91 |
| any person who wants to key well. | 47 | 94 |

|   1   |   2   |   3   |   4   |   5   |   6   |

**Application B9,** *continued*

Slide 8
## Plan the Closing
Prepare the audience for the closing
Select points you want audience to retain
Bring presentation to natural closure

Slide 9
## Deliver the Presentation
Use body language effectively
Pace presentation appropriately
Use voice effectively
Engage audience
Use humor appropriately
Use visuals effectively
Avoid vocal noise and distracting mannerisms

Slide 10
## Plan the Physical Setting
Comfort factors
Facility size and layout
Equipment considerations
Effectiveness factors

**Select layout with clipart or picture of workstation environment.**

Slide 11
## Facilitate Discussion
Ensure that everyone understands the question
Balance and control audience participation
Handle poor or obnoxious questions tactfully

**Select layout with clipart or picture.**

Slide 12
## Presented by
*Your Name*
Training Specialist
E-mail:  kstone@speak.com
Web address:  www.speak.com

**Part 2:  Notes pages**
Key speaker notes provided at right for Slides 2 and 7.

**Part 3:  Print presentation**
1. Print audience handout for the entire presentation. Use the 2x3 thumbnails.
2. Print speaker notes for Slides 2 and 7.
3. Print the presentation title slide and the last slide. These pages will be used as the front and back cover for the handout pages.
4. Save the presentation as **app-b9p3**.

**Notes for Slide 2 (Presentation Components)**

What are three key components of an effective presentation?  (Wait for audience response.)

Briefly describe the three to be discussed today:
    Content (includes opening, body, close)
    Delivery
    Physical Setting

**Notes for Slide 7 (Prepare Effective Visuals)**

Who is the star of the presentation?  The presenter or the visual?

Then why use visuals?
Retention rate increased:
    Wharton Research Center retention study:
    Verbal only—7% retention rate
    Verbal with visuals—38% retention rate

# Join/Split, Insert/Delete Cells

**LESSON 57**

**57a • 6'**

## GETTING started

Key each pair of lines 3 times at a controlled rate. DS between 6-line groups.

### SKILLBUILDING WARMUP

direct reaches

1 June and my brother, Bradly, received advice from junior umpires.

2 My bright brother received minimum reward for serving many years.

adjacent reaches

3 Clio and Trey were sad that very few voters were there last week.

4 Western attire was very popular at the massive auction last week.

double letters

5 Tommie Bennett will go to a meeting in Dallas tomorrow afternoon.

6 Lee will meet Joanne at the swimming pool after accounting class.

| 1 | 2 | 3 | 4 | 5 | 6 | 7 | 8 | 9 | 10 | 11 | 12 | 13 |

---

**57b • 12'**

**NEW FUNCTION**

## Join/split cells

Cells can be joined together to make a larger cell, or they can be split into more cells. Cells can be joined and split horizontally and vertically.

**To join cells:**

1. Select the cells to be joined.
2. Click the **Table** button; choose *Join,* then *Cell.*

**To split cells:**

1. Place the insertion point in the cell to be split; select the cells if more than one.
2. Click the **Table** button; choose *Split,* then *Cell.* The Split Cell dialog box displays.
3. To split the cells into more columns, click the **Columns** button and specify the number of columns to be created. Click the **Rows** button to split the cells into more rows.

### Drill I

1. Create a 2-column, 4-row table.
2. Join Cells A1 and B1.
3. Select Cells B2, B3, and B4. Split the cells into two columns.
4. Key the table as shown below.
5. Position the insertion point in the last cell (C4) and press **TAB** to add a row.
6. Add: **Service and supplies sales 82,385,023   91,404,573**

| PRODUCT LINE SALES COMPARISON | | |
|---|---|---|
| **Product Line** | **1999** | **2000** |
| Hardware sales | $180,485,284 | $195,210,357 |
| Software sales | 136,947,201 | 128,794,203 |

APPLICATION

*Slides and handouts for a presentation*

## Time schedule

Assemble materials ..... 3'
Timed production ...... 40'
Final check;
 compute *n-pram* ....... 7'

### Part 1: Prepare slides

Use the information below and on the next page to prepare a new presentation using the *Polo* master from the *Design* category.

1. Choose the appropriate slide layout shown; add appropriate clipart or photo.
2. Use the slide transition effect *Sweep to Center*.
3. Animate bulleted lists as follows:
   • All slides:
       Fly In, Left to Right.
   • Slide 1: None.
   • Slide 5: None.
   • Slide 6: None.
4. Rearrange slides to follow outline presented in Slide 2. Move Slide 11, *Facilitate Discussion*, after Slide 8, *Plan the Closing*.
5. Save as **app-b9**. Do not close. Go on to Part 2.

---

Slide 1
### CREATING EFFECTIVE PRESENTATIONS
Macon Civic Club
October 30, 200-

Slide 2
### Presentation Components
Presentation content
    Effective opening
    Well-organized body with illustrations
    Effective closing
    Controlled Q/A Session
Effective delivery
Conducive physical setting

Slide 3
### Plan the Opening
Set the tone for the entire presentation
Use a short opening to get attention quickly
Establish credibility
Establish rapport with audience
Engage the audience

Slide 4
### Prepare an Interesting Message
Illustrate
Use variety
Consider audience interests
Avoid overkill with details

Slide 5
### Include Projected Visuals
    Transparencies
    Computer visuals
    Slides
    Video

Slide 6
### Include Nonprojected Visuals
    Models, products, or other objects
    Handouts
    Flip chart

Slide 7
### Prepare Effective Visuals
Select visuals that support rather than replace you
Use visuals you can control
Limit the use of visuals that dominate the presentation

**Select layout with clipart. Choose appropriate clipart such as a person using a visual in a presentation.**

**57b,** *continued*

Apply what you have learned about joining and splitting cells.

## Drill 2

1. Create a 2-column, 4-row table.
2. Join Cells A1 and B1.
3. Select Cells B2, B3, and B4. Split into two columns.
4. Select Cells A2, A3, and A4. Join to form one cell.
5. Place the insertion point in Cell A2. Split into three columns.
6. Place the insertion point in Cell B2 (now the second column). Split into two rows. (Your table should look like the table shown below.)

| | | | | |
|---|---|---|---|---|
| | | | | |
| | | | | |

**57c ● 10'**

**NEW FUNCTION**

## Drill

1. Follow instructions 1-3 of Drill 1, 57b, to create the table at the right.
2. Key the table.
3. Position the insertion point in the last cell (C4) and press **TAB** to add a row.
4. Key: **Presentation software 4,367,650 8,986,317**
5. Position the insertion point in Row 3. Click **Table**, then **Insert**. Click the **Rows** button and choose *Before*. Click **OK**.
6. Key: **Word processing software 85,974,216 91,574,319**
7. Position the insertion point in Row 5 (Graphics software); delete the row. Click **Table,** then **Delete** and **OK**.

## Insert and delete rows

**To insert a row:**

1. Click at the position where the new row is to appear.
2. Click **Table**, then **Insert**.
3. Click the **Rows** button; enter the number of rows to be inserted.
4. Indicate whether the additional rows are to be placed before (above) or after (below) the insertion point by clicking on the appropriate button. Then click **OK**
5. To add a row below the last row, press **TAB** in the last cell.

**To delete a row:**

1. Click the insertion point in the row that is to be deleted.
2. Click **Table,** then **Delete**.
3. Indicate the number of rows to be deleted. Click **OK**.

| SOFTWARE APPLICATION SALES | | |
|---|---|---|
| **Product Line** | **1999** | **2000** |
| Spreadsheet software | $63,829,000 | $71,385,210 |
| Graphics software | 12,847,927 | 10,274,287 |

*Prepare speaker notes*

1. With *app-b6* open, go to Speaker Notes.
2. Select Slide 2; click **Insert Text from Slide**.
3. Repeat for Slides 3 and 5.
4. For Slide 4, insert the text on slide and edit as shown at the right.
5. Save as **app-b7**.

| Decision Factor | More Formal | Less Formal |
| --- | --- | --- |
| Stakes | High | Low |
| Audience disposition | Hostile | Friendly |
| Complexity | Complex | Simple |
| Audience size | Large | Small |
| Audience rank/status | High | Low |
| Repeat performance | Likely | One time |
| Organization norms | Traditional | Casual |

## Printing

As you prepare a presentation, you will need to print (1) the slides, (2) the speaker notes, and (3) a handout or notes for your audience. You may choose to print all slides, the current slide, or a range of slides.

**To print slides and speaker notes:**

1. From the File menu, choose *Print*.
2. Select *Full document* or *Current view*.
3. Select what you want to print: Slides or speaker notes.
4. Enter a range of slides if all slides are not desired.
5. Click **OK**.

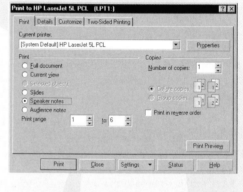

**To print the audience handout:**

1. Click **File**, **Print**, then click the radio button for **Audience notes**.
2. From the Customize tab, click **Thumbnails**. Click the button to the right of Thumbnails. Click and drag across and down the grid to select layout; e.g., 3x3, or 2x4, etc.).
3. Click **Print**.

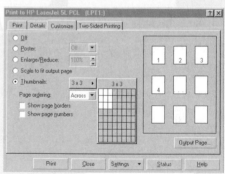

*Print audience handout and selected slides*

1. Open *app-b7*. Print Slides 2-3.
2. Print audience handouts as thumbnails in the format 2x3.
3. Close *app-b7*.

words

## 57d ● 22'

Adjust column widths; shade the heading row 20%; center tables vertically and horizontally.

**Document 1**
1. Create a 2-column, 6-row table.
2. Join the cells (A1 and B1) in Row 1.
3. Split the cells B2-B6 into two columns.
4. Key the table and save.

| SAFETY AWARDS | | | |
|---|---|---|---|
| Award Winner | Department | Amount | 9 |
| Josephine C. Schlictman | Engineering | $2,500 | 18 |
| Christopher J. Westmoreland | Marketing | 2,000 | 26 |
| Marjorie T. Stankiewicz | Purchasing | 1,500 | 35 |
| Frederico P. Hernandez | Research | 1,000 | 42 |

**Document 2**
Retrieve Document 1; add Rows 4 and 8 (shown in italic), and delete Row 6 as shown at right.

| SAFETY AWARDS | | | |
|---|---|---|---|
| Award Winner | Department | Amount | 9 |
| Josephine C. Schlictman | Engineering | $2,500 | 18 |
| *Robert R. Bauerschmidt* | *Maintenance* | *2,250* | 26 |
| Christopher J. Westmoreland | Marketing | 2,000 | 35 |
| ~~Marjorie T. Stankiewicz~~ | ~~Purchasing~~ | ~~1,500~~ | |
| Frederico P. Hernandez | Research | 1,000 | 43 |
| *Franklin T. Cousins* | *Security* | *500* | 49 |

**Document 3**
**Challenge document**
Create the table shown at right.

| CANADA GEOGRAPHICAL INFORMATION | | | | | |
|---|---|---|---|---|---|
| Key Islands | | Key Mountains | | Key Lakes | |
| Island | Sq. Miles | Mountain | Height | Lake | Sq. Miles |
| Baffin | 195,928 | Logan | 19,524 | Superior | 31,700 |
| Victoria | 83,897 | St. Elias | 18,008 | Huron | 23,000 |
| Ellesmere | 75,767 | Lucania | 17,147 | Great Bear | 12,095 |
| Newfoundland | 42,031 | Fairweather | 15,300 | Great Slave | 11,030 |
| Banks | 27,038 | Waddington | 13,104 | Erie | 9,910 |
| Devon | 21,331 | Robson | 12,972 | Winnipeg | 9,416 |

## Slide Sorter view

**Slide Sorter view** provides miniature versions of all slides in the presentation. These miniature versions make excellent handouts when printed. In this view, you can add animation and transition effects as well as position your slides in a different order.

1. With *app-b5* open, click **Slide Sorter** view.
2. Drag Slide 3 and move it between Slides 1 and 2. Your slides will be in the order shown at right.
3. Select Slides 2–6 and apply the *Blinds*, *Vertical* transition.
4. Go to Slide Editor view. In Slides 2–6, animate bullets using *Fly In* effect and *Left to Right* direction.
5. Save as **app-b6**. Keep the presentation open.

Transition

Direction of the slide transition

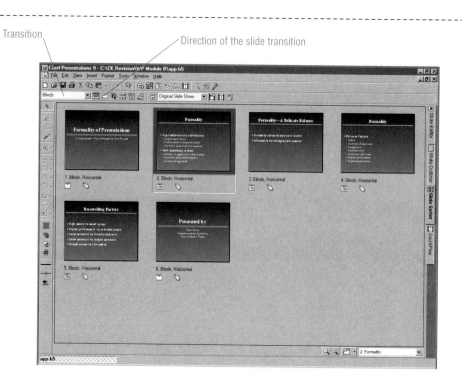

## Speaker Notes

The **Speaker Notes** feature is used for keying the speaker's notes. Display the slide you want to write notes for. If you are in Slide Sorter View, click the desired slide.

**To create speaker notes:**

1. Click **Format, Slide Properties, Speaker Notes**.

2. Key your notes in the Speaker Notes text box or click **Insert Text** from Slide to use notes from the current slide. Use the arrows to move back or forward to notes on other slides.

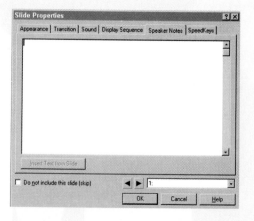

# Assessment

## GETTING started

each line 3 times SS; DS
between 3-line groups

### SKILLBUILDING WARMUP

| | | |
|---|---|---|
| alphabet | 1 | Jacob Kazlowski and five experienced rugby players quit the team. |
| figures | 2 | E-mail account #82-4 is the account for telephone (714) 555-6039. |
| double letters | 3 | Anne will meet with the committee at noon to discuss a new issue. |
| easy | 4 | The men may pay my neighbor for the work he did in the cornfield. |

| 1 | 2 | 3 | 4 | 5 | 6 | 7 | 8 | 9 | 10 | 11 | 12 | 13 |

## 58b ● 10'

### SKILLBUILDING

**Assess straight-copy skill**
Take a 3' and a 5' writing; determine *gwam*; proofread and circle errors.

all letters             *gwam*   3' | 5'

|  | 3' | 5' |
|---|---|---|
| Whether any company can succeed depends on how well it fits | 4 | 2 | 44 |
| into the economic system.   Success rests on certain key factors | 8 | 5 | 47 |
| that are put in line by a management team that has set goals for | 13 | 8 | 49 |
| the company and has enough good judgment to recognize how best to | 17 | 10 | 52 |
| reach those goals.   Because of competition, only the best orga- | 21 | 13 | 55 |
| nized companies get to the top. | 23 | 14 | 56 |
| A commercial enterprise is formed for a specific purpose; | 27 | 16 | 58 |
| that purpose is usually to equip others, or consumers, with | 31 | 19 | 61 |
| whatever they cannot equip themselves.   Unless there is only one | 36 | 21 | 63 |
| provider, a consumer will search for a company that returns the | 40 | 24 | 66 |
| most value in terms of price; and a relationship with such a com- | 44 | 27 | 68 |
| pany, once set up, can endure for many years. | 47 | 28 | 70 |
| Thus our system assures that the businesses that manage to | 51 | 31 | 73 |
| survive are those that have been able to combine successfully an | 56 | 33 | 75 |
| excellent product with a low price and the best service--all in a | 60 | 36 | 78 |
| place that is convenient for the buyers.   With no intrusion from | 64 | 39 | 80 |
| outside forces, the buyer and the seller benefit both themselves | 69 | 41 | 83 |
| and each other. | 70 | 42 | 84 |

| 3' | 1 | 2 | 3 | 4 |
| 5' | 1 | 2 | 3 |

# APPLICATION

**B4**

*Create presentation in Slide Outliner view*

1. Create a new presentation in Slide Outliner view.
2. After you key the outline, click **Format**, **Master Gallery**. Apply the *Darkblue* master from the Color category.
3. Change Slide 5 to the Title layout as follows:
   a. In Slide Editor view, go to Slide 5.
   b. Click the **Select Layout** button on the toolbar.
   c. Click **Title** and **OK**.
4. Save the presentation as **app-b4**.

**Slide 1—Title slide**

> Title: **FORMALITY OF PRESENTATIONS**
>
> Subtitle: A Continuum
> Very Informal to Very Formal

**Slides 3 and 4—Bulleted list (break where appropriate; repeat title)**

> Title: **Formality**
>
> Decision Factors
> - Stakes
> - Audience disposition
> - Complexity
> - Audience size
> - Audience rank/status
> - Repeat performance
> - Organization norms
>
> Reconciling Factors
> - High stakes vs. small group
> - Repeat performances vs. informal norms
> - Large audience vs. friendly audience
> - Small audience vs. hostile audience
> - Formal norms vs. low stakes

**Slide 2**

> Title: **Formality— A Delicate Balance**
>
> - Formality enhances audience control
> - Informality encourages participation

**Slide 5—Title slide**

> **Presented by**
>
> *Your Name*
> Communication Specialist
> *Your School's Name*

# APPLICATION

**B5**

*Working in Slide Outliner view*

1. Open *app-b4*; save as **app-b5**.
2. In Slide Outliner view, position the insertion point at the end of text of the second slide; press ENTER. A space is added to insert copy.
3. Press SHIFT+TAB to move the copy higher in the organizational hierarchy.
4. Key the title and text shown at the right as Slide 3. Choose *Bulleted List* as the slide layout.
5. Save again; do not close.

**Formality**

- Rigid adherence to conventions
  - Conservative dress
  - Professionally designed visuals
  - Carefully controlled environment
- How something is done
  - Manner as opposed to what is done
  - Carefully controlled behavior
  - Structured approach

## 58c ● 34'

**FORMATTING**

Center tables horizontally and vertically. Use the mouse to adjust column widths.

**Document 1**

**Document 2**
1. Right-align Columns B, C, and D.
2. Shade the Total row 10%.

**Document 3**
1. Create a 3-column, 9-row table.
2. Join the cells in Row 1 for the title.
3. Split Cells B3-B9 into two columns.
4. Split Cells C3-C9 into two columns.
5. Shade Row 1 20%.
6. Alignment:
   Headings, center
   Column A, left
   Columns B & D, right
   Columns C & E, decimal

**Document 4**
Retrieve Document 1 and add the information at the right as Row 1 and Row 6 to keep the time in correct order (total words, 58).

### INTERVIEW SCHEDULE

### Conference Room 1

| | |
|---|---|
| 10:00-10:50 a.m. | Alice Salva, Marketing Manager |
| 11:00-11:50 a.m. | Roger Eason, Advertising Director |
| 12:15-1:45 p.m. | Catered Lunch with Sales Team |
| 2:00-3:30 p.m. | Ginger Fogler, Vice President of Marketing |

(4, 7, 17, 28, 38, 49)

### ESTIMATES ON KITCHEN CABINETRY

| Kitchen Component | VSP Kitchens | Designs by Pat | Euro Image |
|---|---|---|---|
| Cabinetry | $34,475 | $22,100 | $38,350 |
| Granite countertops | 8,150 | 7,950 | 10,275 |
| Halogen lighting | 1,450 | 1,600 | 1,800 |
| Appliances (allowance) | 12,000 | 12,000 | 12,000 |
| Total | $56,075 | $43,650 | $62,425 |

(6, 18, 24, 32, 39, 48, 54)

| INTERNATIONAL EXPORTS | | | | |
|---|---|---|---|---|
| **Exports** | **1999** | | **2000** | |
| **Goods and Services** | **$ Millions** | **% of Total** | **$ Millions** | **% of Total** |
| Agriculture | 3,798 | 8.8 | 4,783 | 9.5 |
| Mining | 23,587 | 54.6 | 25,261 | 50.4 |
| Manufacturing | 11,582 | 26.8 | 15,438 | 30.8 |
| Other Goods | 410 | 1.0 | 518 | 1.0 |
| Services | 3,791 | 8.8 | 4,155 | 8.3 |
| Total | 43,168 | 100.0 | 50,155 | 100.0 |

(4, 8, 21, 27, 33, 41, 46, 52, 58)

| | |
|---|---|
| 9:00-9:50 a.m. | Mark Baker, Project Manager |
| 3:45-4:30 p.m. | Jan Mason, Human Resources Manager |

# Views and Printing

**Working with different views**

In Lessons B1 and B2, you created presentations in Slide Editor view and then looked at them in each of the views available in *Presentations*. In this lesson, you will do more extensive work in the various views.

**Slide Outliner view**

An **outline** is a summary of key points. In *Presentations*, the outline consists of titles and main text from each slide. Slide Outliner view is especially useful in organizing a presentation. Presentations can be created and edited in Slide Outliner view, or an outline can be imported from another source such as a *WordPerfect* outline.

**To create slides in Slide Outliner view:**

1. Begin a new presentation; then click **Slide Outliner** to display the Slide Outliner screen.

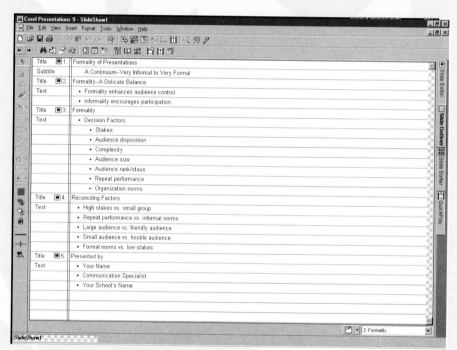

2. Key the title of the first slide; press ENTER.
3. Key the subtitle of the slide and press ENTER, or press ENTER to skip the subtitle. Press CTRL+ENTER to begin the next slide.
4. Key the title and all points on the next slide; press ENTER after each bulleted item. Press TAB after the first bulleted item to move down a level (to the right) or SHIFT+TAB to move up a level (to the left).
5. Repeat Steps 2-4 to complete the presentation.

## Objective Assessment

Answer the questions below to see if you have mastered the content of this module.

1. A vertical list of information is called a _____.

2. A horizontal array of information is called a _____.

3. To move to a previous cell of keyed information in a table, press _____.

4. To center a table horizontally, click the Table button, then select _____.

5. The _____ feature contains preformatted styles that can be applied to tables.

6. The preformatted style _____ will print the table without gridlines.

7. *WordPerfect* defaults to _____ decimal places.

8. Click _____ from the Table drop-down menu to access shading.

9. Cells can be _____ together to make a larger cell, or cells can be _____ into more cells.

10. To delete a row, place the insertion point in the row to be deleted, and then click the _____ button and select _____.

## Performance Assessment

1. Create a 2-column, 9-row table.
2. Join Cells A1 and B1.
3. Split Cells B2-B9 into two columns.
4. Center, bold, and shade all headings 10%.
5. Align columns as marked. Adjust Digits after decimal in Column C to keep % symbol on the same line.
6. Adjust column widths. Center table.
7. Print the table.
8. Delete the Communications row.
9. Add a row for the Management Department that has 1,298 majors and an 8.45% growth rate. Position in alphabetical order.
10. Save and Print.

| COLLEGE OF BUSINESS ADMINISTRATION | | |
|---|---|---|
| **Department** | **Majors** | **Growth Rate** |
| Accounting | 945 | 3.65% |
| Banking, Finance, and Insurance | 1,021 | 2.17% |
| Communications | 326 | -2.5% |
| Economics | 453 | 1.4% |
| International Business | 620 | 14.74% |
| Management Science | 1,235 | 11.8% |
| Marketing | 1,357 | 10.38% |

↑ Left-align      ↑ Right-align    ↑ Decimal-align

**Application B3,**
*continued*

Slide 1—Title slide

> **PERCEPTION**
>
> Process Through Which
> Information Is Selected,
> Organized, and Interpreted

Slide 2

> **Understanding Perception**
>
> ■ Perception is selective
>   - Information is filtered in
>   - Information is screened out

Slide 3

> **Understanding Perception**
>
> ■ People bring to a situation
>   - Values
>   - Experiences
>   - Cultural differences
>   - Motives
>   - Expectations

Slide 4

> **Understanding Perception**
>
> ■ Perceptual frame of reference
>   determines
>   - How one perceives information
>   - How one interprets information

Slide 5

> **Factors Affecting Perception**
>
> ■ Presentation style
> ■ Dress and general appearance
> ■ Level and type of language used
> ■ Formality of presentation
> ■ Way controversy is handled
> ■ Negotiation style

Slide 6—Title slide

> **Presented by**
>
> Peggy Walters
> Training Manager
> Hess and Associates

**Slides with clipart illustrated. Clipart may vary.**

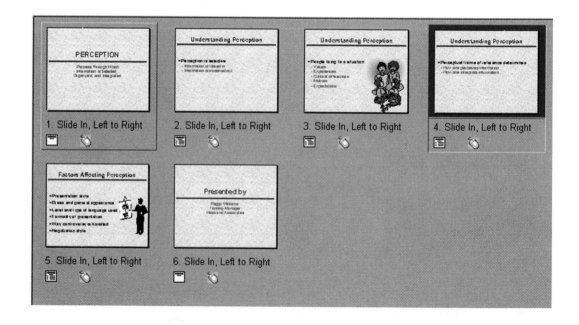

# Assessment

## GETTING started

each line 3 times SS; DS
between 3-line groups

### SKILLBUILDING WARMUP

| | | |
|---|---|---|
| alphabet | 1 | Jayne promised to bring the portable vacuum for next week's quiz. |
| figures | 2 | Our main store is at 6304 Grand; others, at 725 Mayo and 198 Rio. |
| 1st finger | 3 | After lunch, Brent taught us to try to put the gun by the target. |
| easy | 4 | He may make a profit on corn, yams, and hay if he works the land. |

| 1 | 2 | 3 | 4 | 5 | 6 | 7 | 8 | 9 | 10 | 11 | 12 | 13 |

## SKILLBUILDING

**Assess
straight-copy skill**
Key a 3' and a 5' writing;
proofread and circle errors;
determine *gwam* for both
writings.

  all letters

*gwam* 3' | 5'

|  | 3' | 5' |
|---|---|---|
| At a recent June graduation ceremony, several graduates were | 4 | 2 | 43 |
| heard discussing the fact that they had spent what they thought | 8 | 5 | 46 |
| was a major part of their lives in school classrooms. They esti- | 13 | 8 | 48 |
| mated the amount of time they had been in elementary school, in | 17 | 10 | 51 |
| high school, in college, and in graduate school had to be about | 21 | 13 | 54 |
| nineteen or twenty years. | 23 | 14 | 55 |
| Indeed, two decades is a significant span of time. Even if | 27 | 16 | 57 |
| little additional effort is used seeking education, about a | 31 | 19 | 59 |
| quarter of a person's life will have been spent on learning ac- | 35 | 21 | 62 |
| tivities. Graduation is a time for looking at the past and the | 39 | 24 | 65 |
| present and analyzing how they can be merged to form a future. | 44 | 26 | 67 |
| And thus begins The Search. | 45 | 27 | 68 |
| The Search begins with introspection--attempting to sort out | 50 | 30 | 71 |
| and pinpoint all that has gone before, to identify purpose behind | 54 | 32 | 73 |
| the years of effort and expense, to focus it all on some goal. | 58 | 35 | 76 |
| If encouraged to name the goal, we call it, probably for lack of | 63 | 38 | 78 |
| a more definitive name, Success. We desire to be successful. | 67 | 40 | 81 |
| But what is "success"? | 68 | 41 | 82 |

3' | 1 | 2 | 3 | 4 |
5' | 1 | 2 | 3 |

## APPLICATION B2

*Transition and animation*

1. Prepare a new slide presentation (click **Corel Presentations Slide Show** and **Create**).
2. From the Nature category, select *Clouds* master.
3. Choose *Blinds*, *Vertical* as the transition for all slides.
4. For Slides 2–4, animate bulleted lists using *Fly In* effect and *Left to Right* direction.
5. Add graphics to Slides 3 and 4.
6. Save the presentation as **app-b2**; do not close.
7. View the presentation by clicking the **QuickPlay** view button.

**Slide 1 (Title slide)**

> **SOCCER CLINIC**
>
> Sponsored by
> Vernon Futbol Club

**Slide 2 (Bulleted list)**

> **Soccer Facts**
>
> - Earlier versions of game existed over 2500 years ago
> - Most popular spectator sport
> - Fastest-growing participative sport

**Slide 3 (Text and graphic)**

> **Equipment Needs**
>
> - Uniform
> - Socks
> - Shinguards
> - Shoes
> - Ball
> - Athletic bag

**Slide 4 (Bulleted list with graphic)**

> **Game Rules**
>
> - Time limits
> - Direct kick
> - Indirect kick
> - Goal kick
> - Corner kick
> - Penalty kick

## Slides with subpoints

**Subpoints** on a slide refer to the second level of paragraph points. To have subpoints under bulleted text, place the insertion point in the text line of the bulleted item you want to change. Press TAB to move the bulleted item down a level (to the right) or SHIFT+TAB to move the bulleted item up a level (to the left). When you press ENTER, the next line will be at the same level as the line before. Transitions that are added to the bulleted items will also affect the lower-level bulleted items.

## APPLICATION B3

*Animate subpoints*

1. Create a presentation using the *Parchment* background from the *Theme* category.
2. Choose *Slide In* transition effect with *Left to Right* direction; apply to all slides.
3. For Slides 2-5, animate bulleted lists using the *Curve In* effect and *Left and Up* direction.
4. Add clipart to Slides 3 and 5.
5. Save the presentation as **app-b3**; do not close.
6. Play the presentation. Check that all of the points and subpoints animate.

## 59c ● 32'

### Assess document skills
**Time schedule:**
Assemble materials  . . . .  2'
Timed production  . . . . .  25'
(Key documents in order; proofread and correct errors as you work.)
Final check  . . . . . . . . . .  5'
(Proofread and circle any remaining errors. Calculate *g-pram*—total words keyed divided by 25'.)

### Document 1
**Editing exercise**
Use the following format:
DS
TM: 1.5"
LM: 1.5"
RM: 1"
Make the revisions marked in the document.

---

No More Waiting  (14 pt)  3

(12 pt) How often do you sit by the phone waiting for a call?  14

You can't make calls because you might miss your call.  25

Adding to your frustration, a friend calls to talk for only  37

*ital.*
one minute.  Of course, that one minute is when your other  49

caller choses to dial your number.  Unfortunately, you have  61

no way of knowing that you have missed the long-awaited  73

call.  You return to your waiting and still anticipate ing the  84

call. ¶ Put a n end to missing calls with Call Waiting.  You  96

can enjoy the pleasure of using your phone at any # time.  107

When another call comes in, you can answer the second call  119

with out hanging up on the first one.  What are you waiting  131

for ?  Dial 555-2379 and start enjoying no more waiting.  142

---

### Document 2
**Letter in block format**
Key this average-length letter in block format.

---

January 28, 200- | Mr. Patrick Horton | 1873 Lindsey Ave. | Fair Haven, NJ  14
07704-3821 | Dear Patrick  19

Thank you for visiting with me and the other faculty from Helmings  32
Community College who attended Career Day at your high school  44
on January 20, 200-.  We are very pleased that you are interested in a  59
degree in business technology.  65

The faculty and I commend you for your thorough search of academic  79
programs by browsing colleges' home pages on the Internet.  Currently,  94
our home page has been visited by over two thousand prospective stu-  107
dents.  We are very happy to count you among our new students.  120

Since our visit last week, I have forwarded your name and address to the  135
following offices:  admissions, financial aid and scholarships, recruiting,  150
honors programs, and extracurricular programs.  You will be receiving  164
information from these groups in the next few weeks.  Be sure to read  178
the materials carefully, watching specifically for application deadlines.  193

Please call me at 555-0039 for an appointment to schedule your fall  206
classes.  208

Sincerely | Lahitia Graeter | Business Instructor | xx  218

## Transition effects

**Transitions** move one slide off the screen and bring the next slide on. Slides can move in from the left or the top, they can fade out, or they can dissolve into the next slide. Transitions must be chosen with care. Keep in mind that the content of the presentation is more important than having text elements "flying" across the screen. If the transition is distracting, the impact of your presentation is lost.

**To add transitions while you are creating a slide:**

1. In Slide Editor view, right-click and select *Transition* from the Quick menu.
2. Click the effect desired to transition from one slide to the next, e.g., **Sweep**.
3. Select the direction of transition, e.g., *Left to Right*.
4. Click **OK** to apply to the current slide, or click **Apply to all slides in slide show** and **OK** to apply the transition to all slides.

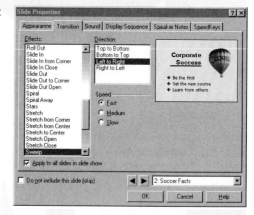

## Animation

When a computer is used to project visuals, the bulleted list can be displayed one point at a time and graphics can enter upon clicking the mouse. Adding movement to text and objects is called **animation**.

**To animate bulleted text:**

1. In Slide Editor view, right-click the bulleted text area and click **Object Animation** from the Quick menu.
2. From the Bullet Animation tab, select *Animate object across screen* as the animation type.
3. Choose the desired animation effect and the desired direction.
4. Click the option **Display one at a time**.
5. Click **OK** to apply to the current slide or check **Apply to All**.

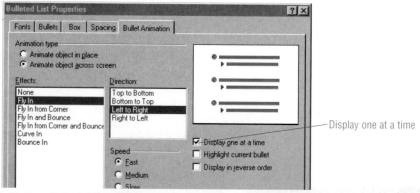

**Document 3**
**3-column table**

1. Use 10-point type. Center a 3-column, 9-row table.
2. Join cells in Row 1 for titles. Key **EMPLOYMENT RESOURCES** and press ENTER.
3. Key **April 200-**.
4. Key the addresses *without* underlines. Do not space within the addresses. Press the Space Bar or TAB following the last letter in the address. *WordPerfect* will automatically convert the address to a hypertext link.
5. Adjust column widths to allow text in Columns A and B to fit on one line.
6. Shade Row 1. Print.
7. Add **FedWorld** in alphabetical order.
8. Center table vertically and horizontally.
9. Print.

**Technology review**

Internet addresses are automatically converted to hypertext links. If you are connected to the Internet, double-clicking on the Internet address will automatically take you to the Web site.

| EMPLOYMENT RESOURCES | | | 4 |
|---|---|---|---|
| April 200- | | | 6 |
| **Title** | **Address** | **Description** | 12 |
| American Employment Weekly | http://branch.com/aew/aew.html | Employment tabloid with ads from the Sunday edition of 50 leading newspapers | 23 / 29 / 35 / 39 |
| Datamain | http://www.datamain.com | Allows applicants to fill out a structured resume or search an online job center | 49 / 53 / 57 / 61 |
| Help Wanted | http://helpwanted.com | Searchable index of openings compiled from companies that have paid to be listed | 89 / 93 / 97 / 102 |
| Job Center | http://www.jobcenter.com | Employment service for professionals with database searching | 114 / 118 / 121 |
| Job Trak | http://www.jobtrak.com | Largest online job listing service in the United States | 132 / 136 / 139 |
| Job Web | http://www.jobweb.org | Employment information, job listings, tips, and more | 147 / 151 / 156 |
| Online Career Center | http://www.occ.com | Career center and employment databank | 166 / 171 |

*FedWorld*    http://www.fedworld.gov    *Bulletin board of job listings from the federal government* — 72 / 76 / 78

**Document 4**
**Interoffice memo**

**TO:** Rosa Garcia | **FROM:** John David Schoenholtz | **DATE:** Current |    13
**SUBJECT:** Internships Available    20

Two internships are still open for senior business technology majors for the fall semester. Companies requesting student interns are Fountain Insurance Agency and Heights-McDonnell Telecommunication Ltd. Both companies have agreed to pay the interns minimum wage for 90 hours.    34 / 47 / 59 / 72 / 76

Please post the enclosed flyer that announces the positions with contact names and phone numbers. I would also appreciate your taking a few minutes in your first class meeting to announce these openings and to share the benefits of completing an internship during the senior year. Please note that students must have a 3.0 GPA to enroll in the internship course.    90 / 103 / 117 / 131 / 145 / 149

xx | Enclosure    152

## Slide Layout, Transition, and Animation

**Selecting a slide layout**

In *Presentations 9*, slides consist of a layout and a background. Different layouts can be used for slides. You can design a layout or use a template (as in Lesson B1) to add interesting features to a presentation. You can also create a background or choose a master from the Master Gallery. *Presentations 9* includes 40 backgrounds with the standard installation.

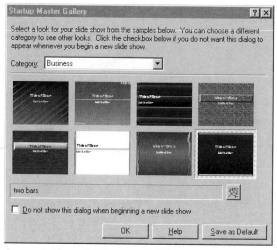

**Presentations 9: Master Gallery**

**Drill 1**   **Adding a graphic**

1. Choose the *Corel Presentations Side Show* option from the PerfectExpert dialog box. Click **Create**.

2. In the Startup Master Gallery dialog box, choose *Design* as the category; then click the *adobe* master. Click **OK**.

3. To select a layout, click the **New Slide** button on the toolbar; select *Bulleted List*. Click **OK**.

4. Key the title: **Style**.

5. Add the text shown below to the text box.

   • **How are you perceived?**

   • **How do you want to be perceived?**

**Tip:** If you have trouble selecting the entire image, press CTRL+A to select all of it.

6. Click **Insert** menu, **Graphics**, and then **Clipart**. From the Clipart tab, choose an appropriate clipart image.

7. Click and drag the clipart to the desired position on the slide. Close the Scrapbook. Drag the corner handles to size the clipart.

8. Save the slide as **b2-d1**.

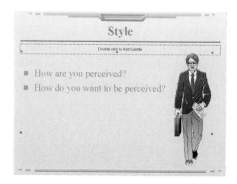

## LESSON 60

# Assessment

60a ● 6'

**G**ETTING
**s t a r t e d**

each line 3 times SS; DS
between 3-line groups

SKILLBUILDING WARMUP

alphabet  1  Jack Voxall was amazed by the quiet response of the big audience.
fig/sym  2  Our #3865 clocks will cost K & B $12.97 each (less 40% discount).
shift  3  In May, Lynn, Sonia, and Jason left for Italy, Spain, and Turkey.
easy  4  It is the duty of a civic auditor to aid a city to make a profit.

| 1 | 2 | 3 | 4 | 5 | 6 | 7 | 8 | 9 | 10 | 11 | 12 | 13 |

60b ● 11'

## SKILLBUILDING

**Assess
statistical-copy skill**
Key a 3' and a 5' writing; circle
errors; determine *gwam*.

  all letters/figures

*gwam*  3'  5'

Now and then the operation of some company deserves a closer | 4 | 2 41

look by investors.  For example, Zerotech Limited, the food, oil, | 8 | 5 44

and chemical company, says in its monthly letter that it will be | 13 | 8 46

raising its second-quarter dividend to 85 cents a share, up from | 17 | 10 49

79 3/4 cents a share, and that a dividend will be paid July 12. | 21 | 13 51

This fine old area firm is erecting an enviable history of | 25 | 15 54

dividend payment, but its last hike in outlays came back in 1987, | 30 | 18 56

when it said a share could go above 65 cents.  Zerotech has, how- | 34 | 21 59

ever, never failed to pay a dividend since it was founded in | 38 | 23 61

1937.  The recent increase extends the annual amount paid to | 42 | 25 64

$5.40 a share. | 43 | 26 65

In this monthly letter, the firm also cited its earnings for | 47 | 28 67

the second quarter and for the first half of this year.  The net | 52 | 31 70

revenue for the second quarter was a record $1.9 billion, up 24.2 | 56 | 34 72

percent from a typical period just a year ago.  Zerotech has its | 61 | 36 75

main company offices at 9987 Nicholas Drive in Albany. | 64 | 38 77

3' | 1 | 2 | 3 | 4 |
5' | 1 | 2 | 3 |

1. Key the following 4 slides using the *Default* master from the *Color* category. Slide 1 uses Title layout by default. Choose *Bulleted List* layout when you add Slides 2, 3, and 4.

Slide 1 (Title slide)

> **CRITICAL CAREER SKILLS**
>
> Technical Skills
> Interpersonal Skills
> Conceptual Skills

Slide 2 (Bulleted list)

> **Technical Skills**
>
> ◆ Design an effective multimedia presentation
> ◆ Deliver an effective multimedia presentation

Slide 3 (Bulleted list)

> **Interpersonal Skills**
>
> ◆ Get along with others
> ◆ Behave diplomatically
> ◆ Communicate effectively

Slide 4 (Bulleted list)

> **Conceptual Skills**
>
> ◆ Identify the big picture
> ◆ Identify how your job fits into the big picture
> ◆ Design presentation that meets audience needs

2. Save the presentation as **app-b1**.
3. View the entire presentation in each of the 4 views:
   - Click **Slide Outliner**.
   - Click **Slide Sorter**.
   - Click **Slide Editor**. Click the slide tabs at the bottom of the slide to move from one slide to the next.
   - Click the arrow next to the text box at the bottom of the screen to see a complete listing of all slides created.
   - Click the first tab labeled **1: Critical Career Skills**. This places you at the beginning of the slide show.
   - Click the **QuickPlay** tab to view the slides as they will appear when projected on the screen. To advance through the slide show, use the left mouse button, Space Bar, or right arrow key. To go back to the previous slide, use the left arrow key, Backspace key, or right mouse button.

**Assess reports**
**Time schedule:**
Assemble materials . . . . . 2'
Timed production . . . . . . 25'
  (Key documents in order;
  proofread and correct errors
  as you work.)
Final check . . . . . . . . . . . 6'
  (Proofread and circle any
  remaining errors. Calculate
  *g-pram*—total words keyed
  divided by 25'.)

**Document I**
**Unbound report**
Format and key the unbound
report at the right.
- DS the report.
- Format main, side, and
  paragraph headings appropriately. Divide main heading into two lines.
- Indent direct quotation;
  bold and italicize as shown.

COPYRIGHT LAW: IMPLICATIONS FOR STUDENTS AND TEACHERS          11

The subject of copyright law is an area of much attention today. The          25
technological advancements in the areas of software, CD-ROMs with          38
sight and sound clips, videotaping, and electronic publishing are only          52
the beginning of questions being raised. There is also a need to          66
understand the Copyright Act of 1976. Groups will continue to work          79
toward change of copyright laws to broaden the use of these new          92
media. This report will present information about the Copyright Act of          106
1976 and identify implications of the copyright law related specifically          121
to students and teachers.          126

Copyright Act of 1976          131

The Copyright Act of 1976 states that things to be copyrighted include          145
"original works of authorship fixed in any tangible medium of          157
expression." Hard copy is only one form of many types of media.          171
Other media include software stored on floppy disk or hard drive,          184
sound recordings, movie productions, still photographs stored on CD-          197
ROM, and the list grows as the technology advances. Publishers have          211
interpreted this copyright law as they print the following statement on          225
copyrighted materials:          230

> **ALL RIGHTS RESERVED.** *The text of this publication, or*          241
> *any part thereof, may not be reproduced or transmitted in any*          254
> *form or by any means, electronic or mechanical, including*          265
> *photocopying, recording, storage in an information retrieval*          277
> *system, or otherwise, without the prior written permission of*          290
> *the publisher.*          293

Implications for Students and Teachers          301

Students and teachers are two groups often facing decisions regarding          315
copyright infringements. For this reason, these groups should be          328
aware of the following situations where the copyright law is prevalently          343
violated.          345

Plagiarizing. Using the work of another without citation is a major          359
offense. Manuscript style manuals clearly delineate the proper manner          373
to cite work borrowed from another. Student term papers as well as          386
faculty manuscripts submitted for publication in journals should          399
include appropriate documentation.          407

Copying music. The composers of the music and the lyrics are pro-          420
tected by copyright law. The copyright protects these individuals' abil-          434
ities to earn profit by disallowing copying of music. For that reason,          449
music directors are required to purchase the needed number of origi-          462
nals for the group.          467

## Develop a presentation

Once the master has been selected, you are ready to design the individual slides for the presentation. *Presentations* provides seven frequently used layouts to ensure efficiency and consistency.

**To develop a presentation:**

1. Double-click in the **Title** box and key the main title.
2. Double-click in the **Subtitle** box and key the subtitle.
3. Click the **New Slide** button on the toolbar to display the New Slide dialog box.

4. Select one of the 7 slide layouts. This layout will be applied to the number of slides keyed in Step 5.
5. Key the number of slides required in the Number to add text box. Click **OK**.

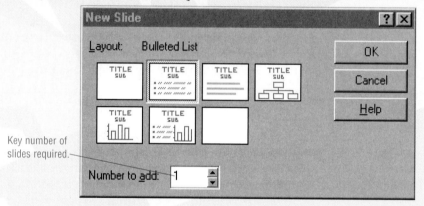

**Note:** To easily and quickly add one slide at a time, click the Down arrow next to the **Insert New Slide** button at the bottom of the document screen. Click a layout for the slide.

6. To delete unwanted slides, click the **Slide Sorter** view button at the right of the slide. Select the unwanted slide and press DELETE. Return to Slide Editor view by clicking **Slide Editor**.
7. Key the slide.
8. Repeat Steps 3-7 each time you wish to insert and key a new slide.

Using copied software.  Using software for which a license has not been
issued has become a common violation of the copyright law.  While some
software is labeled public domain, other software is copyrighted and a
license is required.  Make a policy never to pirate software.  Be sure all
software being used at home or at the office has been officially licensed
and is legal.

Photocopying copyrighted materials.  Copying a textbook in part or in its
entirety is a violation most people do without considering it as an infringement.  Consequently, public copiers often have displayed the text of the
copyright law in an effort to warn offenders.  Again, by allowing entire textbooks or parts of books to be photocopied, the offender is depriving the
authors and publishing companies of income.  Consider the effect on
today's and future originators if the copyright law did not prohibit copying
in this manner.

Using copyrighted materials without permission.  When using graphics in
presentation handouts and/or electronic presentations, students and
teachers are often using cartoons and other graphics without seeking permission from the owner.  Presenters need to know that many graphics in
printed and in electronic media are copyrighted.  Permission to use these
copyrighted materials is possible by submitting a request to the owner.  A
fee for a one-time use may be assessed.  Using a cartoon without permission becomes more complicated when the violator receives remuneration
for the presentation or submits the manuscript for publication.

Conclusion

Because technology has broadened the areas of copyright infringement, it
is very important for students and teachers to be knowledgeable of possible copyright violations.  Be sure to give credit to authors or creators for
their copyrighted work.  If you want to reproduce or reprint portions or
perhaps use a cartoon in a presentation, always write to the appropriate
individual for written permission.

## REFERENCES

**Document 2**
**Leftbound report**
Reformat Document 1 as a
leftbound report.

Bayless, Marsha L., Debbie D. DuFrene, and Florence E. Elliott-Howard.
    "Sound and Sight:  Legal Dimensions of Multimedia."  *1995 South-
    west Administrative Services Association Proceedings.*  Phoenix,
    December 1995.

Ricks, Betty R., Ann J. Swafford, and Kay E. Gow.  *Information and Image
    Management.*  3d ed.  Cincinnati:  South-Western Publishing Co.,
    1992.

U.S. Constitution, art. 1, sec. 8, cl. 8.

words column:
481
495
509
524
539
542

557
572
587
603
617
631
646
650

664
678
692
706
721
736
751
765
778

780

794
809
824
839
853
860

863

877
890
903
906

920
933
934

942

## Main window

The main window for *Presentations* includes many of the features that are already familiar to you. The Menu bar and toolbar serve the same functions as in *WordPerfect*. The Property bar displays directly below the toolbar. The Tool Palette, which allows you to add shapes, fill, charts, and other graphics, displays at the left of the screen. A tab is added below the screen for each slide in the presentation. Either the tabs or list of slides at the right allow you to move easily among slides.

Menu bar

Toolbar

Property bar

Tool Palette

Slide views

Slide tabs

List of slides

## Views

Located at the right of the slide are the View buttons. Use the views as follows:

1. **Slide Editor:** View, create, and modify individual slides in a slide show. The Slide Editor view shows the slide as it will appear when it is presented or printed.
2. **Slide Outliner:** Create or view a slide show in outline form.
3. **Slide Sorter:** Display a miniature of each slide for sorting purposes.
4. **QuickPlay:** Display slides as they will appear when projected on the screen, starting with the current slide.

## Online Help

**Online Help** is a very useful tool in learning how to use *Presentations*. The same Help techniques that you used in *WordPerfect* apply to *Presentations*. Click **Help** on the Menu bar, and then click **Ask the PerfectExpert**. Key your question or topic, and click **Search** to produce a list of topics. Select one of the topics and click **Display**.

## **A**ctivity

*ten*

### Key table with data extracted from the Internet

Searching the Internet for current stock quotes is quick and easy. The information can be transferred into a *WordPerfect* table.

**Practice**
1. Key the table. Center headings and apply 20% fill to Row 1. Save as **Activity10**.
2. Log on to the Internet. Click in the *Location, Address*, or *Netsite* box. Key **msn.com** and press ENTER. The Microsoft home page displays. Scroll down the page to find the stock quotes.
3. Key the first company symbol from the table in the *get quote* box. Click *get quote*.
4. Write down the quotes for Last and Change.
5. Key the next symbol in the *Enter Symbol* box at the top of the page. Click *Enter*. Repeat for each company.
6. Exit the Internet. Return to *WordPerfect* to key the numbers in Columns C and D. Right-align the numbers. Save and print.

### HIGH-TECH STOCK PERFORMANCE

#### Quotes for Current Date

| Symbol | Name | Last | Change |
|---|---|---|---|
| IBM | International Business Machines Corporation | | |
| INTC | Intel Corporation | | |
| MSFT | Microsoft Corporation | | |
| NSCP | Netscape Communications Corporation | | |
| ELNK | Earthlink Network, Inc. | | |
| AOL | America Online, Inc. | | |
| COSFF | Corel Corporation | | |

**Starting
Presentations**

# Getting Started

1. Click the **Start** button. Select *Programs, WordPerfect Office 2000*, then click **Corel Presentations 9**. The PerfectExpert dialog box displays.

2. To create a new presentation, click the **Create New** tab. Click **Corel Presentations Slide Show**, then **Create**.

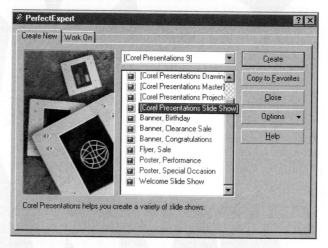

(To open an existing presentation, click the **Work On** tab and select the desired file.)

3. The Startup Master Gallery displays. The Gallery allows you to choose from several different master categories. For this lesson, we will use the *Default* master from the *Color* category (the green background) and click **OK**.

4. The title slide displays in Slide Editor view. The title slide layout varies depending on the master selected.

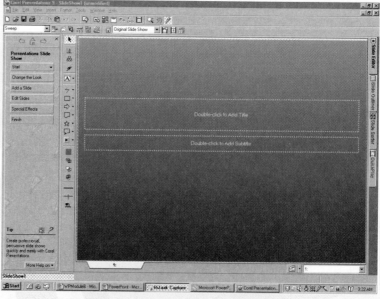

*Corel Presentations 9:* **Main window**

**A**ctivity

*eleven*

## Update table with data extracted from the Internet

Changing currency rates is another area in which the Web can be used to update a table in a *WordPerfect* document.

**Practice**

1. Open *55d-d2*. Replace the date in the heading with the current date. Save as **Activity11**.
2. Log on to the Internet. Key **x-rates.com** in the *Location* or *Address* box and press ENTER. The Exchange Rates home page displays.
3. Click the *Exchange rates* down arrow. Select *United States Dollar*.
4. Click the **Table** button, then click **Submit**.
5. Copy the data from Columns B and C for each currency listed in *55d-d2*. Exit the Internet.
6. Open **Activity11** in *WordPerfect*. Use Typeover mode to replace the numbers in the table with the current numbers. Save and print.

**A**ctivity

*twelve*

## Map a trip

The Maps hyperlink provided by several search engines will search for a specific route and provide an overview map and turn-by-turn maps with text.

**Practice**

1. Click the **Search** button in your Web browser. Browse the search engines to locate the hyperlink for *Maps*; click to open.
2. Your destination city is Asheville, North Carolina. Enter your home city and state as the starting point. Search for a turn-by-turn map with text. Print the directions. What is the total distance? _____ What is the estimated time? _____.
3. You are having a party and need to give guests directions to your home. Using the Excite search engine, go to *Maps* and choose *Map a U.S. Address*. Enter your street address, city, and state, and click **Map it!** Print and trim the map to fit in your party invitation.
4. Use *Maps* from the AltaVista search engine to create a map of your city. Use *Fancy Features* and enter your phone number. Print the map.

**A**ctivity

*thirteen*

## Use a comprehensive search engine

A comprehensive search engine can help you locate information quickly on the Web. The All-in-One Web site is a compilation of search tools found on the Internet, including such categories as People, News and Weather, and Other Interesting Searches/Services.

**Practice**

1. Open the All-in-One Web site (http://www.AllOneSearch.com).
2. From the *People* category:
   a. Use Bigfoot to find the e-mail address for (*provide a name*).
   b. Use Ahoy! To find the home page for (*provide a name*).
3. From the *News and Weather* category:
   a. Use Pathfinder Weather Now to find your current weather.
   b. Use one of the news searches to find news articles about (*provide current event*).
4. From the *Desk Reference* category:
   a. Find the area code for Jackson, Mississippi _____; Cincinnati, Ohio _____.
   b. Find a quotation from *Bartlett's Quotations* about (*provide the topic*).
5. From the *Other Interesting Searches/Services* category:
   a. Convert the U.S. dollar to Canadian dollar _____.
   b. Find a recipe for red velvet cake (*or your recipe choice*).

# PRESENTATIONS

**B**

*module*

## OVERVIEW

### Creating effective presentations

Effective business presentations generally are supported by carefully designed visuals. Good visuals can be prepared using word processing software; however, using presentation software is more efficient and effective.

*Corel Presentations 9* software provides the tools necessary to design and produce a very professional presentation. In addition, *Presentations* makes it easy to integrate materials from other software such as *WordPerfect* and *Quattro Pro*. The reverse is also true; you can create material in *Presentations* and bring it into other software such as *WordPerfect*.

Your keyboarding activities in this module focus on preparing presentation documents using *Presentations* software.

Presentation documents include slides, handouts, speaker's notes, and outlines.

**Slides:** Documents that can be projected, such as overhead transparencies, 35mm slides, or computer-projected visuals.

**Handouts:** Documents that contain smaller, printed versions of the slides in the presentation.

**Speaker's notes:** Documents that contain a miniature slide on each page plus notes that a speaker can use in making the presentation.

**Outlines:** Documents that provide the title and main text of the slides without the graphics or formatting used on the slide.

## OBJECTIVES

1. Apply your keyboarding, formatting, and word processing skills.

2. Work with few *specific* directions.

# Selkirk Communications, Project

Selkirk Communications is a training company that is relocating its office from Spokane, Washington, to Nelson, Canada. As an administrative assistant, you will prepare a number of documents using many of the formatting and word processing skills you have learned throughout Lessons 31–60. Selkirk Communications uses the block letter format and unbound report style.

**Document 1**  SC
**Invitation**
Format this document attractively. Use a different font for the main heading and callouts (PLACE, TIME, etc.). Vary font size. DS between listed items; position the document attractively on the page. Save as **m8-d1**.

|                                                                                      | words |
|--------------------------------------------------------------------------------------|-------|
| **OPEN HOUSE**                                                                       | 2     |
| **PLACE:**  Selkirk Communications                                                   | 8     |
| 1003 Baker St.                                                                       | 11    |
| Nelson BC V1L 5N7                                                                    | 15    |
| **TIME:**  1:00-4:00 p.m.                                                            | 20    |
| **DATE:**  Saturday and Sunday, April 27 and 28                                      | 29    |

Selkirk Communications is excited to open its tenth international communications office in downtown Nelson. Please plan to attend the Open House.

Come in and meet our friendly staff. Learn how we can help meet your training needs.

Selkirk Communications specializes in:
* Instructor-Led Training in Our Classroom or Your Facility
* Newsletters Designed to Meet Your Needs
* Authorized Training Center for *Microsoft Office* and *Corel WordPerfect*
* Oral and Written Communication Refresher Courses

43
57
58
72
76
84
96
104
118
128

# Integrating Computer Applications

The Executive Committee's new Productivity Enhancement Program resulted in standardizing all computer software applications for the company in all locations. The Training and Development Team, at the request of the Executive Committee, developed a training program designed to help all employees learn how to integrate applications available in the standardized suite and to use electronic mail and the Internet.

The Productivity Enhancement Program specifies that each employee must develop in-depth skill in at least two applications, basic skill in the other applications, and be able to produce a compound document—that is, a document that includes elements from multiple software applications in the suite. Employees must also be able to use electronic mail. The Productivity Enhancement Program specifies that most internal documents will be distributed electronically.

To meet the needs of all employees, the Training and Development Team structured the Integrating Computer Applications training program in three phases.

Assessment provides employees who already have developed skill in an application to demonstrate that competence without taking the training module. Two levels of assessments—basic skill and in-depth skill—are available for each application. Each computer-administered and scored assessment contains three versions. An employee who does not successfully complete the assessment in three tries or who elects not to take the assessment option must take the training module for that application. Assessments are also used at the conclusion of training modules.

Development follows assessment. Two options are available for developing skill in the various applications. Employees may sign up for regular training classes or may elect to use the new computer-based training programs (CBT) to develop the skill. The advantage of using the CBT program is that it can be completed at your own workstation. A combination of both instructor-led training and the CBT program may be the best alternative for most employees. An assessment must be completed at the end of each training session to demonstrate the level of skill attained on each software application. Assessment applies to both CBT and instructor-led training.

Integration is the final phase of the program. The integration program accomplishes two objectives—teaching employees how to prepare documents that use objects from the various applications in the suite and standardizing the format for frequently used documents. Cross-functional teams use actual work samples in the integration phase. Detailed information about the integration phase will be provided at least three weeks prior to the training so that participants can assemble the appropriate documents for the training session.

## Document 2
## Block letter

1. Add an appropriate saluta-tion.
2. This letter includes the company name. Key it a DS below the complimentary closing in ALL CAPS. QS to the writer's name.
3. To format a numbered list:
   a. Key I and the period, then press **TAB**. Key the first item and press ENTER.
   b. The next number will appear automatically.
   c. After you have keyed the last listed item and pressed ENTER, back-space to delete the unwanted number.

February 8, 200- | Chamber of Commerce | 225 Hall St. | Nelson BC V1L          13
5X4 | CANADA          15

**Selkirk Communications** will be relocating its headquarters from          32
Spokane, Washington, to downtown Nelson on April 1.  We are an inter-          46
national communications company, offering the following services:          59

1. Written and oral communications refresher workshops          70
2. Customized training on-site or in our training center          82
3. Mail-order newsletters          87
4. Computer training on popular business software          97
5. Individualized or group training sessions          106

I  would like to attend the Nelson Chamber of Commerce meeting in          119
March to share some of the exciting ways we can help Chamber members          133
meet their training needs.  Is there time available for us on your March          147
agenda?  Please contact Anthony Baker, public relations coordinator, at          162
our Nelson office at (604) 555-1093.          169

Selkirk Communications will be holding an open house during the month          183
of April, and we will be inviting you and the Nelson community to attend.          198
We look forward to becoming actively involved with the business com-          212
munity of Nelson.          216

Yours truly | SELKIRK COMMUNICATIONS | Richard R. Holmes, President          229

## Document 3
## Memorandum

To add bullets:

1. Key the items.
2. Select the items.
3. Click **Insert**, then **Outline/Bullets & Numbering**.
4. Click the **Bullets** tab.
5. Choose *Bullet List* from the bullet options shown.
6. Click **OK**.

**TO:** Marilyn Smith, Public Relations Media Assistant | **FROM:** Anthony          14
Baker, Public Relations Coordinator | **DATE:** February 16, 200- |          26
**SUBJECT:** Electronic Presentation          33

Richard Holmes has been invited to introduce our company at the March          47
15 meeting of the Nelson Chamber of Commerce.  Please prepare a 20-          60
minute electronic presentation for this meeting by extracting the key          74
points from Richard's speech, which is attached.          84

As you prepare the presentation, remember these key points:          96

- Write phrases, not sentences, so that listeners focus on the key points.          111
- Use parallel structure and limit wraparound lines of text.          124
- Create *builds* to keep the audience alert.          133
- Add transitions between slides (suggest fade in and out).          145
- Add graphics and humor--we want them to remember us.          156

Please have the presentation ready for Richard to review by February 24.          171
After he has made his revisions and the presentation is final, print the          186
presentation as a handout. | xx | Attachment          194

## APPLICATION

*Announcement with TextArt
and Drop Cap*

1. Key the information as a flyer. Use landscape orientation; all margins 1".
2. Use a TextArt shape and shadow of your choice to format the first line of the flyer.
3. Use 18-point Times New Roman font for other text.
4. Use a drop cap to begin both ¶s.
5. Save as **app-a12**; print.

**Tour of Facilities** ——————— Apply TextArt.

**Saturday, October 15**

Use drop cap.

Basketball Coaches Eddie Nelson and Nancy Hudson invite you to join them for a tour of the new practice facility and television studios. Tours begin at 2:30, 3:30, and 5:00 p.m. Please join all the basketball coaching staff and players for refreshments in the Trophy Room before or after your tour.

Use drop cap.

Football Coach Brad Reaves invites you to join him for a tour of the new Zone Club and the Executive Club in the Stadium. Tours begin at 2:00, 3:00, and 4:00. Please join all the football coaching staff and players for refreshments in the Captain's Room before or after your tour.

## APPLICATION

1. Create the illustration shown at the right.
2. Add text to the rectangular shape; use black fill, and change font color to white.
3. Draw the plaque from the basic shapes and add text.
4. Use the clipart illustrated or a similar one.
5. Group the objects; move them to the approximate horizontal and vertical center of the page.
6. Save as **app-a13**; print.

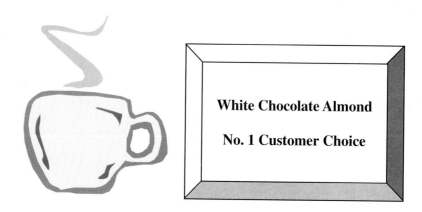

**Cocoa Flavor of the Year**

**White Chocolate Almond**

**No. 1 Customer Choice**

## APPLICATION

The document you will key is shown on p. 399. Follow the step-by-step directions shown at the right for this application. Your solution may look different than the one on p. 399.

1. Use 1" side margins; use TextArt to create a banner similar to the one shown on p. 399.
2. Key the document "Integrating Computer Applications" on the next page.
3. Insert a clipart picture that would be appropriate for a computer training class. Size it to be approximately 2" high and 2" wide. Position it at the horizontal and vertical center of the page. Wrap text around the clipart.
4. Add a border around the clipart.
5. Print a copy and save the document as **app-a14**.

**LESSON A5**     *WORK WITH GRAPHICS AND DROP CAPS*     398

**Note:** Word counts for missing parts have been added to appropriate lines.

## Document 4
**Table**

1. Format the purchase order as a 4-column table.
2. Join the cells in Row 1. Key the main heading and sub-heading in Row 1.
3. Center, shade, and bold the column headings.
4. Calculate the total price for each item.
5. Shade the last row; join the cells in the first three columns (A9, B9, and C9).
6. Calculate the total; center table.

## Document 5
**Block letter**

1. Insert Document 4 table in this order letter using Copy and Paste.
2. Use the current date.
3. Add an appropriate salutation.
4. Format the company name in closing lines in ALL CAPS.
5. Make adjustments in vertical space that allow the letter to print on a letterhead.

## Document 6
**Table**

This table will be used by the president in one of his workshops.

1. Keep the type size large. Select an attractive format for the table or shade Row 1 20% and the remainder of Column A 10%. No lines.
2. Add at least 2 words that you frequently misspell.
3. Supply the correct spelling in Column B.

|  |  |  | words |
|---|---|---|---|
| **PURCHASE ORDER** | | | 3 |
| *(Current date)* | | | 7 |

| Quantity | Description | Unit Price | Total Price | words |
|---|---|---|---|---|
| | | | | 15 |
| 2 | Ergonomic Comfort computer chairs | $455.00 | | 26 |
| 2 | Slide-out keyboard shelf | 54.00 | | 33 |
| 36 | 3 1/2" high-density/double-sided formatted disks | 1.99 | | 46 |
| 1 | 10-ream carton laser printer paper (20 lb.) | 54.25 | | 57 |
| 3 | HP LaserJet Series 4 toner cartridge #92298A | 145.89 | | 69 |
| 2 | Address labels 1" x 2 5/8", white, #5160 | 24.95 | | 80 |
| | Total | | | 83 |

West Coast Office Supplies — 9

3245 Granville St. — 12

Vancouver BC V6B 5Z8 — 17

Please ship the following items, which are listed in — 32
your current office supplies catalog. — 39

**Insert the table here (Document 4)**

Please bill this to our account number 4056278. This — 50
order is urgent; therefore, ship it overnight by Loomis. — 62

Yours truly — 64
Selkirk Communications — 69

Allan Burgess, Purchasing Agent — 75

Frequently Misspelled Words — 6

Correct Spelling — 11

| Misspelled | | words |
|---|---|---|
| recieve | | 14 |
| accomodate | | 19 |
| convience | | 23 |
| similiar | | 27 |
| to (meaning also) | | 31 |
| congradulations | | 38 |
| envelop | | 41 |
| inclosure | | 45 |

## Drop cap

**Drill 3**

1. Key the paragraph at right, applying the drop cap.
2. Save as **a5-d3**; print.

**To create a drop cap:**

1. Click anywhere in the paragraph.
2. Click **Format** menu, **Paragraph**, **Drop Cap**.

**D**rop Cap is a special effect that presents the first letter of a paragraph in large or enhanced text that drops down for one or more lines. Drop caps are created from the Paragraph option on the Format menu. The first letter of this paragraph is formatted as a drop cap.

**Drill 4**

1. Key the paragraph.
2. Apply Drop Cap. Then right-click the **P** and select *Drop Cap*; click *Make the first whole word a drop cap*.
3. Select the letters *PS*; apply a bold scipt font (e.g., French Script MT).
4. Save as **a5-d4** and print.

*PS* (Pommery Springs) is the name of a Limited Liability Corporation created to manage a new residential development consisting of four home sites. The development fits into a special zoning category, Subdivision Without Roads, which permits up to seven homes to be built and serviced by one private driveway. The type of driveway used in a Subdivision Without Roads is left up to the developer. County standards apply to roads in subdivisions with more than seven homes.

## APPLICATION

1. Format the announcement. Use landscape orientation; 1.5" top margin; 1" side and bottom margins.
2. TextArt specifications:
   **TextArt Box 1**
   Main heading:
   Shape—Row 3, Shape 4
   Shadow—2D Options tab; Row 1, Shadow 2
   Justification—Center
   **TextArt Box 2**
   Key the 5 remaining lines DS.
   Shape—Plain (Row 1, Shape 1)
   Shadow—none (center shadow)
   Justification—Center
3. Add an extra thick border around the page.
4. Save as **app-a11**; print.

words

**Document 7**
**Standard memo with table**

After keying table, sort items in alphabetical order. Format the table attractively.

| | | | |
|---|---|---|---|
| **TO:** | All Staff, Spokane Branch | | 6 |
| **FROM:** | Marilyn Josephson, Office Manager | | 14 |
| **DATE:** | Current | | 19 |
| **SUBJECT:** | American versus Canadian Spelling | | 28 |

All correspondence addressed to our Canadian office should now include  42
Canadian spelling. Some of the differences are shown in the following  56
table. We'll need to get a list of other words that differ as well.  70

| U.S. Spelling | Canadian Spelling | |
|---|---|---|
| | | 77 |
| counseling | counselling | 81 |
| honor | honour | 84 |
| endeavor | endeavour | 88 |
| defense | defence | 91 |
| center | centre | 94 |
| check (meaning money) | cheque | 99 |
| color | colour | 102 |
| marvelous | marvellous | 106 |
| z | "zed" | 107 |

**Document 8**
**Multiple-page report with table and appendix**

1. Format the report as a DS unbound report. Proofread carefully; not all errors are marked.
2. Use the Table menu to format the table.
3. Use full justification.
4. Include the agenda as an appendix in the report. (See the directions, p. 185.)
5. Prepare a title page. Assume that the report was prepared for **Nelson Chamber of Commerce** by **Richard R. Holmes, President**. Date the report **March 15**.

PROPOSAL FOR COMMUNITY GOALS CONFERENCE  8

The Steering Committee for the chamber of commerce com-  19
munity enhancement proposes the sponsorship of a goals con-  31
ference for all citizens of Nelson. This recommendation is  43
based on research data compiled from conferences sponsored  55
in other cities similar to Nelson. Also, the recommendation  66
is supported by the committee's combined experience in work-  79
ing with varied groups of citizens and a commitment to  90
progress. The reports presents a proposed outline for a  101
goals conference.  105

Purpose of Conference  109

The purposes of this conference are (1) to improve educa-  121
tion, economic development, youth services, and recreation and  133
(2) to reduce crime in the Nelson and district. All members  145
of the community will be invited to attend this conference and  157

## Grouping and Ungrouping Objects

### Objects

Often graphic illustrations include several different drawing objects. The objects can be grouped so that you can move, size, and edit them as one unit.

**To group graphics:**

1. Select the graphics to be grouped by holding down the SHIFT key and clicking each object.
2. Right-click one of the selected graphics; click **Group**.
3. To ungroup, right-click a grouped object and click **Separate**.

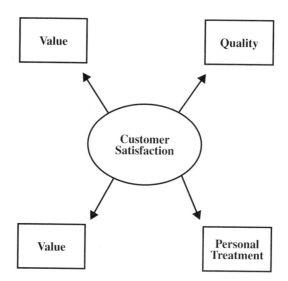

**Drill 2**

1. Draw a rectangle as shown above. Choose *None* for Fill.
2. Copy the rectangle and click **Paste** three times to create three additional boxes. Position the boxes approximately as shown.
3. Draw an oval in the center.
4. Right-click the objects and add the text shown.
5. Add four arrows to the drawing. You can find arrows in the Line category of shapes. **Tip:** You can draw one arrow, then copy and rotate it.
6. Hold down the SHIFT key and click each object to select it.
7. Right-click one of the objects and click **Group**.
8. Select the entire illustration and drag it to another position. Note that all components move at one time.
9. Save the illustration as **a5-d2** and print.

contribute to ~~the~~ the achievement of these goals. A Publicity com- | 170

mittee will be resonsible for informing the community. | 181

## Goals Conference Format | 186

    The Steering Committee recommends that the confence be | 197

held at Marion Hall, ~~Canadian International College (CIC)~~ on ~~March~~ May 18, | 211

200-, from 9:30 a.m. to 4:00 p.m.  Facilities can be | 222

reserved by calling Patzy Frazier at (606) 555-3789. | 233

    The conference would begin with an opening session and | 244

should inlcude introductions of key leaders in the community | 256

as well as Chamber of Commerce officers.  The keynote | 267

speaker should be a prominent state leader who has vision for | 279

quality communities. | 284

    Following the opening sessions, participants will | 294

choose from one of the following five breakout groups: edu- | 306

cation, youth services, ~~education~~ recreation, economic development, | 317

~~youth services, recreation~~ and crime.  Breakout sessions | 323

will be directed by facilitators trained in working with | 335

diverse groups. *Groups will brainstorm and then set goals and prepare plans for achieving the specific goals of the conference. The sessions will run for one hour.* ~~Lunch will follow and be served in the Banquet Room of the college. The afternoon sessions will be a repeat of the workshops so that participants may attend different sessions.~~ | 345, 355, 366, 368

Recommended facilitators include: team leaders and the following | 381

| Team | Team Leaders | Facilitators | |
|---|---|---|---|
| | | | 387 |
| Education | Dale Coppage, Nelson BC | Ellen Obert, Spokane, WA | 399 |
| Youth Services | Lawrence Riveria, Portland, OR | Jack Jones, Vancouver BC | 413 |
| Recreation | Bradley Greger, Nelson BC | Carlos Pena, Calgary AB | 425 |
| Economic Development | Jon Guyton, Nelson BC | Harvey Lewis, Nelson BC | 439 |
| Crime | Monica Brigham, Toronto ON | Shawn McNullan, NC | 450 |

**Shapes**

# Work with Graphics and Drop Caps

The drawing tools of *WordPerfect 9* enable you to add a variety of interesting shapes and graphic features to enhance a document. You can access shapes and other graphic objects from the Insert menu or by displaying the Graphics toolbar.

**Drill 1**

1. Click the **Insert** menu and choose *Shapes*, then *Basic*. Choose a shape marked with an arrow at the right and click **OK**. Position the crosshairs where you want the shape to appear; then click and drag to draw the shape. Draw each of the 4 shapes marked at right.

2. Click a sizing handle and drag to size each shape as shown below.

3. Right-click the rectangle to display the shortcut menu; select *Add Text*. Key the word **Confidential** in 14-pt. bold font. Right-click again. Click **Edit Box** and select *None* for Fill.

4. Double-click the "no" symbol (top right shape below); select red color fill.

5. Double-click the oval and change the fill color to light gray. Click the **Line** tab and choose a thick border line—about 3 points—under *Width*. Click **OK**. Right-click the oval; click **Rotate Shape** and drag a sizing handle to rotate the oval.

6. Double-click the hexagon; add a 4-point line around it. Click the **Shadow** tab and add a shadow.

7. Save as **a5-d1** and print.

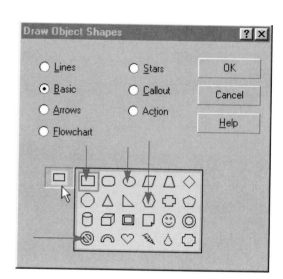

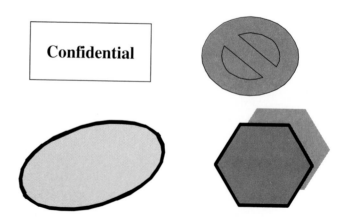

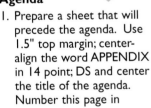

words

After the first breakout sessions, participants will join    462
for lunch in the H. L. Calvert Union Building.  The Steering    474
Committee recommends that Mayor Alton johnson address the    486
topic of meeting educational challenges of the next century.    498
reppat of the morning breakout sessions will begin at 1:30 p.m.    512
This repeat will allow participants to contirube to antoher    524
topic.  In the closing session breakout facilitators will    536
present the goals and plans to the audience.    546

Sponsors    547

The Steerting Committee has discussed the sponsorhsip of    559
a goals conference with a number of partners in the Nelson    570
area.  The following organizations have agreed to serve as    582
sponsors:  Nelson Economic Development Foundation, Bank of    594
Canada, Northeast Bottling Company, and Bank of Nelson, and    605
Farthington's Clothiers.    610

Summary    612

The Steering Committee strongly recommends this goals    623
conference.  The committee will be avilable at the Camber    635
of commerce meeting to answer any questions.    644

To begin numbering pages at other than page 1, choose *Set Value* from the *Select Page Numbering Format* dialog box (click **Format**, **Page**, **Numbering**). Enter the beginning number in the *Set page number* box.

**Document 9
Agenda**

1. Prepare a sheet that will precede the agenda.  Use 1.5" top margin; center-align the word APPENDIX in 14 point; DS and center the title of the agenda.  Number this page in sequence.
2. Format the agenda using the Table menu; do not include lines.  Add a row between items so the agenda appears DS.

Goals Conference Agenda    5

| | | |
|---|---|---|
| 9:30 a.m.-9:45 a.m. | Welcome | 11 |
| 9:45 a.m.-10:15 a.m. | Opening Remarks | 19 |
| | Overview of Community Quality | 25 |
| | Initiative | 27 |
| | Purpose of Goals Conference | 33 |
| | Process | 34 |
| | Introduction of Community Leaders | 41 |
| | and Chamber Officers | 45 |
| 10:15 a.m.-10:35 a.m. | Refreshment Break | 54 |
| 10:35 a.m.-12 noon | Breakout Sessions: | 62 |
| 12 noon-1:00 p.m. | Lunch | 79 |
| | Speaker on Educational Challenges | 86 |
| | of the 21st Century | 90 |
| 1:00 p.m.-2:30 p.m. | Goals Setting Workshops | 98 |
| 2:30 p.m.-2:45 p.m. | Refreshment Break | 106 |
| 2:45 p.m.-4:00 p.m. | Presentation of Goals | 115 |

1. Design the flyer to enhance readability from a distance. Use 1" side margins, landscape orientation, and 14-point Arial font, bold, except for TextArt.
2. Key **ICA** as TextArt with upward slant positioned at left (size to about 1.75" x 2"). Add a shadow (2D Options tab). Add a thick border.
3. Key **Training Schedule** as plain text TextArt (use 1st shape option); size to extend to right margin. Add a shadow.
4. Key a 4-column, 12-row table. Using SpeedFormat, apply Row Fill Columns style; adjust column widths to fit text on one line.
5. Key time note a DS below table.
6. Save as **app-a10** and print.
7. Save the document again as a Web page.

| Application | Level | Dates | Location |
|---|---|---|---|
| Word Processing | Basic skill training | 8/6, 8/9, 8/15 | Training Room 124 |
| Word Processing | In-depth skill training | 8/8, 8/12, 8/21 | Training Room 124 |
| Spreadsheet | Basic skill training | 8/7, 8/13, 8/22 | Training Room 226 |
| Spreadsheet | In-depth skill training | 8/14, 8/16, 8/20 | Training Room 226 |
| Database | Basic skill training | 8/19, 8/23, 8/27 | Training Room 226 |
| Database | In-depth skill training | 8/8, 8/12, 8/21 | Training Room 226 |
| Presentation | Basic skill training | 8/7, 8/16, 8/22 | Training Room 124 |
| Presentation | In-depth skill training | 8/14, 8/23, 8/27 | Training Room 124 |
| E-mail & Internet | Comprehensive | 8/26, 8/29, 8/30 | Training Room 128 |
| Integrated Applications | Comprehensive | 9/9, 9/11, 9/13, 9/17 | Training Room 124 |

Time: 8:30–12:30—except Integrated Applications extends to 4:00.

## VIEWS on... Desktop Publishing

What is the difference between a high-end word processing program and desktop publishing (DTP) software? For one thing, the page layout ability of DTP is more extensive and flexible. DTP software can handle much larger files that include full-color pictures.

Many businesses are creating DTP departments to publish brochures, flyers, and catalogs using DTP software or publishing software integrated in the *WordPerfect Office* suite. The learning curve is steeper for DTP compared to word processing. However, good design is the most important part of creating any document. Your eyes need to flow naturally through the document and not get confused with too many fonts, graphic elements, or words.

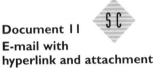

## Document 10
### Table with hyperlinks

1. Key the table at the right using 11 pt font. *WordPerfect* will convert the Web site address to a hyperlink when you strike the Space Bar or **TAB** at the end of each address.
2. Bold headings.
3. Apply 20% shading to Row 1.
4. Save as **Nelson**.

## Document 11
### E-mail with hyperlink and attachment

1. Log on to your e-mail from *WordPerfect*.
2. Address the memo to **All Selkirk Employees**.
3. Subject: **Consider Relocating to Nelson**.
4. Key the memo at right.
5. Select *Nelson and Area Communities Connect*.
6. Click the **Hyperlink Create** button. (If the button is not displayed, select *View, Toolbars*, then *Hyperlink Tools*.)
7. The Hyperlink Properties dialog box displays. Key **http://www.kics.bc.ca** in the *Document/Macro* box. Click **OK**.
8. When finished with the memo, click the **Attachment** button in your e-mail.
9. Select *3 1/2 Floppy (A:)* in the **Look in** box.
10. Select *Nelson*, then *Attach*. *Nelson* now appears in the Attach box.
11. Save as **m8-d11**.

**NELSON, CANADA**

**Web Site Information**

| Subject | Name of Site | Web Site Address |
|---|---|---|
| Nelson and surrounding area | Nelson Area Communities Connect | http://www.kics.bc.ca |
| Schools | School District 81 Fort Nelson | http://www.schdist81.bc.ca |
| City of Nelson | City of Nelson | http://www.city.nelson.bc.ca |
| Library | Nelson Municipal Library | http://www.kics.bc.ca/~library |
| Newspaper | Nelson Daily News | http://www.sterlingnews.com/Nelson/home.html |
| Sports | Nelson World Mid-Summer Curling Bonspiel | http://www.midsummerbonspiel.nelson.bc.ca |

As you are all aware, the Board of Directors voted at the November 27, 1999 meeting to move the corporate headquarters of Selkirk Communications from Portland, OR to Nelson, BC.

Nelson is surrounded by the Selkirk Mountains and sits on the shores of Kootenay Lake. Its heritage, charm, and stunning scenery create the quintessential small-town setting. The city, with a population of 9,500, has a unique mix of urban sophistication and rural ambiance.

We would like you to consider relocating with us to Nelson. To help acquaint you with the area, please take the time to view Nelson and Area Communities Connect. (Double-clicking on the underlined text will take you to this Web site.) Additional information about Nelson can be found in the Web sites listed in the attachment to this memo.

xx

Attachment

# APPLICATION

## A8

1. Key the table. Adjust column widths.
2. Create a bar chart of your choice. Do not display a title.
3. Save as **app-a8**. Print.

| Blood Type | % of Population |
|---|---|
| O+ | 38.4 |
| O- | 7.7 |
| A+ | 32.3 |
| A- | 6.5 |
| B+ | 9.4 |
| B- | 1.7 |
| AB+ | 3.2 |
| AB- | .7 |

# APPLICATION

## A9

1. Key the title in 36-point Arial, bold. Insert a .07-point custom line a DS below the heading.
2. Create a 3-column, 2-row table for the registration information. Format the table in No Lines No Border style.
3. Key the text in Row 1 and insert appropriate clipart in Row 2.
4. Insert a dashed line and the scissors from Iconic Symbols as shown.
5. Use the Horizontal line feature for the name and address section. Press TAB to key the second word in the line.
6. Center the page vertically.
7. Save as **app-a9**. Print.

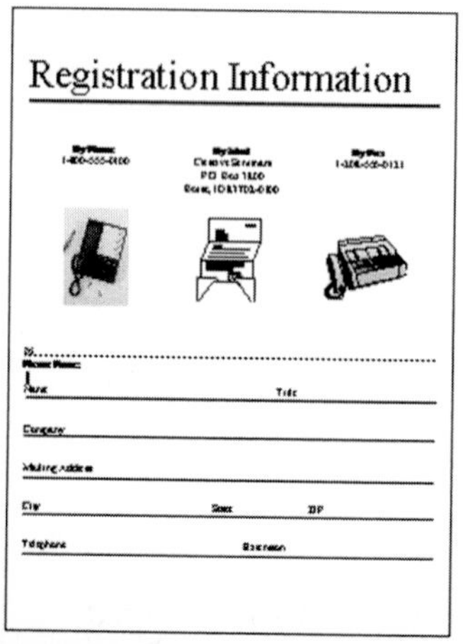

# Registration Information

| **By Phone**<br>1-800-555-0100 | **By Mail**<br>Creative Seminars<br>P.O. Box 3800<br>Boise, ID 83702-0100 | **By Fax**<br>1-208-555-0121 |
|---|---|---|
|   |  |   |

✂ - - - - - - - - - - - - - - - - - - - - - - - - - - - - - - - - - - - - - - - - - - -

**Please Print:**

Name                                                Title
_____

Company
_____

Mailing Address
_____

City, State, ZIP
_____

Telephone                                         Ext.
_____

E-mail Address
_____

The thumbnail preview in the bottom-left is a duplicate miniature of the Registration Information form.

Registration Information

By Phone
1-800-555-0100

By Mail
Creative Seminars
P.O. Box 3800
Boise, ID 83702-0100

By Fax
1-208-555-0121

By
Please Print:
Name                    Title
Company
Mailing Address
City            State        ZIP
Telephone            Extension

# Level 3

# DOCUMENT MASTERY

## OBJECTIVES

### Keyboarding

To key approximately 50 *wam* with good accuracy.

### Formatting Skills

To master basic word processing functions and learn advanced functions. To apply those functions to two-page letters, memos, tables, and reports.

### Communication Skills

To produce error-free documents and apply language arts skills.

# APPLICATION

## A6

1. Key the document at right, including the table.

2. Use 16-point bold for the title. QS below the title. Add a Thick Top/Bottom border a DS above and below title.

3. Insert a 3-D pie chart. Key the data from the table, using *Legend* and *Pie 1* columns.

4. Click the legend. Change the font to 18 point.

5. Right-click **Title of Chart** and select *Hide Title*.

6. Right-click a slice of the pie and select *Display Labels*. On the Position tab, choose Outside Percent.

7. Position the chart at the right of the table. Save as **app-a6**. Print.

## DO YOU HAVE MORE FREE TIME THAN YOU THINK?

It often seems that we don't have any free time. Many of us feel we're working longer hours with less time for family, friends, and fun. A recent hour-by-hour time study by a market research firm in Illinois shows Americans are working slightly less and playing more on the average. If the numbers don't match your calendar, it's probably because the statistics reflect company layoffs across the country, early retirement, and an aging population.

Completing a personal time study of your own may not be a bad idea. Once you know where your time goes, you can figure out how to get some of it back.

| Activity | Time |
|---|---|
| Sleeping | 450 |
| Working | 184 |
| Watching TV | 154 |
| Eating | 77 |
| Reading | 43 |
| Grocery Shopping | 16 |
| Exercising | 15 |

**Chart will be positioned here—Step 3.**

# APPLICATION

## A7

1. Key the announcement as marked.

2. Key the dates and locations as a 2-column table without lines or borders. DS above and below the table.

3. Insert a handshake image from the clipart scrapbook, the CD-ROM, or the Internet.

4. Move image before the conference dates and names.

5. Size image to fit.

6. Save as **app-a7**. Print.

 *Use Times New Roman*

Let's Meet — *36-pt. bold*
DS
Upcoming Conferences — *24-pt. bold*
DS
When you're in town and we're in town, come visit us at our convention booth. We'd love to talk. *18-pt. center*
DS

**April 8-12**
American Research
for Education
*New York, NY*
DS

**April 17-20**
National Music
Educators' Conference
*Kansas City, MO*

**April 28-May 3**
Association for
International Reading
*New Orleans, LA*

**June 9-13**
National Computing
Association
*Minneapolis, MN*

*12-pt. type*

Teachers' Annuity and Insurance Association
4530 Fifth Ave.
New York, NY 10017-3206

*14-pt. bold*

DS

# SKILLBUILDING

## OBJECTIVES

1. Improve keyboarding skill.
2. Improve composition and editing skills.

## LESSON 61

# Skillbuilding

### 61a • 5'

## GETTING started

Key each line 3 times SS (slowly, faster, slowly); DS between 3-line groups; repeat selected lines if time permits. (Use these directions for all skillbuilding warmups.)

### 61b • 10'

## SKILLBUILDING

**Improve keyboarding technique**

each pair of lines 3 times; DS between 6-line groups

### 61c • 5'

## SKILLBUILDING

**Build straight-copy skill**
Key two 1' writings at your top rate; key a 1' writing at your control rate.

**Copy difficulty**
Average difficulty reflects these controls: 1.5 syllables per word, 5.7 characters per word, and 80% familiar words.

### SKILLBUILDING WARMUP

alphabet 1 Benji Vazquez was prepared for the very difficult marketing exam.
fig/sym 2 About 25% of my team (8,460) earned the average salary ($19,637).
adjacent reaches 3 Ty was the guy people wanted in government; he responded quickly.
easy 4 My neighbor may tutor the eight girls on the theory and problems.
| 1 | 2 | 3 | 4 | 5 | 6 | 7 | 8 | 9 | 10 | 11 | 12 | 13 |

**balanced hand:** *think* and *key* words as units

5 The auditor may suspend work for a neighbor if the city pays him.
6 The rich widow paid for the chapel and the dock down by the lake.

**one hand:** key words letter by letter at a steady rate

7 In my opinion, I deserved better grades on my tests on abstracts.
8 We saw Jimmy West trade sweaters at a great craft bazaar at noon.

**combination**

9 The girls tasted the tea from the cafe and had the fish and crab.
10 Their dog ran past the cat to jump in my lap and nap by the pool.
| 1 | 2 | 3 | 4 | 5 | 6 | 7 | 8 | 9 | 10 | 11 | 12 | 13 |

**A** all letters

Image is very important to success on the job. Packaging does make a difference. A messy letter or report, a disorganized office, or a poorly groomed employee all make a bad impression. The quickest way to make a good impression is to present a professional image. You can be a good example for others to follow.

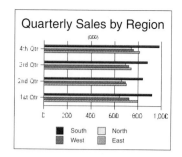

Quarterly Sales by Region

1. Create a horizontal bar chart using the sales data from the 4 quarters in Drill 1. Eliminate the final 3 zeros and the comma separator for all sales data (example: East 800 700 740 810).

2. Use the title **Quarterly Sales by Region** and the subtitle (000). To create a subtitle, right-click the area just below the title and select *Display Subtitle*. Double-click **Subtitle** and key (000) in the text box. In the Font Sizes box on the property bar, select 18 point. Click in the document to return to it.

3. Click the chart to select it. The Graphics toolbar displays. Click the **Border Style** button and choose a *Thin* border.

4. Save the chart as **a4-d4** and print.

### Create a chart from a table

You can use the data in a table to create a chart, without having to rekey the data in the datasheet. The top row (Row 1) and the first column (Column A) in the table will be used as data labels in the chart that is created.

For most types of charts, you can simply click the insertion point in the table and then click Insert, Chart and a chart will display. For some types, such as pie charts, you will need to cut and paste the data from the table to the datasheet.

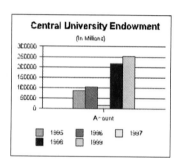

Central University Endowment

**Drill 5**

1. Key the table shown below.

2. With the insertion point in the table, click **Insert**, **Chart**, and choose a vertical bar chart.

3. Format the chart with a title and subtitle.

4. Save the document as **a4-d5** and print.

### CENTRAL UNIVERSITY ENDOWMENT
(In Millions)

| Year | Amount |
|------|--------|
| 1995 | $86,000 |
| 1996 | $103,000 |
| 1997 | $148,000 |
| 1998 | $217,000 |
| 1999 | $254,000 |

## 61d ● 14'

### COMMUNICATION

**Build composing/ editing skills**

1. Use 1.5" top margin; DS; 1" or default side margins.
2. Compose a 4- or 5-sentence ¶ to complete the statement at the right.
3. Edit the ¶, correcting all errors and adding the following title, centered in ALL CAPS and bold. DS below the title.
   **Preparing for My Career**
4. Proofread: Mark errors.
5. Edit: Make corrections.

Computer skills are critical in most business jobs today. Therefore, I will prepare for my career by . . .

## 61e ● 16'

### SKILLBUILDING

**Improve speed**

1. Key two 1' writings on each ¶.
2. Key one 3' writing.
3. Key one 5' writing.

**Optional:** Practice both ¶s as a guided writing. (See inside back cover for directions.)

**Goal:** 4 gwam increase

| | | | gwam |
|---|---|---|---|
| 1/4' | 1/2' | 3/4' | 1' |
| 8 | 16 | 24 | 32 |
| 9 | 18 | 27 | 36 |
| 10 | 20 | 30 | 40 |
| 11 | 22 | 33 | 44 |
| 12 | 24 | 36 | 48 |
| 13 | 26 | 39 | 52 |

all letters                                                    *gwam*  3' | 5'

Ethics is a complex topic to deal with in business. Nor-   4 | 2 | 37

mally, recognizing things that are legally wrong is not very   8 | 5 | 39

hard. The answers to ethical questions, however, are not always   12 | 7 | 42

obvious. Many people do not think it is unethical to use the   16 | 10 | 44

copier that belongs to the company to make a personal copy, but   21 | 12 | 47

most people do think it is unethical to make a thousand personal   25 | 15 | 49

copies on the copy machine. In truth, the principle is the same.   29 | 18 | 52

The difference is in the degree or extent of the abuse.   33 | 20 | 54

An equally perplexing issue relates to others with whom you   37 | 22 | 56

work. Should you blow the whistle when you know someone else is   41 | 25 | 59

doing something wrong? Reporting the actions of others may be   45 | 27 | 62

the right thing to do, but it involves a major amount of risk.   50 | 30 | 64

You may not have judged the situation accurately. Even if you   54 | 32 | 67

are correct, the person may attack you personally.   57 | 34 | 69

3' | 1 | 2 | 3 | 4 |
5' | 1 | 2 | 3 |

**Drill 2**

1. Insert the default chart.
2. Right-click each part of the chart—legend, bars, x-axis labels, y-axis labels, title—to see what options display on the pop-up menu.

## Modify charts

You can modify a chart by right-clicking it to display the pop-up menu. Different pop-up menus appear when you click different parts of the table. Below are some terms you should be familiar with when working with charts:

**x-axis:** identifies items along the horizontal bottom of the chart

**y-axis:** identifies items along the vertical side of the chart

**legend:** labels the information placed in columns or rows of the datasheet

**data label:** names or defines data in Row 1 or Column A of the datasheet

The Chart toolbar also gives you many options for modifying the chart, such as changing the chart type.

## To change chart type:

The Data Chart Gallery button allows you to choose from the many chart types available.

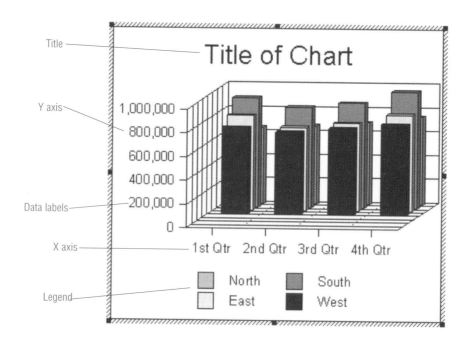

**Drill 3**

Create a pie chart using the total sales figures for the year in the table shown on p. 389.

1. Click **Insert** menu, **Chart**. Click the **Data Chart Gallery** button on the Chart toolbar and select the *3-D pie chart*.
2. Delete the sample text that appears under *Labels 1* in the datasheet, including the Pie Title.
3. Key the sales for the year for each region in the *Pie 1* column. (Refer to the table in Drill 1, p. 389.) Close the datasheet.
4. Double-click the pie; then right-click a slice and select *Display Labels*.
5. From the Data Labels (Pie) dialog box, select *Outside* Percent. Click **OK**.
6. Double-click the title and key **Annual Sales by Region**. Change the font to 36 point.
7. Save the chart as **a4-d3** and print.

# Skillbuilding

**62a ● 5'**

**GETTING started**

### SKILLBUILDING WARMUP

| | | |
|---|---|---|
| alphabet | 1 | Jacky was given a bronze plaque for the extra work he did for me. |
| fig/sym | 2 | Order 12 pairs of #43 skis at $76.59 each for a total of $919.08. |
| 3d/4th fingers | 3 | Zane, Sally, and Max quit polo to swim six laps and work puzzles. |
| easy | 4 | Claudia and I do handiwork at both the downtown and lake chapels. |

| 1 | 2 | 3 | 4 | 5 | 6 | 7 | 8 | 9 | 10 | 11 | 12 | 13 |

**62b ● 10'**

## SKILLBUILDING

**Improve response patterns**

lines 5–16 once; DS between 4-line groups; work at a controlled rate; repeat drill

**direct reaches:** reaches with the same finger; keep hands quiet

5 brand much cent numb cease bright music brief jump special carved
6 create mumps zany mystic curve mummy any checks brag brunch after
7 Bradley broke his left thumb after lunch on a great hunting trip.
8 After having mumps, Cecil once saw June excel in a funny musical.

**adjacent reaches:** keep fingers curved and upright

9 were junior sad yuletide trees polo very join safe property tweed
10 tree trio trickle tripod quit excess was free easy million option
11 Gwen and Sumio are going to be quite popular at the Western Club.
12 Fred said we were going to join the guys for polo this afternoon.

**double letters:** strike keys rapidly

13 dill seem pool attic miss carry dragged kidded layoff lapped buzz
14 commend accuse inner rubber cheer commission football jazz popper
15 Tammy called to see if she can borrow my accounting book at noon.
16 Lynnette will meet with the bookseller soon to discuss the issue.

| 1 | 2 | 3 | 4 | 5 | 6 | 7 | 8 | 9 | 10 | 11 | 12 | 13 |

**62c ● 5'**

## SKILLBUILDING

**Inventory straight-copy skill**

Key two 1' writings to improve speed. Proofread; circle errors; determine *gwam*.

 all letters

Products are protected by patents and trademarks, but often
cheap imitations of the products exist on the market.  The consumer may pay for the quality of the brand name but unknowingly
may receive a product of inferior quality.  If the price of a
product seems too good to be true, analyze the product carefully.
It may just be a fake.

# Work with Charts

Reading a graphical interpretation of a group of numbers is easier than reading the numbers. *WordPerfect* makes it easy to create a chart from a table or spreadsheet or by keying the data in the Datasheet. In this lesson, you will learn to create simple but effective charts. Later, you will learn to create and edit charts within *Quattro Pro*.

**To create a chart:**

1. Click **Chart** on the Insert menu. The datasheet appears with default data in the cells. A sample chart displays, which is based on the data in the datasheet cells. The Chart toolbar also displays.

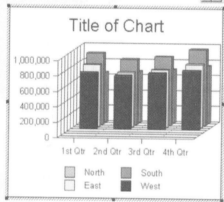

2. Key the data you wish to include in each cell.
3. Click **Title of Chart** in the chart. A property bar will appear at the top of the document screen. Click in the text box, key the title, and press ENTER.
4. Close the datasheet, or click in the *WordPerfect* document to return to it.

**Drill 1**

1. Click **Insert** menu, **Chart**.

2. From the table at the right, key only the data for the 4 quarters in the cells of the datasheet. Do not key the Year data.

3. Click **Title of Chart** and key **Sales by Region**. Close the datasheet.

4. Save the document as **a4-d1** and print. Your chart should look similar to the one shown above.

| Region | 1st Qtr | 2nd Qtr | 3rd Qtr | 4th Qtr | Year |
|--------|---------|---------|---------|---------|------|
| North | 640,000 | 660,000 | 690,000 | 740,000 | 2,730,000 |
| South | 920,000 | 840,000 | 880,000 | 980,000 | 3,620,000 |
| East | 800,000 | 700,000 | 470,000 | 810,000 | 3,050,000 |
| West | 725,000 | 690,000 | 720,000 | 760,000 | 2,895,000 |

## COMMUNICATION

**Build editing skills**
1. Use 1.5" top margin; default side margins; DS.
2. Key the ¶, correcting errors as you key—including the 5 unmarked errors. Center the heading in ALL CAPS and bold. DS below the title.
3. Proofread.

MY WEEKEND PROJECT

My supervisor ask me to ~~carefully~~ read the book, Creating a Very good Impression, and to summarise the key points in each chapter. She want to use some ideas form it in a training program entitled Excellance in Customer Service. Since my dead line is next friday, I plan to spent some time read the book this week end.

## SKILLBUILDING

**Inventory/build straight-copy skill**
1. Key two 1' writings on each ¶.
2. Key one 3' writing.
3. Key one 5' writing.

**Optional:** Practice as a guided writing.

| | | | gwam |
|---|---|---|---|
| 1/4' | 1/2' | 3/4' | 1' |
| 8 | 16 | 24 | 32 |
| 9 | 18 | 27 | 36 |
| 10 | 20 | 30 | 40 |
| 11 | 22 | 33 | 44 |
| 12 | 24 | 36 | 48 |
| 13 | 26 | 39 | 52 |

all letters

|  | gwam | 3' | 5' |

Who is a professional?  The word can be defined in many ways.  Some may think of a professional as someone who is in an exempt job category in an organization.  To others the word can denote something quite different; being a professional denotes an attitude that requires thinking of your position as a career, not just a job.  A professional exerts influence over her or his job and takes pride in the work accomplished.

Many individuals who remain in the same positions for a long time characterize themselves as being in dead-end positions. Others who remain in positions for a long time consider themselves to be in a profession.  A profession is a career to which you are willing to devote a lifetime.  How you view your profession is up to you.

gwam rates (3' / 5'):
4 | 2 | 32
8 | 5 | 35
12 | 7 | 37
17 | 10 | 40
21 | 13 | 43
25 | 15 | 45
28 | 17 | 47
32 | 19 | 49
36 | 22 | 52
40 | 24 | 54
45 | 27 | 57
49 | 29 | 59
50 | 30 | 60

3' | 1 2 3 4
5' | 1 2 3

15. Position a thick, light gray horizontal line across Column 2 on pp. 2-5, as shown on p. 377. (Click **Insert**, **Line**, **Custom Line**; select the line style and color in the Create Graphics Line dialog box; then click **OK**.)

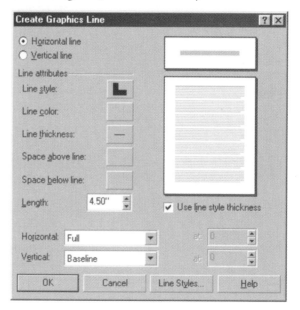

16. Use Flush Right to align the heading *Design Elements*; apply Arial 16-point font and bold.

17. Key the remainder of the document following the same procedures.

18. In the shaded box illustrating typeface styles on p. 2 of the article, apply the font illustrated to each sentence in the box.

19. Print the document and save it as **app-a3**.

# APPLICATION

1. Open *design1* and save it as **design2**.
2. Make the format changes suggested at the right.

1. Change the side margins to .75" and the gutter spacing to .5".
2. Add a footer on each page with **Document Design** at the left margin and the page number at the right margin.

# APPLICATION

*Challenge*

1. Open *design2* and save it as **design3**.
2. Reformat the document using a design of your choice.

# Skillbuilding

**LESSON 63**

## 63a ● 5'

### GETTING started

**SKILLBUILDING WARMUP**

| | | |
|---|---|---|
| alphabet | 1 | Jack Meyer analyzed the data by answering five complex questions. |
| fig/sym | 2 | On May 15, my ZIP Code will change from 23989-4016 to 23643-8705. |
| 1st/2d fingers | 3 | June Hunter may try to give Trudy a new multicolored kite to fly. |
| easy | 4 | Dickey may risk half of the profit they make to bid on an island. |

| 1 | 2 | 3 | 4 | 5 | 6 | 7 | 8 | 9 | 10 | 11 | 12 | 13 |

## 63b ● 9'

### SKILLBUILDING

**Improve keyboarding technique**

each pair of lines 3 times; DS between 6-line groups; key at a controlled rate

home row

5 Dallas Klass had a dish of salad; Sal Lad also had a large salad.

6 Daggard Fallak was a sad lad; all Dag had was a large salad dish.

third row

7 Two or three witty reporters who tried to write quips were there.

8 Trey or Roy wrote two reports that were quite proper for a paper.

first row

9 Zam Benjamin came back to visit six vacant zinc mines and a cave.

10 Benjamin Zinc, a very excited man, made money on six new banners.

| 1 | 2 | 3 | 4 | 5 | 6 | 7 | 8 | 9 | 10 | 11 | 12 | 13 |

## 63c ● 7'

### SKILLBUILDING

**Build straight-copy skill**

Key two 1' writings and one 3' writing at your control rate.

all letters                                                                              gwam   3'

One of the most important skills needed for success on the     4 | 42

job is listening.  However, this is a skill that takes hours of    8 | 46

practice.  You can maximize your effectiveness by learning and    12 | 50

using techniques for effective listening.  People can listen two    17 | 55

or three times faster than they can talk.  Use the difference be-    21 | 59

tween the rate at which a person speaks and the rate at which you    25 | 63

can listen to review what the person has said and to identify the    30 | 68

main ideas communicated.  This active style of listening helps    34 | 72

you avoid the tendency to tune in and out of a conversation.    38 | 76

3' | 1 | 2 | 3 | 4 |

### Step-by-step directions

1. Set margins (top and bottom 1"; side .5")

2. Key the text for the banner heading; use an em dash. Press ENTER 3 times to allow space for shading and for normal paragraph spacing.

3. Select the heading and apply Arial 22-point font and bold. Center the heading horizontally.

4. Position the insertion point immediately below the banner. Select the paragraph marker (Click **View**, **Show ¶** to see the markers). Shade the line 20% (**Format**, **Paragraph**, **Border/Fill**, **Fill** tab, **20%**, **Apply**, **OK**).

> If you have trouble with Step 4, come back to this step after you have defined the columns. ∎

5. Set spacing between paragraphs:
From the Format menu, click **Paragraph**, **Format**. Set *Spacing between paragraphs* at 1.5 lines. Press ENTER only once at the end of each paragraph.

6. Position the insertion point in the space below the shading (the next paragraph) and define the column format. Select *Newspaper* columns; Column 1–2"; Space–1"; Column 2–4.5".

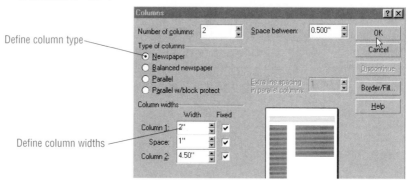

Define column type

Define column widths

7. Press ENTER several times to position the first line of text in Column 1.

8. Key the text; apply 11-point Arial font and bold.

9. Press ENTER several times again. Either enter all text in Column 1 now, estimate the approximate placement, and adjust the text later; or move to the next column (CTRL+ENTER) and key Column 2. Then later you can position the insertion point in Column 1 and add the remaining text.

10. Key the remainder of the text in Column 2; remember to apply Arial font and bold to the headings.

11. Single-space the items in the bulleted list because no item extends beyond 1 line. Select the list and change *Spacing between paragraphs* to **1** in the Paragraph Format dialog box.

12. After you have keyed the last paragraph on p. 1, choose *New Page* from the Insert menu.

13. Position the insertion point in Column 1 on p. 1, and key the remaining text in Column 1 if you have not already done so. If you have keyed the text, check the position to see if it needs to be adjusted; then return to p. 2.

14. Press ENTER several times; then key the text in Column 1 or move to the next column (CTRL+ENTER).

## COMMUNICATION

### Improve composition skills

1. Use 1.5" top margin; default side margins; DS.
2. Center the title in ALL CAPS and bold. DS below the title.
3. Proofread; correct the 5 unmarked errors in the copy and complete the two ¶s that have been started.
4. Proofread and edit your work.

## SKILLBUILDING

### Measure straight-copy skill

1. Key two 3' writings.
2. Key two 5' writings.

### APPEARANCE INFLUENCES FIRST IMPRESSIONS

First impressions are usually made in the initial seconds of contact. Even though first impressions are made very quick, they tend to be long-lasting impressions. Appearence is a key factor that influence first impressions; therefore, a good appearance is very important. This principal should be applied to both the appearance of a person and of an document.

I can enhance my personal appearance by . . . *(Add three or four sentences.)*

I can enhance the appearance of documents I prepare by . . . *(Add three or four sentences.)*

  all letters                     gwam 3' | 5'

|  |  |  |
|---|---|---|
| Individuals who conduct interviews often make snap judg- | 4 | 2 | 41 |
| ments. In fact, the decision to hire or not to hire an applicant | 8 | 5 | 43 |
| is usually made in the first five minutes of the interview. The | 12 | 7 | 46 |
| rest of the time is used to verify that the decision made was the | 17 | 10 | 49 |
| correct one. The wisdom of making a decision so early should be | 21 | 13 | 51 |
| questioned. When a quickly made decision is analyzed, generally | 25 | 15 | 54 |
| the result is that the decision is influenced heavily by the | 30 | 18 | 56 |
| first impression the person makes. | 32 | 19 | |

You can learn to make a good first impression in an interview; all you have to do is be on time, dress appropriately, shake hands firmly, establish eye contact, relax, smile, and show that you have excellent communication skills. Doing all of this may seem very difficult, but it really is not. Making a good impression requires careful planning and many hours of practice. Practice gives you the confidence you need to be able to do the things that make an excellent impression.

(36, 40, 44, 48, 53, 57, 61, 64, 7)

```
3' |    1    |    2    |    3    |    4    |
5' |      1      |      2      |      3      |
```

**Drill 1**

1. Open *a2-crown* from the Formatting Template. Save it as **a2-d1**.
2. Position the insertion point in a column, and change format to 4 equal columns with .25" spacing between them.
3. Adjust the position of the clipart if necessary; position it with the center approximately in the space between columns, next to the first mention of the Eagle Award.
4. Preview the document using Two Pages view (**View** menu); note that it does not fit on one page.
5. Place the insertion point at the top of Column 1. Turn Hyphenation on.
6. Check to ensure that the newsletter fits on one page.

**APPLICATION**

1. Review the contents of "DOCUMENT DESIGN— AN ART AND A SCIENCE," pp. 376–380.
2. Use the document specifications and the step-by-step directions at the right and on pp. 387 and 388 to key and format the article.
3. Save the document as **design1**.

Use Reveal Codes to show formatting while you key the document. This technique is helpful if you are accustomed to spacing twice after punctuation at the end of a sentence.

You may also use the Find and Replace function to search for a period followed by 2 spaces and replace with a period followed by 1 space. ■

## Document specifications

The document specifications that follow were used to create the article "DOCUMENT DESIGN—AN ART AND A SCIENCE," illustrated on pp. 376–380.

| Format |
| --- |
| **Margins:**  Top and bottom 1"; side .5". |
| **Header:**  Banner—bold, CAPS, and 22-point Arial font, centered horizontally; use 1 line space below the banner. |
| **Columns:**  Column 1:  2"; gutter (space between columns): 1"; Column 2:  4.5". |
| Text |
| **Column 1 text:**  Arial; 11 point; bold. |
| **Column 2 text:**  Times New Roman; 11–point font. |
| **Headings:**  Arial; 11 point, bold; *except* use 16-point Arial, bold, flush right for header below top border. |
| **Lists:**  Diamond bullets; SS lists with l-line items; DS between items if an item in the list extends beyond 1 line.  DS above and below a list. |
| **Spacing:**  Set paragraph spacing for 1.5 lines between paragraphs.  (See Step 5, p. 387.)  Use *one space* after end-of-sentence punctuation. |
| **Text:**  Use italic for titles and foreign words; use symbols and special characters (em dash, etc.) rather than typewriter characters. |
| Design Elements |
| **Banner:**  Shade the line space below the banner (20%). |
| **Page design:**  Column 2—use a thick custom graphic line. |
| **Shaded box (p. 2):**  Use 10% shading. |

# Skillbuilding

## 64a ● 7'

### GETTING started

each pair of lines 3 times;
work at a controlled rate

SKILLBUILDING WARMUP

balanced hand

1 The visitor to the island kept both mementos for a sick neighbor.
2 The auditor may handle the work for them if the city pays for it.

one hand

3 Phillip defeated Lynn in a race on a hilly street in Cedar Acres.
4 My grades in art were bad;  Dave regrets my grade average was bad.

combination

5 Doris and Lily were in debt for the cornfield on this big island.
6 My neighbor and I may fix the bicycle at the garage and trade it.

| 1 | 2 | 3 | 4 | 5 | 6 | 7 | 8 | 9 | 10 | 11 | 12 | 13 |

## 64b ● 15'

### COMMUNICATION

**Improve composition skills**

1. Use 1.5" top margin; DS; center and bold title.
2. Use hanging indent for enumerated items.
3. Proofread; correct the 9 errors in the copy and complete the two ¶s that have been started.
4. Proofread your work.

**IMPROVING DOCUMENT PRODUCTIVITY**

My plan for improve my productivite in producting documents is to focus on time managment and on work organization.  If I can improve both of this factors, my overall productivite will be significant higher.

Time management is important because, at my current rate, each second represents an additional word of the document.  I can manage my time better when I am producing documents by doing the following:

1. *(Add three or four numbered items to complete the previous sentence.)*

Work organisation is important in producing documents because organization not only saves time but also lets me focus attention on accurate work. I can improve my work organisation by doing the following:

1. *(Add three or four numbered items to complete the previous sentence.)*

# Design Documents with Columns

For most documents, hyphenation is not necessary. When text is formatted in narrow columns, however, the right margin is often very uneven because long words wrap to the next line. Hyphenation controls the point at which words wrap. The *WordPerfect* hyphenation feature inserts hyphens automatically. Should words be added to or deleted from the line, *WordPerfect* will automatically remove the hyphen if the word containing a hyphen is no longer at the right margin. You can also insert hyphens manually.

**Hard hyphens** remain regardless of the position of words. **Soft hyphens** are removed automatically if the line ending changes. Both can be inserted manually when text is being keyed.

| Hard Hyphen | CTRL + – (the hyphen key) |
|---|---|
| Soft Hyphen | CTRL + SHIFT + – (the hyphen key) |

**NEW FUNCTION**

**To automatically hyphenate words:**

1. Place the insertion point in the paragraph where you wish hyphenation to begin.
2. From the Tools menu, select *Language*, then *Hyphenation*.
3. Click **Turn hyphenation on**; then click **OK**.

The Hyphenation zone specifies the maximum amount of space between the last word in a line and the right margin. Increase the percentage to hyphenate more words. The larger the Hyphenation zone, the more ragged the right margin will be.

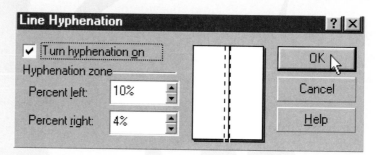

*WordPerfect* may request additional information as it hyphenates the document. Generally, the following options are most acceptable. (Only use these options in this course.)

| Insert Hyphen | Adds a hyphen. |
|---|---|
| Ignore Word | Word wraps to the next line; no hyphenation. |
| Suspend Hyphenation | Discontinues hyphenating during the current procedure. |

## 64c ● 10'

**SKILLBUILDING**

**Improve keyboarding technique**

each set of lines 3 times; DS between 9-line groups; work at a controlled rate

1st/2d fingers
7 junk feet cent give jive truck funny deer hug much bunt tiny very
8 Hunt and Kent, my friends, might buy the bicycle if they find it.
9 Judd might buy the gun for Jennifer if they decide to hunt ducks.

3d/4th fingers
10 saw please low zap plow sap exist quip zero plop was warp swallow
11 Quin saw Paxton as well as Lois at the zoo; Polly was there, too.
12 Does Paul always relax and explore "zany" ideas with Quin or Max?

all fingers
13 quick mixed please walk juice believe haze very young figure tram
14 Quincy and Maxy saw just five zebras on their big trip last week.
15 Zam and Jake required five big boys to explore that aquatic show.

| 1 | 2 | 3 | 4 | 5 | 6 | 7 | 8 | 9 | 10 | 11 | 12 | 13 |

## 64d ● 18'

**SKILLBUILDING**

**Build straight-copy skill**

1. Key two 1' writings on each ¶. Strive to improve *gwam* on the second writing.
2. Key two 5' writings.

all letters                                                                 *gwam*    1' | 5'

    The job market today is quite different than it was a few    12 | 2
years ago.   The fast track to management no longer exists.     24 | 5
Entry-level managers find that it is much more difficult to      36 | 7
obtain a promotion to a higher-level position in management than  49 | 10
it was just a few years ago.   People who are in the market for  61 | 12
new jobs find very few management positions available.   In fact, 74 | 15
many managers at all levels have a difficult time keeping their  87 | 17
current management positions.   Two factors seem to contribute   99 | 20
heavily to the problem.   The first factor is the trend toward  112 | 22
self-managed teams.   The second factor is that as companies    124 | 25
downsize they often remove entire layers of management or an    136 | 27
entire division.                                                140 | 28

    Layoffs are not new;   but, what is new is that layoffs are    12 | 30
affecting white-collar workers as well as blue-collar workers.   24 | 33
Coping with job loss is a new and frustrating experience for many 38 | 35
managers.   A person who has just lost a job will have concerns  50 | 38
about personal security and welfare, and the concerns are com-   63 | 40
pounded when families are involved.   The problem, however, is   75 | 43
more than just an economic one.   Job loss often damages an in-  87 | 45
dividual's sense of self-worth.   An individual who does not have 100 | 48
a good self-concept will have a very hard time selling himself  112 | 50
or herself  to a potential employer.                            120 | 52

1' | 1 | 2 | 3 | 4 | 5 | 6 | 7 | 8 | 9 | 10 | 11 | 12 | 13 |
5' |         1         |         2         |         3         |

*Two-page newsletter with vertical line*

1. Open *app-a1* and save it as **app-a2**. Reformat the newsletter in 3 unequal columns using the Columns dialog box. Column widths:
   Column 1: 1.5"
   Columns 2 and 3: 2.5"
   **Tip:** Clear the *Fixed* check boxes next to Space between columns before changing column widths.

2. Font sizes: body—11 point; headings—12 point.

3. Insert the information at the right as Column 1 of p. 1. Move the first tab on the Ruler to 1" to indent titles.

4. Add a vertical line between columns. DS above and below headings.

5. Set the text of the banner heading to white (**Format, Font, Color, white**). Add solid black fill (100%).

6. In Column 1 of p. 2, insert the title of the newsletter, Page 2, and the date, all in bold.

7. Insert the heading **Students Function as Professional Consultants** for the current article in the "Mail from Employees" column.

8. Use the information below the line at right to compose an article that will fit in the remaining space on p. 2.

9. Add an appropriate heading for your article. Add your name and the title **Production Associate** at the end of your article.

10. Save and print.

---

### Add the information below as Column 1 of p. 1 (see Step 3).

**Current date**

**Newsletter Staff**

Eric Burge
   Editor

Nancy Suggs
Christopher Hess
Anne Reynolds
   Associate Editors

Wayne Martin
   Editorial Assistant

The *Crown Lake News and Views* is a weekly newsletter compiled by the staff of the Human Resources Department, and it is sent to all employees. Employees are invited to share ideas with others by writing a letter to the editor to be included in the "Mail from Employees" column.

---

### Use this information for your composition (see Step 8).

Examples of topics you might select for an article in the "Mail from Employees" column:

- Value of participating in community service activities (write from the perspective of both the employee and the company).

- Invite employees to participate in an activity such as an investment, book, or computer club; an exercise group; a sport; or other area of interest that meets after work once a week. Share benefits of being involved and provide information about the activity.

- Tips for keeping physically fit and why it is important to do so.

- Tips for reducing stress.

- Tips for managing time effectively.

- Tips for traveling on a tight budget.

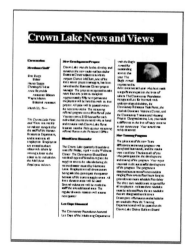

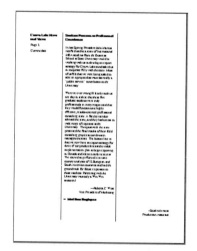

# LETTER AND MEMO MASTERY

## OBJECTIVES

1. Format two-page letters, memos, and e-mails.

2. Learn special letter parts and envelopes.

3. Use Merge to create letters, envelopes, and labels.

4. Improve speed and accuracy.

---

## Block Letter

### 65a • 5'

## GETTING started

1. Read the "Overview of business letters."
2. Divide into teams of three.
3. Study the three letters at right.
   • Record the similarities of the three letter styles.
   • Record the differences.

### Overview of business letters

The business letter is a formal means of communication to persons outside of the organization. Writers communicate effectively through both the message content and the attractive appearance of the document.

Three widely accepted letter styles are **block**, **modified block**, and **simplified block**. A review of the samples below shows that all share similarities with slight variations. It's helpful to learn the basic letter formats, realizing that other variations are also acceptable.

**Block format**

**Modified block format**

**Simplified block format**

---

6. Insert a picture of an eagle from the CD-Rom or download one from the Internet. Size the picture to be about 1.5" wide. Position it at the right side of the column just after the Eagle Award is mentioned in the copy.

7. Insert an envelope symbol from Iconic symbols on the same line and to the left of the heading *Mail from Employees*. Change the symbol to 14 point.

8. Print the document; save it as **app-a1**.

## Lee Daye Honored

The Community Foundation honored Lee Daye of the Marketing Department with the Eagle Award for outstanding service this year. The Eagle Award is presented each year to three citizens who have made a significant impact on the lives of others. The Community Foundation recognized Lee for his work with underprivileged children, the Community Relations Task Force, the Abolish Domestic Violence Center, and the Community Transitional Housing Project. Congratulations, Lee. You made a difference in the lives of many citizens in our community. Your award was richly deserved.

## New Training Program

The pilot test of the new Team Effectiveness training program was completed last month, and the results were excellent. Thanks to all of you who participated in the development and testing of the program. Your input was vital in the successful development of the program. The program is designed as a series of nine modules ranging from two to four hours long to provide maximum schedule flexibility. The three core modules are required for all employees. At least three modules must be selected from the six modules that are designated as electives. Descriptive information and schedules are available from the Training Department and will be posted on the Crown Lake Online Bulletin Board.

## ✉ Mail from Employees

In late spring, President John Marcus notified us that a team of international MBA students from the Business School at State University would be working with us to develop an export strategy for Crown Lake and asked us to cooperate fully with the team. Most of us felt that we were being asked to take on a project that was essentially a "public service" contribution to the University.

Were we ever wrong!!! It only took us one day to realize that these five graduate students were truly professionals in every respect and that they were going to function as a highly effective, results-oriented professional consulting team. A faculty member advised the team, and they had access to a wide range of expertise at the University. This past week the team presented the final results of their field consulting project to the division management team. The bottom line is that we now have an export strategy for three of our product lines and a viable implementation plan to begin exporting to Canada and Mexico early next year. The team also performed extensive country analyses of 12 European and South American countries and laid the groundwork for future expansion to those markets. Partnering with the University was truly a win-win situation!

—Roberta C. West
Vice President of Marketing

## 65b • 10'

**Review of letter parts**

Study the illustration at the right or the one on p. 198 as you read about the letter parts.

**Letterhead:** Company name, address, and telephone number. Often includes fax number and company trademark.

**Dateline:** Current date *or* date letter is mailed.

**Letter address:** Appropriate personal title (*Mr., Ms., Dr., The Honorable*), full name, professional title, company name, and address. Use *Ms.* for women, unless the writer has indicated a preference for *Miss* or *Mrs.* Use the 2-letter state abbreviation and ZIP Code. Key the letter address a QS below the date. Letter addresses may be keyed in ALL CAPS with no punctuation if the letter is sent in a window envelope.

**Salutation:** Appropriate personal title and name (*Dear Senator Smythe* or *Dear Mr. Watts*). Begin a DS below the letter address.

**Body:** The message of the letter. SS the body and DS between paragraphs. Begin the body a DS below the salutation.

**Complimentary close:** Phrase used to close the letter; closings range from informal to formal—*Cordially, Yours truly, Sincerely, Respectfully yours.* Capitalize only the first word. Begin a DS below the body.

**Writer's name and title:** Women often include a preferred personal title (for example, *Ms. Wanda Rainer*). Use a personal title when the first name can be used by either gender (*Mr. Leslie Foster*). Key the name of the writer a QS below the complimentary close.

**Reference initials:** Use lowercase initials for the person who keyed the document (*pt*). If the initials of the originator are included, key them first in uppercase (*CML:pt*). Key initials a DS below writer's name.

**Enclosure notation:** Notice indicating that items are enclosed. Items may be listed (*Enclosure: Check #820*). Key a DS below reference initials.

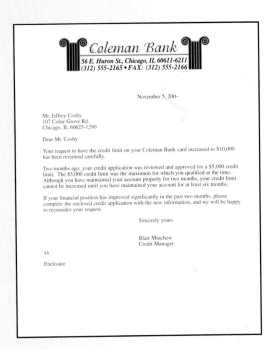

## 65c • 5'

**Letter format guides**

Study the information on letter placement.

**Letter format guides**

- Use default side margins.
- Use 12-point font size for ease of reading. If the letter is long or has several parts, decrease the size to 11 point if doing so will allow the letter to fit on one page.
- Position the dateline at least 2" from the top edge of the paper to allow space for the letterhead. For short letters and average letters, position the dateline by centering the page vertically. For long letters or letters with several features, press ENTER to position the date (see Letter Placement Table).
- View before printing to check vertical placement.

| Letter Placement Table | | |
|---|---|---|
| **Length** | **Date** | **Margins** |
| Short: 1–2 ¶s | Center page | Default |
| Average: 3–4 ¶s | 2.7" or center page | Default |
| Long: 4 or more ¶s | 2.1" (default + 6 hard returns) | Default |

## Wrap text around graphics

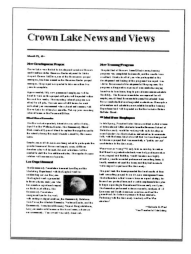

1. Key the informal newsletter at the right using .75" side margins and 10-point Times New Roman font.
2. Place the insertion point below the date. Using the **Columns** button, format the newsletter body in 2 equal-width columns.
3. Select the main heading, and apply bold and 36-point font to create a banner.
4. With the heading selected, click **Format, Paragraph, Border/Fill**. Choose *Thick Top/Bottom* border style to add horizontal lines above and below the heading.
5. DS before each side heading within the newsletter, and use 12-point bold font for the headings.

### To wrap text around graphics:

1. Insert the graphic at the desired position; then place the insertion point over the graphic and click the right mouse button.
2. Select *Wrap* to display the Wrap Text dialog box.
3. Click the wrapping type desired (Square).
4. Click **Wrap text around** style (Left side).
5. Click **OK**.

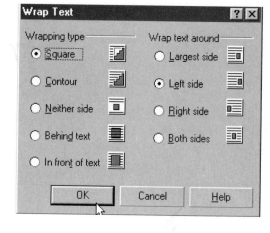

Right-click the graphic; select Wrap

---

# Crown Lake News and Views

## March 25, 200-

### New Development Project

Crown Lake won the bid to develop and construct the new multimillion-dollar Business Center adjacent to Metro Airport. Connie McClure, one of the three senior project managers, has been named as the Business Center project manager. The project is expected to take more than two years to complete. Approximately fifty new permanent employees will be hired to work on this project. All jobs will be posted within the next two weeks. The recruiting referral program is in effect for all jobs. You can earn a $100 bonus for each individual you recommend who is hired and remains with Crown Lake for at least six months. You may pick up your recruiting referral forms in the Personnel Office.

### Blood Drive Reminder

The Crown Lake quarterly blood drive is set for Friday, April 4, in the Wellness Center. The Community Blood Bank needs all types of blood to replace the supplies sent to the islands during the recent disaster caused by Hurricane Lana. Employees in all divisions are being asked to participate this quarter because of the current supply crisis. All three donation sites will be used. Several volunteers will be needed to staff the two additional sites. The regular division rotation will resume next quarter.

**2000 National Technology Association Convention**
**Hospitality Committee**

3501 E. Shea Blvd., Suite 110, Phoenix, AZ 85028-3339
(602) 555-4242 • FAX: (602) 555-4243

Dateline

June 1, 2000
QS

Letter address

Ms. Audra Meaux, President
Meaux Technology, Inc.
2689 Marsalis Ln.
Hot Springs, AR 71913-0345
DS

**Personal title is a courtesy.**

Salutation

Dear Ms. Meaux
DS

Body

Thank you for agreeing to serve as chair of the Hospitality Committee for the 2000 National Technology Association Convention on September 3-6 in Phoenix, Arizona.

The enclosed guidelines outline the responsibilities and timelines of the Hospitality Committee. Please read them carefully and call me at (602) 555-1037 if you have any questions.  You will need about 25 individuals to work with you on this committee.  After you have organized this group, please mail me a complete roster including names, addresses, phone and fax numbers, and e-mail addresses.  I would appreciate having this roster by August 1.

A personal black-and-white photograph is needed for publication in the convention program. Please send me your photo by July 1.

Audra, thank you for your professionalism and willingness to serve.  I look forward to working with you this year.
DS

Complimentary close

Sincerely
QS

**Appropriate closing for business letter**

Ryan Messamore
Vice President of Sales

**Title can be keyed with name—i.e., J. D. Smith, President.**

Reference initials

xx
DS

Enclosure

Enclosure

**Note:** Open punctuation means no punctuation follows the salutation or complimentary close.

BLOCK LETTER FORMAT—OPEN PUNCTUATION

# Work with Columns

## Newsletters

**Newsletters** range from informal documents used to convey "news" to employees to external documents that are relatively formal to communicate information to clients, customers, suppliers, or the general public. Typically, newsletters are written in an informal, conversational style and formatted with banners, newspaper columns, graphic elements, and text enhancements. Newspaper columns differ from columns in a table in that text flows down one column to the top of the next column, whereas in tables, text flows across the columns. Newsletters generally are formatted on standard (8.5" x 11") paper with two to four columns. A simple, uncluttered design with a significant amount of white space is recommended to enhance readability.

## Columns

Columns can be formatted with equal width, or the column widths may vary. Columns can be created and formatted using the Columns button on the toolbar. The Columns button is used to format columns of equal width. The Columns dialog box is used to format columns of unequal width. This dialog box can be accessed either from the Format menu or from the drop-down menu of the Columns button.

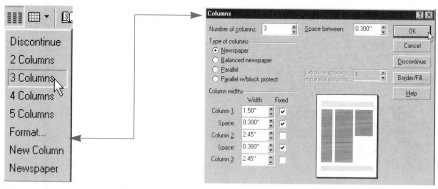

Column format may be set before or after keying the text. Generally, column formats are easier to apply after the text has been keyed.

**To create columns of equal width:**

1. Click the **Columns** button.
2. Select the number of columns.

**To format columns of unequal width:**

1. Access the Columns dialog box (**Columns** button, **Format**).
2. Enter the desired width of columns and spacing between columns (or leave the .5" default spacing). Click **OK**.
3. To keep the width of a column or space between columns the same regardless of margin changes or other column changes, click the Fixed check box.

**To add a vertical line between columns:**

1. Click the **Border/Fill** button in the Columns dialog box.
2. Scroll down the Border Styles until you reach *Column Between*; select it and click **Apply**, then **OK**.

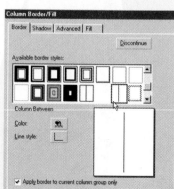

## 65d ● 30'

**Block letter format**
**Document 1**

**Document 2**

Review the block letter format from the model on p. 198. Then key the letter, following the guidelines. Position the dateline by centering the page vertically.

1. Open *paterzo* and print. Save as **65d-d2**.
2. Label the appropriate letter parts on the printout.
3. Write **DS** or **QS** to show correct spacing between parts.
4. Edit the letter parts as indicated in the call-out boxes.

**Document 3**
Format the short letter using block style.

|  | words |
|---|---|
| January 10, 200- │Ms. Denise McWhorter│HandPrints, Inc.│ | 11 |
| 92 E. Cresswell ~~Road~~ Rd.│Selden, NY 11784│Dear Ms. McWhorter | 24 |
| Booth 24, your first choice had been reserved for you | 35 |
| for the annual craft fair on May 15-17. Your booth was ex- | 46 |
| tremely popular last year and we are very pleased to have you | 59 |
| participate in the fair ~~fare~~ again this year. | 67 |
| Our standard agreement from is inclosed. Please sign | 78 |
| the form and return it to us by April 15. Your booths will | 90 |
| have a large table and a minimum of two chairs If you need | 102 |
| anything else for the booth please let us know prior to the | 114 |
| opening of the fair. | 119 |
| Sincerely│Ms. Jennifer A. Reed│President│xx│Enclosure | 129 |

**Document 4**
Format the average letter in block format.

|  | words |
|---|---|
| January 10, 200-│The Honorable Alice Vinicki│P.O. Box 249│Volusia, | 13 |
| FL 32174-3852│Dear Senator Vinicki | 20 |
| Your positive response to deliver the keynote address at the Volusia | 34 |
| Community Goals Conference on Saturday, January 30, was received | 47 |
| with much excitement by the Goals Conference Planning Committee. | 60 |
| Thank you, Senator Vinicki, for your commitment to this community | 74 |
| effort. Mr. Roger Bourgeois, director of the United Planning Institute, | 88 |
| is the lead facilitator of the goals conference and will introduce you at the | 104 |
| opening session beginning at 9 a.m. in the Vinicki Exhibit Hall of | 117 |
| the Volusia Convention Center. | 124 |
| Hotel accommodations have been made for you at the Riverside Suites | 137 |
| for Friday, January 29; confirmation is enclosed. Mr. Bourgeois and I | 151 |
| will meet you at the hotel restaurant at 7:30 a.m. for breakfast and | 165 |
| to escort you to the convention center. A copy of the conference program | 180 |
| and an outline of the issues to be discussed in the various breakout | 194 |
| groups are also enclosed for your review. | 202 |
| We look forward to your address and to your being a key player in our | 216 |
| goals conference. | 220 |
| Respectfully yours│Ms. Le-An Nguyen, President│Chamber of Commerce│ | 234 |
| xx│Enclosures | 236 |

## Desktop Publishing Tips

Designing effective documents requires skill that can be developed through training and experience. An easy first step in developing desktop publishing skill is to examine professionally designed documents—such as textbooks and annual reports—to determine the features that make them both functionally successful and aesthetically pleasing. The second step is to follow a list of guides or tips, such as the ones listed below, that are compiled from comments of experienced desktop publishers and professional printers.

### General Tips

**Personal preferences and habit are weak excuses for poor design.**

◆ Analyze the content and formality of a document before making decisions on design elements.

◆ Opt for a simple, consistent, attractive design that facilitates communication.

◆ Make text flow according to normal reading patterns—from top to bottom and from left to right.

◆ Flow text toward the binding with portrait orientation and away from the binding with landscape orientation.

◆ Use lowercase to enhance readability—limit initial caps or ALL CAPS to headings and special copy that need emphasis.

### Design Element Tips

◆ Select a typeface that clearly distinguishes the letters *O* and lowercase *l* from digits *0* and *1* for technical documents.

◆ Single-space bulleted or numbered lists in which each item is less than one line; space (6 points) before each item when one or more items in the list are longer than one line.

◆ Position header information above the dividing line and footer information below the dividing line when lines are used.

◆ Abandon old typing conventions, such as using two spaces after a colon or a period at the end of a sentence, using the ENTER key to add space before a paragraph, and using underlines rather than italic for titles.

# Letters with Special Features

## 66a ● 5'

### GETTING started

each line 3 times (slowly, faster, slowly); DS between groups; use these directions throughout

| | | |
|---|---|---|
| alphabet | 1 | Josef fixed my lovely wicker chair and my grey quilted bedspread. |
| fig/sym | 2 | The premium (Policy #8193) is $245.67 a year or $20.47 per month. |
| double letters | 3 | Ann called at noon to tell Lee she missed the meeting with Betty. |
| easy | 4 | I pay the city for the right to cut hay in a field the city owns. |

| 1 | 2 | 3 | 4 | 5 | 6 | 7 | 8 | 9 | 10 | 11 | 12 | 13 |

## 66b ● 5'

### NEW FUNCTION

Read about "Date"; then practice entering the current date in the default month-day-year format. Do not save.

### Date

You can easily insert the current date in the letter using the Date command. When the document is saved, the original date remains in the document.

1. Choose *Date/Time* from the Insert menu.

2. Choose the first format option (month, day, year). Click **Insert**.

3. By default, the original date remains in the document when the document is saved. If you want the current date to be updated each time the document is opened, click to add a ✓ in the *Keep the inserted date current* box.

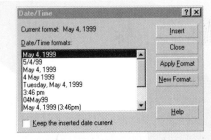

## 66c ● 5'

### FORMATTING

**Letters with special features**

Additional special features help communicate clear and effective messages. Learn the purpose of these features.

**Subject line**

A subject line indicates the main topic of the letter. Subject lines are optional except in simplified block format. Key the subject line a DS below the salutation in either ALL CAPS or initial cap format.

> Ms. Angela Ashmore
> P.O. Box 85
> Starkville, MS 39759-2831
>
> Dear Ms. Ashmore ₍DS₎
> Soccer Camp—May 1-2
>
> A soccer camp for ages 6-12 will be held on May 1-2 at the Davidson Soccer Complex.
>
> Sincerely

**Reference line**

A reference line such as Re: Order No. R1084 directs the reader to source documents or to files. Do not confuse a reference line with a subject line; the purposes are different. Key the reference line a DS below the letter address.

> Route 2, Box 332
> Natchez, MS 39120-1452 ₍DS₎
> Re: Order No. R1084 ₍DS₎
> Dear Mr. Allison
>
> Demand for two of the items (Stock Nos. 3856C and 9257D) that you ordered has been so great that we've had to place

### White Space

The natural tendency in designing documents is to try to save space. White space is not the area to economize, however. A key way to emphasize ideas is to isolate them from other ideas. White space provides the isolation needed to make things stand out on a page. A technique frequently used to emphasize a few critical points is to put the key points in a column (sometimes called a *scanning* column) by themselves surrounded by generous amounts of white space. The extra white space in the column also serves the purpose of reserving space in case a few graphic elements are wider than the text column—they can extend into the blank space of the scanning column.

**White space, a key element of visual design, is often underestimated.**

Documents packed with copy look cluttered and are difficult to read. White space provides an open, uncluttered look that is restful and that leads the reader to important copy that needs emphasis.

### Headings and Layout

Headings follow the same structure as an outline. They are hierarchical and should be ranked from high to low. Headings with the most important content should be positioned above and in a more prominent typestyle than headings with content of lesser importance. Brief headings tend to be more effective than long headings. The key design consideration is consistency. Grammatical structure, as well as typeface and spacing elements, must be consistent for headings of the same level.

*Layout* refers to the careful positioning and spacing of the design elements on a page to create the best visual effect. The number and width of columns influence layout significantly. Column layouts may vary on the same page. Some organizations provide templates and define layout rules for published documents so tightly that document design is purely a science. However, in most organizations, layout rules are not always hard and fast—layout is an art. It is the product of careful experimentation to create the best way to communicate the information contained in a document.

**Less is better than more...**

**Err on the side of too few design elements and too little text rather than too many elements and too much text on a page.**

Many trade-offs exist in designing the layout of a document. For example, consistency and flexibility often conflict. Certain graphic elements may not fit in the space that a consistent layout pattern provides. However, the importance of the content dictates that the consistent layout pattern be modified to accommodate the content.

### Paper

Page size, weight, texture, and finish affect the design of a document. U.S. standard paper is 8.5" x 11"; ISO (international) standard paper is 8.25" x 11.75". The other attributes of paper may vary depending on the printing process, type of document, and cost factors.

## 66d ● 5'

Review and apply the procedures at the right each time you create a letter.

### Proofreading procedures

The final, important step in producing a document is proofreading. Error-free documents send the message that the organization is detail-oriented and competent. Apply these procedures when producing any document.

1. Use Spell Checker.
2. Proofread the document on the screen.
   - Be alert for words that are spelled correctly but are misused, such as your/you, in/on, of/on, the/then, etc.
   - Check letter parts for correctness; be sure special features are present if needed—i.e., enclosure or copy notation.
3. View the document on screen to check placement. Save and print.
4. Check printout with the source copy (textbook).
5. Revise document as needed, save, and print.
6. Proofread the second printout.

## 66e ● 30'

FORMATTING

### Block letters
**Document 1**
**Block letter with subject line**
Use the Date command in this average-length letter.

Apply proofreading procedures.

words

Current date | Mr. Grant S. Cothern | International Enterprises, Inc. |   14
89350 North Oxford Ave. | Braggadorio, MO 63826-0467 | Dear Mr. Cothern   27

Connecting to the Net   32

The questions raised in your letter about connecting to the Internet are   46
shared by millions of business managers.  We at Telecommunication   60
Consultants, Inc. are pleased you have allowed us this opportunity to   74
answer your questions.   78

The costs include *two* installation charges and *two* recurring cost com-   92
ponents for Internet service.  The initial installation consists of a fixed   108
charge for the Internet service provider (ISP) setup and a fixed charge for   123
the telephone company line installation.  The two recurring costs include   138
a monthly charge to the ISP cost, based on line speed, and a monthly   151
charge, based on distance and speed, that is paid to the telephone   165
company.   167

For an organization of 50 or fewer users that does not require speed,   181
modem access is the most cost-effective means of connecting to the   194
Internet.  Other means of access that accommodate many Internet   207
users and allow high performance requirements are also available.  Our   221
representatives are specially trained to design a plan that will allow you   236
to reap the performance you need and remain within your budget.   249
Please call 1-800-555-4NET and begin your connection to the NET.   262

Sincerely yours | Ms. Melissa Galt-Brown | Marketing Manager | xx   274

**Document 2**
**Block letter with reference line**
Use the Date command in this short letter.

Apply proofreading procedures.

Current date | Mr. Yeong Kim | Kim and Associates | 102 Tabor St. |   13
Decatur, AL 35601-4892 | Re:  Order No. 740S913 | Dear Mr. Kim   24

Fifteen TX-400 answering machines were shipped today by Phoenix   37
Express.  Lauren Tartt was granted special approval to ship your order   51
although it exceeds your current credit limit by 30 percent.   64

Please complete and return the credit forms accompanying this letter so   78
that we may consider increasing your current credit limit.  Future orders   93
can then be shipped according to your newly established credit limit.   107

Sincerely | Patrick McReynolds | Credit Manager | xx | Enclosures   119

### Color

Color helps convey vivid images and adds a new dimension to document design. Using color consistently gives a feeling of comfort and helps the reader locate information quickly. Color helps to link elements of a document. Special care needs to be used in selecting colors. The color that displays on a computer screen may look quite different when printed or projected. Often color is a part of a logo, and an exact match is critical.

**Color, used functionally, is a powerful communication tool.**

The color scheme of a document should be simple. A good rule of thumb is to use a maximum of four colors in a document. Graphs with multiple bars or pie segments may require more than four colors and would be an exception. Consistency in the use of color is extremely important.

### Tables and Graphic Elements

Tables and graphic elements should be used when they simplify and clarify information. Limit the use of graphics to those that contribute to the content of a document. A picture often gets the message across quickly and effectively. Too many graphic elements can be distracting and confusing, however. Another important consideration is matching the graphic elements with the tone of a document. A formal document must be matched with a sophisticated (but simple) graphic. Limited use of TextArt can be effective for informal documents such as employee newsletters.

**A picture is worth a thousand words…**

**Too many pictures are as ineffective as too many words.**

Tables are useful in providing large amounts of specific numeric data. Clearly labeled rows and columns help to organize information in a way that facilitates analysis. Charts are particularly useful in documents that contain statistical information. Converting a table to a chart helps the reader grasp the concept quickly and easily.

Using the appropriate chart format for the type of data is critical. As a general rule, use:

- Pie charts to show percentages of a whole
- Line charts to show trends
- Bar charts to compare quantities
- Bilateral bar charts for comparisons with positive and negative data

Effective design of all graphic elements is important. A poorly designed graphic may provide inaccurate or biased information. Careful attention must be paid to the size, placement, and identification of graphic elements in a document. General rules of thumb are to use left or right alignment for graphics within a column, to limit the width of a graphic to the width of the text column when possible, and to identify graphic elements with both a title and number when appropriate.

**Document 3**
**Letter with copy notation**

1. Make this long letter fit on one page by changing the font size to 11 point. Position the dateline for a long letter.
2. Check that all letter parts are included and formatted correctly.
3. Move the last sentence of ¶ 4 to the end of ¶ 1.
4. Send a copy to **Jane Sturdevant**.
5. Print 2 copies.
6. Place a ✔ by the copy notation on the letter to be sent to the person receiving the copy.

**Review:** Key a copy notation a DS below the reference initials or enclosure notation.
**Enclosure**
**c Kathy Cooper**
   **Richard McMillen**

**Document 4**

1. Open *66e-d2*; save as **66e-d4**.
2. Read the letter; then insert an appropriate copy notation.
3. Print 2 copies.
4. Place a ✔ by the copy notation on the letter that will be sent to the third party.

September 1, 200- | 2

*Miss*
Diane Germany | 6
23 South Gate Rd. | 10
Milligan, FL 32537-2819 | 14

Dear Diane | 17

Thank you for stopping by to visit with me last week | 27
at Woodley Community College.  I am very pleased that you | 39
are planning to transfer to Penttila College in our informa- | 51
tion systems technology program.  *Mrs. Sturdevant,* | 61
your business teacher, has shared with me your outstanding | 73
high school and college achievements. | 81

As you requested, I have enclosed an evaluation of your | 107
community college transcript.  Since you plan to complete | 118
your sophomore year at the community college, I would highly | 131
recommend that you complete Principles of Accounting, College | 143
Algebra, a higher level math, and a computer literacy course. | 156
Remember that you may transfer 64 hours; *refer to the top* | 167
*section of the curriculum sheet for core courses.* | 177

*Friday,*
Our department will be planning a special event for prospec- | 189
tive students October 15.  Please place this date on your | 203
calendar and invite your friends to come along as well.  A | 214
well-planned agenda will acquaint you with campus life as | 226
well as a tour of the department and an appointment with | 237
your advisor.  We look forward to your visit to our | 248
department. | 250

Best wishes for an outstanding sophomore year.  Please call | 262
me if you have any questions or if I can help in any way. | 274
We look forward to having you continue this excellent record | 93
at Penttila. | 96

Sincerely | 276

Dr. Seth Olson Associate Professor | 283

Enclosure | 289

## Design Elements

Design elements consist of features used repeatedly and consistently in documents. Design elements include text, typeface, color, tables and graphic elements, white space, headings and layout, and paper.

### Text

The amount of text, the nature of the text, and the purpose for which it is being used influence the design of documents. Long documents require more structure than short documents. Technical, statistical, and complex textual materials require significant amounts of illustration to simplify them. On the other hand, the rigid requirements for a formal report may not be appropriate for an informal newsletter to employees.

**Limit design elements and use them consistently.**

Text itself is often a design element. For example, a company analyzing 20 countries for potential export opportunities might use textual categories as repeated design elements. The analysis of each of the countries might have these segments: political climate, economic conditions, market potential, barriers to entry, and recommendations.

### Typeface

Some organizations prefer to use one typeface for a document; other organizations use compatible typefaces to produce a desired effect. For example, a serif typeface is often used for the body of the document and a sans serif typeface for headings. *Serif* typefaces, such as Times Roman or Times New Roman, have small lines that extend from the main portion of the character. *Sans serif* typefaces, such as Helvetica or Arial, do not have these extenders. Typefaces used for large type or headings, such as Script or Gothic, are generally called *display* typefaces. Script is often used for personal or informal documents and for invitations.

> This typeface, Times New Roman, is a serif typeface.
> This typeface, Arial, is a sans serif typeface.
> *This type face, Vivaldi D, is a display typeface.*

The units of measure for type size are *picas* and *points*. An inch is roughly 6 picas, and a pica contains 12 points or 72 points per inch. A good rule of thumb is to use 10- to 12-point type for the body and 14- to 18-point type for headings. Larger type sizes may be used for banners.

Vertical distance between lines of type (the height of a line) is called *leading*. Leading is set automatically, but it can be adjusted. A rule of thumb is to use 2 points more than the type size for small type.

# Modified Block Letter

## 67a ● 5'

### GETTING started

| | | |
|---|---|---|
| alphabet | 1 | Jo Eizaburo will give them daily price quotations for six stocks. |
| figures | 2 | That room (48' long x 35' wide with 10' ceiling) costs $6,972.50. |
| 3d/4th fingers | 3 | Pam was quick to zap Dex about a poor sample that was on display. |
| easy | 4 | A neighbor may bus the six girls to the lake to fish on the dock. |

| 1 | 2 | 3 | 4 | 5 | 6 | 7 | 8 | 9 | 10 | 11 | 12 | 13 |

## 67b ● 10'

### COMMUNICATION

**Proofreading reinforcement**

1. Open *proof* from the template disk. Save as **67b**.
2. Apply the "Proofreading procedures" reviewed in Lesson 66, p. 201.
3. Compare final copy with a team member to check your work. Mark any errors located.

## 67c ● 27'

### FORMATTING

**Review modified block format**

**Document 1**
1. Read the letter on p. 204.
2. Set a tab at 3.2" on the Ruler. Set 11-point font.
3. Key the long letter in modified block format.
4. Print original without bc.
5. Add bc notation and reprint.

### Modified block format

The modified block format is a variation of the block format. It is "modified" by moving the dateline and the closing lines from the left margin to the center point of the page. Set a tab at the center of the page (3.2") to key the date and closing at center.

To determine the position of the tab at center, subtract the side margin from the center of the paper (4.2" − 1" = 3.2"). A sheet of paper is 8 1/2" wide ÷ 2 = 4.2".

Paragraphs may be indented, but it is more efficient not to indent them. Do not indent paragraphs unless instructed to do so.

### Special feature

**Blind copy notation:** A **copy notation** (c) shows that a copy of the document has been sent to the person named. A **blind copy notation** (bc) indicates that a copy of the document was sent to the person(s) named *without* the recipient's knowledge. A bc notation is not printed on the original. After saving and printing the document for the addressee, add the blind copy notation and reprint for the person(s) who will receive the blind copy.

**Company name:** The company name, an optional letter part, is keyed in UPPERCASE, a DS below the complimentary close; a QS separates the company name from the writer's name. Company names are not commonly used with letterhead stationery.

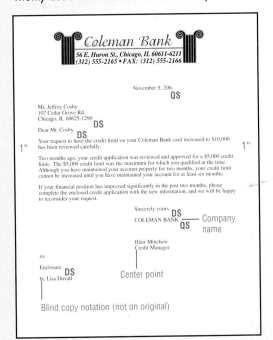

# DOCUMENT DESIGN—AN ART AND A SCIENCE

**Why prepare a document?**

Obviously, a writer expects a document to communicate a message to a specific audience. Likewise, effective document design facilitates communication—it does not simply decorate or make a document look aesthetically pleasing. The science of document design refers to matching the design elements to the message that the document seeks to communicate. The art of document design refers to making a document sensitive to the needs of the audience—giving the document a feeling of being familiar, comfortable, and pleasing to read.

## Desktop Publishing Standards

**Special characters and symbols provide a professional appearance.**

Standards for desktop publishing may vary from standards used in typical document production in a business office. In desktop publishing, only one space follows end-of-sentence punctuation. Traditionally, two spaces follow end-of-sentence punctuation in documents; however, this trend is changing. In typical document production, space between paragraphs is often inserted by striking the ENTER key a second time. In desktop publishing, the Spacing Between Paragraphs option in the Paragraph Format dialog box is used to specify the amount of space before a paragraph. In desktop publishing, special characters such as en and em dashes and spaces, and special symbols such as copyright, trademark, and registered, generally are used.

## Design Objectives

Effective document design accomplishes a number of objectives, such as:

**Templates and style guides ensure consistency.**

- Supports document content
- Adds organizational structure
- Provides a consistent image
- Denotes formality
- Enhances readability
- Emphasizes important points
- Simplifies content presentation
- Compacts copy and optimizes space requirements
- Provides a road map to lead the reader through the document

Document design requires careful planning to accomplish the objectives listed. Many organizations research design carefully and specify standards for all documents published in professional print shops or desktop published internally. They provide employees with templates or grids that serve as guides for the design of documents. Style manuals often are very detailed, and employees follow the directives meticulously. To these organizations, visual design is a key element in corporate identity and image.

# Communication Experts

**999 McArthur Dr.**
**Mt. Morris, MI 48504-4481**
**(810) 555-0101**
**FAX: (810) 555-0111**

November 7, 200-
<sub>QS</sub>

Ms. Jan Kathryn Wheeler, President
Professional Document Designs, Inc.
9345 Blackjack Blvd.
Kingwood, TX 77345-9345
DS

Dear Ms. Wheeler: ——————— **Use a colon, not a comma.**
DS

The format of this letter is called modified block. Modified block format differs from block format in that the date, complimentary close, and the writer's name and title are keyed at the center point.
DS

1"  Paragraphs may be blocked, as this letter illustrates, or they may be indented .5" from the left margin. We suggest using block paragraphs so that an additional tab setting is not needed. However, some people prefer indenting paragraphs.

Although modified block format is very popular, we recommend that you use it only for those customers who request this letter style. Otherwise, we urge you to use block format, which is more efficient, as your standard style.

Another letter style used by some businesses today because of its efficiency is the simplified block letter. Please refer to the model illustrated in the enclosed *Communication Experts Format Guide*. Also, please study carefully the section on protocol in using an appropriate salutation and complimentary close.

Sincerely, ——————— **Use a comma.**
DS

COMMUNICATION EXPERTS ——— Company name
QS

Ms. A. Katina Carter
Communication Consultant

xx

Enclosure
DS

bc Lyndon David, Account Manager

Blind copy
notation

> **Note:** Mixed punctuation means placing a colon after the salutation and a comma after the complimentary close.

## MODIFIED BLOCK LETTER FORMAT—MIXED PUNCTUATION

# DESKTOP PUBLISHING

**A**

*module*

## OVERVIEW

**Desktop publishing** refers to documents published at one's desktop rather than in a professional print shop. The design and layout of publications produced professionally generally include columns, graphic elements, and text enhancements. Professional-looking publications no longer are the sole province of professional printers. Advances in technology and page layout software make it possible to produce professional-looking documents with a personal computer and a laser printer. Today, those same design elements can be incorporated into documents produced using sophisticated word processing software.

Businesses use desktop publishing to produce many different types of publications such as newsletters, brochures, product descriptions, announcements, invitations, advertising flyers, catalogs, proposals, reports, and technical or training manuals.

Producing documents at the desktop rather than sending them to professional print shops usually results in saving significant amounts of time and money. Producing documents internally also streamlines the process of revising and distributing documents.

To achieve a professional appearance, principles of good design and layout must be applied consistently throughout a document. Read carefully the article "DOCUMENT DESIGN—AN ART AND A SCIENCE," on pp. 376–380. This article provides the background information needed in this module. All of your keyboarding activities in this module focus on applying principles of effective design to document production.

**67c,** *continued*

**Document 2**
**Modified block letter**

1. Use the Date command.
2. Format the subject line properly.
3. Provide appropriate complimentary close. **Alexandria H. Skiwski, Technical Manager** is the sender of the letter.
4. Include the company name, **PARRISH TECHNOLOGY SERVICES,** in the closing lines.
5. Send a blind copy notation to **Todd West, Account Manager**.

*Current date | Mr. Jamie Kurman, Jr. | P.O. Box 7390 | Counderspot, PA* — 15
*16315-0985 | Dear Mr. Kurman: | Scanner Recommendations* — 24

*Your assessment, Mr. Kurman, is right on target. The payback period for a* — 39
*scanner would be about six months. We are pleased to provide you with our* — 54
*recommendations.* — 58

*Your test generation software handles both text and graphics; therefore, an* — 73
*intelligent OCR should be purchased. The enclosed analysis provides speci-* — 88
*fications, price information, and our recommendations for both the scanner* — 103
*and the software.* — 107

*Please call us at 1-800-555-6639 to schedule a demonstration of the OCR* — 121
*scanner. We look forward to hearing from you.* — 131

closing — 149

**Document 3**
**Change letter format**

Change *67b* to a modified block letter.

1. Open *67b* and save as **67c-d3**.
2. Clear default tabs.
3. Set a left tab at 3.2" from the Tab Set dialog box.
4. Click the insertion point at the beginning of each line to be formatted at center. Press TAB.
5. Save and print.

**67d ● 8'**

**NEW FUNCTION**

## Convert Case

**Convert Case** allows you to change the capitalization of text that has already been keyed. This handy function will save you time. To use it, select the text to be changed, and then choose *Convert Case* from the *Edit* menu. The Convert Case menu displays:

| | |
|---|---|
| **Lowercase:** | Changes all letters to lowercase. |
| **Uppercase:** | Changes all letters to uppercase. |
| **Initial Capitals**: | Capitalizes the first letter of each selected word. |

**Drill**

1. Open *case* from the template disk. Revise the lines as shown at right.
2. Save as **67d**.

1.  Add the side heading facilities and equipment.
2.  Cindy Sturzenberger is chairman and ceo.  *person*
3.  Britt Burge, president, ASSOCIATED TRAVEL SERVICES, *title case* formerly present of Ast
4.  D.M. POMMERT, ASSOCIATES *president / title case*
5.  ms. margarita valadez *title case* 1130 confederation dr. *title case* saskatoon sk s71 4k5 CANADA *all caps*

## Document 15
### Two-page block letter

Open *a1-lettr* (containing the message of the letter) from the Formatting Template. Save it as **p3-d15**. Follow steps at right.

1. Format the document as a two-page block letter, adding a header for the second page.
2. Add a salutation, subject line, closing, and other necessary letter parts.
3. Use Cut and Paste to reverse ¶s 1 and 2.
4. Key the table below so that it follows ¶ 3. Bold and center column headings.
5. Prepare the envelope.

Letter address:
```
Mr. and Mrs. Hunter Cunningham
901 Cedar St.
Shreveport, LA 71107-3845
```

Subject: `New Rates Become Effective July 1, 200-`

Sender: `Celia Ricchetti, Manager`

| *Level of Service* | *Current Rate* | *New Rate (July 1, 200-)* |
|---|---|---|
| Economy Basic | $11.50 | $14.00 |
| Satellite Basic | $27.95 | $31.95 |

## Document 16
### Letter with label

1. Key in block style with open punctuation.
2. Add appropriate salutation and complimentary closing. Add your name as the writer.
3. Prepare Avery address label 5160. Print on plain paper.

Current date | Ms. Shifa Chow | P.O. Box 5115 | Pascagoula, MS 39581-5115

Thank you for your confidence in my ability to serve Cedar Ridge Wellness Connection as office manager. Yes, I accept your offer of the position.

As we agreed in our telephone conversation, I will report to work at 8 a.m. on Monday, September 2. I understand that the first six months will be a probationary period. After successfully completing this trial period, I will be designated as a permanent employee. Future performance reviews will be regularly administered in January.

Thank you, Ms. Chow, for this opportunity. I look forward to working with your company.

## Document 17
### Report with references

1. Open *fcc* from the Formatting Template.
2. Insert the table from Document 13 where indicated.
3. Key footnotes and references.
4. Insert page numbers.
5. Design a cover page. Include the logo and apply a page border. Use larger fonts to make this page readable and attractive.

Footnotes
p. 1, ¶3, 2d sentence:
   [1]Jacqueline Parsons, *Public Utilities Justified* (New York: American Writers' Press, 1999), p. 115.
p. 2, last sentence:
   [2]William Alexander, "Effect of FCC Reform on Telephone Rates," *FCC Journal*, Spring 2000, <www.fcc.gov.journal>, 2 March 2000.

### REFERENCES

Parsons, Jacqueline. *Public Utilities Justified.* New York: American Writers' Press, 1999.

Alexander, William. "Effect of FCC Reform on Telephone Rates." *FCC Journal.* Spring 2000. <www.fcc.gov.journal> (2 March 2000).

# Modified Block and Special Features

## GETTING started

### SKILLBUILDING WARMUP

| | | |
|---|---|---|
| alphabet | 1 | Jim Winnifred, the proud quarterback, got criticized excessively. |
| fig/sym | 2 | Pat paid $85.90 each ($171.80) for 2 tickets in Row #34 on May 6. |
| double letters | 3 | Will the committee have access to all the books at noon tomorrow? |
| easy | 4 | Jake, their neighbor, paid for the right to fish on the big dock. |

| 1 | 2 | 3 | 4 | 5 | 6 | 7 | 8 | 9 | 10 | 11 | 12 | 13 |

68b ● 5'

## FORMATTING

### Special letter formats

Study the illustrations to learn to format special features of business letters.

**Mailing notations**

A notation such as FACSIMILE, OVERNIGHT, CERTIFIED, SPECIAL DELIVERY, or REGISTERED provides a record of how the letter was sent. Other notations such as CONFIDENTIAL or PERSONAL indicate how the recipient should treat the letter.

Key special notations in ALL CAPS at the left margin a DS below the dateline. On the envelope, key notations that affect postage right-aligned below the stamp (about line 1.3"). Key envelope notations that pertain to the recipient below the return address.

**Attention line**

The attention line directs a letter to a specific person, position, or department within a company. The attention line is the first line of the letter address. The correct salutation is *Ladies and Gentlemen*.

**Business envelopes**

The preferred format for envelopes is ALL CAPS, block format, and no punctuation (see figure below). Note how mailing notations and an attention line are formatted for envelopes.

---

April 2, 200- DS

CONFIDENTIAL DS

Dr. Spencer A. Blakeney
Golden Triangle Clinic
P.O. Box 10984
Tullahoma, TN 37388-1267

Dear Dr. Blakeney

---

December 14, 200- DS

CERTIFIED DS

Attention Division 2 Manager
Clinard Security Services
207 Hollyhill Ave.
Downers Grove, IL 60515-0357

Ladies and Gentlemen

---

Dwight Reed
389 Highway 17
Maysville, KY 41056-2332

CONFIDENTIAL

33 USA

CERTIFIED

ATTENTION DIVISION 2 MANAGER
CLINARD SECURITY SERVICES
207 HOLLYHILL AVE
DOWNERS GROVE IL 60515-0357

**Cable entry into telephony.**  The new law forbids local authorities to require that a cable company obtain an additional franchise agreement in order to enter the telephone business.

**Infrastructure sharing**.  Telcos are required to provide information about their switched network to any "qualifying carrier."  Potential competitors, including cable, need the information in order to connect their network with the telcos' network.

### Cable

The Federal Communications Commission is acting to increase competition to cable TV by approving additional Direct Broadcast Satellite (DBS) capacity for competitors to MCI.  Despite increases in the number of DBS subscribers, cable TV systems remain the dominant supplier in the multichannel video program distribution (MVPD) market.  Consequently, consumers should benefit from the increased competition that will lead to increased program offers and options and/or lower prices in the marketplace for multichannel video programming.

**Rate deregulation.**  The new law deregulates cable rates for the extended basic tier (MTV, Lifetime, ESPN, etc.) in three years.  Equipment rates will remain regulated under the bill.  The bill also eliminates the single subscriber's ability to initiate a rate review at the FCC.  A review can be initiated with a single complaint by a local franchising authority, city official, or state regulator.

A cable system is also free from rate regulation when "a telephone company offers cable service by any means that is comparable to the competing cable system."

**Signal scrambling for indecent programming.**  Cable operators are required to scramble, at no cost, the audio and video of any programming that the subscriber deems unsuitable for children.  The bill also requires a block on the audio and video of sexually explicit programming.

**Set-top boxes.**  The new law insures consumers' ability to purchase set-top boxes in retail stores.  Cable companies and others that provide multichannel video services may also provide set-top boxes, but the price may not be subsidized by subscription fees.  FCC has the authority to suspend its rules temporarily to "promote new or improved technology or services."

### Online Services

The bill, for the first time, attempted to give the federal government the power to regulate the Internet and online services.  It would have prohibited the use of interactive computer services to make or make available an indecent communication to minors.  However, on June 26, 1997, the Supreme Court ruled the bill to be unconstitutional except for its prohibitions against obscenity and child pornography.  Equally important, the Court granted full First Amendment rights to speakers on the Internet.

Before completing the drills, check that your printer can handle envelopes.

## Envelopes

An envelope can be generated whether a letter is displayed or not. A return address is required when a letterhead envelope is not used.

**To generate an envelope:**

1. With the letter displayed, choose *Format*, then *Envelope*. The envelope with letter address displays below the letter.

2. To print a return address, key it in the upper left corner at Ln .25" and Pos .25". To add a notation to the recipient such as CONFIDENTIAL or PLEASE FORWARD, key the notation **DS** below the return address.

3. Select the mailing address, convert to UPPERCASE, and remove punctuation.

4. Key mailing notations flush right (ALT-F7) at approximately Ln 1.3". Save and print.

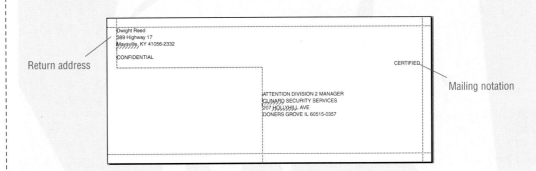

Return address

Dwight Reed
389 Highway 17
Maysville, KY 41056-2332

CONFIDENTIAL

CERTIFIED

ATTENTION DIVISION 2 MANAGER
CLINARD SECURITY SERVICES
207 HOLLYHILL AVE
DONERS GROVE IL 60515-0357

Mailing notation

### Drill I

1. Open *67c-d1*. Generate an envelope.

2. Save as **68c-d1** and print if possible.

### Drill 2

1. Open *67c-d2*.

2. Generate an envelope. Add the notation **OVERNIGHT** to the envelope.

3. Save as **68c-d2** and print.

### Drill 3

Key the envelope at right (no letter is displayed). DS after return address and key **PLEASE FORWARD**. Save as **68c-d3**.

Catherine Gordon
3731 Donavon Rd.
Sterling, VA 22170-1167

PLEASE FORWARD

MR BLAKE HOUSTON AGENT
ALAMAR REALTORS INC
101 BECKER ST
CHEROKEE AL 35611-0101

# DEREGULATION OF THE COMMUNICATIONS INDUSTRY

1. Key the report SS. Use a 1.5" top margin and default side margins.
2. Key the title in bold, all caps, 14 point.
3. In ¶ 2, select the text *Communications Decency Act* and create a hyperlink to www.epic.org.
4. On p. 2, under the side heading *Cable*, select the text *Federal Communications Commission* and create a hyperlink to www.fcc.gov.
5. Insert a page number at the top right of the second page.

The most all-encompassing revision of communications regulation over the past 60 years was signed into law on February 8, 1996 by President Clinton. Implementation of many portions of the legislation is awaiting action by the Federal Communications Commission, which may initiate as many as 80 separate rule-making proceedings. The Commission has provided a tentative schedule of the orders and rule makings necessary to implement the bill.

The law is subject to court challenges. The first major legal challenge to the Act resulted in a victory for opponents of government regulation of the Internet. On June 25, 1997, the Supreme Court ruled that the Communications Decency Act was unconstitutional. This act would have prohibited the transmission of "indecent" or "patently offensive" material over the Internet.

### Telephony

The demand and use of telephone services has increased tremendously over the years. It is now the norm for more than 68 million Americans to have a mobile phone. They make calls on a service that costs 40 percent less than it did three years ago. Calling friends and family across the nation has become less and less expensive as the choice of providers has risen and the AT&T monopoly's hold on the market has weakened.

The telecommunications industry is rapidly changing, and it is changing for the better. This transformation was unleashed by competition and fueled by technology. The phone lines and airwaves are the springboard into the 21st century. They will launch America into a New Economy, one based on the free flow of information, a highly skilled workforce, and a rapidly changing world.

**Telephone and cable buyouts.** The new law bars telephone companies from buying cable systems in markets of fewer than 35,000 people. An exemption exists for markets of 50,000 or less with only one cable system. Telcos and cable companies are also barred from having more than 10 percent financial stake in each other. Joint ventures between cable systems and telcos are also prohibited in their own markets. The bill contains a general exemption if the cable company or telco can show financial hardship.

**Telco provision of video programming.** The bill eliminates the ban on telcos' providing video programming on their own service areas. The telco will be regulated by the technology it chooses to deliver video programming. For example, if it builds a cable system, it will be regulated under cable rules. The law also created a new entity called an "open video system." The open video system must provide two-thirds of its capacity to unaffiliated programmers but does not need a local franchise in order to operate.

*Technology Review*
**Inserting page numbers**

1. Position the insertion point on the first page of the report.
2. Click the **Format** menu; choose *Page*, then *Numbering*.
3. Change the Position to Top Right. Click **OK**.
4. Click **Format**, **Page**, then **Suppress**. Place a check mark in the Page numbering check box. Click **OK**.

## FORMATTING

**Modified block letters**

**Document 1**

1. Format the average-length letter in modified block format; use mixed punctuation.
2. Add reference line:
   **Re: Order No. S3835**
   **Note:** Raise the dateline because the special features push the letter too low on the page. Use good judgment.
3. Include the company name, **TIME+ SOFTWARE INC.**, in the closing lines.
4. Generate an envelope.

Current date | CERTIFIED | Dr. Carol Metzger, Instructor | Merritt Business   15
College | 319 North Jackson St. | Jacksonville, FL 32256-0319 | Dear Dr.   32
Metzger:   34

Your TIME+ personal manager software was shipped to you this morning   48
by next-day air service. We realize that your time is valuable, and   62
installing incorrect software is not a good use of your time. However, we   77
are glad to learn that your students benefited from your demonstration of   91
the software.   94

Easy-to-follow instructions for installing the new software over the cur-   109
rent software are enclosed. You will also note on your copy of the invoice   124
that you were billed originally for the TIME software. The TIME+ software   139
is $99 more; however, we are pleased to provide it at no extra cost to you.   155

An additional bonus for choosing TIME+ is the monthly newsletter,   168
*Managing Time with TIME+.* You should receive your first copy by the first   183
of the month.   186

Sincerely yours, | Ms. Veronica Scrivner | Customer Service Manager | xx |   198
Enclosure | c Eric Shoemaker   204

**Document 2**

1. Format the average-length letter in modified block format; use mixed punctuation.
2. Supply the correct salutation.
3. Generate an envelope with mailing notation.

Did you use the Date command to enter the current date?

Current date | CONFIDENTIAL | Merritt College | Attention Ms.   16
Louise Brown, Director | 750 East Wolfe Rd | Vienna, Wv   22
26105-0750   25

Thank you for the opportunity to participate as an   38
employer in your internship program. *one of your technology majors,* Paul Zieger worked 90   56
hours this summer, and was an excellent *addition* to our   67
department. His final project was an interactive tutorial of   80
the Merritt College library. This tutorial provides an   91
electronic tour of the library, including the layout of the   103
library *its holdings,* and specific directions on locating certain materials.   119
Paul has agreed to work for us part-time during the fall   130
semester. Our initial plans *are* for him to work with faculty   143
in setting up and conducting private demonstrations for classes.   156
In addition, he will write a second tutorial for the graduate   168
library. *Please send another excellent intern next semester.*   181
Sincerely | Daniel E. Romano, Director | Library Services | xx   192

Document 11
Table

Key the table. Use 14 point
for the main heading. Apply
20% fill to Row 1.

# RADIO BROADCASTING
## Multiple Ownership

| *The following local market restrictions would be imposed to ensure that no one person or entity will gain a monopoly of the radio broadcasting market:* | |
|---|---|
| 45 or more stations | No person or entity may own more than 8 radio stations of which not more than 5 may be in the same service (AM or FM). |
| 30 to 44 stations | No person or entity may own more than 7 radio stations of which not more than 4 may be in the same service (AM or FM). |
| 15 to 29 stations | No person or entity may own more than 6 radio stations of which not more than 4 may be in the same service (AM or FM). |
| 14 or fewer stations | No person or entity may own more than 5 radio stations of which not more than 3 may be in the same service (AM or FM). Additionally, no individual or entity may have an interest in more than 50 percent of the stations in the market. |

**Document 12**

**Table**

Key the table. Apply 10% fill
to Row 1. Center Columns
B and C.

**Document 13**

**Table with decimals**

1. Key the main heading in
   Row 1; use 14 point and
   bold. Do not adjust column width.
2. Decimal-align Columns B
   and C. Adjust the number
   of digits after decimal so
   the numbers appear centered in the column.

*Technology Review*

**Tables**

1. Key the table with all
   numbers and text left-
   aligned.
2. Select the column to be
   decimal-aligned. Click
   **Table**, **Format**, then
   the **Column** tab.
   Change **Align contents
   in cells, Horizontal** to
   **Decimal Align**.
3. Increase digits after
   decimal until numbers
   appear centered in the
   column. Click **Apply**,
   then **OK**.

## NEVADA ACCESS NUMBERS

| City | State | Telephone Number | Connection Speed |
|---|---|---|---|
| Reno | NV | 702-555-0120 | up to 28.8K |
| Reno | NV | 702-555-0134 | up to 56K, V.90 |
| Reno | NV | 702-555-0107 | V.34+, K56flex-V.90 |
| Las Vegas | NV | 702-555-0163 | up to 28.8K |
| Las Vegas | NV | 702-555-0187 | up to 56K |
| Las Vegas | NV | 702-555-0156 | V.34+, K56flex-V.90 |

## PICC RATE INCREASES

| Federal PICC Recovery | First Line | Additional Line |
|---|---|---|
| Primary Residence | $0.53 | $1.50 |
| Single-Line Business | $0.53 | $2.75 |
| Multi-Line Business | $2.75 | $2.75 |
| ISDN | $15.00 | $13.50 |

# Simplified Block Letter

## 69a • 5'

### GETTING started

each line 3 times (slowly, faster, slowly); DS between 3-line groups; repeat selected lines if time permits

| | | |
|---|---|---|
| alphabet | 1 | Buzz quickly gave them an explanation justifying your withdrawal. |
| figures | 2 | I read pages 135-183 of Chapter 4 and pages 267-290 of Chapter 6. |
| shift key | 3 | Don G. Lamb lives near A. Hay on S. Park Road in La Paz, Bolivia. |
| easy | 4 | Jane may pay for the sorority emblems and for the enamel emblems. |

| 1 | 2 | 3 | 4 | 5 | 6 | 7 | 8 | 9 | 10 | 11 | 12 | 13 |

## 69b • 10'

### SKILLBUILDING

**Timed writing**
Key a 3' and a 5' writing.

all letters                                                                    *gwam*   3' | 5'

If you wish to advance in your career, you must learn how to   4 | 2 | 37
make good decisions.   You can develop decision-making skills by   8 | 5 | 39
learning to follow six basic steps.   The first three steps help   13 | 8 | 42
you to see the problem.   They are identifying the problem, ana-   17 | 10 | 44
lyzing the problem to find causes and consequences, and making   21 | 13 | 47
sure you define the goals that your solution must meet.   25 | 15 | 49

Now, you are ready to solve the problem with the last three   29 | 17 | 52
steps. They include finding alternative solutions to the prob-   33 | 20 | 54
lem, analyzing each of the alternatives carefully to locate the   37 | 22 | 57
best solution, and putting the best solution into action. Once   41 | 25 | 59
you have implemented a plan of action, check to make sure that   46 | 27 | 62
it meets all of your objectives.   If it does not, then determine   50 | 30 | 64
if the problem is with the solution or with the way it is being   54 | 33 | 67
implemented.   Always keep all options open.   57 | 34 | 69

3' | 1 | 2 | 3 | 4 |
5' | 1 | 2 | 3 |

## 69c • 35'

### FORMATTING

**Simplified block letter with postscript**
Read the information at the right and study the model on the next page.

**Document 1**
Key the long letter on p. 210 in simplified block format. Change font size to 11 point. Proofread; correct errors.

**Simplified block format**
The simplified block format is a variation of the block format. All lines begin at the left margin. This format differs from other letter formats in that the salutation and the complimentary close are omitted. A subject line is required and is keyed a DS below the letter address. The simplified format is used effectively when the letter is addressed to a company rather than to an individual or when the addressee's name is unknown.

**Special feature**
**Postscript.** A postscript, generally used to emphasize information, is keyed a DS below the last notation in a letter. Do not begin with the label "PS." Do not indent the postscript unless paragraphs in the letter are indented.

Ms. Susana Berquist | 842 Devonshire Rd. | Huntington Beach, CA 92646-1203

WorldWide Telecom, a telecommunications company for the 21st century, offers high-quality long-distance services at competitive pricing. WW Telecom has been in the telecommunications business since 1986 and has earned the reputation of being the highest-quality network provider with an excellent record of customer service.

Telecommunications is a multibillion-dollar industry that remains in a continuous state of evolution. It is the fastest-growing industry in this decade, and in its 100+ years has never experienced a down quarter. The passage of the 1996 Telecommunications Reform Act will result in greater competition between companies with many new and diversified products.

Now is the perfect time to explore a career with WW Telecom. The industry is growing, WW Telecom is growing, and your future is calling. Please call me to arrange for an interview.

Yours truly | Melissa Armstrong | Human Resources

Mr. Ronald VonAllman | 9012 Mack Avenue | Seattle, WA 20916-0402

Thank you for your recent letter inquiring about minimum hardware requirements for using our Internet service. The minimum requirements are as follows:

- Windows 95 or 98
- 486 or faster processor
- 16 MB of RAM
- 20 MB or more of free hard disk space
- 28.8K modem (higher preferred)

Please call me if your hardware meets the minimum requirements; I will immediately send you a copy of our Internet software and provide you free unlimited access for 30 days. I am confident that you will be happy with our service and will continue the subscription.

Also, please call me if you have additional questions or concerns.

Sincerely | Jerome Cordova | Customer Service

# Communication Experts
**999 McArthur Dr.**
**Mt. Morris, MI 48504-4481**
**(810) 555-0101**
**FAX: (810) 555-0111**

March 20, 200- <sub>QS</sub>

Professional Document Designs, Inc.
9345 Blackjack Blvd.
Kingwood, TX 77345-9345 <sub>DS</sub>

Subject line  Simplified Block Letter Format ——— **Subject line replaces the salutation.** <sub>DS</sub>

The format of this letter is called simplified block letter format.  This letter style is similar to block format in that all lines are positioned at the left margin.  However, the simplified block format does **not** contain a salutation or a complimentary close.  A subject line is required with this style.  As the label implies, a subject line indicates the main topic of the letter.  The key words contained in a subject line help administrative support staff to sort and route incoming mail and to code documents for storage and retrieval.

The simplified block format is especially useful when the name or title of the receiver of the letter is unknown.  For example, a person writing for hotel reservations likely would not know the name of the reservation clerk.  With simplified block style, the letter can be addressed to the hotel, and the subject line should indicate that the letter is a request for reservations.

In some simplified letter styles, the subject line is preceded and followed by a triple space.  Please note that a double space precedes and follows the subject line in this letter.  We have eliminated the use of triple spacing in document formats to simplify the processing of documents.  As you will note, the simplified block letter format is one of the recommended formats in the enclosed *Communication Experts Format Guide*. <sub>QS</sub>

——— **Complimentary close is omitted.**

Ms. A. Katina Carter
Communication Consultant

xx <sub>DS</sub>
Enclosure <sub>DS</sub>

Postscript  Try this simplified format soon—especially when you do not know the receiver's name or title.

1"   (left)    1"   (right)

SIMPLIFIED BLOCK LETTER FORMAT

**Document 6**
**Memorandum with distribution list**

Key the memo. Add the distribution list at the end of the memo.

**Document 6**
**Memorandum with distribution list**

Key the memo. Add the distribution list at the end of the memo.

*Technology Review*
**Distribution list**

Key the distribution list in alphabetical order at the first default tab.

**TO:** Area Reps—Distribution List | **FROM:** Customer Support | **DATE:** February 1, 200- | **SUBJECT:** Tips for Sales Reps

Here is some information to share with your clients. Please feel free to duplicate and distribute the attached page to potential customers.

A recent study shows that one-third of all customers do not know who their long distance carrier is. The same study also shows that another one-third do not know what rates they are paying for long-distance service. This lack of customer awareness means that millions of people can benefit from a WW Telecom representative who will show them how they can save money on their long-distance bills.

xx
DS

Attachment
DS

Distribution List
    Aurora Brown
    James Caldwell
    Eric Fong
    Lisa Manning
    Tom VonSoosten

**Document 7**
**Flyer**

1. Design an attractive one-page flyer using the information at the right.
2. Insert a page border.
3. Insert the file **logo-wwt** in the upper-left corner.
4. Use bold, italic, and various font sizes to make the brochure attractive and readable.

# WW Telecom
# Long-Distance Service

WW Telecom is the 6th-largest long-distance company in the United States.

WW Telecom is the fastest-growing carrier.

WW Telecom offers a flat rate of 8 cents per minute, 24 hours a day, 7 days a week. Customers can save up to 30% by switching to WW Telecom.

WW Telecom offers substantial discounts on international calling.

WW Telecom offers the first 15 minutes of each month for 2 cents per minute to your chosen international country.

There is no charge to switch customers from their present long-distance carrier to WW Telecom. If customers are not completely satisfied with the services of WW Telecom, there is no charge to return them to their previous carriers.

**Document 8**
**E-mail with attachment**

1. Send the memo you created in Document 6 as an e-mail to your instructor. Delete the distribution list at the end of the memo.
2. Include Document 7 as an attachment.

## 69c, continued

**Document 2**

1. Key the long letter in simplified block format.
2. Add a certified mail notation.
3. Generate an envelope.
4. Proofread; correct errors.

**Document 3**
**Challenge activity**

1. Open *thornburg*. Save as **69c-d3**.
2. Format the long letter in simplified block format.
3. Use the Date command.
4. Supply an appropriate subject line.
5. Send a blind copy to **Matthew Theberge**.
6. Make the last paragraph of the letter a postscript.
7. Three errors (subject/verb, hyphen, comma) need to be corrected.

**Optional:** Generate an envelope.

November 15, 200-|Attention Frequent Flyer Service Center|Atlanta    15
International Airport|P.O. Box 84410|Department 129|Atlanta, GA    28
30320-8441    30

Request for Redemption of Frequent Flyer Award    40

Please redeem an award of 30,000 miles from my frequent flyer account    54
#2521-70442.  Award #D731 is being redeemed as a round-trip ticket to    68
Honolulu, Hawaii, with a departure on Thursday, February 15, and a    81
return on Monday, February 19, 200-.  Flight information is listed below:    96

**Thursday, February 15**    100
Depart Jackson, Mississippi    106
7:10 a.m.    108
Flight #5315    110

**Monday, February 19**    114
Depart Honolulu, Hawaii    119
6:05 p.m.    121
Flight #178    124

Please mail a certificate to the business address listed on the letterhead.    139
Your agent, Azida Hamff, has instructed me to submit this certificate to    154
an airline agent by December 15 to receive my airline tickets.  I will be    168
sure to follow these instructions and look forward to benefiting from my    183
first frequent flyer award.    189

Dr. Frances Hamilton, Professor|xx|bc Robert Heflin, Travel Department    203

# *on...* Protocol in Addresses

Specific protocol is demanded of letter writers as they compose appropriate letter addresses and salutations.

Use a courtesy title before the recipient's name or a professional title after the name.  Do not use both.

| | | |
|---|---|---|
| Ms. Rachel Lindsey | not | Rachel Lindsey |
| Dr. William Jones or William Jones, M.D. | not | Dr. William Jones, M.D. |
| Dr. Susan Chain or Susan Chain, Ph.D. | not | Dr. Susan Chain, Ph.D. |
| The Honorable Steven Combs | not | Mr. Steven Combs |

The women's movement challenges us to ask why we distinguish between married and single women when we don't make the distinction in men.  As a result, the use of *Miss* and *Mrs.* has decreased.  Just as we use *Mr.* for men, *Ms.* is becoming the preferred title by many women.  However, if you know that a woman has a different preference, use it.

**Document 5**
**Modified block letter**

1. Read the information on keying a modified block letter at the right.
2. Change the top margin to .6".
3. Insert the file **letterhd-wwt**.
4. Set a left tab at 3.2".
5. Key the letter; print.

*Technology Review*
**Change bullet style**

1. Key the list of items to be bulleted at the left margin.
2. Select the list.
3. Click **Insert** menu, then **Outline/ Bullets & Numbering**. Click the **Bullets** tab.
4. Select the desired bullet style and click **OK**.

.6" top margin

 *WorldWide* **Telecom**

*5280 Technology Drive, Irvine, CA 92674-2900*
*(949) 555-1000 fax (949) 555-1001*
*www.wwtelecom.com*

January 15, 200-

Ms. Melinda Washington
Blue Ride Enterprises
55 Cresinda Blvd.
Mt. Vernon, WA 03789-9876

Dear Ms. Washington

This is an example of a *modified block letter* that is used by WW Telecom. Some of our managers prefer to use this style because they feel that this letter has a more balanced look.

To key a modified block letter:
• Change the top margin.
• Insert the letterhead.
• Set a tab at 3.2" (Format menu, Line, Tab Set, click Clear All, key 3.2 in the Tab position box, click Set and Close).
• Key the letter. Press TAB before keying the dateline and the writer's name and title/department.

I am enclosing a brochure produced by our department, *WW Telecom Document Formats*. This contains directions for formatting most documents used by our company. If you have questions or need assistance, I can be reached at the Help Desk at extension 510.

Cordially

Douglas Ramkey
Help Desk Manager

xx

Enclosure

# Memos with Numbers and Bullets

**70a • 7'**

## Ｇ ETTING
## s t a r t e d

each pair of lines 3 times;
DS; work at a controlled rate

direct
reaches
1 Barbie browses at many music and ceramic places on Second Avenue.
2 Junior received maximum respect by being humble, not by bragging.

adjacent
reaches
3 Very  popular  artists  read  poetry  to  the  very  sad  group  of  people.
4 A  few  important  people  were  scoring  points  at  the  policy  session.

| 1 | 2 | 3 | 4 | 5 | 6 | 7 | 8 | 9 | 10 | 11 | 12 | 13 |

**70b • 10'**

## NEW
## FUNCTION

## Bullets ≣▾     Numbering ≣▾

Numbered and bulleted lists are commonly used to emphasize information in books, newspaper and magazine articles, and presentations.  Use numbers if the list is a sequence of steps or points.  Use bullets or symbols if the items have no particular order.

**Tip:**  If you key a number and a period and press TAB, *WordPerfect* automatically turns on Numbering.  The next number in sequence will appear when you press ENTER

- To add bullets or numbers, key the list without bullets or numbers.  DS between items.  Select the list and click the **Bullets** button or **Numbering** button.
- To change the style of bullets or numbers, click the down arrow.
- To convert bullets to numbers or vice versa, select the items to change and click the **Bullets** or **Numbering** button.
- To add or remove a single item, click the **Bullets** or **Numbering** button.

### Drill 1
1. Key the text at right without the numbers.
2. Select text to be numbered.
   - Click **Numbering** button.
   - Change to DS.
3. Key **Press PAUSE button** as the second item.
4. Save as **70b-d1** and print.
5. Change the numbers to bullets.

### Drill 2
1. Key the document without bullets.
2. Select document and apply bullets.
3. Delete the bullet before the first line, "MATERIALS FOR OCTOBER...."
4. Center-align the title.  Print.
5. Change the bullets to numbers.
6. Save as **70b-d2**.

#### DIRECTIONS FOR SENDING LONG-DISTANCE FAX

1. Enter telephone number--e.g., 916015553584 (9 is for outside line).
2. Enter long-distance credit card number--e.g., 269830.
3. Turn originals face down and place in tray.  Press Start button to begin scanning.
4. Check message line to verify transmission.

- **MATERIALS FOR OCTOBER 3 BOARD MEETING**
- Minutes
- Directory
- Audit report
- Officer and committee reports
- Site selection report

**Document 4**
**Block letter**
1. Read the letter at the right.
2. Change the top margin to .6".
3. Insert the file **letterhd-wwt**.
4. Key the letter.

*Technology Review*
**Enumerations**
1. Key the list of enumerated items at the left margin. Do not key the numbers.
2. Select the enumerated text and click the **Numbering** button.
3. To move the enumerated text closer to the numbers, select the text and drag the tab on the Ruler from 1.5" to 1.25".

*WorldWide* **Telecom**

*5280 Technology Drive, Irvine, CA 92674-2900*
*(949) 555-1000 fax (949) 555-1001*
*www.wwtelecom.com*

Dateline
January 15, 200-
QS

Letter address
Mr. John Doe
101 Main St.
Atlanta, GA 50258-3377
DS

Salutation
Dear Mr. Doe
DS

Welcome to WorldWide Telecom!  You will find that the managers and executives at WW Telecom prefer to use two letter styles: block and modified block.
DS

Body
This letter is keyed in *block letter style*.  Managers who use this style prefer it for its simplicity and ease of use.  All letter parts begin at the left margin.  The spacing between letter parts has been marked to serve as a guide for you.  After keying the letter, adjust the amount of blank lines between the letterhead and the date to give the letter a balanced look.

Follow these steps to insert the letterhead in each letter.
1. Begin each letter by changing the top margin to .6".
2. Click the Insert menu, File, then letterhd-wwt.
3. Click Insert.  The letterhead displays.

I wish you well as you begin your career here at WW Telecom.
DS

Complimentary close
Sincerely
QS

Writer's name
Title
Laura Brady
Administrative Assistant
DS

Reference initials
xx

**FORMATTING**

## REVIEW MEMO FORMAT

Messages sent between individuals or offices within an organization are called **interoffice memorandums**, or **memos** for short. When these interoffice messages are sent electronically, they are called **e-mail**. Memos include a heading, a body, and one or more notations. Addresses are not required, and use of default margins and tabs makes memos a streamlined, efficient means of communication.

When memos are sent to more than one person, list their names after **TO:**. Organizations may choose to list in alphabetical order or in rank order. For readability, key the names on separate lines. However, it is acceptable to key names across the line of writing. When sending the memo to many people, refer to a distribution list at the end of the memo. Example: **TO:** Task Force Members—Distribution list below.

**Memo format**
1. Use default side margins and 1.5" top margin; use 12 point.
2. Key the form headings in bold.
3. The recipient's and sender's job titles are optional. Personal titles are generally not used. Tab once or twice to align the data that follow the headings.
4. DS headings; DS between ¶s. SS the body.
5. Include reference initials, enclosure notations, or attachments when appropriate.

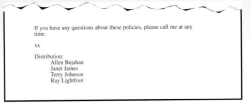

If you have any questions about these policies, please call me at any time.

xx

Distribution:
Allen Bejahan
Janet James
Terry Johnson
Ray Lightfoot

---

**Document 1**
See next page.

**Document 2**
1. Format the list using the Numbering button. DS between items.
2. Add a blind copy notation to **Laura Read**.

words

**TO:**    Production Planning Committee | **FROM:**    Chad Donahoe | **DATE:** 12
October 20, 200- | **SUBJECT:**    November 5 Meeting                             22

The Production Planning Committee is scheduled in the Board Room at 1:30     35
p.m. on November 5.   Final decisions must be made on three renovation       50
issues:                                                                      52

1. The expansion of Line 3 to accommodate the new products that have         66
   been added to the current product line.                                   74

2. The complete renovation of the Gilbert Plant.                             84

3. The retooling necessary to use the new technology recommended for         98
   the Jefferson Plant.                                                      102

Please review the attached material that supplements the material you       116
already have received. | xx | Attachment                                    126

**Document 3**
Alphabetize the names of the recipients. List each on a separate line in sequence.

**TO:** Lashone Taylor, Stephen Hover, and Reba Ingram-Burkley | **FROM:** 13
Cary Molloy | **DATE:**    Current | **SUBJECT:**    Installation of Electronic 28
Publishing System                                                            31

The new electronic publishing system will be installed next week. Training   46
on the system is scheduled for Thursday and Friday of next week.             59
Because learning the new system is important to everyone, all employees      73
must participate in the two-day training program.                            83

**Document 3
Memorandum**

1. Read the memorandum at the right before keying.
2. Apply general procedures from p. 365.
3. Insert the file **letterhd-wwt** at the top of the page. Add the words **Interoffice Communi-cation** at the right margin as shown.

Interoffice Communication

 *WorldWide* **Telecom**

*5280 Technology Drive, Irvine, CA 92674-2900*
*(949) 555-1000 fax (949) 555-1001*
*www.wwtelecom.com*

**TO:** Mr. Carl Troung
Ms. Ronda Wimmer
<sub>DS</sub>

**FROM:** Leslie Eiber
<sub>DS</sub>

**DATE:** January 27, 200-
<sub>DS</sub>

**SUBJECT:** Use of Memorandums at WW Telecom
<sub>DS</sub>

1"
side
margins
A memorandum is an informal written communication sent within the company. A memorandum begins 1.5" from the top (press Enter three times), uses default left and right margins, and uses default tabs.
<sub>DS</sub>

If a memorandum is sent to more than one person, list their names, as shown above. The names should be listed in alphabetical order. If the memo is sent to three or more people, refer to a distribution list that is keyed at the end of the memo.
<sub>DS</sub>

Some of our managers also use the memorandum format to send informal communica-tions outside the company. In these cases, they may choose to attach the letterhead for company identification.
<sub>DS</sub>

xx

**70c,** *continued*

**Document 1**
1. Key the headings in bold.
2. DS between items in the list of criteria. Then select the list and add bullets.

**Acme Technologies**

**Interoffice Memo**

**TO:**    Distribution List
<sub>DS</sub>

**FROM:**    Acme Mexican-American Achievers Committee
<sub>DS</sub>

**DATE:**    April 15, 200-
<sub>DS</sub>

**SUBJECT:**    Mexican-American Achievers
<sub>DS</sub>

Default side margins

For the past three years Acme has nominated a deserving Mexican-American staff member to be honored as a Mexican-American Achiever. This career development program seeks to expose, educate, and enlighten young adults to various opportunities found in the corporate sector. Adult Mexican-American Achievers serve as volunteer counselors, tutors, confidants, and advisors to youth. It is expected that honorees volunteer one year of service to the program.

Mara Pena was the first recipient for Acme. Lydia Valquez was the recipient the second year, and last year Acme sponsored an At Large participant chosen by the Youth in Business Association (YBA). This year we should like to nominate an Acme staff member.

The nominating criteria established by the YBA are as follows:

- A current Acme employee (Mexican-American) who has been employed for at least two years.

- An individual who is willing to volunteer at least one year of service to the program.

- An individual recently completing a special leadership role by representing our company on a community service project.

Please make your nomination on the attached form and forward it to Human Resources by **Thursday, April 20**.
<sub>DS</sub>

xx
<sub>DS</sub>
Attachment
<sub>DS</sub>
Distribution List:

Tab ⟶ Samuel Gibbs
Angela Sansing
Collin Sheridan
Joan Wang

## General procedures for Project 3

1. Unless the directions specify otherwise, save each document using the project number and the document number. For example, Document 3 would be saved as **p3-d3**, Document 4 as **p3-d4**, etc.
2. Refer to the Technology Reviews in the left margin for tips on completing many of the documents.
3. After completing each document, proofread and check spelling. Refer to the Reference Guide at the back of the book for questions on document format. Use Zoom to check document layout.

**Document 1**
**Create logo for World-Wide Telecom**

1. Click the **Insert** menu, then choose *Object*. Click **Create from File** and browse to locate the file *world* on your Formatting Template. Click **Insert**, then **OK**.
2. Right-click the image and select *Wrap*. Click **In front of text**, then **OK**.
3. Right-click the image again and choose *Size*. Set the height and width at 1.25". Click **OK**. Move the graphic to the top left margin.
4. Press ENTER to move the insertion point 1/3 of the way down the graphic. Tab or space over to the right side of the graphic. Key **WorldWide Telecom** in bold and italic.
5. Select **W**, **W**, and **Telecom** and change to 20 point.
6. Save as **logo-wwt** and close.

**Document 2**
**Create letterhead**

1. In a new document screen, change the top margin to .5" (**Format**, **Margins**).
2. Click the **Insert** menu, then **File**. The Insert File dialog box displays.
3. Choose *logo-wwt*, and click **Insert**.
4. On the line below *WorldWide Telecom*, key an underscore that extends to the right margin.
5. Press ENTER to place the insertion point on the next line. Choose right justification. Key **5280 Technology Drive**, **Irvine**, **CA 92674-2900** in bold and italic. Press ENTER and key **(949) 555-1000 fax (949) 555-1001** in bold and italic. Press ENTER and key **www.wwtelecom.com** in bold and italic.
6. Press ENTER 4 times. Change justification to left. Turn off bold and italic.
7. Save as **letterhd-wwt**.

 *WorldWide* **Telecom**

*5280 Technology Drive, Irvine, CA 92674-2900*
*(949) 555-1000 fax (949) 555-1001*
*www.wwtelecom.com*

# Memo Template

## 71a • 5'

### GETTING started

alphabet 1 Zack Javis quietly left the big x-ray room and went to play golf.

figures 2 The shelter fed 64 men, 59 women, and 78 children at 12:30 today.

adjacent reaches 3 Wendy Depuy was pointing to a new polo field where we were going.

easy 4 Diana, a neighbor, may tutor the girl if the usual tutor is sick.

| 1 | 2 | 3 | 4 | 5 | 6 | 7 | 8 | 9 | 10 | 11 | 12 | 13 |

## 71b • 10'

### SKILLBUILDING

**Build straight-copy skill**

1. Key two 1' writings on each ¶. Strive to improve *gwam* on the second writing.
2. Key one 3' writing.

all letters *gwam* 3' | 5'

Most people have good intentions, but they rarely find time    4 | 2 | 46

to convert those good intentions into action. They wonder how    8 | 5 | 49

some very busy individuals frequently can find adequate time to    12 | 7 | 51

do extra little things for others who are not as fortunate as    17 | 10 | 54

they are. The answer is quite simple; those individuals care    21 | 12 | 56

enough to make helping others a major priority in their sched-    25 | 15 | 59

ules. Relatively few people are so organized that they have time    29 | 18 | 61

to do everything that they might like to do. Most people, how-    34 | 20 | 64

ever, manage to find time to do the things they truly want to do.    38 | 23 | 67

What factors distinguish those individuals who are able to    42 | 25 | 69

turn their good intentions into actions from those who simply    46 | 27 | 71

have good intentions? Some people believe that growing up in a    50 | 30 | 74

family that has a tradition of helping others is a major factor.    54 | 33 | 77

Yet, key differences in attitude exist among children who grew up    59 | 35 | 79

in the same family. Perhaps the only factor that is different is    63 | 38 | 82

that some people think helping others is a nice thing to do,    67 | 40 | 84

while others find that they get more joy when they give to others    72 | 43 | 87

than when they receive.    73 | 44 | 88

3' | 1 | 2 | 3 | 4 |
5' | 1 | 2 | 3 |

# WORLDWIDE TELECOM

## OBJECTIVES

Review memos, letters, tables, and reports with references.

Create a logo and letterhead with clipart.

Design a flyer.

## OVERVIEW

***WorldWide Telecom*** Welcome to WorldWide Telecom! WorldWide Telecom is one of the fastest-growing companies in North America. WW Telecom markets leading telecommunications products and services throughout the world. WW Telecom offers competitive long-distance, paging, and Internet services.

You are the administrative assistant, working at WW Telecom headquarters located in Irvine, California. You will be creating support documents for the marketing representatives. The marketing representatives are located throughout the United States. Most of them work out of an office in their home and therefore are required to generate their own documents. You will be creating a packet containing sample document formats for the marketing reps to follow. The first thing you will do is create a logo that the marketing representatives can use to insert into various documents and promotional materials. Then you will use the logo to create a letterhead for the representatives to use.

## Using a template

A **template** is a blueprint for the text, graphics, and formatting in a document. The software provides templates for frequently formatted documents such as letters and memos. The memo template includes the heading, a code for automatically inserting the current date, and other special formatting such as graphic lines.

# Memo

To:        [To]
From:      [From]
Date:      [Date]
Subject:   [Subject]

This is the body of the memo.

> The software formats the template. The heading information is entered in a dialog box.

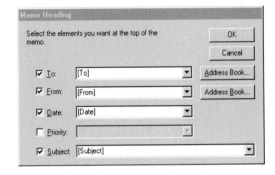

**To use a template:**

1. Click **New from Project** from the File menu.
2. Choose **Memo**, then click **Create** on the Create New tab.
3. When the preformatted memo displays, click the **Fill in Heading Info** button. Do not enter your personal information. Click **OK** and close the Address Book dialog box.
4. Enter the information in the Memo Heading text boxes (To, From, Date, Subject). See dialog box above right. Click **OK**. The completed memo heading displays.
5. Select the text "This is the body of the memo." Key the memo body and save.

Click to close.

**Memo template**

**Document 1**
1. Follow the steps to access the *Memo* template.
2. Press ENTER once between ¶s to DS.

words

| | | |
|---|---|---|
| **TO:** | Wayne Eastman | 4 |
| **FROM:** | Lynn Broome | 8 |
| **DATE:** | Current | 12 |
| **SUBJECT:** | Templates | 16 |

A template is a master copy for all documents of a certain type. Templates   31
include prestored margins and other formats typical of that document.   46
Frequently the template automatically adds space between paragraphs   59
each time you press Enter. Templates are designed for common types of   73
documents such as letters, memos, reports, and fax cover sheets.   87

Refer to pages 208-223 of the enclosed software manual for instructions   101
on using templates. Also, note the section on creating your own templates.   116

Enclosure   119

# Level 5

# INTEGRATED APPLICATIONS

**71d,** *continued*

## Document 2

1. Follow the steps to access the *Memo* template.
2. Key the list. Then select it, set a left tab at 1.25" to decrease the spacing between the numbers and the text, and apply the Numbering feature.
3. Indent the italicized message from the left margin.

### Challenge

Select the sample voice message; insert a border and 10% fill around the message.

**TO:**  All Employees | **FROM:**  Cory Johnson | **DATE:**  (Insert next Monday's  12
date) | **SUBJECT:**  Guidelines for Voice Mail Greeting  21

Recording an appropriate voice mail greeting is very important as we pro-  36
vide our clients with excellent and friendly service.  Please study the fol-  51
lowing essential parts of an effective voice mail greeting and then study the  67
sample greeting shown below:  73

1. State your name.  77
2. Include the day and date you are recording the greeting.  89
3. Describe why you are not available to take the call.  101
4. Request caller to leave a message or directions for obtaining personal  115
   assistance.  118
5. Provide an approximate time when the call will be returned.  131

*Hello, this is Cory Johnson's voice mail.  It's Monday, (Insert date), and I am*  147
*in a meeting until 3:30.  After the tone, please leave your name, phone num-*  162
*ber, and a detailed message.  I will return your call before 5 p.m. today.  For*  178
*immediate assistance, press 0 now.  Thank you.*  188

In addition to recording an appropriate message, it is equally important  203
that you update the greeting each day.  Also check for voice mail messages  218
throughout the day and remember to return calls as promised in the  232
greeting.  234

## Document 3
### Challenge

1. Use the *Memo* template.
2. Correct the 3 errors in word choice. Proofread and correct all errors.
3. Alphabetize the distribution list.
4. Indent each name to the first tab.

When memos are sent to several individuals, list each of their names below the memo as a distribution list. Names may be listed in alphabetical order or in order of rank within the organization.

TO:  Distribution List | FROM:  B. Edward Grant, Credit man-  12

ager | DATE:  Current | SUBJECT:  Revision of Form Letters  24

All form letters have been reviewed, revised, and approved  36

for general use.  You will receive a (ewn) copy within a few  45

days of the correspondence manual.  55

     Special thanks are do each of you for your help on  65

this important project.  The consultant were most comple-  77

mentary of the excellent corporation they received and of  89

the quality of your suggestion for *improving* improvement of the let-  99

ters.  101

xx | Distribution List: | Valerie Lancaster  Philip | Frank Hopper,  113

Jr | J.T. McTaggart | Tommy Bishop | Lamont Loftis  *alphabetize names*  122

## Project, *continued*

### Merged letter of transmittal

Use Merge to prepare a letter for each member of the board of directors. This letter will accompany the business plan.

1. Create the data file for the names and addresses below. Complete names, job titles, and company information for each board member are found in Appendix I. Save as **pommery.dat**.

2. Create the form document using the letter at the right. Save as **pommery.frm**.

3. Merge the documents and print. Save the merged letters as **Proj2-letters**.

**Option:** Create a Pommery letterhead using the clipart *ATLANTIS.wpg* from the Scrapbook. Insert the letterhead into the form file before merging the letters.

**Jeansonne and White**
Pommery Air Service, Inc.
P.O. Box 8473
Hopkins, SC 29061-8473

**Bass**
3829 Quincy Ave.
Denver, CO 80237-2756

**Davis**
3979 El Mundo
Houston, TX 64506-2877

**Burge**
3958 Highland Dr.
Sterling, CO 80751-1211

**Perkins**
7463 St. Andrews
Dallas, TX 75205-2746

**Hess**
3744 Main St.
Oakdale, LA 71463-5811

*Table 4. Stock Ownership*

| Groups | Shares | % of Stock Issued |
|---|---|---|
| Employees | 586,268 | 20.9 |
| Senior officers | 353,146 | 12.6 |
| Outside directors | 651,700 | 23.3 |
| Business community | 640,000 | 22.8 |
| Founders | 571,540 | 20.4 |
| Total | 2,802,654 | 100.0 |

Dear

The Pommery Air Service Business Plan is attached. Please review the plan carefully and be ready to vote on final approval at the board meeting next Friday. Note that this item appears on the agenda sent to you last week.

If you have any questions prior to the meeting, please call me. All of the changes recommended by the board at the last meeting have been implemented in the plan.

Sincerely,

Your name
Senior Staff Assistant

Attachment

### Table of contents
Include all headings and page numbers.

### Title page
Format an attractive title page. Use clipart to insert a jet airplane from the Travel or Transportation category. Be creative with the design as long as the title page is in good taste. Use current date. Omit the Prepared for/Prepared by sections.

72

# Electronic Mail

## GETTING started

each set of lines twice; DS between groups; work at a controlled rate

balanced hand
1 pair slam their cork pay men cut burn turn jam worn lent pan slap
2 Diana may pay for the bush the men cut down if they fix the sign.

one hand
3 were plum freeze junk crave hunk zebra lump grave loop trace milk
4 Jill Pummo saw my bad grades; we agree I deserved a better grade.

combination
5 zebra polo their clay goals slap traces link face mane plum tight
6 Fred fears the high tax rate may decrease the profit of the firm.

| 1 | 2 | 3 | 4 | 5 | 6 | 7 | 8 | 9 | 10 | 11 | 12 | 13 |

## 72b ● 40'

### FORMATTING

**Electronic mail**

Follow these directions for completing documents in Lesson 72.

*Without Internet access:* Complete documents as memos.

*With an e-mail address:* Complete the documents in your software and send.

*With Internet access but no e-mail address:* Instructor will assist you in setting up a free e-mail address.

**Electronic mail**

**Electronic mail (or e-mail)** is an informal message that is sent by one computer user to another computer user. To be able to send or receive e-mail, you must have an e-mail address, an e-mail program, and access to the Internet.

**Heading:** Key accurately the e-mail address of the receiver and supply a specific subject line. The date and your e-mail address will display automatically.

**Attachments:** Documents can be sent electronically by attaching the document file to the recipient's e-mail message. The attached file can then be opened and edited by the recipient.

**Body:** Single-space (SS) the body and DS between paragraphs. Do not indent ¶s.

**Formatting:** Do not add bold or italic or vary fonts. Do not use uppercase letters for emphasis. Use emoticons or e-mail abbreviations with caution (e.g., :-) for "wink" or BTW for *by the way*).

These addresses will receive a copy of the message.

## E-Mail

You can enter multiple e-mail addresses.

To: cryder@tech.com

cc: drowe@tech.com
   kforbes@tech.com

Subject: March Staff Development

Attachment: Agenda.doc

Directions to attach will vary with e-mail software.

**Message:**

The March staff development session will be held on Thursday, March 5, at 2 p.m. in the fifth floor conference room. Please allow two hours in your schedule for this important program entitled "Appropriate Use of E-mail."

Table 1. Efficiency of Pommery Air Service

| Efficiency Measure | Pommery | National Average |
|---|---|---|
| Load factor | 62% | 58% |
| ASM | 10¢ | 14¢ |
| Yield | 16¢ | 12¢ |
| On-time performance | 88% | 94% |

Table 2. Key Personnel *

| Officer | Position | Compensation | Stock Options |
|---|---|---|---|
| C. Jeansonne | CEO | $124,000 | 90,000 shares |
| M. White | President and COO | 106,500 | 75,000 shares |
| C. Walker | V.P. Operations | 85,000 | 50,000 shares |
| L. Coker | V.P. Marketing | 85,000 | 50,000 shares |
| P. Ray | CFO | 85,000 | 50,000 shares |

* Refer to Appendix 2 for biographical sketches.

Table 3. 2001, 2002, and 2003 Pro-Forma Statement of Income

| | 2001 | 2002 | 2003 |
|---|---|---|---|
| Operating Revenue | $44,438,400 | $61,466,400 | $78,874,400 |
| Operating Expense | 41,144,600 | 53,190,000 | 68,898,400 |
| Operating Profit/(Loss) | 3,293,800 | 8,276,400 | 9,976,000 |
| Non-Operating Expense | (671,200) | (709,800) | (1,673,600) |
| Net Income/(Loss) | $2,622,600 | $7,566,600 | $8,302,400 |
| Cost Per ASM | .1019 | .0721 | .0868 |
| Yield | .1647 | .1621 | .1575 |
| Operating Margin | 7.4% | 13.5% | 12.6% |

*Table 4 on next page*

## 72b, continued

### Document 1
**E-mail message**

1. Key the e-mail message to your instructor.
2. Key the subject line as **Assignment 3**.
3. Send the message.

**Task 1:** List five things to consider when choosing an appropriate e-mail password.

1. Do not choose a password that is named after a family member or a pet.
2. Do not use birth dates as a password.
3. Choose a combination of letters and numbers; preferably, use UPPERCASE and lowercase letters, e.g., TLQ6tEpR.
4. Do not share your password with anyone.
5. Do not write your password on paper and leave by your computer.

**Task 2:** List five things to consider when composing e-mail.

1. Do not use bold or italic or vary fonts.
2. Do not use UPPERCASE for emphasis.
3. Use emoticons or e-mail abbreviations with caution (e.g., :) for smile or BTW for by the way).
4. Write clear, concise messages that are free of spelling and grammatical errors.
5. Do not send an e-mail in haste or anger. Think about the message carefully before pressing the Send button.

### Document 2
**E-mail message with attachment**

1. Key the e-mail message (*right*) to your instructor and to one student in your class.
2. Key the subject line as **Activity Report**.
3. Attach the template file *activity*.
4. Send the message.

I have completed the Activity Report required for this year's competitive events. The file Activity.doc is attached to this e-mail for your review. Please add the names of the members initiated at the February meeting and review the listing of awards received by our members. Revise the file as needed.

After you have proofread the report, please print a laser copy and give to Brenda Jones for inclusion in the national project notebook. I would also appreciate your e-mailing me the revised file for my historian records.

Remember, the reports must be postmarked by March 1.

### Document 3
**Compose e-mail**

1. Compose an e-mail message to your instructor.
2. Copy the message to one student in your class.
3. Key the subject line **Inappropriate Use of E-Mail**.
4. Send the message.

### Document 4
**Compose e-mail**

1. Compose an e-mail message to three students in your class that states you are attaching new guidelines for a voice mail greeting. Be sure to order names alphabetically.
2. Key the subject line **Guidelines for Voice Mail Greeting**.
3. Attach the file *71d-d2*.
4. Send the message.

# Project, *continued*

airline industry. The emphasis on football events has created a special niche that contributes significantly to the load factor and, in turn, reduces costs.

**Insurance.** Aircraft insurance rates have increased significantly over the past year for the entire industry. The average increase for the industry was 15 percent. Pommery lowered its insurance rates from $32,750 per month to $27,875 per month. These savings were obtained by changing the mix of underwriters and by reducing the amount of business handled by underwriters in the United States and transferring that business to quality, lower-cost underwriters in Europe.

## Pro-Formas—2001-2003

Pro-formas for 2001, 2002, and 2003 are based on the addition of two jet aircraft within the next 18 months. Revenue and expenses are in current dollars.

*(Insert Pro-Forma Statement of Income from the next page. Label the pro-formas Table 3.)*

## Ownership

Five million common shares have been authorized. Of the authorized shares, 2,802,654 shares have been issued. Common stock ownership is diverse as noted in the following groupings (Table 4).

*(Insert Table 4 from p. 362 here.)*

## Capital Requirements

Pommery is actively seeking $4.5 million in additional capital in the form of equity financing. The additional capital is required for expansion, acquiring two jet aircraft, retiring debt, and improving the information technology system.

## Appendix 1
## Board of Directors

All members of the board of directors have served in that capacity since Pommery Air Service, Inc. was founded in January 1999.

**Cyndi Jeansonne, Chair and CEO**—Founder of the company. Previously served as Executive Vice President with responsibility for marketing for Oklahoma Charter Service.

**Michael White, President and COO**—Co-founder of the company. Previous experience as Vice President of Airline Operations with Southern Airways and Manager of Flight Operations with Texas Charter Service.

**Natalie Bass, Airline Consultant, RTA and Associates**—Senior partner of RTA and Associates for ten years; held position of Chief Pilot of Federated Package Service for six years.

**Herman Davis, Chief Financial Officer, Financial Securities, Inc.**—CFO for seven years; former investment analyst specializing in the airline industry.

**Britt Burge, President, Associated Travel Services**—Two years as President of ATS; former owner of a chain of 14 travel agencies.

**Joseph Wayne Perkins, Senior Vice President, River Industries**—Former Executive Vice President of Bank Services, Inc.; director on several company and civic organization boards.

**Kimberly Hess, Professor, Business Administration, Central University**—Prolific author and known widely for work in economic development; director on several company and civic organization boards.

## Appendix 2
## Key Personnel

All of the senior officers have served as senior officers since Pommery Air Service, Inc. was founded in January 1999.

*(Copy Jeansonne and White information from Appendix 1)*

**Charles Walker, Vice President, Operations**—Twenty years of experience in airline operations and flight operations at four airlines.

**Leslie Coker, Vice President, Marketing**—Six years as a brand manager for Westfield Imports and four years in Event Management for WorldWide Travel, Inc.

**Patrick Ray, Chief Financial Officer**—Co-founder. Previous experience includes seven years as Managing Partner of Ray and Associates, Inc.

# Two-Page Letters and Memos

**73a ● 7'**

### GETTING started

each set of lines 3 times;
DS between 9-line groups;
work at a controlled pace

1 free join day five nut gain hunt mint cut tray five cry trick but

*1st/2d fingers* 2 Much can be said about a velvet jacket Yvonne just bought for me.

3 Brady just found a very well cut diamond that he may give to Kim.

4 was pale six zoo quip saw lap soup zone slap wrap loop well pools

*3d/4th fingers* 5 Polly was at Warsaw Plaza at the quilt show; Wilson placed sixth.

6 Stella will sell wax for Vasquez as we open a booth to sell soup.

7 quip zoo bay rusty plaza sixty very draft wind jackets much great

*all fingers* 8 Javis analyzed the problem and fixed the switch quickly for Gwen.

9 Brooks gave a major quiz which caused anxiety for lots of people.

| 1 | 2 | 3 | 4 | 5 | 6 | 7 | 8 | 9 | 10 | 11 | 12 | 13 |

**73b ● 5'**

## FORMATTING

**Second-page heading**
Read the information at the right and study the examples.

**Second-page heading**
Often letters and memos must be continued on to a second page. For identification purposes, the second and following pages should include the recipient's name, the page number, and the date. This information is keyed as a header. A DS separates the header from the body of the document.

When dividing a paragraph between two pages, be certain that at least two lines of the paragraph appear on each page. Use the Widow/Orphan option of Keep Text Together to prevent the first and last lines of a paragraph from being divided between pages. Do not separate the closing lines from the body.

1" set by software

The Honorable Katie Chatham
Page 2
Current date
**DS**

We look forward to your being our guest
on April 4 at the Unity Goals Conference
and to your sharing your insight with us.

Sincerely

Ryan Walker

xx

**Second page of letter with header**

1" set by software

Carson Mulhern
Page 2
Current date
**DS**

Please review the applications by Friday
of next week. Indicate that you have
reviewed each application by crossing out
your name on the login sheet attached to
each file.

xx

**Second page of memo with header**

## Project, *continued*

promising results and are being evaluated as part of the growth strategy.

## Operating Plan

Pommery is headquartered in Hopkins, South Carolina, with its corporate offices and principal operations located in a new office building at One Pommery Lane. A second facility that houses ground and flight operations is located in the Southside Airport Complex.

**Facilities and equipment.** Present facilities meet the operational needs of Pommery currently and for the projected growth over the next three years. Computer equipment is minimally adequate. The Technology Task Force has studied the issues pertaining to the updating of computer equipment. The Task Force makes its final recommendations for upgrading computer equipment at the next board meeting. The board supported the preliminary recommendations, and the implementation plan is expected to be approved at the next board meeting.

**Operational efficiency.** Airline performance frequently is judged by four major statistics:

- Load factor—percentage of seats filled on a flight

- ASM—cost per available seat mile

- Yield—available seat miles flown divided into revenues

- On-time performance

Some analysts indicate that these airline industry statistics do not translate directly to charter air service. They prefer to use cost per seat block hour. The stage length of flights and the number of passengers significantly affect the price negotiated on charter flights; therefore, either of the standards used provides a reasonable measure of efficiency. Obviously, statistics for charter service are not comparable to those of scheduled airline passenger service. However, they provide a relatively stable measure of efficiency when compared to other charter air service operations.

**Competitive cost analysis.** Pommery compares favorably to the charter air service industry on a national scale when traditional measures of efficiency are applied (Table 1).

*(Insert Table 1 from p. 361 here.)*

**Operational certification.** Pommery is fully certified and meets all regulatory requirements. Certificates of airworthiness are maintained for all aircraft. The company is committed to safety and high standards of maintenance.

## Board of Directors and Key Personnel

The board of directors consists of seven members: Cyndi Jeansonne—Chair and Chief Executive Officer; Michael White—President and Chief Operating Officer; Natalie Bass—Airline Consultant, RTA and Associates; Herman Davis—Chief Financial Officer, Financial Securities, Inc.; Britt Burge—President, Associated Travel Services; Joseph Wayne Perkins—Senior Vice President, River Industries; and Kimberly Hess—Professor of Business Administration, Central University. Brief biographical sketches are contained in Appendix 1.

Key company officers are listed in Table 2 along with their titles, compensation, and number of stock option shares.

*(Insert Table 2 from p. 361 here.)*

## Workforce

Pommery employs 126 full-time employees and a variable number of part-time and contract workers. Significant training has been provided, and all employees participate in an ongoing training and quality development program.

## Financial Plan

Pommery's fiscal year coincides with the calendar year. Pommery earned its first profit in October 1999—a profit of $28,500. The 1999 and 2000 audit statements are provided as a supplement to the business plan. In 1999 the average cost per seat block hour was $25. In 2000 this figure improved to an average cost per seat block hour of $22.50.

**Seasonality.** Charter air service business parallels the seasonality of passenger airline service to some degree. Charter air service business peaks in March as does the entire airline industry. Event charter service helps to combat the weak fourth quarter that is prevalent in the

POMMERY AIR SERVICE, INC., PROJECT 2 **359**

## Header

The Header function places information at the top of each page in a document. In a two-page letter or memo, the header consists of the name of the receiver, page number, and date. The header is keyed at the beginning of the document; however, it should not appear on the first page of the document. To cause the header not to print on the first page, suppress it on page 1.

By default, headers print 1" from the top edge of the paper, and a double space is inserted below the header. You can change the distance between the header and document from the toolbar.

**Drill**

1. Open *stewart*. Save as **73c**.
2. Create the header for the three-page letter to Mr. Henry T. Stewart. Suppress the header on the first page.
3. Use Zoom to view the document. Click **Next Page/Previous Page** to view all three pages.
4. Print.

### To create a header:

1. Click **Insert**, then **Header/Footer**. The Headers/Footers dialog box displays. Header A is the default.
2. Click **Create**. The Headers icons display at the right end of the toolbar.

3. Key the receiver's name and press ENTER.
4. Key **Page** followed by a space. Click **Page Numbering** button on the toolbar, then **Page Number**. Press ENTER.
5. Key the date or use the Date feature (Insert, Date/Time).
6. Click the **Close** (Close editor) button.

### To suppress the header on page 1:

From the Format menu, click **Page**, then **Suppress**. Choose *Header A* and click **OK**.

### To prevent widow/orphan lines:

Click **Format, Keep Text Together**. Place a check in the Widow/Orphan box.

**Two-page letter with header**

**Document I**

1. Open *hightower*. Save as **73d-d1**.
2. Key the remainder of the letter shown at right.
3. Use the Date command.
4. Enter the header and suppress it on p. 1.
5. Include **FACSIMILE** as the mailing notation.
6. Add **Account USC3828GB** as the reference line.

**References**:
Reference line, p. 200
Mailing notation, p. 206
Postscript, p. 209

Our market tests indicate a great deal of interest in a tailgating package. 12
The cost for a box lunch for four is $20. The lunch will include chicken, 24
potato salad, corn on the cob, rolls, and a brownie. We could add High- 36
tower napkins, plates, plastic utensils, and souvenir mugs and sell the 45
package for $30. 55

Please review our preliminary design sketches. We will contact you in a 65
few days for your reaction to the design samples. By then, we should have 77
the final results of our marketing tests. 85

We plan to visit with you three weeks prior to the game to provide an 99
update on all of our marketing activities. 106

Sincerely yours | Ms. Kathy Hossain, Manager | xx | Enclosures | This 119
game will be a bright spot for your team and your financial standing. 132
(header and notations) 150

## Project, *continued*

Pommery cannot and should not try to compete with the major passenger airlines for numerous reasons. They also agree that Pommery cannot compete with the small, local charter services because of the cost structure involved in providing jet air service exclusively.

### The Service

Pommery provides event charter flights and contract charter flights throughout the United States. About 85 percent of the flights originate east of the Mississippi River, and almost 65 percent of flights originate in the Southeast.

**Event charter flights.** These flights are called event charters because they exist to transport passengers to attend specific events that are occurring. The range of events spans from those that occur one time or once in a significant period of time to regularly scheduled events. Examples of one-time events include charters to attend Olympic events, Mardi Gras, or a world-class art exhibition or musical production.

Seasonal events are those that occur regularly during a specified period of time. Athletic events comprise a high percentage of seasonal events. Charter flights to a ski resort or to a nearby city on weekends during the season to watch professional football, basketball, or baseball games would be an example. The flight is made available to a number of participating travel agency partners who reserve a number of seats on these charter flights for their clientele.

Regularly scheduled charters include special packages (usually weekends) to fixed destinations such as Las Vegas, a Gulf Coast casino and resort, or a country music/golf weekend in Myrtle Beach. These events are generally marketed through participating travel agency partners.

**Contract charter flights.** Contract charter flights often overlap with event charter flights. The primary difference is that the contract charter flights are with specific organizations or individuals. For example, a contract may be issued with an athletic department to take its football team and band to a game. The contract is with that athletic department. On the other hand, an event charter flight may go to the same football game with passengers from several travel agency partners and an alumni group.

Companies also use charter flights to take groups to conventions, meetings, and other business activities. Travel agencies often contract for charter flights between destinations on vacation packages.

**Supplementary services.** Meal and beverage services are frequently contracted, in addition to the transportation package. For example, box meals and cold drinks on the return flight after the game are usually a part of athletic charter flight packages. Equipment handling is also a part of the package. Tickets, convention packages, and other services provided usually are arranged through travel partners when they are part of a charter flight contract.

### Market Analysis

The Southeast market was targeted first because of limited jet charter service available in the geographic area. Another determining factor was the intense interest in and support of athletics, particularly college football in the Southeast. Successful charters to games at other institutions created demand from those institutions for their travel schedule. The most profitable section of the market stems from the athletic connections.

**Emerging markets.** An emerging market is being created by women's athletic programs. This market is fueled by the current gender equity emphasis in college athletics. Court decisions and athletic regulations focus on equal treatment of men's and women's sports. Other emerging markets are the resort (particularly tennis, golf, beach, and ski resorts) and casino charters that are arranged by the resorts to bring in customers at a relatively low cost.

**Competition.** Only one other charter air service in the Southeast competes in the same niche market in which Pommery competes with all jet service. Several smaller charter air service companies try to compete with relatively large turboprop aircraft. The market clearly demands jet service. Pommery's market share is conservatively estimated to be 65 percent of the market in the Southeast.

**Market expansion.** The real challenge is to increase the size of this niche market through promotional activities and strategic alliances with travel partners. Pilot projects have produced

**73d,** *continued*

## Two-page memos with hyperlink
### Document 2
1. Key the memo below using bullets for the enumerated items.
2. Use the Header feature. Suppress the header on the first page.
3. Turn on Widow/Orphan protection.
4. Key a copy notation to **Gregory Fletcher**.
5. Select the text *User's Direction* and create a hyperlink to http://www.its.com/interactivetesting/user/directions.

### Document 3
*Revise Document 1:*
1. Change bullets to numbers.
2. Use cut and paste or drag-and-drop editing to move Item 3 between Items 7 and 8 (as numbered below). The list will be renumbered automatically.

**Function review**

**To insert Hyperlink:**
1. Select the text or object to be displayed as a hyperlink.
2. Click **Hyperlink** button. Click **Create Link**.
3. Key filename or Web address or browse for filename or Web site.
4. Click **OK**.

words

**TO:** Leigh Wilkerson | **FROM:** Sara Coover | 8
**DATE:** Current | **SUBJECT:** System Design 17

Thank you for the extensive feedback you 26
have given me on the features of the new ver- 35
sion of our interactive testing system. We 43
appreciate your willingness to participate in 53
the Beta test and spending a significant 61
amount of time comparing the features of the 70
version you have been using for the past two 79
years with those of the new version. Your 87
analysis will be very helpful to all of our sales 97
staff. 99

I spent several hours with five members of the 108
system design team to determine which 117
aspects of the design should be featured in 126
the promotional materials. As a result, the 134
following eight features will be promoted dur- 142
ing the first phase: 147

1. A comprehensive security system that 154
enables a test administrator to limit access 163
to each segment of the database on a need- 172
to-know basis. 2. Easy-to-use menus for all 180
program execution and online, context- 188
sensitive, interactive help support. 3. Effective 197
utility programs that enable the test adminis- 206
trator to import and export data and to main- 215
tain the integrity of the database. 4. A 223
sophisticated, full-featured word processing 232

words

component that is fully integrated in the inter- 241
active testing system. 5. Table-driven printer 250
support that enables the system to interface 259
with virtually all printers currently on the 268
market. 6. The ability to provide scoring keys 277
for multiple test versions and to accept item 286
statistics from both batch and interactive test 296
scoring systems. 7. A mechanism for acquir- 304
ing, storing, and integrating graphics material 313
with test items used in both printed and inter- 322
active tests. 8. A report generation capability 331
for data structures such as classification data 340
as well as for standard reports. 347

Perhaps the most important technical change 356
in the design of the system is the ease with 365
which the system can be customized to meet 373
the needs of the specific user. The database 382
administrator can access a work screen to 391
modify the titles given to many of the data 400
structures so that they will correspond to the 409
general terminology of the user's organization. 419

As a valuable participant in the Beta test, we 429
need your feedback concerning the document 438
User's Directions posted on our Web site. 447
Please review this Web document and e-mail 455
me your comments at scoover@its.com. 462

xx 475

## EXECUTIVE SUMMARY

Pommery Air Service, Inc. is a charter air service headquartered in Hopkins, South Carolina. Pommery's mission is:

- To provide its charter customers with safe, reliable jet transportation, quality service, outstanding value, and low costs.

- To provide an environment for its employees that fosters teamwork and customer focus and rewards integrity and productivity.

- To deliver superior value to its shareholders.

### The Company

Pommery Air Service, Inc., a Delaware corporation founded in January 1999, currently has a fleet of four 737 jet aircraft. Pommery provides air service to almost 60,000 passengers per month. The mix is almost equally divided among business trips, athletic functions, and leisure travel.

An experienced, highly competent management team leads Pommery Air Service, Inc. Management emphasizes teamwork, empowerment, and productivity. Employee stock options provide incentives to employees to focus on quality and profitability.

Pommery Air Service, Inc. became profitable in its tenth month of existence and continues to be profitable. The company operates as a lean, efficient organization. Costs per available seat mile (ASM) have dropped from 14 cents to 10 cents. Yield per revenue passenger mile (RPM) increased from 12 cents to 16 cents.

### The Market

Pommery Air Service, Inc. provides charter flights to destinations throughout the United States. The primary market, however, is defined by origination point rather than destination point. Approximately 65 percent of all flights originate in the Southeast. The secondary market by origination point is the Northeast.

### The Services

Pommery Air Service, Inc. provides two types of charter services: event charter flights and contract charter flights. Event charter flights range from one-time events, to seasonal events, to regularly scheduled events. Charter flights are contracted by an individual, company, or organization. Contract charter flights provide service to one location or may be a key component of a travel package.

Both event and contract charter flights include an array of services depending on the needs of the customer. Supplementary services available with both charter and event flights include: meal and beverage services; local transportation; event tickets; side trips; conference facilities, including logistical support; and a host of special activities.

### The Strategy

Pommery Air Service, Inc. strives to become the dominant air charter service in the eastern United States. Pommery's core competencies involve providing safe, high-quality jet air services that are cost-effective. All other services provided are designed to facilitate and enhance the continual development of the core competencies.

To implement this strategy, Pommery Air Service, Inc. must expand. Expansion requires the addition of two jet aircraft within 18 months. Expansion is contingent upon obtaining $4.5 million in additional capital.

## POMMERY AIR SERVICE, INC.

### Business Plan

Pommery Air Service, Inc. (Pommery), since it was founded as a Delaware corporation in January 1999, has operated as a niche player in the charter air segment of the airline industry.

### Industry

Three distinct segments comprise the charter air service industry:

- Small, local charter operations designed to provide point-to-point transportation for groups of fewer than 20 people in turboprop aircraft.

- Occasional charter flights provided by major passenger airlines.

- Small niche markets that target specific types of clientele.

Pommery operates exclusively in the third segment of the industry, offering contract charter flights and event charter flights. The overall charter air service industry is highly competitive. The most intensive competition exists in the other two segments of the charter air service. Pommery's board of directors and management agree that

## 74a ● 5'

### GETTING started

each line 3 times (slowly, faster, slowly); DS between 3-line groups; repeat selected lines if time permits

## 74b ● 10'

### SKILLBUILDING

**Assess straight-copy skill**

Key one 3' or one 5' writing. Circle errors; determine *gwam*.

alphabet 1 Jeffrey quickly packed a dozen boxes of goods and gave them away.
figures 2 We will meet in Building 870, Room 69, at 12:45 p.m. on March 30.
direct reaches 3 Brecken hunted in many places for those recent surveys on hunger.
easy 4 Did the six big bowls, six mementos, and eight maps fit in a box?
| 1 | 2 | 3 | 4 | 5 | 6 | 7 | 8 | 9 | 10 | 11 | 12 | 13 |

 all letters                    *gwam*   3'  5'

How are letters and other documents produced in the modern    4   2 52
office?  They are prepared in a number of ways.  Just a few years    8   5 54
ago, with rare exceptions, a document was composed by a manager   13   8 57
who either wrote it in longhand or dictated it.  Then, one of the   17 10 60
office staff typed it in final form. Today, the situation is   21 13 62
quite different. Office staff may compose and produce various   25 15 65
documents, or they may finalize documents that were keyed by   29 18 67
managers.  In some cases, managers like to produce some or all of   34 20 70
their documents in final form.   36 22 71

Many people question how this dramatic change in the way   40 24 73
documents are prepared came about.  Two factors can be cited as   44 26 76
the major reasons for the change.  The primary factor is the   48 29 78
extensive use of computers in offices today.  A manager who uses   52 31 81
a computer for a variety of tasks may find it just as simple to   57 34 83
key documents at the computer as it would be to prepare them for   61 37 86
office personnel to produce.  The other factor is the increase in   65 39 89
the ratio of office personnel to managers.  Today, one secretary   70 42 91
is very likely to support as many as six or eight managers.   74 44 94
Managers who share office staff find that they get much quicker   78 47 96
results by finalizing their own documents when they compose them.   82 49 99

3' | 1 | 2 | 3 | 4 |
5' | 1 | 2 | 3 |

OBJECTIVE

Integrate formatting and word processing skills.

# Pommery Air Service, Inc.

## Project Scenario

As Senior Staff Assistant, you have been asked to finalize the business plan that the Executive Committee has been preparing for several weeks (pp. 357–362). Format the complete report as one document following the guidelines below. Save as **project2**.

1. **Report format:** SS; leftbound; full-justified. **Font size:** Title and centered headings: 16 point; side headings: 12 point; report body: 11 point. Bold all headings.

2. **Page numbering:** Use Roman numerals for the preliminary pages; use Arabic numbers for the body. Print the page number on the first page of the body. (**Note:** Use the Numbering command rather than the Number option on the Headers/Footers toolbar because you must have the option of changing the page number *value* from 5 to 1 and number *style* from Roman to Arabic on the first page of the body.)

3. **Tables:** Use Column Fill Header style for tables. Use 10-point font, if necessary, to fit information in a table. Adjust columns, center tables. Spell out names and abbreviated titles, if necessary (obtain information from the Appendix).

4. **Preliminary pages:** Create a title page, table of contents, and executive summary.
   **Paging:** Create a new page for each Appendix.

5. **Headers:** Insert a graphic line on all pages except the title page, using the Horizontal Line option on the Header/Footer feature bar.

6. **Footers:** Insert a graphic line again. Beneath the line, key **Pommery Air Service, Inc.** at the left margin. Close the Headers/Footers toolbar and insert the page number at the right margin on *all* pages except the title page. See example below. **Challenge:** Remember to change the page number value and style on the page 1 of the body.

---

Pommery Air Service, Inc.         ii

## 74c ● 35'

### Assess production

**Time schedule:**

Assemble materials . . . . . 3'
Timed production . . . . . . 25'
Check; compute *n-pram* . . 7'

1. When directed to begin, key each document. Proofread; correct errors. Work for 25'.
2. Proofread carefully; correct errors; compute *n-pram* (total words keyed minus penalty divided by 25').

### Document 1

Key the average letter using block letter style, open punctuation.

### Document 2

Key the short letter using modified block letter style, mixed punctuation.

### Document 3

Key the memo (*bottom right*).

### Document 4

**Two-page letter**

1. Open *collins* from the template disk. Save as **74c-d4**.
2. Insert Date command.
3. Change the document to 12 point.
4. Add reference line: **Re: Customer No. 2348**.
5. Change numbers to bullets.
6. Insert second-page header.

### Document 5

**E-mail**

1. Rekey Document 3 as an e-mail message to your instructor.
2. Attach the file you prepared for Document 2 above.
3. Send the message.

---

January 30, 200- | CERTIFIED MAIL | Miss Shea Patterson | 43 University — 13
Dr. | Lacombe, LA 70445-2536 | Dear Shea — 21

Congratulations! Because of your outstanding academic record and leadership potential in your teaching profession, you have been selected for membership in Pi Omega Pi, the honorary society for undergraduate business education majors. Being selected for membership in Pi Omega Pi is the highest honor that a student of business education can achieve. — 35 50 64 78 92

A formal initiation ceremony will be held on Tuesday, February 13, at 4 p.m. in Room 252 of the T. S. McKinney Building. Please complete the enclosed form and return it to me by Friday, February 9. A one-time initiation fee of $40 is also due by the initiation. — 106 120 135 145

Shea, I am delighted that you have been selected as a Pi Omega Pi member and look forward to your initiation on February 13. — 159 171

Sincerely | Michael Taylor, President | xx | Enclosure | c Dr. Zimiko Tayyar — 184

---

May 1, 200- | Mr. Marvell Hodges | 503 County Lake Rd. | Clinton, MS — 13
39056-0503 | Dear Mr. Hodges: — 18

Over seventy-five teachers have preregistered to participate in the Electronic Presentation Workshop scheduled for August 8-9 at Ferguson Community College. We are very pleased with the overwhelming response to this offering. — 32 46 60 64

The workshop will begin at 8 a.m. and conclude by 5 p.m. each day. Please come to Room T38 of the Continuing Education Building. You may make your housing reservation today by calling (601) 555-3842. I look forward to an outstanding learning experience. — 77 92 107 116

Sincerely, | Andrew David Smith | Associate Professor | xx — 126

---

**TO:** Technology Task Force | **FROM:** Clifford F. McCrory, Chair | **DATE:** — 14
October 20, 200- | **SUBJECT:** School Board Recommendations — 25

Our professional staff finalized the Technology Task Force report requesting approval of four major technology enhancements for K-14. A draft copy is enclosed for your review. Please make any corrections and return the draft to us within one week so that the final report can be prepared. — 40 55 69 83

The report will be sent special delivery to each school board member no later than Monday. This deadline must be followed if the item is to appear on the November 15 agenda. If we do not hear from you within one week, we will assume that you accept the draft as submitted. | xx | Enclosure — 98 113 127 141

**Document 2**
**Table with sort**

1. Key the table; center column headings.
2. Right-align numbers in Columns B, C, and D. Center table horizontally. Save as **120b-d2a**; print.
3. Insert these rows in alphabetical order:

   **Hawaii  500  1,452  5,951**
   **New York  2,152  2,920**
   **12,892**
4. Sort the table by dollar amounts shown in Column D in descending order. Save as **120b-d2b**; print.
5. Add a row at the bottom of the table. Key **USA Average** in Column A. Calculate the average cost for Columns B, C, and D.
6. Apply Currency format without decimals where appropriate.
7. Apply Header Fill Single style; key $ for first data row. Save as **120b-d2c**; print.

**Document 3**
**Agenda**

Format the headings of the agenda in proper format. Key the names flush right. Insert leaders as marked.

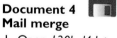

**Document 4**
**Mail merge**

1. Open *120b-d4data*. Select *120b-mrg.frm* as the form document.
2. Add your name and address as a new record; amount paid, $200.
3. Merge and print.

**Document 5**
**Labels**

Create mailing labels (5160) for *120b-d4data*. Sort by State, then City, and then LastName. Merge and print.

## AVERAGE ANNUAL COLLEGE TUITION

| State | Community Colleges | Public 4-year | Private 4-year | words |
|-------|-------------------:|--------------:|---------------:|------:|
| | | | | 6 |
| | | | | 11 |
| | | | | 17 |
| Arizona | 734 | 1,819 | 6,076 | 23 |
| California | 365 | 2,388 | 12,748 | 29 |
| Connecticut | 1,520 | 3,476 | 15,704 | 35 |
| Florida | 1,112 | 1,784 | 9,941 | 40 |
| Maine | 2,137 | 3,131 | 15,383 | 45 |
| Massachusetts | 2,441 | 4,163 | 15,685 | 52 |
| Ohio | 2,164 | 3,265 | 11,782 | 56 |
| South Dakota | 3,430 | 2,338 | 8,574 | 63 |
| Texas | 680 | 1,504 | 8,410 | 67 |
| Vermont | 2,877 | 5,532 | 15,032 | 72 |

STANDARDS OF ACCREDITATION MEETING — 7

June 5, 200- — 10

Agenda — 11

Welcome and Introductions ———————— Tina D. Rosebrook — 20
Introduce Speakers and Participants — 27
Describe Meeting Objectives — 33
Standards of Accreditation ———————— Robert Kavanaugh — 41
Characteristics of Accreditation — 48
Interpretation of Accreditation Standards — 56
Lunch — 58
"Total Quality Management" ——————— Albert C. Palms — 66
Critical Areas ———————— Linda Winberg — 72
Issues Related to Accreditation — 79
The Appeals Process — 82

## Objective Assessment

Answer the questions below to see if you have mastered the content of this module.

1. The major differences between block, modified block, and simplified block are: (a) Block is keyed
_____; (b) modified block has _____;
and (c) simplified block _____.

2. What is the correct salutation written to the attention of Ms. Sarah Gray at Mountain Inn Resort? _____

3. For A–F below, circle which letter part appears first.

   **A.** reference line or attention line          **B.** subject line or reference line

   **C.** reference initials or enclosure          **D.** salutation or subject line

   **E.** mailing notation or dateline          **F.** attention line or company name

4. Write a second-page header for a letter written today to Mr. Mark McMullan.



5. A _____ notation shows that a copy of the document was sent to the person(s) named without the recipient's knowledge.

## Performance Assessment

1. Open *testing*.
2. Key the list shown at right after the fourth ¶; do not key numbers. DS between items. Then use Numbering feature to insert numbers.
3. Read the memo carefully to determine where to insert the following side headings; bold.

   **Packaging Options**
   **Key Features**
   **Marketing Preview**

4. Use the Header feature in the second-page memo heading.
5. Proofread carefully. The following errors are contained in the memo:
   • possessive noun
   • parallel construction
   • number style

1. Test items may be entered either by keying the items using the macros provided with the system or by scanning items from printed copy.

2. Word processing features are fully integrated with numerous attributes including bold, underline, italic, large fonts, superscripts, and subscripts.

3. The system has graphics capabilities that enable users to scan, create, maintain, and modify high-resolution graphic images.

4. The system associates graphic images with items both for printing test items and to present items for interactive testing.

5. A current default record allows the test administrator to set system parameters for the test, reducing the data that test-takers must enter.

6. The system allows either test administrators or users to enter parameters to produce scaled scores, percent-correct scores, and percentiles.

7. The scoring module automatically produces item analyses and other industry standard statistical analyses and interfaces with a variety of statistical software packages.

8. The system has a complete score-reporting mechanism that allows the user to select standard report formats or to custom design reports.

# Administrative Document Assessment

## 120a ● 17'

### G ETTING
### started

1. Use Skillbuilding Warmup lines on p. 349.
2. Key a 3' and a 5' writing from 118b, p. 349.

## 120b ● 33'

### FORMATTING

**Time schedule:**

Preparation . . . . . . . . . . . . 3'
Timed production . . . . . . . 25'
Final check. . . . . . . . . . . . 5'
Follow the same directions as in 117c on p. 347.

**Document 1**
**Minutes**

Key the heading lines below in proper format. Apply bullets as directed in the draft.

**Sterling Heights Community Hospital**
**August 10, 200-**
**Advisory Board Meeting Minutes**

|  | words |
|---|---|
|  | heading 17 |

Presiding:  *bold*  Jacinto A. Campo, Administrator — 25

Participants:  Shawn Hartman, Assistant Administrator; — 36
Terry Olson, Community Relations; John Kaplan, Director of — 48
Marketing; Ron Volson, Human Resources; Lisa Summons, — 59
Director of Education; Susan Phillips, Director of Nursing — 71

Board Members: *bold*  *lc titles*  Vincent Perez, City of Sterling Heights; — 82
Captain Wayne Anderson, Wayne County Sheriff Station; — 93
Robert Le, American Heart Association; Cynthia Cross, — 104
Buxton Medical Supplies; Nancy Ricardo, General Motors — 115
Corp. — 116

Administrator Jacinto Campo welcomed all new board members — 128
and guests to the first official advisory board meeting. — 140
Introductions were made around the table. — 

*gave*
All advisory committee members and participants *a* toured *of* — 155
the hospital guided by Jacinto Campo. Facility improve- — 162
*and*
ments were discussed during the tour. Areas targeted for — 176
remodeling this year were also pointed out. — 

Bylaws for the advisory board were distributed and — 186
*#*
discussed. Mr. Campo expressed the hospitals *commitment* desire to get *being* — 200
involved in the community. *The advisory board input will be critical.* — 215

*Bullet these items*

Current hospital projects were discussed: Bears — 225
Program, MOMS, Hospital feedback methods. — 241
*(maternal Obstetrical Medical Services)*

Plaques were presented to each of the advisory board — 250
members and pictures were taken. The next advisory board — 262
meeting is scheduled for . *October 16, 200-*. — 270

# Activity

*fourteen*

## Research for Hospitality Committee for the National Technology Association Convention on April 3-6 in Phoenix, Arizona

Ms. Audra Meaux, Chair of the Hospitality Committee (see letter on p. 198), has asked you to do some research on the Internet for the Hospitality Committee. This large convention will be held at the Phoenix Civic Plaza Convention Center. Participants will stay in numerous hotels in the Phoenix, Scottsdale, and Tempe area. Information on rates and locations has already been prepared. Ms. Meaux is located in Hot Springs, Arkansas.

### Instructions

1. Compile information that Ms. Meaux can use for a Chat Room session or a teleconference with the Hospitality Committee. Locate information in the following categories:
   - Facts about cities (Phoenix, Scottsdale, Tempe)
   - Transportation: airlines, rental cars, etc. serving area
   - Restaurants
   - Entertainment: parks, golf or other sports, zoo, museums, cultural activities, clubs, etc.
   - Specialties of area: native crafts, scenic areas
   - Maps of area

2. Make a list of additional categories and subcategories of information available for participants and families. Print the most important or best information in each category.

3. Prepare a list of Web addresses for each subcategory of information with a very brief description of what is found at that address.

4. Locate information on the Phoenix Pride Commission and the list of Points of Pride.

5. Organize your information in a memo addressed to Ms. Meaux.

## REPETITIVE STRESS INJURIES

The study of *ergonomics* shows hand-arm alignment to be the center of keyboard repetitive stress injuries (RSI). Misalignment causes muscles to become overworked, causing stress and fatigue in the hands and arms. Whether you're a butcher, court stenographer, landscaper, concert pianist, or computer operator, if you want to cure aching fingers, hands, arms, and back, do not resort to splints, wrist rests, stretching exercises, or surgery. The problem is not with the piano, the computer, the cash register, or the meat cleaver; the problem is with the way people move. The finger, the hand, and the arm must move as a unit.

In the business environment, repetitive stress injuries have mushroomed to afflict everyone from secretaries to executives with hurting muscles, tendons, and nerves. In fact, more than 60 percent of all workplace illnesses are caused by repetitive stress injuries—a cost of as much as $20 billion a year for U.S. businesses.[1]

### Position Yourself Properly

Preventing tired wrists and hands is really a matter of taking charge of your posture and computer work environment. Awkward posture while keying, poorly positioned equipment and furniture, and failure to change your keying or sitting position can add to wear and tear on your wrists and hands.

**Hand position.** Keep your wrists and hands straight. When you work with straight wrists and fingers, the nerves, muscles, and tendons stay relaxed and comfortable. Therefore, they are less likely to develop the strains and pains that are often associated with keying.

**Posture.** Your posture at the computer affects the position of your wrists and hands. If you lean your body forward *(flexion)* or backward *(extension)* or if you slouch, your wrists and hands also adapt by becoming flexed or extended. Slouching causes the nerves, muscles, and tendons that support your wrists and hands to become tense and strained.

1. Sit up straight; face the computer straight-on.
2. Hold your head at a slight downward tilt to avoid straining muscles in your neck and shoulders.

3. Keep hands and wrists straight while keying.
4. Touch your keys lightly; this keeps your wrists and fingers relaxed.
5. Keep your feet flat and pointed toward the workstation.

### Adjust Your Workstation

Your office furniture is adjusted properly if you are able to easily maintain a straight wrist, hand, and back posture.

1. Adjust keyboard tray to desk height so that your wrists and hands are straight while keying.
2. Adjust screen height so that the top of it is at about eye level.
3. Adjust chair height and seat back so that you can key with straight wrists and hands.
4. Position your keyboard so that your wrists and forearms are straight.

The Internet contains many ergonomic resources that can provide you with tips on healthy computing. The following is a list of a few sources to investigate:

Insert the file *table*.

Footnote

[1]"Ergonomics Defined." <http://www.teos-inc.com/about.htm>, 12 April 1999, p. 1.

### REFERENCES

"Ergonomics Defined." <http://www.teos-inc.com/about.htm> (12 April 1999).

Larson, Mary. *Comfortable Computing for Your Wrists and Hands.* Liberty Insurance Company, 1997.

Woods, Patricia Mason. "Is Your Job Making You Sick?" *Essence.* Vol. 29, No. 5, pp. 46-48.

# Activity
## fifteen

### Research stocks for your investment club

You have joined an investment club. Each member is asked to research and present ten stocks to the club for consideration.

**Instructions**

1. Search ten stocks with no more than three stocks in any one of the following sectors: technology, financials, energy, healthcare, or retail. The club considers the following criteria in analyzing the stock:

   • P/E—The price/earnings ratio (often listed under fundamentals) should be no more than 60.

   • Price—Today's opening price should be no more than $100 and no less than $10 per share.

   • At least one and preferably two analysts have rated the stock as a "buy."

   • The volume traded should be at least 100,000 shares in a day.

   Possible Web sites to use (not limited to these sites):
   www.Quicken.com
   www.pathfinder.com
   www.dowjones.com
   www.msnbc.com
   www.cnnfn.com

2. Complete the following table for the ten stocks you select. Add footer or a footnote with the date the information was compiled and with a note saying all stocks met the volume criteria.

| Company | Symbol | Sector | Opening Price | P/E Ratio | Name of analyst rating as buy |
|---------|--------|--------|---------------|-----------|-------------------------------|
|         |        |        |               |           |                               |
|         |        |        |               |           |                               |
|         |        |        |               |           |                               |
|         |        |        |               |           |                               |
|         |        |        |               |           |                               |
|         |        |        |               |           |                               |
|         |        |        |               |           |                               |
|         |        |        |               |           |                               |
|         |        |        |               |           |                               |
|         |        |        |               |           |                               |

# Report Assessment

## SKILLBUILDING WARMUP

alphabet 1 Jax Zwanka and my friends plan to go back to that quaint village.

fig/sym 2 I paid $59.75 ($5.69 a yard) for 10 1/2 yds. of #34 cotton (80%).

shift key 3 Don, Jan, Sue, Tim, Lee, Ty, and I will go to see Tien and Chien.

easy 4 Kent and Clay may fix fish or lamb for the neighbors at the lake.

| 1 | 2 | 3 | 4 | 5 | 6 | 7 | 8 | 9 | 10 | 11 | 12 | 13 |

119b ● 12'

## SKILLBUILDING

**Assess statistical rate**
Key one 3' and one 5' writing.

 all letters/figures

*gwam* 3'| 5'

|  | | |
|---|---|---|
| Significant changes are currently occurring in the labor force. | 4 | 3 39 |
| The greatly publicized baby boom generation is aging. | 8 | 5 41 |
| In 1975, roughly 25% of the labor force was in the 16- to 24- | 12 | 7 44 |
| year-old age group. By the year 2000, an estimated 16% to 18% of | 16 | 10 46 |
| the labor force will be between 16 and 24 years of age; and the | 21 | 12 49 |
| largest group will be those 35 to 50 years old. Approximately | 25 | 15 51 |
| 25% of the force will consist of new entrants. | 28 | 17 53 |
| Another key change is the number of women entering the | 32 | 19 55 |
| labor force. By 2000, nearly 50% of the workforce will be | 36 | 21 58 |
| female. The number of women professionals has doubled since | 40 | 24 60 |
| 1974. Of all the professionals in the labor force, 51% are women | 44 | 26 63 |
| and 49% are men. The types of jobs women seek have also changed | 48 | 29 66 |
| drastically. Many women actively seek positions that were for- | 53 | 32 68 |
| merly male-dominated positions. One thing is quite clear: The | 57 | 34 71 |
| workforce of 2000 will be very different from that of 1975. | 61 | 36 74 |

3' | 1 | 2 | 3 | 4 |

5' | 1 | 2 | 3 |

119c ● 33'

## FORMATTING

**Time schedule:**

Preparation . . . . . . . . . . . . 3'

Timed production . . . . . . . 25'

Final check . . . . . . . . . . . 5'

**Leftbound report**

1. DS report.
2. Key the footnote using the footnote information at the end of the report.
3. Insert the file *table* below the last paragraph. Format entries in 10-point type.
4. Place the references on a separate page, using the correct format.
5. Prepare a title page.
6. Prepare a table of contents that includes all headings, the table heading, and reference page.

# TABLE AND TAB MASTERY

## OBJECTIVES

1. Review tables and tabs.

2. Use alternate table formats, math, and sort.

3. Convert tables to text, and draw tables.

4. Insert tabs in tables.

5. Improve speed and accuracy.

**module** **11**

---

# Table Review

## 75a • 5'

### GETTING started

Key each line 3 times (slowly, faster, slowly); DS between 3-line groups. Use these directions for all Skillbuilding Warmups in this module.

| | | |
|---|---|---|
| alphabet | 1 | Jennifer quickly packed a dozen boxes of food and gave them away. |
| figures | 2 | Ted bought 240 shares of stock at 89.75 and sold them for 136.25. |
| direct reaches | 3 | Bryce opened a brown bag of mulch, dumping much of it on my desk. |
| easy | 4 | Claudia did pay for eight antique bowls and also for six emblems. |

| 1 | 2 | 3 | 4 | 5 | 6 | 7 | 8 | 9 | 10 | 11 | 12 | 13 |

## 75b • 15'

**Table review**

Review creating and formatting simple tables. Complete Drills 1–3. To review these procedures in greater detail, refer to Lessons 54–57 or Software Training Manual, pp. A13–14.

### Create and format a simple table

Tables consist of columns, rows, and cells. Columns are vertical lists of information labeled alphabetically from left to right (A, B, C, etc). Rows are arranged horizontally and are numbered from top to bottom. Cells are the intersection of a row and column. Each cell has an address that consists of the column letter and the row number. The first cell is A1, the second cell in Row 1 is B1, etc.

Tables are created using the Table command on the Insert menu or the Table QuickCreate button. Click Table QuickCreate, hold down the left mouse button, and drag across and down until you have the desired number of table columns and rows. When you release the mouse button, the table is inserted in your document. The table you create will spread from the left to the right margin, with all columns being of equal width.

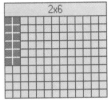

Table QuickCreate

words

Newport Beach, CA *14 pt.*

Sand and Surf Hotel      *right align*     *14 pt.*    Tustin, CA    403

680 Beach ~~Boulevard~~ *Blvd.*    Best Suites Hotel    411

*bold & italic*    92 Hotel Circle    417

8/22, 8/23                      10/17, 10/18    422

Sincerely|Arnold C. Chan|Marketing Director|xx|Enclosure: Brochure    471

---

**Document 2**
**Interoffice memorandum**
Key the document in standard memorandum format.

| | | words |
|---|---|---|
| **TO:** | GENESCO Employees | 5 |
| **FROM:** | Lena Gabadon, RN, Occupational Health Nurse | 15 |
| **DATE:** | Current | 19 |
| **SUBJECT:** | Safety Tip of the Month | 26 |

Moving around whenever possible during the work hours can help ward off   40
tension.  The reduction in stress and the exercise will, of course, keep you   56
in better physical condition.  Try incorporating some of these tips into your   71
workday:   73

**Document 3**
1. Open the *Memo* template in *WordPerfect*.
2. Fill in the headings.
3. Copy the body of the memo from Document 2. Change the bullets to enumerations.

- Use the stairs rather than the elevator to move between floors.   87
- Take a 15-minute break every two hours.  Use the time to walk outside.   102
- Exercise your legs by rotating your ankles whenever possible.   115
- Extend your legs while sitting to increase circulation.   126
- Force a yawn to relax facial muscles and to release tension in other   141
  parts of your body.   145

Stop by and see me in the infirmary if you have questions or call me at   159
extension 329.   162

---

opening 3

**Document 4**
**Modified block letter**
Use the current date; supply the salutation, a facsimile notation, and a copy notation for **Ralph Manz**.

Mr. M. Ljupco Kralev|RCP Dexion Trading|Boulevard Avnoj 75-2-22|   16
91000 Skopje|MACEDONIA   20

Hopefully, you had a pleasant trip back to Macedonia.  We enjoyed meet-   38
ing you, and we look forward to working with you.  Our schedules will be   52
finalized this week, and we will fax that information to you.   65

Our understanding is that our first visit will be for the purpose of going   80
with you to various companies to determine needs for management devel-   94
opment and training.  We would then use that information to develop an   108
appropriate program that you could implement in your Human Resources   122
Development Center.  We would also work out arrangements to provide fac-   136
ulty to teach the program that we design.   145

**Document 5 (Optional)**
**E-mail message**
Compose an e-mail message to your instructor. Attach **Document 1**.

We are excited about the ideas you proposed, and we believe we can help   159
you develop and staff an excellent program that will be very successful.  We   175
look forward to hearing from you soon.   183

Sincerely | Peggy Coker   187

closing 191

**75b,** *continued*

Click the right mouse button in the table to access features such as Size Column to Fit or Row/Column Indicators. ▨

When the insertion point is clicked in the table, a table toolbar displays at the top of the screen. If you click the Table button, a drop-down menu appears giving options for formatting the table. For example, to display the column letters and row numbers, select *Row/Col Indicators.* The Table menu also displays if you right-click in the table.

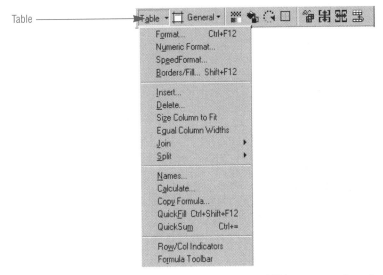

Table menu and toolbar

## Formatting a table

Tables are created, keyed, and then formatted.

• To format cells, select the cells and assign the format. Bold, font size, spacing, type font, alignment, and other formats are applied in this manner.

• Center the table horizontally, click the *Table* button, then *Format, Table* tab, *Table position on page, Center.*

• Adjust the column width to fit the data. Use the mouse or Size Column to Fit (*Table* button, *Size Column to Fit*).

**Drill 1**

Review creating a table and applying formats, including shading.
*Reference:* Pages 151–152, 155, 157, 160, 162, or Software Training Manual, pp. TM13–TM14.

1. Create a 3 x 3 table.

2. In Row 1, key **Name, Address,** and **Telephone Number** in Cells A1–C1.

3. Key the information for three of your friends in the table. After keying the data for your second friend, press Tab to add another row.

4. Select Row 1; apply bold to the headings.

5. Click the **Borders/Fill** command on the Table menu. Click the **X** next to Fill. Apply 10% Fill to Row 1.

6. Center-align headings in Row 1.

7. Save as **75b-d1** and print.

**Drills 2 and 3**

Review adjusting the column width and centering the table.
*Reference:* Page 156, or Software Training Manual page TM14.

1. Open *75b-d1.* Save as **75b-d2.**

2. Adust column widths using the mouse.

3. Center the table horizontally.

4. Save again and print.

5. Open *75b-d1* again and adjust column widths using Size Column to Fit. Save as **75b-d3.**

## 118c ● 35'

### FORMATTING

**Time schedule:**

Preparation . . . . . . . . . 3'
Timed production . . . . 25'
Final check. . . . . . . . . . 7'

**Document 1**
**Two-page letter**

1. Key the two-page letter in block format.
2. Obtain the letter address from the business card.
3. Bold, italicize, and format text as shown.

**Northwest Insurance Corporation**

Ms. Maria Carillo
**Marketing Specialist**

Telephone: (714) 555-4325
FAX: (714) 555-5432
E-mail: Mcarillo@NIC.com

5250 Jamboree Ave.
Irvine, CA 90630-0934

---

Do you feel lost because your competitors and/or associates are using terms such as the *italic* information superhighway, cyberspace, Internet, *and* World Wide Web? Did you know that your competitors are linking with other business associates around the world for the cost of a local phone call? Are you aware that they are marketing their products and services worldwide for less than $50 a month?

Don't be left out! Learn to use the high technology and use it to your advantage. Enroll in the Internet For Beginners Workshop *— all caps throughout*. This is a 12-hour hands-on workshop that will teach you everything you need to know to be a productive Internet user ~~in your office~~. As the workshop ~~title states, this workshop~~ *designed* is for people who have ~~never~~ *little or no* had telecommunications experience.

You will learn ~~how~~ to use electronic mail effectively. You will receive hands-on experience sending and receiving messages via e-mail. E-mail can save your company money and slash your long-distance phone charges.

The workshop is taught by experts *You will begin by learning* ~~who will start by teaching you basic~~ telecommunications vocabulary and terminology. *and you will receive* ~~They will provide you with a~~ 50 page glossary that you can use for a handy desk reference. You will learn about the Internet and its many practical applications ~~that can be used in your office~~. Each student will be ~~provided with computer~~ time and connection *ed* to the Internet. Your instructor will walk you through the steps to access information that will enhance your work environment.

Your organization will receive a 20% group discount if ~~three~~ *3* or more participants enroll in the workshop at the same location. ~~The workshop can be tailored to the needs of your organization~~ if 12 or more participants enroll. One of our corporate trainers will perform a needs analysis study at your organization and custom design the curriculum for your office.

This two-day seminar is offered from 9:00 a.m. - 3:30 p.m. The Internet For Beginners Workshop will be offered at two convenient locations near you. *Insert locations here — next page*

The Internet is a powerful business tool—one you cannot afford to be without! Call our toll-free number today to enroll, 1-800-555-1234. *All major credit cards are accepted.*

42
60
78
96
103
122
138
152
168
170
274
291
299
186
203
221
228
244
256
327
334
343
369
385
398
440
457

## FORMATTING

Follow the guides at the right for all tables in this module. Key Documents 1–6. Use a 1.5" top margin.

## REVIEW TABLE FORMAT

- Use a standard top margin (1.5") or center the table vertically.
- Center the main heading in UPPER-CASE and bold. Headings may be positioned above the table or within the table. Key the secondary heading and column headings in bold, capitalizing all important words.

- Create and key the table.
- Center the table horizontally and adjust column widths.
- Shade and align rows and columns as instructed.
- DS above and below a table within a document.

words

**Document 1**

1. Center-align column headings. Center-align Column B.
2. Adjust width using the mouse; center table horizontally.
3. Shade Row 1 20%.
4. Save as **75c-d1**.

**WOLFANGEL REAL-ESTATE SALES** —— Main heading    6

**October Sales Leaders** —— Secondary heading    10

| Agent | Sales $ | Office | |
|-------|---------|--------|---|
| Jacqueline C. Zahradnik | 3,869,451 | Lakeshore Boulevard | 25 |
| Katherine Ann Harrington | 2,564,081 | Lexington Heights | 36 |
| Michael T. Wang | 1,975,392 | Center City | 43 |

(row: Agent / Sales $ / Office = 14)

**Document 2**

1. Center column headings.
2. Right-align figures in Columns C and D. Center-align Column B.
3. Center table horizontally. Use Size Column to Fit to adjust column widths.
4. Apply 10% shading to Row 1.
5. Save as **75c-d2**.

| Employee | I.D. | Hardware | Software | |
|----------|------|----------|----------|---|
| Alexander, J. | R492 | $105,134,384 | $1,868,553,280 | 16 |
| Courtenay, W. | R856 | 79,364,091 | 1,384,319,500 | 25 |
| Holsonback, E. | C845 | 27,386,427 | 1,098,237,260 | 33 |

(header row = 6)

in heading    20

**Document 3**
**Memo with table**

1. Format a memo to **Jane Greenbaum** from **Angela Atwater**, regarding the **Installation of Equipment**. Use the current date.
2. Center column headings; center-align text in C2–C5 and D2–D5. (Table will have lines.)
3. Save as **75c-d3**.

The workstations have arrived and will be installed in a few days. The    35
tentative schedule for delivery is shown below:    44

| Employee | Location | Date | Time | |
|----------|----------|------|------|---|
| R. Judy | Annex 3B | May 8, 200- | 9:00 a.m. | 58 |
| C. Flores | RC 280 | May 8, 200- | 1:00 p.m. | 65 |
| B. Lott | Annex 3C | May 11, 200- | 9:00 a.m. | 73 |
| M. Rogers | RC 282 | May 11, 200- | 1:00 p.m. | 81 |

(header row = 50)

Please call me immediately if this schedule is not satisfactory. We have very    97
limited flexibility, but we will try to accommodate any changes needed.    112

# Correspondence Assessment

**GETTING started**

## SKILLBUILDING WARMUP

alphabet 1 Zack Q. Davis just left a very brief message with six nice poems.

figures 2 Jan bought 27 toys at $3.98 each, a total of $107.46 plus 5% tax.

adjacent reaches 3 We are going to build a store on a very quiet point west of here.

easy 4 Tod and I may visit the ancient chapel and then go to the island.

| 1 | 2 | 3 | 4 | 5 | 6 | 7 | 8 | 9 | 10 | 11 | 12 | 13 |

118b ● 10'

## SKILLBUILDING

### Assess straight-copy skill

1. Key one 3' writing and one 5' writing.
2. Circle errors; determine *gwam*.

 all letters

*gwam* 3' | 5'

|  |  |  |
|---|---|---|
A successful organization tries to put the right employee in | 4 | 2 | 51
the right job. The process of selecting employees raises many | 8 | 5 | 53
questions that frequently are very perplexing. A key issue | 12 | 7 | 56
that must be balanced deals with the rights of the individual | 16 | 10 | 58
who is seeking a position and the rights of the organization that | 21 | 12 | 61
is hiring a person to fill a position. Laws specify the types of | 25 | 15 | 64
information that can be asked in the hiring process to ensure | 29 | 18 | 66
that bias is not a factor in hiring. However, most firms do | 33 | 20 | 69
strive to be fair in the hiring process. The issue that many | 37 | 22 | 71
employers struggle with is how to determine who will be the | 41 | 25 | 73
right employee for a particular job that is available. | 45 | 27 | 76

The ability to predict an individual's performance on the | 49 | 29 | 78
job is very important. Assessing an individual in the hiring | 53 | 32 | 80
process to determine how he or she will perform on the job, | 57 | 34 | 83
however, is a very difficult task. Most techniques measure the | 61 | 37 | 85
potential or the way that a person can perform, but the way a | 66 | 39 | 88
person can perform may differ drastically from the way the person | 70 | 42 | 90
will perform when he or she is hired. Past performance on a job | 74 | 45 | 93
may be the best measure of future performance, which is why firms | 79 | 47 | 96
seek individuals with experience. | 81 | 49 | 97

3' | 1 | 2 | 3 | 4 |
5' | 1 | 2 | 3 |

**Review tables**

## Insert and delete rows and columns

Rows and columns can be inserted and deleted within a table. The insertion point must be in the appropriate position in the table. Rows can easily be inserted at the end of a table by positioning the insertion point in the last cell and pressing TAB.

Click the right mouse button in the table to choose Insert or Delete.

| Insert row | Rows are added before (above) or after (below) the insertion point. Position the insertion point above or below where the new row is to be inserted. From the Table menu, choose *Insert,* enter the number of rows, then choose *Before* or *After.* |
|---|---|
| Insert column | Columns are added left or right of the insertion point. Position the insertion where the new column is to be added. From the Table menu, click **Insert**, then click the button next to *Columns*, and choose *Before* to add a new column to the left of the insertion point or *After* to add a column to the right of the insertion point. |
| Delete row | Click the insertion point in the row to be deleted. From the Table menu, choose *Delete*, then *Rows*. |
| Delete column | Click the insertion point in the column to be deleted. From the Table menu, choose *Delete*, then *Columns*. |

words

**Document 4**

1. Center column heads, bold, and apply 10% shading.
2. Right-align number columns.
3. Save as **75c-d4** and print.

**SEMINAR REGISTRATION**                                       4

| Registrant | Seminar | Airport | Guest | |
|---|---|---|---|---|
| Bates, Georgina | $1,350.00 | $ 69.00 | $  45.95 | 19 |
| Brewer, Peggy M. | 1,000.00 | 34.50 | 0 | 26 |
| Nickels, Suzanne T. | 1,100.00 | 0 | 0 | 33 |
| Rogers, Arlene C. | 1,350.00 | 34.50 | 0 | 39 |
| Stimpkin, Lawrence | 1,200.00 | 138.00 | 137.85 | 48 |
| Vasquez, Carlos | 1,350.00 | 69.00 | 45.95 | 55 |

**Documents 5–6**

1. Edit *75c-d4*, inserting and deleting rows as noted at right.
2. Save as **75c-d5** and print.
3. Edit *75c-d5* by deleting Column D. Adjust column width and center table horizontally. Save as **75c-d6**.

*Delete Row 5, beginning "Rogers, Arlene C."*

*Add the following entries in alphabetical order:*

| | | | |
|---|---|---|---|
| *Wellington, Lucas* | *1,250.00* | *34.50* | *45.95* |
| *Krammer, Merri* | *1,350.00* | *69.00* | *45.95* |

**117c,** *continued*

**Document 1**
**Action minutes**
Key the action minutes for the **Document Standards Committee** meeting held on **April 29, 200-.**

**Presiding:** Rufus Harris | **Participants:** Sabrina S. Perkins, Shaquala   25
O'Daniel, Troy Temple, Ryan Wilkes, Roy Glen, and Suzanne Finley   38

The Senior Management Committee approved the standard formats for   52
minutes of meetings, and the Document Standards Committee has estab-   65
lished the procedures to be used in implementing these formats.   78

The Document Standards Committee will communicate to all employees   91
that action minutes will be the standard minutes for all meetings *except* for   106
meetings of the board of directors and formal meetings so designated by   120
the Senior Management Committee. Roy Glen and Suzanne Finley will   133
prepare and send official notification by May 1.   143

The action minutes will contain the heading illustrated in this document,   158
a summary of each agenda item stating the decision made or action taken,   172
the person responsible for the item, and the date due if applicable. Action   188
minutes should be limited to one page when possible.   198

Shaquala O'Daniel and Troy Temple will prepare and distribute the illus-   212
trations of the standard formats for both action and traditional minutes for   227
the *Document Standards Manual* by May 15.   235

**Document 2**
**Mail merge**
1. Create the form document and data file. Insert appropriate merge codes in the form document.
2. Sort by ZIP Code in ascending order.
3. Create envelopes; delete punctuation.

**Document 3**
**Mailing labels**
1. Open the data file for Document 2 and create mailing labels ( Avery 5160).
2. Sort by ZIP Code in ascending order.

**Form document**

Congratulations on your FIELD(Semester) FIELD(Year) graduation from Lexus University. We join you in celebration of this outstanding achievement.

Your university experiences can continue if you join the Lexus Alumni Association. Alumni meetings and socials provide numerous opportunities to network with former classmates and alumni, to attend special interest seminars that will enrich you both personally and professionally, and to contribute to the future of Lexus by your participation. Visit our Web page at www.lexus.edu/alumni to see the many possibilities for our alumni.

Don't be left out, FIELD(FirstName)! Complete and return the enclosed form to receive additional information on becoming a Lexus Alumni member.

Sincerely yours | Zachary Kirkpatrick, President | Lexus Alumni Association

**Data file**

| Title | FirstName | LastName | Address | City | State | ZIP | Semester | Year |
|-------|-----------|----------|---------|------|-------|-----|----------|------|
| Ms. | Linda | Thomas | 2161 Mazo Dr. | Dana Point | CA | 92629 | Fall | 2000 |
| Mr. | Patrick | Moy | 96 Abbott Rd. #24 | Artesia | MI | 48255 | Spring | 2001 |
| Miss | Leigh | Douglas | 3555 Jackson St. | Dana Point | CA | 92628 | Spring | 2001 |

# Table Review and Landscape Orientation

LESSON 76

**76a ● 10'**

**GETTING started**

**Troublesome pairs**

each line once, concentrate
on keying the reach correctly;
DS between groups

i 1 sit in said did dirk city kid fin its lit iris wit hit ilk simmer
e 2 gem ewe men eke ever me le hen cede key led fen eye be pen leader
i/e 3 pie lei piece feign mein feint neigh lie reign die veil vein diem
i/e 4 Either Marie or Liem tried to receive eight pieces of cookie pie.

w 5 new jaw awe win we was awe away hew saw flaw law wan pew wit wavy
o 6 to onto rot job coho sox box oboe wok roe out oil dot tote oriole
w/o 7 ow wows how won worn now woe wool mow row work cow woke flows low
w/o 8 Women won't want to work now; we are worn out after woeful worry.

s 9 sans is ants sons has sun spas his six bus asps skis its spy sobs
l 10 el let la alp lot lilt led elk lab old lily fly lip ilk loll milk
s/l 11 also slow else sly false slaw sells slag sails sly sled slip slam
s/l 12 Slater tells us Elsie is also slightly slow to slip off to sleep.

| 1 | 2 | 3 | 4 | 5 | 6 | 7 | 8 | 9 | 10 | 11 | 12 | 13 |

**76b ● 10'**

**NEW FUNCTION**

**Document**

1. Change paper size orientation to landscape.
2. Key the table below.
3. Format attractively; center the page vertically. Save as **76b**.

## Landscape orientation

*WordPerfect* assumes that you will be printing your document on standard 8.5" x 11" paper in portrait orientation. To print a wide document on a standard sheet of paper, you must choose landscape orientation. **Landscape** orientation positions the document horizontally on the paper (11" x 8.5").

**To change the paper to landscape orientation:**

1. From the Format menu, choose *Page*, then *Page Setup*.

2. On the Size tab, click the **Landscape** button. Notice that the illustration in the preview box changes from portrait to landscape. Click **OK**.

| Provider | Telephone | E-Mail Address | Setup Fee | Monthly Fee | |
|---|---|---|---|---|---|
| Second Extension | (231) 555-0183 | info@secexten.com | $30 | $18 | 11 / 23 |
| Future Network Solutions | (784) 555-0105 | sales@futurenet.com | 25 | 10 | 36 |
| Advance Computer Networks | (408) 555-0162 | info@advance.com | 10 | 20 | 50 |
| Cyberspace Networking | (909) 555-0130 | info@cybersp.com | 35 | 22 | 62 |
| Southwest Access Systems | (586) 555-0170 | sales@swestac.com | 40 | 30 | 75 |
| IntraCorp. Networks | (714) 555-0159 | info@intracor.com | 30 | 25 | 87 |

# Assessment

## 117a • 5'

### GETTING started

alphabet 1 Jacque Wakes examined the zone map carefully before approving it.

figures 2 Lee authorized payment of Invoices #2783 ($196) and #1946 ($508).

double letters 3 Tommy and Sammy will do bookkeeping for the committees this week.

easy 4 Jake paid an auditor to fix eight problems and dispel the theory.

| 1 | 2 | 3 | 4 | 5 | 6 | 7 | 8 | 9 | 10 | 11 | 12 | 13 |

## 117b • 10'

### SKILLBUILDING

**Assess straight-copy skill**

Key one 3' or one 5' writing. Circle errors; determine *gwam*.

 all letters

| | gwam | 3' | 5' |
|---|---|---|---|

An effective job search requires very careful planning and a lot of hard work. Major decisions must be made about the type of job, the size and the type of business, and the geographic area. Once all of these basic decisions have been made, then the complex task of locating the ideal job can begin. Some jobs are listed in what is known as the open job market. These positions are listed with placement offices of schools, placement agencies, and they are advertised in newspapers or journals.

4 | 2 | 42
8 | 5 | 45
13 | 8 | 48
17 | 10 | 50
21 | 13 | 53
25 | 15 | 55
30 | 18 | 58
33 | 20 | 60

The open market is not the only source of jobs, however. Some experts believe that almost two-thirds of all jobs are in what is sometimes called the hidden job market. Networking is the primary way to learn about jobs in the hidden job market. Employees of a company, instructors, and members of professional associations are some of the best contacts to tap the hidden job market. Much time and effort are required to tap these sources, but the hidden market often produces the best results.

37 | 22 | 62
41 | 25 | 65
46 | 27 | 67
50 | 30 | 70
54 | 32 | 72
58 | 35 | 75
63 | 38 | 77
66 | 40 | 80

3' | 1 | 2 | 3 | 4 |
5' | 1 | 2 | 3 |

## 117c • 35'

**Assess production**

**Time schedule:**

Assemble materials . . . . . . 3'
Timed production . . . . . . . 25'
Final check; compute
*n-pram* . . . . . . . . . . . . . . 7'

1. Organize your supplies.

2. When directed to begin, key the three documents on p. 348 for 25'.

3. Proofread carefully; correct errors; compute *n-pram* (total words keyed - penalty ÷ 25').

words

### Join and split cells
See Function Review below.

### Document 1
1. Create a 3-column, 5-row table.
2. Select Cells B2–B5 and split the cells into 2 columns. Do the same with C2–C5.
3. Join A1 and A2. Press ENTER to key **Division** on the second line.
4. Right-align numbers. Save as **76c-d1**.

### Document 2
1. Create a 3-column, 7-row table.
2. Join the cells in Row 1 and then A2 and A3. Split B3–B7 and C3–C7 into 4 columns.
3. Key the main heading in 14 point and the secondary heading in 12 point.
4. Shade, bold, and center column headings.
5. Save as **76c-d2**.

### Document 3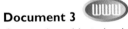
Create the table in landscape orientation. Format and key as shown.

**Function review**
**Join cells**
Table menu, Join, Cell

**Split cells**
Table menu, Split, Cell

### Internet option for Document 3:
1. Log on to the Internet and follow the directions below the table.
2. Key the data from the Internet in the table.

Two cells merged into one

Two columns split into four

**ALBANY STATE COLLEGE**

**1999-00 Enrollments**

| Division | Fall Semester | | Spring Semester | |
|---|---|---|---|---|
| | Male | Female | Male | Female |
| Business and Computer Science | 1,025 | 985 | 843 | 760 |
| Fine Arts and Humanities | 915 | 1,164 | 685 | 723 |
| Science and Engineering | 2,200 | 1,002 | 1,450 | 645 |

4
8
14
21
30
39
48

**FLY AWAY SPECIALS**

**April 1-May 25, 200-**

| Destination | First Class | | Coach Class | |
|---|---|---|---|---|
| | One Way | Round Trip | One Way | Round Trip |
| Mexico City, Mexico | $499 | $   899 | $399 | $599 |
| London, England | 650 | 1,000 | 450 | 800 |
| Singapore | 620 | 1,100 | 395 | 610 |
| New Zealand | 710 | 1,350 | 410 | 799 |

4
8
13
23
34
43
51
59

| Destination | Day 1 | | Day 2 | | Day 3 | | Comments |
|---|---|---|---|---|---|---|---|
| | Hi | Lo | Hi | Lo | Hi | Lo | |
| San Diego, California | | | | | | | |
| Las Vegas, Nevada | | | | | | | |
| Chicago, Illinois | | | | | | | |
| Miami, Florida | | | | | | | |

### Internet option
1. Go to www.weather.com.
2. Enter **San Diego** in the box *Enter a city or Zip,* and click **Go**. When given a choice between Texas or California, select *San Diego, California.*
3. Scroll down the screen to view the 5-day forecast. Write down the highs and lows for the next 3 days as well as comments such as "partly cloudy."
4. Repeat Steps 2 and 3 for each city.

**Letter and envelope styles**

Circle the correct response for each pair.

Letter address:

1.  a.  Shawn Davis
        2603 Boyd Rd.
        Morrow, GA 30260-9805

    b.  Mr. Shawn Davis
        2603 Boyd Rd.
        Morrow, GA 30260-9805

2.  a.  Ms. Jane Flint
        Flint Telecommunications
        Fasanenstrasse 5
        D-10625 Berlin 12
        GERMANY

    b.  Ms. Jane Flint
        Flint Telecommunications
        Fasanenstrasse 5
        D-10625
        Berlin 12, Germany

Envelope:

3.  a.  MRS JOYCE T SALTERS
        BOX 4150
        DECATUR MS 39327-4150

    b.  Mrs. Joyce T. Salters
        Box 4150
        Decatur, MS 39327-4150

4.  a.  Miss Carole Johnson
        2006 Fifth St.
        Dallas, TX

    b.  MISS CAROLE JOHNSON
        2006 FIFTH ST
        DALLAS TX 75221-2006

Closing lines:

5.  a.  Sincerely yours,

    b.  Sincerely Yours,

---

116f ●

**Proofreading**

Key the memo at right. Correct the following unmarked errors:

3 spelling
1 number
1 possessive
3 punctuation
1 consistency

**TO:** All Staff | **FROM:** Connie S. Lockhart, Staff Development Coordinator | **DATE:** Current | **SUBJECT:** WordPerfect's Tools Enhance Communication

This weeks staff development corner highlights 3 elements of *WordPerfect's* Tools menu that will enhance communication in the documents you produce. These valuable tools are Spell Checker, Thesaurus, and QuickCorrect.

**Spell Checker.** Always check spelling after keying a document to correct keying errors. Then proofread carefully for errors in word choice content and accuracy

**Thesaurus.** Enhance the quality of a document by chosing an alternate word. The first draft may include the word <u>disagreement</u>. The thesaurus suggests the word <u>misunderstanding</u>, which provides a more positive tone.

QuickCorrect. This feature automatically corrects common spelling errors, capitalization at the beginning of sentences, names of days of the week, or CAPS LOCK keying errors. Add your own entries to assist in automatic corection.

# SpeedFormat and Sort

## 77a • 5'

### GETTING started

alphabet 1 Jamie quickly apologized for submitting the complex reviews late.

figures 2 Chapters 7, 18, 19, and 23 had 65 pages; the others had 40 pages.

shift key 3 Amy, Ty, Jo, Ann, Lee, Al, and Bob may go to El Paso or San Jose.

easy 4 Claudia and my neighbor may fix duck, lamb, and panfish for them.

| 1 | 2 | 3 | 4 | 5 | 6 | 7 | 8 | 9 | 10 | 11 | 12 | 13 |

## 77b • 8'

### SKILLBUILDING

**Build straight-copy skill**

1. Key two 1' writings at your top rate; key a 1' writing at your control rate.
2. Key a 5' writing from *82b*, p. 249. Work for control.

 all letters

*gwam* 1'

Technology is bringing about many changes in offices. Smart    12 | 101
managers recognize that not only will the technology be new, but    25 | 114
also the way work is done will be changed. These managers in-    38 | 126
volve all workers in the planning of the changes. They offer to    51 | 139
train those who need it, and they let all workers know what the    63 | 152
impact of the technology will be on their jobs. Smart managers    76 | 165
help workers to be change agents, rather than change resisters.    89 | 178

1' | 1 | 2 | 3 | 4 | 5 | 6 | 7 | 8 | 9 | 10 | 11 | 12 | 13 |

## 77c • 5'

### FUNCTION REVIEW

**Document**

1. Key the table; do not apply formats. Spell out *applications* in Row 5.
2. Apply the Row Fill Header style.
3. Center the table horizontally. Use Size Column to Fit.
4. Save as **77c**.

Character formats such as bold or shading can be added *after* a style is applied. ▨

### SpeedFormat

The **SpeedFormat** feature lets you format a table using a preset style. Styles with shading in the last row or column are well suited for tables that contain totals. Key the table without adding formats. Then choose *SpeedFormat* from the Table menu. Choose a style from the Available styles list box. Click **Apply**, then **Close** to return to the table.

### CLASS SCHEDULE

| Class | Teacher | Location | Time |
|---|---|---|---|
| Algebra | Dr. Yamaguchi | 222 Lee Hall | 9:00-10:00 a.m. |
| English | Dr. Riswell | 385 Humanities | 10:00-11:00 a.m. |
| Keyboarding | Dr. Patel | 489 Business | 11:00 a.m.-12:00 p.m. |
| Computer Apps. | Dr. Kalinowski | 145 Business | 1:00-2:00 p.m. |

# Employment Test

116a ●

Industry requires basic skills of entry-level employees. Although industry today is rarely testing for spelling, grammar, punctuation, and simple mathematical skills, you can be assured that you will be expected to have a mastery of these valuable skills. Test yourself on the following sample test.

116b ●

**Spelling**

Write the correct spelling for the frequently misspelled words at the right.

congradulations _____

convience _____

thesarus _____

grammer _____

priviledge _____

maintance _____

restaraunt _____

fax (spelled out) _____

to (meaning also) _____

116c ●

**Word choice**

Circle the correct response.

1. The school board must (accept, except) the Supreme Court ruling.
2. The difficult decision was (among, between) the three of us.
3. The young defense lawyer (cited, sighted, sited) three lawsuits.
4. "I (complement, compliment) you on your creativity," he stated.
5. How much (farther, further) must the group travel tomorrow?
6. Wesley counted (fewer, less) errors than the French teacher counted.
7. Are you sure (its, it's) agreeable with your grandparents?
8. The (personal, personnel) were asked to report to work at 8 a.m.
9. The keyboarding class designed their own (stationary, stationery).
10. Congratulations! You have (passed, past) the first round of tests.

116d ●

**Math**

Calculate the amounts at the right.

1. What is 30 percent of 2,696? _____
2. Change 12 percent to a decimal. _____
3. Change .25 to a percentage. _____
4. Change .065 to a percentage. _____
5. Compute the correct amounts for each blank below:

| Units | Unit Cost | | Total Cost |
|-------|-----------|---|------------|
| 6 | 2.95 | | _____ |
| 29 | 19.65 | | _____ |
| | | Subtotal | _____ |
| | | Sales tax 7% | _____ |
| | | Total | _____ |

## Sort in tables

*WordPerfect* can sort information in a table either alphabetically or numerically. Information can be sorted in either ascending or descending order. **Ascending order** means from A to Z, or 1 to 10. **Descending order** means from Z to A, or 10 to 1.

To learn about Sort, refer to the Sort dialog box at right and the table in Document I as you read the following paragraphs.

**To do a simple sort:**
1. Select the entire table except for the column headings.
2. From the Tools menu, choose *Sort*.
3. In the Sort by list, choose *First cell in a table row*. Click **Sort**.

**To change keys:**
*WordPerfect's* default is to sort by the first cell in a table row (see Sort dialog box). However, you may customize your sort by setting new keys, or sorting rules. The **key** determines the priority in which data will be sorted. In Document 1, to sort according to state, you would change the Column box to **5**, since the state is keyed in the fifth column. To sort according to ZIP Code, change the Column box to **6**.

1. Click the **Edit** button on the Sort dialog box.
2. Choose the appropriate keys (sorting rules):
   **Key:** Indicate the priority for sorting.
   **Type:** Choose *Alphabetic* or *Numeric*.
   **Sort order:** Choose *Ascending* or *Descending*.
   **Column:** Key the number of the column to be sorted.
3. Click **OK** and then **Sort**.

**77e ● 25'**

FORMATTING

### Sort tables
Do *not* close Document I until you finish Document 3.

**Document I**
Key the table; save as **77e-dI**; print but do not close.

**Document 2**
Document *77e-dI* should be displayed.
1. Sort by Last Name in ascending order.
2. Check yourself: In the Edit Sort dialog box, compare the key to Key I in the second dialog box above.
3. Save as **77e-d2**. Do not close the document.

**AREA REPRESENTATIVES**

| Last Name | First Name | Initial | City | State | ZIP |
|---|---|---|---|---|---|
| Guddy | Allen | A | Seattle | WA | 93006 |
| Castille | Lorraine | W | Minneapolis | MN | 55455 |
| Strauss | Karla | C | Omaha | NE | 65532 |
| Golla | Patricia | B | San Francisco | CA | 95476 |
| Leuenberger | Michael | W | Chicago | IL | 60672 |
| Lepak | Gary | L | Laredo | TX | 76549 |
| McDowell | Ashley | M | Dallas | TX | 75543 |
| Le | Trinh | M | Oxnard | CA | 93321 |
| Goddard | Denise | X | San Francisco | CA | 95436 |
| Woodbury | Sally | D | Durham | NC | 23498 |
| Slater | Joseph | T | New Bern | NC | 23653 |
| Uribe | Ornella | B | Del Rio | TX | 78890 |

**FORMATTING**

**Follow-up letters**

### Follow-up letters

Successful job hunters understand the importance of writing winning resumes and application letters. Additionally, they understand the value of writing follow-up letters. They may write any or all of the following letters:

• Follow-up letter to companies that have not responded to the resume (mailed two weeks to one month later).

• Thank-you letter after the interview.
• Thank-you letter to references.
• Job acceptance or job refusal letters.

Key these letters on quality paper, use acceptable letter style, and proofread to ensure an error-free document.

---

**Document 1**
**Follow-up letter**

1. Open *letterhead*. Save as **115c-d1**.
2. Key in block letter style.

| | words |
|---|---|
| Current date│Mr. Bennett Cortese│*Financial News*│706 North Pineville | 14 |
| St.│Woodstock, VA 22664-0038 | 20 |
| | |
| Dear Mr. Cortese | 23 |

Recently I applied as a junior graphic designer at *Financial News*. Since `38` writing to you, I have additional qualifications that I wish to report to you. `54`

My enclosed resume has been updated to include my recent first-place `68` award in the College Graphic Design Category of the National Collegiate `82` Graphic Design Association. This award, the most prestigious award pre- `97` sented by NCGDA, was established to recognize the excellent work of the `111` most aspiring graphic design student. I am most honored to have received `126` this distinction by academia. `132`

Mr. Cortese, I would like the opportunity to discuss with you the valuable `147` contributions I can make to your newspaper. Please write or call me at `161` (601) 555-4977.│Sincerely│Janna M. Howard│Enclosure `172`

---

**Document 2**
**Thank-you letter**

1. Open *letterhead*. Edit the letterhead design; resave as *howard*.
2. Address the thank-you letter to Mr. Cortese (Document 1). Save as **115c-d2**.

**Document 3**
**Thank you to reference**

1. Open *howard*.
2. Insert the file *thank-you* from the formatting template. Save as **115c-d3**.

| | opening 23 |
|---|---|

Thank you for taking time to talk with me about the position as junior `37` graphic designer at *Financial News*. `45`

I appreciated the comprehensive tour and explanation of the Graphic `58` Design Department. This group of professionals is very fortunate to be `73` equipped with the most up-to-date technological equipment and software `87` and the staff development support. Consequently, your subscribers are `101` the real winners. `105`

Mr. Cortese, I would like the opportunity to work at *Financial News* and to `120` contribute to the popularity and success of this outstanding newspaper. I `135` am eagerly awaiting your call.│Sincerely│Janna M. Howard `146`

# Performing multiple sorts

Sometimes you may need to sort by more than one criteria. For example, you could sort by ZIP Code (those with the same ZIP Code will be sorted according to last name). To sort by more than one criteria, you must add a key. Key 1 would be for the ZIP Code column (6) and Key 2 would be for the Last Name column (1).

### Document 3
### Multiple sorts

Document *77e-d2* should be displayed.

1. Sort the document in ascending order by State, then City, then Last Name. Follow the instructions at right to add the second and third keys.
   - Key 1: State (Column 5)
   - Key 2: City (Column 4)
   - Key 3: Last Name (Column 1)
2. Save as **77e-d3**.

## To add a key:

1. To keep the heading row from being included in the sort (you cannot select all the cells for the multiple sort), click in the heading row. Click **Table** menu, **Format**, **Row** tab. Click **Header row**, **Apply**, and **OK**. Sort will recognize Row 1 as a header row and will not include it in the sort.

2. Click the **Add Key at End** button in the Edit Sort dialog box.

3. Indicate the column to be sorted, the Type, and the Sort order.

4. Click **OK**. The Sort dialog box displays.

5. Click **Sort**.

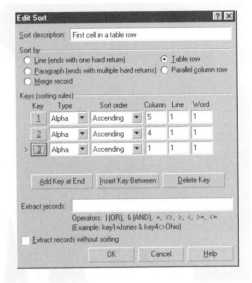

### Document 4

1. Key the table at the right.
2. Sort the document in ascending order according to Department, then Employee.
3. Save as **77e-d4**. Print. Do not close.

### Document 5

1. Sort the table in *77e-d4* according to Department in descending order; then according to Years of Service in descending order.
2. Save as **77e-d5**. Print.

words

## DATALINE CORPORATION

### Personnel Department

| Employee | Department | Years of Service | |
|---|---|---|---|
| Carter, Jill | Accounting | 25 | 21 |
| Dahlia, Karl | Maintenance | 18 | 27 |
| Anderson, Rebecca | Human Resources | 7 | 34 |
| Kahalla, Ahli | Maintenance | 21 | 40 |
| Quinton, Roger | Accounting | 6 | 45 |
| Stanton, Victoria | Human Resources | 9 | 53 |
| Jarvis, Kevin | Accounting | 12 | 58 |
| Larson, Sharon | Accounting | 2 | 64 |
| Takaki, William | Accounting | 20 | 70 |
| Smith, Lisa | Maintenance | 1 | 75 |
| Nguyen, Vo | Human Resources | 3 | 81 |

(words column: 4, 8, 16)

# LESSON 115

# Employment Letters

## 115a • 5'
## GETTING started

| | | |
|---|---|---|
| alphabet | 1 | Jimmy Kloontz required extra help with lunch for five big groups. |
| figures | 2 | Flight 1975 was due at 10:53; it arrived at Gate 28 at 12:46 p.m. |
| 3d/4th fingers | 3 | Alan was quite glad that Max told Sal about the six jazz players. |
| easy | 4 | Did he fish with Pamela by the island or in the lake by the dock? |

| 1 | 2 | 3 | 4 | 5 | 6 | 7 | 8 | 9 | 10 | 11 | 12 | 13 |

## 115b • 20'
## FORMATTING

**Application letters**
Read the information at the right.

### Application letter
The purpose of an application letter is to obtain an interview. Application letters vary, depending on how you learned of the position. You want to show that your skills match the position requirements. A good strategy for writing an application letter is to:

- Establish a point of contact if possible.
- Specify the type of job you are seeking.
- Interpret your major qualifications in terms of employer benefits.
- Request an interview.

Plain paper or personal stationery—never an employer's letterhead—may be used for an application letter. Your application letter must include your return address. You can create your own letterhead or use the personal business letter format, keying your address immediately above the date. Block, modified block, or simplified format may be used.

**Document 1**
**Application letter**
1. Open *letterhead*. Save as **115b-d1**.
2. Position the insertion point at the end of the document (CTRL + END). Key in block style with open punctuation. Address to:
   **Mr. Bennett Cortese**
   *Financial News*
   **706 North Pineville St.**
   **Woodstock, VA 22664-0038**
3. Add appropriate salutation.
4. Save again; print.

**Document 2**
**Personal stationery**
1. Create your own personal stationery.
2. Save as **Your Name-ltrhd**.

| | words |
|---|---|
| opening | 23 |

My college degree in office systems technology and my graphics design job experience in the United States and Japan qualify me to function well as a junior graphic designer for your newspaper.

As a result of my comprehensive four-year program, I am skilled in the most up-to-date office suite packages as well as the latest version of desktop publishing and graphics programs. In addition, I am very skilled at locating needed resources on the Internet. In fact, this skill played a very important role in the design award that I received last month.

My technical and communication skills were applied as I worked as the assistant editor and producer of the *Cother Alumni News*. I understand well the importance of meeting deadlines and also producing a quality product that will increase newspaper sales.

After you have reviewed the enclosed resume as well as my design samples located on my Web page at www.netdoor.com/~jhoward, I would look forward to discussing my qualification and career opportunities with you at *Financial News*.

Sincerely | Janna M. Howard | Enclosure

| | |
|---|---|
| | 38 |
| | 53 |
| | 62 |
| | 76 |
| | 91 |
| | 106 |
| | 121 |
| | 136 |
| | 150 |
| | 164 |
| | 179 |
| | 188 |
| | 201 |
| | 217 |
| | 233 |
| | 234 |
| | 241 |

# Formulas in Tables

## 78a ● 10'

### GETTING started

each group 3 times; work at a controlled rate

1st/2d fingers

1 dirt nut fun drum try buy been curt very hunt bunt rent cent jump
2 We think Julio may give Ruth a ring Sunday if she will accept it.
3 My name is Geoffrey, but I very much prefer Jeff on this nametag.

3d/4th fingers

4 was pill look zoom loop west low loose quiz walk saw wax box zeal
5 Paul Velasquez was at a popular plaza quilt shop when he saw Sal.
6 Sal was at a Palawan zoo; he was also at Wuxi Plaza for six days.

| 1 | 2 | 3 | 4 | 5 | 6 | 7 | 8 | 9 | 10 | 11 | 12 | 13 |

## 78b ● 12'

### NEW FUNCTION

### Formulas in tables

*WordPerfect* can add, subtract, multiply, and divide numbers in a table using formulas. If changes are made later to the numbers, the answer can be recalculated.

Using the Formula Bar is an easy way to perform many math calculations. (See the next page.) Click the **Table** button and then select *Formula Toolbar*. Some of the options on this bar are listed here.

**QuickFill:** Continues a pattern of incrementing values (such as months of the year or days of the week) across a row or down a column.

**QuickSum:** Calculates the sum of the values in cells above or to the left of the insertion point.

**Copy formula:** Copies a formula to other cells.

**To copy a formula:**
1. Place the insertion point in the cell that contains the formula to be copied.
2. Click the **Copy Formula** button.
3. Indicate the number of times the formula is to be copied either down or to the right.

**To recalculate a total:**
If you change a number after a total has been obtained, click in the cell containing the answer, and the answer will be recalculated automatically.

### Document I
1. Key the table at the right.
2. Use QuickSum to obtain the totals in Row 5.
3. Center the table horizontally and apply Size Column to Fit.
4. Save as **78b-dI** and print.

words

**FIRST QUARTER PAYROLL**

4

| Employee | January | February | March | |
|----------|---------|----------|-------|---|
| Berchov, Katrina | 2000 | 2045 | 2010 | 11 |
| Craxton, Tenton | 1600 | 1585 | 1650 | 18 |
| Patel, Rajeh | 2100 | 1785 | 1920 | 25 |
| Total | | | | 31 |
| | | | | 32 |

## Document 2
### Unbound report

1. Use 1.5" top margin and default side margins: DS.
2. SS bulleted list and *Keywords* section.
3. Save as **114b-d2**.

## Document 3
### Scannable resume

1. Open *114b-d1*.
2. Convert this traditional resume to a scannable resume using information from *114b-d2*. Add blank lines between sections and/or different information.
3. Use the keywords shown in *114b-d2*.

## Document 4

Prepare a scannable resume using your own data.

## Document 5
### On the Internet

1. Browse the Internet for guides to effective resume writing.
   - www.ceweekly.wa.com/helpful/grw.html
2. Search for Career WEB's database of career opportunities and employers.
   - www.cweb.com

# WRITING AN ELECTRONIC (SCANNABLE) RESUME

Many companies are using electronic applicant-tracking systems to process the large volume of resumes being submitted for job openings. Applicants may submit electronic resumes (resumes read by the computer) via e-mail or post to corporate Web pages or job banks on the Internet. Printed resumes received for job openings are scanned into the database using OCR scanners.

After the resumes are stored in the electronic tracking system, the system compares the electronic resumes to a list of keywords listed in the job descriptions. A ranked report is generated showing the number of matches for each keyword. The applicants with the higher ranking or largest number of keyword matches are considered for the position(s).

## Format Requirements

To ensure readability, certain formatting is required for resumes that are scanned into electronic applicant-tracking systems. When formatting an electronic resume, remember these format guidelines:

- Use at least 1" margins.
- Use simple typefaces that are clear and easy to scan. Choose at least a 10-point font but do not exceed 14 point.
- Do not use fancy formatting, such as italics, underlining, graphic lines or boxes, etc.
- Use solid bullets (•).
- Include blank lines between sections of the resume.
- Do not fold the resume or staple the resume.

## Content Requirements

As a scannable resume requires certain format changes, it requires content changes as well. Most importantly, the scannable resume must include a section titled Keywords or Keyword Summary. Position the keyword summary after the objective section. Be sure to capitalize the first word of each keyword and separate with a period. Begin with the most important keyword and move to the least important. The example below illustrates a Keywords section added to a traditional resume.

### Keywords

Graphic design position. Bachelor's degree in office systems technology and graphic design. Cother University. 3.8 GPA. Graphic Designers' Society. Intern work experience. Japanese fluency. Traveled Japan. Enjoy photography. Computer proficiency. Windows, Macintosh. Software applications. WordPerfect, Quattro Pro, Presentations, Paradox, Internet, Netscape, Web design, HTML programming, PageMaker, HyperStudio, Adobe Photoshop, CorelDraw. Database creation. Newsletter design. Communication skills. Team player. Creative. Willing to relocate.

**78b,** *continued*

**Document 2**

1. Open *78b-d1.*
2. Insert the "Total" column as shown.
3. Click **QuickSum** to insert the total in E2.
4. Click the **Copy Formula** button.
5. Click the Down button and key **3** in the times box; click **OK.**
6. Save as **78b-d2.** Print.

**Document 3**

1. Open *78b-d1.*
2. Change the number in B2 to 4,000; then click in B5 to recalculate the total.
3. Change the number in D4 to 2,500; click in D5 to recalculate.
4. Save as **78b-d3.** Print.

**78c ● 25'**

**NEW FUNCTION**

## FIRST QUARTER PAYROLL

| Employee | January | February | March | Total |
|---|---|---|---|---|
| Berchov, Katrina | 2000 | 2045 | 2010 | |
| Craxton, Tenton | 1600 | 1585 | 1650 | |
| Patel, Rajeh | 2100 | 1785 | 1920 | |
| Total | | | | |

## Writing a formula

You can write your own formulas to add, subtract, multiply, divide, or average numbers in a table. A formula includes the cell address and the math symbol. For example, B2–C2 means subtract the value of Column C, Row 2 from Column B, Row 2.

**To enter a formula:**

1. Place the insertion point in the cell that will contain the formula.
2. Display the Formula Toolbar.
3. Enter the formula to the right of the blue check mark.
4. Click on the blue check mark to enter the formula. The answer is inserted in the cell.

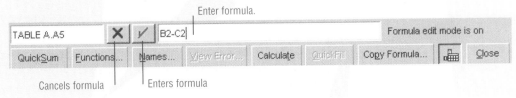

The following symbols can be used in formulas.

| Operation | Symbol | Example |
|---|---|---|
| Addition | + | B2+C2 |
| Subtraction | – (hyphen) | B2–C2 |
| Multiplication | * | B2*C2 |
| Division | / | B2/C2 |
| Average | Place parentheses ( ) around the part of the calculation to be performed first. | (B2+C2+D2+E2)/4 |

# JANNA M. HOWARD —— 18 pt. Arial

**Temporary Address (May 30, 2000)** —— 12 pt. Arial
587 Birch Cir.
Clinton, MS 39056-0587
(601) 555-4977
**E-mail: jhoward@netdoor.com**

**Permanent Address**
328 Fondren St.
Orlando, FL 32801-0328
(407) 555-3834
**Web page: www.netdoor.com/~jhoward**

| | |
|---|---|
| **CAREER OBJECTIVE** | To obtain a graphic design position with an opportunity to advance to a management position. |
| **SUMMARY OF ACHIEVEMENTS** | Bachelor's degree with double major in office systems technology and graphics design; proficient in computer environments and major software applications. Related work experience in three organizations, including internship in foreign country. Speak Japanese and enjoy photography. |
| **EDUCATION** | **B.S.  Office Systems Technology and Graphics Design** (double major), Cother University, Mobile, Alabama.  May 2000.  Grade-point average: 3.8/4.0.  Served as president of Graphic Designers' Society. |

12 pt. Arial
(left column)

**SPECIAL SKILLS**

| | |
|---|---|
| Environments: | *Microsoft Windows*® and *Macintosh*® |
| Software: | *WordPerfect Suite 2000*®, *Netscape*®, *CorelDraw*®, *PageMaker*®, *HyperStudio*®, *PhotoShop*®, *Illustrator*®, *Freehand*® |
| Language: | BASIC and HTML |
| Keyboarding skill: | 70 words per minute |
| Foreign language: | Japanese |
| Travel: | Japan (two summers working as a graphic design intern) |

**EXPERIENCE**

**Cother University Alumni Office**, Mobile, Alabama.  Assistant editor and producer of the *Cother Alumni News*, 1998 to present.
- Design layout and production of six editions; met every publishing deadline.
- Received the "Cother Design Award."
- Assisted editor in design of Alumni Office Web page (http://www.cu.edu/alumni/).

**Cother Library**, Mobile, Alabama.  Student assistant in Audiovisual Library, 1997-1998.
- Created *Audiovisual Catalog* using computerized database.
- Prepared monthly and yearly reports using database.
- Designed brochure to promote library services (http://www.cu.edu/~jhoward/samples/brochure).

**REFERENCES**

Request portfolio from Cother University Placement Office.

11 pt. Times New Roman (right column)

RESUME

**78c,** *continued*

### Documents 1-2

1. Key the table at the right.
2. Shade Row 1 10%. Shade Column D, 20%. Adjust column widths.
3. In D2, enter a formula to calculate Net Profit (Gross Revenues - Expenses). Copy the formula to D3–D5.
4. Right-align the figures in Columns B–D.
5. Save as **78c-d1**.
6. Add a Total row to *78c-d1*. Calculate the totals and net profit. Save as **78c-d2**.

### Document 3

1. Open *78c-d1*; save as **78c-d3**.
2. Change the numbers in the cells as follows and recalculate the Net Profit:

   C3  312,000
   B4  575,000
   C5  350,000

### Document 4

1. Key the table.
2. Enter a formula in F2 to calculate the Average Score. Copy the formula to F3–F6.
3. Center the numbers in Columns B–F.
4. Change the format to Row Fill Header.
5. Save and print.

### AJAX  INCORPORATED
#### Eastern Division

| Quarter | Gross Revenues | Expenses | Net Profit | words |
|---|---|---|---|---|
| | | | | 4 |
| | | | | 7 |
| | | | | 16 |
| First | 320,000 | 260,000 | | 20 |
| Second | 480,000 | 302,000 | | 25 |
| Third | 510,000 | 365,000 | | 29 |
| Fourth | 495,000 | 358,000 | | 34 |

### ELECTROPHYSIOLOGY 102
#### Fall 200-

| Student | Test 1 | Test 2 | Test 3 | Test 4 | Average Score | words |
|---|---|---|---|---|---|---|
| | | | | | | 4 |
| | | | | | | 6 |
| | | | | | | 16 |
| Baxton, C. | 83 | 87 | 89 | 88 | | 21 |
| Daruma, L. | 92 | 95 | 90 | 93 | | 25 |
| Contreras, S. | 79 | 80 | 65 | 75 | | 31 |
| Perez, A. | 87 | 85 | 91 | 90 | | 35 |
| Quan, P. | 90 | 89 | 93 | 95 | | 39 |

## 78d ● 3'

### SELF ✔
### check

Answer the True/False questions at the right to see if you have mastered the material presented in this lesson.

T   F

1. To add a column of numbers quickly, click the Number Type button on the Formula toolbar.

2. To recalculate a total, click the QuickSum button.

3. To add a single row of numbers, write a formula and enter it in the Formula box.

4. To obtain the quotient of C5 and D5 in cell E5, the formula would be E5 = C5 x D5.

5. To quickly add a row at the end of a table, choose Insert from the Table menu.

# GETTING started

alphabet 1 Mavis quickly fixed her car so we could go play jazz with a band.

figures 2 Jayne asked 492 men, 180 women, and 376 children 1,925 questions.

3d/4th fingers 3 I gave him my opinion on a great estate tax case we read at noon.

easy 4 Did a man sign a form and pay for the right to fish on the docks?

| 1 | 2 | 3 | 4 | 5 | 6 | 7 | 8 | 9 | 10 | 11 | 12 | 13 |

## FORMATTING

## Resumes

### Document 1

1. Format the resume on p. 341. Adjust the text so that it fits on one page (11-point font or smaller margins).
2. Select Arial (sans serif font) for the identification section and the headings. Select Times New Roman (serif font) for the text of the resume.
3. Format the body using Indent or as a two-column table. Set a tab in Column 2 for the list of software.
4. Save as **114b-d1**.

---

**Function review:**
Insert, Symbol, ®

---

**Resume**

A **resume** is a summary of your qualifications; it is the sole basis for the interviewer's decision to invite you for an interview. Prior to preparing a resume, complete a self-analysis, identifying your career goals and job qualifications.

Most resumes contain some or all of the following information:

- **Identifying information:** Include your name, telephone number, and address. You may also include your e-mail address and Internet address. Students may need to list both a temporary and a permanent address.

- **Career objective:** Specify the type of position you are seeking. Let the employer know you have a specific career goal.

- **Summary of achievements:** Summarize what you believe are your most important achievements. Emphasize special skills such as foreign languages, computer skills, or any unique job skills.

- **Education:** List diplomas or degrees earned, schools attended, and dates. Include information such as majors and grade-point averages when it is to your advantage to do so.

- **Experience:** Provide job titles, employers, dates of employment, a brief description of the positions, and major achievements. Emphasize achievements rather than activities. Use active voice and concrete language; for example, "Handle an average of 200 customer orders a week." List information in the same order for each position.

- **Honors and activities:** Demonstrate leadership potential and commitment. Give specific examples.

- **References:** Indicate how to obtain references. Usually a separate list of references is given to the interviewer upon request.

Items within the sections of the resume are arranged in reverse chronological order (most recent experiences listed first).

Which section is presented first? From your self-analysis, you will determine which one of your qualifications is the strongest. If work experience is stronger than education, then present this section first. A recent college graduate would present education first.

A major consideration in preparing an effective resume is the overall attractiveness of the resume. Use high-quality paper, print on laser printer using effective layout design that will allow your resume to appear professionally created. However, do not overdo.

# LESSON 79

# Number Format; Insert File

## 79a • 5'

### GETTING started

Key the drill twice; DS between 2-line groups.

adjacent keys
1 Trey and Guy Walker were going to join us for a very quick snack.
2 Where were Mario, Guy, and Luis going after the water polo class?

fig/sym
3 Jay paid Invoice #2846 ($3,017.35) and Invoice #7925 ($8,409.16).
4 I caught 20 halibut (69.5# average) and 37 trout (4.81# average).

easy
5 He may shape the clay bowl in a form, or he may shape it by hand.
6 Helene may suspend the formal audit if their firm pays a penalty.

alphabet
7 Zacke was an example of a very quiet but charming and fair judge.
8 Quincy Ziff worked very hard to build just six wellness programs.

| 1 | 2 | 3 | 4 | 5 | 6 | 7 | 8 | 9 | 10 | 11 | 12 | 13 |

## 79b • 5'

### NEW FUNCTION

## Insert file

Using **Insert file**, a stored file can be inserted into another document. This function is especially useful in combining new information with previously stored information.

**To insert file:**

1. Place the insertion point where you want to insert the file.
2. Click **File** on the Insert menu.
3. Select the file you wish to insert.
4. Click **Insert**.

## Changing the number format

If your table contains numeric data, sometimes you may need to change the format of the numbers. When inserting a sum or using another formula, the number format may differ from the numbers you have keyed.

**To change the number format:**

1. Click **Numeric Format** from the Table menu.
2. Choose the *Cell*, *Column*, or *Table* tab.
3. Select the desired format. Check the format in the preview box.
4. Change the number of decimal places if necessary. The default is zero.

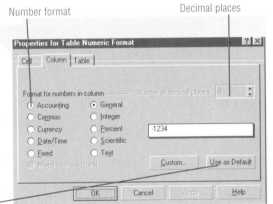

Number format

Decimal places

Set changes as the default

## Edit data file

Sometimes you will want to edit an existing record. The easiest way to do this is to open the data file and click the Quick Entry button on the Merge bar. Click in any field to edit the text in the field.

**To add a new record**, click the New Record button in the Quick Data Entry dialog box and enter the data in each field.

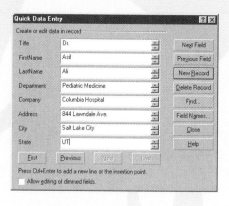

113d ● 25'

**Edit Merge**
**Document 1**
**Merge letters**
Open *111c-data*, created in Lesson 111. Save as **113d-data**. Make the updates listed at the right.

1. Mr. Bell now works for **Prestage Technology Company**. Ms. Richards' new ZIP Code is **53073-4321**.

2. Add two new records:

   **Mr. William Chambers**        **Ms. Eleanor Kubly**
   **Adrian Florists**             **Kubly and Ross Associates**
   **1456 W. 18 St.**              **356 Hammond Ave.**
   **Milwaukee, WI 53213-2264**    **Milwaukee, WI 53221-6814**

3. Sort by LastName in ascending order. Save the data file.

4. Insert merge fields for envelopes. Merge; print the letters and envelopes.

**Documents 2 and 3**
**Labels**

### Document 2 File folder labels

1. Create file folder labels with company name (5066-File Folder) for **111d-data**.
2. Sort by Company; ascending order. Edit in UPPERCASE.
3. Save the merged labels as **113d-d2**. Print.

### Document 3 Name badges (Optional)

1. Use records in *lrn-data* to create name badges for the Lakeland Conference on Women in Employment (111b).
2. Select *Avery label 5095—Name Badge*. Format attractively.

**FORMATTING**

**Document 1**

1. Key table. Enter a formula in B8 that calculates the average of the column.
2. Change the Numeric format to Integer.
3. Apply 20% shading to Row 8.
4. Center and bold column headings. Adjust column widths.

## LARSON DISTRIBUTION

### Regional Office Employees

| Regional Office | Number of Employees |
|---|---|
| Seattle | 16 |
| San Diego | 22 |
| Denver | 12 |
| Chicago | 24 |
| Atlanta | 11 |
| Newark | 10 |
| Average Number of Employees | |

**Document 2**

1. Send the memo to **Gary Bunzel**, from **Alice Baldwin**. Add a subject line. Use current date.
2. Key the table without the $ or commas. Add a row for the Total.
3. Sort the Cost column in descending order.
4. Use a formula for total.
5. Change numeric format to *Commas* and *zero* Digits after the Decimal in Column C.
6. Format attractively. Add the $ in Rows 2 and 7.

The changes you requested on the structural drawings that we transmitted to you on September 4 have been evaluated, and new costs have been figured. We have based cost estimates on the unit price schedule in Exhibit C of the original contract, No. AT-129.

| Work Order No. | Engineer Specs. | Costs |
|---|---|---|
| AT-PP-3 | 703-1437 | $ 6,114 |
| AT-R2-21 | 83-730 | 58,832 |
| AT-W-11 | 3382-82 | 8,266 |
| AT-MJ-07 | 7739-9 | 3,053 |
| AT-SM-5 | 4983-03 | $ 63,283 |

Contact me if you wish to discuss the items in this quotation

**Document 3**

1. Key the memo using the *Memo* template. Insert the table *folder* from the template disk where indicated.
2. Save as **79c-d3**. Check the placement of the table.

**TO:**       Royal Canadian Employees

**FROM:**    Alan Nottingham

**DATE:**    June 22, 200-

**SUBJECT:**  Company Forms

The CIS Department has downloaded the most widely used forms onto the hard drive of your computer. Below is a list of the forms, the filename the form is stored under, and the subdirectory in which the form is stored.

*Insert file "folder"*

If you need additional help in retrieving these forms, please call me at extension 617.

# More About Merge

## Envelopes for merged letters

Envelopes or address labels can be merged from the data file as the files are merged.

When printing envelopes, you will need to know the type of envelope feeder your printer uses. With labels, you will need to know the kind of label. In this lesson, you will create #10 envelopes (standard business envelopes) along with the merged letter.

**Drill**

1. Open *lrn-mrg* and *lrn-data* that you created in **111b**.
2. Create envelopes following the steps at the right.
3. Save as **113a**.
4. Print the envelopes only.

### To create envelopes from Merge:

1. Open the form document. Click **Merge** on the Merge bar.
2. Click **Envelopes** from the Perform Merge dialog box.
3. Click the **Insert Field** button. Select the appropriate fields for the envelope address. Add spaces between fields as necessary. Close the dialog box.

FIELD(Title)FIELD(FirstName)FIELD(LastName)
FIELD(Department)
FIELD(Company)
FIELD(Address)
FIELD(City)FIELD(State)FIELD(Zip)

**Figure 1**   Merge fields in an envelope

4. Click **Continue Merge** on the Merge bar.
5. Click **Merge**. The envelopes appear in the file after the merged letters.
6. Edit the envelopes for UPPERCASE and no punctuation.

## Merge labels

The data file is often used for merging letters, registration forms, envelopes, and numerous types of labels. Once you select the desired label format you want to create, fields are inserted from the data file.

**Drill**

1. Open *111c-data*.
2. Select Avery 5160 address label.
3. Merge and print. Save as **113b**.

### To create labels from merge:

1. Open data file. Click **Go to Form**. Click **Create** from the Associate dialog box. A blank document screen displays for the new form document.
2. Choose *Format* menu, *Labels*. Choose a label and click **Select**.
3. Click **Insert Field** from the Merge bar. Insert the appropriate fields for a mailing label. Your screen will look similar to Figure 1 above.
4. Click **Merge**; then **Merge**.
5. Save the merged labels.

## Adjust row height

The height of some rows in a table may need to be changed—either increasing the height for emphasis or decreasing the depth. After changing the cell height, you may need to center the text within the cell to make it attractive.

**To adjust row height:**

1. Position the insertion point on the bottom line of the row.
2. When the mouse turns to a two-headed arrow, hold down the left mouse button and drag the line to the desired height.

**To center text within a cell:**

1. With the insertion point in the cell to be formatted, click the **Table** button; select *Format*, then the *Cell* tab.
2. Choose *Center* for the Vertical alignment. Click **Apply**, then **OK**.

**Drill**

1. Create a 5-column, 10-row table.
2. Join Rows 1, 2, and 7. Format these rows in the fonts noted.
3. Right-align numbers.
4. Adjust height of Rows 1, 2, and 7. Then center the text vertically and horizontally in these rows.
5. Save as **79e**.

| Quarterly Sales Report | | | | | |
|---|---|---|---|---|---|
| Atlanta Office | | | | | |
| **Representative** | **1st** | **2nd** | **3rd** | **4th** | 20 pt. bold — 16 pt. bold — 14 pt. bold |
| Robinson | 10,000 | 12,000 | 9,000 | 11,000 | |
| Mason | 8,000 | 6,000 | 10,000 | 9,000 | |
| Alexander | 12,000 | 10,000 | 11,000 | 9,000 | |
| Dallas Office | | | | | 16 pt. bold |
| Smith | 7,000 | 9,000 | 8,000 | 9,000 | |
| Jones | 11,000 | 8,000 | 9,000 | 7,500 | |
| Rajeih | 9,000 | 11,000 | 8,000 | 10,000 | |

# *on...* the Mobile Office

The "mobile" office refers to a work environment other than the traditional office to which employees report to perform work on a daily basis. Sometimes the mobile office is described as work anywhere, anytime.

The concept of telecommuting or working in the mobile office has been around for many years, but it is usually applied to employees such as sales representatives who work out of their cars or homes. Today, technology makes it very feasible for many different types of employees to work away from the traditional office.

The equipment typically required includes a computer with appropriate software, a modem, a laser printer, a fax machine, a separate telephone line, electronic mail, and voice mail. Companies often furnish the equipment to employees, which generally costs far less than providing office facilities for employees.

Working in a mobile office requires employees to work without direct supervision, coordinate their own activities, assume responsibility for their own work, and be self-starters. The benefits include flexibility, reduced commute time, and savings on business attire.

**NEW
FUNCTION**

**Drill 1**

1. Open *lrn-data*. Filter records as follows:
   Field: **State**
   Condition 1: **UT**
2. Merge and print. Save as **112d-d1**.

**Drill 2**

1. With *lrn-data* open, filter to merge records with a ZIP Code of 84110.
2. Merge and print. Save as **112d-d2**.

112e • 14'

FORMATTING

**Mail merge**

1. Open *diverse*, a letterhead, from the Formatting Template. Save as **112e-mrg**.
2. Create the data file at right in a new document window and save as **112e-data**.
3. Select *112e-mrg* as the form document. (*Hint:* Key *.* to view all files. Answer *Yes* to *Change the file type to Merge Form File?*)
4. Enter the form document, inserting the merge fields. Supply salutation.
5. Sort by ZIP Code in descending order.
6. Merge; save as **112e**.

# Filter data records

Filtering data records prior to merging the form document and the data file allows you to select a specific set of data records to merge. For example, you can create a target mailing to individuals in a specific state or ZIP Code.

**To filter records:**

1. Be sure the form document and data file are set up.
2. From either the form document or the data file, click **Merge** on the Merge bar.
3. Click **Select Records**. *Specify conditions* should be checked in the Select Records dialog box.
4. Click the down arrow and choose the appropriate data field (e.g., State).
5. Key the data you will use for the first condition (e.g., UT). Click **OK** and then **Merge**.

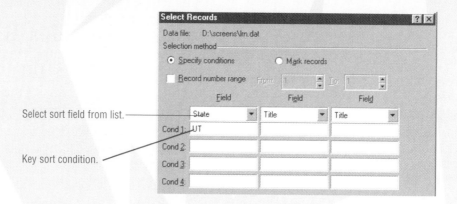

Data file

| Company | Address | City | State | ZIP | FirstName | LastName |
|---------|---------|------|-------|-----|-----------|----------|
| FitTight Tools, Inc. | 335 W. Main St. | Milwaukee | WI | 53203 | John | Powers |
| Bowers Tools, Inc. | 39897 Saratoga | Milwaukee | WI | 53217 | Sara | Smith |
| Warner CompuTec Co. | 112 W. Main St. | Milwaukee | WI | 53220 | Todd | Swenson |

**Form document**

(Insert Date code.)

FIELD (Company)

FIELD (Address)

FIELD (City), FIELD (State) FIELD (ZIP)

We have been notified that a discrimination problem involving FIELD (Title) FIELD (FirstName) FIELD (LastName) exists at your worksite.

Please contact the Diverse Employment Opportunities Commission office each weekday at 608-555-1273. You have 30 days from the date of this letter to reply.

Sincerely | Paul Vellucci, Jr., Director

# Rotate and Skew Text

## 80a ● 5'

## GETTING started

alphabet 1 Zack Bigg may require extra help with dinner for just five teams.
fig/sym 2 The desk (72" x 46" x 28") weighs 105 pounds and costs $3,190.75.
double letters 3 Gregg Mann will meet us at the pool before the committee meeting.
easy 4 Jane may go with them to the authentic burial chapel at the lake.

| 1 | 2 | 3 | 4 | 5 | 6 | 7 | 8 | 9 | 10 | 11 | 12 | 13 |

## 80b ● 7'

## SKILLBUILDING

**Build/measure straight-copy skill**
Key either a 3' or a 5' timing.

 all letters                                             *gwam* 3' | 5'

What characterizes the life of an entrepreneur?  Those who     4 | 2 | 43
have never owned their own businesses may think owning a business   8 | 5 | 46
means being your own boss, setting your own hours, and making a   13 | 8 | 48
lot of money.  Those who have run their own businesses are quick   17 | 10 | 51
to report that owning a business may be exciting and challenging;   21 | 13 | 54
but it also requires hard work, long hours, and personal sacri-   26 | 15 | 56
fice.  A good idea is not the only prerequisite for a successful   30 | 18 | 59
business.  A little luck even helps.                           32 | 19 | 60

Many small businesses are operated as businesses from the   36 | 22 | 63
initial stages.  However, some small businesses that turn out to   41 | 24 | 65
be successful are just hobbies in the early stages.  The entre-   45 | 27 | 68
preneur has a job and uses the income from it to support the   49 | 29 | 70
hobby.  When the hobby begins to require more and more time, the   53 | 32 | 73
entrepreneur has to choose between the job and the hobby.  The   57 | 34 | 75
decision is usually based on finances.  If enough money can be   62 | 37 | 78
made from the hobby or can be obtained from another source, the   66 | 39 | 80
hobby is turned into a business.                               68 | 41 | 82

3' | 1 | 2 | 3 | 4 |
5' | 1 | 2 | 3 |

# Sort and Filter Records

112a • 5'

## G E T T I N G
## s t a r t e d

112b • 8'

technique 1 Zola's optional plans of using buzz saws and axes were plausible.

2 Brazil has various exotic cocoa, coconut, and banana concoctions

easy 3 The official amendment may be a problem for their firm to handle.

4 The sigh of this man was audible as the big dog got on the boxes.

| 1 | 2 | 3 | 4 | 5 | 6 | 7 | 8 | 9 | 10 | 11 | 12 | 13 |

Take one 5' writing on 107c.

112c • 13'
**NEW
FUNCTION**

## Sort data records

Sorting records determines the order in which the records are merged. You might sort records in ZIP order, Last Name order, or City order. Occasionally, a multiple sort is needed to sort first by one field and then a second field. For example, merged name badges or registration letters might be sorted first by state, then by city, and then last name. A new key, or set of sorting rules, is added for each sort order. Records are sorted either in **ascending order** (from A to Z *or* 1, 2 …) or **descending order** (Z to A *or* 100, 99, etc.).

### To sort records:

The form document should be set up and the data file selected (see 111b for directions).

1. From the data file, click **Tools, Sort**. The Sort dialog box displays with *First word in a merge data file* selected.
2. Click the **Edit** button.
3. Enter the number of the field to sort by under *Field*. To find the field number, count the fields in the data file until you get to the one you want.
4. Choose either *Ascending* order or *Descending* order. Click **OK** and then **Sort**.
5. Save the data file after sorting.
6. Complete merge in usual manner.

In each drill, use *lrn-mrg* (Lesson 111b) as the data file and *lrn-data* as the form document.

### Drill 1

1. Open data file.
2. Sort by ZIP (field 9) in ascending order. Resave *lrn-mrg*.
3. Merge with form file.
4. Print. Save as **112c-d1**.

### Drill 2

1. Open data file; complete a multiple sort: **State**, then **City**, then **Last Name**. Resave data file.
2. Merge with form document.
3. Print. Save as **112c-d2**.

### Drill 3

1. Sort in descending order by **ZIP**. Resave.
2. Merge with form document and save as **112c-d3**. Do not print.

### To do a multiple sort:

Click **Add Key at End** in the Edit Sort dialog box. A second key is added. Repeat steps 3 and 4 above, entering the field number and sort order of the second field key.

Key 1 is the first order or level of sort

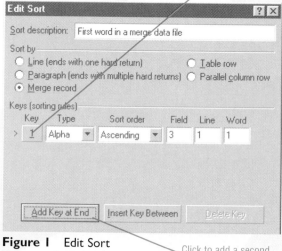

**Figure 1**   Edit Sort

Click to add a second sort order

## Rotate text in table

You will learn some creative ways to enhance the appearance of a table. The tables below are eye-catching because of the vertical row at the left of the table. The text inside the row has been rotated 90 degrees (from horizontal to vertical). Three rotation options are available: 90 degrees, 180 degrees, or 270 degrees. Each time you click the button, the text rotates 90 degrees.

**To rotate text:**

Key the text. Click the **Rotate Cell** button until the text displays in the direction desired.

**To center text within the cell:**

Click **Table** menu, **Format**, **Cell** tab. Under Align cell contents, choose *Horizontal Center* and *Vertical Center*. Click **Apply** and **OK**. Option: Click the Vertical Alignment button on the Table property bar; click the Justification button for horizontal alignment.

If you edit text that has been rotated, the table disappears and a Text Box Editor displays. Edit the text in the pane. Then close the box and return to the table.

**Document 1**

1. Create a 3-column, 6-row table.
2. Key and format the text in Columns B and C.
3. Join the cells in Column A. Key **New Videos** in bold.
4. Rotate the text in Column A to the position shown. Center the text horizontally and vertically in the cell. Apply 20% shading.
5. Center the table horizontally. Adjust all column widths.
6. Save as **80c-d1**.

| New Videos | Video Title | Release Date |
|---|---|---|
| | Job Search Techniques & Sources | 2-15-2000 |
| | Searching for Jobs on the Internet | 4-1-2000 |
| | The Successful Job Interview | 4-15-2000 |
| | Getting That Promotion | 4-15-2000 |
| | Love the Job or Leave It | 4-30-2000 |

**Document 2**

1. Create a 3-column, 6-row table. Join B1 and C1 and key the table.
2. Join the cells in Column A.
3. Key **Registered Nurses** in bold.
4. Rotate text. Align at bottom vertically; center horizontally. Shade 20%.
5. Center the table horizontally. Adjust column widths.
6. Save as **80c-d2**.

| Registered Nurses | JASONVILLE MEMORIAL HOSPITAL | |
|---|---|---|
| | Staff Assignments | |
| | Employees | Assignment |
| | Susan Boyd | Operating Room |
| | Lisa Rogers | Intensive Care Unit |
| | William Smith | Outpatient |
| | Jean Alexander | Radiology |

3. Click **Merge**. The merged letters will appear on the screen as a new document with a page break between letters.

4. Save your letters as **111b** and print.

5. Close the document. The form file, which was behind the merged file, appears. Close the form file and then the data file.

## 111c • 20'

**Merge document**

1. Create the data file for a merge. Save the file as **111c-data**.
2. Create the form file, inserting the merge codes for the variables. Supply an appropriate salutation. Save as **111c-mrg**.
3. Merge the data file and form file.

| Field names | Record 1 | Record 2 | Record 3 |
| --- | --- | --- | --- |
| Title | Mrs. | Mr. | Ms. |
| FirstName | Paje | William | Luwanda |
| LastName | Vang | Bell | Richards |
| Company | Bellflower Plastics | Thornton Chemicals | Rosemont Florists |
| Address | 56899 Glendale Rd. | 345 Coldspring Rd. | 885 N. Third St. |
| City | Milwaukee | Waukesha | Pewaukee |
| State | WI | WI | WI |
| ZIP | 55989-3456 | 88765-3569 | 77883-4321 |

Form file

(Insert letter address merge fields.)

Thank you for submitting your proposal to American Studies Association for enacting a more culturally diverse employment program for city workers.

American Studies Association continually strives to work with city governments in three area counties to provide work environments that value diversity. The goal, of course, is to employ persons that reflect differences in age, lifestyle, and interests. Different people solve problems differently, and that leads to better decisions.

You may be contacted, (Title) (LastName), to serve on the special Council for Managing Diversity that is being established in our three-county region. Again, thank you for letting us know what you are doing to ensure diversity at (Company).

Sincerely | Hunter Nyiri, Director | xx

## 80d • 20'

### NEW FUNCTION

**Document 1**

1. Open *speedpro* from the Formatting Template. Save as **80d-d1**.
2. Apply Left Up skewing to Column A.
3. Save again. The table should look similar to the one shown.

**Document 2**

1. Open *speedpro* again. Save as **80d-d2**.
2. Change the numeric format to **Currency** with **0** digits.
3. Apply Right Down skew.
4. Save.

**Document 3**

1. Open *speedpro* again. Save as **80d-d3a**.
2. Apply Top Left Skewing.
3. Increase width of Row 1 until all column headings are visible. Save.
4. Change the skewing to Left Up – Top Left.
5. Increase angle of top tow to –60. Adjust height as necessary. Save as **80d-d3b**.

*Reference*: Adjust Row Height, p. 242.

## Skewing table cells

For added impact in tables, the top row and left and right columns can be skewed or slanted to enhance the appearance. Skewing changes the angle of the text. Care must be taken, however, that the table is still easy to read. The angle of the skew can be changed.

**To skew cells:**

1. Click **Table** menu, **Format**. Click the **Skew** tab.
2. Choose the part of the table to be skewed/direction of skew from the Skew Settings box.
3. Click **Apply** and **OK**.

**To change the skew:**

1. With the Skew tab displayed, click the **More** button.
2. Click the spin boxes to adjust the angle. Note that separate settings are available for rows and columns.
3. Click **OK**, then **Apply** and **OK**.

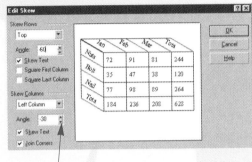

Edit angle of skew.

SPEEDPRO COMPUTERS

| Model | | CPU | RAM | Price |
|---|---|---|---|---|
| 575 | | | | |
| 5100 | | Pentium 166 Mhz | 16 MB | $   560.00 |
| 5120 | | Pentium 200 Mhz | 16 MB | 650.00 |
| 6100 | | Pentium 300 Mhz | 32 MB | 795.00 |
| 6125 | | Pentium II 300 Mhz | 32 MB | 1,450.00 |
| 7000 | | Pentium II 400 Mhz | 64 MB | 1,750.00 |
| | | Pentium III500 Mhz | 64 MB | 2,800.00 |

SPEEDPRO COMPUTERS

| | CPU | RAM | Price |
|---|---|---|---|
| 575 | | | |
| 5100 | Pentium 166 Mhz | 16 MB | $   560.00 |
| 5120 | Pentium 200 Mhz | 16 MB | 650.00 |
| 6100 | Pentium 300 Mhz | 32 MB | 795.00 |
| 6125 | Pentium II 300 Mhz | 32 MB | 1,450.00 |
| 7000 | Pentium II 400 Mhz | 64 MB | 1,750.00 |
| | Pentium III 500 Mhz | 64 MB | 2,800.00 |

5. Point to **Title** and double-click to enter that field. Press the SPACE BAR once. Double-click **FirstName**; press the SPACE BAR again. Double-click **LastName** and press ENTER.

   Continue to enter the letter address. Press the SPACE BAR to insert a space between fields. Insert punctuation as necessary between fields or at the end of a field.

6. Key the rest of the letter. Click **Close** in the dialog box when all merge codes have been inserted.

7. Check the spelling of the document.

8. Save the form file as **lrn-mrg**. The extension *.frm* is added automatically. Do not exit the form document.

DATE

FIELD(Title) Space FIELD(FirstName) Space FIELD(LastName)

FIELD(Department)

FIELD(Company)

FIELD(Address)

FIELD(City) Comma Space FIELD(State) Space FIELD(ZIP)

Dear Space FIELD(Title) Space FIELD(LastName):

Thank you for agreeing to present your paper titled FIELD(Speech) at the Lakeland Conference on Women in Employment to be held at the Omni Hotel in Milwaukee on March 15. Your presentation is scheduled for FIELD(Time) in the Blue Room. You may expect approximately 300 participants.

You are also invited to attend a dinner buffet in your honor on Friday afternoon at 5 p.m. We would appreciate your returning the enclosed reply card if you plan to join us at this special event.

FIELD(Title) FIELD(LastName), we look forward to your presentation and to your outstanding contribution to our program.

Sincerely yours (Enter 4 times) |Ms. Melody Wilson |Program Coordinator | xx

**Step 3: Complete the merge**

Now that the data file and form file have been prepared, you are ready to combine them into three letters.

1. With the form document displayed, click **Merge** on the Merge bar.

2. The Perform Merge dialog box displays. Observe that the Form document displays *Current Document* because you left *lrn-mrg* on the screen. *Lrn-data* is displayed in the Data Source box. Output shows *New Document*.

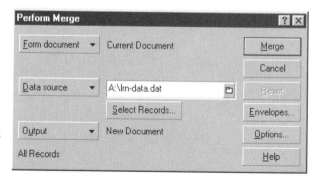

**81a • 5'**

**GETTING started**

## SKILLBUILDING WARMUP

| | | |
|---|---|---|
| alphabet | 1 | Jeff made Buzzy walk six hours to visit a quaint shopping center. |
| fig/sym | 2 | I paid $51.79 to ship the large executive desk (86" x 42" x 30"). |
| one hand | 3 | Barbara, as you are aware, gave Jim Millin a bad grade on a test. |
| easy | 4 | Pamela's goal is to bid for the ancient oak chapel on the island. |

| 1 | 2 | 3 | 4 | 5 | 6 | 7 | 8 | 9 | 10 | 11 | 12 | 13 |

**81b • Optional**

**SKILLBUILDING**

**Build straight-copy skill**

1. Key two 1' writings at your top rate.
2. Key a 1' writing at your control rate.

all letters                                                    gwam  2'

Most men and women in executive positions accept travel as a     6 | 50
part of corporate life.  At the same time, executives try to keep  13 | 57
time spent on the road to a minimum.  Top management usually     19 | 63
supports the efforts to reduce travel time as long as effective-  25 | 70
ness is not jeopardized.  One of the reasons for support is that  32 | 76
it is quite expensive for executives to travel.  Other reasons   38 | 82
are that traveling can be tiring and frequently causes stress.   44 | 89

2' | 1 | 2 | 3 | 4 | 5 | 6 |

**81c • 10'**

**Tabs**

Review setting tabs on the Ruler. Reference: Lesson 41 or TM10.

**Documents 1 and 2**

1. On the Ruler, set left, center, right, and decimal tabs as indicated.
2. Tab to key the first column.
3. Save as **81c-d1** and **81c-d2**.

Document 1

| Stafford | Phoenix | 10,000.00 | 36 months |
|---|---|---|---|
| Pell | San Francisco | 3,000.00 | 36 months |
| EEOG | Washington, D.C. | 14,000.00 | 48 months |
| Work Study | Atlanta | 8,000.00 | 9 months |

Left 1.5"    Center 3.5"    Decimal 5.25"    Right 7.0"

Document 2

| Apricot | P-525 | 1,895.00 | 560 |
|---|---|---|---|
| LSI | RX-1005 | 2,225.00 | 1,050 |
| Regent | Q-9498 | 1,530.00 | 850 |
| Quattro | M-43 | 2,950.00 | 2,000 |

Left 1.5"    Center 3.5"    Decimal 5.5"    Right 7.25"

6. Save the changes to your disk as **lrn-data**. The extension *.dat* will be added automatically, identifying the file as a data file. Should this extension get deleted accidentally, simply add it to the filename.

7. Review the file on your screen, looking for the following:

   • FIELDNAMES code is at the top of the document.

   • ENDFIELD follows each field. Does each record have 11 fields?

   • ENDRECORD follows each record. Do you have 3?

   • Hard Page code [HPg] separates each record.

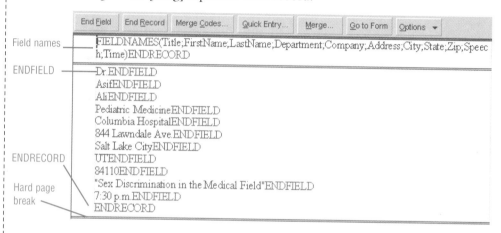

Field names — FIELDNAMES(Title;FirstName;LastName;Department;Company;Address;City;State;Zip;Speech;Time)ENDRECORD

ENDFIELD — Dr.ENDFIELD
AsifENDFIELD
AliENDFIELD
Pediatric MedicineENDFIELD
Columbia HospitalENDFIELD
844 Lawndale Ave.ENDFIELD
Salt Lake CityENDFIELD
ENDRECORD UTENDFIELD
84110ENDFIELD
Hard page break "Sex Discrimination in the Medical Field"ENDFIELD
7:30 p.m.ENDFIELD
ENDRECORD

Review the Data file Merge bar below. If you wish to get back to the Quick Data Entry dialog box, click the Quick Entry button. If you need to add codes, use the End Field or End Record buttons.

Data File Merge bar

### Step 2: Create the form document

The next step is to prepare the form document and insert merge fields to indicate the variables. You can key the form document by choosing *Merge* from the Tools menu and then clicking the **Create Document** button. However, if your data file is still open, simply click the **Go to Form** button on the Merge bar. *WordPerfect* then creates a link between the data file in the window and the new form document.

1. With the *lrn-mrg* data file displayed, click the **Go to Form** button on the Merge bar. The Associate dialog box appears.

2. Click **Create**. A new window displays. (Notice that the *Go to Form* button has been replaced by the *Go to Data* button.)

3. Position the insertion point for the letter dateline. Click the **Date** button on the Merge Bar. A red Date code automatically updates the date each time you merge the document.
   Press ENTER 4 times to position the insertion point for the letter address.

4. Click the **Insert Field** button on the Merge bar. The Insert Field Name or Number dialog box identifies the data file and lists the names of the fields.

## Dot tabs

A **leader** is a series of dots that leads the eye to the next column. Leaders are used in documents such as tables of contents, agendas, and financial documents. Leaders are created by setting a dot tab. Dot tabs can be set on the Ruler or from the Tab Set dialog box. The tab positions for this lesson are for the Ruler (absolute).

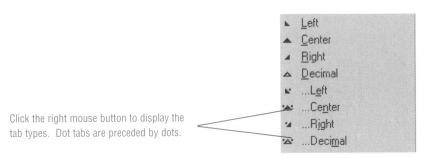

Click the right mouse button to display the tab types. Dot tabs are preceded by dots.

**Document 1**

1. Using the Ruler, clear all tabs. Then set a dot right tab at 7.25" for the second column; set DS.
2. Press TAB after each name; note that the leaders extend to the text.
3. Save as **81d-d1**.

Dot right 7.25"

John Sneider . . . . . . . . . . . . . . . . . . . . . . . . . . . . . . . . . . . . . .President

JoAnn Rouche . . . . . . . . . . . . . . . . . . . . . . .Vice President, Education

Janice Weiss  . . . . . . . . . . . . . . . . . . . .Vice President, Membership

Lotus Fijutisi . . . . . . . . . . . . . . . . . . . . . . .Chief Financial Officer

Loretta Russell  . . . . . . . . . . . . . . . . . . . . . .Recording Secretary

**Document 2**

1. Using the Ruler, set a right tab at 7.25". Set DS.
2. Key the column headings. Press ENTER.
3. Set a dot left tab at 6.75".
4. Key player name at left margin. Press TAB to insert leaders and again for last column.
5. Save as **81d-d2**.

| | Right 7.25" |
|---|---|
| **Player and Position** | **Points** |

| | Dot left 6.75" | |
|---|---|---|
| Nathaniel Hartwell—Small Forward . . . . . . . . . . . . . . . . . . . | | 220 |
| Cedric McCoy—Power Forward . . . . . . . . . . . . . . . . . . . . . . | | 250 |
| Robert Marschink—Center . . . . . . . . . . . . . . . . . . . . . . . . | | 190 |
| Joseph Manning—Point Guard . . . . . . . . . . . . . . . . . . . . . . | | 90 |
| Barry English—Shooting Guard . . . . . . . . . . . . . . . . . . . . . . | | 130 |

## Tabs in tables

Tabs can also be set within cells of a table. Text can be indented with a left tab, or numbers can be aligned at specific positions in cells by setting a decimal or right tab. Set a decimal tab if the numbers include decimals. Generally, it is easier to key the table and then set the tabs and align the text. Tabs can be set either on the Ruler or in the Tab Set dialog box. Using the Ruler is generally easier because your document is displayed.

**To set tabs in a table:**

1. Click in the cell where the tab will be set. Display the Ruler.
2. Clear all tabs.
3. Set the tab for the desired setting. (Tab settings provided are for the Ruler.)
4. Press CTRL + TAB at the beginning of the number to align the numbers in each cell.

**To create the data file:**

1. Select *Tools*, then *Merge*. The Merge dialog box displays.
2. Click the Create Data button. The Create Data File dialog box displays. You can manipulate the position of the fields or add and delete fields from this dialog box.
3. Enter each field name listed below in the Name a field box. Press ENTER after each entry. Click **OK** after entering all the field names.

Title
FirstName
LastName
Department
Company
Address
City
State
ZIP
Speech
Time

4. The Quick Data Entry dialog box displays with all the field names you have entered. Key the variables for Records 1–3 below.

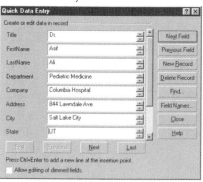

- Press ENTER after each variable.
- Do not space after keying the variable.
- Press CTRL + ENTER to add a line to a field.
- Use the Previous Field and Next Field buttons to move between fields to edit them.
- Press ENTER after the last field to complete the record.

| Field names | Record 1 | Record 2 | Record 3 |
|---|---|---|---|
| Title | Dr. | Dr. | Dr. |
| FirstName | Asif | Sharon | Jan |
| LastName | Ali | Abdul-Rahman | Doenier |
| Department | Pediatric Medicine | Orthopedic Surgery | OB/GYN Clinic |
| Company | Columbia Hospital | St. Mary's Hospital | St. Luke's Hospital |
| Address | 844 Lawndale Ave. | 4456 W. Lake Dr. | 3854 Sheridan Rd. |
| City | Salt Lake City | Milwaukee | Chicago |
| State | UT | WI | IL |
| ZIP | 84110 | 53221 | 60650 |
| Speech | "Sex Discrimination in the Medical Field" | "Women in the Medical Field" | "Recruiting Women in the Medical Field" |
| Time | 8:30 p.m. | 7:30 p.m. | 8 p.m. |

5. After keying the last record, click **Close**.

**81e,** *continued*

**Document 1**
**Tabs in table**

1. Key the table. Do not adjust column widths.
2. Center column headings.
3. On the Ruler, set a decimal tab in Cell B2 at position 4.5".
4. Press CTRL + TAB before each number to align the numbers in Columns B and C.

| City | Population | Registered Voters | |
|------|------------|-------------------|---|
| | | | 7 |
| Grand Blanc | 14,000 | 9,000 | 12 |
| Mt. Chester | 3,500 | 995 | 16 |
| Port Alexandria | 117,500 | 83,000 | 22 |
| Seaside | 1,853,000 | 792,000 | 27 |

**Document 2**
**Tabs in tables**

1. Key the heading outside the table. Key the table without formats. Insert the ⋆ from Iconic Symbols.
2. After the table is keyed, click in A2. Set a left tab at 1.25" on the Ruler.
3. Align A2–A8 and A10–A13 at the tab. Cells A1 and A9 should remain at the left margin.
4. Center-align Columns B and C.
5. Bold all headings.
6. Center the table horizontally. Adjust column widths using Size Column to Fit.
7. Using SpeedFormat, apply No Lines No Border style.
8. Center the page vertically.

LIST OF FREQUENTLY CALLED NUMBERS    7

| Place/Doctor | Speed# | Number | |
|--------------|--------|--------|---|
| | | | 13 |
| Children's Hospital | ⋆08 | 555-3822 | 19 |
| Davidson Pharmacy | ⋆07 | 555-~~1111~~ 7763 | 26 |
| Health Department | ⋆13 | 555-9874 | 32 |
| Heritage General Hospital | ⋆10 | 555-1283 | 40 |
| Northside Drive Pharmacy | ⋆12 | 555-3682 | 47 |
| Police Department | ⋆00 | 555-~~0087~~ 0891 | 53 |
| Westland Circle Pharmacy | ⋆01 | 555-8267 | 61 |
| Referring Physicians | | | 65 |
| Kozuma, Sam | *02 | 555-2145 | 70 |
| Sandhu, Al | *03 | 555-5765 | 75 |
| Nichols, Tom | *14 | 555-9321 | 79 |
| Rivera, Karen | *15 | 555-0428 | 85 |

**Document 3**
**Challenge**

1. Key the table; use QuickSum to obtain the totals.
2. Select all cells with numbers and change the numeric format to **Currency** with **2** decimal places.
3. Align the column headings at center and the numbers at the decimal.
4. Skew the cells. Choose Left Down.
5. Adjust column widths.

PARACOMMUNICATIONS, INC.    5

Quarterly Payroll Expenses    10

| Office | Salary | Fringe Benefits | Contributions | |
|--------|--------|-----------------|---------------|---|
| | | | | 19 |
| Riverside | 93600.58 | 15310.99 | 1900.25 | 26 |
| Pasadena | 1231400 | 32010.45 | 22500 | 33 |
| Northridge | 28431 | 8450 | 950 | 38 |
| Total | | | | 39 |

# Merge

Merge is an easy way to create a new document by combining information from two other documents. Use merge to personalize form letters, print labels, or address envelopes.

To create a merged document, you must merge a form file with a data file. The **form document** contains the message that remains the same for each person and the *merge fields* that indicate where to print the variables from the data file. The **data file** contains the names, addresses, or other variables that will change in each document.

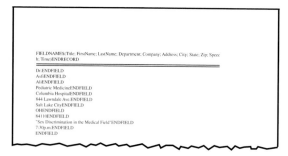

**Form Document**

**Final Document**

**Data File**

Three steps are required to create a merged document:

1) Set up the data file;  2) create the form document;  3) merge the data file and form document. The Merge dialog box will guide you.  Follow the steps to create your first merged document.

### Step 1:  Set up the data file

The data file includes the variables that will be merged with the form document. You can either open an existing file or create a new data file. You can also obtain the variables from a database file.  Become familiar with these new terms:

**Merge codes:**  Codes that instruct *WordPerfect* during the merge.

**Record:**  The variables for one individual.  ENDRECORD marks the end of a record.

**Merge field:**  Separate variables for each record.  ENDFIELD marks the end of a field.

# LESSON 82

# Review

**82a • 5'**

**G**ETTING
**started**

## SKILLBUILDING WARMUP

| | | |
|---|---|---|
| alphabet | 1 | David quickly won six big money prizes as the jockey of the year. |
| fig/sym | 2 | Please bill me for the supplies ($2,871.50) and fees ($1,394.65). |
| double letters | 3 | Lynn will call Tommy before the committee meets tomorrow at noon. |
| easy | 4 | Pamela may be the auditor for the endowment of the island chapel. |

| 1 | 2 | 3 | 4 | 5 | 6 | 7 | 8 | 9 | 10 | 11 | 12 | 13 |

**82b • 10'**

## SKILLBUILDING

**Build straight-copy skill**
Key a 1' and a 3' writing at your control rate.

 all letters                                          *gwam*   1'   3'

|  |  |  |
|---|---|---|
| The technology used in offices today requires employees to | 12 | 4 | 58 |
| be flexible and to be willing to learn new ways to accomplish the | 25 | 8 | 62 |
| work that they do.  Too often workers try to adapt the new tech- | 38 | 13 | 66 |
| nology to the old procedures rather than modify the way they do | 51 | 17 | 70 |
| work to maximize the advantages of the technology.  Although most | 64 | 21 | 75 |
| people think they can adapt to change very easily, the truth is | 77 | 25 | 79 |
| that change is very frustrating for most people.  The majority of | 90 | 30 | 83 |
| the changes in offices caused by technology are difficult to make | 103 | 34 | 88 |
| because many things have to change at the same time.  A change in | 116 | 39 | 92 |
| hardware or software requires changes in the way work is done as | 129 | 43 | 97 |
| well as learning to use the new software or hardware.  These | 141 | 47 | 101 |
| changes might be easier to implement if they could be made gradu- | 154 | 51 | 105 |
| ally rather than simultaneously. | 161 | 54 | 107 |

1' | 1 | 2 | 3 | 4 | 5 | 6 | 7 | 8 | 9 | 10 | 11 | 12 | 13 |
3' |     1     |        2        |        3        |        4        |

## 110c ● 35'

**Labels**

Print the labels on plain paper.

**Document 1**

**Single-address label**

1. Open *wheeler*. Copy the letter address.
2. In a New Blank Document screen, select *Avery 5163* address label.
3. Paste the address on the label. Select the address and convert it to UPPERCASE. Delete all punctuation.
4. Save as **110c-d1**. Print.

**Document 2**

**File-folder label**

Prepare file-folder labels for members of your class. Key in Index order: LAST NAME, FIRST NAME, MI. Use file-folder label Avery 5266.

**Document 3**

Prepare three different address labels: your address, your instructor's, and your parents'. Use any address label. Print.

**Document 4**

1. Prepare address labels using Avery 5163 for the persons listed below. Use proper address format. Assume they all live in Colorado Springs, CO.
2. Print all of the labels.

| | | | |
|---|---|---|---|
| Cox, John & Paula | 2000 Meadowlark Ln. | 80931-9874 | 555-0188 |
| Chang, Tao Chou | 110 Park Lane Rd. | 80933-0985 | 555-4689 |
| Gordon, Ronald | Route 2, Box 92 | 80935-4321 | 555-2238 |
| Luhanga, Lena | 609 Seville Place | 80934-5431 | 555-0997 |
| Maeda, Koji | 40 Holtsinger Ave. | 80914-9874 | 555-2506 |
| Nolen, Chris | 606 Lincoln St. | 80913-4327 | 555-8662 |
| Vinson, G. T. | 2710 Hillside Dr. | 80914-9874 | 555-8765 |

**Document 5**

**Name badges**

1. Begin a new document. Prepare a name badge for *Doe, John* using Avery 5395.
2. Select the name, and then center it and apply 36-point font. Center the name vertically on the badge by pressing ENTER before the name.
3. Create a second badge with your name. Use two lines for your name if it is long.

**Document 6**

**Custom badges**

1. From the Label dialog box, click **Create**.
2. Key the description **3 x .7 label**.
3. Change the Label size to width, 3"; height, .7".
4. Change the number of labels per page to 12 rows, 2 columns. Click **OK**.
5. Select the *3 x .7* label from the list box.
6. Key labels for John Doe and for yourself. Print.

FORMATTING

**Review**
**Document 1**

1. Key the table. Apply the Header Fill Single style. Center table horizontally and apply Size Column to Fit.
2. Save as **82c-d1a**. Print.
3. Sort in ascending order by Employee. Save as **82c-d1b**. Print.
4. Sort in ascending order by Department, then by Employee. Save as **82c-d1c**. Print.

### GOLDEN HANDSHAKE CANDIDATES

| Employee | Department | Hire Date |
|---|---|---|
| Thayer, Jeffrey | Information Systems | 8/21/75 |
| Stevenson, Allison | Human Resources | 7/27/72 |
| Lew, Richard | Marketing | 6/15/76 |
| Gore, Rajah | Information Systems | 8/16/76 |
| Castillo, Maria | Human Resources | 10/23/74 |
| Husaan, Miram | Information Systems | 12/2/72 |
| Nelson, Barbara | Marketing | 3/16/74 |
| Wallace, Reggie | Human Resources | 8/10/75 |

*words: 6, 12, 20, 29, 35, 43, 51, 60, 67, 75*

**Document 2**

1. Key the memo heading information. Then set a dot left tab at 6.75" and a right tab at 7.25".
2. Save as **82c-d2**.

**TO:** Marc L. Howard | **FROM:** Judith R. Baysmith | **DATE:** Current | **SUBJECT:** Reprints of Training Manuals

Our supply of training manuals is low. Please reprint the following manuals in the quantities indicated:

Dot left tab | Right tab

*Positive Customer/Client Service* . . . . . . . . . . . . . . . . . . . . 5,000
*Communicating with Power* . . . . . . . . . . . . . . . . . . . 300
*Teamwork—The Key to Productivity and Job Satisfaction* . . . . . . 1,875
*Career Strategies for Women in Management* . . . . . . . . . . . . . 750

We are totally out of the *Executive Secretary Program* manuals. However, we want to update the manual before it is reprinted. We will get the new copy to you within a few days.

*words: 15, 22, 36, 43, 51, 57, 69, 78, 93, 108, 114*

**Document 3**

1. Change the page orientation to landscape. Key the table.
2. Right-align the numbers in Columns C, D, E, and F.
3. Insert a formula in F3 that sums D3 and E3. Repeat for F4–F7.
4. Change the numeric format of Column F to **Commas** with **0** decimal places.
5. Save and print. Your document will not align as the one at the right.

### LAUREL SYSTEMS INCORPORATED

| Employee | Manager | Budget | Revenue Generated | | Total |
|---|---|---|---|---|---|
| | | | Office Systems | Publishing | |
| Anderson, John | Jackson | 1,256,840 | 315,875 | 257,931 | |
| Cheng, Lai Ling | Mendoza | 1,205,874 | 524,764 | 560,871 | |
| Nozaki, Mary | Larson | 1,283,764 | 75,384 | 28,760 | |
| Schultz, Timothy | Jackson | 895,962 | 265,987 | 329,841 | |
| Takasuchi, Ken | Larson | 1,249,085 | 82,150 | 25,075 | |

*words: 6, 9, 20, 30, 40, 49, 59, 68*

# Labels

**G**ETTING
s t a r t e d

Use Skillbuilding Warmup on p. 321.

110b ● 10'

**N E W
F U N C T I O N**

## Labels

Address labels are often needed when mailing documents that will not fit in a #10 envelope or documents that should not be folded. Labels are also prepared for file folders, nametags, and disks.

**To create a label:**

1. Choose *Labels* from the Format menu.

2. From the Labels list box, select the label you will be using. Click **Select**. Label types and numbers that are identified in the software correlate directly with the commercial paper labels that you put in the printer. (Note that the label is described in Label Details.)

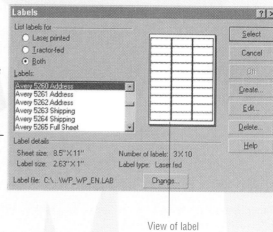

View of label

3. Key the label in the template provided. Use these keystrokes for labels:

| | |
|---|---|
| CTRL + ENTER | Moves to the next label. |
| ENTER | Ends a line of text within a label. |
| ALT + PgDn or ALT + PgUp | Moves to the next or previous label. |
| CTRL + g | Moves to a specific label. |

## Printing labels

To print a single copy of all labels, simply print in the usual manner. Sometimes you may only want to print specific labels or a range of labels.

**Drill**

In a New Blank Document screen, access the Labels dialog box. Scroll though the options to see the labels that are available.

**To print specific labels:**

1. Click **Print**, then choose *Multiple Pages* tab.
2. Select page(s), then type the number of each label or a range of labels.

| Type: | To Print: |
|---|---|
| 2 | Label 2 |
| 1,3,5 | Labels 1, 3, and 5 |
| 3  8 | Labels 3 and 8 (a space between 3 and 8) |
| -5 | Beginning of the document through Label 5 |
| 5- | Label 5 through the rest of the document |

3. Click **Print**.

## 83a ● 5'

### GETTING started

alphabet 1 Jacqueline Katz made extra money by singing with the five groups.
figures 2 I sold 27 roses, 10 irises, 68 lilies, 54 tulips, and 39 orchids.
space bar 3 If she may go with me to a lake, I may do all of the work and go.
easy 4 The girls got the bicycle at the land of enchantment at the lake.

| 1 | 2 | 3 | 4 | 5 | 6 | 7 | 8 | 9 | 10 | 11 | 12 | 13 |

## 83b ● 7'

### SKILLBUILDING

**Assess straight-copy skill**

Key one 5' writing.

all letters                                              *gwam*  3' | 5'

Employees who work together as a team are more effective    4 | 2 39
than those who work solo.   This concept is known as synergy.   8 | 5 42
Synergy simply means that the joint action exceeds the sum of  12 | 7 44
individual actions.   The results are not just in the quantity of  16 | 10 47
work; major gains in quality result when people work together as  21 | 12 49
a team.   Teamwork is critical for success.                24 | 14 51

What characterizes an excellent team member?   An excellent  28 | 17 53
team member understands the goals of the team and will place team  32 | 19 56
values above her or his individual objectives.   An excellent team  36 | 22 59
member helps to determine the most effective way to reach the  40 | 24 61
goals that were set by the group and will help to make each  44 | 27 63
decision that affects the group.   Above all, an excellent team  49 | 29 66
member will support a decision made by the team.   Each member  53 | 32 68
must understand her or his role and respect the roles of others.  57 | 34 71
Every member of a team must share in both victory and defeat.  61 | 37 74

3' |    1    |    2    |    3    |    4    |
5' |       1       |       2       |       3       |

## 83c ● 38'

### FORMATTING

**Assess production**

**Time schedule:**
Assemble materials . . . . .   5'
Timed production . . . . . .   25'
Final check . . . . . . . . . .   8'
When directed to begin, work for 25'. Correct all errors. Determine *n-pram*.

**Good organization enhances productivity.**
1. Check that the printer is turned on and supplied with paper.
2. Clear a space in your work area to place completed documents face down so that they will remain in the proper sequence.
3. Move quickly from one document to the next.

evening when people of the community can come together to socialize 185
and share their support of the schools of Okemos.  Also, this event 199
enables our chapter to raise funds to carry out projects for the next 213
school year," Sinago added. 219

    Artwork by Stephen Kimbrell, Douglas Aylward, Noor Hashim, 233
Anissa L. Hatfield, and Eugene Burrell will be auctioned during 246
the Friday night event.  "The artwork for this year's auction is quite 260
impressive," Sinago said.  "Many of the artists have gained national 274
recognition and have won numerous awards at local, state, and 287
national levels." 290

    In addition to the artwork to be auctioned, the talents of local stu- 304
dents will be highlighted.  A variety of entertainment, including 317
pianists, violinists, a string orchestra, and choral ensemble, is also 332
scheduled to begin at 7 p.m. 338

    The annual Celebration of the Arts is open to the public. 350
Reservations may be made by calling 555-3498.  Tickets will also be 363
available at the door. 368

### 369

**Document 2**
**Two-page news release**
1. Open *southridge* from the Formatting Template.
2. Save as **109c-d2**.
3. Key a footer for first page.
4. Key a header for second page.

**Document 3**
**Compose news release**
1. Use the information at the right to compose a news release. Add ¶ about Suarez Development Corp. Use Lesson 109b to develop the ¶.
2. Edit the release and correct errors. The release date is November 1. **Shelby Merchant** is the contact person.

Suarez will provide three $5,000 scholarships a year to students to study real estate or finance at any Tennessee college or university of the student's choice. Seniors from all public and private schools will be eligible. An independent selection committee will be established to screen applicants and select recipients. The State Department of Education has been asked to work with Suarez in developing the criteria to be used.

# on... News Releases

Public relations experts realize that to get their news printed, they must transmit news releases using the preferred method of the particular news media. Because weekly newspapers may prefer one method and local radio stations another, organizations are transmitting news releases in various ways. These transmissions may include

- mailing hard copies of news releases through traditional mail,
- faxing news releases,
- sending news releases as e-mail, and
- transmitting news releases electronically via modem connection.

Organizations are using other creative means to communicate their news, including posting to electronic services for news media, responding to media postings for news, and posting news releases on their own company Web pages.

**83c,** *continued*

**Document I**
**Sort table**
1. Format as a table; 1.5" top margin. Italicize foreign words.
2. Adjust column width manually.
3. Apply Row Fill Header style.
4. Save as **83c-d1a**. Print table.
5. Sort alphabetically by country in ascending order.
6. Save as **83c-d1b**. Print.

| | | words |
|---|---|---|
| *International Greetings* | | 5 |
| Country | Method of Greeting | 10 |
| Greece | Embrace and kiss both cheeks or shake hands. | 21 |
| Argentina | Shake hands and slightly nod head. Women may also kiss each other on the cheek, and men may embrace. | 32 / 39 / 43 |
| United States | Firm handshake. | 49 |
| Australia | Handshake between men. A man may shake a woman's hand only if she extends her hand first. | 59 / 67 / 69 |
| Thailand | Place both hands together at chest and bow slightly (the *wai*). | 79 / 84 |
| Belgium | Shake hands with a quick shake and light pressure. | 96 |
| Saudi Arabia | Shake hands. Males may also extend the left hand to the other's right shoulder, then kiss the left and right cheeks. | 108 / 117 / 122 |
| Chile | Shake hands and kiss the right cheek. | 131 |
| Russia | Shake hands. Older people may use the traditional three kisses on the cheeks. | 140 / 147 / 149 |
| Portugal | Shake hands with a warm, firm shake. | 158 |
| China | Nod, slightly bow, or shake hands. | 167 |
| Japan | Bow as low and long as the other person. | 176 |
| Fiji | Smile and flick up the eyebrows or shake hands. | 187 |
| India | Bend gently with palms together below chin (the *namaste*). | 196 / 200 |
| France | Shake hands. | 204 |

## FORMATTING

**Two-page news release**
Study the information and illustrations at the right.

Similar to other two-page documents, a two-page news release includes a header on the second page; the first page includes a footer. Note these points about a two-page release:

- Key the footer **-more-** at the bottom of the first page.
- Key a header on the second and subsequent pages. The header consists of a one-word "slug line," usually the first word of the subject line followed by a slash and page number (i.e., Celebration/2).
- Key **# # #** or **-30-** after the last line of a release to indicate the end of the news release.

In addition to the artwork to be auctioned, the talents of local students will be highlighted. A variety of entertainment, including pianists, violinists, a string orchestra, and choral ensemble, is also scheduled to begin at 7 p.m.

-more-

**Page 1 footer**

Celebration/2

The annual Celebration of the Arts is open to the public. Reservations may be made by calling 555-3498. Tickets will also be available at the door.

###

**Page 2 header**

**To create footer for first page:**
1. From the Insert menu, choose *Header/Footer*.
2. Select *Footer A*. Click **Create**.
3. Center **-more-**.
4. Position insertion point on page 2 and suppress Footer A (**Format** menu, **Page**, **Suppress**, **Footer A**).

**To create header for second page:**
5. Position insertion point on p. 2.
6. Select *Header A* in the Headers/Footers dialog box and click **Create**.
7. Key the first word of the subject line and **/**; click the **Page Numbering** button and select *Page Number*.

**Figure 1**    Header/Footer Property bar

**Document 1**
**Two-page news release**
1. A news release form has been created for you. Open *ppfe*. Save it as **109c-d1**.
2. Key the two-page news release.
3. Once the document is keyed, create a footer for the first page and a header for page 2.
4. Save again. Print.

(Document 1, *continued*)

| | words |
|---|---|
| Contact Person:  Sherry Sinago | 3 |
| Current date | 6 |
| For Release:  Immediately | 8 |

CELEBRATION TO BENEFIT SCHOOLS — 14

OKEMOS, MI—The Okemos Chapter of Parents' Partnership for — 25
Education will hold its annual Celebration of the Arts, Friday from — 40
7:30 to 11 p.m. at the Talbert Hotel. — 47

Participants will have an opportunity to enjoy an hors d'oeuvres — 60
buffet, see excellent musical and dramatic entertainment by students — 74
of Okemos Schools, view award-winning student artwork, and bid on — 87
artwork by locally and nationally known artists. — 97

An annual fundraising event for the Okemos Chapter of Parents' — 110
Partnership for Education, Celebration of the Arts serves several key — 124
purposes, according to organizers. — 131

"The Celebration of the Arts provides an opportunity to showcase — 144
the superior quality of talent that is being nurtured in the Okemos — 158
Schools," said Chapter President Sherry Sinago. "It also provides an — 172

words

**Document 2**
**Sort table**

1. Key table; apply the Row Fill Columns style. Center table horizontally. Adjust column widths. Save as **83c-d2a** and print.
2. Sort alphabetically by Country in ascending order.
3. Save as **83c-d2b** and print.
4. Sort in descending order by Unit, then in ascending order by Country. Save as **83c-d2c** and print.

## CURRENCY UNITS OF VARIOUS COUNTRIES

| Country | Unit | |
|---------|------|---|
| Italy | Lira | 12 |
| Austria | Schilling | 16 |
| Norway | Krone | 18 |
| Belgium | Franc | 21 |
| Portugal | Escudo | 24 |
| Canada | Dollar | 27 |
| Russia | Ruble | 30 |
| Denmark | Krone | 33 |
| Spain | Peseta | 35 |
| France | Franc | 38 |
| Sweden | Krona | 41 |
| Germany | Deutsche Mark | 45 |
| Switzerland | Franc | 48 |
| Greece | Drachma | 51 |
| Turkey | Lira | 54 |
| Holland | Guilder | 57 |

*(Country / Unit header row: 10)*

**Document 3**
**Formulas**

1. Key the table; apply Column Fill Header style. Right-align Columns B–F. Save as **83c-d3a**.
2. Total the numbers in each column.
3. Insert a column to the right of the table. Label it **Average**. Enter a formula in G2 to calculate the average; copy it to other rows.
4. Change the numeric format to **Commas** with **0** decimal places.
5. Center the table horizontally and apply Size Column to Fit.
6. Save as **83c-d3b** and print.

## U.S. RESIDENTS TRAVELING OVERSEAS

### (In Thousands)

| Destination | 1990 | 1991 | 1992 | 1993 | 1994 | |
|-------------|------|------|------|------|------|---|
| Western Europe | 7,979 | 6,215 | 2,929 | 7,217 | 7,786 | 26 |
| Eastern Europe | 304 | 334 | 527 | 667 | 708 | 33 |
| Caribbean | 3,230 | 3,456 | 3,241 | 3,574 | 3,630 | 41 |
| South America | 911 | 1,133 | 1,102 | 1,231 | 1,488 | 50 |
| Central America | 608 | 566 | 942 | 924 | 762 | 57 |
| Middle East | 528 | 290 | 782 | 838 | 889 | 63 |
| Far East | 2,542 | 2,570 | 2,730 | 2,570 | 3,267 | 71 |
| Oceania | 576 | 537 | 511 | 564 | 581 | 77 |
| Total | | | | | | 78 |

*(Title row: 7; subtitle: 10; header row: 17)*

# News Releases

**109a ● 10'**

## GETTING started

1. Prepare the news release form shown.
2. Save as **suarez**.

---

**SUAREZ CORPORATION** —— 18 pt.

**1986 Briarwood Cir.** —— 12 pt.

**Memphis, TN 38116-1986**

Horizontal line

**(901) 555-6032** | **(901) 555-2833 FAX**

DS

**NEWS RELEASE**                                     **Contact Person:**

DS

**For Release:**                         Right tab 7.5" on the Ruler

---

**109b ● 20'**

## FORMATTING

### News release

Read the information at the right. Then key the document below.

### News release

A **news release** conveys information an organization wishes to publish. An organization prepares a news release for a newspaper or other news media.

A news release states the most important information first. Then if it needs to be shortened, it can be cut from the end. A subject line may be suggested. When possible, the maximum length is one page.

### Format

• Use default side margins.
• Include the current date and the release date.
• Include the name of a contact person to assist the publisher in verifying facts.
• Begin ¶ 1 with the city (UPPERCASE) and then the state abbreviation.

---

**SUAREZ CORPORATION**
**1986 Briarwood Cir.**
**Memphis, TN 38116-1986**

(901) 555-6032                              (901) 555-2833 Fax

**NEWS RELEASE**                          **Contact Person:** Barbara Hatten
April 30, 200-
**For Release:** Immediately

SUAREZ ACQUIRES LOCAL COMPANY

   MEMPHIS, TN—Suarez Corporation announced today that it acquired Cumberland Printing Services. Jonah Suarez, president, indicated that Hugh Strahan, president of Cumberland, will serve as vice president of Suarez Corporation. All Cumberland employees will transfer to Suarez.

   The acquisition marks Suarez's entry into the office services arena. Suarez will offer complete desktop publishing and printing services as well as introduce a full range of multimedia services.

                          ###

---

### Document
### One-page news release

1. Open *suarez* prepared in 109a. Save as **109b**. Add text following "For Release" and "Contact Person."
2. Key the news release at the right.
3. Save again; print.

|  | words |
|---|---|
| Contact Person: Barbara Hatten \| Current date \| For Release: Immediately \| SUAREZ MOVES HEADQUARTERS | 10 |
|  | 14 |
| MEMPHIS, TN—The Suarez Corporation announced today that it is consolidating its statewide offices and moving its headquarters to Memphis. The company has leased space in the Davenport Building until its Churchill Tower can be built. | 26 |
|  | 40 |
|  | 54 |
|  | 61 |
| Suarez employs 785 people. Of the 785 employees, 300 are expected to transfer to Memphis. During the next 15 months, Suarez expects to hire 500 employees in sales, administrative support, accounting, engineering, architectural, and management areas. | 73 |
|  | 88 |
|  | 103 |
|  | 112 |
| Suarez develops projects through the South. Its primary focus is commercial real estate development. Suarez has already developed 3 shopping centers in the Hammond area and 25 in the state. | 125 |
|  | 139 |
|  | 150 |
| ### | 151 |

## Objective Assessment

Answer the questions below to see if you have mastered the content of this module.

1. Default tabs are set every _____.

2. List the two orientations in which a document may be printed: _____ and _____.

3. The _____ feature will add numbers above or to the left.

4. Use the _____ _____ command to repeat a formula.

5. _____ are often used in documents to guide the eye from one column to the next.

6. To align text in a table at a left or right tab, press _____ + _____.

7. To add a row at the end of the table, place the insertion point in the last cell and press _____.

8. *WordPerfect* allows you to sort _____ and _____ in both ascending and descending order.

9. _____ contains preformatted styles that can be applied to tables.

10. The _____ feature automatically adjusts the widths of the columns.

## Performance Assessment

### Document 1
### Table with totals

1. Format the title in 14 point and bold.
2. Calculate totals in Column E and Row 8.
3. Right-align numbers. Change the numeric format to **Commas** with **0** decimal places.
4. Center the table horizontally and apply Size Column to Fit.
5. Save as **ck11-d1** and print. Do not close.

### Documents 2 and 3
### Sort in tables

1. Sort *ck11-d1* by Total per Person in descending order.
2. Save as **ck11-d2** and print.
3. Sort by Total per Person in ascending order.
4. Save as **ck11-d3** and print.

| A-1 ELECTRONICS First Quarter Sales | | | | |
|---|---|---|---|---|
| **Salesperson** | **January** | **February** | **March** | **Total per Person** |
| Cheryl Ignasio | 17,000 | 11,000 | 15,000 | |
| Patrick Manning | 21,500 | 19,000 | 23,000 | |
| Hillary Salinas | 19,500 | 18,000 | 21,000 | |
| Alex Trombley | 25,000 | 22,500 | 27,700 | |
| Doan Vu | 26,000 | 24,300 | 28,900 | |
| Total Sales | | | | |

**Document 3**
Use a 1" or 1.5" top margin, depending on the length of the minutes.

words

**SALES KICK-OFF MEETING**          5
**July 1, 200-**          7

**Action Minutes**          10

**Presiding:**  Susan Easley          15

**Participants:**  Jim Crabtree, J. F. Lee, Samantha VonKohn, Susan Wren,          29
Bill Rockel, and Tony Rigdon          35

President Easley summarized the results for the year and commended the          49
Southern Region for attaining its goals.  She presented 93 President's Club          64
awards (list attached).          69

Bill Rockel, national sales manager, presented the new directions and the          84
marketing strategies to attain the goals set.  A 20 percent increase in over-          100
all sales is the target for the year.          107

Samantha VonKohn, vice president of human resources, presented the new          122
compensation plans and announced that dental coverage is now provided.          136

Attachment          138

**Document 4**

SYSTEMS FOR EMPLOYMENT TRAINING   *} Bold and Center*          6
March 1, 200-  _DS_          9
Action Minutes          12

Presiding:  Cynthia Housely _DS_          18
Participants:  Janete Garriga, Diane Rodgers, Cary Tabb,          29
Nancy Riser, Ricky Boler, W. C. Wax, Jr., and Anne Stokes          41

Cynthia Housely welcomed the group and announced that          52
Systems Training, Inc. was the host for the meeting.  In          63
addition, Systems invited the group to serve as consultants          75
in the development of computer-based training systems.          86

*Cary Tabb*
~~Anne Stokes~~ presented a summary of his workplace analysis; a          98
copy is attached.  He summarized that the primary jobs ~~that~~          109
~~were~~ being targeted today were entry-level workers in the          120
medical, clerical, and basic services area.  The skills          131
required fit in the broad categories of technical job          141
skills, communication skills, interpersonal skills, and          153
workplace dynamics.          157

Ricky Boler reported on *three* ~~3~~ pilot programs.  His report          169
showed that all three programs showed initial promise.  The          181
computer-based programs were far more successful than the          192
traditional programs.  A report will be completed in ~~2~~ *two*          204
weeks; and Ricky will mail a copy to all participants.          215

^ *Attachment*          217

# REPORT MASTERY

## OBJECTIVES

1. Format business reports with preliminary pages.

2. Format reports with endnotes, footnotes, and hyperlinks.

3. Extend skillbuilding speed and accuracy.

## LESSON 84

## Skillbuilding/Editing

### 84a ● 5'

**GETTING started**

each line 3 times SS; DS between 3-line groups

### SKILLBUILDING WARMUP

| | | |
|---|---|---|
| alphabet | 1 | Buzz McGuy worked at a very quaint shop just six miles from here. |
| figures | 2 | A 42-acre track of land has a 5,086 ft. frontage on Highway 3791. |
| direct reaches | 3 | Joycelyn is a young bright nurse in a zany brown checked uniform. |
| easy | 4 | Claudia did sign both forms for the auditor and paid the penalty. |

| 1 | 2 | 3 | 4 | 5 | 6 | 7 | 8 | 9 | 10 | 11 | 12 | 13 |

### 84b ● 8'

**SKILLBUILDING**

Key each pair of lines 3 times; rekey any lines that were difficult to key.

1st row
5 Zack will wax the five cabs to be used by the civic club members.
6 Vivian's bunny munched many bunches of carrots and nine cabbages.

2d row
7 Jackson said that Haskins made good grades in all of his classes.
8 Sally Davis saw me after she called all her classmates last week.

3d row
9 Were these top-quality reporters equipped to work out the detail?
10 The quiet reporter, Rhett Roper, quipped that her tips were tops.

4th row
11 Invoice #95786 (2/10, n/30) included interest ($29,040 @ 8%/mo.).
12 He received a check (#7209) for $1,865.34 that was dated 12/24/99!

| 1 | 2 | 3 | 4 | 5 | 6 | 7 | 8 | 9 | 10 | 11 | 12 | 13 |

## 108e ● 30'

**Agenda and action minutes**

Study the information at the right. Then key Documents 1-4.

Summary-type documents such as agendas, minutes, and itineraries are generally formatted similar to reports. An **agenda** is a list of items that will be covered at a meeting. Items are often numbered for longer meetings, especially with attachments relating to specific agenda items. Use 1" or 1.5" top margin, depending on the length of the document. Use default side and bottom margins.

In an agenda, names are aligned flush right with leaders. For action minutes, drag the left indent marker to align headings that wrap to two or more lines.

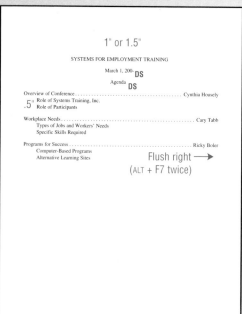

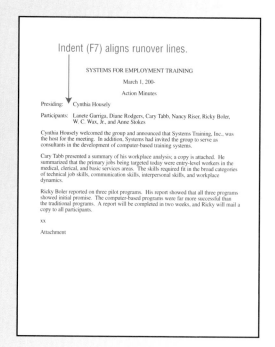

**Documents 1-2**

Format the agendas, using a 1.5" top margin.
Use Flush Right to align the names.

words

**CONVENTION PLANNING COMMITTEE** — 6
**October 15, 200-** — 9

**Agenda** — 11

Welcome . . . . . . . . . . Faye Jones, President — 17

Goal Setting . . . . . . . . Planning Committee — 23
    Attendance — 25
    Trade Show — 28

Development of Theme . . Planning Committee — 36

Program Topics. . . . . A. L. Ty, Program Chair — 43

words

**PTA Meeting** — 2
**November 8, 200-** — 6

**Agenda** — 7

Welcome . . . . . . . . Jane Windham, President — 14

Remarks . . . . . . . . . Janet Smith, Principal — 20

Reports . . . . . . Wilma Cook, Superintendent — 27
    Public School Partnerships — 32
    Bond Referendum Update — 37

Program . . . . . . . . . . Second Grade Classes — 42

## SKILLBUILDING

**Build straight-copy skill**
1. Key three 1' writings at your top rate.
2. Key two 3' writings at your control rate.

*all letters*                                                              *gwam* 1'  3'

Technical, human, and conceptual skills are the three types      12  4 35
of skills all supervisors are expected to have.  The skills are  25  8 40
quite different, and they vary in importance depending on the    37 12 44
level of the supervisor in an organization.  Technical skills    50 16 48
refer to knowing how to do the job.  Human skills relate to      62 20 52
working with people and getting them to work as a team.  Concep- 74 25 56
tual skills refer to the ability to see the big picture as well  87 29 60
as how all the parts fit together.                               94 31 63

```
1' | 1 | 2 | 3 | 4 | 5 | 6 | 7 | 8 | 9 | 10 | 11 | 12 | 13 |
3' |     1     |       2       |        3        |       4       |
```

84d ● 25'

**NEW FUNCTION**

## Go To

The **Go To** function is useful to move quickly to a specific location on a specific page in a document.  For example, you can move to a table, to a specific range of cells within a table, to a bookmark, or to a column.  The options depend upon the format of the document.

1. With a document open on the screen, choose *Go To* from the Edit menu.
2. Click the item you wish to access in the Go to what box.
3. Enter the appropriate number in the Enter number text box. (The name of the text box changes depending on the item chosen.)
4. Click **Go To**.

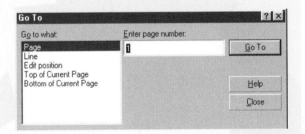

**Drill 1**

Open *meade* from the template disk.  Save it as **84d**.  You will use it in Drills 1, 2, and 3.  Follow the steps at the right.

Use the Go To function to practice moving to the following locations:

1. Page 4          After moving to page 4, the status line reads: "Pg _____, Ln _____."
2. Footnote 1      The insertion point is on page_____.
3. The next table  The title of the table is _____.
4. Page 1          The title is on page 1, line _____.

**Drill 2**

File *84d* should be displayed.

1. Use the Go To function to move to the table.
2. Use Cut and Paste to move the table immediately above the side heading

"Outpatient Expansion Proposed."

3. Print only p. 3 of the report (Print dialog box).  Do not save.

# LESSON 108

# Agenda and Action Minutes

**108a ● 5'**

## GETTING started

### SKILLBUILDING WARMUP

alphabet 1 My objectives were analyzed very quickly during that proxy fight.

figures 2 We need 240 orchards, 1,396 roses, 287 carnations, and 510 tulips.

shift 3 Pat, Ty, Max, Al, and Rod took the test;  Jan, Ben, and I did not.

easy 4 The panel may blame us for the toxic odor problems on the island.

| 1 | 2 | 3 | 4 | 5 | 6 | 7 | 8 | 9 | 10 | 11 | 12 | 13 |

**108b ● 10'**

## NEW FUNCTION

### Flush Right

**Flush Right** inserts leaders and automatically aligns text at the right margin.  Flush Right is appropriate when the data in the right column consists of text rather than digits.

### Drill

Key the text at the left margin and press ALT + F7 twice.

Pitcher . . . . . . . . . . . . . . . . . . . . . . . . . . . . . . . . . . . Matthew Daniel
First base . . . . . . . . . . . . . . . . . . . . . . . . . . . . . . . . . . John D. Forde
Second base . . . . . . . . . . . . . . . . . . . . . . . . . . . . . . . . Jeff Watson
Third base . . . . . . . . . . . . . . . . . . . . . . . . . . . . . . . . Miquel Sanchez
Shortstop . . . . . . . . . . . . . . . . . . . . . . . . . . . . . . . . Patrick Johnson

**108c ● 5'**

## FORMATTING

**Review Indent**

Indent establishes a temporary left margin at tab positions.

1. Key the headings in bold, then press **F7** to indent. In the second heading, the text will wrap to the first tab.
2. DS to key the ¶.

Tab

**Presiding:** → Cynthia Housely

**Participants:**  Lanete Garriga, Diane Rodgers, Cary Tabb, Nancy Riser, Ricky Boler, W. C. Wax, Jr., and Anne Stokes

↑ Press F7 to indent second line to tab (Pos 2").

Cynthia Housely welcomed the group and announced that Systems Training, Inc. was the host for the meeting.  In addition, Systems had invited the group to serve as consultants in the development of computer-based systems.

**108d ●**

## SKILLBUILDING

Take three 1' timings. Try to complete the ¶.

 all letters/figures                                    *gwam*  1'

   Some  people  may  debate  that  quality  is  more  vital  than      12
quantity.   They  also  may  argue  that  poor  work  can't  be  justified   25
by  merely  increasing  a  worker's  output.   However,  if  a  minimum     38
quantity  can't  be  produced,  then  the  standard  of  quality  may  not   51
have  any  real  significance  in  the  market.   Perhaps  the  best  view   64
is  one  that  expects  high  quality  yet  recognizes  a  need  for  a  mini-  77
mum  of  output.                                                          79

| 1 | 2 | 3 | 4 | 5 | 6 | 7 | 8 | 9 | 10 | 11 | 12 | 13 |

**84d,** *continued*

## Find and Replace

The **Find** function is used to locate specific text or codes in a document. The **Replace** function will replace text or codes with different material. *WordPerfect's* default is to search forward from the insertion point, although this can be changed in the Options menu. The drop-list arrows in the text boxes display previously specified text or codes; this allows you to repeat a previously used search.

### To find text:

1. Choose *Find and Replace* from the Edit menu.
2. Key the item(s) to be located in the Find text box.
3. Click the **Find Next** button to locate the first occurrence of the text.

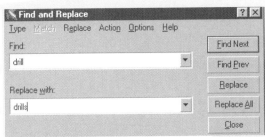

### Other Find Options

To find formatting codes such as margins, click the **Type** drop-down list. To repeat a previous search, click the drop-list arrows in the text box to display previous searches. To find only text that matches in case, font type, or codes such as bold or italic, key the text you want to find in the Find text box and select *Match*. Choose from one of the options.

### To replace text:

1. Key the new text in the Replace with text box. If you wish to delete the text and not replace it, leave <Nothing> in the Replace with text box.

2. Click **Replace** to replace the text and to search for the next occurrence. When the find and replace is complete, a dialog box displays indicating no more matches. If you do not wish to replace the selected text, click the Find Next button to continue.

3. To replace every occurrence of the text without being prompted at each occurrence, click **Replace All**.

4. Return to your document by clicking **Close**.

When keying the word you wish to find, do *not* space after the word or *WordPerfect* will not locate the word when it appears at the end of a sentence. See "Meade" in Drill 3.

### Drill 3

1. File *84d* should be displayed.
2. Open the Find and Replace dialog box. Click each menu to review the options.
3. First find each instance of the words in the first column at right.
4. Then find and replace the words with the ones shown in the second column.
5. Ensure that all instances of the words were replaced; then print the file without saving it.

| Find | Replace with |
|---|---|
| 1. Meade | Meade-Enright |
| 2. doctors | physicians |
| 3. projected | estimated |
| 4. Left margin 1.5" code | 1" |

### Drill 4

1. Open *report* from the formatting template. Save as **84d-d4**.
2. Find each occurrence of "Typeface."
3. Find each occurrence of "Typeface"; match the case.
4. Find each occurrence of "Brochure"; match the case.
5. Find and replace each occurrence of "brochure" with "announcement." Do not match the case.

## SKILLBUILDING

**Build straight-copy skill**

1. Key two 3' writings (strive to increase speed).
2. Key one 5' writing at your control rate.

  all letters                                                                          *gwam*  3' | 5'

|   |   |   |
|---|---|---|

Rightsizing is a word that brings fear to many people be- 4 | 2 | 54
cause it is frequently associated with layoffs. Just a few 8 | 5 | 56
years ago, companies added layers of management. Today, the 12 | 7 | 59
trend is quite different; companies are getting rid of layers of 16 | 10 | 61
management. They often describe themselves as becoming "lean and 21 | 12 | 64
mean." Two extremely complex issues must be addressed. One key 25 | 15 | 66
issue is the number of employees who must cope with job loss. 29 | 17 | 69
The other key issue is managing a company with a new structure 33 | 20 | 72
and with employees who fear that they may be in the next group of 38 | 23 | 74
workers on the list to be eliminated. 40 | 24 | 76

Coping with job loss is never easy. Usually it damages an 44 | 27 | 78
employee's self-concept. Some people respond to the situation by 49 | 29 | 81
becoming very angry. Often those who survived the layoff have 53 | 32 | 83
similar problems. Many feel guilty that they still have a job, 57 | 34 | 86
and they no longer trust the company. These reactions are very 61 | 37 | 88
normal, but they do not solve the problem. Both those employees 66 | 39 | 91
who have lost their jobs and those who remain in the company must 70 | 42 | 94
focus their efforts on the future rather than bemoan the past. 74 | 45 | 96
One lesson they should learn is that their careers are too valu- 79 | 47 | 99
able to entrust to the company to manage. Each person must 83 | 50 | 101
be responsible for managing his or her own career. 86 | 52 | 103

3' | 1 | 2 | 3 | 4
5' | 1 | 2 | 3

107d ● 15'

## COMMUNICATION

**Compose as you key**

Assume you are a department manager. Compose a memo to Maxine stating in one or two paragraphs how you think members of your department will react to the program.

107e ● 5'

## SKILLBUILDING

**Review ten-key pad**

Go to the Open Screen of *Numeric Keypad.* Complete this drill.

---

### Wellness Program

Maxine Findlay of the Human Resources Department has contracted to use without charge the facilities at Xavier's gym. This privilege is an extension of the wellness policy your company adopted last January.

| a | b | c | d | e |
|---|---|---|---|---|
| 54 | 456 | 500 | 664 | 506 |
| 78 | 86 | 900 | 870 | 764 |
| 12 | 31 | 102 | 718 | 224 |

## LESSON 85

**85a ● 5'**

### GETTING started

each line 3 times SS; DS
between 3-line groups

alphabet 1 Vicky quizzed us about the way we plan on adjusting the tax form.
fig/sym 2 Pay the $846.59 invoice (#47536 with 2/10, n/30 terms) on 8/1/99.
adjacent reaches 3 Teresa and Mario were going to read about the great polo players.
easy 4 Rick may fix fish for us at the lake, or he may make a lamb dish.

| 1 | 2 | 3 | 4 | 5 | 6 | 7 | 8 | 9 | 10 | 11 | 12 | 13 |

**85b ● 10'**

### SKILLBUILDING

**Specific finger drills**
Key each pair of lines twice;
rekey any lines that were
difficult to key.

1st/2d 5 Hunter threw that bag out after Trey brought the china back here.
6 Braden and Joyce bought five large blueberry bushes for the yard.

2d/3d 7 Dick and Louis will call six legislators from the Sixth District.
8 Did Lois lose her new gold locket this week before she left home?

3d/4th 9 Was Zam planning to play polo or squash with Alexis last weekend?
10 Alexis Zimple was too lazy to plan and write six short proposals.

| 1 | 2 | 3 | 4 | 5 | 6 | 7 | 8 | 9 | 10 | 11 | 12 | 13 |

**85c ● 12'**

### SKILLBUILDING

**Build straight-copy skill**
1. Key two 1' writings on
each ¶. Strive to increase
keystroking speed.
2. Key one 5' writing; proofread; circle errors; determine *gwam*.

all letters                                          *gwam*    1' | 5'

Working at home is not exactly a new phenomenon, but the con-    12 | 2 | 47
cept is growing quite rapidly.   For many years, people have worked    26 | 5 | 50
at home.   In most instances, they were self-employed and operated    39 | 8 | 52
a business from their homes.   Today, the people who work at home    52 | 10 | 55
fit into a variety of categories.   Some own their own businesses;    65 | 13 | 58
others bring extra work home after the workday ends.   A key change    79 | 16 | 60
is the large group of people who are employed by huge organizations    92 | 18 | 63
but who work out of home offices.   These employees are in jobs that    106 | 21 | 66
include sales, creative, technical, and a host of other categories.    120 | 24 | 69

The real change that has occurred is not so much the numbers    12 | 26 | 71
of people who are working at home and the variety of jobs, but the    26 | 29 | 74
complex tools that are now available for doing the job.   Technology    39 | 32 | 76
has truly made the difference.   In many cases, clients and customers    53 | 35 | 79
are not even aware that they are dealing with individuals working    66 | 37 | 82
at home.   Computers, printers, fax machines, telephone systems,    79 | 40 | 84
and other office equipment enable the worker in the home to function    93 | 42 | 87
in the same way as workers in a typical business office.    104 | 45 | 89

| 1' | 1 | 2 | 3 | 4 | 5 | 6 | 7 | 8 | 9 | 10 | 11 | 12 | 13 |
| 5' | | 1 | | | 2 | | | 3 | | | | | |

# ADMINISTRATIVE AND EMPLOYMENT DOCUMENTS

## OBJECTIVES

1. Format agendas, minutes, itineraries, news releases, and labels.

2. Create mail merge documents.

3. Compose and format employment documents.

3. Assess employment skills.

## LESSON 107 — Skillbuilding

### 107a ● 5'

**GETTING started**

Key each line 3 times (slowly, faster, slowly); repeat selected lines if time permits. Follow these directions for all Skill-building Warmups in this module.

### 107b ● 10'

**SKILLBUILDING**

Key each set of specific rows (third and first row) twice.

Reach to the first and third rows with a minimum of hand movement; keep hands quiet.

### SKILLBUILDING WARMUP

alphabet 1 Buzz McGuy worked at a very quaint shop just six miles from here.

figures 2 Is that 1240- x 1375-foot lot 26 miles out on Highway 689 or 793?

adjacent reaches 3 Porter and Guy were quite sad; we quickly tried to cheer them up.

easy 4 Chan may go to the land of enchantment on the island by the lake.

| 1 | 2 | 3 | 4 | 5 | 6 | 7 | 8 | 9 | 10 | 11 | 12 | 13 |

**third row**

5 We refused to support your ideas to greet the trio of protesters.

6 Peter tested his theory of selling quality ideas to his superior.

7 We were to report at a ferry to people who had written the story.

8 Your pewter is too twisted to put out for your top people to use.

9 Tip is our top reporter for writing up the story of the oil pipe.

**first row**

10 Mendez came in a cab for a minimum of six dozen zinnias and mums.

11 My bunny munched five dozen boxes of beans and a bin of cabbages.

12 Boxing can be viewed at varied time zones on Mayfoxx Cablevision.

13 Numerous local ZIP Codes were available for box-address mailings.

14 Much to the concern of Vivian, boxcars occupy the condemned zone.

| 1 | 2 | 3 | 4 | 5 | 6 | 7 | 8 | 9 | 10 | 11 | 12 | 13 |

## Thesaurus

The **Thesaurus** function is an online reference that enables the user to look up the definitions of words and to replace words with synonyms, antonyms, or related words.

**To use Thesaurus:**

1. Select the word you wish to replace.
2. Choose *Thesaurus* from the Tools menu.
3. Click the Options box and select *Auto Look Up* and synonyms (the defaults) if they are not checked.
4. Click the **+** (plus) next to the definition to display a list of synonyms.
5. Choose a suitable word; then click **Replace**. (Note the definition displays.)
6. To replace another word, select the word and click **Look Up**.

Always read the entire sentence to see if it needs to be edited when a word has been replaced. For example, if you replace "suitable" with "appropriate" in the ¶ at the right, you must change the article *a* to *an*. ■

**Drill**

1. Key the ¶ as it appears; DS.
2. Replace each bold word with a suitable alternative.
3. Read the sentence with replacements to be sure they make sense.

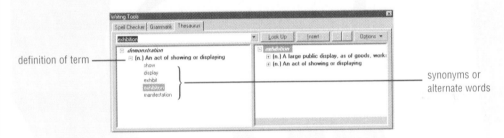

definition of term —

synonyms or alternate words

A thesaurus is a **handy** reference. If you **often** overuse **particular** words, the online thesaurus is useful in finding appropriate substitutes. To learn to use the Thesaurus function, key this paragraph as it appears. Then use Thesaurus to look up the words in bold and select a **suitable** word from the list **supplied**.

85e ● 13'

**FORMATTING**

**Reinforcement**

**Document 1**
**Unbound report**

1.5" top margin; default side and bottom margins; SS and block ¶s; DS between ¶s. Heading: bold; 14-point type.

**Document 2**
**Leftbound report**

Reformat the report as a leftbound report. Use the thesaurus to replace "employees" with another word. Use 1.5" top and left margins; default right and bottom margins. DS; indent ¶s.

Block SS ¶s; indent DS ¶s. ■

### TELECOMMUTING

Employees of Madison, Inc. requested the option to telecommute on a part-time basis. A survey of employees indicated that 20 percent of the employees would work at home a minimum of two days per week if the option were available. About 10 percent of the employees would prefer to work at home five days per week.

*(Key the two paragraphs from the timed writing in 85c here.)*

Employees estimated the cost of equipping each home office to be $2,000. They believe that staggering the days in which telecommuting employees report to the office would save enough rent to offset the equipment costs. These costs would have to be validated prior to making a final decision.

## Objective Assessment

Answer the questions below to see if you have mastered the content of this module.

1. The Clipart Scrapbook can be accessed through the _____ button on the _____ toolbar.

2. To select a graphic, _____.

3. _____ appear around the perimeter of a graphic when it is selected.

4. To keep the original proportions of a graphic when resizing it, drag the _____ of the graphic.

5. In a report, the preliminary page numbers are formatted with _____ numerals.

6. Using the Border/Fill feature, you can place borders around _____ or _____.

7. What feature may identify possible errors in subject/verb agreement? _____

8. What type of column would you use to format a document in two columns of equal length?
   _____

9. To return the insertion point to a specific location the next time you open the document, you would insert a/an
   _____.

10. Use a/an _____ to mark several positions within a document.

## Performance Assessment
### Unbound report with newspaper columns
1. Format the main heading as a TextArt banner.
2. Format the report into two balanced columns. SS the body.
3. Prepare a title page for **Riko Lin** by **you** as **Manager of Human Resources**; use current date.

|  | words |
|---|---|
| **OUTSOURCING—THE OTHER SIDE** | 6 |

This report summarizes a study that was 14
requested by the Executive Committee to 22
determine the downsides of outsourcing, if 30
any. A careful review of the current literature 40
and interviews with executives in a number of 49
companies involved in outsourcing provided 58
the data for this report. The full report docu- 67
ments all sources used. 72

The trend of companies to purchase from out- 81
siders those products and services previously 90
produced by their own employees has a num- 99
ber of disadvantages. This trend certainly cre- 108
ates tensions between unions representing 117
workers and management. In fact, union 125
strikes precipitated by outsourcing virtually 134
shut down several major companies, resulting 143
in losses far greater than the savings gener- 152
ated by outsourcing. Outsourcing may be a 160
key factor in energizing labor unions. 169

Numerous other problems surfaced during the 177
interviews. A number of companies reported 186
that the savings promised far exceeded the sav- 196
ings actually generated. One large organiza- 205
tion reported that the 38 percent savings the 214
consultants estimated "conservatively" turned 223
out to be 8 percent savings. Several executives 233
indicated that production problems also sur- 242
faced and caused significant delays in deliveries. 252
The view on quality was mixed. 258

The attitude of employees whose jobs were not 268
eliminated by outsourcing concerned execu- 276
tives most. They reported worrying about a 285
fragmented workforce that distrusted manage- 294
ment. If in the long run outsourcing produces 303
an adversarial relationship between employees 312
and managers, the gain may, in fact, be a loss. 322

# Report Format Review

## GETTING started

alphabet 1 Eve Quinn played my saxophone for a jazz group about once a week.

figures 2 Each of the 169 trucks held 27.50 tons of timber at $43.80 a ton.

double letters 3 Lynn will call a committee meeting at noon to discuss the issues.

easy 4 Jane may go to the lake with the auditor, and Haley may fix fish.

| 1 | 2 | 3 | 4 | 5 | 6 | 7 | 8 | 9 | 10 | 11 | 12 | 13 |

86b ● 15'

**NEW FUNCTION**

**Function review**

## Keep Text Together and Page Numbering

Documents longer than one page require that additional codes be inserted at the beginning of the first page. These codes ensure that text flows properly between pages and that pages are numbered properly. **Widow/Orphan** prevents single lines of text from being left at the bottom of a page or being carried to the top of a continuing page. **Block Protect** keeps text together that should not be separated (i.e., side heading and ¶ that follows).

### To use Keep Text Together

#### Widow/Orphan:

1. From the Format menu, choose *Keep Text Together*.
2. Click the box under **Widow/Orphan** to place a check mark in the box, and then click **OK**.

#### Block protect:

1. Select the text to keep together.
2. Click to check the **Block protect** box.

### To insert page numbers:

1. From the Format menu, choose *Page*, then *Numbering* to display the Select Page Numbering Format dialog box.
2. Click the **Position** box and select a page number position (i.e., Top Right). Click **OK**.

### Suppress

Page numbers print on each page of the document. Since you do not want a number to print on the first page, insert the Suppress code. Suppress can also be used for headers and footers.

### To use Suppress:

1. Choose *Format, Page,* then *Suppress*.
2. Put a check mark in the Page numbering box.

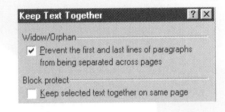

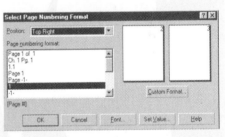

**Drill I**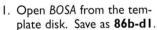

1. Open *BOSA* from the template disk. Save as **86b-d1**.

2. Insert page numbers at the top right; suppress the number on the first page.

3. Select the heading "Recommendations" and the ¶ that follows. Apply Block protect.

4. Turn on Widow/Orphan.

5. Make "Developers" a separate page.

6. Verify report format.

**106c,** *continued*

**Document 1,** *continued*

**Title page**

4. Format a title page as part of the report; use graphic dividers or a simple graphic element and the following information:

**Prepared for Wesley Wren**
**Prepared by you** as **Project Director**
**Current date**

**Table of contents**

5. Prepare a table of contents as part of the same report.
6. Number table of contents page **ii**.

**Document 2**
**Memo with bookmark**

1. Key the memo.
2. Copy the table from *106c-d1*, including its title. Insert the table at the point noted.

TO:  Study Participants

FROM:  Your name

DATE:  Current

SUBJECT:  Outsourcing Study Results

Thank you very much for participating in the survey we conducted on Outsourcing Human Resources functions. We were very pleased with the outstanding response rate on the survey —350 out of the 500 surveys were returned for a 70 percent response.

This memo provides the information that we promised to share with you. Only 3 percent of the respondents indicated that they outsourced all human resources functions, and 14 percent had not outsourced any of their human resources functions. Table 1 provides information about the functions outsourced and the level of satisfaction experienced.

(Insert bookmark, outsource, here.)

Most companies indicated they had difficulty quantifying the cost savings generated by outsourcing. Therefore, the study generated very little cost data.

Thank you again for participating in the study. We hope the information supplied will be of value to you.

**86b,** *continued*

Read the information at the right; then key Drill 2.

In *WordPerfect 9*, the en dash (–) is comparable to two hyphens; the em dash (—) is comparable to three hyphens. ■

## Symbols and special characters

Symbols and special characters not shown on the keyboard may be inserted in a document from the Symbol command on the Insert menu. Examples of special characters from the Typographic Symbols character set are listed below:

Em Dash — En Dash – Copyright © Registered ® Trademark ™

### To insert symbols and special characters:

1. Position the insertion point where the symbol or special character is to be inserted.
2. Choose *Symbol* from the Insert menu.
3. Review the sets of symbols that are available.
4. Select the set and symbol desired.
5. Click **Insert and Close**.

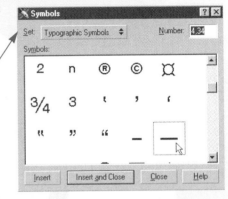

### Drill 2

Key the lines below using the symbols shown.

1. Roberts—Dining at Its Best (em dash)
2. Pages 22–28 (en dash)
3. *Seasons of Love*©
4. RavenWood™
5. Certified Document Processor®

6. ❏ Yes ❏ No
7. See ¶2.
8. Mark it 25¢.
9. ☞ Yes, send it today.
10. ☺ No, don't cancel my order.

**86c ● 30'**

FORMATTING

**Three-page leftbound report**

### Document 1

1. Read the report on pp. 262–263; pay particular attention to the content that gives guides for formatting reports.
2. Format the leftbound report (1.5" left margin; default top, right, and bottom margins; full justification; use 12-point font).
3. On first page, press ENTER to position the insertion point at about 1.5"; key the main heading.
4. Select the heading and change the font to 14-point type; apply bold.
5. Insert page numbers at the top right; suppress the page number on the first page; use Widow/Orphan.

6. Key the remainder of the report; format the headings as illustrated. Page and line breaks will be different than illustrated.
7. Use the special characters (em dash, en dash, etc.) when appropriate.
8. Preview the document before printing to see that the page numbers display on the second and succeeding pages. If any headings are left alone at the bottom of the page, apply Block protect.
9. Print and save the document.

### Document 2

1. Reformat Document 1 as a double-spaced unbound report. Remember to change the left margin to 1" and to indent ¶s. DS between bulleted items.

2. Preview the document; check to ensure that headings are not left alone at the bottom of the page.

percent had not outsourced any of the human resources functions. The 380
specific function outsourced varied widely as did the quality rating 394
assigned by the company (Table 1). 401

**Table 1. Human Resources Functions Outsourced**[2] 441

| Function | Outsourced (%) | 3 | 2 | 1 | |
|---|---|---|---|---|---|
| Benefits design and administration | 42 | 28 | 36 | 36 | 457 |
| Compensation | 26 | 18 | 25 | 57 | 462 |
| Employee services | 46 | 32 | 29 | 39 | 468 |
| Health and safety | 28 | 25 | 35 | 40 | 474 |
| Payroll | 68 | 70 | 16 | 14 | 478 |
| Recordkeeping and administration | 74 | 72 | 18 | 10 | 487 |
| Recruiting and hiring | 24 | 28 | 24 | 48 | 494 |
| Training | 80 | 65 | 20 | 15 | 498 |

Training, recordkeeping, and payroll were the functions outsourced the 512
most by companies. These same functions also received the highest qual- 526
ity ratings. 529

Most companies had difficulty quantifying the cost savings generated by 544
outsourcing the various human resources functions. Companies that still 558
have mainframe computers reported limited savings by outsourcing pay- 572
roll. Companies that no longer have mainframe computers reported much 586
higher savings from outsourcing payroll. 595

The greatest cost savings reported were from outsourcing the training 609
function. The primary reason attributed to the savings in training was 623
that the wide range of expertise needed made it impractical to hire staff 638
in all of the areas. Universities and consulting firms could provide the 653
expertise needed at a lower cost than the companies could. 665

**Conclusions and Recommendations** 671

Success with outsourcing varies dramatically. At this time, the only func- 686
tion recommended for outsourcing is training. Further study is needed 700
before a decision on outsourcing other functions can be made. 712

---

[2]Quality rating percentage applies only to those organizations that outsourced the function. Scale: 3 = very satisfied; 2 = satisfied; 1 = not satisfied.

# FORMATTING GUIDES FOR REPORTS (14 pt.)
DS

Business reports are used internally and externally. Managers often delegate the preparation of internal reports to subordinates; therefore, most reports go up to higher ranks in the organization. External reports often are used to secure business or to report on business that has been conducted for a client. Since reports can have a significant impact on an organization's business and on an individual's upward career mobility, they are usually prepared with care. The following factors must be considered in formatting reports:

- Placement—spacing, margins, and pagination
- Headings—main, side, and paragraph
- Documentation—endnotes, footnotes, internal citations, and references
- Report assembly—preliminary pages, body of report, and appendices

## Placement

1.5"

Left
margin

Effective report design requires many decisions about each of the factors just listed. A few basic guides can be applied to assist in making good formatting decisions.

**Spacing.** Reports may be formatted using either single or double spacing. Commercially prepared reports are generally single-spaced using many typesetting features. The desktop publishing capabilities of word processing software enable employees to prepare reports similar to those prepared professionally. Therefore, the trend is to single-space reports, to use full justification, and to incorporate desktop publishing features in the report.

**Margins.** Reports may be formatted with default or 1" top, side, and bottom margins. A half inch of extra space is provided in the top margin (1.5") for the first page of the report and for major sections that begin on a new page. Extra space is required for binding. Most reports are bound at the left (1.5" left margin); a few are bound at the top (1.5" top margin).

**Pagination.** The way a report is paginated depends on the binding and the preference of the writer. Usually, leftbound and unbound reports are paginated at the top right margin, and topbound reports are paginated at the center bottom margin. However, other positions are acceptable. Arabic numerals (1, 2, 3) are used for the body of the report and the appendix; lowercase Roman numerals (i, ii, iii) are used for preliminary pages. The body of the report starts with page 1, but it is not numbered.

## Headings

Topical headings or captions introduce the material that follows and provide structure in a report. Position, capitalization, font size, and attributes, such as bold and italic, indicate levels of importance. Headings also set segments of copy apart and make the copy easier to read. The spacing before and after headings depends on the font and attributes used.

LEFTBOUND REPORT

FORMATTING

**Assess reports**
**Time schedule:**
Assemble materials . . . . . . 3'
Timed production  . . . . . . 25'
Final check;
   compute *n-pram*  . . . . . . 7'

**Document 1**
**Leftbound report with footnotes**
1. SS; 12-point font; full justification; number pages.
2. Format the table in Column Fill Header style. Center-align Columns B, C, D, and E.
3. Save the document as **106c-d1**. See steps 4–6 on p. 320.

(*Document 1 continued on next page.*)

## OUTSOURCING HUMAN RESOURCES

The Human Resources Department currently manages all human resources functions, including:

- Benefits design and administration
- Compensation
- Employee services
- Health and safety
- Payroll
- Recordkeeping and administration
- Recruiting and hiring
- Training

### To Outsource or Not?

The purpose of this study is to analyze the company's entire human resources operation to determine the feasibility and desirability of outsourcing human resources functions to organizations that specialize in providing those functions. Relevant criteria used in determining the feasibility or desirability of outsourcing included cost, efficiency, quality, impact on employees outside the human resources function, and impact on company strategy.

### Supporting Data

Both primary and secondary data were used in the analysis. Published sources were reviewed to determine the issues that needed to be addressed and to serve as a basis for developing a short questionnaire to solicit information from other companies. This survey was also designed to identify approximately 10 highly successful companies that could be used for benchmarking purposes. In-depth interviews were conducted with all of the "benchmark" companies. Surveys were mailed to 500 randomly selected companies with human resources departments of 10 or more professional staff members.[1]

### Findings

Of the 500 surveys mailed, 350 (70 percent) usable surveys were returned. The most surprising response was that over 75 percent of all companies had examined 1 or more human resources functions to determine if the function(s) should be outsourced. Only 3 percent of the companies reported outsourcing all human resources functions, and 14

---

[1]The company list used was provided by Martin & Martin Human Resources Consultants, Inc., http://www.martin.martin.com, October 1999.

17
24
31
34
38
42
44
51
56
58
63
76
91
105
120
135
149
153
156
170
183
198
213
227
240
256
270
296
298
310
325
338
352
366

## Documentation

Most writers give credit when they use the work of others. Quotes or extensive use of published material should be referenced. In business, many employees feel that the internal reports they use as references belong to the company; therefore, referencing is not important. Employees should keep in mind, however, that referencing helps the reader locate more complete information than the report contains. Reports can be documented in several ways.

**Endnotes and footnotes.** A superior number or other reference mark inserted at the point of reference serves as an indicator that the source is provided at the bottom of the page or at the end of the section or document in numerical order. The only difference between footnotes and endnotes is in the position of the reference information. Footnotes are positioned at the bottom of each page, whereas endnotes are positioned at the end of the document. They serve the same purpose and are formatted in the same way.

**Internal citations.** Internal citations provide source information within the body of the report. The name(s) of the author(s), publication date, and the page numbers are separated by commas and enclosed in parentheses before the terminal punctuation, as illustrated in this sentence (VanHuss, 2000, 10-12). Now that footnotes and endnotes are just as easy to format as internal citations, the use of internal citations is declining.

**References.** The reference list at the end of the report contains all references whether quoted or not in alphabetical order by author name. The names of authors, the title of publication, the name and location of the publisher, and the publication date make up the reference. References are single-spaced with a double space between items. Book and periodical titles are formatted in italic.

## Report Assembly

The components of a business report vary depending on the formality of the report. Reports generally are assembled in three separate segments. Generally, the body of the report is prepared first; then, the material to be appended; and, finally, the front matter.

**Preliminary pages.** A title page, letter of transmittal, table of contents, and executive summary are often placed at the beginning of a report. Other pages may be added. The title page makes the initial impression for the report; therefore, it deserves special attention. An effective title page is formatted attractively and contains the title of the report, who the report was prepared for, who the report was prepared by, and the date.

**Body of the report.** The body of the report varies widely depending on the type of report. Reports frequently contain enumerated items, tables, charts, and graphics. Organizations usually have style guides for the various types of reports commonly used.

**Appendices.** Materials that support a report such as questionnaires, biographical sketches, and large tables are placed at the end of the report in a section called the appendix. The material may be segmented into several different appendices and may be preceded by a page naming the appendix.

# Assessment

**106a • 5'**

## GETTING started

each line 3 times SS; DS
between 3-line groups

| | | |
|---|---|---|
| alphabet | 1 | Zoeby quickly moved to join experienced teams before withdrawing. |
| fig/sym | 2 | Building #3 has 9,620 sq. ft. (9 rooms) & costs the city $81,745. |
| 3d/4th fingers | 3 | Lizza or Paula saw a sad polo pony that was for sale last August. |
| easy | 4 | Sid and Pam may go to an island on a bicycle to fish on the dock. |

| 1 | 2 | 3 | 4 | 5 | 6 | 7 | 8 | 9 | 10 | 11 | 12 | 13 |

**106b • 10'**

## SKILLBUILDING

**Assess straight-copy skill**
Key two 3' or one 5' writing; proofread; circle errors; determine *gwam*.

all letters                                                                *gwam*  3' | 5'

Sports are very big business today; that is, those sports competi-   4 | 3 | 62
tions in which men participate are very big business.  What about    9 | 5 | 65
sports for women?  At the professional level, women have made real  13 | 8 | 67
progress in golf and tennis; they, as well as their sponsors, can   18 | 11 | 70
make big money in both of these events.  The other sports for women 22 | 13 | 73
still are not considered to be major revenue sports.  The future    26 | 16 | 75
may be much better, however, because sports for women at all levels 31 | 19 | 78
are gaining in popularity.  Programs that are designed to help      35 | 21 | 81
young girls develop their athletic skills and interest are having   40 | 24 | 83
an impact.  The result is that girls now expect to play for organ-  44 | 26 | 86
ized clubs as well as in school programs just as boys do.  Club     48 | 29 | 88
sports often will lead to varsity teams.                            51 | 31 | 90

Many people wonder how much impact the current emphasis on          55 | 33 | 92
gender equity will have on sports at the college level.  Most       59 | 35 | 95
people agree that this new emphasis is very positive for women.     63 | 38 | 97
Some people feel, though, that it either has had or could have a    68 | 41 | 100
negative impact on sports for men.  They believe that resources     72 | 43 | 103
that would have been spent on sports such as football, basketball,  77 | 46 | 105
and baseball for men are now being spent on the Olympic sports for  81 | 49 | 108
women.  Overall, most people believe that both men and women who    85 | 51 | 111
have the ability to excel in an athletic event as well as in the    90 | 54 | 113
classroom should have the opportunity and should be encouraged to   94 | 56 | 116
do so.  Success for both women and men is better than success for   98 | 59 | 118
either.                                                             99 | 59 | 119

3' | 1 | 2 | 3 | 4 |
5' | 1 | 2 | 3 |

# Leftbound Report

## 87a • 5'

### GETTING started

each line 3 times SS; DS between 3-line groups

alphabet 1 Jack and I analyzed the data by answering five complex questions.

fig/sym 2 Bids for that new room (30' 6" x 24' 8") were $4,157 and $3,975.80!

shift key 3 Ty, Jo, Ron, Paul, Ann, Juan, Sue, and Lee may go to Rome in May.

easy 4 Diana's neighbor may turn the giant dish by hand to dismantle it.

## 87b • 5'

### Function review
Review and apply the procedures at the right each time you create a hyperlink.

### Drill
1. Key the table at the right.
2. Display the Hyperlink Tools toolbar (View menu, Toolbars, Hyperlink Tools). Use it to help you navigate.
3. Select the text in the first column and hyperlink to the file or site in the second column.
4. Save table as **87b**.

**To create a hyperlink:**

1. Select the text or graphic to be displayed as a hyperlink.
2. Display Hyperlink Tools toolbar. Click **Hyperlink Create** button.
3. Select a file or Web page to be linked by using one of the following methods:
   a. Key the filename or Web address in the Document/Macro entry box.
   b. Click the folder icon to locate the desired filename.
   c. Click the **Browse Web** button if the Web address is not known. When you locate the desired file or Web page, click **Select**. Click **OK**.

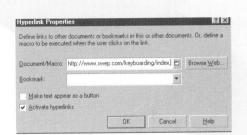

| 86c-d1 | This hyperlink is to the WordPerfect file 86c-d1 that I created in the previous lesson. |
| Weather report | Hyperlink to the Web page http://www.weather.com. |

## 87c • 5'

### Function review

### Change page number format

Preliminary pages are normally formatted with lowercase Roman numerals at the bottom of the page. In this lesson, you will key a title page and a table of contents. Title pages are counted but not numbered. Thus, the table of contents will be the second page (ii) of the report.

**To change number format:**

1. Select *Page*, then *Numbering* from the Format menu.
2. Select the Page numbering format (*i*).
3. Select the position of the page number (*Bottom Center*) in the Position box.
4. Click the **Set Value** button and change page number if necessary.

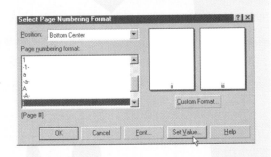

**Document 6**
**Transmittal memo**

**Document 7**
**Challenge**

1. Reformat Document 5 as a two-column report.
2. Change margins to .4" side margins and 1" top and bottom margins.
3. Change to 10-point type.
4. Create the main heading as a banner using TextArt.
5. Adjust the table to fit in one column.
6. Balance columns on the second page.

TO: Loan Committee, Board of Directors    8

FROM: Donald S. King, Loan Officer    15

DATE: March 20, 200–    19

RE: Line of Credit Request— Custom Painting, Inc.    29

Please review the attached loan report submitted on behalf of    41
Mrs. Alyssa Mendez, owner of Custom Painting, Inc. All necessary    55
financial data are summarized in the report. Financial    66
statements and tax documents are available in the file.    77
Based on the financial strength of the borrower, the continued    90
improvement in the financials, and the strong debt-to-    101
worth ratio, I recommend that you approve this request    112
for a $100,000 line of credit for working capital for Custom    124
Painting, Inc. as presented. Michael J. Marshall concurs    135
with this recommendation and has noted his concurrence on the    148
loan application in the file.    154
xx/Attachment    157

## 104-105d • 5'

**SELF** ✔
**c h e c k**

Answer the True/False questions at the right to see if you have mastered the material presented in this lesson.

T  F

1. To return the insertion point to a specific location in the document, set a bookmark.

2. To balance newspaper columns, insert a page break at the end of the text.

3. A paragraph border can be added to a heading by positioning the insertion point in the heading and selecting Horizontal line from the Graphics toolbar.

4. To change the number of columns from two to one, delete the [Col Def] code in Reveal Codes.

5. To include a banner heading in a two-column document, define the columns before the banner.

## Title page and table of contents

### Drill 1

Format the title page at the right. Use 14 point for the title and 12 point for other information. Bold text. Center the page vertically. Return 8 times between parts.

### Drill 2

Format the table of contents as page **iii** of a left-bound report. Set tabs as follows on the Ruler: 2" left; 7" dot right; 7.4" right.

Spacing for a table of contents can vary depending on the length of the document. A very short table of contents might have all items double-spaced. ▓

### Title page

The title page of a report should contain:

- Concise title of the report
- Name and title of the individual or the organization for whom the report was prepared
- Name and title of the individual preparing the report
- Date the report was completed

Format the title page attractively. Usually, the text is aligned horizontally, and the page is centered. However, other attractive formats are also used.

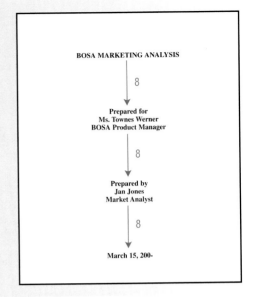

BOSA MARKETING ANALYSIS

8

Prepared for
Ms. Townes Werner
BOSA Product Manager

8

Prepared by
Jan Jones
Market Analyst

8

March 15, 200-

About 1.5" top margin

Bold, 14-point type → **TABLE OF CONTENTS**

7" dot right   7.4" right

| | |
|---|---|
| Letter of Transmittal | ii |

Default margin

1.5" left margin

| | |
|---|---|
| Executive Summary | iv |
| Placement | 1 |
| Spacing | 1 |
| Margins | 1 |
| Pagination | 1 |
| Headings | 2 |
| Documentation | 2 |
| Endnotes and footnotes | 2 |
| Internal citations | 2 |
| References | 2 |
| Report Assembly | 2 |
| Preliminary pages | 2 |
| Body of the report | 3 |
| Appendices | 3 |

2" left

12-point type

iii —— Number preliminary pages with lowercase Roman numerals.

**Document 5**
**Unbound loan report with footnotes**

1. Use default margins; SS; bold headings.
2. In the table, right-align Columns B, C, and D; adjust column widths; center table. Select the entire table and apply Block protect to prevent it from dividing on 2 pages (Format, Keep Text Together).
3. Number pages.

words

| | | words |
|---|---|---|
| **SUNSHINE BANK** | | 3 |
| **Internal Loan Report** | | 7 |

Mrs. Alyssa Mendez, owner of Custom Painting, Inc., presented a request for the renewal of the $100,000 working capital line of credit for Custom Painting, Inc.

16
26
35
39

**Request Details**

42

The loan officer and Custom Painting, Inc. tentatively negotiated a price of Wall Street Journal prime interest rate plus 1 percent with a maturity of 1 year and a $250 renewal fee for the $100,000 request for the working capital line of credit. The line will be secured by accounts receivable of Custom Painting, Inc. and fully guaranteed by Mrs. Mendez, owner of Custom Painting, Inc. Based on total receivables of $267,000 (as of October 31, 1999), the bank will have a loan to value of 37 percent.

51
60
69
78
87
97
106
116
125
134
144

In addition to this request, the borrower has three other loans with Sunshine Bank:

153
160

- A $13,000 term loan secured by an automobile

170

- Two real estate loans of $150,000 and $130,000 (in the names of Paul and Alyssa Mendez)

179
188

Both real estate loans are secured by a first and second mortgage, respectively, on real estate valued at $480,000. The $480,000 represents a combination of two appraisals: $280,000, dated March 4, 1999; and $200,000, dated August 16, 1999.[1]

197
206
215
223
232
292

**Financial Information—Custom Painting, Inc.**

301

To support the request for credit, the borrower provided year-end reviewed financial statements for Custom Painting, Inc. and a current personal financial statement, dated March 1, 2000. The financial highlights for the corporation for the past three years are summarized in Table 1.

310
320
329
338
348
358

[1]The real estate loans are secured by the same property with a total value of $480,000. The owners originally intended to separate this property into two tracts, each having a separate building. Due to tax reasons, the borrower opted to keep the property as one tract.

words

**Table 1. Financial Highlights, Custom Painting, Inc.** 369

| | 1997 | 1998 | 1999 | |
|---|---|---|---|---|
| | | | | 372 |
| Revenues | $1,390,000 | $1,470,000 | $1,586,000 | 380 |
| Net Profit | 2,000 | 3,000 | 53,000 | 386 |
| Total Assets | 426,000 | 391,000 | 422,000 | 394 |
| Total Liabilities | 145,000 | 107,000 | 85,000 | 402 |
| Net Worth | 281,000 | 284,000 | 337,000 | 409 |
| Working Capital | 211,000 | 273,000 | 307,000 | 417 |
| Current Ratio | 3:1 | 5:1 | 15:1 | 422 |
| Quick Ratio | 13:1 | 4:1 | 13:1 | 427 |
| Debt-to-Worth | .52:1 | .38:1 | .25:1 | 434 |

**Analysis**

436

Revenues increased to $1.6 million in 1999, a 7 percent increase from the previous year. Cost of goods sold ($1.2 million) decreased from 84 percent in 1998 to 78 percent in 1999. All ratios improved significantly from 1998 to 1999, with emphasis on improved net worth and working capital and dramatic strengthening of the current ratio and the debt-to-worth ratio.

445
455
465
474
484
492
502
510

With a net profit after taxes of $53,000 and depreciation of $13,000, the borrower had $66,000 in traditional cash flow to accommodate $5,000 in current maturity of long-term debt. This change produces a coverage ratio of 13X.

519
527
537
546
555

**Financial Information—Personal**

562

Mrs. Mendez provided a personal financial statement reflecting total assets of $994,000 compared to total liabilities of $371,000, leaving a net worth of $623,000. Assets are centered in:

571
581
591
600

- $2,000 cash

603

- $614,000 real estate

608

- $300,000 Custom Painting, Inc.

614

All liabilities are in real estate debt. A current review of the guarantor's personal credit bureau reflects limited debt and all satisfactory accounts.

625
633
642
646

Mr. and Mrs. Mendez own two commercial buildings currently financed by Sunshine Bank. The buildings are currently fully leased to a business owned by their son. Mrs. Mendez agreed to provide updated lease contracts so that the bank could ascertain cash flows. The file will be updated as soon as they are provided.

654
664
674
684
693
702
709

**Leftbound report**

Save each document as a separate file.

**Document 1**

1. DS; 1.5" left margin; defaults for other margins; begin first page on about 1.5".
2. At the end of ¶1, key **Visit http://www. longterminsurance.com for more information**. Create a hyperlink.
3. Number pages in the upper right; suppress the page number on the first page.

**Document 2**

Format a title page using the following information:

Title of report

Prepared for: **All Employees**

Prepared by you as: **Vice President of Human Resources**

**Current date**

**Document 3**

Prepare a table of contents. DS the entries because this table of contents is very short. Number the page **ii** in bottom-center position. Include all headings in the table of contents.

---

LONG-TERM CARE INSURANCE  *Bold, 14-point type, center*   5

Long-term care insurance is *now* available to all employees.   17
This coverage can be included *as one of the options* in the flexible benefits package   34
provided by the company, or it can be purchased through the   46
optional coverage package. About ~~twenty-five~~ *(use figures)* percent of all   57
people will need long-term care at some point in their   68
lives. Long-term care can be ~~extremely~~ expensive--more then   78
$50,000 per year for nursing home care and as much as $10,000   90
per year for *home* care ~~provided in the home~~.   95

**Coverage Provided**   99

The coverage *provided* under the plan offered by the company   111
*is* ~~are~~ available to employee*s* spouses, dependents, and parents   123
*and grandparents* of both employees and spouses. The coverage includes health   138
care and personal service care for individuals suffering from   151
chronic disease or from a long-term disability.   161

**Health care.** The type of health care provided includes   172
basic skilled care and intermediate nursing care. Other   183
types of health care are covered through the company's regular   196
health insurance program.   201

**Personal service care.** Custodial care is provided for   212
individuals who are unable to perform day-to-day living   223
activities without assistance. Personal service care can be   236
*(list items; use bullets; indent each one)*
provided in several types of facilities: a traditional   247
nursing home, a day-care center for adults, the individual's   260
home, a relative's home, ~~or~~ a skilled nursing unit.   270

Cost of Plan Offered   274

The plan selected for long-term care is available in   285
*use figures*
per-day benefits ranging from fifty to one hundred fifty dol-   293
lars. The cost of the benefit varies depending on the levels   304
of coverage selected, the number of individual*s* covered by an   316
employee, the ages of individuals covered, and other types of   329
*disability*
coverage carried by the employee. A benefits counselor can   343
*specific*
provide the details for each employee interested in the plan.   357

**Document 4
Memo report**

1. Open *105* and save as **105c-d4**. Use default margins; SS.
2. Center table; adjust columns if necessary.
3. Copy the bookmark *canadian_sites* from file *105c-d1* and insert where noted in the copy.
4. Insert bullets for the list of U.S. beta sites and then sort alphabetically in ascending order.
5. Check spelling and grammar; correct errors.
6. Add a header for the second page.
7. Check that side headings and paragraphs divide at appropriate positions.

Functions applied:
Sort
Header/Footer
Grammatik
Spell Checker
Widow/Orphan

TO:    EC   *Replace with Executive Committee throughout the document.*    5

FROM:   Marla Alvarez    9

DATE:   Current    14

SUBJECT:   Status of Version 7.0 Beta Test    22

*Replace with Computer Applications Assessment throughout document.*

The Version 7.0 Beta test of the CAA software began the first week of this month as    44

scheduled.  The decision of the EC to launch the Beta test in Canada prove to be a very    66

good one.  Both the number of test segments administered and the number of participants    84

exceeded the team's projections provided to the EC.    98

Test Design    100

The new modular design of the 5 modules with 6 equivalent versions of a 15-minute test    117

resulted in 120 test segments that need to be validated. *(Table 1)*    131

*merge cells*   DS    *merge cells*   *bold heads*

**Table 1.  Test Module Design**    137

| Application | Basic | | Power | | Total |
|---|---|---|---|---|---|
| | Objective | Concurrent | Objective | Concurrent | |
| Word processing | 6 | 6 | 6 | 6 | X |
| Spreadsheet | 6 | 6 | 6 | 6 | X |
| Database | 6 | 6 | 6 | 6 | X |
| Presentations | 6 | 6 | 6 | 6 | X |
| Integrated Suite | 6 | 6 | 6 | 6 | X |
| Total | X | X | X | X | X |

143
151
157
161
165
170
176
180

*Add total in cells marked with x.*

In the CAA Version 7.0 Beta test in Canada, the project team projected that 80 of the seg-    204

*replace with en dash.*

ments would be taken by 5/10 Canadian participants.  The psychometrician directing the    221

validation effort insisted that each segment be taken twice with a minimum interval of    239

~~one~~ 1 week between administratons so that a test/retest ~~analysis~~ *reliability measure* could be used.    257

Each test segment was taken by a minimum of 10 participants in a test/retest situation.    274

The total number of participants exceeded 750.    284

*Insert bookmark here (canadian-sites)*

The Version 7.0 Beta testing in the United States begins next week.  The sites selected    302

include: New York, San Francisco, Chicago, New Orleans, Atlanta, Denver, Dallas,    318

Kansas City, Portland, and Cincinnati. *Use bulleted list in alphabetic order for cities.*    326

*Test Schedule*    329

The test schedule extend for ~~three~~ 3 weeks.  Final results should be available in approxi-    346

mately ~~one~~ 1 month.    349

# Reports with Footnotes/Endnotes

## GETTING started

each line 3 times SS; DS
between 3-line groups

### SKILLBUILDING WARMUP

| | | |
|---|---|---|
| alphabet | 1 | Jack Quin refused to buy frozen vegetables except wild mushrooms. |
| fig/sym | 2 | He bought an old truck in 1986 for $2,457 and sold it for $3,200. |
| space bar | 3 | I may buy one or more pipes for him to see if I can go to a shop. |
| easy | 4 | Chan may go to the land of enchantment on the island by the lake. |

| 1 | 2 | 3 | 4 | 5 | 6 | 7 | 8 | 9 | 10 | 11 | 12 | 13 |

## FORMATTING

**Footnotes/endnotes and references**

**Endnotes and footnotes:** Earlier you learned to format textual citations for documentation. In this lesson you will learn to format endnotes and footnotes to document the source of materials. Both endnotes and footnotes indicate the reference cited in the text with a superscript (…[1]). The first line of footnotes is indented 0.5" from the left margin. The complete reference is single-spaced with a DS between references.

Footnotes are positioned at the bottom of the same page as the reference cited (Figure 1). An endnote is placed at the end of the document on a separate page titled NOTES.

The NOTES page has the same top and side margins as the first page of the report and is numbered in sequence with the preceding page. Bold NOTES and follow with a DS.

**References:** A complete listing of references *consulted* in the preparation of the document (which includes the works *cited* in the notes) are listed on a reference page (Figure 2). The page may be titled **REFERENCES** or **BIBLIOGRAPHY**. References cited are listed alphabetically by author surnames. The first line begins at the left margin; all other lines are indented. DS between entries. Use the same top margin as the first page of the report.

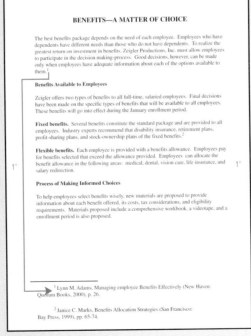

**Figure 1**   Footnotes at the bottom of page

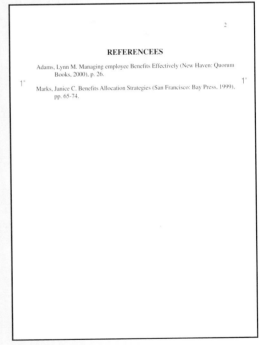

**Figure 2**   Reference page

## 104-105c ● 70'

**Document 1   Two-column unbound report**

1. Change to 11-point font and 1" margins for top, sides, and bottom.
2. Format report title as a banner heading across both columns; use 14-point type; main heading in UPPERCASE; subtitle in Initial Capitals; use bold and appropriate spacing for all headings.
3. SS report; two balanced newspaper columns.
4. Create a bookmark named **canadian_sites** for the heading "Test Administration" through the bulleted list of sites.
5. Save the document as **105c-d1**.

**Document 2   Three-column report**

1. Reformat Document 1 as a three-column balanced newspaper report. Change font to 10-point type.
2. Add a border to the heading and use 10% fill; add a line before and after the heading.

**Document 3   Three-column report**

1. Remove the border, extra lines, and shading from the heading in Document 2. Align heading at the left.
2. Insert a clipart image of Canada or a world map, such as *MISC0028*, below the report main heading. Move it to align flush right, even with the main heading.

words

| | |
|---|---|
| **COMPUTER APPLICATIONS ASSESSMENT** | 7 |
| **Version 7.0 Beta Test—Canada** | 13 |

The Version 7.0 Beta test of the Computer Applications Assessment was administered at six sites in Canada to verify the functionality of the testing software and to validate five application test modules. The testing software consists of programs designed to administer, score, and report results of document-oriented tests for application programs. — 21, 30, 40, 50, 59, 67, 77, 83

Data from the survey of senior human resources executives, conducted for us by Korsgaard and Associates, and the survey of training managers, conducted for us by Werner and Associates, indicated that test module configuration must facilitate the design of tests to be used in employment screening and in industry training programs. Both surveys pinpointed the following design factors considered to be critical in the decision to purchase a testing system: — 93, 102, 111, 118, 128, 137, 146, 156, 166, 176

- Tests must be available to assess skills at a minimum of two mastery levels. — 185, 192

- Test administrators must be able to select either objective or concurrent software tests. — 201, 210

- Test length must accommodate varying time requirements ranging from 15 minutes to an hour for each level of an application. — 218, 226, 236

**Test Design** — 238
The Version 7.0 Beta test of the application modules was structured at two levels of proficiency—basic and power. The basic level requires mastery of frequently used software functions. Tests at each level contain both objective and concurrent software assessment items. Modules were structured into 15-minute — 247, 256, 265, 274, 283, 292, 301

words

tests that could be administered as separate tests or combined for longer time frames. — 310, 319

**Test Administration** — 323
The Beta test was administered in six Canadian sites: — 332, 334

- Calgary — 336
- Montreal — 338
- Quebec — 340
- Toronto — 342
- Vancouver — 344
- Winnipeg — 346

Using an identification number, Beta test participants logged on the interactive testing system. Each test was administered to a minimum of ten participants. Some participants took tests for several different applications. A complete log report is available. — 355, 364, 373, 382, 392, 399

**Software Concerns** — 403
Participants and the test administrator logged all software problems. The log is attached to this report. Several minor software problems were reported. Only two major system failures were noted. One was attributed to a virus on the computer, and the other was caused by improper installation of the software. — 412, 421, 431, 440, 449, 458, 466

**Functionality Assessment** — 471
The new features of the assessment software performed very effectively. All participants completed an evaluation form, and administrators also provided feedback on the system. The results were analyzed, and a summary of the data was prepared. Overall, the new features of the system facilitate both test administration and test taking. Both test administrators and test takers felt that the new features provide a real incentive for upgrading to the 7.0 version software. — 479, 489, 498, 507, 516, 525, 534, 544, 553, 563, 566

## Footnotes

A footnote consists of a reference in the text (superior number) and the footnote positioned at the bottom of the page. When you enter a footnote, *WordPerfect* does several things automatically:

- Inserts the superior figure in the text and in the footnote.
- Positions the footnote correctly at the bottom of the page.
- Adds a divider line to separate the footnote from other text on the page.
- Indents the footnote 0.5" from the left margin.
- Adds a blank line between footnotes.
- Renumbers the footnotes if footnotes added or deleted.

Click inside the footnote text area or choose *Edit* from the Footnote/Endnote dialog box. To delete a note, delete the reference number in the body of the document. ■

**To create a footnote:**

1. Position the insertion point where the footnote reference number will be inserted. Do not key the number in the text; the software inserts the footnote number automatically.
2. Click **Insert** menu, then **Footnote/Endnote**.
3. Click **Create**.
4. Key the footnote text. Do not key the number or DS below the footnote.
5. Click outside the footnote area or click the **Close** button on the property bar.

The Footnote Property Bar appears when you are in the footnote area. The buttons enable you to move between footnotes. The Close button returns you to the regular body of the report.

— Close

### Drill I

1. Key the paragraph, adding the three footnotes.
2. Insert a hard page break and create a Reference page for all three sources in proper reference format. Number the reference p. 2 in the upper right corner.
3. Save as **88c-d1**. Print.

Robin McGee set the school record for points in a game—47.[1]  He holds six statewide records.  This makes him one of the top ten athletes in the school's history.[2]  He expects to get a basketball scholarship at an outstanding school.[3]

_____

[1]Roy Anderson,  *High School Athletic Association Records*  (Minneapolis: Sports Press, 1999), p. 41.

[2]Monica King,  "Top Ten Athletes,"  *Graduate Education Journal*, Spring 2000, <http://www.gej.edu/athletes/topten.htm>, 25 April 2000.

[3]Robin McGee, <rmg3@umt.edu>,  "Basketball Scholarship."  E-mail to Matthew P. Crowson, <mpcrowson@umt.edu>, 7 March 2000.

### REFERENCES

Book→ Anderson, Roy.  *High School Athletic Association Records*.  Minneapolis: Sports Press, 1999.

Online Journal → King, Monica.  "Top Ten Athletes."  *Graduate Education Journal*.  Spring 2000.  <http://www.gej.edu/athletes/topten.htm> (25 April 2000).

E-mail → McGee, Robin.  <rmg3@umt.edu>.  "Basketball Scholarship."  E-mail to

### To create columns:

1. Click the **Columns** button on the toolbar and select the number of columns.

2. Click **Format** on the drop-down list to display the Columns dialog box. Choose the type of column.

3. To change the spacing between columns, click the up/down arrows in the Space between box to increase or decrease the spacing. Default spacing between columns is .5".

4. The default width of columns is equal column width. Use the arrows in the Column width box to change the width of one or more columns.

5. Press CTRL + ENTER to end one column and begin keying in the next column.

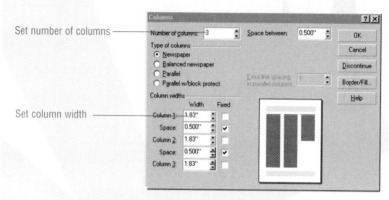

Set number of columns ——

Set column width ——

### To create a banner:

A banner is a heading that spans several columns. To format a banner, key the banner text first and then create the columns to be used in the document. Apply center alignment, large font, border, and fill to the banner text as desired.

### Drill 1—Format entire document in two columns

1. Key the heading **Working with Newspaper Columns** and the five ¶s on p. 310. Use 11-point font.
2. Center the main heading. Apply 24-point font.
3. Click the insertion point in the first paragraph. Create 2 columns.
4. Save as **105b-d1**.
5. View the document to see how the columns are positioned on the page.

### Drill 2—Balance the columns

1. Place the insertion point in ¶ 1. From the Columns dialog box (Columns, Format), change the type of column to Balanced Newspaper.
2. View the document to see how the columns are positioned on the page.

### Drill 3—Add a border to the banner

1. Add a double-line border around the title and 10% fill (Format, Paragraph, Border/Fill).
2. Preview; then print the document.
3. Preview; save as **105b-d3**; print.

### Drill 4—Change column format to three columns

1. Position the insertion point in one of the columns.
2. Click **Columns** button and change to three columns.
3. Preview the document. Save as **105b-d4**.

The endnote feature positions the endnote flush with the left margin. In order to indent the endnote, which is the traditional format, you would need to enter them manually and not use the endnote feature.

## Drill 2

1. Rekey the paragraph from Drill 1 on p. 268.
2. Enter the references as endnotes rather than as footnotes. (Note: A divider line is not entered or keyed.)
3. Enter a hard page break immediately before the endnotes.
4. Center **NOTES** in bold at about 1.5" top margin.
5. See the illustration at the right for an example.

## Endnotes

The major difference between footnotes and endnotes is that you put endnotes on a page by themselves at the end of the document. You must add a page (hard page break), number it, and give it a heading called NOTES.

*WordPerfect* places the endnote number at the left margin. Space twice after the period following the number of the endnote and key the endnote. Select *Draft* from the View menu to hide the endnotes on screen. Select *Page View* to see the endnotes as they are keyed. *WordPerfect* does these endnote steps automatically:

- Inserts a superior figure in the text and a number in the endnote. Do not key the number.
- Positions the endnote at the end of the document.
- Adds a blank line between endnotes.
- Renumbers the endnotes if editing changes cause endnotes to be added or deleted.

### To create an endnote:

1. Insert endnotes as they occur within the report. Position the insertion point where the endnote reference number will be inserted.
2. Click **Insert** menu, then **Footnote/Endnote**.
3. Click the **Endnote Number** button; then **Create**.
4. Key the endnote text. Do not press ENTER. The endnote appears at the end of the document. (The endnote will move down as you key more copy.)
5. Click outside the endnote area or click **Close** on the Footnote Property bar.

### To edit an endnote:

6. Click inside the endnote text area or choose *Edit* from the Footnote/Endnote dialog box.
7. To delete a note, delete the reference number in the body of the document

### To prepare a **NOTES** page:

Insert a new page break (CTRL + ENTER) below the last line of the report. Center **NOTES** with an approximate 1.5" top margin; DS, 12 point. The page is numbered in the upper right corner.

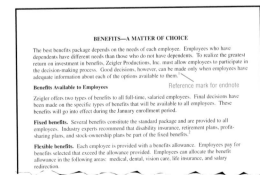

**Figure 3**   Report with endnotes

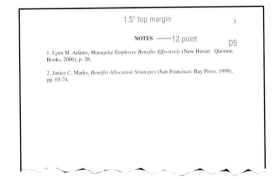

**Figure 4**   NOTES page

# Business Report with Columns

## GETTING started

each line 3 times SS; DS between 3-line groups

### SKILLBUILDING WARMUP

| | | |
|---|---|---|
| alphabet | 1 | Rex Patey quickly moved to a new zone just before the group came. |
| figures | 2 | Vi paid $19.50 for Seats 7 and 8; Pat paid $26 for Seats 3 and 4. |
| 1st/2d fingers | 3 | Guy tried to come to my rescue before going to work this morning. |
| easy | 4 | Jay and I may go with eight girls to fish on the docks by a lake. |

| 1 | 2 | 3 | 4 | 5 | 6 | 7 | 8 | 9 | 10 | 11 | 12 | 13 |

## Columns

Most documents you have keyed up to this point have been one-column documents—that is, the text extended from the left margin to the right margin. The tables that you keyed in earlier modules positioned text in two or more columns. Newspaper columns provide another way of positioning more than one column of text on a page. These columns of text are called **newspaper columns** because they are formatted the way a newspaper is formatted. Text is read down one column, then up to the top of the next column, then down that column until all text has been read.

Newspaper columns by default are of equal width with 0.5" between the columns. However, columns can be formatted with varying widths. They can also have a line drawn between the columns. When text formatted in newspaper columns is less than a page long, the columns are balanced—that is, the text is divided about equally among the columns on the page.

Generally, columns have a **banner heading**—that is, a heading that spans or is centered over all the columns. A banner is keyed before the Columns feature is turned on. The appearance of the banner can be enhanced by adding a border around it and shading over it (Format, Paragraph, Border/Fill).

The number of columns can easily be changed. To increase or decrease the number of columns, position the insertion point in a column. Then click the Columns button on the toolbar and select the number of columns desired. To change the spacing between the columns, click **Format** on the drop-down list that displays when you click Columns.

*WordPerfect* places a [Col Def] code in the document that contains the columns. To remove the columns, delete the [Col Def] code from the Reveal Codes screen.

**COMPUTER APPLICATIONS ASSESSMENT**
Version 7.0 Beta Test--Canada

The Version 7.0 Beta test of the Computer Applications Assessment was administered at six sites in Canada to verify the functionality of the testing software and to validate five application test modules. The testing software consists of programs designed to administer, score, and report results of document-oriented tests for application programs.

Data from the survey of senior human resources executives, conducted for us by Korsgaard and Associates, and the survey of training managers, conducted for us by Werner and Associates, indicated that test module configuration must facilitate the design of tests to be used in employment screening and in industry training programs. Both surveys pinpointed the following design factors considered to be critical in the decision to purchase a testing system:

- Tests must be available to assess skills at a minimum of two mastery levels.
- Test administrators must be able to select either objective or concurrent software tests.
- Test length must accommodate varying time requirements ranging from 15 minutes to an

hour for each level of an application.

**Test Design**

The Version 7.0 Beta test of the application modules was structured at two levels of proficiency—basic and power. The basic level requires mastery of frequently used software functions. Tests at each level contain both objective and concurrent software assessment items. Modules were structured into 15-minute tests that could be administered as separate tests or combined for longer time frames.

**Test Administration**

The Beta test was administered in six Canadian sites:

- Calgary
- Montreal
- Quebec
- Toronto
- Vancouver
- Winnipeg

Using an identification number, Beta test participants logged on the interactive testing system.

Each test was administered to a minimum of ten participants. Some participants took tests for several different applications. A complete log report is available.

**Software Concerns**

Participants and the test administrator logged all software problems. The log is attached to this report. Several minor software problems were reported. Only two major system failures were noted. One was attributed to a virus on the computer, and the other was caused by improper installation of the software.

**Functionality Assessment**

The new features of the assessment software performed very effectively. All participants completed an evaluation form, and administrators also provided feedback on the system. The results were analyzed, and a summary of the data was prepared. Overall, the new features of the system facilitate both test administration and test taking. Both test administrators and test takers felt that the new features provide a real incentive for upgrading to the 7.0 version software.

## FORMATTING

**Document 1**
**Leftbound report**
**with footnotes**

1. Format the leftbound report SS. Use 14-point font and CAPS for main heading.
2. In ¶ 1, select the text *Zeigler Productions, Inc.* Create a hyperlink to http://www.zeigler.com.
3. Insert the file *benefits* from the template disk where indicated.
4. Format the table as shown.
5. Insert page numbers in the top-right position; suppress on p. 1.
7. Save as **88d-d1**.

Insert a file: **Insert** menu, **File**, filename.

*Benefits—A Matter of Choice*

The best benefits package depends on the needs of each employee. Employees who have dependents have different needs than those who do not have dependents. To realize the greatest return on investment in benefits, Zeigler Productions, Inc. must allow employees to participate in the decision-making process. Good decisions, however, can be made only when employees have adequate information about each of the options available to them.[1]

*Benefits Available to Employees*

Zeigler offers two types of benefits to all full-time, salaried employees. Final decisions have been made on the specific types of benefits that will be available to all employees. These benefits will go into effect during the January enrollment period.

*Fixed benefits.* Several benefits constitute the standard package and are provided to all employees. Industry experts recommend that disability insurance, retirement plans, profit-sharing plans, and stock-ownership plans be part of the fixed benefits.[2]

*Flexible benefits.* Each employee is provided with a benefits allowance. Employees pay for benefits selected that exceed the allowance provided. Employees can allocate the benefit allowance in the following areas: medical, dental, vision care, life insurance, and salary redirection.

*Process of Making Informed Choices*

To help employees select benefits wisely, new materials are proposed to provide information about each benefit offered, its costs, tax considerations, and eligibility requirements. Materials proposed include a comprehensive workbook, a videotape, and a decision worksheet. A special telephone help desk to answer questions during the enrollment period is also proposed.

(Insert the file *benefits* here.)

(continued on p. 271)

**Document 5**
**Memo**

1. Key the memo, correcting grammar errors.
2. Copy the word processing training schedule from *103-d2* and paste it at the end of the memo.
3. Note that the column heads were not part of the copy; therefore, you will need to insert a row and add the headings. Bold the headings.
4. Check grammar.
5. Save and print Document 5.

TO:        All Employees                                                         4

FROM:    Lynn Maybury, Training Manager                          11

DATE:    Current                                                              16

SUBJECT:    Word Processing Training                              23

The word processing training program has been finalized. The          35
module are divided into three levels—novice, proficient, and          47
power. Novice users includes those who are likely to use word          60
processing infrequently or who have little experience with our          72
previous word processing software. Proficient users are those          85
whom are likely to use word processing frequently or who have          97
considerable experience with our previous word processing software.   111
Power users are those who need to be able to apply all software       124
functions and too troubleshoot problems.                            132

Our trainers will be happy to talk with you about your par-          144
ticular needs and make recommendations for the level of skill        156
you should attain. They will also answer any questions you may        169
have about the training program.                                    176

The word processing training schedule follows:                      185

**102-103c ● 5'**

**SELF ✔**
**check**

Answer the True/False questions at the right to see if you have mastered the material presented in this lesson.

T  F

1. To create a bookmark, click Bookmark on the Edit menu.
2. A QuickMark saves your place in a document.
3. Only one QuickMark can be inserted into a document.
4. Insert a file in an open document by clicking on the Insert menu, then File.
5. Several bookmarks can be inserted in a document by naming each bookmark.

**88d,** *continued*

**Document 2**
**Title page**
Prepare a title page with the following information. Save as **88d-d2**.
> Prepared for: **Ms. Virginia Covington**
> Prepared by: **Your name, Project Director**
> **Current date**

**Document 3**
**Table of contents**
1. Set left margin at 1.5". Set tabs on the Ruler: 2" left, 7" dot right, and 7.4" right.
2. Prepare a table of contents that includes all headings and the appropriate page numbers. Number the page **ii**.
3. Assemble the report:
   Title page
   Contents
   Report

**Document 4**
1. Reformat the report as an unbound report.
2. Delete the footnotes in Document 1 and enter the reference information as endnotes; create a NOTES page.

*Costs of the New Program*

*A complete projection of all costs was prepared by the benefits specialists and is available in the Human Resources Department. A summary of the projected costs per employee follows:*

| Component | Cost per Employee |
|---|---|
| Print materials | $ 2.50 |
| Videotape | 3.75 |
| Help desk | 1.95 |
| Enrollment process | 2.25 |
| Total | $ 10.45 |

*The costs compare very favorably to the costs incurred four years ago when major changes were made in benefits. The cost at that time was $9.75 per employee.*

Footnote/Endnote text

*[1]Lynn M. Adams, Managing Employee Benefits Effectively (New Haven: Quorum Books, 2000), p. 26.*

*[2]Janice C. Marks, Employee Benefits Allocation Strategies (San Francisco: Bay Press, 1999), pp. 65-74.*

Reference text

*Adams, Lynn M. Managing Employee Benefits Effectively. New Haven: Quorum Books, 2000.*

*Marks, Janice C. Employee Benefits Allocation Strategies. San Francisco: Bay Press, 1999.*

**Document 2**
1. Key the table as a new document.
2. Use the Column Fill Header format. Italicize column headings. Leave a blank row before each application as shown.
3. Save as **103b-d2**. Print and close the file.

**Document 3**
1. Open Document 1 (*103b-d1*).
2. Insert file *103b-d2* at the end of Document 1.
3. Select the content you just inserted (file *103b-d2*) and create a selected bookmark named *Master Schedule*.
4. Select all information under the heading *Training Areas and Levels* and create a selected bookmark named *Training Areas*.
5. Close and save the document.

**Document 4**
1. Compose a brief memo to your instructor with the following message: *Here is the information you requested about the training areas and schedules.*
2. Insert the selected bookmark *Training Areas*.
3. Insert the selected bookmark *Master Schedule*.
4. Print Document 4; save as **103b-d4**.

## MASTER TRAINING SCHEDULE*

### Computer Applications

| *Application* | *Novice* | *Proficient* | *Power* | |
|---|---|---|---|---|
| **Word Processing** | January 7 | January 14 | January 21 | 26 |
| | March 3 | March 10 | March 17 | 32 |
| | May 6 | May 13 | May 20 | 36 |
| | November 5 | November 12 | November 19 | 43 |
| **Spreadsheet** | January 9 | January 16 | January 23 | 51 |
| | March 5 | March 12 | March 19 | 57 |
| | June 10 | June 17 | June 24 | 61 |
| | November 3 | November 10 | November 17 | 68 |
| **Presentation Software** | January 27 | February 3 | February 10 | 80 |
| | March 18 | March 25 | April 8 | 85 |
| | July 8 | July 15 | July 22 | 89 |
| | November 24 | December 8 | December 10 | 96 |
| **Database** | January 29 | February 5 | February 12 | 105 |
| | March 20 | March 27 | April 10 | 110 |
| | August 7 | August 14 | August 21 | 116 |
| | November 26 | December 9 | December 16 | 123 |
| **Network Communications** | February 11 | February 18 | February 25 | 135 |
| | April 7 | April 14 | April 21 | 140 |
| | September 9 | September 16 | September 23 | 148 |
| | December 11 | December 18 | December 22 | 155 |
| **Project Management** | February 13 | February 20 | February 27 | 164 |
| | April 9 | April 16 | April 23 | 171 |
| | October 9 | October 16 | October 23 | 178 |
| | December 1 | December 8 | December 15 | 184 |

*Each training session is a three-hour module and is offered twice on each date scheduled. The morning session begins at 8:45 and ends at 11:45. The afternoon session begins at 1:15 and ends at 4:15. At least two trainers are scheduled for each session.

Other column values: 5, 10, 17

200
217
234
236

# LESSON 89 — Working with Long Reports

## 89a • 5'

### GETTING started

each line 3 times SS; DS between 3-line groups

| | | |
|---|---|---|
| alphabet | 1 | Zam injured five fingers, but he produces excellent quality work. |
| fig/sym | 2 | Lauren shipped a 46.5# box (32 x 18 x 10) for $19.75 on 10/27/99. |
| direct reaches | 3 | Barb, Tony, and Huey got many great bargains at decreased prices. |
| easy | 4 | We may visit a chapel and an antique mall when we go to the town. |

| 1 | 2 | 3 | 4 | 5 | 6 | 7 | 8 | 9 | 10 | 11 | 12 | 13 |

## 89b • 5'

### FORMATTING

**Sequence of a long report**

In previous lessons, you have created sections of reports and saved them each as individual documents. In this lesson, you will learn to prepare a long report as one document, with the preliminary pages numbered with lower-case Roman numerals and the body of the report numbered with Arabic numbers. Numbers are suppressed on the title page and the first page of the body.

Business reports frequently include an Executive Summary, which provides an overview of the main points of the report. If an appendix is included, it follows the body. The report is sequenced in the order listed:

1. Title page
2. Transmittal memo
3. Table of contents
4. Executive summary
5. Body of the report
6. Appendix

## 89c • 20'

### NEW FUNCTION

### Page number value

The starting page number value may not always be 1. Page value is an option of the Numbering command.

**To change the value of a page number:**

1. From the Format menu, choose *Page*, then *Numbering*.
2. Click the **Set Value** button. Change the number to the desired page value.
3. Click **OK**.

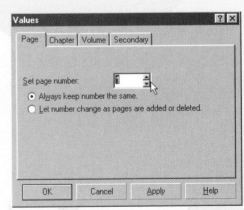

**Document 1  Unbound report**
1. SS; use 14-point title and 12-point side headings; bold all headings; use appropriate spacing before and after headings.
2. Run Grammatik. (Ignore passive sentences.)
3. Save the document as **103b-d1**.

words

**MASTER TRAINING SCHEDULE**     5
**Computer Applications**     9

The Senior Executive Committee charged the   18
Training Department with developing a new,   27
comprehensive computer application training   35
program and a one-year master training   43
schedule in anticipation of the forthcoming   52
productivity mandates.  The Senior Executive   61
Committee approved the preliminary work,   69
which includes a major technology upgrade,   78
completed by the Productivity Enhancement   86
Task Force.  The first phase of the training   95
program focuses on computer applications used   104
in the corporate offices.   110

**Training Areas and Levels**   115
The Productivity Enhancement Task Force   123
identified six areas of computer application   132
upgrades that would be installed and available   141
to all employees; thus, new training programs   151
must be in place by the time the installation is   160
completed.   These areas include:   167

- Word processing (WP)   172
- Spreadsheet (SS)   176
- Presentations (PS)   180
- Database (DB)   183
- Network communications (NC)   189
- Project management (PM)   194

Specialized programs will be available only to   204
selected departments needing the applications;   213
therefore, they are not included in the master   222
training plan.  After reviewing all training pro-   232
gram evaluations from the past year, the   240
Training Department agreed that training pro-   249
grams for each application should be struc-   258
tured into three levels:   263

- Novice—employees who are likely to use an   272
  application infrequently or who have had   280

little experience with the previous version   289
of the application.   293

- Proficient—employees who are likely to use   302
  an application frequently or who have had   311
  considerable experience with the previous   319
  version of the application.   325

- Power—employees who have advanced   332
  computer skills or need to have advanced   340
  computer skills.   344

**Training Requirements**   348
The Productivity Enhancement Task Force   356
goals endorsed by the Senior Executive   364
Committee specify that each employee must   372
complete the entire training program within   381
one year of installation.   Departments must   390
meet the following requirements:   397

- All employees in the department must be   405
  trained as a minimum at the novice level in   414
  each of the six required application areas.   423

- All employees in the department must be   431
  trained at the proficient level in at least two   441
  of the six required application areas.   449

- Each department must have at least two   457
  employees trained at the proficient level in   466
  each of the six required application areas.   475

- Each department must have at least one   483
  employee trained at the power level in each   492
  of the six required application areas.   500

**Training Modules**   504
The entire training program has been cus-   512
tomized for the corporate offices. All depart-   521
ment managers submitted documents for use   530
in the development of the training modules.   539

Each module contains segments of computer-   547
based training and segments of instructor-led   556
training. The instructor-led segments are used   566
to introduce and to close each module. These   575
segments are conducted in the Computer   583
Training Center. The computer-based training   592
segments may be completed either in the   600
Computer Training Center or at the employee's   609
workstation.   The master training schedule   618
follows.   619

**Drill 1**

In this drill, you will change the page number format in a document. To save time, you will work with a document that has already been keyed. It includes a title page, transmittal memo, contents, and a report. The document has no hard page breaks, so it all runs together. You will insert the page breaks at the proper locations, format the document, and then enter the page numbers. You will then check the drill to be sure that you have formatted it correctly.

1. Open the file *BOSA2* on the template disk. Save it as **89c-d1**.
2. Insert a hard page break below the last line of the title page, transmittal memo, table of contents, and before the final paragraph headed "DEVELOPERS."
3. Click **DEVELOPERS**. Check the status line at the end of the document. It should read "Pg 6."
4. Position the first line of the memo, contents, and body of the report on about Ln 1.5".
5. Number the preliminary pages:
   a. Move the insertion point to the Home position (CTRL + HOME).
   b. Access page numbering.
   c. Change the number format to lowercase Roman (*i*).
   d. Change the position to *Bottom Center*.
   e. Suppress the page number on the title page.
6. Number the body of the report:
   a. Move the insertion point to the first page of the body (main heading, BOSA MARKETING ANALYSIS). The status line should read "Pg 4."
   b. Access page numbering.
   c. Change the starting value from 4 to *1*.
   d. Change the format from lowercase Roman to numbers (*1*).
   e. Change the position from Bottom Center to *Top Right*.
   f. Suppress the page number on the first page of the body.

**Check Drill 1**

Preview the document in Drill 1. Check to see that:

1. The title page is on a page by itself, and the status line reads "Pg 1."
2. The transmittal memo is on a page by itself, and the status line reads "Pg 2."
3. The table of contents is on a page by itself, and the status line reads "Pg 3." The document reads "iii."
4. The table is positioned on the page with text before and after it, and the status line reads "Pg 2" when you click the insertion point in the table.
5. "Developers" section is on a new page, and the status line reads "Pg 3." The page number is in the upper right.
6. Increase the Zoom percentage so that you can read the page numbers. Check to see that pages are numbered correctly. Move the insertion point to the first page of the body of the report. Turn on Widow/Orphan protection. Apply Block protect to any side headings that may separate from the paragraph that follows. Print.

**Drill 2**

In this drill you will key a short document, then enter the page numbers when you are finished. Follow the steps at the right and at the top of p. 274.

1. From the View menu, choose *Draft*. You will be able to see the hard page breaks as you key this drill.
2. Key **TITLE PAGE**; insert a hard page break.
3. Key **Page ii, Transmittal Memo**. Insert a hard page break.
4. Key **Page iii, Table of Contents**. Insert a hard page break.
5. Key **Body of the Report, page 1**. Insert a hard page break.

*(continued on next page)*

## Bookmarks and QuickMarks

**Bookmarks** and **QuickMarks** mark specific locations in a document so that you can access them quickly. Although similar, these features serve different purposes.

A document can have only one QuickMark. It saves your place so that when you open the document, you will automatically go to the location of the insertion point the last time you saved the document. A QuickMark is not named, and you can only have one per document.

Conversely, you can have multiple bookmarks as long as each has a separate name. Bookmarks can be used to select text and insert it in another document or to create cross references and indexes.

**To set a QuickMark:**
1. From the Tools menu, click **Bookmark**.
2. To return to the QuickMark upon opening the file, click to place a check mark in both boxes at the bottom of the dialog box: **Set QuickMark on file save** and **Go to QuickMark on file open**.

**To create and go to a bookmark:**
1. Position the insertion point where the bookmark is desired.
2. Click **Tools**, **Bookmark**, **Create**.
3. Key the bookmark name and click **OK**.
4. To find the bookmarked place, click the **Edit** menu, then **Go To**. Select **Bookmark**, then the bookmark name, and click **Go To**.

**To create a bookmark with selected text:**
1. Select the text you want to include.
2. Click **Tools**, **Bookmark**, **Create**.
3. Key the bookmark name and click the **Selected Bookmark** check box, then **OK**.

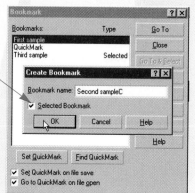

**To insert a selected bookmark into another document:**
1. Place the insertion point in the document containing the bookmark.
2. Click **Tools**, **Bookmark**; choose the name of the selected bookmark and click **Go To & Select**. (The contents of the bookmark will be highlighted in the document.)
3. Click **Copy** button on the toolbar.
4. Position the insertion point where you want to insert the contents of the bookmark. Click the **Paste** button.

### Drill

1. Key the three ¶s at the right. Save as **102a**.
2. Position the insertion point at the beginning of the first ¶; create a bookmark named **sample1**.
3. Select the second ¶; create a selected bookmark named **sample2**.
4. Create a QuickMark at the end of the third ¶.
5. Close the document.
6. Open the document; check that the insertion point is at the end of the third ¶.
7. Go to and select **sample2**; insert the contents in a new document.

### Drill

This first paragraph is used to illustrate how to create a bookmark so that you can access this position in the document quickly. It simply marks the position but does not select the text.

This second paragraph is used to illustrate how to create a bookmark with selected text so that you can access the content and paste it in another document easily.

This third paragraph has a QuickMark at the end of it so that when you open the document, you will be at the same position you were when you closed it.

**Drill 2,** *continued*

6. Key **Body of the Report, page 2**. Your document should look similar to the one below.
7. On the title page, insert page numbers as lowercase Roman numerals. Suppress on the title page.
8. On Report, Page 1, change the Number value to *1*, change the position of the page number, change the number style to Numbers, and suppress the page number on the first page.

TITLE PAGE

Page ii, Transmittal Memo

Page iii, Table of Contents

Body of the Report, page 1

Body of the Report, page 2

**89d ● 20'**

FORMATTING

**Edit report**
Open *ComTech* and save as **89d**. Complete the steps at the right.

**Functions applied:**
Convert Case, Copy/Paste, Find and Replace, Go To, Keep Text Together, Spell Checker, Thesaurus.

1. Insert the following right-aligned footer on all but the first page: **Edited by** (*your name*).
2. Number pages appropriately.
3. Change line spacing to double.
4. Change the font size as follows:
   - 14 point for the title
   - 11 point for the report
   - 12 point for side headings
5. Use Widow/Orphan protection to ensure that one line of a ¶ is not left at the bottom or top of a page.
6. Use Block protect, if necessary, to avoid having a heading left alone at the bottom of a page.
7. Find all occurrences of *CCI* and replace with *Corporate Communications Institute*.
8. Spell out *Corp.* (Corporation) each time it is abbreviated.
9. Convert all side headings from UPPERCASE to Initial Capitals.
10. Move the ¶ with the heading **TRAINING** immediately above **PROJECT MANAGEMENT**.
11. Use the Thesaurus to find an appropriate substitute for the word "primary" in the second ¶. Indicate the word you chose: _____.
12. Use Spell Checker to correct errors in the document.
13. Prepare a title page and table of contents for the report.

*Title page:* Create a title page for the report. Assume that it was prepared by you for your class and instructor.

*Contents:* Create a Contents page using the side and paragraph headings in the report. Indent the paragraph headings to the first default tab. Set a dot right tab and a right tab for the page numbers. The dot tab should precede the right tab by about 1/2". Number the contents as page **ii**.

14. Save again and print.
15. Copy the two ¶s with the heading **The Project** to a new document. Save as **89d-d2** and print.

## 101c ● 25'

**FORMATTING**

**Document 1
Report with graphic and border**

1. Enter the heading **Trend Analysis Report** in TextArt, 20-point font. Apply the first selection in TextArt.
2. Insert a Heavy bottom border: on the Border tab of the Paragraph Border/Fill dialog box, choose *Thin Bottom* border, then *Heavy line* style.
3. Insert clipart or a picture. Align the image to the right of the heading.
4. Key the subheading **Market Trends** in 16 point. Add a border and fill. Reverse out text (Format menu, Font, Color white).
5. DS between ¶s. Apply bullets after you have keyed all ¶s.
6. Insert an image of your choice below the last ¶.
7. Key the last line in script. Use a heavy bottom border.
8. Save as **101c-d1**.

**Document 2
Challenge**

1. Open *87e-d1*.
2. Delete page numbers.
3. Add a bottom border as a header on each page.
4. Add a top border as a footer. Below the border, key **BOSA Marketing Analysis** aligned at the left; insert Arabic page numbers at the right.
5. Save as **101c-d2**.

---

Apply TextArt

Add graphic here.

DS

## Market Trends

☑ The population in the metropolitan area is growing both in the college's service area and in the demographic segments that represent the greatest market enrollment penetration.

☑ The metropolitan area continues to add employment opportunities at a growth rate of 22 percent, but the area economy suffers from some of the same insecurities about the future as do other areas.

☑ Information technology is creating more customer potential and new demands for the delivery of coursework as well as generating new opportunities for competitors to enter this education market.

☑ The pace of change is forcing people at all levels of the economy to learn new skills at the same time people are being asked to work harder—and sometimes hold more than one job.

☑ The new school improvement plan has not taken shape as quickly as anticipated, but a move toward mastering skills and testing for proficiencies—not rote knowledge—is gaining momentum.

*Add graphic here.*

*Understanding our community to prepare for our future.*

LESSON 101    BORDERS AND TEXTART

90-91 ● 45'

FORMATTING

## Business report with executive summary

**Overview:** The report includes a title page, transmittal memo, contents, executive summary, body, and appendix. The entire report will be saved as one file (**90**). You will key the executive summary, the body, and the appendix; create the preliminary pages; and finally, number the pages.

### Step 1: Create executive summary

1. Format as an unbound report; DS. Use 1.5" top margin. Use proper format for headings.
2. The executive summary and the pages that precede it will be numbered with Roman numerals. Do not number pages until the entire report is completed.

An executive summary restates the purpose of the report, findings, conclusions, and recommendations. It is formatted as a preliminary page. ■

### Step 2: Format body

1. Key the report.
2. Insert file *forms* from your template disk. Check the format; adjust as necessary.
3. Use Numbering for enumerated items. SS each item; DS between items.

# Long Business Report

words

## EXECUTIVE SUMMARY — 4

A survey of the forms used by Hess and Glenn, Inc. showed — 15
that 89 percent of the forms were paper-based forms and 11 — 27
percent were electronic forms. Forms come from a variety — 39
of sources, and no centralized control system is in place to — 51
manage the forms. A new system for managing and con- — 61
trolling forms has been developed, and the office man- — 72
ager has been charged with implementing the system. — 83

The system focuses on analyzing current forms and — 93
designing new forms, converting paper-based forms to elec- — 104
tronic forms, and inventorying forms. The system will — 115
reduce costs and improve efficiency and effectiveness. — 127

## FORMS DESIGN, MANAGEMENT, CONTROL, AND CONVERSION — 137

The survey of forms used by Hess and Glenn, Inc. indicates — 148
that paper-based forms are used extensively throughout the — 160
organization. The survey identified 154 paper-based forms, — 172
including 9 continuous forms, 134 flat sheets, and 11 unit — 184
sets. Nine (5.8%) of the forms were initiated in the past — 196
three months; 14 (9.1%) were revised versions of "old" forms; — 208
and the remainder (85.1%) were reprints of forms used in — 220
the past. Most of the forms are used companywide. Only 20 — 232
online forms were identified in the survey. — 241

*[Insert "forms" from the template disk here.]*

## TextArt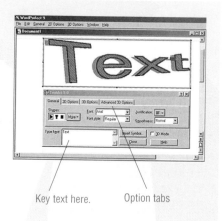

**TextArt** is a useful—even fun—application that allows you to manipulate and add special effects to text. TextArt provides an interesting way to add banners to documents, such as newsletters or reports that are formatted in columns. It can also be used to prepare letterhead or note pages for casual memos. With TextArt you can add features such as textured fills and 3-D effects. TextArt was used to create the banner shown below. The second example illustrates 3-D effects for the same banner.

*This Banner uses TextArt*

*This Banner is in 3D Mode*

### To use TextArt:

1. Display the Graphics toolbar (*View*, *Toolbars*, *Graphics*) and click the **TextArt** button.

2. Select the desired shape; click **More** for additional shapes.

3. Click in the text box and key the text desired.

4. Click the **2D Options** tab to add color and other options.

5. Click **3D Mode** to turn on 3D Mode.

6. Click **Close** to insert the image.

Key text here.    Option tabs

### Drill 1  Create your name in TextArt

1. Click the **TextArt** button; select a style; click **OK**.

2. Key your full name in the text area.

3. Print your banner.

### Drill 2  Add 3D effects

1. With your banner selected, click **3D Mode**, then the **3D Options** tab.

2. Choose one of the preset rotations.

3. Print your banner.

### Drill 3  Add color and pattern

1. With your banner selected, click the **2D Options** tab (deselect 3D mode), then **Pattern** button. Select the desired pattern, pattern color, and text color.

2. Print your banner if you have a color printer available.

### Drill 4  Review

1. Create a banner with the following heading: **Notes from (your first name)**.

2. Select the style, 3D effect, and color of your choice.

**Step 3: Format appendix**
After keying the body of the report, prepare the appendix.

**Appendix**
1. Key the headings. Then create a 3-column table. Display the Ruler. Adjust Columns A and B so they are about .5" wide. Delete all tabs. Set a left tab about .5" from the left edge of Column C. Make all adjustments before keying text in the table.
2. Key the checklist using 11-point font; 1.5" top margin.

To create check boxes in Columns A and B, click **Insert**, **Symbol**; then select ❏ from Iconic Symbols. Use CTRL + TAB to move to the tab within Column C.

words

| | | | | words |
|---|---|---|---|---|
| | | **APPENDIX** *14 pt.* | | 2 |
| | | **CHECKLIST FOR EVALUATING FORMS** | | 8 |
| | | Place a check mark "Yes" or "No" at *left* in response to each item. | | 21 |

*Column A*  *Column B*  *Column C*

| Yes | No | | Need for the Form | |
|---|---|---|---|---|
| | | | | 26 |
| ❏ | ❏ | 1. | Does the expected use of the *form* justify the cost of designing and producing it? | 41 / 44 |
| ❏ | ❏ | 2. | Does the form contain information collected on other forms? | 58 |
| ❏ | ❏ | 3. | Can the (info) on the proposed form be combined with or replaced by another form? | 73 / 77 |
| ❏ | ❏ | 4. | Has the *form* been authorized? | 85 |
| | | | **Content of the Form** | 89 |
| ❏ | ❏ | 5. | Is all information contained on the form necessary? | 101 |
| ❏ | ❏ | 6. | Does the form request all necessary information? | 112 |
| ❏ | ❏ | 7. | Are related items grouped together? | 121 |
| ❏ | ❏ | 8. | Is the information sequenced to facilitate word flow? | 133 |
| ❏ | ❏ | 9. | Is the easy-to-read? *form* | 140 |
| | | | **Design of the Form** | 144 |
| ❏ | ❏ | 10. | Can the form be created electronically? | 154 |
| ❏ | ❏ | 11. | Are the instructions provided adequate? | 163 |
| ❏ | ❏ | 12. | Is the space provided on the form adequate? | 174 |
| ❏ | ❏ | 13. | Can the form be printed on standard-sized paper? | 186 |
| ❏ | ❏ | 14. | Are multiple copies required? | 193 |
| ❏ | ❏ | 15. | Does the format facilitate completion of the form? | 205 |
| ❏ | ❏ | 16. | Is the form attractive and professional looking? | 217 |
| | | | **Overall Effectiveness** | 221 |
| ❏ | ❏ | 17. | Does the form do what it was designed to do? | 232 |
| ❏ | ❏ | 18. | Can the objective of the form be accomplished in a better way? | 246 |

After you have inserted the check boxes in the first row of Columns A and B, copy the two check boxes to the clipboard and paste them in other rows. ■

# Borders and TextArt

## Borders

**Borders** are graphic lines that enclose text, pictures, or clipart. Borders are added to enhance appearance or to provide emphasis. Reports often have simple graphic lines at the top and bottom of the page.

**To add a border to text:**

1. Place the insertion point in the line of text to which you will add a border.
2. Choose *Format, Paragraph, Border/Fill*.
3. On the Border tab, select the desired border style and click **Apply border to current paragraph only**. Click **Apply**.
4. On the Fill tab, select the fill style and *Apply*. Click **OK**.

**Drill 1**

1. Display the Paragraph Border/Fill dialog box.
2. Experiment inserting border lines of various styles and weights.
3. Click the **Fill** tab. Experiment adding shading.
4. Do not save.

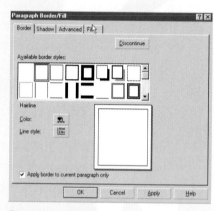

**Figure 1**   Border dialog box

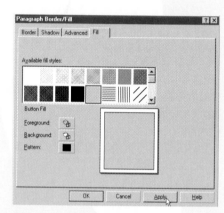

**Figure 2**   Fill dialog box

**Drill 2**

1. Key the text at the right. Insert the bullet from the Typographic Symbols character set (**Insert** menu, **Symbol**).
2. Add a single border. Add space above and below the names by positioning the insertion point at the beginning and end of the line and pressing ENTER. Center-align the copy within the border.
3. Select the text, copy it, and paste it below the border. Then add a double border. Press ENTER before and after the text and center-align. Add 20% fill. Save as **101a**.

Csiszar and VanHuss, LLC • 3847 Veterans Rd. • Columbia, SC 29209-3827

Csiszar and VanHuss, LLC • 3847 Veterans Rd. • Columbia, SC 29209-3827

Csiszar and VanHuss, LLC • 3847 Veterans Rd. • Columbia, SC 29209-3827

**Step 4: Create preliminary pages**
- Go to the Home position (CTRL + HOME).
- Insert a hard page break. Go to the top of the document again. The status line should read *Pg1*.
- Create the title page using the information below. Center the page vertically.
- Create the other preliminary pages, inserting a hard page break after the memo and contents.

### Title page

The report is prepared by **you** as a **Forms Design Consultant**; prepared for **Hess and Glenn, Inc**.

### Transmittal memo

Compose a memo to All Employees (each person will receive a copy of the report) from you. Subject: Forms Design Report Thank the employees for being so cooperative in helping you complete your analysis. Point out that you believe the new system will help improve both the efficiency and the effectiveness of the entire organization. Encourage employees to try to put as many forms as possible online.

### Table of contents

Prepare a table of contents. Include all headings. Set tabs for the contents (1.5" left, 7.0" dot right, 7.4" right).

**Step 5: Number pages**
- With the insertion point in the title page, number the preliminary pages using lowercase Roman numerals. Suppress the number on the title page.
- Move the insertion point to the first page of the body. Number the body of the report, including the appendix, using Arabic numbers. Suppress the number on the first page of the body.

**Step 6: Proofread and preview**
Preview to check top margins and page numbering before printing.

---

**90-91 ● 5'**

**SELF** ✓

**check**

Answer the True/False questions to see if you have mastered the material presented in this lesson.

T   F

1. A hard page break is inserted by pressing CTRL + HOME.

2. Check boxes are inserted by selecting *Character* in the Graphics menu.

3. Within a document, pages must be numbered with either Roman or Arabic numerals.

4. Preliminary pages are formatted with lowercase Roman numerals.

5. An executive summary summarizes the report and is formatted as the last page of the report.

## FORMATTING

**Document 1**

1. Insert an appropriate graphic image.
2. Center-align the image.
3. Format the announcement as marked.
4. Save as **100c-d1**.
5. Move the image between the heading lines and the paragraph.
6. Move the image below the last line of the text.
7. Print the version of the document you like the best—graphic at the top, in the middle, or at the bottom.

```
              Jazz Band Concert
                      DS
              Thursday, June 11, 200-
         SS   8 p.m.
              Student Center Auditorium
                      QS
     Come join the Jazz Band as it plays favorites from the
60s, 70s, and 80s.  Listen to the band's smooth sounds playing
selections from the John Tesh Project, Manhattan Transfer,
Chicago, and Windham Hill.
```

*Arial 36 pt.*

*Arial 18 pt.*

**Document 2**

1. Create the announcement at the right. Insert a graphic of your choice, Then repeat it across the page.
2. Format the table using Single Lines style.
3. Use a font style and size of your choice. Space text attractively.

**Document 3**
**Compose an announcement**

Create an announcement for a club or organization to which you belong. Include a graphic and wrap text next to it. Use a large size font to make it attractive and pleasing to read.

## Benson Employees' Credit Union

Insert and repeat graphic.

### Offers the following rates for financing cars:

| 1999 and Newer Cars | Time | Interest Rate |
|---------------------|----------|---------------|
| 100% Financing | 48 months | 6.00% APR |
| 100% Financing | 60 months | 6.25% APR |
| 90% Financing | 72 months | 6.50% APR |

All interested members welcome to apply
May 10-June 7.
For further details and application, visit us at
www.benson.org.

# Review Long Reports

## LESSON 92

**92a • 5'**

### GETTING started

each line 3 times SS; DS
between 3-line groups

### SKILLBUILDING WARMUP

| | | |
|---|---|---|
| alphabet | 1 | Mark was checking just six books quickly to verify the zip codes. |
| fig/sym | 2 | We paid only $2,975.63 ($2.13) for 1,400 of the 80-page booklets. |
| adjacent reaches | 3 | Porter and Guy were quite sad; we quickly tried to cheer them up. |
| easy | 4 | Rowland may fix a ham and corn dish, or he may fix lamb for them. |

| 1 | 2 | 3 | 4 | 5 | 6 | 7 | 8 | 9 | 10 | 11 | 12 | 13 |

---

**92b • optional**

### SKILLBUILDING

**Build straight-copy skill**
Key one 3' and one 5' writing
at your control rate.

 all letters                                                    *gwam*   3'   5'

| | 3' | 5' |
|---|---|---|
| Most people today have become very health conscious. Some | 4 | 2 | 52 |

Most people today have become very health conscious. Some    4  2  52
individuals worry about the bad effects of a diet that contains    8  5  55
far too much fat and a life style that does not include very much    13  8  57
exercise. However, many of those people never get past the stage    17  10  60
of worrying. Others just try to find a quick solution to the    21  13  63
problem. They try zany diets and easy exercise programs. The    25  15  65
real solution is to get in the habit of eating correctly and doing    30  18  68
exercise on a regular basis. The results are well worth the effort.    34  21  70

The combination of exercising on a regular basis and eating    38  23  73
properly produces much better results than either of these activi-    43  26  76
ties can produce by itself. An effective diet includes food from    47  28  78
all of the major food groups. Eating food that has a very high    51  31  81
fiber content and a very low fat content can help to prevent a    56  33  83
number of diseases. Not eating a meal to save a few calories is    60  36  86
not a very good idea. A good exercise program has several important    65  39  89
characteristics. Each session lasts approximately twenty minutes    69  41  91
and occurs at least three times a week. Also, the activity should    73  44  94
be fast enough to increase your heart rate. Walking at a fast pace    78  47  97
is one of the best and one of the most desirable activities that    82  49  99
you can do.    83  50  100

| 3' | 1 | 2 | 3 | 4 | |
| 5' | 1 | 2 | 3 | |

# LESSON 100

# Announcements with Graphics

## 100a ● 5'

## GETTING started

each line 3 times SS; DS
between 3-line groups

### SKILLBUILDING WARMUP

alphabet 1 Quick, lively jumps of a gray fox will amaze both giddy children.
figures 2 The 164 copies (priced at $18.75) may be shipped on May 29 or 30.
outside 3 Lowell gave his old football jersey to a happy young man at camp.
easy 4 Vivian may wish to make an apricot gown for the big civic social.

| 1 | 2 | 3 | 4 | 5 | 6 | 7 | 8 | 9 | 10 | 11 | 12 | 13 |

## 100b ● 15'

**Function review**

## Dragging text and graphics

You can move graphics using the Cut and Paste commands in the same way you would text. A quicker method, however, is to drag with the mouse.

### To drag text or graphics:

1. Select the text or graphic to be moved.
2. Hold down the left mouse button and move the mouse. When the pointer changes to the move arrow, drag the text or image to the desired position and release the mouse button.

### To copy graphics:

Select the graphic, hold down the CTRL key, and drag and drop the graphic.

**Drill 1  Copy graphics**

1. Select 2 pictures (such as the dog and cat) or download 2 from the Internet. Position the pictures side by side.
2. Size the pictures to be approximately the same size.

3. Copy and move the pictures so that you have 4 pictures positioned as shown at the right.

**Drill 2  Drag text**

1. Key the following:
   **We plan to visit on May 1 with Leslie Lee**.

2. Select text: *on May 1*. Drag the selected text to move it after *Leslie Lee*.

3. The text should now read:
   **We plan to visit with Leslie Lee on May 1**.

*WordPerfect* has several tools to help you enter text correctly. You have already learned to use Spell-As-You-Go (underlines words in red that aren't in the *WordPerfect* dictionary), QuickCorrect (automatically corrects some errors as you key), Spell Checker and Thesaurus. Now you will learn to use Grammatik and Grammar-As-You-Go.

## Grammatik

The **Grammatik** feature identifies possible errors in grammar, punctuation, or style. The errors are displayed in a sentence box with suggestions for improving or correcting the sentence. You can choose to ignore or to change the sentence as suggested. Grammatik is a writer's tool, but only a tool. You, the writer, must always proofread the final document for errors in grammar, punctuation, word usage, and style.

Grammatik will also let you change the style of checking. For example, to check passive voice, you could select "Very Strict" but to check only basic grammar rules, you could pick "Quick Check." Grammatik will also provide statistical information such as the number of syllables per word, words per sentence, and reading grade level. For these additional options, choose the Options button.

### Drill 1

1. Key Drill 3 exactly as it appears in Communication Workshop 4, page A11 (in the Appendix). Do not correct the errors as you key.
2. Using Grammatik, correct the errors that need to be corrected.
3. Proofread the document and correct the errors that Grammatik did not locate. You should find 5 more errors (3 punctuation errors and two misused or misspelled words). Remember, Grammatik is a tool; you are the expert.

### Drill 2

1. Key Drill 4 on page A11 exactly as it appears. Do not correct the errors as you key.
2. Use Grammatik to correct errors.
3. Proofread and locate the errors that Grammatik did not locate.
4. Did you find 3 additional errors (quite, want, then)?

**To use Grammatik:**

1. With a document displayed on the screen, click **Tools**, then **Grammatik**.
2. When an error displays in the box, do one of the following:
   - Select a replacement from the Replacement list box; then click **Replace**.
   - Edit the text manually by clicking the insertion point on the error in the document window; then key the correct text. Click **Resume**.
   - Ignore the problem by clicking **Skip Once** or **Skip All**.

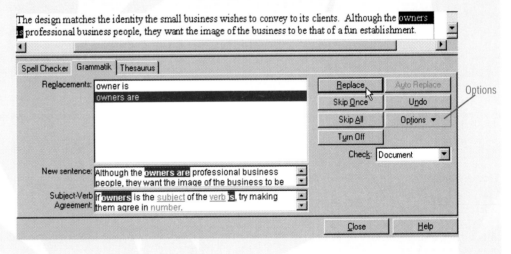

## Grammar-As-You-Go

**Grammar-As-You-Go** underlines words or phrases that might be incorrect. It includes the checking features of Spell-As-You-Go. When the insertion point is in a word that is misspelled or is a grammar error, that word is shown correctly in the text box at the right of the Property Bar. This feature is referred to as Prompt-As-You-Go. Prompt-As-You-Go must be enabled first, however. Click **Tools**, then **Proofread**, then **Prompt-As-You-Go**. Then click **Grammar-As-You-Go**, and both grammar and spelling errors will be identified as you key.

**Document 1**

1. Open *partyshop-ltrhd*; save as **99b-d1**.
2. Key the letter at the right using the letterhead you created. Use block format and current date. Use the following address:

**Ms. Marianna Gilcrest**
**Gilcrest and Associates**
**P.O. Box 3957**
**Columbia, SC**
    **29201-3957**

Dear Ms. Gilcrest

The design of the letterhead illustrated on this page matches the identity the small business wishes to convey to its clients. Although the owners are not professional people, they want the image of the business to be that of a fun establishment.

The letterhead contains the following design features:

- Clipart—The clip inserted is the Party clip from the Special Occasions category. It is aligned at the left so that text can be inserted on the right side.

- The name of the business was keyed using the Vivaldi font in bold with a font size of 36 points.

- The address and telephone/fax lines were keyed using the same Vivaldi with a font size of 12 points.

- A horizontal line was then positioned below the text to separate the letterhead from the remainder of the page that will be used for correspondence.

- The top margin was changed to .5 inches so that the letterhead would not take up an excessive amount of space.

Incidentally, the letter is keyed in 12 point Times New Roman font. Please let me know what you think of this design.

Sincerely   (Your name)   Graphic Designer

**Document 2**

Key a second letter to Ms. Gilcrest using *pommery-ltrhd*. Revise the letter as directed at the right to match the description of Pommery Springs, LLC.

1. Change last sentence of ¶ 1 to: *Although the owners are professional people, they want the development to have the feel of a basic residential community.*
2. Delete the first bulleted item.
3. In the second bulleted item, change the font and size to: *Arial* and *14 point.*
4. In the third bulleted item, change the font to *Arial.*

**Documents 3 and 4**

**Document 3**
Compose a letter to Ms. Gilcrest describing the design elements you used in the first letterhead you created on your own (*letterhead-bus*).

**Document 4**
Modify the letter to Ms. Gilcrest to describe the letterhead you created as *letterhead-personal*.

**FORMATTING**

**Leftbound report**

**Overview:** The report includes a title page, transmittal memo, contents, and notes page. Prepare and save the preliminary pages and the body of the report as one file. Number pages appropriately. SS report; leftbound format.

*Bold* **GUIDES FOR PREPARING MEETING DOCUMENTATION** *14-point type*

The procedures used to prepare support documents for meetings in the Moss Springs Company were reviewed during the productivity analysis that was *just* completed. The type of support documents used, *the format,* and the way in which they were prepared varied widely throughout the company. The primary documents used were meeting notices, agendas, handouts, visual aids, and minutes. The following guides were compiled *as a result* on the basis of the productivity review.

**Annual Meeting**

The following quote from the Moss Spring Company Policy *Italic* Manual contains the policy for the documentation of the Annual Meeting:

*block indent; single-space*

The annual Meeting of the Moss Springs Company shall be held within 3 months of the end of the fiscal year. The Corporate Secretary shall mail to all who are eligible to attend the meeting a notice and agenda *30* thirty days prior to the meeting. The Corporate Secretary shall prepare a verbatim record of the meeting and provide each member of the Board of Directors with a copy of the minutes within two weeks of the meeting. The minutes shall be a part of the permanent records of the Moss Springs Company.

**Other Meetings**

*stet*

Meetings ~~other than the annual meeting~~ will be held at the discretion of the Board of Directors and the appropriate company managers. Documentation for regular and "called" meetings of the Board *is* ~~as~~ described in the following paragraphs.

**Support Documents**

The Senior *Management* Committee required that an agenda be distributed prior to all formal meetings of committees and of staff at the departmental level or higher. Minutes must be prepared and distributed to all participants after the meeting.

**99a,** *continued*

When a graphic is inserted in a document, it aligns at the left automatically. Text that you key will wrap around both sides of the image by default. You can change the way text wraps around the graphic in the Wrap Text dialog box.

1. Set a .5" top margin.
2. Insert *prty0002.wpg* from the Special Occasions, Misc. category in the Scrapbook.
3. Click to select the clipart and drag the sizing handles to enlarge it slightly.
4. With the clip selected, position the pointer over the clip and right-click the mouse to display the pop-up menu.
5. Click **Wrap**, then **Square** wrapping type, and then Wrap text around **Right side**.

**Document 2**
**Letterhead with wrapped text and line**

Follow the steps to create the letterhead shown in Figure 3. You will format the clipart so that text will wrap to the right of it. If you do not have the clipart shown, substitute an appropriate clip.

• Insert a graphic.
• Wrap text to the right of graphic.
• Insert graphic line.
• Insert date to be updated automatically.

 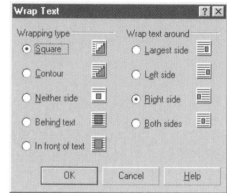

**Figure 3**

6. Position the insertion point on the right side of the clipart. Key the company name as follows:

**The Party Shop** ———————— 36 pt. Vivaldi, bold, centered

**2386 Crown Lake Drive     Hopkins, SC 29061-8476**
                                                                                    12 pt., centered
**Telephone:  (803) 555-0137     FAX: (803) 555-0139**

7. Insert a horizontal line below the address.
8. Leave two or three blank lines below the horizontal line. Change to the default font (Times New Roman, 12 pt.), insert the date, and check "Keep the inserted date current."
9. Press ENTER to position the insertion point for the letter address. Save the document as **partyshop–ltrhd**. When it is opened, the inside address can be keyed immediately.

**Documents 3 and 4**
**Create personal letterhead**

**Document 3**

Design a letterhead with a very professional appearance using your name and address. The style should be such that you could use it for correspondence such as applying for a part-time job or internship. Save as **letterhead-bus**.

**Document 4**

Design a letterhead using clipart and your name and address. You plan to use this letterhead for corresponding with friends. Be creative and select something that you think would be fun to use. Save as **letterhead-personal**.

**Minutes**

The Administrative Manager developed the following procedures to to implement the policy on maintaining appropriate minutes. The Senior Management Committee met and approved these
procedures for immediate implementation.

**Agenda**

The agenda should contain the date, time, and meeting
place. It also should contain a listing of all topic to be
discussed during the meeting. Distribution of the agenda should
allow adequate time for participants to prepare for the meeting. *preparation*

**Verbatim minutes.** The Annual Meeting will be recorded and
a verbatim transcript of the meeting will be prepared by the
Corporate Secretary. Verbatim minutes are costly and will be *; therefore, they*
used only for the Annual Meeting.

**Detailed minutes.** A detailed record will be maintained of
the *regular* monthly meetings and of special meetings of the Board of
Directors. The minutes should provide identifying information
and a *comprehensive* summary of the discussion and action taken on all agenda
items.

**Action minutes.** Action minutes, consist *ing* of identifying
information *and* a brief summary of decisions made and of key
views expressed. *will be used for most meetings* The emphasis should be on decisions, assignment of responsability, and action planned for the future.

**Visual aids.** Visual aids can be used to heighten interest,
to present information quickly, and to enhance participants
understanding. The use of visual aids is ~~required~~ *recommended* at all meetings. Guides for preparing and using effective aids are contained in the procedures manual and should be consulted as
needed.

**Handouts.** Handouts should be prepared when they will
enhance understanding at a meeting or when participants need a
file copy of ~~the~~ information. *presented during a meeting* Handouts should be produced only
when the information justifies the *preparation* cost.

# Letterheads with Graphics

**Creating letterheads**

The design of letterheads ranges from very simple with a few word processing attributes to complex following very strict visual identity specifications. Logos are usually registered as trademarks, and managers protect trademarks by mandating that they be used exactly (color, position, type size, design) as they are registered. In this lesson, you will create letterheads using basic design elements. Note these features of the letterheads in the figures below:

• Both include a graphic line.

• The second example includes a graphic with text wrapped squarely to the right of it.

• The date was inserted as a field so that each time the letterhead is opened, the current date is inserted automatically.

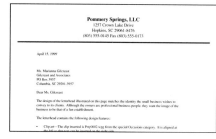

**Figure 1** Letterhead with graphic line

**Figure 2** Letterhead with text wrapped to right of the graphic

**Document 1**
**Letterhead with graphic line**

Create the Pommery Springs, LLC letterhead shown.

1. Set a .5" top margin.

2. Key the company name using center alignment, bold, and 14-pt. Arial:

   Pommery Springs, LLC.

3. Key the company address in 12-pt. bold.

   1257 Crown Lake Drive
   Hopkins, SC 29061-8476
   (803) 555-0145  Fax (803) 555-0173

4. Press ENTER after the address. Insert a horizontal line (click 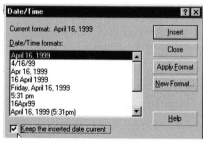, the **Horizontal Line** button on the Graphics toolbar).

5. Leave two or three blank lines after the horizontal line. Change to the default font for the letter (Times New Roman, 12 pt.).

    Horizontal lines are inserted from margin to margin. To extend the line, click it and drag a sizing handle. ■

6. Change justification to left. Insert the date and set it to update automatically (check "Keep the inserted date current").

7. Press ENTER 4 times to position the letter address.

8. Save the document as **pommery-ltrhd**. When it is opened, the letter address can be keyed immediately.

Date/Time dialog box:
Current format: April 16, 1999
Date/Time formats:
April 16, 1999
4/16/99
Apr 16, 1999
16 April 1999
Friday, April 16, 1999
5:31 pm
16Apr99
April 16, 1999 (5:31pm)
☑ Keep the inserted date current
Insert | Close | Apply Format | New Format... | Help

**92d,** *continued*

1. Insert file *support* before the Standardized format section.
2. Insert a hyperlink at the end of the last sentence of the body of the report as noted. The link is to file *92-forms* on your template disk.
3. Format the endnotes on a separate NOTES page. (**Reference**: p. 269).
4. Add the preliminary pages.
5. Number all the pages of the report.
6. Check grammar and spelling.
7. Save again and print.

(Insert the file *support* from your template disk here.)

**Standardized format.** Standard format N for all documents *have* has been developed and ~~included~~ *placed* in the proce⌐dures manual.  The Annual Meeting Minutes Books contains copies of minutes of previous Annual Meetings; the same format is to be used for the minutes of each Annual Meeting. #**Forms.** The preparation of support documents can be simplified with the use of *electronic* forms.  Templates for preparing agendas and for recording action minutes can be downloaded from the *online* forms file.

  A:\92-Forms

Use this information to prepare the Notes page.

*1 Anil Wasu, <Awassu@ProdCon.com>, "Enhancing Productivity: The Moss Springs Company." E-mail to Patrick Ray, <PatRay@gwm.sc.edu>, 6 December 1999, p. 2.*

*2 Moss Springs Company Policy Manual, (Chicago, 1999), p. 42.*

*3 Mary Anderson, Effective Meetings (Boston: Bay Publishing Co., 1999), pp. 74-86.*

# *on...* Using FTP to Download Files

**NEWS**

File Transfer Protocol (FTP) provides an easy and fast way to move files from one computer to another over the Internet.  Most browsers allow you to access FTP servers in the same way that you access World Wide Web (HTTP) servers.  FTP server sites typically contain directories that are linked to subdirectories that are displayed by clicking on the directory icon.  Files are posted in the subdirec-

tories.  A file can be viewed or downloaded. To upload files to an FTP site, you must have write access to the FTP server.

Both private and public FTP sites are available.  Private sites require a password to access the sites;  public sites typically do not.  Many public sites can be located by searching for FTP sites.

## Banners, dividers, and decorators

Graphics are useful in separating segments of a document or in adding attractive elements to a title page.  Figure 1 below was created using clipart (*Banner1.wpg*) from the Awards category; Figure 2 was created using a banner from the Star shapes category.  Clipart objects such as you used in the announcement above can also be used on title pages.

**Figure I**

**Figure 2**

**Documents 2 and 3**

1. Use the information at right to create a title page. Insert a clipart banner similar to the one in Figure 1. Save as **98c-d2**.
2. Use the same information to create a second title page.  Use Star shapes on the toolbar to insert a banner similar to the one in Figure 2.
3. Copy the first banner and create a new one at the bottom of the page. Save as **98c-d3**.

### Designing Effective Title Pages

**Prepared for**
**The XYZ Company**

**Prepared by**
**Your name**

**Current date**

**Document 4**

1. Key the announcement, applying the proofreaders' marks.  Key the dates and locations as a 2-column table without lines. DS outside the table.
2. Insert a handshake image.
3. Move the image before the conference dates and names.
4. Size the image to fit the page.
5. Save as **98c-d4**.

*Use Times*

**Let's Meet** — 36-pt. *bold*
DS
**Upcoming Conferences** — 24-pt. *bold*
DS

When you're in town and we're in town, come visit us at our ] 18-pt. center convention booth.  We'd love to talk.
DS

| | |
|---|---|
| **April 8-12** | **April 28-May 3** |
| American Research for Education | Association for International Reading |
| *New York, NY* | *New Orleans, LA* |
| DS | |
| **April 17-20** | **June 9-13** |
| National Music Educators' Conference | National Computing Association |
| *Kansas City, MO* | *Minneapolis, MN* |

] 12-pt. type

TS

Teachers' Annuity and Insurance Association ] 14-pt. bold
4530 Fifth Ave.
New York, NY 10017-3206

# Assessment

## SKILLBUILDING WARMUP

| | | |
|---|---|---|
| alphabet | 1 | Zack quit just six months before Pawley revealed a big discovery. |
| fig/sym | 2 | We bought 4 modems (28,800) @ $79.15 each for a total of $316.60. |
| double letters | 3 | Rebecca Lee called a meeting of all our bookkeepers in Tennessee. |
| easy | 4 | Did Pamela pay for a rug in an ancient chapel and an enamel bowl? |

| 1 | 2 | 3 | 4 | 5 | 6 | 7 | 8 | 9 | 10 | 11 | 12 | 13 |

93b ● 10'

**SKILLBUILDING**

**Assess straight-copy skill**

Key two 3' or one 5' writing;
proofread; circle errors;
determine *gwam*.

all letters

| | gwam | 3' | 5' |
|---|---|---|---|

Lifetime employment is a concept that was quite popular just a    4 | 3 | 43
couple of decades ago. A worker often took a job with the full    8 | 5 | 46
intent of staying in that same job for years. Workers felt that    13 | 8 | 48
good performance and loyalty would ensure that the company would    17 | 10 | 51
return their loyalty and retain them for their entire careers.    21 | 13 | 54
Today, few people believe that organizations are very likely to    26 | 15 | 56
provide lifetime work for very many people. In fact, most people    30 | 18 | 59
plan their careers knowing that they may have to embark on five    34 | 21 | 61
or six careers before they retire.    37 | 22 | 63

The concept that is most likely to replace lifetime employment    41 | 24 | 65
is lifetime employability. This concept is very different in that    45 | 27 | 68
it means that each person must be responsible for his or her own    50 | 30 | 71
career. The company should provide the worker with the opportunity    54 | 33 | 73
to continue to learn new skills so that he or she will be employable    59 | 35 | 76
in another job if the current one goes away. Learning how to con-    63 | 38 | 79
tinue learning and keeping up to date are critical career skills    68 | 41 | 81
today.    68 | 41 | 82

| 3' | 1 | 2 | 3 | 4 |
| 5' | | 1 | 2 | 3 |

93c ● 35'

FORMATTING

**Assessment: reports**
**Time schedule:**
Assemble materials ..... 3'
Timed production ...... 25'
Compute *n-pram* ....... 7'

**Leftbound report with footnotes**
Create the entire report as one document, including the title page and contents.
1. Format the report SS; full justification; number pages.
2. In the table, center and bold column heads; right-align numbers in Column B; adjust column widths; center table.

**Title page**
3. Format title page with the following information:
   Prepared for **Kenneth Ravens** by **you** as **Project Director**; **current date**.

**Table of contents**
4. Create contents. Number as page **ii**.

### Shapes

*WordPerfect* provides preset shapes on the Graphics toolbar. You can create basic shapes such as circles, lines, rectangles, and polygons, as well as arrows, stars, callouts, and more.

**To insert a shape:**

1. Position the insertion point where you want the shape to appear.
2. Click the down arrow next to a shape category button on the Graphics toolbar to see the available shapes. Click a shape.
3. The pointer turns into a cross. Drag down and to the right until the shape is the desired size.
4. Hold down the CTRL key while you draw a line to insert straight horizontal, vertical, or diagonal lines. Hold down SHIFT while you draw a rectangle to create a square.
5. Click outside the shape to return to the document window.

**Drill**

1. Display the Graphics toolbar. Click the down arrows to review the various shapes.
2. Click the down arrow next to the star shape and select the first banner in the bottom row.
3. Drag the crosshairs until the diameter of the banner is about 2".

98c ● 30'

**FORMATTING**

**Document 1**

1. Center-align announcement.
2. Insert a picture from the Clipart Scrapbook.
3. Enlarge the picture.
4. Key the announcement.
5. Center the page.
6. Save as **98c-d1**; print.

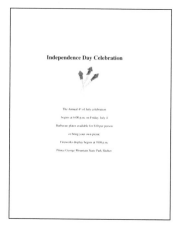

Independence Day Celebration ——— 14 pt., bold

Add clipart here.

The annual 4th of July celebration

begins at 6:00 p.m. on Friday, July 4.

Barbecue plates available for $10 per person

or bring your own picnic.

Fireworks display begins at 9:00 p.m.

Prince George Mountain State Park Shelter

## ADVERTISING ON THE INTERNET

This study was conducted to determine the desirability of developing a strategy for Pat's Place to begin advertising on the World Wide Web, the main marketing network of the Internet. Several factors were considered:

- Internet advertising by competitors
- Site development strategies
- Estimated cost of developing a Web site

### Competitive Advertising on the Internet

Of 450 randomly selected firms in the industry that were surveyed, 216 (48 percent) responded. Of those that responded, 97 (45 percent) had advertised on the Internet. About 40 percent of the firms not advertising on the Internet were considering advertising on it within a year or two.

Firms advertising on the Internet reported mixed results. Many indicated that it was too early to evaluate the success of their advertising because they were still trying to determine the best way to use the Internet. Most of the companies were using the equivalent of reprints of catalogs and other promotional materials.

### Site Development Strategies

Firms in the industry generally had developed their own Web site. Advertising experts interviewed believe that site development is critical to the success of cyberspace advertising and that the poor results reported could be attributed to poorly developed Web pages. Benchmarking companies in a range of industries produces better results than using only the industry of a company.[1]

Three types of strategies for developing a Web site predominate: in-house development, the use of traditional full-service advertising agencies, and the use of the new cyberagencies that specialize in interactive marketing.

**In-house development.** The obvious advantage of in-house development is lower costs. The primary disadvantage is that most organizations have limited expertise in developing effective Web sites. A review of the literature indicates that about 50 percent of all Web sites currently in use were developed by employees of the company.[2]

**Traditional full-service agencies.** The key advantage of using the traditional advertising agency that handles other advertising for a company is that the Internet advertising can be an integral part of the company's total advertising plan. The primary disadvantage is that the traditional agency is not likely to have much expertise in cyberadvertising. About 25 percent of the Web sites in use were developed by traditional advertising agencies.

**Cyberagencies.** These agencies specialize in interactive advertising on the Internet. The advantage they have over traditional agencies is the level of expertise in this new field. The disadvantages are lack of knowledge about the company and making interactive advertising an integral part of the company's total advertising.

Experts point out that cyberadvertising will be effective only when it is integrated into the mainstream advertising media such as radio, television, and print media. A joint venture of traditional agencies and cyberagencies may offer the greatest promise for using the Internet effectively.

### Web Site Development Costs

The following table shows the projected costs of developing a Web site and advertising materials:

| Developer | Estimated Cost |
|---|---|
| In-house development team | $ 60,000 |
| Traditional agency | 150,000 |
| Cyberagency | 200,000 |

### Recommendations

Pat's Place should consider advertising on the Internet. However, further study is needed to determine the best strategy to do so.

Footnote text:

[1]Mark Levinson, "Benchmarking Internet Advertising," *The Small Business Journal* (March 1999), p. 28.
[2]Mary Stackhouse, *Web Site Development* (Chicago: Seiver, Inc., 1999), pp. 44-45.

# Graphics

Clipart, pictures, shapes, TextArt, charts, and scanned images are graphic elements that add interest to documents such as announcements, invitations, reports, and newsletters. You can find these graphic elements easily by displaying the Graphics toolbar (View menu, Toolbars, Graphics). In this lesson, you will learn to work with clipart and shapes.

Clipart

Draw shapes and lines

## Clipart

*WordPerfect* contains a scrapbook of clipart—pictures stored in the software—that can be inserted in documents. The *WordPerfect* suite contains thousands of clipart images, but only a limited number of images may have been copied to the network or local drive. You may have to access the *Corel Office 2000* CD-ROM for some of the clips. The Internet button on the Scrapbook dialog box launches your Web browser. Additional images may be downloaded from the Corel Web site. If you do not have a clip that is used in this text, substitute an appropriate clip.

**Drill**

1. Go to the Clipart Scrapbook and insert the binoculars (*BINOCLR.WPG*). Substitute another image if you do not have this one.

2. Select another image of your choice and insert it.

3. Resize the first picture you inserted to make it smaller.

4. Resize the second picture you inserted to make it larger.

**To insert clipart:**

1. Position the insertion point where you wish to insert the clipart.

2. To select art from the *WordPerfect* Clipart Scrapbook, click the **Clipart** button on the Graphics toolbar.

3. Scroll through the Scrapbook and choose the clipart you wish to use. Click and drag it into the document.

4. Close the Scrapbook dialog box.

**To size clipart:**

1. Click the graphic to select it. Eight handles (small boxes) appear.

2. Resize the graphic:

   • To keep the original proportions, position the pointer on the right bottom corner of the graphic until the pointer changes to a diagonal double-pointed arrow. Drag it up and to the left to make the graphic smaller or down and to the right to make it larger.

   • To distort or change the proportion, drag a middle handle.

Diagonal pointer

**To move clipart:**

1. Select the image.

2. Hold down the left mouse button and drag to the new location.

## Objective Assessment

Answer the questions below to see if you have mastered the content of this module.

1. _____ are references at the bottom of a page; _____ are placed at the end of the document.

2. The preferred way to format titles of publications is to use _____.

3. The Go To function is found in the _____ menu.

4. The default in the Find and Replace feature is to search _____ from the position of the insertion point.

5. The Thesaurus feature can be accessed through the _____ menu.

6. To create an em dash, select _____ from the Insert menu.

7. A footnote or endnote is displayed when the document is being keyed in _____ view.

8. Preliminary pages of a report are numbered using _____ numerals.

9. To center text vertically on a title page, select _____ from the _____ menu.

10. To change the page numbering sequence, click Format, Page, Numbering, then _____.

## Performance Assessment

### Unbound report with footnotes

DS; insert footnotes; number pages appropriately. *Title Page:* Prepared for **Patrick Schultz** by **you** as **Apartment Manager**; **current date**. Save the entire report as **ckpt12**.

### POMMERY PLACE APARTMENTS
### Annual Report

All goals for the rental and maintenance of Pommery Place Apartments have been met or exceeded for this calendar year. The apartments continue to attract and maintain an excellent tenant population.

### Revenue Generation

Revenue produced from Pommery Place exceeded the revenue from the previous year by 14 percent.[1] The increase was produced from several sources.

**Occupancy rate.** Pommery Place Apartments currently has a 100 percent occupancy rate and has maintained that rate with the exception of one two-week period in March. The tenant who signed a lease for G in the townhouse building was transferred and moved out of town before occupying the apartment. The transfer clause of the lease was invoked, and the apartment was rented and occupied two weeks later.

**Rent increases.** The leases on 24 units were renewed, and the monthly rent was increased $25 per unit. The minimum monthly rent is now $500 on the garden apartments and $625 on the townhouses.

### Expense Reduction

Expenses incurred this year were 15 percent below those of the last two years.[2] The expense reduction can be attributed to the correction of the plumbing problems that existed during the past two years and the low turnover rate. The painting, carpet cleaning, and general maintenance that are done between tenants were minimal this year. Advertising costs were also minimal because of the low turnover and quick rental.

### Projections for Next Year

The outlook for next year is outstanding. The time required to rent a unit averages three to five days. Occasionally, prospective tenants stop in at the office and ask to be put on a waiting list. Turnover is expected to be very low, and no major maintenance problems are anticipated.

Footnote text:
[1] *Pommery Place Annual Report,* 1999, p. 2.
[2] *Pommery Place Annual Reports,* 1998 and 1999, p. 4.

## SKILLBUILDING

Key each line at a comfortable rate. Practice difficult lines.

5  On June 11 and July 11, 11 men and 11 women worked 11 hours each.
6  Al received Invoice 22RC22 on May 22 and paid $225.22 on June 22.
7  The 33 boys visited 3 girls at 3:30 p.m. on May 3 at 33 Oak Road.
8  The 44 men found 44 sections of 4' pipe required before 4:44 p.m.
9  On June 15, 55 women ran over 25 miles in 2 hours and 55 minutes.
10  The 66 players shot 6,666 free throws in 66 minutes and made 666.
11  The 7 rooms were 17' 7" wide and 7' 7" long with 17' 7" ceilings.
12  Those 8 coaches made 88 trips averaging 88 miles each in 88 days.
13  The 9 boys packed 9 boxes weighing 99 pounds in 9 hours on May 9.
14  Was the value listed at $10,000,000 or $20,000,000 on October 20?

| 1 | 2 | 3 | 4 | 5 | 6 | 7 | 8 | 9 | 10 | 11 | 12 | 13 |

## SKILLBUILDING

1. Key two 1' writings on each ¶.
2. Key three 5' writings; proofread; circle errors; determine *gwam*.

all letters

gwam   1'|  5'

People come in many sizes and shapes.  Thus, a workstation     12 | 2 |44
designed for the average person will not fit all people.  A     24 | 5 |46
workstation should be designed for the person who will use it.     37 | 7 |49
If more than one person will use it, then it must be adjustable     49 | 10 |51
to meet the needs of each person who will use it.  Ergonomics is     62 | 12 |54
the term used to describe human factors engineering.  Today,     75 | 15 |56
desks, chairs, keyboards, and video display terminals are avail-     87 | 17 |59
able with a number of features that can be adjusted to accommo-     100 | 20 |61
date the person who will use the furniture or equipment.     112 | 22 |64

Just because furniture or equipment has adjustable features     12 | 25 |66
does not mean that the people using the furniture or equipment     24 | 27 |69
will adjust it properly.  Too often they do not.  Maximum return     37 | 30 |71
from the money spent on ergonomic furniture is dependent on how     50 | 32 |74
the furniture is used, and comfort may not be the best guide for     63 | 35 |76
making adjustments.  Many people have habits that may cause them     76 | 38 |79
to adjust furniture in an improper way.  They need to be told and     89 | 40 |82
taught what will work best.     95 | 41 |83

1' | 1 | 2 | 3 | 4 | 5 | 6 | 7 | 8 | 9 | 10 | 11 | 12 | 13 |
5' |       1       |       2       |       3       |

# Level
# 4

# ENHANCING

# DOCUMENT

# FORMAT

## Keyboarding

To key approximately 55 *wam* with good accuracy.

## Word Processing Skills

To learn advanced functions.

## Formatting Skills

To apply advanced functions to sophisti-cated documents, including documents with graphics and columns, and adminis-trative and employment documents.

## Communication Skills

To produce error-free documents and apply language arts skills.

# GRAPHIC ENHANCEMENTS

## OBJECTIVES

1. Build keyboarding skill.

2. Format documents with graphics and other design enhancements.

3. Format reports in columns.

---

## LESSON 97

# Skillbuilding

### 97a ● 7'

## GETTING started

Key each line 3 times SS; DS between 3-line groups. Follow this procedure throughout Module 14.

**SKILLBUILDING WARMUP**

alphabet 1 Dixie Vaughn acquired that prize job with a firm just like yours.

figures 2 Send me Files 43 and 67 by March 21; my official number is 91085.

one hand 3 Jim regarded a decrease in gas rates on a pump as a tax decrease.

easy 4 When did the city auditor pay the proficient firm for a big sign?

| 1 | 2 | 3 | 4 | 5 | 6 | 7 | 8 | 9 | 10 | 11 | 12 | 13 |

### 97b ● 5'

## SKILLBUILDING

**Build straight-copy skill**

Key two 1' writings at your top rate; key a 1' writing at your control rate.

 all letters

            4        8       12
The format of a document is quite important to organizations

     16        20       24
because it affects image. An effective format does not have to

     28        32       36
be complex. It just has to look professional and be easy to

     40        44       48
read. To have a consistent image, always use a standard format.

| 1 | 2 | 3 | 4 | 5 | 6 | 7 | 8 | 9 | 10 | 11 | 12 | 13 |

# SKILLBUILDING

### Lessons 94-96

## LESSON 94

### 94a • 15'

## GETTING started

1. Key lines 1–4 three times SS; DS between 3-line groups.
2. Take a 1' writing on line 4.
3. Take two 1' writings on each of the remaining lines. Try to match or exceed your *gwam* on line 4.

# Skillbuilding

### SKILLBUILDING WARMUP

alphabet 1 Why did Jackson Velasquez quit playing six days before that game?

figures 2 The score at half was 59 to 47; it is 102 to 98 with 3' 06" to go.

direct reaches 3 Ervn, a brown bunny, jumped to the center of a huge serving bowl.

easy 4 A neighbor on the island owns the mangy dog in the downtown mall.

script 5 *You must be able to speak and write effectively to be successful.*

statistical 6 My CEO gave an 18- to 20-minute talk to 6 or 7 groups of 35 to 49.

rough draft 7 I use ~~graphics~~ soft ware to prepare an project good visual slides.

| 1 | 2 | 3 | 4 | 5 | 6 | 7 | 8 | 9 | 10 | 11 | 12 | 13 |

### 94b • 10'

## SKILLBUILDING

**Build/assess script-copy skill**
1. Key two 1' writings.
2. Key one 5' writing. Proofread; circle errors; determine *gwam*.

 all letters

*gwam* 1' | 5'

*A comment often made by managers in various types of organizations is that many of the young people they hire know the subject area that they studied in school very well, but they usually have very weak communication skills. Few, if any, good jobs exist today that do not require the ability to listen, read, write, and speak effectively. Too often, these basic skills are taken for granted. Students may be told that these skills are very important, but the skills are not always taught and seldom are they reviewed in classes. Students often believe they already have the skills. They do not exert much effort to continue improving the basic skills they will need on the job each day. Time spent on these skills is a good investment.*

| | 1' | 5' |
|---|---|---|
| | 12 | 2 | 32 |
| | 27 | 5 | 35 |
| | 41 | 8 | 38 |
| | 55 | 11 | 41 |
| | 71 | 14 | 44 |
| | 86 | 17 | 47 |
| | 100 | 20 | 50 |
| | 114 | 23 | 53 |
| | 129 | 26 | 56 |
| | 144 | 29 | 59 |
| | 149 | 30 | 60 |

## 96c • 15'

### SKILLBUILDING

**Improve keyboarding technique**

each set of lines 3 times; DS between 6-line groups

## 96d • 15'

### SKILLBUILDING

**Build/assess straight-copy skill**

1. Key three 1' writings on each ¶.
2. Key one 5' writing or two 3' writings. Proofread; circle errors; determine *gwam*.

| | | |
|---|---|---|
| 1st/2d fingers | 5 | Becky and Joyce visited with me on the first day they moved here. |
| | 6 | Hunter and Kristin met with three or four members this afternoon. |
| 2d/3d fingers | 7 | Wesley Desselle was seeking more knowledge about an English test. |
| | 8 | Did Edward excel in window sales this week like he did last week? |
| 3d/4th fingers | 9 | Alex was too lazy to study for quizzes or exams in world history. |
| | 10 | Paul has six small poodles and a few wild animals on a sun porch. |

| 1 | 2 | 3 | 4 | 5 | 6 | 7 | 8 | 9 | 10 | 11 | 12 | 13 |

all letters                                                        *gwam*  3'| 5'

|  | 3' | 5' |
|---|---|---|
| How much power is adequate?  Is more power always better | 4 | 2 50 |
| than less power?  People often raise the question in many differ- | 8 | 5 52 |
| ent instances.  Regardless of the situation, most people seem to | 12 | 7 55 |
| seek more power.  In jobs, power is often related to rank in an | 17 | 10 57 |
| organization, to the number of people reporting to a person, and | 21 | 13 60 |
| to the ability to spend money without having to ask someone with | 25 | 15 63 |
| more power.  Most experts indicate that the power a person has | 30 | 18 65 |
| should closely match the responsibilities (not just duties and | 34 | 20 68 |
| tasks) for which he or she can be held accountable. | 37 | 22 70 |
| Questions about power are not limited to jobs and people. | 41 | 25 72 |
| Many people ask the question in reference to the amount of power | 45 | 27 75 |
| or speed a computer should have.  Again, the response usually | 50 | 30 77 |
| implies that more is better.  A better approach is to analyze how | 54 | 32 80 |
| the computer is to be used and then try to match power needs to | 58 | 35 82 |
| the types of applications.  Most people are surprised to learn | 62 | 37 85 |
| that home computer buyers tend to buy more power than buyers in | 67 | 40 87 |
| offices.  The primary reason is that the computers are used to | 71 | 43 90 |
| play games with extensive graphics, sound, and other media appli- | 75 | 45 93 |
| cations.  Matching the needs of the software is the key. | 79 | 47 95 |

3' | 1 | 2 | 3 | 4 |
5' | 1 | 2 | 3 |

**LESSON 96**     SKILLBUILDING                                    292

## Improve keyboarding technique

Key each set of lines twice; DS between 4-line groups; key one-hand words letter by letter; key balanced-hand words as units.

**balanced hand**

8 pens turn fur slam pay rifle worn pan duck ham lap slap burn girl
9 Andy Clancy, a neighbor, may visit at the lake and at the island.

**one hand**

10 read ploy create kiln crate plum were pony cats jump severe hump
11 Phillip, as you are aware, was a reader on deferred estate cases.

**combination**

12 did you we spent pony street busy jump held severe pant exert due
13 Were profits better when we were on Main Street than Duck Street?

| 1 | 2 | 3 | 4 | 5 | 6 | 7 | 8 | 9 | 10 | 11 | 12 | 13 |

## Build/assess straight-copy skill

1. Key three 1' writings on each ¶.
2. Key one 5' writing or two 3' writings. Proofread; circle errors; determine *gwam*.

all letters                                                                    *gwam* 3' | 5'

What do you think about when you hear individuals being ................ 4 | 2 | 50
called student athletes? Many people think only of the very ............ 8 | 5 | 52
visible football or basketball players who attract a lot of ............ 12 | 7 | 55
attention and often get special treatment on campus. Few people ........ 16 | 10 | 57
think about the large numbers of young men and women who put in ........ 20 | 12 | 60
long hours working and training to be the very best they can be ........ 25 | 15 | 62
in a wide variety of sports. These students may never receive .......... 29 | 17 | 65
any type of recognition in the news media, and they do not ............. 33 | 20 | 67
attract large crowds to watch them perform. They frequently ............ 37 | 22 | 70
excel in both academic and athletic performance. ...................... 40 | 24 | 72

What does a student athlete in one of the less visible ................. 44 | 26 | 74
sports with very little opportunity to become a professional ........... 48 | 29 | 76
athlete gain from the significant investment of time and ef- ........... 52 | 31 | 79
fort in a sport? To be successful in a sport, a student must ........... 56 | 34 | 81
be organized, be an effective time manager, and have self- ............. 60 | 36 | 83
confidence. An athlete learns that teamwork, ethical conduct, .......... 64 | 38 | 86
and hard work are a major part of success in any type of en- ........... 68 | 41 | 88
deavor. The skills do not apply just to sports; they also apply ........ 72 | 43 | 91
to jobs and to life. Most important of all, these individuals ......... 77 | 46 | 93
are doing what they really enjoy doing. ............................... 79 | 47 | 95

3' | 1 | 2 | 3 | 4 |
5' | 1 | 2 | 3 |

# LESSON 96

# Skillbuilding

## 96a ● 5'

### GETTING started

each line 3 times SS; DS between 3-line groups

**SKILLBUILDING WARMUP**

| | | |
|---|---|---|
| alphabet | 1 | Vasquez wrote the chilling poem about the jinx of five dark days. |
| fig/sym | 2 | Call Lee at (803) 555-1296 tonight or at (714) 555-4096 tomorrow. |
| double letters | 3 | Jeff will meet Lynn tomorrow at the swimming pool for his lesson. |
| easy | 4 | Did the six big bowls, six mementos, and eight maps fit in a box? |

| 1 | 2 | 3 | 4 | 5 | 6 | 7 | 8 | 9 | 10 | 11 | 12 | 13 |

## 96b ● 15'

### SKILLBUILDING

**Build/assess rough-draft copy skill**

1. Key two 1' writings on each ¶ at your top rate.
2. Key two 3' writings at your control rate.
3. Proofread; circle errors; determine *gwam*.

**A** all letters

|  | gwam | 1' | 3' |
|---|---|---|---|

~~Many~~ *Most* people in the early stages of a career — 9 | 3 | 55

think of advancing to high^er positions within the — 19 | 6 | 59

organization. *A small number of* ~~Fewer and fewer~~ (positions) *stat* are — 28 | 9 | 62

available at the higher levels to handle the large — 38 | 13 | 65

number of people wanting to move up. Therefore — 48 | 16 | 68

not all employees can move up at a steady rate. — 58 | 19 | 72

Periods exist in which a^n employee stays at the same — 68 | 23 | 75

level. Reaching a level and not being able to — 78 | 26 | 78

move upward is called "plateauing." — 85 | 28 | 81

Quite often, plateauing is the product of the — 9 | 31 | 84

way an organization is structured. College teach- — 19 | 35 | 87

ers for example, who attain a full professorate — 29 | 38 | 90

reach a plateau. They are at the *highest* ~~top~~ level and — 39 | 41 | 94

can not be promoted unless they change careers. — 49 | 45 | 97

An individual can also reach a plateau by mas- — 58 | 48 | 100

tering the content of a job so *well* ~~good~~ that it no — 67 | 51 | 103

longer is a challenge. — 72 | 52 | 104

# Skillbuilding

## 95a • 5'

### GETTING started

each line 3 times SS; DS between 3-line groups

### SKILLBUILDING WARMUP

alphabet 1 Jeffery quickly packed a dozen boxes of goods and gave them away.

figures 2 The 764 class meets from 9:10 to 9:55 in Room 3284 in Building 7.

adjacent reaches 3 Guy and Sam said we were going to the polo match with ten people.

easy 4 Claudia may fix the problem with the turn signals on the bicycle.

| 1 | 2 | 3 | 4 | 5 | 6 | 7 | 8 | 9 | 10 | 11 | 12 | 13 |

## 95b • 10'

### SKILLBUILDING

**Improve skill transfer**
Key two 1' writings on each line; compare speed on various types of copy.

5 Most work environments require employees to be effective team members.

6 Good interpersonal skills are necessary for effective team membership.

7 Team decisions are usually better decisions that individuals decisions.

8 The team training session (#284-97) meets from 8:30 to 4:15 on May 26.

| 1 | 2 | 3 | 4 | 5 | 6 | 7 | 8 | 9 | 10 | 11 | 12 | 13 |

## 95c • 12'

### SKILLBUILDING

**Build/assess statistical-copy skill**

1. Key two 1' writings on each ¶ at your top rate.
2. Key two 3' writings at your control rate.
3. Proofread; circle errors; determine *gwam*.

 all letters/figures

*gwam* 1' | 3'

Even though investments in real estate do not have the same tax advantage that they had some years ago, they still can be sound investments.  An example would be a 12-unit apartment building that costs $485,625.  Assume that $450,000 was financed at 9.75% interest.  Amortized over 30 years, the debt service would be $3,865.  Other outlays would be about $1,235 for a combined monthly outlay of $5,100.

If the 12 units rented for $475 per month each or a total rent of $5,700, the apartments would have a positive cash flow at just 90% occupancy.  The apartments would appreciate quickly, and the initial outlay of $35,625 would be worth a great deal plus the tax benefits.  Of course, the risks must be considered carefully before you invest your money.

| | 1' | 3' |
|---|---|---|
| | 12 | 4 | 54 |
| | 24 | 8 | 58 |
| | 36 | 12 | 63 |
| | 49 | 16 | 67 |
| | 62 | 21 | 71 |
| | 74 | 25 | 75 |
| | 81 | 27 | 77 |
| | 12 | 31 | 81 |
| | 25 | 35 | 86 |
| | 38 | 40 | 90 |
| | 51 | 44 | 94 |
| | 62 | 48 | 98 |
| | 70 | 50 | 101 |

1' | 1 | 2 | 3 | 4 | 5 | 6 | 7 | 8 | 9 | 10 | 11 | 12 | 13 |
3' | 1 | 2 | 3 | 4 |

**Improve keyboarding technique**

each set of lines 2 times; DS between 4-line groups

1st
9 Zam and six lazy men visited Cecil and Bunn at a bank convention.
10 Zane, much to the concern of Bev and six men, visited their zone.

2d
11 Jill said she wished that she had fed Dale's dog a lot less food.
12 Jake Hall sold the glass flask at a Dallas "half-off" glass sale.

3d
13 Did either Peter or Trey quip that reporters were out to get you?
14 Either Trey or Peter tried to work with a top-quality pewter toy.

4th
15 18465 97354 12093 87541 09378 34579 74629 45834 28174 11221 27211
16 02574 29765 39821 07623 17659 20495 39481 10374 32765 77545 22213

| 1 | 2 | 3 | 4 | 5 | 6 | 7 | 8 | 9 | 10 | 11 | 12 | 13 |

95e ● 15'

**Build/assess straight-copy skill**

1. Key three 1' writings on each ¶.
2. Key one 5' writing or two 3' writings. Proofread; circle errors; determine *gwam*.

all letters                                                        *gwam*   3' | 5'

Students, for decades, have secured part-time jobs to help           4 | 2 52
pay for college expenses. Today, more students are gainfully         8 | 5 54
employed while they are in college than ever before. Many of        12 | 7 57
them are employed because their financial situation requires that   17 | 10 59
they earn money. Earnings from jobs go to pay for tuition,          21 | 12 62
books, living costs, and other necessities. Some work so that       25 | 15 64
they can own cars or buy luxury items; others seek jobs to gain     29 | 17 67
skills or to build their vitas. These students are aware that       33 | 20 69
many organizations prefer to hire a person who has had some type    38 | 23 72
of work experience than one who has had none.                       41 | 24 74

Students often ask if the work experience has to be in              44 | 27 76
exactly the same field. Obviously, the more closely related the     49 | 29 78
experience, the better it is. However, the old adage, anything      53 | 32 81
beats nothing, applies. Regardless of the types of jobs students    57 | 34 84
have, they can demonstrate that they get to work regularly and on   62 | 37 86
time, they have good human relations skills, they are organized     66 | 40 89
and can manage time effectively, and they produce good results.     70 | 42 91
All of these factors are very critical to employers. The bottom     75 | 45 94
line is that employers like to use what you have done in the past   79 | 47 97
as a predictor of what you will do in the future.                   82 | 49 99

3'  | 1 | 2 | 3 | 4 |
5'  | 1 | 2 | 3 |

# Contents

| CHOOSING A UNIVERSITY—COMPARISON FACTORS | | |
| Your Name | | |
| Factor | Choice #1 | Choice #2 |
| --- | --- | --- |
| Student Enrollment | 10,000 | 4,000 |
| Tuition (semester) Residents Out-of-state | $1,800 $3,500 | $1,750 $5,000 |

**Job Search**

You will be graduating next semester and will need a full-time job. You want to use the Internet as one element of your job search. Conducting a job search on the Internet is new to you.

**Instructions**

1. Browse the following Web sites to learn about job searches using the Internet. (You are not limited to these Web sites.)

www.dbm.com/jobguide     www.monsterboard.com
www.monster.com     www.careeravenue.com
www.careermosaic.com     www.occ.com
www.ajb.dni.us     www.joboptions.com
www.telecomjobs.www     classified.yahoo.com

Use the following categories to guide your exploration:

- Job openings (for which you are qualified) in preferred location(s)
- Salaries and other benefits
- Company information (including locations, types of business, stock listing, company opinions)
- Sample resumes
- Posting a resume

2. Print the following: (1) one list of current openings in desired positions/locations, (2) information about one company, (3) two sample resumes that are posted, and (4) one set of guidelines for posting a resume.

# appendix A

# FILE MANAGEMENT

**Windows Explorer**

Files can be managed by using a program called *Windows Explorer*. To access *Windows Explorer*, click *Start,* point to *Programs,* and click *Windows Explorer. Windows Explorer* provides a very convenient way to set up folders (directories) and subfolders (subdirectories). Folders and subfolders can be set up on your hard disk drive or on a floppy disk. The example shown below provides folders for a keyboarding and an English class.

**Creating folders and subfolders**

Note that each folder has two subfolders—Classwork and Homework. To create the folders, click 3½ Floppy (A:), then click File. From the cascading menu, click New and then Folder. Key English as the name of the folder. Then repeat the process and name the new folder Keyboarding.

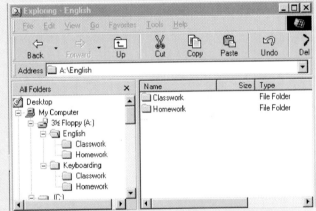

To create the subfolders for the folder named English, click English, then New, and then Folder. Name the folder Classwork. Repeat the process, naming the new folder Homework. To create the subfolders for Keyboarding, click Keyboarding, then New, and then Folder. Name the folder Classwork. Repeat the process, naming the new folder Homework.

### Drill 1

**Using *Windows Explorer***

1. Insert your storage disk into Drive A or B.

2. Click **Start.**  Highlight *Programs.*  Click **Windows Explorer.**

3. Maximize the *Explorer* window. If Desktop is not the top object in the All Folders pane, click on the up scroll arrow until it is displayed.

4. If a plus sign (+) displays beside the My Computer icon, click the **+** to extend its sublevels.

5. Click on **3 1/2" Floppy** (**A:** or **B:**).

6. From the View menu, click **List** to display the contents of the folder in numerical and alphabetical order.

### Drill 2

**Create folders for this book**

1. From the File menu, choose *New,* then *Folder.*  A new folder icon labeled New Folder displays in the Contents pane.

2. Enter the folder name **Module 4** and press ENTER.  A new folder appears on your disk.

3. Repeat Steps 1 and 2 to create new folders labeled Module 5, Module 6, Module 7, Module 8, and Appendix.

# appendix D

# INTERNET ACTIVITIES

## Activity sixteen

### Selection of an Ergonomic Chair

You are employed in a Fortune 500 company in Atlanta, Georgia. One of your responsibilities is to make decisions that ensure a comfortable and productive environment for the 250 office employees employed by your company. You have already attended seminars on ergonomics and realize the importance of comfortable employees who can produce well in their environments.

#### Instructions

1. Today your task is to order office chairs. Search the Internet for ergonomic concerns associated with an office chair and the criteria for purchasing an ergonomic office chair.

2. Prepare a short unbound report entitled **THE ERGONOMIC OFFICE CHAIR**. Develop your report as follows:

   • Present information on the physical problems that result from employees using an inappropriate office chair.

   • List criteria to consider when choosing an ergonomic chair.

## Activity seventeen

### College Selection

You would like to pursue a degree in _____ (you supply the degree) at a four-year college or university. You have narrowed your choice to two colleges/universities.

Choice #1 _____     Choice #2 _____

#### Instructions

1. When selecting a college/university, you should consider such factors as location, tuition, room and board, degree program, student organizations, recreational activities, winning football team, etc.

2. Prepare a table entitled **CHOOSING A UNIVERSITY—COMPARISON FACTORS** (see Sample on p. A22). Key your name as the subtitle.

   • Create a three-column table. In Column A, list factors that will weigh in your choice of a college/university.

   • Key the names of your school choices as headings for Columns B and C.

   • Key the facts for each college/university in the appropriate cell.

## Selecting folders/ directories and files

Only one folder/directory can be selected at a time in the left pane. Multiple files or folders can be selected in the right pane. To select multiple files or folders listed in consecutive order, click on the first object to be selected, hold down the SHIFT key, and click the last object to be selected. The entire group of folders or files is now highlighted.

To select files or folders that are scattered throughout the Contents pane/content list area, hold down the CTRL key while you click each of the desired objects.

## Deleting and renaming folders

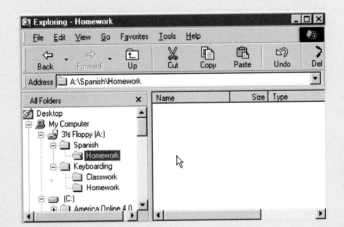

If you change your English class to a Spanish class, you could simply rename the folder. Click on the English folder, then click File, and then Rename. Key Spanish. In your Spanish class, you do not need the subfolder named Classwork. Click the subfolder Classwork, then click File, and then Delete. Respond Yes to the inquiry, *Are you sure you want to remove the folder Classwork and all its contents?*

Files and folders can be moved by dragging them from one position to another. They can be copied by pressing CTRL and dragging the file to the new position.

## Moving and copying files

As you create more files, you probably will need to create additional folders or directories and then rearrange existing files by moving or copying them into the new folders/directories. When a file is copied, the original file remains in place, and another copy of the file is placed at the destination. When a file is moved, the original file is removed from its original location and placed at the destination.

- Folders and files are moved by dragging the object from the Contents pane to its destination. If you drag a folder on the same disk, it will be moved. If you drag a file to another disk (from Drive A to C), it will be copied.

- To copy a file/folder, use the CTRL key while dragging the file.

- To move a file/folder, use the SHIFT key.

The file or folder that is to be copied is referred to as the **source copy**; the location where the copy is to be moved is called the **destination**. Folders and files that are moved or copied by mistake can be restored to their original location by using Undo in the Edit menu.

**Drill 5**

Review pronoun case in the Reference Guide. Key the sentences correcting errors as you go. Save as **cw3-d5**.

1. Marie and me have volunteered to work on the committee.
2. It is she who received the free airline ticket.
3. It was not me who sent in the request.
4. Give the assignment to George and I.
5. She has more time available than me for handling this project.
6. Did you see Cheryl and he at the opening session?


**Drill 6**
**Pronoun and antecedent agreement**

Key the sentences correcting all errors in pronoun agreement. Save as **cw3-d6**.

1. Each student must have their own data disk.
2. Several students have his or her own computer.
3. Some of the employees were happy with their raises.
4. Neither Chris nor Joseph wants to do their share.
5. The company has not decided whether they will make profit sharing available.
6. The jury has reached their decision; it will be announced at 10 a.m.


**Drill 7**
**Word usage**

Key the sentences and select the proper word choice. Save as **cw3-d7**.

1. Please *accept/except* all contributions *accept/except* those of perishable foods.
2. His *advice/advise* was to *accept/except* all forms *accept/except* those that arrive late.
3. Can we have *counsel/council* present at the Dayton City *Council/Counsel* meeting tomorrow?
4. The high school *principal/principle* based her decision on sound *principals/principles*.
5. According to the report *cited/sighted*, no prints were found at that *sight/site*.
6. Did the Woodward High Advisory *Council/Counsel* select my *Principals/Principles of Accounting* text?
7. *It's/Its* true that the bird found at the *sight/site* had lost *it's/its* eye.


**Drill 8**
**Word usage**

Key the sentences, inserting the correct word choice. Save as **cw3-d8**.

1. *Access/excess* steps are required to *access/excess* and *adapt/adopt* the data.
2. Did they *adapt/adopt* new procedures for *accessing/assessing* data from the system?
3. They need to study the map *farther/further* before they drive any *farther/further*.
4. We *hear/here* what you are saying; we want to explore this *farther/further*.
5. Lynn and I did not *know/no* that we *passed/past* the exam.
6. We know from *passed/past* experience that *know/no* news is good news.
7. Merry indicated that she did not *know/no* that the bill was *passed/past* due.
8. The *coarse/course*-weave fabric *complemented/complimented* the decor in the den.

## Managing files with *WordPerfect*

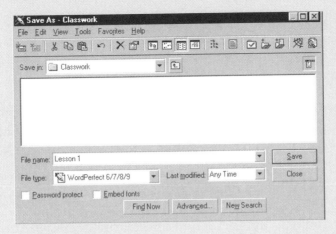

Files are most often managed with application software, such as *WordPerfect*. To save your first document in the Classwork subfolder, click File on the Menu bar; then click Save As to display the Save As dialog box. In the Save in box, click Drive A; then double-click the Keyboarding folder; then click the Classwork subfolder.

In the File name box, replace the * with the filename Lesson 1. Click Save to save the file. Use the same procedure to save another new document named Lesson 2.

## Filenaming conventions

Selecting appropriate filenames is extremely important. Files that are named in a logical, systematic manner are easier to locate than files that are named in a haphazard way. Filenames can be 255 characters long, including spaces. A period is used to separate the filename from the extension. *WordPerfect* automatically adds a *wpd* extension to indicate that the file is a *WordPerfect* document. The following symbols cannot be used in a filename: * + = [ ] : ; " < > ? / \ |.

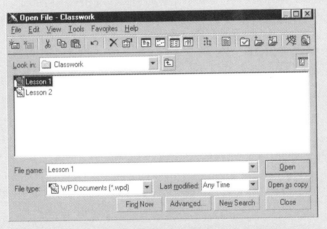

Note from the preceding example that using a logical system of folders, subfolders, and filenames makes it easy to find files when you need them. If you needed to find the first lesson that you did as classwork in your keyboarding class, it would be logical and easy to remember to look in the Keyboarding class folder, then in the Classwork subfolder, and then for Lesson 1. Files can be opened by clicking File on the Menu bar and then clicking Open.

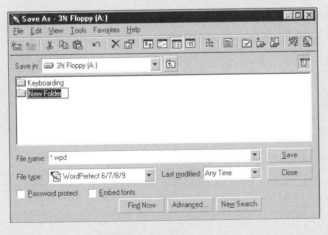

New folders can also be created from the Save As dialog box by clicking on the right mouse button. When the pop-up menu displays, click New, then click Folder. The folder can then be named in the same way that you named folders using *Windows Explorer*.

# COMMUNICATION WORKSHOP 3

**Drill 1**
**Introductory elements**

Review using commas after an introductory word, phrase, or clause in the Reference Guide of this text. Key the sentences at right inserting correct punctuation. DS between each. Save as **cw3-d1**.

1. Apparently the FastTrack courier service is no longer in business.
2. If the company's network crashes tonight you will need to reboot.
3. Because training is convenient soon we will all be able to be proficient users.
4. If you are not satisfied with the results after reviewing the template return it to us for a full refund.
5. If you will check the Bullets and Numbering option on the Format menu you will find the option for creating a simple outline.

**Drill 2**

Review the comma rules in the Reference Guide. Key the sentences inserting correct punctuation. DS between each. Save as **cw3-d2**.

1. AB Creations which is located near Exit 15 will host a meeting for new students.
2. I know Michael that you prefer to use your own software.
3. Glenn arrived in Honolulu Hawaii on Monday June 9.
4. My manager Douglas Denny got his MBA from Western College.
5. You will learn to work with both spreadsheet and word processing software and then you will link files between the two programs.
6. Please include your Internet address Paul on all future correspondence (name@lwpco.com).
7. Effective Friday October 29 the number for technical support will change.
8. Al Rosa and Terry will attend the conference in Anchorage Alaska.

**Drill 3**
**Apostrophes**

Review the rules on apostrophes in the Reference Guide. Key the sentences; correct all errors. DS between items. Save as **cw3-d3**.

1. Mary Thomas, my neighbors sister, will take care of my son.
2. The assistant gave him the instructors telephone number.
3. The announcers microphone is never shut off.
4. His father-in-laws home will be open for touring next week.
5. Two hours time is not sufficient to set up the exhibit.
6. Someones car lights have been left on.

**Drill 4**

Key the message as a memo to **Janie McDermott** from you regarding the **Magnolia Conference Center Facility**. Use the current date. Insert correct punctuation and capitalization. Save as **cw3-d4**.

This past week I visited the magnolia conference center facilities in isle of palms south carolina as you requested. bob bremmerton group manager was my host for the visit.

Magnolia offers many advantages for our leadership training conference. The prices are reasonable the facilities are excellent and the location is suitable. In addition to the beachfront location tennis and golf packages are part of the group price.

# appendix B

## SKILLBUILDING WORKSHOP 2

**Drill 1**
**Compare skill sentences**

1. Take a 1' writing on line 1; determine *gwam* and use this score for your goal as you take two 1' writings each on lines 2 and 3.

2. Take a 1' writing on line 4; determine *gwam* and use this score for your goal as you take two 1' writings each on lines 5 and 6.

1 Did the visitor on the bicycle signal and turn to the right?
2 The 17 girls kept 30 bushels of kale and 29 bushels of yams.
3 *The hen and a lamb roam down the field of rocks to the corn.*
4 The penalty she had to pay for the bogus audit is a problem.
5 Handle 10 ducks, 46 fish, and 38 hams for the island ritual.
6 *We got the usual quantity of shamrocks for Pamela to handle.*
| 1 | 2 | 3 | 4 | 5 | 6 | 7 | 8 | 9 | 10 | 11 | 12 |

**Drill 2**
**Review number and symbol reaches**

Key each line twice SS; DS between 2-line groups; repeat difficult lines.

1 The inn opened at 6789 Brentt; rooms are $45 (May 12 to July 30).
2 I paid $1.56 for 2% milk and $97 for 48 rolls of film on June 30.
3 Order #4567-0 (dated 2/18) was shipped on May 30 to Spah & Erven.
4 Send Check #3589 for $1,460--dated the 27th--to O'Neil & Company.
5 Ann's 7% note (dated May 13) was just paid with a check for $285.
6 Send to The Maxi-Tech Co., 3489 D Drive, our Bill #10 for $25.67.
7 I wrote "Serial #1830/27"; I should have written "Serial #246/9."
| 1 | 2 | 3 | 4 | 5 | 6 | 7 | 8 | 9 | 10 | 11 | 12 | 13 |

**Drill 3**
**Improve keying techniques**

Concentrate on each word as you key it; key each group twice; DS between 3-line groups.

direct reaches

1 runny cedar carver brunt numbs humps dunce mummy arbor sects hymn
2 Irvyn jumped over a clump of green grass; he broke my brown pump.
3 My uncle Cedric carved a number of brown cedar mules in December.

adjacent reaches

4 trios where alert point buyer spore milk sands sagas treads ports
5 There were three points in Porter's talk on the ports of Denmark.
6 Has Bert Welker prepared loin of pork as her dinner on Wednesday?

double letters

7 glass sells adder offer room sleek upper errors inner pretty ebbs
8 The committee soon agreed that Bess's green wool dress looks odd.
9 Three sweet little moppets stood happily on a green grassy knoll.
| 1 | 2 | 3 | 4 | 5 | 6 | 7 | 8 | 9 | 10 | 11 | 12 | 13 |

# COMMUNICATION WORKSHOP 2

**Drill I**
**Review use of the apostrophe**
1.5" top margin; default side margins; use bold and indent as shown; center the title

### USING AN APOSTROPHE TO SHOW POSSESSION

1. Add **'s** to a singular noun not ending in **s**.

2. Add **'s** to a singular noun ending in **s** or **z** sound if the ending **s** is pronounced as a syllable; as, Sis's lunch, Russ's car, Buzz's average.

3. Add **'** only if the ending **s** or **z** is awkward to pronounce; as, series' outcome, ladies' shoes, Delibes' music, Cortez' quest.

4. Add **'s** to a plural noun that does not end in **s**; as, men's notions, children's toys, mice's tracks.

5. Add only **'** after a plural noun ending in **s**; as, horses' hoofs, lamps' shades.

6. Add **'s** after the last noun in a series to show joint possession of two or more people; as, Jack and Judy's house; Peter, Paul, and Mary's song.

7. Add **'s** to each noun to show individual possession of two or more persons; as, Li's and Ted's tools, Jill's and Ed's races.

**Drill 2**
**Review use of quotation marks**
1.5" top margin; default side margins; indent examples to the first tab

### SPACING WITH QUOTATION MARKS

**Use quotation marks:**

after a comma or a period; as,
"I bought," she said, "more paper."

before a semicolon; as,
She said, "I have little money"; she had, in fact, none.

before a colon; as,
He called these items "fresh":  beans, peas, and carrots.

after a question mark if the quotation itself is a question; as,
"Why did you do that?" he asked.

before a question mark if the quotation is not a question; as,
Why did he say, "I will not run"?

## Drill 4
### Build production skill

1. Key 1' writings (18 *gwam*) on the letter parts, arranging each line in correct block format. Ignore top margin requirements.

2. Return 5 times between drills.

1   May 15, 200- | Mr. Brad Babbett | 811 Wier Ave., W. | Phoenix, AZ 83018-8183 | Dear Mr. Babbett

2   May 3, 200- | Miss Lois J. Bruce | 913 Torch Hill Rd. | Columbus, GA 31904-4133 | Dear Miss Bruce

3   Sincerely yours | George S. Murger | Assistant Manager | xx | Enclosures: Warranty Deed | Invoice

4   Very cordially yours | Marvin J. Cecchetti, Jr. | Assistant to the Comptroller | xx | Enclosures

## Drill 5
### Reach for new goals

1. From the second or third column at the right, choose a goal 2-3 *gwam* higher than your best rate on either straight or statistical copy.

2. Take 1' writings on that sentence; try to finish it the number of times shown at the top of the goal list.

3. If you reach your goal, take 1' writings on the next line. If you don't reach your goal, use the preceding line.

|  | words | 1' timing 6 times gwam | 1' timing 5 times gwam |
|---|---|---|---|
| Do they blame me for the goal? | 6 | 36 | 30 |
| The 2 men may enamel 17 oboes. | 6 | 36 | 30 |
| The auditor may handle the problem. | 7 | 42 | 35 |
| Did the 4 chaps focus the #75 lens? | 7 | 42 | 35 |
| She did vow to fight for the right name. | 8 | 48 | 40 |
| He paid 10 men to fix a pen for 3 ducks. | 8 | 48 | 40 |
| The girl may cycle down to the dormant field. | 9 | 54 | 45 |
| The 27 girls paid their $9 to go to the lake. | 9 | 54 | 45 |
| The ensign works with vigor to dismantle the auto. | 10 | 60 | 50 |
| Bob may work Problems 8 and 9; Sid did Problem 40. | 10 | 60 | 50 |
| The form may entitle a visitor to pay for such a kayak. | 11 | 66 | 55 |
| They kept 7 panels and 48 ivory emblems for 29 chapels. | 11 | 66 | 55 |

| 1 | 2 | 3 | 4 | 5 | 6 | 7 | 8 | 9 | 10 | 11 |

## Drill 6
### Improve concentration

Set a right tab at 5.5" for the addresses. Key the Internet addresses in Column 2 exactly as they are listed. Accuracy is critical.

| | |
|---|---|
| The paperless guide to New York City | http://www.mediabridge.com/nyc |
| A trip to outer space | http://spacelink.msfc.nasa.gov |
| Search engine | http://webcrawler.com |
| Government printing office access | http://www.access.gpo.gov/index.html |
| MarketPlace--corporate information | http://www.mktplace.com |
| Touchstone's PC-cillin virus scan | http://www.antivirus.com |

## Drills 3 and 4
### Capitalization

Key the salutations and complimentary closings, using correct capitalization. Number each item and DS between each.

**Reference:** RG1

**Drill 3**

1. ladies and gentlemen
2. dear mr petroielli
3. dear sir or madam
4. dear service manager
5. dear reverend schmidt
6. dear mr. fong and miss landow
7. dear mr. and mrs. green
8. dear senator kukanis

**Drill 4**

1. very sincerely yours
2. yours truly
3. very truly yours
4. sincerely yours
5. cordially yours
6. respectfully yours
7. sincerely
8. very sincerely yours

## Drill 5
### Letter addresses

Apply correct capitalization, number expression, and abbreviations in the letter addresses. Assume capitalization in letter addresses in Items 7 and 8 is correct. Key each address at the left margin; return 4 times between addresses.

**Reference:** RG5 for correct two-letter state abbreviations.

1. mr. aaron farrell
   223 east 3 street
   ft. wright, kentucky 41001-1420

2. ms. andrea phfehler
   412 morris road
   la jolla, california 92037-3310

3. mr. hoyt warner
   vice president of operations
   elgin manufacturing co.
   364 east 42nd street
   ypsilanti, michigan 48197-2211

4. mr. carlos rodriquez
   manulife international, inc.
   491 Paseo de la Cruz
   Mexico City 06500
   MEXICO

5. mr. scott veith
   p.o. box 175976
   orem, utah 84057-2399

6. ms. carol henson
   alger inc., suite 248
   pueblo, colorado 84001-6243

7. mr adam dabdoub
   1130 confederation drive
   Quebec City PG G1J2G3
   CANADA

8. mr. d. l. foust
   foust travel inc., suite 38
   779 cascade
   Calgary AB T3E 0R5
   CANADA

## Drill 6
### Composition

DS the ¶, inserting a proper noun in each blank and applying correct capitalization and number expression.

last _____ , my friend _____ and I had a holiday, so we decided to make the most of our day and take a bicycle trip to _____. before leaving, we stopped at _____ to purchase some high-energy foods to sustain us on our trip. we packed our saddle bags and left about _____ o'clock, traveling _direction_ on _____ street. although we were not on a sightseeing trip, we did pass _____ and _____. by _____ p.m., we returned home exhausted from our journey of _____ miles.

## Drill 7
### Assess skill growth: straight copy

1. Key 1' writings on each ¶ of a timing. Note that ¶s within a timing increase by 2 words.

   **Goal:** to complete each ¶.

2. Key a 3' timing on the entire writing.

 To access writings on *MicroPace Pro*, key **W** and the timing number. For example, key **W8** for *Writing 8*.

 Timings are also available as Diagnostic Writings in *Keyboarding Pro*.

|  | gwam |  |
|---|---|---|
|  | 1' | 3' |

**Writing 8:** 34, 36, 38 *gwam*

|  | 1' | 3' |
|---|---|---|
| Any of us whose target is to achieve success in our professional | 13 | 4 |
| lives will understand that we must learn how to work in harmony | 26 | 8 |
| with others whose paths may cross ours daily. | 35 | 12 |
| We will, unquestionably, work for, with, and beside people, just | 13 | 16 |
| as they will work for, with, and beside us. We will judge them, | 26 | 20 |
| as most certainly they are going to be judging us. | 38 | 24 |
| A lot of people realize the need for solid working relations and | 13 | 28 |
| have a rule that treats others as they, themselves, expect to be | 26 | 33 |
| treated. This seems to be a sound, practical idea for them. | 40 | 37 |

**Writing 9:** 36, 38, 40 *gwam*

|  | 1' | 3' |
|---|---|---|
| I spoke with one company visitor recently; and she was very much | 13 | 4 |
| impressed, she said, with the large amount of work she had noted | 26 | 9 |
| being finished by one of our front office workers. | 36 | 12 |
| I told her how we had just last week recognized this very person | 13 | 16 |
| for what he had done, for output, naturally, but also because of | 26 | 21 |
| its excellence. We know this person has that "magic touch." | 38 | 25 |
| This "magic touch" is the ability to do a fair amount of work in | 13 | 29 |
| a fair amount of time. It involves a desire to become ever more | 26 | 34 |
| efficient without losing quality--the "touch" all workers should | 39 | 38 |
| have. | 40 | 38 |

**Writing 10:** 38, 40, 42 *gwam*

|  | 1' | 3' |
|---|---|---|
| Isn't it great just to untangle and relax after you have keyed a | 13 | 4 |
| completed document? Complete, or just done? No document is | 25 | 8 |
| quite complete until it has left you and passed to the next step. | 38 | 13 |
| There are desirable things that must happen to a document before | 13 | 17 |
| you surrender it. It must be read carefully, first of all, for | 26 | 22 |
| meaning to find words that look right but aren't. Read word for | 39 | 26 |
| word. | 40 | 26 |
| Check all figures and exact data, like a date or time, with your | 13 | 31 |
| principal copy. Make sure format details are right. Only then, | 26 | 35 |
| print or remove the work and scrutinize to see how it might look | 39 | 39 |
| to a recipient. | 42 | 40 |

| 1' | 1 | 2 | 3 | 4 | 5 | 6 | 7 | 8 | 9 | 10 | 11 | 12 | 13 |
|---|---|---|---|---|---|---|---|---|---|---|---|---|---|
| 3' |  | 1 |  |  | 2 |  |  | 3 |  |  | 4 |  |  |

# appendix C

## COMMUNICATION WORKSHOP 1

**Drill 1**
**Capitalization**
Key the sentences, correcting all capitalization errors. Number each item and DS between them.
**Reference:** RG1

1. mara will visit glacier national park and vancouver, british columbia, this fall.

2. eric and kate bought 6 notebooks. each notebook holds 350 pages.

3. mohammed is striving to earn his mba in six years at columbia university.

4. i saw the quote in section c of the *times* regarding the governor of ohio.

5. joseph lutke earned his cpa and was promoted to vice president of finance on monday, april 3.

6. the production department will meet march 3 in the wells conference room.

7. robin is enrolled in accounting 101; lee is in a marketing class.

8. complimentary closings range from informal (cordially yours, sincerely yours, sincerely) to formal (very truly yours, yours very sincerely).

9. we told them smart write is a registered trademark of holt, inc.

10. george is the leading sales representative in the western region.

**Drill 2**
**Number expression**
Key each phrase, applying correct number expression. Number each item.
**Reference:** RG1

1. class of about 450 students

2. prize of one thousand dollars

3. Was it three percent or five percent?

4. nine o'clock meeting that was extended beyond noon

5. 2 days to check on about one hundred fifty thousand returns

6. three two-foot strips

7. 26th of May is when

8. two boxes of letterhead and twelve reams of paper

9. building listed near $2.5 million

10. received three hundred calls the first day

11. Francis gave only $.75.

12. invited six girls and twelve boys

13. Over $2,000,000 was raised.

14. will be working until 6 o'clock for 4 days

15. only 5 of the 35 members

16. 3 of us will be here all day.

17. with a ten percent budget cut planned for the 1st of next year

18. paid fifty dollars for 8 tickets at two p.m.

19. a $50 value

20. 1 of the 12-poster sets plus a 64-page user's guide

**Drill 8**
**Guided writing:**
**improve speed/accuracy**
Key as 1' guided writings, working for either speed or control.

**Optional:** Key as a 3' writing.

To access writings on *MicroPace Pro*, key **W** and the timing number. For example, key **W11** for Writing 11.

**Writing 11**

|   |   |   |   |
|---|---|---|---|
| • | 4 | • | 8 | • | 12 |

Anyone who expects some day to find an excellent job should    4 | 34

begin now to learn the value of accuracy.  To be worth anything,    8 | 38

completed work must be correct, without question.  Naturally, we    13 | 43

realize that the human aspect of the work equation always raises    17 | 47

the prospect of errors; but we should understand that those same    20 | 51

errors can be found and fixed.  Every completed job should carry    26 | 56

at least one stamp; the stamp of pride in work that is exemplary.    30 | 60

**Writing 12**

No question about it:  Many personal problems we face today    4 | 34

arise from the fact that we earthlings have never been very wise    8 | 38

consumers.  We haven't consumed our natural resources well; as a    13 | 43

result, we have jeopardized much of our environment.  We excused    17 | 47

our behavior because we thought that our stock of most resources    20 | 51

had no limit.  So, finally, we are beginning to realize just how    26 | 56

indiscreet we were; and we are taking steps to rebuild our world.    30 | 60

**Writing 13**

When I see people in top jobs, I know I'm seeing people who    4 | 34

sell.  I'm not just referring to employees who labor in a retail    8 | 38

outlet; I mean those people who put extra effort into convincing    13 | 43

others to recognize their best qualities.  They, themselves, are    17 | 47

the commodity they sell; and their optimum tools are appearance,    20 | 51

language, and personality.  They look great, they talk and write    26 | 56

well; and, with candid self-confidence, they meet you eye to eye.    30 | 60

3' | 1 | 2 | 3 | 4 |

**Drill 7**
**Tab and numbers**
Key each line once; operate TAB with left little finger without pausing. Set 4-space inter-column tabs.

| | | | | | | | | | |
|---|---|---|---|---|---|---|---|---|---|
| 1 | route | 497 | savor | 2149 | incur | 8637 | flute | 4975 | motor | 7959 |
| 2 | taken | 518 | under | 7633 | piano | 0816 | juror | 7749 | marks | 7148 |
| 3 | vigor | 485 | zebra | 1354 | cover | 3943 | value | 4197 | amend | 1736 |
| 4 | ozone | 919 | yacht | 6136 | fixed | 4823 | havoc | 6149 | ninth | 6865 |
| 5 | kudos | 873 | banjo | 5167 | urban | 7451 | wrote | 2495 | jeans | 7316 |
| 6 | scuba | 237 | timer | 5873 | cough | 3975 | total | 5951 | while | 2689 |

| 1 | 2 | 3 | 4 | 5 | 6 | 7 | 8 | 9 | 10 | 11 | 12 | 13 |

**Writing 20**

 all letters

|  | gwam | 3' | 5' |
|---|---|---|---|

The kinds of leisure activities you choose constitute your life style and, to a great extent, reflect your personality. For example, if your daily activities are people oriented, you may balance this by spending your free time alone. On the other hand, if you would rather be with people most of the time, your socialization needs may be very high. At the other end of the scale are people who are engaged in machine-oriented work and also enjoy spending leisure time alone. These people tend to be rather quiet and reserved.

Every individual needs a certain amount of relaxation to remain physically and mentally alert. However, what one person finds relaxing may be just the opposite for another person. For example, one person may like to read a good book; another may find that reading causes nervousness and fatigue. The same holds true for the person who enjoys sports. Studies have shown that jogging may be quite good for a person who enjoys it but may be detrimental to another person who does not enjoy it.

Experts have noted that the proper balance of leisure, relaxation, and recreation is almost essential for individuals who live and work in a highly automated world. This balance is necessary if each person is to be productive in handling the everyday pressure and stress of life. Because every person has unique needs that are met in a variety of ways, one must properly assess all of the day's activities if the maximum benefit is to be gained from each day of life.

gwam 3'/5':
4 2 62
8 5 65
12 7 67
17 10 70
21 13 72
25 15 75
29 18 77
33 20 80
35 21 81
39 23 83
43 26 86
48 29 89
52 31 91
56 34 94
61 36 96
65 39 99
69 41 101
72 43 103
76 46 106
81 48 108
85 51 111
89 53 113
93 56 116
98 59 118
100 60 120

3' | 1 | 2 | 3 | 4 |
5' | 1 | 2 | 3 |

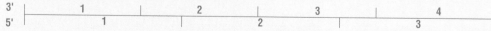

# SKILLBUILDING WORKSHOP 3

**Drill I**
**Variable rhythm patterns**

each line twice SS; DS between 2-line groups; rekey difficult lines

**Fluency** (key phrases and words, not letter by letter)

1 it is | it is he | to us | am due | by the man | an end | by the body | go with
2 cut the firm | due to the | go to the end | did pay us | form a half firm
3 they wish us to go | kept the man down | held the box down | cut the ox

4 Did the busy men dismantle the shamrock ornament for the visitor?
5 The key to the eighth problem is to spell rogue and theory right.
6 When Jane and I go to the city, we may visit the chapel and mall.

7 The auditor had problems with the theory to make a profit for us.
8 Diane did rush the lapdog to the city when it bit their neighbor.
9 If the altos are on key, they may enrich the chant in the ritual.

| 1 | 2 | 3 | 4 | 5 | 6 | 7 | 8 | 9 | 10 | 11 | 12 | 13 |

**Control** (key at a steady but not fast pace)

10 we saw | ad in | as my | we are | on him | ate up | we act ill | add gas to oil
11 age was | you are only | jump on art | my faded nylon | red yolk | few were
12 best care | you read | tax base | after we oil | saw data | agreed rate was

13 Water and garbage rates fell after my rebates were added in July.
14 Acres of wet grass and poppy seeds were tested for zebras to eat.
15 Jo ate the lumpy beets and sweet tarts but craved a stewed onion.

16 Jimmy saw a cab in my garage; I was awarded it in an estate case.
17 Dad feared we'd pay extra estate taxes after debts were assessed.
18 Rebates on oil, added to decreases in taxes, affect oil reserves.

| 1 | 2 | 3 | 4 | 5 | 6 | 7 | 8 | 9 | 10 | 11 | 12 | 13 |

**Variable-rhythm sentences** (vary pace with difficulty of words)

19 Dad attested to the fact that the barbers paid the auditor's tax.
20 Giant oaks and sassafras trees edged the east lane of the street.
21 Holly may join us by the pool to meet the eight big team members.

22 Did you get sufficient green material to make the eight sweaters?
23 All crates of cabbages were saved after I agreed to make payment.
24 Both visitors were totally enchanted as they watched the regatta.

| 1 | 2 | 3 | 4 | 5 | 6 | 7 | 8 | 9 | 10 | 11 | 12 | 13 |

**Drill 6**
**Number reaches**
Key each line at a comfortable rate; practice difficult lines.

1 My staff of 11 worked 11 hours a day from May 11 to June 11.
2 Her flight, PW 222, lands at 2:22 p.m. on Thursday, June 22.
3 We 3, part of the 333rd Corps, marched 33 miles on August 3.
4 Car 444 took Route 4 east to Route 44, then 4 miles to Aden.
5 The 55 wagons traveled 555 miles in '55; only 5 had trouble.
6 Put 6 beside 6; result 66. Then, add one more 6 to get 666.
7 She sold 7,777 copies of Record 77, Schubert's 7th Symphony.
8 In '88, it took 8 men and 8 women 8 days to travel 88 miles.
9 The 9 teams, 9 girls and 9 boys, depart on Bus 999 at 9 a.m.
10 Million has six zeros; as, 000,000. Ten has but one; as, 0.

| 1 | 2 | 3 | 4 | 5 | 6 | 7 | 8 | 9 | 10 | 11 | 12 | 13 |

**Writing 19**

 all letters

|  | gwam | 3' | 5' |
|---|---|---|---|

Planning, organizing, and controlling are three of the — 4 | 2 | 65
functions that are familiar to all sorts of firms. Because these — 8 | 5 | 68
functions are basic to the managerial practices of a business, — 12 | 7 | 71
they form the very core of its daily operations. Good managerial — 17 | 10 | 73
procedures, of course, do not just occur by accident. They must — 21 | 13 | 76
be set into motion by people. Thus, a person who plans to enter — 25 | 15 | 78
the job market, especially in an office position, should study — 30 | 18 | 81
all of the elements of good management in order to apply those — 34 | 20 | 83
principles to her or his work. — 36 | 22 | 85

Leadership is another very important skill for a person — 40 | 24 | 87
to develop. Leaders are needed at all levels in a business to — 44 | 26 | 89
plan, organize, and control the operations of a firm. A person — 48 | 29 | 92
who is in a key position of leadership usually is expected to ini- — 52 | 31 | 95
tiate ideas as well as to carry out the goals of a business. — 57 | 34 | 97
Office workers who have developed the qualities of leadership are — 61 | 37 | 100
more apt to be promoted than those without such skills. While — 65 | 39 | 102
leadership may come naturally for some people, it can be learned — 70 | 42 | 105
as well as be improved with practice. — 72 | 43 | 106

Attitude is an extremely important personality trait that — 76 | 46 | 109
is a big contributor to success in one's day-to-day activities. — 80 | 48 | 111
Usually a person with a good attitude is open-minded to the ideas — 85 | 51 | 114
of others and is able to relate with others because he or she has — 89 | 53 | 117
an interest in people. Thus, one's attitude on the job often — 93 | 56 | 119
makes a great difference in whether work gets done and done — 97 | 58 | 122
right. Because teamwork is a part of many jobs, developing a — 101 | 61 | 124
good attitude toward work, people, and life seems logical. — 105 | 63 | 126

3' | 1 | 2 | 3 | 4 |
5' | 1 | 2 | 3 |

**Writing 14**
To access these writings on *MicroPace Pro* software, key **W** and the writing number. For example, key **W14** for Writing 14.

 all letters                                        *gwam*  3' | 5'

Much of the cost of hiring a new employee is clear:    3 | 2 | 40
Recruiting trips, placement fees, and advertising expenses are    8 | 5 | 43
much higher than ever before. Recruiting, even when successful    12 | 7 | 46
and free of problems, accounts for only part of the cost. The    16 | 10 | 48
lower productivity rate of a new employee while she or he is    20 | 12 | 51
being trained is a hidden cost factor. The time lag between when    25 | 15 | 53
a person is hired and when that person actually becomes produc-    29 | 17 | 56
tive may frequently extend from six to ten months.    32 | 19 | 58

As expensive as the cost of recruiting and training is,    36 | 22 | 60
the investment is very worthwhile if an employee is kept produc-    40 | 24 | 63
tive and remains with the company. A large number of poor em-    44 | 27 | 65
ployees who stay on the job become uninspired about their jobs.    49 | 29 | 68
Such people are retirees in residence. The workers who may feel    53 | 32 | 70
that their expectations have not been realized begin to do just    57 | 34 | 73
enough to get by and find the greatest challenge and fulfillment    62 | 37 | 75
in finding new ways to avoid work.    64 | 38 | 77

3' | 1 | 2 | 3 | 4
5' | 1 | 2 | 3

 all letters                                        *gwam*  3' | 5'

Telephone conference calls have been used for years. Today,    4 | 2 | 47
graphic data can also be conveyed over telephone lines to enhance    3 | 5 | 50
the calls. Two types of devices are used to send the data. The    10 | 8 | 52
first type is an electronic blackboard. The terminal, although    17 | 10 | 55
it does look like a blackboard, is really used to send written    21 | 13 | 57
material over telephone lines to a screen. The second type is a    26 | 15 | 60
digitized graphics tablet. The graphics tablet looks very much    30 | 18 | 63
like a tablet of art paper. An image is formed on a pressure-    34 | 20 | 65
sensitive surface, and the data is entered into the computer.    38 | 23 | 68

Conference calls may not be as effective as face-to-face    42 | 25 | 70
meetings, but they are far less expensive than the travel    47 | 28 | 73
required for many face-to-face meetings. The time workers spend    51 | 31 | 75
away from the office while they are traveling is also costly.    55 | 33 | 78
The key to success in using conference calls is to select    59 | 35 | 80
carefully the type of meeting to be conducted by a call. The    63 | 38 | 83
primary objectives of many types of meetings can be attained    67 | 40 | 85
through conference calls, especially if the calls are enhanced by    72 | 43 | 88
utilizing terminals to transmit graphic data.    75 | 45 | 89

5' | 1 | 2 | 3

**Writing 15**

## Drill 5
### Double letters and Space Bar
Key each group twice; keep thumb curved and close to the Space Bar.

**Double letters**

1 Anne Sneed was keen at assessing the needs of our swimming class.
2 Three raccoons, mammals with ringed tails, scurry under the tree.
3 We will attach Emma's current address to the anniversary balloon.
4 Kenny called Anne as soon as the ballots arrived from Cincinnati.

**Space Bar**

5 Did the six men bid for the car?  Les and I saw Ken put in a bid.
6 If it is time to pay Jen for the oak hen, then let Jason pay Jen.
7 Did Pam say she may copy the forms in a day or two for all of us?
8 Who won the match?  I nominated two:  Mr. Fuji Kitts and E. Chaz.

| 1 | 2 | 3 | 4 | 5 | 6 | 7 | 8 | 9 | 10 | 11 | 12 | 13 |

## Writing 18

 all letters

|  | *gwam* | 3' | 5' |
|---|---|---|---|

Many people find that creative thinking can be nurtured 　— 4 | 2 | 66
with effort.  One way to do this is to find multiple solutions to — 8 | 5 | 68
a problem.  Alternatives to a problem should be sought out when — 12 | 7 | 71
there seems to be only one possible solution as well as when a — 17 | 10 | 73
solution has already been found.  The more ideas generated, the — 21 | 13 | 76
more options there may be.  If a person can identify the options — 25 | 16 | 79
that are available and experiment with them, then possibly he or — 30 | 18 | 81
she can come up with several other options.  This approach — 33 | 20 | 84
fosters new ideas and stimulates the creative thinking process. — 38 | 23 | 86

Another way to be creative is to try to relate present — 41 | 25 | 88
events to past events and define common elements that can be ap- — 46 | 27 | 91
plied to a current problem.  This method of relating a past expe- — 50 | 30 | 93
rience to a current event, even though the situations may be very — 54 | 33 | 96
different, helps a person find a connecting link between things — 59 | 35 | 99
or concepts.  The point is to find the similarities between what — 63 | 38 | 101
has happened previously and what is taking place at the present — 67 | 40 | 104
time.  By finding a connection between the elements, a person may — 72 | 43 | 106
discover new ways to analyze and solve problems. — 75 | 45 | 108

A creative individual does not just give up if a problem — 79 | 47 | 111
seems too difficult to solve.  A person who sticks to a problem — 83 | 50 | 113
also is more likely to succeed in solving it than the individual — 87 | 52 | 116
who gives up and goes on to other things.  Brainstorming may also — 92 | 55 | 119
be constructive in finding alternatives.  All in all, being cre- — 96 | 58 | 121
ative doesn't mean you have to solve a problem by yourself, that — 100 | 60 | 124
the solution must be found immediately, or that unique solutions — 105 | 63 | 126
must be found. — 106 | 63 | 127

| 3' | 1 | 2 | 3 | 4 |
|---|---|---|---|---|
| 5' | 1 | 2 | 3 | |

**Drill 2
Tab and numbers**

Key each line once; operate TAB with left little finger without pausing. Set 4-space intercolumn tabs.

| | | | | | | | | | |
|---|---|---|---|---|---|---|---|---|---|
| 1 | route | 497 | savor | 2149 | incur | 8637 | flute | 4975 | motor | 7959 |
| 2 | taken | 518 | under | 7633 | piano | 0816 | juror | 7749 | marks | 7148 |
| 3 | vigor | 485 | zebra | 1354 | cover | 3943 | value | 4197 | amend | 1736 |
| 4 | ozone | 919 | yacht | 6136 | fixed | 4823 | havoc | 6149 | ninth | 6865 |
| 5 | kudos | 873 | banjo | 5167 | urban | 7451 | wrote | 2495 | jeans | 7316 |
| 6 | scuba | 237 | timer | 5873 | cough | 3975 | total | 5951 | while | 2689 |

| 1 | 2 | 3 | 4 | 5 | 6 | 7 | 8 | 9 | 10 | 11 | 12 | 13 |

**Drill 3
Variable rhythm patterns**

each line twice SS; DS between 2-line groups; rekey difficult lines. Use 1" margins or 65-space line.

**Fluency** (key phrases and words, not letter by letter)

1 When Bo's dog bit a neighbor, he rushed the cur to a city kennel.
2 When the alto is on key, she will enrich the chant of the ritual.
3 She will visit the island town with eight men from the coal firm.

**Control** (key at a steady but not fast pace)

4 My crew in the reserve regattas exceeded the minimum set by Dave.
5 Ed darted to the bazaar to get poppy seeds for the zebras to eat.
6 We reversed the monopoly opinion after Polly presented the facts.

| 1 | 2 | 3 | 4 | 5 | 6 | 7 | 8 | 9 | 10 | 11 | 12 | 13 |

**Writing 16**

all letters                                                                     *gwam*   3' | 5'

|  | 3' | 5' |
|---|---|---|
| At no other time in history than the present day has there | 4 | 2 | 61 |
| been such a great concern for eye care. This increased in- | 8 | 5 | 63 |
| terest in vision and the need for good eye care has resulted, in | 12 | 7 | 66 |
| part, from the wide use of computers. With such a variety of | 16 | 10 | 68 |
| uses for computers, vast numbers of people are using visual dis- | 21 | 12 | 71 |
| play terminals on a daily basis. Each year finds more and more | 25 | 15 | 73 |
| people using the technology mainly because it makes work easier | 29 | 17 | 76 |
| and enhances leisure activities. | 31 | 19 | 77 |
| If you spend long hours using a computer, you should un- | 35 | 21 | 80 |
| derstand some of the problems involved in using the display ter- | 39 | 24 | 82 |
| minal. If some of these problems are recognized, good judgment | 44 | 26 | 85 |
| in utilizing display terminals can be applied. For example, com- | 48 | 29 | 87 |
| fort in front of the screen is important to avoid fatigue. A | 52 | 31 | 90 |
| screen should be at eye level, about the same distance from you | 56 | 34 | 92 |
| as you would hold a book. Reference material should be as close | 61 | 36 | 95 |
| to the screen as possible to minimize head and eye movements. | 65 | 39 | 97 |
| Of equal importance to you as a computer user is screen | 69 | 41 | 100 |
| light intensity, which should be three to four times greater than | 73 | 44 | 102 |
| room lighting. Also, never place your screen toward a window or | 77 | 46 | 105 |
| a bright light where glare forces you to strain your eyes. A | 82 | 49 | 107 |
| general rule to follow when using computers is to take a short | 86 | 51 | 110 |
| break every hour, even if only for five minutes. Adhering to | 90 | 54 | 112 |
| this very sensible practice on a regular basis will be beneficial | 94 | 57 | 115 |
| to your eyes and will add to your productivity. | 97 | 58 | 117 |

3' | 1 | 2 | 3 | 4 |
5' | 1 | 2 | 3 |

**Drill 4**
**Adjacent keys and direct reaches**
Key each group twice.

Keep fingers upright (not slanted) over the keys. ■

**Direct reaches**

1 Barb saw hybrids at the fairgrounds--hydrangea, hyacinth, grapes.
2 Unless I get two discounts, any price for brass is not a bargain.
3 Volumes of excellent municipal records were a target for thieves.
4 The brilliant young graduate counted a hundred brochures for Jim.

**Adjacent reaches**

5 Opal went to Salem to buy Ervan a poster and play her new guitar.
6 San Diego was a possible site for opening a pony and saddle shop.
7 The poinsettia was a popular potted flower at the yuletide sales.
8 Ty transferred to a guidance position to join Wendy in the Yukon.

| 1 | 2 | 3 | 4 | 5 | 6 | 7 | 8 | 9 | 10 | 11 | 12 | 13 |

**Writing 17**

 all letters

*gwam* 3' | 5'

An essential part of analyzing a career option is to de-  4  2  65
termine the type and extent of education that are required for a  8  5  67
selected career.  A main factor to consider about an education is  12  7  70
how long it will take to get the skills that are needed to com-  17  10  73
pete successfully for a job.  This factor includes any other  21  12  75
training that may be essential at the outset of employment.  Be-  25  15  78
cause jobs change, also assess how an educational program is  29  17  80
structured to meet work changes.  31  19  81

Many people choose a career without considering how well  35  21  84
they may be suited for it.  For example, a person who is outgoing  39  24  86
and enjoys being around people probably should not select a  43  26  89
career that requires spending long hours working alone.  A job  48  29  91
that requires quick, forceful action to be taken probably should  52  31  94
not be pursued by a person who is shy and contemplative. Just  56  34  96
because one has an aptitude for a specific job does not mean he  60  36  99
or she will be successful in that job.  Thus, be sure to weigh  65  39 101
individual personality traits before making a final career  69  41 104
choice.  69  42 104

Money and inner satisfaction are the two leading reasons  73  44 106
why most people work.  For most persons, the need for money  77  46 109
translates into food, shelter, and clothing.  Once the basic  81  49 111
needs of a person are met, satisfaction is the greatest motivator  85  51 114
for working.  To the average person, a job is satisfying if he or  90  54 117
she enjoys the work, likes the people associated with the work,  94  56 119
and feels a sense of pride in a job well done.  Because you may  98  59 122
not be the average person, analyze yourself to discover what will  103  62 124
provide job satisfaction.  104  63 125

3' | 1 | 2 | 3 | 4 |
5' | 1 | 2 | 3 |

# reference guide

## Capitalize

1. First word of a sentence and of a direct quotation.

   We were tolerating instead of managing diversity.

   The speaker said, "We must value diversity, not merely recognize it."

2. Names of proper nouns—specific persons, places, or things.

   *Common nouns:* continent, river, car, street
   *Proper nouns:* Asia, Mississippi, Buick, State St.

3. Derivatives of proper nouns and geographical names.

   American history   English accent   German food
   Ohio Valley        Tampa, Florida   Mount Rushmore

4. A personal or professional title when it precedes the name or a title of high distinction without a name.

   Lieutenant Kahn   Mayor Walsh        Doctor Welby
   Mr. Ty Brooks      Dr. Frank Collins  Miss Tate
   the President of the United States

5. Days of the week, months of the year, holidays, periods of history, and historic events.

   Monday, June 8      Labor Day        Renaissance

6. Specific parts of the country but not compass points that show direction.

   Midwest        the South        northwest of town

7. Family relationships when used with a person's name.

   Aunt Helen        my dad        Uncle John

8. Noun preceding a figure except for common nouns such as *line, page,* and *sentence.*

   Unit 1    Section 2    page 2    verse 7    line 2

9. First and main words of side headings, titles of books, and works of art. Do not capitalize words of four or fewer letters that are conjunctions, prepositions, or articles.

   *Computers in the News*        *Raiders of the Lost Ark*

10. Names of organizations and specific departments within the writer's organization.

    Girl Scouts                    our Sales Department

## Number expression
### General guidelines

1. Use **words** for numbers *one* through *ten* unless the numbers are in a category with related larger numbers that are expressed as figures.

   He bought three acres of land.  She took two acres.
   She wrote 12 stories and 2 plays in the last 13 years.

2. Use **words** for approximate numbers or large round numbers that can be expressed as one or two words. Use **numbers** for round numbers in millions or higher with their word modifier.

   We sent out about three hundred invitations.
   She contributed $3 million dollars.

3. Use **words** for numbers that begin a sentence.

   Six players were cut from the ten-member team.

4. Use **figures** for the larger of two adjacent numbers.

   We shipped six 24-ton engines.

### Times and dates

5. Use **words** for numbers that precede *o'clock* (stated or implied).

   We shall meet from two until five o'clock.

6. Use **figures** for times with *a.m.* or *p.m.* and days when they follow the month.

   Her appointment is for 2:15 p.m. on July 26, 2000.

7. Use **ordinals** for the day when it precedes the month.

   The 10th of October is my anniversary.

### Money, percentages, and fractions

8. Use **figures** for money amounts and percentages.  Spell out *cents* and *percent* except in statistical copy.

   The 16% discount saved me $145; Bill, 95 cents.

9. Use **words** for fractions unless the fractions appear in combination with whole numbers.

   one-half of her lesson        5 1/2        18 3/4

*(continued)*

# Basic grammar

## Use a singular verb

1. With a **singular subject**. (The singular forms of to be include: am, is, was. Common errors with to be are: you was, we was, they was.)
   The man works hard. He is angry; she was late.
2. With most **indefinite pronouns**: another, anybody, anything, everything, each, either, neither one, everyone, anyone, nobody.
   Each of the candidates has been critical.
   Neither of the boys is able to attend.
3. With **singular subjects** joined by or/nor, either/or, neither/nor.
   Neither your grammar nor punctuation is correct.
   Either Jody or Jan has your dish.
4. With a **collective noun** (family, choir, herd, faculty, jury, committee) that acts as one unit.
   The jury has reached a decision.
   The council is in an emergency session.
   But:
   The faculty have their assignments. (Each has his/her own assignment.)
5. With words or phrases that express periods of time, weights, measurements, or amounts of money.
   Fifteen dollars is what he earned.
   Two-thirds of the money has been turned in.
   One hundred pounds is too much.

## Use a plural verb

6. With a **plural subject**.
   The students are working hard.
   The lights are turned off at five o'clock.
7. With **compound** (two or more) **subjects** joined by *and*.
   Success and notoriety come with the award.
   Carbohydrates and fats are important to your diet.
8. With **some, all, most, none, several, few, both, many,** and **any** when they refer to more than one of the items.
   All of my friends have seen the movie.
   Some of the teams have won two or more games.

## Addresses

10. Use **words** for street names First through Tenth and ordinals for streets above Tenth. Use **figures** for house numbers other than number **one**. (If street name is a number, separate it from house number with a dash.)
    One Lytle Place Second Ave. 142--534 St.

# Pronoun case

## Use the nominative case

1. When the pronoun acts as the **subject** of a verb.
   Jim and I went to the movies.
   Mike and she were best friends.
2. When the pronoun is used as a **predicate pronoun**. (The verb be is a linking verb; it links the noun/pronoun to the predicate.)
   It was she who answered.
   It was he who left.

## Use the objective case

1. When the pronoun is used as a **direct** or **indirect** object.
   Jill invited us to the meeting.
   The printer gave Bill and me the tickets to the game.
2. When the pronoun is an **object of the preposition.**
   I am going with you and him.
   This issue is between you and me.

## Agreement of pronoun and antecedent

The **antecedent** is the word the pronoun refers to.
The antecedent must agree with the pronoun in **person** (first, second, third), **gender** (feminine, masculine, neuter), and in **number** (singular or plural).

1. The antecedent must agree with the pronoun in **person.**
   Someone had left his or her computer on the plane.
   The ash tree has lost its leaves.
2. The antecedent must agree with the pronoun in **gender.** (neuter when gender of antecedent is unknown).
   Gail said that she liked her doll.
   The chair sits firmly on its legs.
   The dog looked for its master for days.
3. The antecedent must agree with the pronoun in **number.** If the antecedent of a pronoun is singular, use a singular pronoun. If the antecedent is plural, use a plural pronoun.
   All members of the class paid their dues.
   Each of the Scouts brought his sleeping bag.

## Proofreading procedures

Proofread documents so that they are free of errors. Error-free documents send the message that you are detail-oriented and a person capable of doing business. Apply these procedures after you key a document.

1. Use Spelling.

2. Proofread the document on screen to be sure that it makes sense. Check for these types of errors:
   - Words, headings, and/or amounts omitted.
   - Extra words or lines not deleted during the editing stage.
   - Incorrect sequence of numbers in a list.

3. Preview the document on screen using the Print Preview feature. Check the vertical placement, presence of headers or footers, page numbers, and overall appearance.

4. Save the document again and print.

5. Check the printed document by comparing it to the source copy (textbook). Check all figures, names, and addresses against the source copy. Check that the document style has been applied consistently throughout.

6. If errors exist on the printed copy, revise the document, save, and print.

7. Verify the corrections and placement of the second printed copy.

## Proofreaders' marks

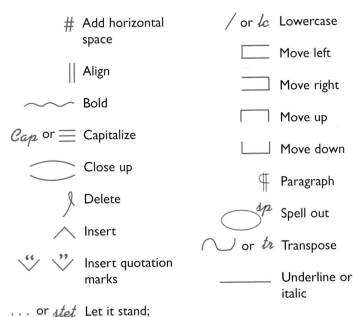

| | |
|---|---|
| # | Add horizontal space |
| ‖ | Align |
| ∼ | Bold |
| *Cap* or ≡ | Capitalize |
| ⌣ | Close up |
| ⅄ | Delete |
| ∧ | Insert |
| ⌄ ⌄ | Insert quotation marks |
| . . . or *stet* | Let it stand; ignore correction |

| | |
|---|---|
| / or *lc* | Lowercase |
| ⌐ | Move left |
| ¬ | Move right |
| � | Move up |
| ⌊ | Move down |
| ⁋ | Paragraph |
| *sp* | Spell out |
| ∿ or *tr* | Transpose |
| ___ | Underline or italic |

## Word division

With the use of proportional fonts found in current word processing packages, word division is less of an issue. Occasionally, however, you will need to make decisions on dividing words, such as when using the Columns function.

The following list contains generally accepted guidelines for dividing words.

1. Divide words between syllables only; therefore, do not divide one-syllable words.

2. **Short words:** Avoid dividing short words (five letters or fewer).

   area          bonus          since          ideal

3. **Double consonants:** Divide words with double consonants between the double letters unless the root word ends with the double letters. In this case, divide after the second consonant.

   mis- sion     trim- ming     dress- ing     call- ing

4. **One-letter syllables:** Do not divide after a *one-letter* syllable at the *beginning* of a word or before a *one-* or *two-letter* syllable at the end of a word; divide after a *one-letter* syllable within a word.

   enough        abroad         starter        friendly
   ani- mal      sepa- rate     regu- late

5. **Two single-letter syllables:** Divide between two single-letter syllables within a word.

   gradu- ation                 evalu- ation

6. **Hyphenated words:** Compound words with a hyphen may be divided only after the hyphen.

   top- secret   soft- spoken   self- respect

7. **Figures:** Avoid dividing figures presented as a unit.

   #870331       190,886        1/22/99

8. **Proper nouns:** Avoid dividing proper nouns. If necessary, include as much of the proper noun as possible before dividing it.

   Thomas R./Lewiston        *not* Thomas R. Lewis/ton
   November 15,/ 2000         *not* November/ 15, 2000

# Punctuation

## Use an apostrophe

1. To make most singular nouns and indefinite pronouns possessive (add **apostrophe** and **s**).

   computer + 's = computer's   Jess + 's = Jess's

   anyone's   one's   somebody's

2. To make a plural noun that does not end in s possessive (add **apostrophe** and **s**).

   women + 's = women's   men + 's = men's

   children + 's = children's   deer + 's = deer's

3. To make a plural noun that ends in s possessive. Add only the **apostrophe**.

   boys + ' = boys'   managers + ' = managers'

4. To make a compound noun possessive or to show joint possession. Add **apostrophe** and **s** to the last part of the hyphenated noun.

   son-in-law's   Rob and Gen's game

5. To form the plural of numbers and letters, add **apostrophe** and **s**. To show omission of letters or figures, add an **apostrophe** in place of the missing items.

   7's   A's   It's   I add'l

## Use a colon

1. To introduce a listing.

   The candidate's strengths were obvious:   experience, community involvement, and forthrightness.

2. To introduce an explanatory statement.

   Then I knew we were in trouble:  The item had not been scheduled.

## Use a comma

1. After an introductory phrase or dependent clause.

   After much deliberation, the jury reached its decision.

   If you have good skills, you will find a job.

2. After words or phrases in a series.

   Mike is taking Greek, Latin III, and Chemistry II.

3. To set off nonessential or interrupting elements.

   Troy, the new man in MIS, will install the hard drive.

   He cannot get to the job, however, until next Friday.

4. To set off the date from the year and the city from the state.

   John, will you please reserve the center in Billings, Montana, for January 10, 2000.

5. To separate two or more parallel adjectives (adjectives could be separated by *and* instead of a comma).

   The loud, whining guitar could be heard above the rest.

6. Before the conjunction in a compound sentence. The comma may be omitted in a very short sentence.

   You must leave immediately, or you will miss your flight.

   We tested the software and they loved it.

7. Set off appositives and words of direct address.

   Karen, our team leader, represented us at the conference.

   Paul, have you ordered the CD-ROM drive?

## Use a semicolon

1. To separate independent clauses in a compound sentence when the conjunction is omitted.

   Please review the information; give me a report by Tuesday.

2. To separate independent clauses when they are joined by conjunctive adverbs (however, nevertheless, consequently, etc.).

   The traffic was heavy; consequently, I was late.

3. To separate a series of elements that contain commas.

   The new officers are Fran Pena, president; Harry Wong, treasurer; and Muriel Williams, secretary.

## Use a dash

1. To show an abrupt change of thought.

   Invoice 76A—which is 10 days overdue—is for $670.

2. After a series to indicate a summarizing statement.

   Noisy fuel pump, worn rods, and failing brakes—for all these reasons I'm trading the car.

## Use italic or underline

1. With titles of complete literary works.

   College Keyboarding   Hunt for Red October

2. To emphasize special words or phrases.

   What does professional mean?

## Use a hyphen

1. To show end-of-line word division.

2. In many compound words—check a dictionary if unsure.
   - Two-word adjectives before a noun:

     two-car family
   - Compound numbers between twenty-one and ninety-nine.
   - Fractions and some proper nouns with prefixes/suffixes.

     two-thirds   ex-Governor   all-American

## Use an exclamation point

After emphatic interjections or exclamatory sentences.

Terrific!   Hold it!   You bet!   What a great surprise!

# Addressing procedures

When generating an envelope from a letter displayed on the screen, delete the punctuation and convert the address to ALL CAPS format before printing the envelope. An envelope can also be generated when a letter is not displayed. Business letters are usually mailed in envelopes that have the return address pre-printed; return addresses are printed only for personal letters or when letterhead envelopes are not available.

When preparing an envelope using an electronic typewriter or some other technology, follow the spacing guidelines below:

**Small envelope.** On a No. 6 3/4 envelope, place the address near the center—about 2 inches from the top and left edges. Place a return address in the upper left corner (line 2, 3 spaces from left edge).

**Large envelope.** On a No. 10 envelope, place the address near the center—about line 14 and .5" left of center. A return address, if not preprinted, should be keyed in the upper left corner (see small envelope).

An address must contain at least three lines; addresses of more than six lines should be avoided. The last line of an address must contain three items of information ONLY: (1) the city, (2) the state, and (3) the ZIP Code, preferably a 9-digit code.

Place mailing notations that affect postage (e.g., REGISTERED, CERTIFIED) below the stamp position (line 8); place other special notations (e.g., CONFIDENTIAL, PERSONAL) a DS below the return address.

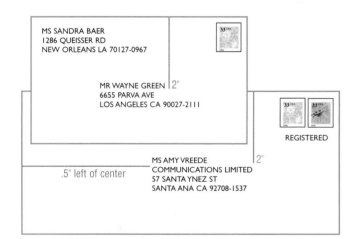

# Folding and inserting procedures

## Large envelopes (No. 10, 9, 7 3/4)

| Step 1 | Step 2 | Step 3 |
|---|---|---|

**Step 1:** With document face up, fold slightly less than 1/3 of sheet up toward top.

**Step 2:** Fold down top of sheet to within 1/2" of bottom fold.

**Step 3:** Insert document into envelope with last crease toward bottom of envelope.

## Small envelopes (No. 6 3/4, 6 1/4)

| Step 1 | Step 2 | Step 3 |
|---|---|---|

**Step 1:** With document face up, fold bottom up to 1/2" from top.

**Step 2:** Fold right third to left.

**Step 3:** Fold left third to 1/2" from last crease and insert last creased edge first.

## Window envelopes (full sheet)

| Step 1 | Step 2 | Step 3 |
|---|---|---|

**Step 1:** With sheet face down, top toward you, fold upper third down.

**Step 2:** Fold lower third up so address is showing.

**Step 3:** Insert document into envelope with last crease toward bottom of envelope.

# Two-letter state abbreviations

| | | | | |
|---|---|---|---|---|
| Alabama, AL | Guam, GU | Massachusetts, MA | New York, NY | Tennessee, TN |
| Alaska, AK | Hawaii, HI | Michigan, MI | North Carolina, NC | Texas, TX |
| Arizona, AZ | Idaho, ID | Minnesota, MN | North Dakota, ND | Utah, UT |
| Arkansas, AR | Illinois, IL | Mississippi, MS | Ohio, OH | Vermont, VT |
| California, CA | Indiana, IN | Missouri, MO | Oklahoma, OK | Virgin Islands, VI |
| Colorado, CO | Iowa, IA | Montana, MT | Oregon, OR | Virginia, VA |
| Connecticut, CT | Kansas, KS | Nebraska, NE | Pennsylvania, PA | Washington, WA |
| Delaware, DE | Kentucky, KY | Nevada, NV | Puerto Rico, PR | West Virginia, WV |
| District of Columbia, DC | Louisiana, LA | New Hampshire, NH | Rhode Island, RI | Wisconsin, WI |
| Florida, FL | Maine, ME | New Jersey, NJ | South Carolina, SC | Wyoming, WY |
| Georgia, GA | Maryland, MD | New Mexico, NM | South Dakota, SD | |

## Letter parts

**Letterhead.** Company name and address. May include other data.

**Date.** Date letter is mailed. Usually in month, day, year order. Military style is an option (day/month/year: 17/1/99).

**Letter address.** Address of the person who will receive the letter. Include personal title (Mr., Ms., Dr.); name; professional title; company; and address.

**Salutation.** Greeting. Corresponds to the first line of the letter address. Usually includes name and courtesy title; use Ladies and Gentlemen if letter is addressed to a company name.

**Body.** Message. SS; DS between paragraphs.

**Complimentary close.** Farewell, such as Sincerely.

**Writer.** Name and professional title. Women may include a personal title.

**Initials.** Identifies person who keyed the document (for example, tr). May include identification of writer (ARB:tr).

**Enclosure.** Copy is enclosed with the document. May specify contents.

**Copy notation.** Indicates that a copy of the letter is being sent to person named.

### Envelope

```
IMAGE MAKERS
5131 Moss Springs Rd.
Columbia, SC 29209-4768


                    MS MARY BERNARD PRESIDENT
                    BERNARD IMAGE CONSULTANTS
                    4927 STUART AVE
                    BATON ROUGE LA 70808-3519
```

### Block letter (open punctuation)

```
Professional Office Consultants, Inc.
584 Castro St.
San Francisco, CA 94114-2201
415-555-8725
415-555-8775 (FAX)
```

Dateline: January 17, 200-
DS

Letter address:
Ms. Amanda Castillo, Office Manager
Telekct Corporation
24 Technology Dr.
Irvine, CA 92865-9845
DS

Salutation: Dear Ms. Castillo
DS

Body:
Thank you for selecting Professional Office Consultants, Inc. to assist with the setup of your new corporate office. You asked us for a recommendation for formatting business letters. We highly recommend the block letter style because it is easy to read.

This letter is keyed in block format. As you can see, all lines begin at the left margin. Most letters can be keyed using default side margins and then centered vertically on the page for attractive placement. The block letter format is easy to key because tabs are not required.

We think that you will be happy using the block letter format. Over 80 percent of businesses today are using this same style.
DS

Complimentary close: Sincerely
QS

Writer's: Anderson Cline
Title: OA & CIS Consultant
DS

Reference initials: tr

### Modified block letter (mixed punctuation)

```
IMAGE MAKERS
5131 Moss Springs Road
Columbia, SC 29209-4768
(803) 555-0127
```

October 27, 200-

Ms. Mary Bernard, President
Bernard Image Consultants
4927 Stuart Ave.
Baton Rouge, LA 70808-3519

Dear Ms. Bernard:

The format of this letter is called modified block. Modified block format differs from block format in that the date, complimentary close, and the signature lines are positioned at the center point.

Paragraphs may be blocked, as this letter illustrates, or they may be indented from the left margin. We suggest you block paragraphs when you use modified block style so that an additional tab setting is not needed. However, some people who use modified block format prefer indented paragraphs.

Although modified block format is very popular, we recommend that you use it only for those customers who request this letter style. Otherwise, we urge you to use block format, which is more efficient, as your standard style.

Both formats are illustrated in the enclosed Image Makers Format Guide. Please note that the block format is labeled "computer compatible."

Sincerely,

Patrick R. Ray
Communication Consultant

tr

Enclosure

Copy notation: c Scot Carl, Account Manager

### Letter placement table

| Length | Dateline position | Margins |
| --- | --- | --- |
| Short: 1-2 ¶s | Center page or 3" | Default |
| Average: 3-4 ¶s | Center page or 2.7"* | Default |
| Long: 4+ ¶s | 2.1" (default + 6 hard returns) | Default |

Default margins or a minimum of 1".

*Raise date to 2" if several extra features are included.

## Personal business letter

**Janna M. Howard**
**587 Birch Cir.**
**Clinton, MS 39056-0587**
**(601) 555-4977**

Current date

> The return address may be keyed immediately above the date, or you may create a personal letterhead as shown here.

Mrs. Linda Chandler
*Financial News*
32 North Critz St.
Hot Springs, AR 71913-0032

Dear Mrs. Chandler

My college degree in office systems technology and my graphics design job experience in the United States and Taiwan qualify me to function well as a junior graphic designer for your newspaper.

As a result of my comprehensive four-year program, I am skilled in the most up-to-date office suite packages as well as the latest version of desktop publishing and graphics programs. In addition, I am very skilled at locating needed resources on the information highway. In fact, this skill played a very important role in the design award that I received last month.

My technical and communication skills were applied as I worked as the assistant editor and producer of the *Cother Alumni News*. I understand well the importance of meeting deadlines and also in producing a quality product that will increase newspaper sales.

After you have reviewed the enclosed resume, I would look forward to discussing my qualifications and career opportunities with you at *Financial News*.

Sincerely

Janna M. Howard

Enclosure

**Personal business letter**

## Resume

**JANNA M. HOWARD**

**Temporary Address (May 30, 2000)**
587 Birch Cir.
Clinton, MS 39056-0587
(601) 555-4977
E-mail: jhoward@netdoor.com

**Permanent Address**
328 Fondren St.
Orlando, FL 32801-0328
(407) 555-3834
Web page: www.netdoor.com/~jhoward

| | |
|---|---|
| **CAREER OBJECTIVE** | To obtain a graphic design position with an opportunity to advance to a management position. |
| **SUMMARY OF ACHIEVEMENTS** | Bachelor's degree with double major in office systems technology and graphics design; proficient in computer environments and major software applications. Related work experience in three organizations, including internship in foreign country. Speak Japanese and enjoy photography. |
| **EDUCATION** | **B.S. Office Systems Technology and Graphics Design** (double major), Cother University, Mobile, Alabama. May 2000. Grade-point average: 3.8/4.0. Served as president of Graphic Designers' Society. |

**SPECIAL SKILLS**

| Environments: | *Microsoft Windows*® and *Macintosh*® |
|---|---|
| Software: | *WordPerfect Suite 2000*® *Netscape*®, *CorelDraw*®, *PageMaker*®, *HyperStudio*®, *PhotoShop*®, *Illustrator*®, *Freehand*® |
| Language: | BASIC and HTML |
| Keyboarding skill: | 70 words per minute |
| Foreign language: | Japanese |
| Travel: | Japan (two summers working as a graphic design intern) |

**EXPERIENCE**

**Cother University Alumni Office**, Mobile, Alabama. Assistant editor and producer of the *Cother Alumni News*, 1998 to present.
- Design layout and production of six editions; met every publishing deadline.
- Received the "Cother Design Award."
- Assisted editor in design of Alumni Office Web page (http://www.cu.edu/alumni/).

**Cother Library**, Mobile, Alabama. Student assistant in Audiovisual Library, 1997-1998.
- Created *Audiovisual Catalog* using computerized database.
- Prepared monthly and yearly reports using database.
- Designed brochure to promote library services (http://www.cu.edu/~jhoward/samples/brochure).

**REFERENCES** — Request portfolio from Cother University Placement Office.

**Resume**

## Standard memo

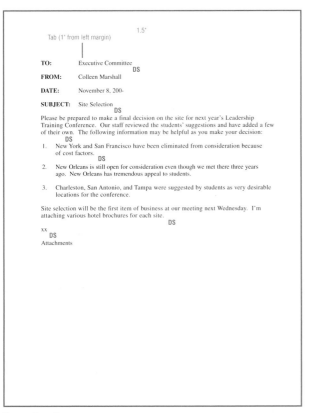

1.5"
Tab (1" from left margin)

TO:      Executive Committee
DS
FROM:    Colleen Marshall

DATE:    November 8, 200-

SUBJECT: Site Selection
DS
Please be prepared to make a final decision on the site for next year's Leadership Training Conference. Our staff reviewed the students' suggestions and have added a few of their own. The following information may be helpful as you make your decision:
DS
1. New York and San Francisco have been eliminated from consideration because of cost factors.
DS
2. New Orleans is still open for consideration even though we met there three years ago. New Orleans has tremendous appeal to students.

3. Charleston, San Antonio, and Tampa were suggested by students as very desirable locations for the conference.

Site selection will be the first item of business at our meeting next Wednesday. I'm attaching various hotel brochures for each site.
DS
xx
DS
Attachments

**Standard memo**

## Standard memo with distribution list

1.5"
Tab (1" from left margin)

TO:      Team Leaders
DS
FROM:    Form Paragraph Task Force

DATE:    Current

SUBJECT: Initial Meetings with Task Force

The task force assigned the responsibility for developing form paragraphs to use in key departments of our company plans to work in your department beginning two weeks from today. Please assign two representatives from your department to coordinate the work with us.
DS
The procedure that the Executive Committee asked us to follow is to collect samples of typical correspondence, meet with departmental representatives to collect additional information, and then to prepare a draft of the form paragraphs for review. After we receive your feedback on the draft copy, we will schedule a meeting to finalize the paragraphs.

Matthew Redfern has been assigned as the task force coordinator for your department. Please direct all communications about the project to him.
DS
xx
DS
Distribution List:
    Nestor Garcia, Claims
    Roberta Layman, Underwriting
    Rosa Romero, Agency Services
    Diana Wang, Business Services

**Standard memo with distribution list**

## Special letter parts/features

**Attention line.** Directs the letter to a specific title or person within the company. Positioned as the first line of letter address; the salutation is *Ladies and Gentlemen*.

**Company name.** Company name of the sender is keyed in ALL CAPS a DS below complimentary close; may be used when plain paper rather than letterhead is used or when the document is in the nature of a contract.

**Enumerations.** Hanging indent format; block format may be used if paragraphs are not indented.

**Mailing notation.** Provides record of how the letter was sent (FAC-SIMILE, CERTIFIED, REGISTERED) or how the letter should be treated by the receiver (CONFIDENTIAL). DS below date.

**Postscript.** Used to emphasize information; DS below last line of copy.

**Reference line.** Directs the reader to a source document such as an invoice. DS below letter address.

**Second-page heading.** Addressee's name, page number, date arranged in block format about 1" from the top edge. Second sheet is plain paper of the same quality as letterhead.

**Subject line.** Indicates topic of the letter; DS below salutation at left margin. It may be keyed in ALL CAPS or cap-and-lowercase.

## Simplified block format

Communication Concepts, Inc.
178 S. Prospect Ave. ■ San Bernardino, CA 92410-4567 ■ (714) 186-7934

August 13, 200-
DS

Dr Carl Visquel
3A2 Old Murfreesboro Rd
Nashville, TN 37217-8902
DS

Simplified Block Letter Format
DS

This letter is arranged in simplified block format. Several differences distinguish this format from the block and modified block styles.

The salutation is omitted; it is replaced by a subject line. The subject line is keyed below the letter address. A double space is left above and below it.

The letter format is further streamlined by the omission of the complimentary close. The writer's name and title (or department) are keyed a quadruple space below the body of the letter. The name and title are placed on the same line.

Notice that the letter address of this letter is keyed in the style recommended by the U.S. Postal Service for OCR processing: ALL-CAP letters with no punctuation. As with the other letter formats, it would also be appropriate to use cap-and-lowercase letters with punctuation for the letter address.

Many organizations have decided to use this particular style. Their opinion is that the salutation and complimentary close serve little purpose and are obsolete. Other organizations still prefer the traditional block or modified block format.
DS

Mrs. Caroline Martinez, Word Processing Specialist
DS

xx

## Second-page heading
## Enumerated items (hanging indent format)

1"

Mr. Jason Artis
Page 2
April 9, 2000-
DS

You will need to perform the following steps:
1. Review the sample projects and proposed guidelines.
2. Determine the specific responsibilities of the project manager and put these in writing.

Thank you, Mr. Artis, for your cooperation. It is always a pleasure working with you.

Very truly yours

## Attention line/Subject line

Samantha's Fashions
422 Main St. ■ Wichita KS 67202-1304 ■ (316) 125-3342

March 15, 200-

Attention Fashion Buyer
Amason Fashion Mart
4385 Pelan Dr.
Hays, KS 67601-2863
DS

Ladies and Gentlemen
DS

FALL FASHION CAMPAIGN
DS

The demand for two of the items that were sent last week was

## Company name

Thank you for your order; we appreciate your business.

Your order should be shipped via Pony Express within the next two weeks.
DS

Sincerely
DS

STYLES BY REX
QS

Ms. Ellen Turnquist
General Manager

n

## Mailing notation/Reference line

MUSIC BY MAIL
3716 Handley Dr.
New Haven, CT
06513-2297
(203) 156-8975

March 15, 200-
DS

CERTIFIED MAIL
DS

Mr. John West, Buyer
Tainal Music Center
4385 Dove Ave.
Rigby, ID 83442-1244
DS

Re: Order No. R-3855
DS

Dear Mr. West

The items that you ordered last week were sent by overnight

## Envelope with mailing notation

Turner Roofing Co.
10318 Rearview Ave.
Dayton, OH 45029-1927

CERTIFIED MAIL

MR JACK BROWN
QUALITY TRAINING ASSOCIATES
28 REVINA DR
ATLANTA GA 30346-9105

## Postscript

Sincerely
QS

Ms. Rae Mathias, President
DS

pr
DS

The cashmere sweaters will be shipped by air to you just as soon as our stock is replenished. You will find them well worth the wait.

# Standard unbound report and outline format

**Margins:** *Top* 1.5" for first page and reference page; 1" for succeeding pages; *Side* 1" or default; *bottom* 1".

**Spacing:** *Educational reports*: DS, paragraphs indented .5". *Business reports*: SS, paragraphs blocked with a DS between.

**Page numbers:** Second and subsequent pages are numbered at top right of the page. DS follows the page number.

**Main headings:** Centered; ALL CAPS; 14 pts.

**Side headings:** Bold; main words capitalized; DS above and below.

**Paragraph headings:** Bold; capitalize first word, followed by a period.

*NOTE:* Larger fonts may also be used for headings.

# Report documentation

**Internal citations:** Provides source of information within report. Includes the author's surname, publication date, and page number (Bruce, 2000, 129).

**Endnotes:** Superior figure keyed at point of reference within report. All sources placed on a separate page at the end of the report in numerical order. Endnotes precede the bibliography or references.

**Bibliography or references:** Lists all references, whether quoted or not, in alphabetical order by authors' names. References may be formatted on the last page of the report if they all fit on the page; if not, list on a separate, numbered page.

---

**EFFECTIVE PRESENTATIONS** DS

I.  PLANNING AND PREPARING PRESENTATIONS DS

   A.  Opening
       1.  Gain attention
       2.  Set the tone
   B.  Body of the Presentation
       1.  Focus on objective
       2.  Organize information
       3.  Prepare support materials
   C.  Closing DS

II. DELIVERING PRESENTATIONS DS

   A.  Delivery Techniques
       1.  Engage audience
       2.  Project voice effectively
       3.  Control environment
   B.  Visuals and Supporting Materials
       1.  Ensure readability
       2.  Use effectively

III. FOLLOW-UP ACTIVITIES

   A.  Discussion and Questions
   B.  Postpresentation Activities

**Outline**

---

1.5"

**BASIC STEPS IN REPORT WRITING** DS

The effective writer makes certain that reports that leave her or his desk are technically correct in style, usable in content, and attractive in format. DS

Side heading — **The First Step** DS

Information is gathered about the subject; the effective writer takes time to outline the data to be used in the report. This approach allows the writer to establish the organization of the report. When a topic outline is used, order of presentation, important points, and even various headings can be determined and followed easily when writing begins.

Default side margins — **The Correct Style**

The purpose of the report often determines the style. Most academic reports (term papers, for example) are double-spaced with indented paragraphs. Most business reports, however, are single-spaced; and paragraphs are blocked. When a style is not stipulated, general usage may be followed.

**The Finished Product**

Most capable writers will refrain from making a report deliberately impressive, especially if doing so makes it less expressive. The writer does, however, follow the outline carefully as a first draft is written. Obvious errors are ignored momentarily. Refinement comes later, after all the preliminary work is done. The finished document will then be read and reread to ensure it is clear, concise, correct, and complete.

**First page of unbound report**

---

2 DS

and thus oxygen becomes a crucial part of any aquatic ecosystem. Dissolved oxygen is derived from the atmosphere as well as from the photosynthetic processes of aquatic plants. Oxygen, in turn, is consumed through the life activities of most aquatic animals and plants (Bruce, 2000, 129). When dissolved oxygen reaches very low levels in the aquatic environment, unfavorable conditions for fish and other aquatic life can develop.

**Conclusion**

The absence of dissolved oxygen may give rise to unpleasant odors produced through anaerobic (no oxygen) decomposition. On the other hand, an adequate supply of oxygen helps maintain a healthy environment for fish and other aquatic life and this supply may help prevent the development of unacceptable conditions that are caused by the decomposition of municipal and industrial waste (Ryn, 1999, 29). DS

**REFERENCES** DS

Book — Beard, Fred F. *The Fulford County Dilemma.* Niagara Falls: Dawn General Press, 1998.

Bruce, Lois L. "Hazardous Waste Management: A History." *State of Idaho Bulletin No. 7312.* Boise: State of Idaho Press, 2000.

Periodical — Ryn, Jewel Scott. "But Please Don't Drink the Water." *Journal of Environmental Science,* Winter 1999, pp. 25-38.

Electronic reference — "Documenting Sources from the World Wide Web." MLA <http://www.mla.org/setstl.htm> (12 July 1999).

**Second page of unbound report**

---

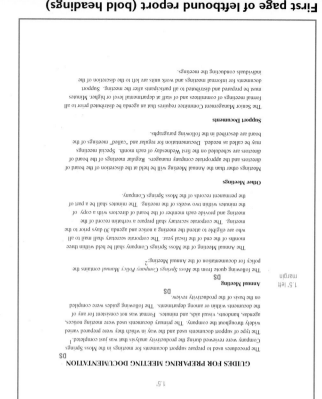

1.5″

## GUIDES FOR PREPARING MEETING DOCUMENTATION
DS

The procedures used to prepare support documents for meetings in the Moss Springs Company were reviewed during the productivity analysis that was just completed.[1] The type of support documents used and the way in which they were prepared varied widely throughout the company. The primary documents used were meeting notices, agendas, handouts, visual aids, and minutes. Format was not consistent for any of the documents within or among departments. The following guides were compiled on the basis of the productivity review.

**Annual Meeting**
DS

1.5″ left margin

The following quote from the *Moss Springs Company Policy Manual* contains the policy for documentation of the Annual Meeting:[2]

The Annual Meeting of the Moss Springs Company shall be held within three months of the end of the fiscal year. The corporate secretary shall mail to all who are eligible to attend the meeting a notice and agenda 30 days prior to the meeting. The corporate secretary shall prepare a verbatim record of the meeting and provide each member of the board of directors with a copy of the minutes within two weeks of the meeting. The minutes shall be a part of the permanent records of the Moss Springs Company.

**Other Meetings**

Meetings other than the Annual Meeting will be held at the discretion of the board of directors and the appropriate company managers. Regular meetings of the board of directors are scheduled on the first Wednesday of each month. Special meetings may be called as needed. Documentation for regular and "called" meetings of the board are described in the following paragraphs.

**Support Documents**

The Senior Management Committee requires that an agenda be distributed prior to all formal meetings of committees and of staff at departmental level or higher. Minutes must be prepared and distributed to all participants after the meeting. Support documents for informal meetings and work units are left to the discretion of the individuals conducting the meetings.

1.5″

### REFERENCES
DS

Anderson, Mary. *Effective Meetings.* Boston: Bay Publishing Co., 1998.

*Moss Springs Company Policy Manual.* Chicago: 1999.

Wasu, Anil. *Enhancing Productivity: The Moss Springs Company.* Chicago: Productivity Consultants, Inc., 1999.

4

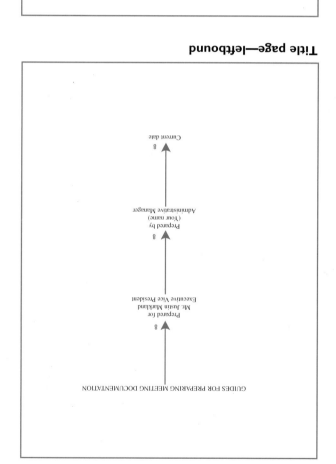

GUIDES FOR PREPARING MEETING DOCUMENTATION

Prepared for
Mr. Justin Markland
Executive Vice President

Prepared by
(Your name)
Administrative Manager

Current date

1.5″

### TABLE OF CONTENTS
DS

iii

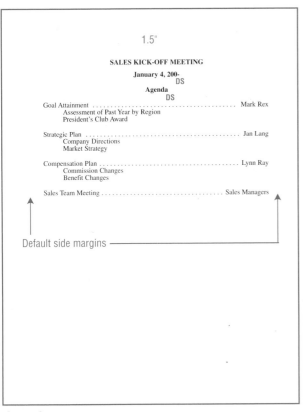

**Agenda**

**SALES KICK-OFF MEETING**

January 4, 200-
DS

**Action Minutes**
DS

**Presiding:**     President Mark Rex

**Participants:**    All Marketing and Sales Staff

President Rex summarized the results for the year and commended Region 3 for attaining its goals. He presented 146 President's Club Awards (list attached).

Jan Long, national sales manager, presented the new directions and the marketing strategies to attain the goals set. A 15 percent increase in overall sales is the target for the year.

Lynn Ray, vice president of human resources, presented the new compensation plans and announced that dental coverage is now provided.

Sales teams met individually.

Default side margins

**Action minutes**

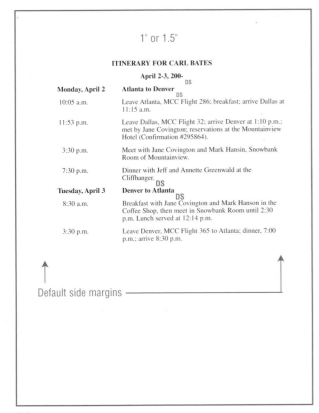

**Itinerary**

Facsimile
**TRANSMITTAL**
▬▬▬▬▬▬▬▬

**To:**     Students

**Fax #:**    (608) 555-4567

**Re:**     Preparation of Fax Cover Sheet

**Date:**    October 27, 200-

**Pages:**    1, including this cover sheet

This document is an example of a fax cover sheet that was prepared using a template file on the software. You will note that in this style of fax, the sender's name, company name, and other related information prints automatically at the bottom of the sheet.

All of the vital information for sending the fax is located in the heading of the fax. Learning to use a template document will save you time.

From the desk of ...

**Marie Ann Jacobs**

**Jacobs Incorporated**
**1701 Eagle Lake Dr.**
**South Bend, IN 47035-1584**

**(812) 555-0626**
**FAX: (812) 555-2306**

**Fax cover sheet (template document)**

# Repetitive stress injury (RSI)

**Repetitive stress injury (RSI)** is a result of repeated movement of a particular part of the body. A familiar example is "tennis elbow." Of more concern to keyboard users is the form of RSI called **carpal tunnel syndrome (CTS)**.

CTS is an inflammatory disease that develops gradually and affects the wrist, hands, and forearms. Blood vessels, tendons, and nerves pass into the hand through the carpal tunnel (see illustration below). If any of these structures enlarge or if the walls of the tunnel narrow, the median nerve is pinched, and CTS symptoms may result.

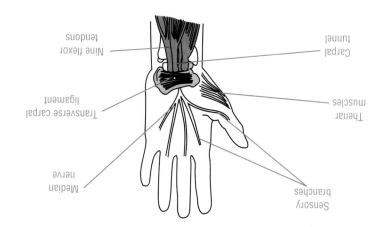

Palm view of left hand

Nine flexor tendons
Carpal tunnel
Transverse carpal ligament
Thenar muscles
Median nerve
Sensory branches

## Symptoms of RSI/CTS

CTS symptoms include numbness in the hand; tingling or burning in the hand, wrist, or elbow; severe pain in the forearm, elbow, or shoulder; and difficulty in gripping objects. Symptoms usually appear during sleeping hours, probably because many people sleep with their wrists flexed.

If not properly treated, the pressure on the median nerve, which controls the thumb, forefinger, middle finger, and half the ring finger (see top right), causes severe pain. The pain can radiate into the forearm, elbow, or shoulder and can require surgery or result in permanent damage or paralysis.

## Causes of RSI/CTS

RSI/CTS often develops in workers whose physical routine is unvaried. Common occupational factors include: (1) using awkward posture, (2) using poor techniques, (3) performing tasks with wrists bent *(see below)*, (4) using improper equipment, (5) working at a rapid pace, (6) not taking rest breaks, and (7) not doing exercises that promote graceful motion and good techniques.

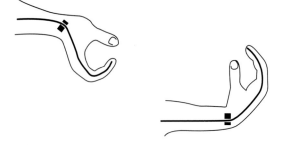

Improper wrist positions for keystroking

Other factors associated with CTS include a person's genetic makeup; the aging process; hormonal influences; obesity; chronic diseases such as rheumatoid arthritis and gout; misaligned fractures; and hobbies such as gardening, knitting, and woodworking that require the same motion over and over. CTS affects over three times more women than men, with 60 percent of the affected persons between the ages of 30 and 60.

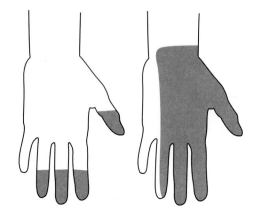

Areas affected by carpal tunnel syndrome

# Finger gymnastics

Brief daily practice of finger gymnastics will strengthen your finger muscles and increase the ease with which you key. Begin each keying period with this conditioning exercise. Choose two or more drills for this practice.

**DRILL 1.** Hands open, fingers wide, muscles tense. Close the fingers into a tight "fist," with thumb on top. Relax the fingers as you straighten them; repeat 10 times.

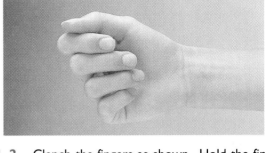

**DRILL 2.** Clench the fingers as shown. Hold the fingers in this position for a brief time; then extend the fingers, relaxing the muscles of fingers and hand. Repeat the movements slowly several times. Exercise both hands at the same time.

**DRILL 3.** Place the fingers and the thumb of one hand between two fingers of the other hand, and spread the fingers as much as possible. Spread all fingers of both hands.

**DRILL 4.** Interlace the fingers of the two hands and wring the hands, rubbing the heel of the palms vigorously.

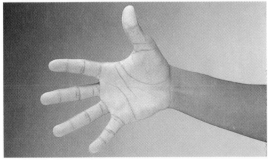

**DRILL 5.** Spread the fingers as much as possible, holding the position for a moment or two; then relax the fingers and lightly fold them into the palm of the hand. Repeat the movements slowly several times. Exercise both hands at the same time.

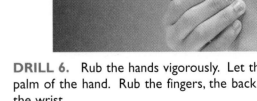

**DRILL 6.** Rub the hands vigorously. Let the thumb rub the palm of the hand. Rub the fingers, the back of the hand, and the wrist.

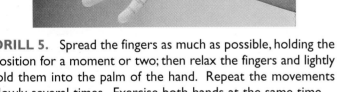

**DRILL 7.** Hold both hands in front of you, fingers together. Hold the last three fingers still and move the first finger as far to the side as possible. Return the first finger; then move the first and second fingers together; finally move the little finger as far to the side as possible.

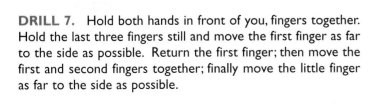

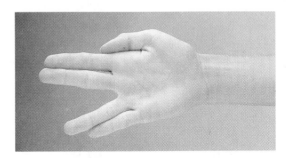

# index

| Function | Menu or Toolbar | Lesson Introduced |
|---|---|---|
| Block protect | Format, Keep Text Together, Block protect | 49, 86 |
| Bold, Italic, Underline | Property bar; Format, Font | 34 |
| Bookmarks, QuickMark | Tools, Bookmark | 102 |
| Borders | Format, Paragraph, Border/Fill | 101 |
| Bullets | Toolbar; Insert, Outline/Bullets & Numbering | 70 |
| Convert Case | Edit, Convert Case | 67 |
| Center page | Format, Page, Center, Current Page | 36 |
| Charts | Insert, Chart | A4 |
| Columns | Toolbar; Format, Columns | 104 |
| Comments | Insert, Comments, Create | F4 |
| Copy | Toolbar; Edit, Copy | 46 |
| Cut | Toolbar, Edit, Cut | 46 |
| Date | Insert, Date/Time | 66 |
| Document Review | File, Document Review | F4 |
| Drop Cap | Format, Paragraph, DropCap | A5 |
| Embed Object | Edit, Paste Special, Paste option | D1 |
| Envelopes | Format, Envelope | 68 |
| Find and Replace | Edit, Find and Replace | 84 |
| Flush Right | ALT + F7 | 108 |
| Font size, Font face | Property bar; Format, Font | 34 |
| Footnotes, Endnotes | Insert, Footnote/Endnote | 88 |
| Go To | Edit, Go To | 84 |
| Grammatik | Tools, Grammatik | 92 |
| Graphics<br>  Insert, edit<br>  Group<br>  Shapes<br><br>  Wrap text | <br>Graphics toolbar, Clipart<br>Hold SHIFT key and select items; right-click an item, Group.<br>Insert, Shapes, Basic, OK, position crosshairs, click and drag.<br>   Option: Graphics toolbar.<br>Select clipart, right click, Wrap, make selections. | <br>98<br>A5<br><br>A5<br>A5 |
| Hanging Indent | Format, Paragraph, Hanging Indent | 45 |
| Hard page break | CTRL + ENTER | 48 |
| Header/Footer | Insert, Header/Footer | 73, 109 |
| Highlighting | Toolbar, Highlight button | F4 |
| Horizontal line | Graphics toolbar, Horizontal line | 99 |
| Hyperlink | Toolbar; Tools, Hyperlink | 87 |
| Hyphenation | Tools, Language, Hyphenation | A2 |
| Indent | F7 key; Format, Paragraph, Indent | 45, 108 |
| Insert file | Insert, File | 79 |
| Insert mode | Insert key; Status bar | 33 |

| Function | Menu or Toolbar | Lesson Introduced |
|----------|-----------------|-------------------|
| Internet Publisher | File, Internet Publisher, New Web Document, Select, Create a blank web document | G1 |
| Justification | Toolbar; Format, Justification | 34 |
| Labels | Format, Labels | 110 |
| Landscape orientation | Format, Page, Page Setup | 76 |
| Leaders/Flush Right | ALT + F7 twice | 108 |
| Line spacing | Format, Line, Spacing | 36 |
| Link Object | Edit, Paste Special, Paste Link | |
| Margins | Format, Margins | 45 |
| Master Document/Subdocuments | File, Document, Subdocument<br>File, Document, Expand Master or Condense Master | F5 |
| Merge<br>  with Paradox | Tools, Merge<br>From Paradox: Tools, Expert, Merge | 111<br>E6 |
| Memo template | File, New from Project, Memo | 71 |
| New blank document | Toolbar; File New | |
| Numbers | Toolbar; Insert, Outline/Bullets & Numbering | 70 |
| Page Numbering | Format, Page, Numbering | 86 |
| Paste | Toolbar; Edit, Paste | 46 |
| Paste Special | Edit, Paste Special, Paste | F2 |
| Print | Toolbar; File, Print | 31 |
| QuickCorrect | Tools, QuickCorrect | 35, F1 |
| QuickWords | Tools, QuickWords | F1 |
| Reveal Codes | View, Reveal Codes | 35 |
| Ruler | View, Ruler | 40 |
| Shapes | Graphics toolbar, shapes buttons | 98 |
| Sort | Tools, Sort | 77 |
| Spell-As-You-Go | Tools, Proofread | 35 |
| Spell Checker | Toolbar; Tools, Spell Checker | 35 |
| Styles<br>  QuickStyle | Toolbar—Select Style down arrow<br>   Select Style down arrow, QuickStyle | F2 |
| Suppress | Format, Page, Suppress | 86 |
| Tables: Basics<br>  Specialized features | Table menu | 53-55<br>77-80 |
| Table of Contents | Tools, Reference, Table of Contents | F3 |
| Tabs<br>  Dot tabs | Ruler; Format, Line, Tab Set<br>Ruler; Format, Line, Tab Set | 41<br>81 |
| TextArt | Graphics toolbar, TextArt | 101 |
| Thesaurus | Tools, Thesaurus | 85 |
| Undo/Redo | Toolbar | TM7 |
| Widow/Orphan | Format, Keep Text Together, Widow/Orphan | 86 |
| Zoom | Toolbar | 39 |